CODE OF FEDERAL
REGULATIONS

Title 21
Food and Drugs

Parts 300 to 499

Revised as of April 1, 2015

Containing a codification of documents
of general applicability and future effect

As of April 1, 2015

Published by the Office of the Federal Register
National Archives and Records Administration
as a Special Edition of the Federal Register

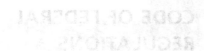

U.S. GOVERNMENT OFFICIAL EDITION NOTICE

Legal Status and Use of Seals and Logos

The seal of the National Archives and Records Administration (NARA) authenticates the Code of Federal Regulations (CFR) as the official codification of Federal regulations established under the Federal Register Act. Under the provisions of 44 U.S.C. 1507, the contents of the CFR, a special edition of the Federal Register, shall be judicially noticed. The CFR is prima facie evidence of the original documents published in the Federal Register (44 U.S.C. 1510).

It is prohibited to use NARA's official seal and the stylized Code of Federal Regulations logo on any republication of this material without the express, written permission of the Archivist of the United States or the Archivist's designee. Any person using NARA's official seals and logos in a manner inconsistent with the provisions of 36 CFR part 1200 is subject to the penalties specified in 18 U.S.C. 506, 701, and 1017.

Use of ISBN Prefix

This is the Official U.S. Government edition of this publication and is herein identified to certify its authenticity. Use of the 0–16 ISBN prefix is for U.S. Government Publishing Office Official Editions only. The Superintendent of Documents of the U.S. Government Publishing Office requests that any reprinted edition clearly be labeled as a copy of the authentic work with a new ISBN.

 U.S. GOVERNMENT PUBLISHING OFFICE

U.S. Superintendent of Documents • Washington, DC 20402–0001

http://bookstore.gpo.gov

Phone: toll-free (866) 512-1800; DC area (202) 512-1800

Table of Contents

Cite this Code: **CFR**

To cite the regulations in this volume use title, part and section number. Thus, **21 CFR 300.50** *refers to title 21, part 300, section 50.*

Explanation

The Code of Federal Regulations is a codification of the general and permanent rules published in the Federal Register by the Executive departments and agencies of the Federal Government. The Code is divided into 50 titles which represent broad areas subject to Federal regulation. Each title is divided into chapters which usually bear the name of the issuing agency. Each chapter is further subdivided into parts covering specific regulatory areas.

Each volume of the Code is revised at least once each calendar year and issued on a quarterly basis approximately as follows:

Title 1 through Title 16..as of January 1
Title 17 through Title 27 ....as of April 1
Title 28 through Title 41 ....as of July 1
Title 42 through Title 50...as of October 1

The appropriate revision date is printed on the cover of each volume.

LEGAL STATUS

The contents of the Federal Register are required to be judicially noticed (44 U.S.C. 1507). The Code of Federal Regulations is prima facie evidence of the text of the original documents (44 U.S.C. 1510).

HOW TO USE THE CODE OF FEDERAL REGULATIONS

The Code of Federal Regulations is kept up to date by the individual issues of the Federal Register. These two publications must be used together to determine the latest version of any given rule.

To determine whether a Code volume has been amended since its revision date (in this case, April 1, 2015), consult the "List of CFR Sections Affected (LSA)," which is issued monthly, and the "Cumulative List of Parts Affected," which appears in the Reader Aids section of the daily Federal Register. These two lists will identify the Federal Register page number of the latest amendment of any given rule.

EFFECTIVE AND EXPIRATION DATES

Each volume of the Code contains amendments published in the Federal Register since the last revision of that volume of the Code. Source citations for the regulations are referred to by volume number and page number of the Federal Register and date of publication. Publication dates and effective dates are usually not the same and care must be exercised by the user in determining the actual effective date. In instances where the effective date is beyond the cutoff date for the Code a note has been inserted to reflect the future effective date. In those instances where a regulation published in the Federal Register states a date certain for expiration, an appropriate note will be inserted following the text.

OMB CONTROL NUMBERS

The Paperwork Reduction Act of 1980 (Pub. L. 96–511) requires Federal agencies to display an OMB control number with their information collection request.

Many agencies have begun publishing numerous OMB control numbers as amendments to existing regulations in the CFR. These OMB numbers are placed as close as possible to the applicable recordkeeping or reporting requirements.

PAST PROVISIONS OF THE CODE

Provisions of the Code that are no longer in force and effect as of the revision date stated on the cover of each volume are not carried. Code users may find the text of provisions in effect on any given date in the past by using the appropriate List of CFR Sections Affected (LSA). For the convenience of the reader, a "List of CFR Sections Affected" is published at the end of each CFR volume. For changes to the Code prior to the LSA listings at the end of the volume, consult previous annual editions of the LSA. For changes to the Code prior to 2001, consult the List of CFR Sections Affected compilations, published for 1949-1963, 1964-1972, 1973-1985, and 1986-2000.

"[RESERVED]" TERMINOLOGY

The term "[Reserved]" is used as a place holder within the Code of Federal Regulations. An agency may add regulatory information at a "[Reserved]" location at any time. Occasionally "[Reserved]" is used editorially to indicate that a portion of the CFR was left vacant and not accidentally dropped due to a printing or computer error.

INCORPORATION BY REFERENCE

What is incorporation by reference? Incorporation by reference was established by statute and allows Federal agencies to meet the requirement to publish regulations in the Federal Register by referring to materials already published elsewhere. For an incorporation to be valid, the Director of the Federal Register must approve it. The legal effect of incorporation by reference is that the material is treated as if it were published in full in the Federal Register (5 U.S.C. 552(a)). This material, like any other properly issued regulation, has the force of law.

What is a proper incorporation by reference? The Director of the Federal Register will approve an incorporation by reference only when the requirements of 1 CFR part 51 are met. Some of the elements on which approval is based are:

(a) The incorporation will substantially reduce the volume of material published in the Federal Register.

(b) The matter incorporated is in fact available to the extent necessary to afford fairness and uniformity in the administrative process.

(c) The incorporating document is drafted and submitted for publication in accordance with 1 CFR part 51.

What if the material incorporated by reference cannot be found? If you have any problem locating or obtaining a copy of material listed as an approved incorporation by reference, please contact the agency that issued the regulation containing that incorporation. If, after contacting the agency, you find the material is not available, please notify the Director of the Federal Register, National Archives and Records Administration, 8601 Adelphi Road, College Park, MD 20740-6001, or call 202-741-6010.

CFR INDEXES AND TABULAR GUIDES

A subject index to the Code of Federal Regulations is contained in a separate volume, revised annually as of January 1, entitled CFR INDEX AND FINDING AIDS. This volume contains the Parallel Table of Authorities and Rules. A list of CFR titles, chapters, subchapters, and parts and an alphabetical list of agencies publishing in the CFR are also included in this volume.

An index to the text of "Title 3—The President" is carried within that volume.

The Federal Register Index is issued monthly in cumulative form. This index is based on a consolidation of the "Contents" entries in the daily Federal Register.

A List of CFR Sections Affected (LSA) is published monthly, keyed to the revision dates of the 50 CFR titles.

REPUBLICATION OF MATERIAL

There are no restrictions on the republication of material appearing in the Code of Federal Regulations.

INQUIRIES

For a legal interpretation or explanation of any regulation in this volume, contact the issuing agency. The issuing agency's name appears at the top of odd-numbered pages.

For inquiries concerning CFR reference assistance, call 202-741-6000 or write to the Director, Office of the Federal Register, National Archives and Records Administration, 8601 Adelphi Road, College Park, MD 20740-6001 or e-mail *fedreg.info@nara.gov*.

SALES

The Government Publishing Office (GPO) processes all sales and distribution of the CFR. For payment by credit card, call toll-free, 866-512-1800, or DC area, 202-512-1800, M-F 8 a.m. to 4 p.m. e.s.t. or fax your order to 202-512-2104, 24 hours a day. For payment by check, write to: US Government Publishing Office – New Orders, P.O. Box 979050, St. Louis, MO 63197-9000.

ELECTRONIC SERVICES

The full text of the Code of Federal Regulations, the LSA (List of CFR Sections Affected), The United States Government Manual, the Federal Register, Public Laws, Public Papers of the Presidents of the United States, Compilation of Presidential Documents and the Privacy Act Compilation are available in electronic format via *www.ofr.gov*. For more information, contact the GPO Customer Contact Center, U.S. Government Publishing Office. Phone 202-512-1800, or 866-512-1800 (toll-free). E-mail, *ContactCenter@gpo.gov*.

The Office of the Federal Register also offers a free service on the National Archives and Records Administration's (NARA) World Wide Web site for public law numbers, Federal Register finding aids, and related information. Connect to NARA's web site at *www.archives.gov/federal-register*.

The e-CFR is a regularly updated, unofficial editorial compilation of CFR material and Federal Register amendments, produced by the Office of the Federal Register and the Government Publishing Office. It is available at *www.ecfr.gov*.

AMY P. BUNK,
Acting Director,
Office of the Federal Register.
April 1, 2015.

THIS TITLE

Title 21—FOOD AND DRUGS is composed of nine volumes. The parts in these volumes are arranged in the following order: Parts 1–99, 100–169, 170–199, 200–299, 300–499, 500–599, 600–799, 800–1299 and 1300 to end. The first eight volumes, containing parts 1–1299, comprise Chapter I—Food and Drug Administration, Department of Health and Human Services. The ninth volume, containing part 1300 to end, includes Chapter II—Drug Enforcement Administration, Department of Justice, and Chapter III—Office of National Drug Control Policy. The contents of these volumes represent all current regulations codified under this title of the CFR as of April 1, 2015.

For this volume, Susannah C. Hurley was Chief Editor. The Code of Federal Regulations publication program is under the direction of John Hyrum Martinez, assisted by Stephen J. Frattini.

Title 21—Food and Drugs

(This book contains parts 300 to 499)

1

CHAPTER I—FOOD AND DRUG ADMINISTRATION, DEPARTMENT OF HEALTH AND HUMAN SERVICES (CONTINUED)

EDITORIAL NOTE: Nomenclature changes to chapter I appear at 59 FR 14366, Mar. 28, 1994, and 69 FR 13717, Mar. 24, 2004.

SUBCHAPTER D—DRUGS FOR HUMAN USE

SUBCHAPTER D—DRUGS FOR HUMAN USE

PART 300—GENERAL

Subpart A [Reserved]

Subpart B—Combination Drugs

Sec.
300.50 Fixed-combination prescription drugs for humans.

Subpart C—Substances Generally Prohibited From Drugs

300.100 Chlorofluorocarbon propellants.

AUTHORITY: 21 U.S.C. 331, 351, 352, 355, 360b, 361, 371.

Subpart A [Reserved]

Subpart B—Combination Drugs

§ 300.50 Fixed-combination prescription drugs for humans.

The Food and Drug Administration's policy in administering the new-drug, antibiotic, and other regulatory provisions of the Federal Food, Drug, and Cosmetic Act regarding fixed combination-dosage form prescription drugs for humans is as follows:

(a) Two or more drugs may be combined in a single dosage form when each component makes a contribution to the claimed effects and the dosage of each component (amount, frequency, duration) is such that the combination is safe and effective for a significant patient population requiring such concurrent therapy as defined in the labeling for the drug. Special cases of this general rule are where a component is added:

(1) To enhance the safety or effectiveness of the principal active component; and

(2) To minimize the potential for abuse of the principal active component.

(b) If a combination drug presently the subject of an approved new-drug application has not been recognized as effective by the Commissioner of Food and Drugs based on his evaluation of the appropriate National Academy of Sciences-National Research Council panel report, or if substantial evidence of effectiveness has not otherwise been presented for it, then formulation, labeling, or dosage changes may be proposed and any resulting formulation may meet the appropriate criteria listed in paragraph (a) of this section.

(c) A fixed-combination prescription drug for humans that has been determined to be effective for labeled indications by the Food and Drug Administration, based on evaluation of the NAS-NRC report on the combination, is considered to be in compliance with the requirements of this section.

[40 FR 13496, Mar. 27, 1975, as amended at 64 FR 401, Jan. 5, 1999]

Subpart C—Substances Generally Prohibited From Drugs

§ 300.100 Chlorofluorocarbon propellants.

The use of chlorofluorocarbons in human drugs as propellants in self-pressurized containers is generally prohibited except as provided by § 2.125 of this chapter.

[43 FR 11317, Mar. 17, 1978]

PART 310—NEW DRUGS

Subpart A—General Provisions

Sec.
310.3 Definitions and interpretations.
310.4 Biologics; products subject to license control.
310.6 Applicability of "new drug" or safety or effectiveness findings in drug efficacy study implementation notices and notices of opportunity for hearing to identical, related, and similar drug products.

Subpart B—Specific Administrative Rulings and Decisions

310.100 New drug status opinions; statement of policy.
310.103 New drug substances intended for hypersensitivity testing.

Subpart C—New Drugs Exempted From Prescription-Dispensing Requirements

310.200 Prescription-exemption procedure.
310.201 Exemption for certain drugs limited by new drug applications to prescription sale.

5

AUTHORITY: 21 U.S.C. 321, 331, 351, 352, 353, 355, 360b–360f, 360j, 361(a), 371, 374, 375, 379e; 42 U.S.C. 216, 241, 242(a), 262, 263b–263n.

EFFECTIVE DATE NOTE: At 79 FR 33087, June 10, 2014, the authority citation for 21 CFR part 310 was revised, effective June 15, 2015. For the convenience of the user, the revised text is set forth as follows:
AUTHORITY: 21 U.S.C. 321, 331, 351, 352, 353, 355, 360b–360f, 360j, 361(a), 371, 374, 375, 379e, 379k–1; 42 U.S.C. 216, 241, 242(a), 262, 263b–263n.

Subpart A—General Provisions

§ 310.3 Definitions and interpretations.

As used in this part:

(a) The term *act* means the Federal Food, Drug, and Cosmetic Act, as amended (secs. 201–902, 52 Stat. 1040 *et seq.*, as amended; 21 U.S.C. 321–392).

(b) *Department* means the Department of Health and Human Services.

(c) *Secretary* means the Secretary of Health and Human Services.

(d) *Commissioner* means the Commissioner of Food and Drugs.

(e) The term *person* includes individuals, partnerships, corporations, and associations.

(f) The definitions and interpretations of terms contained in section 201 of the act shall be applicable to such terms when used in the regulations in this part.

(g) *New drug substance* means any substance that when used in the manufacture, processing, or packing of a drug, causes that drug to be a new drug, but does not include intermediates used in the synthesis of such substance.

(h) The newness of a drug may arise by reason (among other reasons) of:

(1) The newness for drug use of any substance which composes such drug, in whole or in part, whether it be an active substance or a menstruum, excipient, carrier, coating, or other component.

(2) The newness for a drug use of a combination of two or more substances, none of which is a new drug.

(3) The newness for drug use of the proportion of a substance in a combination, even though such combination containing such substance in other proportion is not a new drug.

(4) The newness of use of such drug in diagnosing, curing, mitigating, treating, or preventing a disease, or to affect a structure or function of the body, even though such drug is not a new drug when used in another disease or to affect another structure or function of the body.

(5) The newness of a dosage, or method or duration of administration or application, or other condition of use prescribed, recommended, or suggested in the labeling of such drug, even though such drug when used in other dosage, or other method or duration of administration or application, or different condition, is not a new drug.

(i) [Reserved]

(j) The term *sponsor* means the person or agency who assumes responsibility for an investigation of a new drug, including responsibility for compliance with applicable provisions of the act and regulations. The "sponsor" may be an individual, partnership, corporation, or Government agency and may be a manufacturer, scientific institution, or an investigator regularly and lawfully engaged in the investigation of new drugs.

(k) The phrase *related drug(s)* includes other brands, potencies, dosage forms, salts, and esters of the same drug moiety, including articles prepared or manufactured by other manufacturers: and any other drug containing a component so related by chemical structure or known pharmacological properties that, in the opinion of experts qualified by scientific training and experience to evaluate the safety and effectiveness of drugs, it is prudent to assume or ascertain the liability of similar side effects and contraindications.

(l) *Special packaging* as defined in section 2(4) of the Poison Prevention Packaging Act of 1970 means packaging that is designed or constructed to be significantly difficult for children under 5 years of age to open or obtain a toxic or harmful amount of the substance contained therein within a reasonable time and not difficult for normal adults to use properly, but does not mean packaging which all such children cannot open or obtain a toxic or harmful amount within a reasonable time.

(m) [Reserved]

(n) The term *radioactive drug* means any substance defined as a drug in section 201(g)(1) of the Federal Food, Drug, and Cosmetic Act which exhibits spontaneous disintegration of unstable nuclei with the emission of nuclear particles or photons and includes any nonradioactive reagent kit or nuclide generator which is intended to be used in the preparation of any such substance but does not include drugs such as carbon-containing compounds or potassium-containing salts which contain trace quantities of naturally occurring radionuclides. The term "radioactive drug" includes a "radioactive biological product" as defined in §600.3(ee) of this chapter.

[39 FR 11680, Mar. 29, 1974, as amended at 39 FR 20484, June 11, 1974; 40 FR 31307, July 25, 1975; 46 FR 8952, Jan. 27, 1981; 50 FR 7492, Feb. 22, 1985]

§310.4 Biologics; products subject to license control.

(a) If a drug has an approved license under section 351 of the Public Health Service Act (42 U.S.C. 262 *et seq.*) or under the animal virus, serum, and toxin law of March 4, 1913 (21 U.S.C. 151 *et seq.*), it is not required to have an approved application under section 505 of the act.

(b) To obtain marketing approval for radioactive biological products for human use, as defined in § 600.3(ee) of this chapter, manufacturers must comply with the provisions of § 601.2(a) of this chapter.

[64 FR 56448, Oct. 20, 1999, as amended at 70 FR 14981, Mar. 24, 2005]

§ 310.6 Applicability of "new drug" or safety or effectiveness findings in drug efficacy study implementation notices and notices of opportunity for hearing to identical, related, and similar drug products.

(a) The Food and Drug Administration's conclusions on the effectiveness of drugs are currently being published in the FEDERAL REGISTER as Drug Efficacy Study Implementation (DESI) Notices and as Notices of Opportunity for Hearing. The specific products listed in these notices include only those that were introduced into the market through the new drug procedures from 1938–62 and were submitted for review by the National Academy of Sciences-National Research Council (NAS-NRC), Drug Efficacy Study Group. Many products which are identical to, related to, or similar to the products listed in these notices have been marketed under different names or by different firms during this same period or since 1962 without going through the new drug procedures or the Academy review. Even though these products are not listed in the notices, they are covered by the new drug applications reviewed and thus are subject to these notices. All persons with an interest in a product that is identical, related, or similar to a drug listed in a drug efficacy notice or a notice of opportunity for a hearing will be given the same opportunity as the applicant to submit data and information, to request a hearing, and to participate in any hearing. It is not feasible for the Food and Drug Administration to list all products which are covered by an NDA and thus subject to each notice. However, it is essential that the findings and conclusions that a drug product is a

"new drug" or that there is a lack of evidence to show that a drug product is safe or effective be applied to all identical, related, and similar drug products to which they are reasonably applicable. Any product not in compliance with an applicable drug efficacy notice is in violation of section 505 (new drugs) and/or section 502 (misbranding) of the act.

(b)(1) An identical, related, or similar drug includes other brands, potencies, dosage forms, salts, and esters of the same drug moiety as well as of any drug moiety related in chemical structure or known pharmacological properties.

(2) Where experts qualified by scientific training and experience to evaluate the safety and effectiveness of drugs would conclude that the findings and conclusions, stated in a drug efficacy notice or notice of opportunity for hearing, that a drug product is a "new drug" or that there is a lack of evidence to show that a drug product is safe or effective are applicable to an identical, related, or similar drug product, such product is affected by the notice. A combination drug product containing a drug that is identical, related, or similar to a drug named in a notice may also be subject to the findings and conclusions in a notice that a drug product is a "new drug" or that there is a lack of evidence to show that a drug product is safe or effective.

(3) Any person may request an opinion on the applicability of such a notice to a specific product by writing to the Food and Drug Administration at the address shown in paragraph (e) of this section.

(c) Manufacturers and distributors of drugs should review their products as drug efficacy notices are published and assure that identical, related, or similar products comply with all applicable provisions of the notices.

(d) The published notices and summary lists of the conclusions are of particular interest to drug purchasing agents. These agents should take particular care to assure that the same purchasing policy applies to drug products that are identical, related, or similar to those named in the drug efficacy notices. The Food and Drug Administration applies the same regulatory policy to all such products. In many instances a determination can readily be made as to the applicability of a drug efficacy notice by an individual who is knowledgeable about drugs and their indications for use. Where the relationships are more subtle and not readily recognized, the purchasing agent may request an opinion by writing to the Food and Drug Administration at the address shown in paragraph (e) of this section.

(e) Interested parties may submit to the Food and Drug Administration, Center for Drug Evaluation and Research, Office of Compliance, 10903 New Hampshire Ave., Silver Spring, MD 20993–0002, the names of drug products, and of their manufacturers or distributors, that should be the subject of the same purchasing and regulatory policies as those reviewed by the Drug Efficacy Study Group. Appropriate action, including referral to purchasing officials of various government agencies, will be taken.

(f) This regulation does not apply to OTC drugs identical, similar, or related to a drug in the Drug Efficacy Study unless there has been or is notification in the FEDERAL REGISTER that a drug will not be subject to an OTC panel review pursuant to §§330.10, 330.11, and 330.5 of this chapter.

[39 FR 11680, Mar. 29, 1974, as amended at 48 FR 2755, Jan. 21, 1983; 50 FR 8996, Mar. 6, 1985; 55 FR 11578, Mar. 29, 1990; 74 FR 13113, Mar. 26, 2009]

Subpart B—Specific Administrative Rulings and Decisions

§310.100 New drug status opinions; statement of policy.

(a) Over the years since 1938 the Food and Drug Administration has given informal advice to inquirers as to the new drug status of preparations. These drugs have sometimes been identified only by general statements of composition. Generally, such informal opinions were incorporated in letters that did not explicitly relate all of the necessary conditions and qualifications such as the quantitative formula for the drug and the conditions under which it was prescribed, recommended, or suggested. This has contributed to misunderstanding and misinterpretation of such opinions.

(b) These informal opinions that an article is "not a new drug" or "no longer a new drug" require reexamination under the Kefauver-Harris Act (Public Law 87–781; 76 Stat. 788–89). In particular, when approval of a new drug application is withdrawn under provisions of section 505(e) of the Federal Food, Drug, and Cosmetic Act, a drug generally recognized as safe may become a "new drug" within the meaning of section 201(p) of said act as amended by the Kefauver-Harris Act on October 10, 1962. This is of special importance by reason of proposed actions to withdraw approval of new drug applications for lack of substantial evidence of effectiveness as a result of reports of the National Academy of Sciences—National Research Council on its review of drug effectiveness; for example, see the notice published in the FEDERAL REGISTER of January 23, 1968 (33 FR 818), regarding rutin, quercetin, et al.

(c) Any marketed drug is a "new drug" if any labeling change made after October 9, 1962, recommends or suggests new conditions of use under which the drug is not generally recognized as safe and effective by qualified experts. Undisclosed or unreported side effects as well as the emergence of new knowledge presenting questions with respect to the safety or effectiveness of a drug may result in its becoming a "new drug" even though it was previously considered "not a new drug." Any previously given informal advice that an article is "not a new drug" does not apply to such an article if it has been changed in formulation, manufacture control, or labeling in a way that may significantly affect the safety of the drug.

(d) For these reasons, all opinions previously given by the Food and Drug Administration to the effect that an article is "not a new drug" or is "no longer a new drug" are hereby revoked. This does not mean that all articles that were the subjects of such prior opinions will be regarded as new drugs. The prior opinions will be replaced by opinions of the Food and Drug Administration that are qualified and current on when an article is "not a new drug," as set forth in this subchapter.

[39 FR 11680, Mar. 29, 1974]

§ 310.103 New drug substances intended for hypersensitivity testing.

(a) The Food and Drug Administration is aware of the need in the practice of medicine for the ingredients of a new drug to be available for tests of hypersensitivity to such ingredients and therefore will not object to the shipment of a new drug substance, as defined in § 310.3(g), for such purpose if all of the following conditions are met:

(1) The shipment is made as a result of a specific request made to the manufacturer or distributor by a practitioner licensed by law to administer such drugs, and the use of such drugs for patch testing is not promoted by the manufacturer or distributor.

(2) The new drug substance requested is an ingredient in a marketed new drug and is not one that is an ingredient solely in a new drug that is legally available only under the investigational drug provisions of this part.

(3) The label bears the following prominently placed statements in lieu of adequate directions for use and in addition to complying with the other labeling provisions of the act:

(i) "Rx only"; and

(ii) "For use only in patch testing".

(4) The quantity shipped is limited to an amount reasonable for the purpose of patch testing in the normal course of the practice of medicine and is used solely for such patch testing.

(5) The new drug substance is manufactured by the same procedures and meets the same specifications as the component used in the finished dosage form.

(6) The manufacturer or distributor maintains records of all shipments for this purpose for a period of 2 years after shipment and will make them available to the Food and Drug Administration on request.

(b) When the requested new drug substance is intended for investigational use in humans or the substance is legally available only under the investigational drug provisions of part 312 of this chapter, the submission of an "Investigational New Drug Application" (IND) is required. The Food and Drug Administration will offer assistance to any practitioner wishing to submit an Investigational New Drug Application.

(c) This section does not apply to drugs or their components that are subject to the licensing requirements of the Public Health Service Act of 1944, as amended. (See subchapter F—Biologics, of this chapter.)

[39 FR 11680, Mar. 29, 1974, as amended at 55 FR 11578, Mar. 29, 1990; 67 FR 4907, Feb. 1, 2002]

Subpart C—New Drugs Exempted From Prescription-Dispensing Requirements

§ 310.200 Prescription-exemption procedure.

(a) *Duration of prescription requirement.* Any drug limited to prescription use under section 503(b)(1)(B) of the act remains so limited until it is exempted as provided in paragraph (b) or (e) of this section.

(b) *Prescription-exemption procedure for drugs limited by a new drug application.* Any drug limited to prescription use under section 503(b)(1)(B) of the act shall be exempted from prescription-dispensing requirements when Commissioner finds such requirements are not necessary for the protection of the public health by reason of the drug's toxicity or other potentiality for harmful effect, or the method of its use, or the collateral measures necessary to its use, and he finds that the drug is safe and effective for use in self-medication as directed in proposed labeling. A proposal to exempt a drug from the prescription-dispensing requirements of section 503(b)(1)(B) of the act may be initiated by the Commissioner or by any interested person. Any interested person may file a petition seeking such exemption, which petition may be pursuant to part 10 of this chapter, or in the form of a supplement to an approved new drug application.

(c) *New drug status of drugs exempted from the prescription requirement.* A drug exempted from the prescription requirement under the provisions of paragraph (b) of this section is a "new drug" within the meaning of section 201(p) of the act until it has been used to a material extent and for a material time under such conditions except as provided in paragraph (e) of this section.

(d) *Prescription legend not allowed on exempted drugs.* The use of the prescription caution statement quoted in section 503(b) (4) of the act, in the labeling of a drug exempted under the provisions of this section, constitutes misbranding. Any other statement or suggestion in the labeling of a drug exempted under this section, that such drug is limited to prescription use, may constitute misbranding.

(e) *Prescription-exemption procedure of OTC drug review.* A drug limited to prescription use under section 503(b)(1)(B) of the act may also be exempted from prescription-dispensing requirements by the procedure set forth in §330.13 of this chapter.

[39 FR 11680, Mar. 29, 1974, as amended at 41 FR 32582, Aug. 4, 1976; 42 FR 4714, Jan. 25, 1977; 42 FR 15674, Mar. 22, 1977; 72 FR 15043, Mar. 30, 2007]

§310.201 **Exemption for certain drugs limited by new-drug applications to prescription sale.**

(a) The prescription-dispensing requirements of section503(b)(1)(B) of the Federal Food, Drug, and Cosmetic Act are not necessary for the protection of the public health with respect to the following drugs subject to new drug applications:

(1) *N*-Acetyl-*p*-aminophenol (acetaminophen, *p*-hydroxy-acetanilid) preparations meeting all the following conditions:

(i) The *N*-acetyl-*p*-aminophenol is prepared, with or without other drugs, in tablet or other dosage form suitable for oral use in self-medication, and containing no drug limited to prescription sale under the provisions of section 503(b)(1) of the act.

(ii) The *N*-acetyl-*p*-aminophenol and all other components of the preparation meet their professed standards of identity, strength, quality, and purity.

(iii) If the preparation is a new drug, an application pursuant to section 505 (b) of the act is approved for it.

(iv) The preparation contains not more than 0.325 gram (5 grains) of *N*-acetyl-*p*-aminophenol per dosage unit, or if it is in liquid form not more than 100 milligrams of *N*-acetyl-*p*-aminophenol per milliliter.

(v) The preparation is labeled with adequate directions for use in minor conditions as a simple analgesic.

(vi) The dosages of *N*-acetyl-*p*-aminophenol recommended or suggested in the labeling do not exceed: For adults, 0.65 gram (10 grains) per dose or 2.6 grams (40 grains) per 24-hour period: for children 6 to 12 years of age, one-half of the maximum adult dose or dosage; for children 3 to 6 years of age, one-fifth of the maximum adult dose or dosage.

(vii) The labeling bears, in juxtaposition with the dosage recommendations, a clear warning statement against administration of the drug to children under 3 years of age and against use of the drug for more than 10 days, unless such uses are directed by a physician.

(viii) If the article is offered for use in arthritis or rheumatism, the labeling prominently bears a statement that the beneficial effects claimed are limited to the temporary relief of minor aches and pains of arthritis and rheumatism and, in juxtaposition with directions for use in such conditions, a conspicuous warning statement, such as "Caution: If pain persists for more than 10 days, or redness is present, or in conditions affecting children under 12 years of age, consult a physician immediately".

(2) Sodium gentisate (sodium-2, 5-dihydroxybenzoate) preparations meeting all the following conditions:

(i) The sodium gentisate is prepared, with or without other drugs, in tablet or other dosage form suitable for oral use in self-medication, and containing no drug limited to prescription sale under the provisions of section 503(b)(1) of the act.

(ii) The sodium gentisate and all other components of the preparation meet their professed standards of identity, strength, quality, and purity.

(iii) If the preparation is a new drug, an application pursuant to section 505(b) of the act is approved for it.

(iv) The preparation contains not more than 0.5 gram (7.7 grains) of anhydrous sodium gentisate per dosage unit.

(v) The preparation is labeled with adequate directions for use in minor conditions as a simple analgesic.

11

(vi) The dosages of sodium gentisate recommended or suggested in the labeling do not exceed: For adults, 0.5 gram (7.7 grains) per dose of 2.0 grams (31 grains) per 24-hour period; for children 6 to 12 years of age, one-half of the maximum adult dose or dosage.

(vii) The labeling bears, in juxtaposition with the dosage recommendations, a clear warning statement against administration of the drug to children under 6 years of age and against use of the drug for a prolonged period, except as such uses may be directed by a physician.

(3) Isoamylhydrocupreine and zolamine hydrochloride (N, N-dimethyl-N′-2-thiazolyl-N′-p-methoxybenzyl-ethylenediamine hydrochloride) preparations meeting all the following conditions:

(i) The isoamylhydrocupreine and zolamine hydrochloride are prepared in dosage form suitable for self-medication as rectal suppositories or as an ointment and containing no drug limited to prescription sale under the provisions of section 503(b)(1) of the act.

(ii) The isoamylhydrocupreine, zolamine hydrochloride, and all other components of the preparation meet their professed standards of identity, strength, quality, and purity.

(iii) If the preparation is a new drug, an application pursuant to section 505(b) of the act is approved for it.

(iv) The preparation contains not more than 0.25 percent of isoamylhydrocupreine and 1.0 percent of zolamine hydrochloride.

(v) If the preparation is in suppository form, it contains not more than 5.0 milligrams of isoamylhydrocupreine and not more than 20.0 milligrams of zolamine hydrochloride per suppository.

(vi) The preparation is labeled with adequate directions for use in the temporary relief of local pain and itching associated with hemorrhoids.

(vii) The directions provide for the use of not more than two suppositories or two applications of ointment in a 24-hour period.

(viii) The labeling bears, in juxtaposition with the dosage recommendations, a clear warning statement against use of the preparation in case of rectal bleeding, as this may indicate serious disease.

(4) Phenyltoloxamine dihydrogen citrate (N,N-dimethyl-(a-phenyl-O-toloxy) ethylamine dihydrogen citrate), preparations meeting all the following conditions:

(i) The phenyltoloxamine dihydrogen citrate is prepared, with or without other drugs, in tablet or other dosage form suitable for oral use in self-medication, and containing no drug limited to prescription sale under the provisions of section 503(b)(1) of the act.

(ii) The phenyltoloxamine dihydrogen citrate and all other components of the preparation meet their professed standards of identity, strength, quality, and purity.

(iii) If the preparation is a new drug, an application pursuant to section 505(b) of the act is approved for it.

(iv) The preparation contains not more than 88 milligrams of phenyltoloxamine dihydrogen citrate (equivalent to 50 milligrams of phenyltoloxamine) per dosage unit.

(v) The preparation is labeled with adequate directions for use in the temporary relief of the symptoms of hay fever and/or the symptoms of other minor conditions in which it is indicated.

(vi) The dosages recommended or suggested in the labeling do not exceed: For adults, 88 milligrams of phenyltoloxamine dihydrogen citrate (equivalent to 50 milligrams of phenyltoloxamine) per dose or 264 milligrams of phenyltoloxamine dihydrogen citrate (equivalent to 150 milligrams of phenyltoloxamine) per 24-hour period; for children 6 to 12 years of age, one-half of the maximum adult dose or dosage.

(vii) The labeling bears, in juxtaposition with the dosage recommendations:

(a) Clear warning statements against administration of the drug to children under 6 years of age, except as directed by a physician, and against driving a car or operating machinery while using the drug, since it may cause drowsiness.

(b) If the article is offered for temporary relief of the symptoms of colds, a statement that continued administration for such use should not exceed 3 days, except as directed by a physician.

(5)–(7) [Reserved]

(8) Dicyclomine hydrochloride (1-cyclohexylhexahydrobenzoic acid. β-diethylaminoethyl ester hydrochloride; diethylaminocarbethoxy-bicyclohexyl hydrochloride) preparations meeting all the following conditions:

(i) The dicyclomine hydrochloride is prepared with suitable antacid and other components, in tablet or other dosage form for oral use in self-medication, and containing no drug limited to prescription sale under the provisions of section 503(b)(1) of the act.

(ii) The dicyclomine hydrochloride and all other components of the preparation meet their professed standards of identity, strength, quality, and purity.

(iii) If the preparation is a new drug, an application pursuant to section 505(b) of the act is approved for it.

(iv) The preparation contains not more than 5 milligrams of dicyclomine hydrochloride per dosage unit, or if it is in liquid form not more than 0.5 milligram of dicyclomine hydrochloride per milliliter.

(v) The preparation is labeled with adequate directions for use only by adults and children over 12 years of age, in the temporary relief of gastric hyperacidity.

(vi) The dosages recommended or suggested in the directions for use do not exceed 10 milligrams of dicyclomine hydrochloride per dose or 30 milligrams in a 24-hour period.

(vii) The labeling bears, in juxtaposition with the dosage recommendations, clear warning statements against:

(a) Exceeding the recommended dosage.

(b) Prolonged use, except as directed by a physician, since persistent or recurring symptoms may indicate a serious disease requiring medical attention.

(c) Administration to children under 12 years of age except as directed by a physician.

(9)–(10) [Reserved]

(11) Hexadenol (a mixture of tetracosanes and their oxidation products) preparations meeting all the following conditions:

(i) The hexadenol is prepared and packaged, with or without other drugs, solvents, and propellants, in a form suitable for self-medication by external application to the skin as a spray, and containing no drug limited to prescription sale under the provisions of section 503(b)(1) of the act.

(ii) The hexadenol and all other components of the preparation meet their professed standards of identity, strength, quality, and purity.

(iii) If the preparation is a new drug, an application pursuant to section 505(b) of the act is approved for it.

(iv) The preparation contains not more than 5 percent by weight of hexadenol.

(v) The preparation is labeled with adequate directions for use by external application in the treatment of minor burns and minor skin irritations.

(vi) The labeling bears, in juxtaposition with the directions for use, clear warning statements against:

(a) Use on serious burns or skin conditions or prolonged use, except as directed by a physician.

(b) Spraying the preparation in the vicinity of eyes, mouth, nose, or ears.

(12) Sulfur dioxide preparations meeting all the following conditions:

(i) The sulfur dioxide is prepared with or without other drugs, in an aqueous solution packaged in a hermetic container suitable for use in self-medication by external application to the skin, and containing no drug limited to prescription sale under the provisions of section 503(b)(1) of the act.

(ii) The sulfur dioxide and all other components of the preparation meet their professed standards of identity, strength, quality, and purity.

(iii) If the preparation is a new drug, an application pursuant to section 505(b) of the act is approved for it.

(iv) The preparation contains not more than 5 grams of sulfur dioxide per 100 milliliters of solution.

(v) The preparation is labeled with adequate directions for use by external application to the smooth skin in the prevention or treatment of minor conditions in which it is indicated.

(vi) The directions for use recommend or suggest not more than two applications a day for not more than 1 week, except as directed by a physician.

(13)–(15) [Reserved]

(16) Tuaminoheptane sulfate (2-aminoheptane sulfate) preparations meeting all the following conditions:

(i) The tuaminoheptane sulfate is prepared, with or without other drugs, in an aqueous vehicle suitable for administration in self-medication as nose drops, and containing no drug limited to prescription sale under the provisions of section 503(b)(1) of the act.

(ii) The preparation is packaged with a style of container or assembly suited to self-medication by the recommended route of administration, and delivering not more than 0.1 milliliter of the preparation per drop.

(iii) The tuaminoheptane sulfate and all other components of the preparation meet their professed standards of identity, strength, quality, and purity.

(iv) If the preparation is a new drug, an application pursuant to section 505(b) of the act is approved for it.

(v) The tuaminoheptane sulfate content of the preparation does not exceed 10 milligrams per milliliter.

(vi) The preparation is labeled with adequate directions for use in the temporary relief of nasal congestion.

(vii) The dosages recommended or suggested in the directions for use do not exceed the equivalent: For adults, 5 drops of a 1 percent solution per nostril per dose, and 5 doses in a 24-hour period; for children 1 to 6 years of age, 3 drops of a 1 percent solution per nostril per dose, and 5 doses in a 24-hour period; for infants under 1 year of age, 2 drops of a 1 percent solution per nostril per dose, and 5 doses in a 24-hour period.

(viii) The labeling bears, in juxtaposition with the dosage recommendations:

(a) Clear warning statements against use of more than 5 doses daily, and against use longer than 4 days unless directed by a physician.

(b) A clear warning statement to the effect that frequent use may cause nervousness or sleeplessness, and that individuals with high blood pressure, heart disease, diabetes, or thyroid disease should not use the preparation unless directed by a physician.

(17) [Reserved]

(18) Vibesate (a mixture of copolymers of hydroxy-vinyl chlorideacetate, sebacic acid, and modified maleic rosin ester) preparations meeting all the following conditions.

(i) The vibesate is prepared and packaged, with or without other drugs, solvents, and propellants, in a form suitable for self-medication by external application to the skin as a spray, and containing no drug limited to prescription sale under the provisions of section 503(b)(1) of the act.

(ii) The vibesate and all other components of the preparation meet their professed standards of identity, strength, quality, and purity.

(iii) If the preparation is a new drug, an application pursuant to section 505(b) of the act is approved for it.

(iv) The preparation contains not more than 13 percent by weight of vibesate.

(v) The preparation is labeled with adequate directions for use by external application as a dressing for minor burns, minor cuts, or other minor skin irritations.

(vi) The labeling bears in juxtaposition with the directions for use clear warning statements against:

(a) Use on serious burns and on infected, deep, and puncture wounds unless directed by a physician.

(b) Spraying the preparation near the eyes or other mucous membranes.

(c) Inhaling the preparation.

(d) Use near open flames.

(e) Puncturing the container or throwing the container into fire.

(19) Pramoxine hydrochloride (4-N-butoxyphenyl γ-morpholinopropyl ether hydrochloride) preparations meeting all the following conditions:

(i) The pramoxine hydrochloride is prepared, with or without other drugs, in a dosage form suitable for use in self-medication by external application to the skin, and containing no drug limited to prescription sale under the provisions of section 503(b)(1) of the act.

(ii) The pramoxine hydrochloride and all other components of the preparation meet their professed standards of identity, strength, quality, and purity.

(iii) If the preparation is a new drug, an application pursuant to section 505(b) of the act is approved for it.

(iv) The preparation contains not more than 1.0 percent of pramoxine hydrochloride.

(v) The preparation is labeled with adequate directions for use by external application to the skin for the temporary relief of pain or itching due to minor burns and sunburn, nonpoisonous insect bites, and minor skin irritations.

(vi) The directions for use recommend or suggest not more than four applications of the preparation per day, unless directed by a physician.

(vii) The labeling bears, in juxtaposition with the directions for use, clear warning statements against:

(*a*) Prolonged use.

(*b*) Application to large areas of the body.

(*c*) Continued use if redness, irritation, swelling, or pain persists or increases, unless directed by a physician.

(*d*) Use in the eyes or nose.

(20) [Reserved]

(21) Pamabrom (2-amino-2-methyl-propanol-1-8-bromotheophyllinate) preparations meeting all the following conditions:

(i) The pamabrom is prepared with appropriate amounts of a suitable analgesic and with or without other drugs, in tablet or other dosage form suitable for oral use in self-medication, and containing no drug limited to prescription sale under the provisions of section 503(b)(1) of the act.

(ii) The pamabrom and all other components of the preparation meet their professed standards of identity, strength, quality, and purity.

(iii) If the preparation is a new drug, an application pursuant to section 505(b) of the act is approved for it.

(iv) The preparation contains not more than 50 milligrams of pamabrom per dosage unit.

(v) The preparation is labeled with adequate directions for use in the temporary relief of the minor pains and discomforts that may occur a few days before and during the menstrual period.

(vi) The dosages recommended or suggested in the labeling do not exceed 50 milligrams of pamabrom per dose or 200 milligrams per 24-hour period.

(22) Diphemanil methylsulfate (4-diphenylmethylene-1,1-dimethyl-piperidinium methylsulfate) preparations meeting all the following conditions:

(i) The diphemanil methylsulfate is prepared, with or without other drugs, in a dosage form suitable for use in self-medication by external application to the skin, and containing no drug limited to prescription sale under the provisions of section 503(b)(1) of the act.

(ii) The diphemanil methylsulfate and all other components of the preparation meet their professed standards of identity, strength, quality, and purity.

(iii) If the preparation is a new drug, an application pursuant to section 505(b) of the act is approved for it.

(iv) The preparation contains not more than 2.0 percent of diphemanil methylsulfate.

(v) The preparation is labeled with adequate directions for use by external application to the skin for the relief of symptoms of mild poison ivy, oak, and sumac and other minor irritations and itching of the skin.

(vi) The directions for use recommend or suggest not more than four applications of the preparation per day, unless directed by a physician.

(vii) The labeling bears, in juxtaposition with the directions for use, a clear warning statement, such as: "Caution: If redness, irritation, swelling, or pain persists or increases, discontinue use and consult physician."

(23) Dyclonine hydrochloride (4-butoxy-3-piperidinopropiophenone hydrochloride; 4-*n*-butoxy-β-piperidonopropiophenone hydrochloride) preparations meeting all the following conditions:

(i) The dyclonine hydrochloride is prepared, with or without other drugs, in a dosage form suitable for use as a cream or ointment in self-medication by external application to the skin, or rectally, and contains no drug limited to prescription sale under the provisions of section 503(b)(1) of the act.

(ii) The dyclonine hydrochloride and all other components of the preparation meet their professed standards of identity, strength, quality, and purity.

(iii) If the preparation is a new drug, an application pursuant to section 505(b) of the act is approved for it.

(iv) The preparation contains not more than 1.0 percent of dyclonine hydrochloride.

(v) The preparation is labeled with adequate directions for use:

(*a*) By external application to the skin for the temporary relief of pain and itching in sunburn, nonpoisonous insect bites, minor burns, cuts, abrasions, and other minor skin irritations.

(*b*) [Reserved]

(*c*) In the prevention or treatment of other minor conditions in which it is indicated.

(vi) The labeling bears, in juxtaposition with the directions for use, clear warning statements against:

(*a*) Continued use if redness, irritation, swelling, or pain persists or increases, unless directed by a physician.

(*b*) Use in case of rectal bleeding, as this may indicate serious disease.

(*c*) Use in the eyes.

(*d*) Prolonged use.

(*e*) Application to large areas of the body.

(*f*) Use for deep or puncture wounds or serious burns.

(24) Chlorothen citrate (chloromethapyrilene citrate; *N,N*-dimethyl-*N'*-(2-pyridyl)-*N'*-(5-chloro-2-thenyl) ethylenediamine citrate) preparations meeting all the following conditions:

(i) The chlorothen citrate is prepared, with or without other drugs, in tablet or other dosage form suitable for oral use in self-medication, and containing no drug limited to prescription sale under the provisions of section 503(b)(1) of the act.

(ii) The chlorothen citrate and all other components of the preparation meet their professed standards of identity, strength, quality, and purity.

(iii) If the preparation is a new drug, an application pursuant to section 505(b) of the act is approved for it.

(iv) The preparation contains not more than 25 milligrams of chlorothen citrate per dosage unit.

(v) The preparation is labeled with adequate directions for use in the temporary relief of the symptoms of hay fever and/or the symptoms of other minor conditions in which it is indicated.

(vi) The dosages recommended or suggested in the labeling do not exceed: For adults, 25 milligrams of chlorothen citrate per dose or 150 milligrams of chlorothen citrate per 24-hour period; for children 6 to 12 years of age, one-

half of the maximum adult dose or dosage.

(vii) The labeling bears, in juxtaposition with the dosage recommendations:

(*a*) Clear warning statements against administration of the drug to children under 6 years of age or exceeding the recommended dosage, unless directed by a physician, and against driving a car or operating machinery while using the drug, since it may cause drowsiness.

(*b*) If the article is offered for the temporary relief of symptoms of colds, a statement that continued administration for such use should not exceed 3 days, unless directed by a physician.

(25) [Reserved]

(26) Methoxyphenamine hydrochloride (β-(*o*-methoxyphenyl)-isopropyl-methylamine hydrochloride; 1-(*o*-methoxyphenyl)- 2-methylaminopropane hydrochloride) preparations meeting all the following conditions:

(i) The methoxyphenamine hydrochloride is prepared with appropriate amounts of a suitable antitussive, with or without other drugs, in a dosage form suitable for oral use in self-medication, and containing no drug limited to prescription sale under the provisions of section 503(b)(1) of the act.

(ii) The methoxyphenamine hydrochloride and all other components of the preparation meet their professed standards of identity, strength, quality, and purity.

(iii) If the preparation is a new drug, an application pursuant to section 505(b) of the act is approved for it.

(iv) The preparation contains not more than 3.5 milligrams of methoxyphenamine hydrochloride per milliliter.

(v) The preparation is labeled with adequate directions for use in the temporary relief of cough due to minor conditions in which it is indicated.

(vi) The dosages recommended or suggested in the labeling do not exceed: For adults, 35 milligrams of methoxyphenamine hydrochloride per dose or 140 milligrams of methoxyphenamine hydrochloride per 24-hour period; for children 6 to 12 years of age, one-half of the maximum adult dose or dosage.

(vii) The label bears a conspicuous warning to keep the drug out of the reach of children, and the labeling bears, in juxtaposition with the dosage recommendations:

(*a*) A clear warning statement against administration of the drug to children under 6 years of age, unless directed by a physician.

(*b*) A clear warning statement to the effect that frequent or prolonged use may cause nervousness, restlessness, or drowsiness, and that individuals with high blood pressure, heart disease, diabetes, or thyroid disease should not use the preparation unless directed by a physician.

(*c*) A clear warning statement against use of the drug in the presence of high fever or if cough persists, since persistent cough as well as high fever may indicate the presence of a serious condition.

(27) Biphenamine hydrochloride (β-diethylaminoethyl-3-phenyl-2-hydroxybenzoate hydrochloride) preparations meeting all the following conditions:

(i) The biphenamine hydrochloride is prepared in a form suitable for use as a shampoo and contains no drug limited to prescription sale under the provisions of section 503(b)(1) of the act.

(ii) The biphenamine hydrochloride meets its professed standards of identity, strength, quality, and purity.

(iii) If the preparation is a new drug, an application pursuant to section 505(b) of the act is approved for it.

(iv) The preparation contains not more than 1 percent of biphenamine hydrochloride.

(v) The preparation is labeled with adequate directions for use for the temporary relief of itching and scaling due to dandruff.

(vi) The label bears a conspicuous warning to keep the drug out of the reach of children.

(28) Tyloxapol (an alkylarylpolyether alcohol) and benzalkonium chloride ophthalmic preparations meeting all the following conditions:

(i) The tyloxapol and benzalkonium chloride are prepared, with other appropriate ingredients which are not drugs limited to prescription sale under the provisions of section 503(b)(1) of the act, as a sterile, isotonic aqueous solution suitable for use in self-medication on eye prostheses.

(ii) The preparation is so packaged as to volume and type of container as to

afford adequate protection and be suitable for self-medication with a minimum risk of contamination of the solution during use. Any dispensing unit is sterile and so packaged as to maintain sterility until the package is opened.

(iii) The tyloxapol, benzalkonium chloride, and other ingredients used to prepare the isotonic aqueous solution meet their professed standards of identity, strength, quality, and purity.

(iv) An application pursuant to section 505(b) of the act is approved for the drug.

(v) The preparation contains 0.25 percent of tyloxapol and 0.02 percent of benzalkonium chloride.

(vi) The label bears a conspicuous warning to keep the drug out of the reach of children and the labeling bears, in juxtaposition with the dosage recommendations, a clear warning that if irritation occurs, persists, or increases, use of the drug should be discontinued and a physician consulted. The labeling includes a statement that the dropper or other dispensing tip should not touch any surface, since this may contaminate the solution.

(29) [Reserved]

(b) [Reserved]

[39 FR 11680, Mar. 29, 1974, as amended at 42 FR 36994, July 19, 1977; 52 FR 15892, Apr. 30, 1987; 52 FR 30055, Aug. 12, 1987; 55 FR 31779, Aug. 3, 1990; 57 FR 58374, Dec. 9, 1992; 58 FR 49898, Sept. 23, 1993; 59 FR 4218, Jan. 28, 1994; 60 FR 52507, Oct. 6, 1995; 72 FR 15043, Mar. 30, 2007; 72 FR 67640, Nov. 30, 2007]

Subpart D—Records and Reports

§310.303 Continuation of long-term studies, records, and reports on certain drugs for which new drug applications have been approved.

(a) A new drug may not be approved for marketing unless it has been shown to be safe and effective for its intended use(s). After approval, the applicant is required to establish and maintain records and make reports related to clinical experience or other data or information necessary to make or facilitate a determination of whether there are or may be grounds under section 505(e) of the act for suspending or withdrawing approval of the application. Some drugs, because of the nature of the condition for which they are intended, must be used for long periods of time—even a lifetime. To acquire necessary data for determining the safety and effectiveness of long-term use of such drugs, extensive animal and clinical tests are required as a condition of approval. Nonetheless, the therapeutic or prophylactic usefulness of such drugs may make it inadvisable in the public interest to delay the availability of the drugs for widespread clinical use pending completion of such long-term studies. In such cases, the Food and Drug Administration may approve the new drug application on condition that the necessary long-term studies will be conducted and the results recorded and reported in an organized fashion. The procedures required by paragraph (b) of this section will be followed in order to list such a drug in § 310.304.

(b) A proposal to require additional or continued studies with a drug for which a new drug application has been approved may be made by the Commissioner on his own initiative or on the petition of any interested person, pursuant to part 10 of this chapter. Prior to issuance of such a proposal, the applicant will be provided an opportunity for a conference with representatives of the Food and Drug Administration. When appropriate, investigators or other individuals may be invited to participate in the conference. All requirements for special studies, records, and reports will be published in § 310.304.

[39 FR 11680, Mar. 29, 1974, as amended at 41 FR 4714, Jan. 25, 1976; 42 FR 15674, Mar. 22, 1977]

§ 310.305 Records and reports concerning adverse drug experiences on marketed prescription drugs for human use without approved new drug applications.

(a) *Scope.* FDA is requiring manufacturers, packers, and distributors of marketed prescription drug products that are not the subject of an approved new drug or abbreviated new drug application to establish and maintain records and make reports to FDA of all serious, unexpected adverse drug experiences associated with the use of their drug products. Any person subject to

the reporting requirements of paragraph (c) of this section shall also develop written procedures for the surveillance, receipt, evaluation, and reporting of postmarketing adverse drug experiences to FDA.

(b) *Definitions.* The following definitions of terms apply to this section:

Adverse drug experience. Any adverse event associated with the use of a drug in humans, whether or not considered drug related, including the following: An adverse event occurring in the course of the use of a drug product in professional practice; an adverse event occurring from drug overdose whether accidental or intentional; an adverse event occurring from drug abuse; an adverse event occurring from drug withdrawal; and any failure of expected pharmacological action.

Disability. A substantial disruption of a person's ability to conduct normal life functions.

Life-threatening adverse drug experience. Any adverse drug experience that places the patient, in the view of the initial reporter, at *immediate* risk of death from the adverse drug experience as it occurred, *i.e.*, it does not include an adverse drug experience that, had it occurred in a more severe form, might have caused death.

Serious adverse drug experience. Any adverse drug experience occurring at any dose that results in any of the following outcomes: Death, a life-threatening adverse drug experience, inpatient hospitalization or prolongation of existing hospitalization, a persistent or significant disability/incapacity, or a congenital anomaly/birth defect. Important medical events that may not result in death, be life-threatening, or require hospitalization may be considered a serious adverse drug experience when, based upon appropriate medical judgment, they may jeopardize the patient or subject and may require medical or surgical intervention to prevent one of the outcomes listed in this definition. Examples of such medical events include allergic bronchospasm requiring intensive treatment in an emergency room or at home, blood dyscrasias or convulsions that do not result in inpatient hospitalization, or the development of drug dependency or drug abuse.

Unexpected adverse drug experience. Any adverse drug experience that is not listed in the current labeling for the drug product. This includes events that may be symptomatically and pathophysiologically related to an event listed in the labeling, but differ from the event because of greater severity or specificity. For example, under this definition, hepatic necrosis would be unexpected (by virtue of greater severity) if the labeling only referred to elevated hepatic enzymes or hepatitis. Similarly, cerebral thromboembolism and cerebral vasculitis would be unexpected (by virtue of greater specificity) if the labeling only listed cerebral vascular accidents. "Unexpected," as used in this definition, refers to an adverse drug experience that has not been previously observed (*i.e.*, included in the labeling) rather than from the perspective of such experience not being anticipated from the pharmacological properties of the pharmaceutical product.

(c) *Reporting requirements.* Each person identified in paragraph (c)(1)(i) of this section shall report to FDA adverse drug experience information as described in this section and shall submit one copy of each report to the Central Document Room, Center for Drug Evaluation and Research, Food and Drug Administration, 5901–B Ammendale Rd., Beltsville, MD 20705–1266.

(1) *Postmarketing 15-day "Alert reports".* (i) Any person whose name appears on the label of a marketed prescription drug product as its manufacturer, packer, or distributor shall report to FDA each adverse drug experience received or otherwise obtained that is both serious and unexpected as soon as possible, but in no case later than 15 calendar days of initial receipt of the information by the person whose name appears on the label. Each report shall be accompanied by a copy of the current labeling for the drug product.

(ii) A person identified in paragraph (c)(1)(i) of this section is not required to submit a 15-day "Alert report" for an adverse drug experience obtained from a postmarketing study (whether or not conducted under an investigational new drug application) unless the applicant concludes that there is a reasonable possibility that the drug caused the adverse experience.

(2) *Postmarketing 15-day "Alert reports"—followup.* Each person identified in paragraph (c)(1)(i) of this section shall promptly investigate all serious, unexpected adverse drug experiences that are the subject of these postmarketing 15-day Alert reports and shall submit followup reports within 15 calendar days of receipt of new information or as requested by FDA. If additional information is not obtainable, records should be maintained of the unsuccessful steps taken to seek additional information. Postmarketing 15-day Alert reports and followups to them shall be submitted under separate cover.

(3) *Submission of reports.* To avoid unnecessary duplication in the submission of, and followup to, reports required in this section, a packer's or distributor's obligations may be met by submission of all reports of serious adverse drug experiences to the manufacturer of the drug product. If a packer or distributor elects to submit these adverse drug experience reports to the manufacturer rather than to FDA, it shall submit each report to the manufacturer within 5 calendar days of its receipt by the packer or distributor, and the manufacturer shall then comply with the requirements of this section even if its name does not appear on the label of the drug product. Under this circumstance, the packer or distributor shall maintain a record of this action which shall include:

(i) A copy of each adverse drug experience report;

(ii) The date the report was received by the packer or distributor;

(iii) The date the report was submitted to the manufacturer; and

(iv) The name and address of the manufacturer.

(4) Each report submitted to FDA under this section shall bear prominent identification as to its contents, *i.e.*, "15-day Alert report," or "15-day Alert report-followup."

(5) A person identified in paragraph (c)(1)(i) of this section is not required to resubmit to FDA adverse drug experience reports forwarded to that person

by FDA; however, the person must submit all *followup* information on such reports to FDA.

(d) *Reporting form.* (1) Except as provided in paragraph (d)(3) of this section, each person identified in paragraph (c)(1)(i) of this section shall submit each report of a serious and unexpected adverse drug experience on an FDA Form 3500A (foreign events may be submitted either on an FDA Form 3500A or, if preferred, on a CIOMS I form).

(2) Each completed FDA Form 3500A should pertain only to an individual patient.

(3) Instead of using Form FDA Form 3500A, a manufacturer, packer, or distributor may use a computer-generated FDA Form 3500A or other alternative format (e.g., a computer-generated tape or tabular listing) provided that:

(i) The content of the alternative format is equivalent in all elements of information to those specified in FDA Form 3500A, and

(ii) The format is agreed to in advance by MedWatch: The FDA Medical Products Reporting Program.

(4) FDA Form 3500A and instructions for completing the form are available on the Internet at *http://www.fda.gov/medwatch/index.html.*

(e) *Patient privacy.* Manufacturers, packers, and distributors should not include in reports under this section the names and addresses of individual patients; instead, the manufacturer, packer, and distributor should assign a unique code number to each report, preferably not more than eight characters in length. The manufacturer, packer, and distributor should include the name of the reporter from whom the information was received. Names of patients, individual reporters, health care professionals, hospitals, and geographical identifiers in adverse drug experience reports are not releasable to the public under FDA's public information regulations in part 20 of this chapter.

(f) *Recordkeeping.* (1) Each manufacturer, packer, and distributor shall maintain for a period of 10 years records of all adverse drug experiences required under this section to be reported, including raw data and any correspondence relating to the adverse drug experiences, and the records required to be maintained under paragraph (c)(4) of this section.

(2) Manufacturers and packers may retain the records required in paragraph (f)(1) of this section as part of its complaint files maintained under § 211.198 of this chapter.

(3) Manufacturers, packers, and distributors shall permit any authorized FDA employee, at all reasonable times, to have access to and copy and verify the records established and maintained under this section.

(g) *Disclaimer.* A report or information submitted by a manufacturer, packer, or distributor under this section (and any release by FDA of that report or information) does not necessarily reflect a conclusion by the manufacturer, packer, or distributor, or by FDA, that the report or information constitutes an admission that the drug caused or contributed to an adverse effect. The manufacturer, packer, or distributor need not admit, and may deny, that the report or information submitted under this section constitutes an admission that the drug caused or contributed to an adverse effect.

[51 FR 24479, July 3, 1986, as amended at 52 FR 37936, Oct. 13, 1987; 55 FR 11578, Mar. 29, 1990; 57 FR 17980, Apr. 28, 1992; 62 FR 34167, June 25, 1997; 62 FR 52249, Oct. 7, 1997; 67 FR 9585, Mar. 4, 2002; 74 FR 13113, Mar. 26, 2009]

EFFECTIVE DATE NOTE: At 79 FR 33087, June 10, 2014, § 310.305 was amended by:

a. Removing the word "shall" each time it appears and by adding in its place the word "must";

b. Adding alphabetically in paragraph (b) the definitions of "Individual case safety report (ICSR)" and "ICSR attachments";

c. Revising paragraph (c) introductory text, paragraph (c)(1)(i), and the second sentence of paragraph (c)(3) introductory text; removing the last sentence in paragraph (c)(2), and removing and reserving paragraph (c)(4);

d. Revising paragraph (d); and

e. Redesignating paragraphs (e) through (g) as paragraphs (f) through (h), adding a new paragraph (e), revising newly redesignated paragraph (f), and in newly redesignated paragraph (g)(1) removing "(c)(4)" and adding in its place "(c)(3)", effective June 10, 2015. For the convenience of the user, the added and revised text is set forth as follows:

§ 310.305 Records and reports concerning adverse drug experiences on marketed prescription drugs for human use without approved new drug applications.

*   *   *   *   *

(b) * * *

Individual case safety report (ICSR). A description of an adverse drug experience related to an individual patient or subject.

ICSR attachments. Documents related to the adverse drug experience described in an ICSR, such as medical records, hospital discharge summaries, or other documentation.

*   *   *   *   *

(c) *Reporting requirements.* Each person identified in paragraph (c)(1)(i) of this section must submit to FDA adverse drug experience information as described in this section. Except as provided in paragraph (e)(2) of this section, 15-day "Alert reports" and followup reports, including ICSRs and any ICSR attachments, must be submitted to the Agency in electronic format as described in paragraph (e)(1) of this section.

(1) *Postmarketing 15-day "Alert reports".* (i) Any person whose name appears on the label of a marketed prescription drug product as its manufacturer, packer, or distributor must report to FDA each adverse drug experience received or otherwise obtained that is both serious and unexpected as soon as possible, but no later than 15 calendar days from initial receipt of the information by the person whose name appears on the label. Each report must be accompanied by the current content of labeling in electronic format as an ICSR attachment unless it is already on file at FDA.

*   *   *   *   *

(3) *Submission of reports.* * * * If a packer or distributor elects to submit these adverse drug experience reports to the manufacturer rather than to FDA, it must submit, by any appropriate means, each report to the manufacturer within 5 calendar days of its receipt by the packer or distributor, and the manufacturer must then comply with the requirements of this section even if its name does not appear on the label of the drug product.
* * *

*   *   *   *   *

(4) [Reserved]

*   *   *   *   *

(d) *Information reported on ICSRs.* ICSRs include the following information:

(1) *Patient information.*
(i) Patient identification code;
(ii) Patient age at the time of adverse drug experience, or date of birth;
(iii) Patient gender; and
(iv) Patient weight.

(2) *Adverse drug experience.*
(i) Outcome attributed to adverse drug experience;
(ii) Date of adverse drug experience;
(iii) Date of ICSR submission;
(iv) Description of adverse drug experience (including a concise medical narrative);
(v) Adverse drug experience term(s);
(vi) Description of relevant tests, including dates and laboratory data; and
(vii) Other relevant patient history, including preexisting medical conditions.

(3) *Suspect medical product(s).*
(i) Name;
(ii) Dose, frequency, and route of administration used;
(iii) Therapy dates;
(iv) Diagnosis for use (indication);
(v) Whether the product is a combination product as defined in § 3.2(e) of this chapter;
(vi) Whether the product is a prescription or nonprescription product;
(vii) Whether adverse drug experience abated after drug use stopped or dose reduced;
(viii) Whether adverse drug experience reappeared after reintroduction of drug;
(ix) Lot number;
(x) Expiration date;
(xi) National Drug Code (NDC) number; and
(xii) Concomitant medical products and therapy dates.

(4) *Initial reporter information.*
(i) Name, address, and telephone number;
(ii) Whether the initial reporter is a health care professional; and
(iii) Occupation, if a health care professional.

(5) *Manufacturer, packer, or distributor information.*
(i) Manufacturer, packer, or distributor name and contact office address;
(ii) Telephone number;
(iii) Report source, such as spontaneous, literature, or study;
(iv) Date the report was received by manufacturer, packer, or distributor;
(v) Whether the ICSR is a 15-day "Alert report";
(vi) Whether the ICSR is an initial report or followup report; and
(vii) Unique case identification number, which must be the same in the initial report and any subsequent followup report(s).

(e) *Electronic format for submissions.* (1) Each report required to be submitted to FDA under this section, including the ICSR and any ICSR attachments, must be submitted in an electronic format that FDA can process, review, and archive. FDA will issue guidance on how to provide the electronic submission (e.g., method of transmission, media, file formats, preparation and organization of files).

(2) Each person identified in paragraph (c)(1)(i) of this section may request, in writing, a temporary waiver of the requirements in paragraph (e)(1) of this section. These waivers will be granted on a limited basis for good cause shown. FDA will issue guidance on requesting a waiver of the requirements in paragraph (e)(1) of this section.

(f) *Patient privacy.* Manufacturers, packers, and distributors should not include in reports under this section the names and addresses of individual patients; instead, the manufacturer, packer, and distributor should assign a unique code for identification of the patient. The manufacturer, packer, and distributor should include the name of the reporter from whom the information was received as part of the initial reporter information, even when the reporter is the patient. The names of patients, individual reporters, health care professionals, hospitals, and geographical identifiers in adverse drug experience reports are not releasable to the public under FDA's public information regulations in part 20 of this chapter.

*   *   *   *   *

Subpart E—Requirements for Specific New Drugs or Devices

§ 310.501 Patient package inserts for oral contraceptives.

(a) *Requirement for a patient package insert.* The safe and effective use of oral contraceptive drug products requires that patients be fully informed of the benefits and the risks involved in their use. An oral contraceptive drug product that does not comply with the requirements of this section is misbranded under section 502 of the Federal Food, Drug, and Cosmetic Act. Each dispenser of an oral contraceptive drug product shall provide a patient package insert to each patient (or to an agent of the patient) to whom the product is dispensed, except that the dispenser may provide the insert to the parent or legal guardian of a legally incompetent patient (or to the agent of either). The patient package insert is required to be placed in or accompany each package dispensed to the patient.

(b) *Distribution requirements.* (1) For oral contraceptive drug products, the manufacturer and distributor shall provide a patient package insert in or with each package of the drug product that the manufacturer or distributor intends to be dispensed to a patient.

(2) Patient package inserts for oral contraceptives dispensed in acute-care hospitals or long-term care facilities will be considered to have been provided in accordance with this section if provided to the patient before administration of the first oral contraceptive and every 30 days thereafter, as long as the therapy continues.

(c) *Contents of patient package insert.* A patient package insert for an oral contraceptive drug product is required to contain the following:

(1) The name of the drug.

(2) A summary including a statement concerning the effectiveness of oral contraceptives in preventing pregnancy, the contraindications to the drug's use, and a statement of the risks and benefits associated with the drug's use.

(3) A statement comparing the effectiveness of oral contraceptives to other methods of contraception.

(4) A boxed warning concerning the increased risks associated with cigarette smoking and oral contraceptive use.

(5) A discussion of the contraindications to use, including information that the patient should provide to the prescriber before taking the drug.

(6) A statement of medical conditions that are not contraindications to use but deserve special consideration in connection with oral contraceptive use and about which the patient should inform the prescriber.

(7) A warning regarding the most serious side effects of oral contraceptives.

(8) A statement of other serious adverse reactions and potential safety hazards that may result from the use of oral contraceptives.

(9) A statement concerning common, but less serious side effects which may help the patient evaluate the benefits and risks from the use of oral contraceptives.

(10) Information on precautions the patients should observe while taking oral contraceptives, including the following:

(i) A statement of risks to the mother and unborn child from the use of oral contraceptives before or during early pregnancy;

(ii) A statement concerning excretion of the drug in human milk and associated risks to the nursing infant;

(iii) A statement about laboratory tests which may be affected by oral contraceptives; and

(iv) A statement that identifies activities and drugs, foods, or other substances the patient should avoid because of their interactions with oral contraceptives.

(11) Information about how to take oral contraceptives properly, including information about what to do if the patient forgets to take the product, information about becoming pregnant after discontinuing use of the drug, a statement that the drug product has been prescribed for the use of the patient and should not be used for other conditions or given to others, and a statement that the patient's pharmacist or practitioner has a more technical leaflet about the drug product that the patient may ask to review.

(12) A statement of the possible benefits associated with oral contraceptive use.

(13) The following information about the drug product and the patient package insert:

(i) The name and place of business of the manufacturer, packer, or distributor, or the name and place of business of the dispenser of the product.

(ii) The date, identified as such, of the most recent revision of the patient package insert placed prominently immediately after the last section of the labeling.

(d) *Other indications.* The patient package insert may identify indications in addition to contraception that are identified in the professional labeling for the drug product.

(e) *Labeling guidance texts.* The Food and Drug Administration issues informal labeling guidance texts under §10.90(b)(9) of this chapter to provide assistance in meeting the requirements of this section. A request for a copy of the guidance texts should be directed to the Center for Drug Evaluation and Research, Division of Reproductive and Urologic Products, Food and Drug Administration, 10903 New Hampshire Ave., Silver Spring, MD 20993–0002.

(f) *Requirement to supplement approved application.* Holders of approved applications for oral contraceptive drug products that are subject to the requirements of this section are required to submit supplements under §314.70(c) of this chapter to provide for the labeling required by this section. Such labeling may be put into use without advance approval by the Food and Drug Administration.

[54 FR 22587, May 25, 1989, as amended at 74 FR 13113, Mar. 26, 2009]

§310.502 **Certain drugs accorded new drug status through rulemaking procedures.**

(a) The drugs listed in this paragraph have been determined by rulemaking procedures to be new drugs within the meaning of section 201(p) of the act. An approved new drug application under section 505 of the act and part 314 of this chapter is required for marketing the following drugs:

(1) Aerosol drug products for human use containing 1,1,1-trichloroethane.

(2) Aerosol drug products containing zirconium.

(3) Amphetamines (amphetamine, dextroamphetamine, and their salts, and levamfetamine and its salts) for human use.

(4) Camphorated oil drug products.

(5) Certain halogenated salicylanilides (tribromsalan (TBS, 3,4′,5-tribromosalicylanilide), dibromsalan (DBS, 4′, 5-dibromosalicylanilide), metabromsalan (MBS, 3, 5-dibromosalicylanilide), and 3,3′, 4,5′-tetrachlorosalicylanilide (TC-SA)) as an ingredient in drug products.

(6) Chloroform used as an ingredient (active or inactive) in drug products.

(7) Cobalt preparations intended for use by man.

(8) Intrauterine devices for human use for the purpose of contraception that incorporate heavy metals, drugs, or other active substances.

(9) Oral prenatal drugs containing fluorides intended for human use.

(10) Parenteral drug products in plastic containers.

(11) Sterilization of drugs by irradiation.

(12) Sweet spirits of nitre drug products.

(13) Thorium dioxide for drug use.

(14) Timed release dosage forms.

(15) Vinyl chloride as an ingredient, including propellant, in aerosol drug products.

(b) [Reserved]

[62 FR 12084, Mar. 14, 1997, as amended at 64 FR 401, Jan. 5, 1999]

§ 310.503 Requirements regarding certain radioactive drugs.

(a) On January 8, 1963 (28 FR 183), the Commissioner of Food and Drugs exempted investigational radioactive new drugs from part 312 of this chapter provided they were shipped in complete conformity with the regulations issued by the Nuclear Regulatory Commission. This exemption also applied to investigational radioactive biologics.

(b) It is the opinion of the Nuclear Regulatory Commission, and the Food and Drug Administration that this exemption should not apply for certain specific drugs and that these drugs should be appropriately labeled for uses for which safety and effectiveness can be demonstrated by new drug applications or through licensing under the Public Health Service Act (42 U.S.C. 262 et seq.) in the case of biologics. Continued distribution under the investigational exemption when the drugs are intended for established uses will not be permitted.

(c) Based on its experience in regulating investigational radioactive pharmaceuticals, the Nuclear Regulatory Commission has compiled a list of reactor-produced isotopes for which it considers that applicants may reasonably be expected to submit adequate evidence of safety and effectiveness for use as recommended in appropriate labeling. Such use may include, among others, the uses in this tabulation:

Isotope	Chemical form	Use
Chromium 51 ...	Chromate	Spleen scans.
Do	......do	Placenta localization.
Do	......do	Red blood cell labeling and survival studies.
Do	Labeled human serum albumin.	Gastrointestinal protein loss studies.
Do	......do	Placenta localization.
Do	Labeled red blood cells.	Do.
Cobalt 58 or Cobalt 60.	Labeled cyanocobalamin.	Intestinal absorption studies.
Gold 198	Colloidal	Liver scans.
Do	......do	Intracavitary treatment of pleural effusions and/or ascites.
Do	......do	Interstitial treatment of cancer.
Iodine 131	Iodide	Diagnosis of thyroid functions.
Do	......do	Thyroid scans.
Do	......do	Treatment of hyperthyroidism and/or cardiac dysfunction.
Do	......do	Treatment of thyroid carcinoma.
Do	Iodinated human serum albumin.	Blood volume determinations.
Do	......do	Cisternography.
Do	......do	Brain tumor localization.
Do	......do	Placenta localization.
Do	......do	Cardiac scans for determination of pericardial effusions.
Do	Rose Bengal	Liver function studies.
Do	......do	Liver scans.
Do	Iodopyracet, sodium iodohippurate, sodium diatrizoate, diatrizoate methylglucamine, sodium diprotrizoate, sodium acetrizoate, or sodium iothalamate.	Kidney function studies and kidney scans.
Do	Labeled fats and/or fatty acids.	Fat absorption studies.
Do	Cholografin	Cardiac scans for determination of pericardial effusions.
Do	Macroaggregated iodinated human serum albumin.	Lung scans.
Do	Colloidal microaggregated human serum albumin.	Liver scans.
Iodine 125	Iodide	Diagnosis of thyroid function.
Do	Iodinated human serum albumin.	Blood volume determinations.
Do	Rose Bengal	Liver function studies.
Do	Iodopyracet, sodium iodohippurate, sodium diatrizoate, diatrizoate methylglucamine, sodium diprotrizoate, sodium acetrizoate, or sodium iothalamate.	Kidney function studies.
Do	Labeled fats and/or fatty acids.	Fat absorption studies.
Iron 59	Chloride, citrate and/or sulfate.	Iron turnover studies.
Krypton 85	Gas	Diagnosis of cardiac abnormalities.
Mercury 197	Chlormerodrin	Kidney scans.
Do	......do	Brain scans.

Isotope	Chemical form	Use
Mercury 203 [1] ..	......do	Kidney scans.
Do	......do	Brain scans.
Phosphorus 32	Soluble phosphate ..	Treatment of polycythemia vera.
Do	......do	Treatment of leukemia and bone metastasis.
Do	Colloidal chromic phosphate.	Intracavitary treatment of pleural effusions and/or ascites.
Do	......do	Interstitial treatment of cancer.
Potassium 42 ..	Chloride	Potassium space studies.
Selenium 75	Labeled methionine	Pancreas scans.
Strontium 85	Nitrate or chloride ...	Bone scans on patients with diagnosed cancer.
Technetium 99m.	Pertechnetate	Brain scans.
Do	......do	Thyroid scans.
Do	Sulfur colloid	Liver and spleen scans.
Do	Pertechnetate	Placenta localization.
Do	......do	Blood pool scans.
Do	......do	Salivary gland scans.
Do	Diethylenetri-amine pentaacetic acid (DTPA).	Kidney scans.
Xenon 133	Gas	Diagnosis of cardia abnormalities. Cerebral blood-flow studies. Pulmonary function studies. Muscle bloodflow studies.

[1] This item has been removed from the AEC list for kidney scans but is included as the requirements of this order are applicable.

(d)(1) In view of the extent of experience with the isotopes listed in paragraph (c) of this section, the Nuclear Regulatory Commission and the Food and Drug Administration conclude that such isotopes should not be distributed under investigational-use labeling when they are actually intended for use in medical practice.

(2) The exemption referred to in paragraph (a) of this section, as applied to any drug or biologic containing any of the isotopes listed in paragraph (c) of this section, in the "chemical form" and intended for the uses stated, is terminated on March 3, 1972, except as provided in paragraph (d)(3) of this section.

(3) The exemption referred to in paragraph (a) of this section, as applied to any drug or biologic containing any of the isotopes listed in paragraph (c) of this section, in the "chemical form" and intended for the uses stated, for

which drug a new drug application or a "Investigational New Drug Application" was submitted prior to March 3, 1972, or for which biologic an application for product license or "Investigational New Drug Application" was submitted prior to March 3, 1972, is terminated on August 20, 1976, unless an approvable notice was issued on or before August 20, 1976, in which case the exemption is terminated either upon the subsequent issuance of a nonapprovable notice for the new drug application or on November 20, 1976, whichever occurs first.

(e) No exemption from section 505 of the act or from part 312 of this chapter is in effect or has been in effect for radioactive drugs prepared from accelerator-produced radioisotopes, naturally occurring isotopes, or nonradioactive substances used in conjunction with isotopes.

(f)(1) Based on its experience in regulating investigational radioactive pharmaceuticals, the Nuclear Regulatory Commission has compiled a list of reactor-produced isotopes for which it considers that applicants may reasonably be expected to submit adequate evidence of safety and effectiveness for use as recommended in appropriate labeling; such use may include, among others, the uses in this tabulation:

Isotope	Chemical form	Use
Fluorine 18	Fluoride	Bone imaging.
Indium-113m ...	Diethylenetriamine pentaacetic acid (DTPA).	Brain imaging; kidney imaging.
Do	Chloride	Placenta imaging; blood pool imaging.
Technetium 99m.	Human serum albumin microspheres.	Lung imaging.
Do	Diethylenetriamine pentaacetic acid (Sn).	Kidney imaging; kidney function studies.
Do	......do	Brain imaging.
Do	Polyphosphates	Bone imaging.
Do	Technetated aggregated albumin (human).	Lung imaging.
Do	Disodium etidronate	Bone imaging.

(2) In view of the extent of experience with the isotopes listed in paragraph (f)(1) of this section, the Nuclear Regulatory Commission and the Food and Drug Administration conclude that they should not be distributed under investigational-use labeling when they

25

are actually intended for use in medical practice.

(3) Any manufacturer or distributor interested in continuing to ship in interstate commerce drugs containing the isotopes listed in paragraph (f)(1) of this section for any of the indications listed, shall submit, on or before August 25, 1975 to the Center for Drug Evaluation and Research, Food and Drug Administration, 5600 Fishers Lane, Rockville, MD 20857, a new drug application or a "Investigational New Drug Application" for each such drug for which the manufacturer or distributor does not have an approved new drug application pursuant to section 505(b) of the act. If the drug is a biologic, a "Investigational New Drug Application" or an application for a license under section 351 of the Public Health Service Act shall be submitted to the Center for Biologics Evaluation and Research, Food and Drug Administration, 8800 Rockville Pike, Bethesda, MD 20014, in lieu of any submission to the Center for Drug Evaluation and Research.

(4) The exemption referred to in paragraph (a) of this section, as applied to any drug or biologic containing any of the isotopes listed in paragraph (f)(1) of this section, in the "chemical form" and intended for the uses stated, is terminated on August 26, 1975 except as provided in paragraph (f)(5) of this section.

(5)(i) Except as provided in paragraph (f)(5)(ii) of this section, the exemption referred to in paragraph (a) of this section, as applied to any drug containing any of the isotopes listed in paragraph (f)(1) of this section, in the "chemical form" and intended for the uses stated, for which drug a new drug application or "Investigational New Drug Application" was submitted to the Center for Drug Evaluation and Research on or before August 25, 1975 is terminated on August 20, 1976, unless an approvable notice was issued on or before August 20, 1976, in which case the exemption is terminated either upon the subsequent issuance of a nonapprovable notice for the new drug application or on November 20, 1976, whichever occurs first.

(ii) The exemption referred to in paragraph (a) of this section, as applied to any biologic containing any of the isotopes listed in paragraph (f)(1) of this section in the "chemical form" and intended for the uses stated, for which biologic an application for product license or "Investigational New Drug Application" was submitted to the Center for Biologics Evaluation and Research on or before August 25, 1975 is terminated on October 20, 1976, unless an approvable notice was issued on or before October 20, 1976, in which case the exemption is terminated either upon the subsequent issuance of a nonapprovable notice for the new drug application or on January 20, 1977, whichever occurs first.

(g) The exemption referred to in paragraph (a) of this section, as applied to any drug intended solely for investigational use as part of a research project, which use had been approved on or before July 25, 1975 in accordance with 10 CFR 35.11 (or equivalent regulation of an Agreement State) is terminated on February 20, 1976 if the manufacturer of such drug or the sponsor of the investigation of such drug submits on or before August 25, 1975 to the Food and Drug Administration, Bureau of Drugs, HFD–150, 5600 Fishers Lane, Rockville, MD 20857, the following information:

(1) The research project title;

(2) A brief description of the purpose of the project;

(3) The name of the investigator responsible;

(4) The name and license number of the institution holding the specific license under 10 CFR 35.11 (or equivalent regulation of an Agreement State);

(5) The name and maximum amount per subject of the radionuclide used;

(6) The number of subjects involved; and

(7) The date on which the administration of the radioactive drugs is expected to be completed.

(h) The exemption referred to in paragraph (a) of this section, as applied to any drug not referred to in paragraphs (d), (f), and (g) of this section, is terminated on August 26, 1975.

[39 FR 11680, Mar. 29, 1974, as amended at 40 FR 31307, July 25, 1975; 40 FR 44543, Sept. 29, 1975; 41 FR 35171, Aug. 20, 1976; 41 FR 42947, Sept. 29, 1976; 50 FR 8996, Mar. 6, 1985; 55 FR 11578, Mar. 29, 1990; 64 FR 56449, Oct. 20, 1999]

§310.509 Parenteral drug products in plastic containers.

(a) Any parenteral drug product packaged in a plastic immediate container is not generally recognized as safe and effective, is a new drug within the meaning of section 201(p) of the act, and requires an approved new drug application as a condition for marketing. An "Investigational New Drug Application" set forth in part 312 of this chapter is required for clinical investigations designed to obtain evidence of safety and effectiveness.

(b) As used in this section, the term "large volume parenteral drug product" means a terminally sterilized aqueous drug product packaged in a single-dose container with a capacity of 100 milliliters or more and intended to be administered or used intravenously in a human.

(c) Until the results of compatibility studies are evaluated, a large volume parenteral drug product for intravenous use in humans that is packaged in a plastic immediate container on or after April 16, 1979, is misbranded unless its labeling contains a warning that includes the following information:

(1) A statement that additives may be incompatible.

(2) A statement that, if additive drugs are introduced into the parenteral system, aseptic techniques should be used and the solution should be thoroughly mixed.

(3) A statement that a solution containing an additive drug should not be stored.

(d) This section does not apply to a biological product licensed under the Public Health Service Act of July 1, 1944 (42 U.S.C. 201).

[62 FR 12084, Mar. 14, 1997]

§310.515 Patient package inserts for estrogens.

(a) *Requirement for a patient package insert.* FDA concludes that the safe and effective use of drug products containing estrogens requires that patients be fully informed of the benefits and risks involved in the use of these drugs. Accordingly, except as provided in paragraph (e) of this section, each estrogen drug product restricted to prescription distribution, including products containing estrogens in fixed combinations with other drugs, shall be dispensed to patients with a patient package insert containing information concerning the drug's benefits and risks. An estrogen drug product that does not comply with the requirements of this section is misbranded under section 502(a) of the Federal Food, Drug, and Cosmetic Act.

(b) *Distribution requirements.* (1) For estrogen drug products, the manufacturer and distributor shall provide a patient package insert in or with each package of the drug product that the manufacturer or distributor intends to be dispensed to a patient.

(2) In the case of estrogen drug products in bulk packages intended for multiple dispensing, and in the case of injectables in multiple-dose vials, a sufficient number of patient labeling pieces shall be included in or with each package to assure that one piece can be included with each package or dose dispensed or administered to every patient. Each bulk package shall be labeled with instructions to the dispensor to include one patient labeling piece with each package dispensed or, in the case of injectables, with each dose administered to the patient. This section does not preclude the manufacturer or labeler from distributing additional patient labeling pieces to the dispensor.

(3) Patient package inserts for estrogens dispensed in acute-care hospitals or long-term care facilities will be considered to have been provided in accordance with this section if provided to the patient before administration of the first estrogen and every 30 days thereafter, as long as the therapy continues.

(c) *Patient package insert contents.* A patient package insert for an estrogen drug product is required to contain the following information:

(1) The name of the drug.

(2) The name and place of business of the manufacturer, packer, or distributor.

(3) A statement regarding the benefits and proper uses of estrogens.

(4) The contraindications to use, *i.e.,* when estrogens should not be used.

27

(5) A description of the most serious risks associated with the use of estrogens.

(6) A brief summary of other side effects of estrogens.

(7) Instructions on how a patient may reduce the risks of estrogen use.

(8) The date, identified as such, of the most recent revision of the patient package insert.

(d) *Guidance language.* The Food and Drug Administration issues informal labeling guidance texts under § 10.90(b)(9) of this chapter to provide assistance in meeting the requirements of paragraph (c) of this section. Requests for a copy of the guidance text should be directed to the Center for Drug Evaluation and Research, Division of Reproductive and Urologic Products, Food and Drug Administration, 10903 New Hampshire Ave., Silver Spring, MD 20993–0002.

(e) *Exemptions.* This section does not apply to estrogen-progestogen oral contraceptives. Labeling requirements for these products are set forth in § 310.501.

(f) *Requirement to supplement approved application.* Holders of approved applications for estrogen drug products that are subject to the requirements of this section must submit supplements under § 314.70(c) of this chapter to provide for the labeling required by paragraph (a) of this section. Such labeling may be put into use without advance approval by the Food and Drug Administration.

[55 FR 18723, May 4, 1990, as amended at 74 FR 13113, Mar. 26, 2009]

§ 310.517 Labeling for oral hypoglycemic drugs of the sulfonylurea class.

(a) The University Group Diabetes Program clinical trial has reported an association between the administration of tolbutamide and increased cardiovascular mortality. The Food and Drug Administration has concluded that this reported association provides adequate basis for a warning in the labeling. In view of the similarities in chemical structure and mode of action, the Food and Drug Administration also believes it is prudent from a safety standpoint to consider that the possible increased risk of cardiovascular mortality from tolbutamide applies to all other sulfonylurea drugs as well. Therefore, the labeling for oral hypoglycemic drugs of the sulfonylurea class shall include a warning concerning the possible increased risk of cardiovascular mortality associated with such use, as set forth in paragraph (b) of this section.

(b) Labeling for oral hypoglycemic drugs of the sulfonylurea class shall include in boldface type at the beginning of the "Warnings" section of the labeling the following statement:

SPECIAL WARNING ON INCREASED RISK OF
CARDIOVASCULAR MORTALITY

The administration of oral hypoglycemic drugs has been reported to be associated with increased cardiovascular mortality as compared to treatment with diet alone or diet plus insulin. This warning is based on the study conducted by the University Group Diabetes Program (UGDP), a long-term prospective clinical trial designed to evaluate the effectiveness of glucose-lowering drugs in preventing or delaying vascular complications in patients with non-insulin-dependent diabetes. The study involved 823 patients who were randomly assigned to one of four treatment groups (*Diabetes*, 19 (supp. 2): 747–830, 1970).

UGDP reported that patients treated for 5 to 8 years with diet plus a fixed dose of tolbutamide (1.5 grams per day) had a rate of cardiovascular mortality approximately 2½ times that of patients treated with diet alone. A significant increase in total mortality was not observed, but the use of tolbutamide was discontinued based on the increase in cardiovascular mortality, thus limiting the opportunity for the study to show an increase in overall mortality. Despite controversy regarding the interpretation of these results, the findings of the UGDP study provide an adequate basis for this warning. The patient should be informed of the potential risks and advantages of (name of drug) and of alternative modes of therapy.

Although only one drug in the sulfonylurea class (tolbutamide) was included in this study, it is prudent from a safety standpoint to consider that this warning may also apply to other oral hypoglycemic drugs in this class, in view of their close similarities in mode of action and chemical structure.

[49 FR 14331, Apr. 11, 1984]

§ 310.518 Drug products containing iron or iron salts.

Drug products containing elemental iron or iron salts as an active ingredient in solid oral dosage form, e.g., tablets or capsules shall meet the following requirements:

(a) *Labeling.* (1) The label of any drug in solid oral dosage form (e.g., tablets or capsules) that contains iron or iron salts for use as an iron source shall bear the following statement:

WARNING: Accidental overdose or iron-containing products is a leading cause of fatal poisoning in children under 6. Keep this product out of reach of children. In case of accidental overdose, call a doctor or poison control center immediately.

(2)(i) The warning statement required by paragraph (a)(1) of this section shall appear prominently and conspicuously on the information panel of the immediate container label.

(ii) If a drug product is packaged in unit-dose packaging, and if the immediate container bears labeling but not a label, the warning statement required by paragraph (a)(1) of this section shall appear prominently and conspicuously on the immediate container labeling in a way that maximizes the likelihood that the warning is intact until all of the dosage units to which it applies are used.

(3) Where the immediate container is not the retail package, the warning statement required by paragraph (a)(1) of this section shall also appear prominently and conspicuously on the information panel of the retail package label.

(4) The warning statement shall appear on any labeling that contains warnings.

(5) The warning statement required by paragraph (a)(1) of this section shall be set off in a box by use of hairlines.

(b) The iron-containing inert tablets supplied in monthly packages of oral contraceptives are categorically exempt from the requirements of paragraph (a) of this section.

[68 FR 59715, Oct. 17, 2003]

§ 310.519 Drug products marketed as over-the-counter (OTC) daytime sedatives.

(a) Antihistamines, bromides, and scopolamine compounds, either singly or in combinations, have been marketed as ingredients in over-the-counter (OTC) drug products for use as daytime sedatives. The following claims have been made for daytime sedative products: "occasional simple nervous tension," "nervous irrita-bility," "nervous tension headache," "simple nervousness due to common every day overwork and fatigue," "a relaxed feeling," "calming down and relaxing," "gently soothe away the tension," "calmative," "resolving that irritability that ruins your day," "helps you relax," "restlessness," "when you're under occasional stress . . . helps you work relaxed." Based on evidence presently available, there are no ingredients that can be generally recognized as safe and effective for use as OTC daytime sedatives.

(b) Any OTC drug product that is labeled, represented, or promoted as an OTC daytime sedative (or any similar or related indication) is regarded as a new drug within the meaning of section 201(p) of the Federal Food, Drug, and Cosmetic Act for which an approved new drug application under section 505 of the act and part 314 of this chapter is required for marketing.

(c) Clinical investigations designed to obtain evidence that any drug product labeled, represented, or promoted as an OTC daytime sedative (or any similar or related indication) is safe and effective for the purpose intended must comply with the requirements and procedures governing the use of investigational new drugs set forth in part 312 of this chapter.

(d) Any OTC daytime sedative drug product introduced into interstate commerce after December 24, 1979, that is not in compliance with this section is subject to regulatory action.

[44 FR 36380, June 22, 1979; 45 FR 47422, July 15, 1980, as amended at 55 FR 11579, Mar. 29, 1990]

§ 310.527 Drug products containing active ingredients offered over-the-counter (OTC) for external use as hair growers or for hair loss prevention.

(a) Amino acids, aminobenzoic acid, ascorbic acid, benzoic acid, biotin and all other B-vitamins, dexpanthenol, estradiol and other topical hormones, jojoba oil, lanolin, nucleic acids, polysorbate 20, polysorbate 60, sulfanilamide, sulfur 1 percent on carbon in a fraction of paraffinic hydrocarbons, tetracaine hydrochloride, urea, and wheat germ oil have been marketed as ingredients in OTC drug products for external use as hair growers or for hair loss prevention. There is a lack of adequate data to establish general recognition of the safety and effectiveness of these or any other ingredients intended for OTC external use as a hair grower or for hair loss prevention. Based on evidence currently available, all labeling claims for OTC hair grower and hair loss prevention drug products for external use are either false, misleading, or unsupported by scientific data. Therefore, any OTC drug product for external use containing an ingredient offered for use as a hair grower or for hair loss prevention cannot be considered generally recognized as safe and effective for its intended use.

(b) Any OTC drug product that is labeled, represented, or promoted for external use as a hair grower or for hair loss prevention is regarded as a new drug within the meaning of section 201(p) of the Federal Food, Drug, and Cosmetic Act (the act), for which an approved new drug application under section 505 of the act and part 314 of this chapter is required for marketing. In the absence of an approved new drug application, such product is also misbranded under section 502 of the act.

(c) Clinical investigations designed to obtain evidence that any drug product labeled, represented, or promoted for OTC external use as a hair grower or for hair loss prevention is safe and effective for the purpose intended must comply with the requirements and procedures governing the use of investigational new drugs set forth in part 312 of this chapter.

(d) After January 8, 1990, any such OTC drug product initially introduced or initially delivered for introduction into interstate commerce that is not in compliance with this section is subject to regulatory action.

[54 FR 28777, July 7, 1989]

§ 310.528 Drug products containing active ingredients offered over-the-counter (OTC) for use as an aphrodisiac.

(a) Any product that bears labeling claims that it will arouse or increase sexual desire, or that it will improve sexual performance, is an aphrodisiac drug product. Anise, cantharides, don qual, estrogens, fennel, ginseng, golden seal, gotu kola, Korean ginseng, licorice, mandrake, methyltestosterone, minerals, nux vomica, Pega Palo, sarsaparilla, strychnine, testosterone, vitamins, yohimbine, yohimbine hydrochloride, and yohimbinum have been present as ingredients in such drug products. Androgens (e.g., testosterone and methyltestosterone) and estrogens are powerful hormones when administered internally and are not safe for use except under the supervision of a physician. There is a lack of adequate data to establish general recognition of the safety and effectiveness of any of these ingredients, or any other ingredient, for OTC use as an aphrodisiac. Labeling claims for aphrodisiacs for OTC use are either false, misleading, or unsupported by scientific data. The following claims are examples of some that have been made for aphrodisiac drug products for OTC use: "acts as an aphrodisiac;" "arouses or increases sexual desire and improves sexual performance;" "helps restore sexual vigor, potency, and performance;" "improves performance, staying power, and sexual potency;" and "builds virility and sexual potency." Based on evidence currently available, any OTC drug product containing ingredients for use as an aphrodisiac cannot be generally recognized as safe and effective.

(b) Any OTC drug product that is labeled, represented, or prompted for use as an aphrodisiac is regarded as a new drug within the meaning of section 201(p) of the Federal Food, Drug, and Cosmetic Act, (the act), for which an approved new drug application under section 505 of the act and part 314 of this chapter is required for marketing. In the absence of an approved new drug application, such product is also misbranded under section 502 of the act.

(c) Clinical investigations designed to obtain evidence that any drug product labeled, represented, or promoted for OTC use as an aphrodisiac is safe and effective for the purpose intended must comply with the requirements and procedures governing the use of investigational new drugs set forth in part 312 of this chapter.

(d) After January 8, 1990, any such OTC drug product initially introduced or initially delivered for introduction into interstate commerce that is not in compliance with this section is subject to regulatory action.

[54 FR 28786, July 7, 1989]

§310.529 Drug products containing active ingredients offered over-the-counter (OTC) for oral use as insect repellents.

(a) Thiamine hydrochloride (vitamin B–1) has been marketed as an ingredient in over-the-counter (OTC) drug products for oral use as an insect repellent (an orally administered drug product intended to keep insects away). There is a lack of adequate data to establish the effectiveness of this, or any other ingredient for OTC oral use as an insect repellent. Labeling claims for OTC orally administered insect repellent drug products are either false, misleading, or unsupported by scientific data. The following claims are examples of some that have been made for orally administered OTC insect repellent drug products: "Oral mosquito repellent," "mosquitos avoid you," "bugs stay away," "keep mosquitos away for 12 to 24 hours," and "the newest way to fight mosquitos." Therefore, any drug product containing ingredients offered for oral use as an insect repellent cannot be generally recognized as safe and effective.

(b) Any OTC drug product that is labeled, represented, or promoted for oral use as an insect repellent is regarded as a new drug within the meaning of section 201(p) of the Federal Food, Drug and Cosmetic Act for which an approved new drug application under section 505 of the act and part 314 of this chapter is required for marketing. In the absence of an approved new drug application, such product is also misbranded under section 502 of the act.

(c) Clinical investigations designed to obtain evidence that any drug product labeled, represented, or promoted OTC for oral use as an insect repellent is safe and effective for the purpose intended must comply with the requirements and procedures governing the use of investigational new drugs set forth in part 312 of this chapter.

(d) Any such drug product in interstate commerce after December 17, 1985, that is not in compliance with this section is subject to regulatory action.

[40 FR 25171, June 17, 1985, as amended at 55 FR 11579, Mar. 29, 1990]

§310.530 Topically applied hormone-containing drug products for over-the-counter (OTC) human use.

(a) The term "hormone" is used broadly to describe a chemical substance formed in some organ of the body, such as the adrenal glands or the pituitary, and carried to another organ or tissue, where it has a specific effect. Hormones include, for example, estrogens, progestins, androgens, anabolic steroids, and adrenal corticosteroids, and synthetic analogs. Estrogens, progesterone, pregnenolone, and pregnenolone acetate have been present as ingredients in OTC drug products marketed for topical use as hormone creams. However, there is a lack of adequate data to establish effectiveness for any OTC drug use of these ingredients. Therefore, with the exception of those hormones identified in paragraph (e) of this section, any OTC drug product containing an ingredient offered for use as a topically applied hormone cannot be considered generally recognized as safe and effective for its intended use. The intended use of the product may be inferred from the product's labeling, promotional material, advertising, and any other relevant factor. The use of the word "hormone" in the text of the labeling or in the ingredient statement is an implied drug claim. The claim implied by the use of this term is that the product will have a therapeutic or some other physiological effect on the body. Therefore, reference to a product as a "hormone cream" or any statement in the labeling indicating that "hormones" are present in the product, or any statement that features or emphasizes the presence of a hormone ingredient in the product, will be considered to be a therapeutic claim for the product, or a claim that the product will affect the structure or function of the body, and will consequently cause the product to be a drug.

(b) Any OTC drug product that is labeled, represented, or promoted as a topically applied hormone-containing product for drug use, with the exception of those hormones identified in paragraph (e) of this section, is regarded as a new drug within the meaning of section 201(p) of the act, for which an approved application or abbreviated application under section 505 of the act and part 314 of this chapter is required for marketing. In the absence of an approved new drug application or abbreviated new drug application, such product is also misbranded under section 502 of the act.

(c) Clinical investigations designed to obtain evidence that any drug product labeled, represented, or promoted for OTC use as a topically applied hormone-containing drug product is safe and effective for the purpose intended must comply with the requirements and procedures governing the use of investigational new drugs set forth in part 312 of this chapter.

(d) After March 9, 1994, any such OTC drug product initially introduced or initially delivered for introduction into interstate commerce that is not in compliance with this section is subject to regulatory action.

(e) This section does not apply to hydrocortisone and hydrocortisone acetate labeled, represented, or promoted for OTC topical use in accordance with part 348 of this chapter.

[58 FR 47610, Sept. 9, 1993]

§ 310.531 Drug products containing active ingredients offered over-the-counter (OTC) for the treatment of boils.

(a) Aminacrine hydrochloride, benzocaine, bismuth subnitrate, calomel, camphor, cholesterol, ergot fluid extract, hexachlorophene, ichthammol, isobutamben, juniper tar (oil of cade), lanolin, magnesium sulfate, menthol, methyl salicylate, oxyguinoline sulfate, petrolatum, phenol, pine tar, rosin, rosin cerate, sassafras oil, sulfur, thymol, triclosan, and zinc oxide have been present in OTC boil treatment drug products. There is a lack of adequate data to establish general recognition of the safety and effectiveness of these or any other ingredient for OTC use for the treatment of boils. Treatment is defined as reducing the size of a boil or reducing an infection related to a boil. Treatment has in-

volved the use of "drawing salves" for these purposes. These "drawing salves" contained various ingredients. Based on evidence currently available, any OTC drug product offered for the treatment of boils cannot be considered generally recognized as safe and effective.

(b) Any OTC drug product that is labeled, represented, or promoted for the treatment of boils is regarded as a new drug within the meaning of section 201(p) of the Federal Food, Drug, and Cosmetic Act (the act), for which an approved application or abbreviated application under section 505 of the act and part 314 of this chapter is required for marketing. In the absence of an approved new drug application or abbreviated new drug application, such product is also misbranded under section 502 of the act.

(c) Clinical investigations designed to obtain evidence that any OTC boil treatment drug product is safe and effective for the purpose intended must comply with the requirements and procedures governing the use of investigational new drugs set forth in part 312 of this chapter.

(d) After May 7, 1991, any such OTC drug product that contains aminacrine hydrochloride, bismuth subnitrate, calomel, camphor, cholesterol, ergot fluid extract, hexachlorophene, isobutamben, juniper tar (oil of cade), lanolin, magnesium sulfate, menthol, methyl salicylate, oxyguinoline sulfate, petrolatum, phenol, pine tar, rosin, rosin cerate, sassafras oil, thymol, or zinc oxide initially introduced or initially delivered for introduction into interstate commerce that is not in compliance with this section is subject to regulatory action.

(e) After May 16, 1994, any such OTC drug product that contains benzocaine, ichthammol, sulfur, or triclosan initially introduced or initially delivered for introduction into interstate commerce that is not in compliance with this section is subject to regulatory action.

(f) This section does not apply to drug products that contain benzocaine labeled, represented, or promoted for OTC topical use in accordance with part 348 of this chapter.

[58 FR 60336, Nov. 15, 1993]

§310.532 Drug products containing active ingredients offered over-the-counter (OTC) to relieve the symptoms of benign prostatic hypertrophy.

(a) The amino acids glycine, alanine, and glutamic acid (alone or in combination) and the ingredient sabal have been present in over-the-counter (OTC) drug products to relieve the symptoms of benign prostatic hypertrophy, e.g., urinary urgency and frequency, excessive urinating at night, and delayed urination. There is a lack of adequate data to establish general recognition of the safety and effectiveness of these or any other ingredients for OTC use in relieving the symptoms of benign prostatic hypertrophy. In addition, there is no definitive evidence that any drug product offered for the relief of the symptoms of benign prostatic hypertrophy would alter the obstructive or inflammatory signs and symptoms of this condition. Therefore, self-medication with OTC drug products might unnecessarily delay diagnosis and treatment of progressive obstruction and secondary infections. Based on evidence currently available, any OTC drug product containing ingredients offered for use in relieving the symptoms of benign prostatic hypertrophy cannot be generally recognized as safe and effective.

(b) Any OTC drug product that is labeled, represented, or promoted to relieve the symptoms of benign prostatic hypertrophy is regarded as a new drug within the meaning of section 201(p) of the Federal Food, Drug, and Cosmetic Act (the act), for which an approved application under section 505 of the act and part 314 of this chapter is required for marketing. In the absence of an approved application, such product is also misbranded under section 502 of the act.

(c) Clinical investigations designed to obtain evidence that any drug product labeled, represented, or promoted for OTC use to relieve the symptoms of benign prostatic hypertrophy is safe and effective for the purpose intended must comply with the requirements and procedures governing the use of investigational new drugs set forth in part 312 of this chapter.

(d) After August 27, 1990, any such OTC drug product initially introduced or initially delivered for introduction into interstate commerce that is not in compliance with this section is subject to regulatory action.

[55 FR 6930, Feb. 27, 1990]

§310.533 Drug products containing active ingredients offered over-the-counter (OTC) for human use as an anticholinergic in cough-cold drug products.

(a) Atropine sulfate, belladonna alkaloids, and belladonna alkaloids as contained in Atropa belladonna and Datura stramonium have been present as ingredients in cough-cold drug products for use as an anticholinergic. Anticholinergic drugs have been marketed OTC in cough-cold drug products to relieve excessive secretions of the nose and eyes, symptoms that are commonly associated with hay fever, allergy, rhinitis, and the common cold. Atropine sulfate for oral use as an anticholinergic is probably safe at dosages that have been used in marketed cough-cold products (0.2 to 0.3 milligram); however, there are inadequate data to establish general recognition of the effectiveness of this ingredient. The belladonna alkaloids, which contain atropine (d, dl hyoscyamine) and scopolamine (l- hyoscine), are probably safe for oral use at dosages that have been used in marketed cough-cold products (0.2 milligram) but there are inadequate data to establish general recognition of the effectiveness of these ingredients as an anticholinergic for cough-cold use. Belladonna alkaloids for inhalation use, as contained in Atropa belladonna and Datura stramonium, are neither safe nor effective as an OTC anticholinergic. There are inadequate safety and effectiveness data to establish general recognition of the safety and/or effectiveness or any of these ingredients, or any other ingredient, for OTC use as an anticholinergic in cough-cold drug products.

(b) Any OTC cough-cold drug product that is labeled, represented, or promoted for use as an anticholinergic is regarded as a new drug within the meaning of section 201(p) of the Federal Food, Drug, and Cosmetic Act, for which an approved new drug application under section 505 of the act and part 314 of this chapter is required for marketing. In the absence of an approved new drug application, such product is also misbranded under section 502 of the act.

(c) Clinical investigations designed to obtain evidence that any cough-cold drug product labeled, represented, or promoted for OTC use as an anticholinergic is safe and effective for the purpose intended must comply with the requirements and procedures governing the use of investigational new drugs set forth in part 312 of this chapter.

(d) After the effective date of the final regulation, any such OTC cough-cold drug product that is labeled, represented, or promoted for use as an anticholinergic may not be initially introduced or initially delivered for introduction into interstate commerce unless it is the subject of an approved new drug application.

[50 FR 46587, Nov. 8, 1985, as amended at 55 FR 11579, Mar. 29, 1990]

§ 310.534 Drug products containing active ingredients offered over-the-counter (OTC) for human use as oral wound healing agents.

(a) Allantoin, carbamide peroxide in anhydrous glycerin, water soluble chlorophyllins, and hydrogen peroxide in aqueous solution have been present in oral mucosal injury drug products for use as oral wound healing agents. Oral wound healing agents have been marketed as aids in the healing of minor oral wounds by means other than cleansing and irrigating, or by serving as a protectant. Allantoin, carbamide peroxide in anhydrous glycerin, water soluble chlorophyllins, and hydrogen peroxide in aqueous solution are safe for use as oral wound healing agents, but there are inadequate data to establish general recognition of the effectiveness of these ingredients as oral wound healing agents.

(b) Any OTC drug product that is labeled, represented, or promoted for use as an oral wound healing agent is regarded as a new drug within the meaning of section 201(p) of the Federal Food, Drug, and Cosmetic Act, for which an approved new drug application under section 505 of the act and part 314 of this chapter is required for marketing. In the absence of an approved new drug application, such product is also misbranded under section 502 of the act.

(c) Clinical investigations designed to obtain evidence that any drug product labeled, represented, or promoted for OTC use as an oral wound healing agent is safe and effective for the purpose intended must comply with the requirements and procedures governing the use of investigational new drugs set forth in part 312 of this chapter.

(d) After the effective date of the final regulation, any OTC drug product that is labeled, represented, or promoted for use as an oral wound healing agent may not be initially introduced or initially delivered for introduction into interstate commerce unless it is the subject of an approved new drug application.

[51 FR 26114, July 18, 1986, as amended at 55 FR 11579, Mar. 29, 1990]

§ 310.536 Drug products containing active ingredients offered over-the-counter (OTC) for use as a nailbiting or thumbsucking deterrent.

(a) Denatonium benzoate and sucrose octaacetate have been present in OTC nailbiting and thumbsucking deterrent drug products. There is a lack of adequate data to establish general recognition of the safety and effectiveness of these and any other ingredients (e.g., cayenne pepper) for OTC use as a nailbiting or thumbsucking deterrent. Based on evidence currently available, any OTC drug product containing ingredients offered for use as a nailbiting or thumbsucking deterrent cannot be generally recognized as safe and effective.

(b) Any OTC drug product that is labeled, represented, and promoted as a nailbiting or thumbsucking deterrent is regarded as a new drug within the meaning of section 201(p) of the Federal Food, Drug, and Cosmetic Act (the act) for which an approved application or abbreviated application under section 505 of the act and part 314 of this chapter is required for marketing. In the absence of an approved new drug application or abbreviated new drug application, such product is also misbranded under section 502 of the act.

(c) Clinical investigations designed to obtain evidence that any drug product labeled, represented, or promoted for OTC use as a nailbiting or thumbsucking deterrent is safe and effective for the purpose intended must comply with the requirements and procedures governing the use of investigational new drugs set forth in part 312 of this chapter.

(d) After March 2, 1994, any such OTC drug product initially introduced or initially delivered for introduction into interstate commerce that is not in compliance with this section is subject to regulatory action.

[58 FR 46754, Sept. 2, 1993]

§ 310.537 **Drug products containing active ingredients offered over-the-counter (OTC) for oral administration for the treatment of fever blisters and cold sores.**

(a) L-lysine (lysine, lysine hydrochloride), *Lactobacillus acidophilus*, and *Lactobacillus bulgaricus* have been present in orally administered OTC drug products to treat fever blisters and cold sores. There is a lack of adequate data to establish general recognition of the safety and effectiveness of these or any other orally administered ingredients for OTC use to treat or relieve the symptoms or discomfort of fever blisters and cold sores. Based on evidence currently available, any OTC drug product for oral administration containing ingredients offered for use in treating or relieving the symptoms or discomfort of fever blisters and cold sores cannot be generally recognized as safe and effective.

(b) Any OTC drug product for oral administration that is labeled, represented, or promoted to treat or relieve the symptoms or discomfort of fever blisters and cold sores is regarded as a new drug within the meaning of section 201(p) of the Federal Food, Drug, and Cosmetic Act (the act), for which an approved application under section 505 of the act and part 314 of this chapter is required for marketing. In the absence of an approved application, such product is also misbranded under section 502 of the act.

(c) Clinical investigations designed to obtain evidence that any drug product for oral administration labeled, represented, or promoted for OTC use to treat or relieve the symptoms or discomfort of fever blisters and cold sores is safe and effective for the purpose intended must comply with the requirements and procedures governing the use of investigational new drugs set forth in part 312 of this chapter.

(d) After December 30, 1992, any such OTC drug product initially introduced or initially delivered for introduction into interstate commerce that is not in compliance with this section is subject to regulatory action.

[57 FR 29173, June 30, 1992]

§ 310.538 **Drug products containing active ingredients offered over-the-counter (OTC) for use for ingrown toenail relief.**

(a) Any product that bears labeling claims such as for "temporary relief of discomfort from ingrown toenails," or "ingrown toenail relief product," or "ingrown toenail reliever," or similar claims is considered an ingrown toenail relief drug product. Benzocaine, chlorobutanol, chloroxylenol, dibucaine, tannic acid, and urea have been present as ingredients in such products. There is lack of adequate data to establish general recognition of the safety and effectiveness of these or any other ingredients for OTC use for ingrown toenail relief. Based on evidence currently available, any OTC drug product containing ingredients offered for use for ingrown toenail relief cannot be generally recognized as safe and effective.

(b) Any OTC drug product that is labeled, represented, or promoted for ingrown toenail relief is regarded as a new drug within the meaning of section 201(p) of the Federal Food, Drug, and Cosmetic Act (the act), for which an approved application or abbreviated application under section 505 of the act and part 314 of this chapter is required for marketing. In the absence of an approved new drug application or abbreviated new drug application, such product is also misbranded under section 502 of the act.

(c) Clinical investigations designed to obtain evidence that any drug product labeled, represented, or promoted for OTC use for ingrown toenail relief is safe and effective for the purpose intended must comply with the requirements and procedures governing the use of investigational new drugs set forth in part 312 of this chapter.

(d) After March 9, 1994, any such OTC drug product initially introduced or initially delivered for introduction into interstate commerce that is not in compliance with this section is subject to regulatory action.

(e) This section does not apply to sodium sulfide labeled, represented, or promoted for OTC topical use for ingrown toenail relief in accordance with part 358, subpart D of this chapter, after June 6, 2003.

[58 FR 47605, Sept. 9, 1993, as amended at 68 FR 24348, May 7, 2003]

§ 310.540 **Drug products containing active ingredients offered over-the-counter (OTC) for use as stomach acidifiers.**

(a) Betaine hydrochloride, glutamic acid hydrochloride, diluted hydrochloric acid, and pepsin have been present as ingredients in over-the-counter (OTC) drug products for use as stomach acidifiers. Because of the lack of adequate data to establish the effectiveness of these or any other ingredients for use in treating achlorhydria and hypochlorhydria, and because such conditions are asymptomatic, any OTC drug product containing ingredients offered for use as a stomach acidifier cannot be considered generally recognized as safe and effective.

(b) Any OTC drug product that is labeled, represented, or promoted for use as a stomach acidifier is regarded as a new drug within the meaning of section 201(p) of the Federal Food, Drug, and Cosmetic Act, for which an approved new drug application under section 505 of the act and part 314 of this chapter is required for marketing. In the absence of an approved new drug application, such product is also misbranded under section 502 of the act.

(c) Clinical investigations designed to obtain evidence that any drug product labeled, represented, or promoted as a stomach acidifier for OTC use is safe and effective for the purpose intended must comply with the requirements and procedures governing the use of investigational new drugs set forth in part 312 of this chapter.

(d) After the effective date of the final regulation, any such OTC drug product initially introduced or initially delivered for introduction into interstate commerce that is not in compliance with this section is subject to regulatory action.

[53 FR 31271, Aug. 17, 1988]

§ 310.541 **Over-the-counter (OTC) drug products containing active ingredients offered for use in the treatment of hypophosphatemia.**

(a) Hypophosphatemia is a condition in which an abnormally low plasma level of phosphate occurs in the blood. This condition is not amenable to self-diagnosis or self-treatment. Treatment of this condition should be restricted to the supervision of a physician. For this reason, any drug product containing ingredients offered for OTC use in the treatment of hypophosphatemia cannot be considered generally recognized as safe and effective.

(b) Any drug product that is labeled, represented, or promoted for OTC use in the treatment of hypophosphatemia is regarded as a new drug within the meaning of section 201(p) of the Federal Food, Drug, and Cosmetic Act (the act), for which an approved application under section 505 of the act and part 314 of this chapter is required for marketing. In the absence of an approved application, such product is also misbranded under section 502 of the act.

(c) Clinical investigations designed to obtain evidence that any drug product labeled, represented, or promoted for OTC use in the treatment of hypophosphatemia is safe and effective for the purpose intended must comply with the requirements and procedures governing the use of investigational new drugs set forth in part 312 of his chapter.

(d) After November 12, 1990, any such OTC drug product initially introduced or initially delivered for introduction into interstate commerce that is not in compliance with this section is subject to regulatory action.

[55 FR 19858, May 11, 1990]

§ 310.542 Over-the-counter (OTC) drug products containing active ingredients offered for use in the treatment of hyperphosphatemia.

(a) Hyperphosphatemia is a condition in which an abnormally high plasma level of phosphate occurs in the blood. This condition in not amenable to self-diagnosis or self-treatment. Treatment of this condition should be restricted to the supervision of a physician. For this reason, any drug product containing ingredients offered for OTC use in the treatment of hyperphosphatemia cannot be considered generally recognized as safe and effective.

(b) Any drug product that is labeled, represented, or promoted for OTC use in the treatment of hyperphosphatemia is regarded as a new drug within the meaning of section 201(p) of the Federal Food, Drug, and Cosmetic Act (the act), for which an approved application under section 505 of the act and part 314 of this chapter is required for marketing. In the absence of an approved application, such product is also misbranded under section 502 of the act.

(c) Clinical investigations designed to obtain evidence that any drug product labeled, represented, or promoted for use in the treatment of hyperphosphatemia is safe and effective for the purpose intended must comply with the requirements and procedures governing use of investigational new drugs set forth in part 312 of this chapter.

(d) After November 12, 1990, any such OTC drug product initially introduced or initially delivered for introduction into interstate commerce that is not in compliance with this section is subject to regulatory action.

[55 FR 19858, May 11, 1990]

§ 310.543 Drug products containing active ingredients offered over-the-counter (OTC) for human use in exocrine pancreatic insufficiency.

(a) Hemicellulase, pancreatin, and pancrelipase have been present as ingredients in exocrine pancreatic insufficiency drug products. Pancreatin and pancrelipase are composed of enzymes: amylase, trypsin (protease), and lipase. Significant differences have been shown in the bioavailability of marketed exocrine pancreatic insufficiency drug products produced by different manufacturers. These differences raise a potential for serious risk to patients using these drug products. The bioavailability of pancreatic enzymes is dependent on the process used to manufacture the drug products. Information on this process is not included in an OTC drug monograph. Therefore, the safe and effective use of these enzymes for treating exocrine pancreatic insufficiency cannot be regulated adequately by an OTC drug monograph. Information on the product's formulation, manufacture, quality control procedures, and final formulation effectiveness testing are necessary in an approved application to ensure that a company has the ability to manufacture a proper bioactive formulation. In addition, continuous physician monitoring of patients who take these drug products is a collateral measure necessary to the safe and effective use of these enzymes, causing such products to be available by prescription only.

(b) Any drug product that is labeled, represented, or promoted for OTC use in the treatment of exocrine pancreatic insufficiency is regarded as a new drug within the meaning of section 201(p) of the Federal Food, Drug, and Cosmetic Act (the act), for which an approved application under section 505 of the act and part 314 of this chapter is required for marketing. In the absence of an approved application, such product is also misbranded under section 502 of the act.

(c) Clinical investigations designed to obtain evidence that any drug product labeled, represented, or promoted for OTC use in the treatment of exocrine pancreatic insufficiency is safe and effective for the purpose intended must comply with the requirements and procedures governing the use of investigational new drugs set forth in part 312 of this chapter.

(d) After May 7, 1991, any such OTC drug product that contains hemicellulase initially introduced or initially delivered for introduction into interstate commerce that is not in compliance with this section is subject to regulatory action.

(e) After October 24, 1995, any such OTC drug product that contains pancreatin or pancrelipase initially introduced or initially delivered for introduction into interstate commerce that is not in compliance with this section is subject to regulatory action.

[60 FR 20165, Apr. 24, 1995]

§ 310.544 Drug products containing active ingredients offered over-the-counter (OTC) for use as a smoking deterrent.

(a) Any product that bears labeling claims that it "helps stop or reduce the cigarette urge," "helps break the cigarette habit," "helps stop or reduce smoking," or similar claims is a smoking deterrent drug product. Cloves, coriander, eucalyptus oil, ginger (Jamaica), lemon oil (terpeneless), licorice root extract, lobeline (in the form of lobeline sulfate or natural lobelia alkaloids or *Lobelia inflata* herb), menthol, methyl salicylate, povidone-silver nitrate, quinine ascorbate, silver acetate, silver nitrate, and thymol have been present as ingredients in such drug products. There is a lack of adequate data to establish general recognition of the safety and effectiveness of these or any other ingredients for OTC use as a smoking deterrent. Based on evidence currently available, any OTC drug product containing ingredients offered for use as a smoking deterrent cannot be generally recognized as safe and effective.

(b) Any OTC drug product that is labeled, represented, or promoted as a smoking deterrent is regarded as a new drug within the meaning of section 201(p) of the Federal Food, Drug, and Cosmetic Act (the act), for which an approved application or abbreviated application under section 505 of the act and part 314 of this chapter is required for marketing. In the absence of an approved new drug application or abbreviated new drug application, such product is also misbranded under section 502 of the act.

(c) Clinical investigations designed to obtain evidence that any drug product labeled, represented, or promoted for OTC use as a smoking deterrent is safe and effective for the purpose intended must comply with the requirements and procedures governing the use of investigational new drugs set forth in part 312 of this chapter.

(d) After May 7, 1991, any such OTC drug product containing cloves, coriander, eucalyptus oil, ginger (Jamaica), lemon oil (terpeneless), licorice root extract, menthol, methyl salicylate, quinine ascorbate, silver nitrate, and/or thymol initially introduced or initially delivered for introduction into interstate commerce that is not in compliance with this section is subject to regulatory action. After December 1, 1993, any such OTC drug product containing lobeline (in the form of lobeline sulfate or natural lobelia alkaloids or *Lobelia inflata* herb), povidone-silver nitrate, silver acetate, or any other ingredients initially introduced or initially delivered for introduction into interstate commerce that is not in compliance with this section is subject to regulatory action.

[58 FR 31241, June 1, 1993]

§ 310.545 Drug products containing certain active ingredients offered over-the-counter (OTC) for certain uses.

(a) A number of active ingredients have been present in OTC drug products for various uses, as described below. However, based on evidence currently available, there are inadequate data to establish general recognition of the safety and effectiveness of these ingredients for the specified uses:

(1) *Topical acne drug products.*

Alcloxa
Alkyl isoquinolinium bromide
Aluminum chlorohydrex
Aluminum hydroxide
Benzocaine
Benzoic acid
Boric acid
Calcium polysulfide
Calcium thiosulfate
Camphor
Chloroxylenol
Cloxyquin
Coal tar
Dibenzothiophene
Estrone
Magnesium aluminum silicate
Magnesium sulfate
Phenol
Phenolate sodium
Phenyl salicylate
Povidone-iodine
Pyrilamine maleate
Resorcinol (as single ingredient)

Resorcinol monoacetate (as single ingredient)
Salicylic acid (over 2 up to 5 percent)
Sodium borate
Sodium thiosulfate
Tetracaine hydrochloride
Thymol
Vitamin E
Zinc oxide
Zinc stearate
Zinc sulfide

(2) *Anticaries drug products*—(i) *Approved as of May 7, 1991.*

Hydrogen fluoride
Sodium carbonate
Sodium monofluorophosphate (6 percent rinse)
Sodium phosphate

(ii) *Approved as of October 7, 1996.*

Calcium sucrose phosphate
Dicalcium phosphate dihydrate
Disodium hydrogen phosphate [1]
Phosphoric acid [1]
Sodium dihydrogen phosphate
Sodium dihydrogen phosphate monohydrate
Sodium phosphate, dibasic anhydrous reagent [1]

(3) *Antidiarrheal drug products*—(i) *Approved as of May 7, 1991.*

Aluminum hydroxide
Atropine sulfate
Calcium carbonate
Carboxymethylcellulose sodium
Glycine
Homatropine methylbromide
Hyoscyamine sulfate
Lactobacillus acidophilus
Lactobacillus bulgaricus
Opium, powdered
Opium tincture
Paregoric
Phenyl salicylate
Scopolamine hydrobromide
Zinc phenolsulfonate

(ii) *Approved as of* April 19, 2004; April 18, 2005, *for products with annual sales less than $25,000.*

Attapulgite, activated
Bismuth subnitrate
Calcium hydroxide
Calcium polycarbophil
Charcoal (activated)
Pectin
Polycarbophil
Potassium carbonate
Rhubarb fluidextract

---

[1] These ingredients are nonmonograph except when used to prepare acidulated phosphate fluoride treatment rinses identified in §355.10(a)(3) of this chapter.

(4) *Antiperspirant drug products*—(i) *Ingredients—Approved as of May 7, 1991.*

Alum, potassium
Aluminum bromohydrate
Aluminum chloride (alcoholic solutions)
Aluminum chloride (aqueous solution) (aerosol only)
Aluminum sulfate
Aluminum sulfate, buffered (aerosol only)
Sodium aluminum chlorohydroxy lactate

(ii) *Approved as of December 9, 2004; June 9, 2005, for products with annual sales less than $25,000.*

Aluminum sulfate buffered with sodium aluminum lactate

(5) [Reserved]

(6) *Cold, cough, allergy, bronchodilator, and antiasthmatic drug products*—(i) *Antihistamine drug products*—(A) *Ingredients.*

Methapyrilene hydrochloride
Methapyrilene fumarate
Thenyldiamine hydrochloride

(B) *Ingredients.*

Phenyltoloxamine dihydrogen citrate
Methapyrilene hydrochloride
Methapyrilene fumarate
Thenyldiamine hydrochloride

(ii) *Nasal decongestant drug products*—(A) *Approved as of May 7, 1991.*

Allyl isothiocyanate
Camphor (lozenge)
Creosote, beechwood (oral)
Eucalyptol (lozenge)
Eucalyptol (mouthwash)
Eucalyptus oil (lozenge)
Eucalyptus oil (mouthwash)
Menthol (mouthwash)
Peppermint oil (mouthwash)
Thenyldiamine hydrochloride
Thymol
Thymol (lozenge)
Thymol (mouthwash)
Turpentine oil

(B) *Approved as of August 23, 1995.*

Bornyl acetate (topical)
Cedar leaf oil (topical)
Creosote, beechwood (topical)
Ephedrine (oral)
Ephedrine hydrochloride (oral)
Ephedrine sulfate (oral)
Racephedrine hydrochloride (oral/topical)

(C) Approved as of April 11, 2007; October 11, 2007, for products with annual sales less than $25,000. Any ingredient(s) labeled with claims or directions for use for sinusitis or for relief

of nasal congestion associated with si-
nusitis.

(iii) *Expectorant drug products.*

Ammonium chloride
Antimony potassium tartrate
Beechwood creosote
Benzoin preparations (compound tincture of
  benzoin, tincture of benzoin)
Camphor
Chloroform
Eucalyptol/eucalyptus oil
Horehound
Iodides (calcium iodide anyhydrous, hydroid-
  ic acid syrup, iodized lime, potassium io-
  dide)
Ipecac
Ipecac fluidextract
Ipecac syrup
Menthol/peppermint oil
Pine tar preparations (extract white pine
  compound, pine tar, syrup of pine tar, com-
  pound white pine syrup, white pine)
Potassium guaiacolsulfonate
Sodium citrate
Squill preparations (squill, squill extract)
Terpin hydrate preparations (terpin hydrate,
  terpin hydrate elixir)
Tolu preparations (tolu, tolu balsam, tolu
  balsam tincture)
Turpentine oil (spirits of turpentine)

(iv) *Bronchodilator drug products—*(A)
Approved as of October 2, 1987.

Aminophylline
Belladonna alkaloids
Euphorbia pilulifera
Metaproterenol sulfate
Methoxyphenamine hydrochloride
Pseudoephedrine hydrochloride
Pseudoephedrine sulfate
Theophylline, anhydrous
Theophylline calcium salicylate
Theophylline sodium glycinate

(B) Approved as of January 29, 1996.
Any combination drug product containing theophylline (e.g., theophylline
and ephedrine, or theophylline and
ephedrine and phenobarbital).

(C) Approved as of June 19, 1996. Any
ingredient(s) in a pressurized metered-
dose inhaler container.

(D) Approved as of October 29, 2001.
Any oral bronchodilator active ingredient (e.g., ephedrine, ephedrine hydrochloride, ephedrine sulfate,
racephedrine hydrochloride, or any
other ephedrine salt) in combination
with any analgesic(s) or analgesic-anti-
pyretic(s), anticholinergic, antihistamine, oral antitussive, or stimulant
active ingredient.

(7) *Dandruff/seborrheic dermatitis/psori-
asis drug products.*

Alkyl isoquinolinium bromide
Allantoin
Benzalkonium chloride
Benzethonium chloride
Boric acid
Calcium undecylenate
Captan
Chloroxylenol
Colloidal oatmeal
Cresol, saponated
Ethohexadiol
Eucalyptol
Juniper tar
Lauryl isoquinolinium bromide
Menthol
Mercury oleate
Methylbenzethonium chloride
Methyl salicylate
Phenol
Phenolate sodium
Pine tar
Povidone-iodine
Resorcinol
Sodium borate
Sodium salicylate
Thymol
Undecylenic acid

(8) *Digestive aid drug products—*(i) *Approved as of May 7, 1991.*

Bismuth sodium tartrate
Calcium carbonate
Cellulase
Dehydrocholic acid
Dihydroxyaluminum sodium carbonate
Duodenal substance
Garlic, dehydrated
Glutamic acid hydrochloride
Hemicellulase
Homatropine methylbromide
Magnesium hydroxide
Magnesium trisilicate
Ox bile extract
Pancreatin
Pancrelipase
Papain
Peppermint oil
Pepsin
Sodium bicarbonate
Sodium citrate
Sorbitol

(ii) *Approved as of November 10, 1993.*

Alcohol
Aluminum hydroxide
Amylase
Anise seed
Aromatic powder
Asafetida
Aspergillus oryza enzymes (except lactase
  enzyme derived from *Aspergillus oryzae*)
Bacillus acidophilus
Bean
Belladonna alkaloids
Belladonna leaves, powdered extract
Betaine hydrochloride

Bismuth subcarbonate
Bismuth subgallate
Black radish powder
Blessed thistle (cnicus benedictus)
Buckthorn
Calcium gluconate
Capsicum
Capsicum, fluid extract of
Carbon
Cascara sagrada extract
Catechu, tincture
Catnip
Chamomile flowers
Charcoal, wood
Chloroform
Cinnamon oil
Cinnamon tincture
Citrus pectin
Diastase
Diastase malt
Dog grass
Elecampane
Ether
Fennel acid
Galega
Ginger
Glycine
Hydrastis canadensis (golden seal)
Hectorite
Horsetail
Huckleberry
Hydrastis fluid extract
Hydrochloric acid
Iodine
Iron ox bile
Johnswort
Juniper
Kaolin, colloidal
Knotgrass
Lactic acid
Lactose
Lavender compound, tincture of
Linden
Lipase
Lysine hydrochloride
Mannitol
Mycozyme
Myrrh, fluid extract of
Nettle
Nickel-pectin
Nux vomica extract
Orthophosphoric acid
Papaya, natural
Pectin
Peppermint
Peppermint spirit
Phenacetin
Potassium bicarbonate
Potassium carbonate
Protease
Prolase
Rhubarb fluid extract
Senna
Sodium chloride
Sodium salicylate
Stem bromelain
Strawberry

Strychnine
Tannic acid
Trillium
Woodruff

(iii) Charcoal, activated

(9) [Reserved]

(10) *External analgesic drug products*—
(i) *Analgesic and anesthetic drug products.*

Aspirin
Chloral hydrate
Chlorobutanol
Cyclomethycaine sulfate
Eugenol
Hexylresorcinol
Methapyrilene hydrochloride
Salicylamide
Thymol

(ii) *Counterirritant drug products.*

Chloral hydrate
Eucalyptus oil

(iii) *Male genital desensitizer drug products.*

Benzyl alcohol
Camphorated metacresol
Ephedrine hydrochloride

(iv) *Diaper rash drug products.* Any ingredient(s) labeled with claims or directions for use in the treatment and/or prevention of diaper rash.
(v) *Fever blister and cold sore treatment drug products.*

Allyl isothiocyanate
Aspirin
Bismuth sodium tartrate
Camphor (exceeding 3 percent)
Capsaicin
Capsicum
Capsicum oleoresin
Chloral hydrate
Chlorobutanol
Cyclomethycaine sulfate
Eucalyptus oil
Eugenol
Glycol salicylate
Hexylresorcinol
Histamine dihydrochloride
Menthol (exceeding 1 percent)
Methapyrilene hydrochloride
Methyl nicotinate
Methyl salicylate
Pectin
Salicylamide
Strong ammonia solution
Tannic acid
Thymol
Tripelennamine hydrochloride
Trolamine salicylate
Turpentine oil
Zinc sulfate

41

(vi) *Insect bite and sting drug products.*

Alcohol
Alcohol, ethoxylated alkyl
Benzalkonium chloride
Calamine
Ergot fluidextract
Ferric chloride
Panthenol
Peppermint oil
Pyrilamine maleate
Sodium borate
Trolamine salicylate
Turpentine oil
Zinc oxide
Zirconium oxide

(vii) *Poison ivy, poison oak, and poison sumac drug products.*

Alcohol
Aspirin
Benzethonium chloride
Benzocaine (0.5 to 1.25 percent)
Bithionol
Calamine
Cetalkonium chloride
Chloral hydrate
Chlorobutanol
Chlorpheniramine maleate
Creosote, beechwood
Cyclomethycaine sulfate
Dexpanthenol
Diperodon hydrochloride
Eucalyptus oil
Eugenol
Glycerin
Glycol salicylate
Hectorite
Hexylresorcinol
Hydrogen peroxide
Impatiens biflora tincture
Iron oxide
Isopropyl alcohol
Lanolin
Lead acetate
Merbromin
Mercuric chloride
Methapyrilene hydrochloride
Panthenol
Parethoxycaine hydrochloride
Phenyltoloxamine dihydrogen citrate
Povidone-vinylacetate copolymers
Pyrilamine maleate
Salicylamide
Salicylic acid
Simethicone
Sulfur
Tannic acid
Thymol
Trolamine salicylate
Turpentine oil
Zirconium oxide
Zyloxin

(11) [Reserved]
(12) *Laxative drug products*—(i)(A) *Bulk laxatives.*

Agar
Carrageenan (degraded)
Carrageenan (native)
Guar gun

(i)(B) *Bulk laxatives—Approved as of* March 29, 2007.

Granular dosage forms containing psyllium (hemicellulose), psyllium hydrophilic mucilloid, psyllium seed, psyllium seed (blond), psyllium seed husks, plantago husks, or plantago seed including, but not limited to, any granules that are:
(*1*) Swallowed dry prior to drinking liquid,
(*2*) Dispersed, suspended, or partially dissolved in liquid prior to swallowing,
(*3*) Chewed, partially chewed, or unchewed, and then washed down (or swallowed) with liquid, or
(*4*) Sprinkled over food.

(ii) *Saline laxative.*

Tartaric acid

(iii) *Stool softener.*

Poloxamer 188

(iv)(A) *Stimulant laxatives—Approved as of May 7, 1991.*

Aloin
Bile salts/acids
Calcium pantothenate
Calomel
Colocynth
Elaterin resin
Frangula
Gamboge
Ipomea
Jalap
Ox bile
Podophyllum resin
Prune concentrate dehydrate
Prune powder
Rhubarb, Chinese
Sodium Oleate

(iv)(B) *Stimulant laxatives—Approved as of January 29, 1999.*

Danthron
Phenolphthalein

(C) *Stimulant laxatives—Approved as of* November 5, 2002.

Aloe ingredients (aloe, aloe extract, aloe flower extract)
Cascara sagrada ingredients (casanthranol, cascara fluidextract aromatic, cascara sagrada bark, cascara sagrada extract, cascara sagrada fluidextract).

(13) [Reserved]
(14) *Oral health care drug products (nonantimicrobial).*

Antipyrine

Camphor
Cresol
Dibucaine
Dibucaine hydrochloride
Eucalyptol
Lidocaine
Lidocaine hydrochloride
Methly salicylate
Myrrh tincture
Pyrilamine maleate
Sorbitol
Sugars
Tetracaine
Tetracaine hydrochloride
Thymol

(15) *Topical otic drug products*—(i) *For the prevention of swimmer's ear and for the drying of water-clogged ears, approved as of May 7, 1991.*

Acetic acid

(ii) *For the prevention of swimmer's ear, approved as of August 15, 1995.*

Glycerin and anhydrous glycerin
Isopropyl alcohol

(16) *Poison treatment drug products.*

Ipecac fluidextract
Ipecac tincture
Zinc sulfate

(17) *Skin bleaching drug products.*

Mercury, ammoniated

(18) *Skin protectant drug products*—(i)(A) *Ingredients—Approved as of May 7, 1991.*

Allantoin (wound healing claims only)
Sulfur
Tannic acid
Zinc acetate (wound healing claims only)

(B) *Ingredients—Approved as of* June 4, 2004; June 6, 2005, *for products with annual sales less than $25,000.*

Beeswax
Bismuth subnitrate
Boric acid
Cetyl alcohol
Glyceryl stearate
Isopropyl palmitate
Live yeast cell derivative
Shark liver oil
Stearyl alcohol

(ii) *Astringent drug products.*

Acetone
Alcohol
Alum, ammonium
Alum, potassium
Aluminum chlorhydroxy complex
Aromatics
Benzalkonium chloride

Benzethonium chloride
Benzocaine
Benzoic acid
Boric acid
Calcium acetate (except calcium acetate monohydrate when combined with aluminum sulfate tetradecahydrate to provide an aluminum acetate solution as described in §347.20(b) of this chapter)
Camphor gum
Clove oil
Colloidal oatmeal
Cresol
Cupric sulfate
Eucalyptus oil
Eugenol
Ferric subsulfate (Monsel's Solution)
Honey
Isopropyl alcohol
Menthol
Methyl salicylate
Oxyquinoline sulfate
P-t-butyl-m-cresol
Peppermint oil
Phenol
Polyoxeythylene laurate
Potassium ferrocyanide
Sage oil
Silver nitrate
Sodium borate
Sodium diacetate
Talc
Tannic acid glycerite
Thymol
Topical starch
Zinc chloride
Zinc oxide
Zinc phenolsulfonate
Zinc stearate
Zinc sulfate

(iii) *Diaper rash drug products.*

Aluminum hydroxide
Cocoa butter
Cysteine hydrochloride
Glycerin
Protein hydrolysate
Racemethionine
Sulfur
Tannic acid
Zinc acetate
Zinc carbonate

(iv) *Fever blister and cold sore treatment drug products.*

Bismuth subnitrate
Boric acid
Pyridoxine hydrochloride
Sulfur
Tannic acid
Topical starch
Trolamine
Zinc sulfate

(v) *Insect bite and sting drug products*—(A) *Ingredients—Approved as of November 10, 1993.*

Alcohol
Alcohol, ethoxylated alkyl
Ammonia solution, strong
Ammonium hydroxide
Benzalkonium chloride
Camphor
Ergot fluid extract
Ferric chloride
Menthol
Peppermint oil
Phenol
Pyrilamine maleate
Sodium borate
Trolamine
Turpentine oil
Zirconium oxide

(B) *Ingredients—Approved as of* June 4, 2004; June 6, 2005, *for products with annual sales less than $25,000.*

Beeswax
Bismuth subnitrate
Boric acid
Cetyl alcohol
Glyceryl stearate
Isopropyl palmitate
Live yeast cell derivative
Shark liver oil
Stearyl alcohol

(vi) *Poison ivy, poison oak, and poison sumac drug products—*(A) *Ingredients— Approved as of November 10, 1993.*

Alcohol
Anion and cation exchange resins buffered
Benzethonium chloride
Benzocaine
Benzyl alcohol
Bismuth subnitrate
Bithionol
Boric acid
Camphor
Cetalkonium chloride
Chloral hydrate
Chlorpheniramine maleate
Creosote
Diperodon hydrochloride
Diphenhydramine hydrochloride
Eucalyptus oil
Ferric chloride
Glycerin
Hectorite
Hydrogen peroxide
Impatiens biflora tincture
Iron oxide
Isopropyl alcohol
Lanolin
Lead acetate
Lidocaine
Menthol
Merbromin
Mercuric chloride
Panthenol
Parethoxycaine hydrochloride
Phenol
Phenyltoloxamine dihydrogen citrate

Povidone-vinylacetate copolymers
Salicylic acid
Simethicone
Tannic acid
Topical starch
Trolamine
Turpentine oil
Zirconium oxide
Zyloxin

(B) *Ingredients—Approved as of* June 4, 2004; June 6, 2005, *for products with annual sales less than $25,000.*

Beeswax
Bismuth subnitrate
Boric acid
Cetyl alcohol
Glyceryl stearate
Isopropyl palmitate
Live yeast cell derivative
Shark liver oil
Stearyl alcohol

(19) [Reserved]
(20) *Weight control drug products.*

Alcohol
Alfalfa
Alginic acid
Anise oil
Arginine
Ascorbic acid
Bearberry
Biotin
Bone marrow, red
Buchu
Buchu, potassium extract
Caffeine
Caffeine citrate
Calcium
Calcium carbonate
Calcium caseinate
Calcium lactate
Calcium pantothenate
Carboxymethylcellulose sodium
Carrageenan
Cholecalcierol
Choline
Chondrus
Citric acid
Cnicus benedictus
Copper
Copper gluconate
Corn oil
Corn syrup
Corn silk, potassium extract
Cupric sulfate
Cyanocobalamin (vitamin B_{12})
Cystine
Dextrose
Docusate sodium
Ergocalciferol
Ferric ammonium citrate
Ferric pyrophosphate
Ferrous fumarate
Ferrous gluconate
Ferrous sulfate (iron)

Flax seed
Folic acid
Fructose
Guar gum
Histidine
Hydrastis canadensis
Inositol
Iodine
Isoleucine
Juniper, potassium extract
Karaya gum
Kelp
Lactose
Lecithin
Leucine
Liver concentrate
Lysine
Lysine hydrochloride
Magnesium
Magnesium oxide
Malt
Maltodextrin
Manganese citrate
Mannitol
Methionine
Methylcellulose
Mono- and di-glycerides
Niacinamide
Organic vegetables
Pancreatin
Pantothenic acid
Papain
Papaya enzymes
Pepsin
Phenacetin
Phenylalanine
Phosphorus
Phytolacca
Pineapple enzymes
Plantago seed
Potassium citrate
Pyridoxine hydrochloride (vitamin B_6)
Riboflavin
Rice polishings
Saccharin
Sea minerals
Sesame seed
Sodium
Sodium bicarbonate
Sodium caseinate
Sodium chloride (salt)
Soybean protein
Soy meal
Sucrose
Thiamine hydrochloride (vitamin B_1)
Thiamine mononitrate (vitamin B_1 mono-nitrate)
Threonine
Tricalcium phosphate
Tryptophan
Tyrosine
Uva ursi, potassium extract
Valine
Vegetable
Vitamin A
Vitamin A acetate
Vitamin A palmitate

Vitamin E
Wheat germ
Xanthan gum
Yeast

(21) *Ophthalmic drug products.* (i) *Ophthalmic anesthetic drug products.*

Antipyrine
Piperocaine hydrochloride

(ii) *Ophthalmic anti-infective drug products.*

Boric acid
Mild silver protein
Yellow mercuric oxide

(iii) *Ophthalmic astringent drug products.*

Infusion of rose petals

(iv) *Ophthalmic demulcent drug products.*

Polyethylene glycol 6000

(v) *Ophthalmic vasoconstrictor drug products.*

Phenylephrine hydrochloride (less than 0.08 percent)

(22) *Topical antifungal drug products.* (i) *Diaper rash drug products.* Any ingredient(s) labeled with claims or directions for use in the treatment and/or prevention of diaper rash.
(ii) *Ingredients.*

Alcloxa
Alum, potassium
Aluminum sulfate
Amyltricresols, secondary
Basic fuchsin
Benzethonium chloride
Benzoic acid
Benzoxiquine
Boric acid
Camphor
Candicidin
Chlorothymol
Coal tar
Dichlorophen
Menthol
Methylparaben
Oxyquinoline
Oxyquinoline sulfate
Phenol
Phenolate sodium
Phenyl salicylate
Propionic acid
Propylparaben
Resorcinol
Salicylic acid
Sodium borate
Sodium caprylate
Sodium propionate
Sulfur

Tannic acid
Thymol
Tolindate
Triacetin
Zinc caprylate
Zinc propionate

(iii) Any ingredient(s) labeled with claims or directions for use on the scalp or on the nails.

(iv) *Ingredients.*

Camphorated metacresol
Chloroxylenol
m-cresol
Nystatin

(23) *Internal analgesic drug products—*(i) *Approved as of November 10, 1993.*

Aminobenzoic acid
Antipyrine
Aspirin, aluminum
Calcium salicylate
Codeine
Codeine phosphate
Codeine sulfate
Iodoantipyrine
Lysine aspirin
Methapyrilene fumarate
Phenacetin
Pheniramine maleate
Pyrilamine maleate
Quininé
Salsalate
Sodium aminobenzoate

(ii) *Approved as of* February 22, 1999.

Any atropine ingredient
Any ephedrine ingredient

(24) *Orally administered menstrual drug products—*(i) *Approved as of November 10, 1993.*

Alcohol
Alfalfa leaves
Aloes
Asclepias tuberosa
Asparagus
Barosma
Bearberry (extract of uva ursi)
Bearberry fluidextract (extract of bearberry)
Blessed thistle (cnicus benedictus)
Buchu powdered extract (extract of buchu)
Calcium lactate
Calcium pantothenate
Capsicum oleoresin
Cascara fluidextract, aromatic (extract of cascara)
Chlorprophenpyridamine maleate
Cimicifuga racemosa
Codeine
Collinsonia (extract stone root)
Corn silk
Couch grass
Dog grass extract
Ethyl nitrite

Ferric chloride
Ferrous sulfate
Gentiana lutea (gentian)
Glycyrrhiza (licorice)
Homatropine methylbromide
Hydrangea, powdered extract (extract of hydrangea)
Hydrastis canadensis (golden seal)
Hyoscyamine sulfate
Juniper oil (oil of juniper)
Magnesium sulfate
Methapyrilene hydrochloride
Methenamine
Methylene blue
Natural estrogenic hormone
Niacinamide
Nutmeg oil (oil of nutmeg)
Oil of erigeron
Parsley
Peppermint spirit
Pepsin, essence
Phenacetin
Phenindamine tartrate
Phenyl salicylate
Piscidia erythrina
Pipsissewa
Potassium acetate
Potassium nitrate
Riboflavin
Saw palmetto
Senecio aureus
Sodium benzoate
Sodium nitrate
Sucrose
Sulferated oils of turpentine
Taraxacum officinale
Theobromine sodium salicylate
Theophylline
Thiamine hydrochloride
Triticum
Turpentine, venice (venice turpertine)
Urea

(ii) *Approved as of* February 22, 1999.

Any atropine ingredient
Any ephedrine ingredient

(25) *Pediculicide drug products—*(i) *Approved as of November 10, 1993.*

Benzocaine
Benzyl alcohol
Benzyl benzoate
Chlorophenothane (dichlorodiphenyl trichloroethane)
Coconut oil soap, aqueous
Copper oleate
Docusate sodium
Formic acid
Isobornyl thiocyanoacetate
Picrotoxin
Propylene glycol
Sabadilla alkaloids
Sulfur, sublimed
Thiocyanoacetate

(ii) *Approved as of June 14, 1994.* The combination of pyrethrum extract (formerly named pyrethrins) and piperonyl butoxide in an aerosol dosage formulation.

(26) *Anorectal drug products*—(i) *Anticholinergic drug products.*

Atropine
Belladonna extract

(ii) *Antiseptic drug products.*

Boric acid
Boroglycerin
Hydrastis
Phenol
Resorcinol
Sodium salicylic acid phenolate

(iii) *Astringent drug products.*

Tannic acid

(iv) *Counterirritant drug products.*

Camphor (greater than 3 to 11 percent)
Hydrastis
Menthol (1.25 to 16 percent)
Turpentine oil (rectified) (6 to 50 percent)

(v) *Keratolytic drug products.*

Precipitated sulfur
Sublimed sulfur

(vi) *Local anesthetic drug products.*

Diperodon
Phenacaine hydrochloride

(vii) *Other drug products.*

Collinsonia extract
Escherichia coli vaccines
Lappa extract
Leptandra extract
Live yeast cell derivative
Mullein

(viii) *Protectant drug products.*

Bismuth oxide
Bismuth subcarbonate
Bismuth subgallate
Bismuth subnitrate
Lanolin alcohols

(ix) *Vasoconstrictor drug products.*

Epinephrine undecylenate

(x) *Wound healing drug products.*

Cholecalciferol
Cod liver oil
Live yeast cell derivative
Peruvian balsam
Shark liver oil
Vitamin A

(xi) *Combination drug products.* Any combination drug product containing

hydrocortisone and pramoxine hydrochloride.

(27) *Topical antimicrobial drug products*—(i) *First aid antiseptic drug products.*

Ammoniated mercury
Calomel (mercurous chloride)
Merbromin (mercurochrome)
Mercufenol chloride (ortho-chloromercuriphenol, ortho-hydroxyphenylmercuric chloride)
Mercuric chloride (bichloride of mercury, mercury chloride)
Mercuric oxide, yellow
Mercuric salicylate
Mercuric sulfide, red
Mercury
Mercury oleate
Mercury sulfide
Nitromersol
Para-chloromercuriphenol
Phenylmercuric nitrate
Thimerosal
Vitromersol
Zyloxin

(ii) *Diaper rash drug products.*

Para-chloromercuriphenol
Any other ingredient containing mercury

(28) *Vaginal contraceptive drug products*—(i) *Approved as of October 22, 1998.*

Dodecaethylene glycol monolaurate (polyethylene glycol 600 monolaurate)
Laureth 10S
Methoxypolyoxyethyleneglycol 550 laurate
Phenylmercuric acetate
Phenylmercuric nitrate
Any other ingredient containing mercury

(ii) *Approved as of November 5, 2002.*
Octoxynol 9

(29) *Sunscreen drug products.* (i) *Ingredients.*

Diethanolamine methoxycinnamate
Digalloyl trioleate
Ethyl 4-[bis(hydroxypropyl)] aminobenzoate
Glyceryl aminobenzoate
Lawsone with dihydroxyacetone
Red petrolatum

(ii) Any ingredients labeled with any of the following or similar claims. Instant protection or protection immediately upon application.

Claims for "all-day" protection or extended wear claims citing a specific number of hours of protection that is inconsistent with the directions for application in 21 CFR 201.327.

(30) [Reserved]
(b) Any OTC drug product that is labeled, represented, or promoted for the

uses specified and containing any active ingredient(s) as specified in paragraph (a) of this section is regarded as a new drug within the meaning of section 210(p) of the Federal Food, Drug, and Cosmetic Act (the Act), for which an approved new drug application under section 505 of the Act and part 314 of this chapter is required for marketing. In the absence of an approved new drug application, such product is also misbranded under section 502 of the Act.

(c) Clinical investigations designed to obtain evidence that any drug product labeled, represented, or promoted for the OTC uses and containing any active ingredient(s) as specified in paragraph (a) of this section is safe and effective for the purpose intended must comply with the requirements and procedures governing the use of investigational new drugs set forth in part 312 of this chapter.

(d) Any OTC drug product that is not in compliance with this section is subject to regulatory action if initially introduced or initially delivered for introduction into interstate commerce after the dates specified in paragraphs (d)(1) through (d)(39) of this section.

(1) May 7, 1991, for products subject to paragraphs (a)(1) through (a)(2)(i), (a)(3)(i), (a)(4)(i), (a)(6)(i)(A), (a)(6)(ii)(A), (a)(7) (except as covered by paragraph (d)(3) of this section), (a)(8)(i), (a)(10)(i) through (a)(10)(iii), (a)(12)(i)(A), (a)(12)(ii) through (a)(12)(iv)(A), (a)(14) through (a)(15)(i), (a)(16) through (a)(18)(i)(A), (a)(18)(ii) (except as covered by paragraph (d)(22) of this section), (a)(18)(iii), (a)(18)(iv), (a)(18)(v)(A), and (a)(18)(vi)(A) of this section.

(2) February 10, 1992, for products subject to paragraph (a)(20) of this section.

(3) December 4, 1992, for products subject to paragraph (a)(7) of this section that contain menthol as an antipruritic in combination with the antidandruff ingredient coal tar identified in § 358.710(a)(1) of this chapter. This section does not apply to products allowed by § 358.720(b) of this chapter after April 5, 2007.

(4) February 28, 1990, for products subject to paragraph (a)(6)(iii) of this section, except those that contain ipecac.

(5) September 14, 1993, for products subject to paragraph (a)(6)(iii) of this section that contain ipecac.

(6) December 9, 1993, for products subject to paragraph (a)(6)(i)(B) of this section.

(7) March 6, 1989, for products subject to paragraph (a)(21) of this section, except those that contain ophthalmic anti-infective ingredients listed in paragraph (a)(21)(ii).

(8) June 18, 1993, for products subject to paragraph (a)(21) of this section that contain ophthalmic anti-infective ingredients.

(9) June 18, 1993, for products subject to paragraph (a)(10)(iv) of this section.

(10) June 18, 1993, for products subject to paragraph (a)(22)(i) of this section.

(11) November 10, 1993, for products subject to paragraphs (a)(8)(ii), (a)(10)(v) through (a)(10)(vii), (a)(18)(ii) (except products that contain ferric subsulfate as covered by paragraph (d)(22) of this section and except products that contain calcium acetate monohydrate as covered by paragraph (d)(39) of this section) through (a)(18)(v)(A), (a)(18)(vi)(A), (a)(22)(ii), (a)(23)(i), (a)(24)(i), and (a)(25) of this section.

(12) March 2, 1994, for products subject to paragraph (a)(22)(iii) of this section.

(13) August 5, 1991, for products subject to paragraph (a)(26) of this section, except for those that contain live yeast cell derivative and a combination of hydrocortisone and pramoxine hydrochloride.

(14) September 2, 1994, for products subject to paragraph (a)(26)(vii) and (a)(26)(x) of this section that contain live yeast cell derivative.

(15) September 23, 1994, for products subject to paragraph (a)(22)(iv) of this section.

(16) June 14, 1994, for products subject to paragraph (a)(25)(ii) of this section.

(17) April 19, 2004, for products subject to paragraph (a)(3)(ii) of this section. April 18, 2005, for products with annual sales less than $25,000.

(18) August 15, 1995, for products subject to paragraph (a)(15)(ii) of this section.

(19) October 2, 1987, for products subject to paragraph (a)(6)(iv)(A) of this section.

(20) January 29, 1996, for products subject to paragraph (a)(6)(iv)(B) of this section.

(21) April 21, 1994, for products subject to paragraph (a)(8)(iii) of this section.

(22) April 21, 1993, for products subject to paragraph (a)(18)(ii) of this section that contain ferric subsulfate.

(23) August 23, 1995, for products subject to paragraph (a)(6)(ii)(B) of this section.

(24) October 7, 1996, for products subject to paragraph (a)(2)(ii) of this section.

(25) June 19, 1996, for products subject to paragraph (a)(6)(iv)(C) of this section.

(26) February 22, 1999, for products subject to paragraphs (a)(23)(ii) and (a)(24)(ii) of this section.

(27) [Reserved]

(28) October 22, 1998, for products subject to paragraphs (a)(27) and (a)(28)(i) of this section.

(29) January 29, 1999, for products subject to paragraph (a)(12)(iv)(B) of this section.

(30) November 5, 2002, for products subject to paragraph (a)(12)(iv)(C) of this section.

(31) December 31, 2002, for products subject to paragraph (a)(29)(i) of this section.

(32) June 4, 2004, for products subject to paragraphs (a)(18)(i)(B), (a)(18)(v)(B), and (a)(18)(vi)(B) of this section. June 6, 2005, for products with annual sales less than $25,000.

(33) October 29, 2001, for products subject to paragraph (a)(6)(iv)(D) of this section.

(34) December 9, 2004, for products subject to paragraph (a)(4)(ii) of this section. June 9, 2005, for products with annual sales less than $25,000.

(35) [Reserved]

(36) November 5, 2002, for products subject to paragraph (a)(28)(ii) of this section.

(37) September 25, 2003, for products subject to paragraph (a)(26)(xi) of this section.

(38) October 1, 2007, for products subject to paragraph (a)(12)(i)(B) of this section.

(39) September 6, 2010, for products subject to paragraph (a)(18)(ii) of this section that contain calcium acetate monohydrate, except as provided in § 347.20(b) of this chapter.

(40) December 17, 2012, for products subject to paragraph (a)(29)(ii) of this section. December 17, 2013, for products with annual sales less than $25,000.

[55 FR 46919, Nov. 7, 1990]

EDITORIAL NOTE: For FEDERAL REGISTER citations affecting § 310.545, see the List of CFR Sections Affected, which appears in the Finding Aids section of the printed volume and at *www.fdsys.gov.*

EFFECTIVE DATE NOTE: At 61 FR 9571, Mar. 8, 1996, in § 310.545 in paragraph (a)(6)(ii)(B), the entry for "1-desoxyephedrine (topical)" was stayed until further notice.

§ 310.546 **Drug products containing active ingredients offered over-the-counter (OTC) for the treatment and/or prevention of nocturnal leg muscle cramps.**

(a) Quinine sulfate alone or in combination with vitamin E has been present in over-the-counter (OTC) drug products for the treatment and/or prevention of nocturnal leg muscle cramps, *i.e.*, a condition of localized pain in the lower extremities usually occurring in middle life and beyond with no regular pattern concerning time or severity. There is a lack of adequate data to establish general recognition of the safety and effectiveness of quinine sulfate, vitamin E, or any other ingredients for OTC use in the treatment and/or prevention of nocturnal leg muscle cramps. In the doses used to treat or prevent this condition, quinine sulfate has caused adverse events such as transient visual and auditory disturbances, dizziness, fever, nausea, vomiting, and diarrhea. Quinine sulfate may cause unpredictable serious and life-threatening hypersensitivity reactions requiring medical intervention and hospitalization; fatalities have been reported. The risk associated with use of quinine sulfate, in the absence of evidence of its effectiveness, outweighs any potential benefit in treating and/or preventing this benign, self-limiting condition. Based upon the adverse benefit-to-risk ratio, any drug product containing quinine or quinine sulfate cannot be considered generally recognized as safe for the treatment and/or prevention of nocturnal leg muscle cramps.

(b) Any OTC drug product that is labeled, represented, or promoted for the treatment and/or prevention of nocturnal leg muscle cramps is regarded as a new drug within the meaning of section 201(p) of the Federal Food, Drug, and Cosmetic Act (the act), for which an approved application or abbreviated application under section 505 of the act and part 314 of this chapter is required for marketing. In the absence of an approved new drug application or abbreviated new drug application, such product is also misbranded under section 502 of the act.

(c) Clinical investigations designed to obtain evidence that any drug product labeled, represented, or promoted for OTC use for the treatment and/or prevention of nocturnal leg muscle cramps is safe and effective for the purpose intended must comply with the requirements and procedures governing the use of investigational new drugs set forth in part 312 of this chapter.

(d) After February 22, 1995, any such OTC drug product initially introduced or initially delivered for introduction into interstate commerce that is not in compliance with this section is subject to regulatory action.

[59 FR 43252, Aug. 22, 1994]

§ 310.547 Drug products containing quinine offered over-the-counter (OTC) for the treatment and/or prevention of malaria.

(a) Quinine and quinine salts have been used OTC for the treatment and/or prevention of malaria, a serious and potentially life-threatening disease. Quinine is no longer the drug of choice for the treatment and/or prevention of most types of malaria. In addition, there are serious and complicating aspects of the disease itself and some potentially serious and life-threatening risks associated with the use of quinine at doses employed for the treatment of malaria. There is a lack of adequate data to establish general recognition of the safety of quinine drug products for OTC use in the treatment and/or prevention of malaria. Therefore, quinine or quinine salts cannot be safely and effectively used for the treatment and/

or prevention of malaria except under the care and supervision of a doctor.

(b) Any OTC drug product containing quinine or quinine salts that is labeled, represented, or promoted for the treatment and/or prevention of malaria is regarded as a new drug within the meaning of section 201(p) of the act, for which an approved application or abbreviated application under section 505 of the act and part 314 of this chapter is required for marketing. In the absence of an approved new drug application or abbreviated new drug application, such product is also misbranded under section 502 of the act.

(c) Clinical investigations designed to obtain evidence that any drug product labeled, represented, or promoted for OTC use for the treatment and/or prevention of malaria is safe and effective for the purpose intended must comply with the requirements and procedures governing the use of investigational new drugs set forth in part 312 of this chapter.

(d) After April 20, 1998, any such OTC drug product initially introduced or initially delivered for introduction into interstate commerce that is not in compliance with this section is subject to regulatory action.

[63 FR 13528, Mar. 20, 1998]

§ 310.548 Drug products containing colloidal silver ingredients or silver salts offered over-the-counter (OTC) for the treatment and/or prevention of disease.

(a) Colloidal silver ingredients and silver salts have been marketed in over-the-counter (OTC) drug products for the treatment and prevention of numerous disease conditions. There are serious and complicating aspects to many of the diseases these silver ingredients purport to treat or prevent. Further, there is a lack of adequate data to establish general recognition of the safety and effectiveness of colloidal silver ingredients or silver salts for OTC use in the treatment or prevention of any disease. These ingredients and salts include, but are not limited to, silver proteins, mild silver protein, strong silver protein, silver, silver ion, silver chloride, silver cyanide, silver iodide, silver oxide, and silver phosphate.

(b) Any OTC drug product containing colloidal silver ingredients or silver salts that is labeled, represented, or promoted for the treatment and/or prevention of any disease is regarded as a new drug within the meaning of section 201(p) of the Federal Food, Drug, and Cosmetic Act (the act) for which an approved application or abbreviated application under section 505 of the act and part 314 of this chapter is required for marketing. In the absence of an approved new drug application or abbreviated new drug application, such product is also misbranded under section 502 of the act.

(c) Clinical investigations designed to obtain evidence that any drug product containing colloidal silver or silver salts labeled, represented, or promoted for any OTC drug use is safe and effective for the purpose intended must comply with the requirements and procedures governing the use of investigational new drugs as set forth in part 312 of this chapter.

(d) After September 16, 1999, any such OTC drug product containing colloidal silver or silver salts initially introduced or initially delivered for introduction into interstate commerce that is not in compliance with this section is subject to regulatory action.

[64 FR 44658, Aug. 17, 1999]

PART 312—INVESTIGATIONAL NEW DRUG APPLICATION

Subpart A—General Provisions

312.120 Foreign clinical studies not conducted under an IND.
312.130 Availability for public disclosure of data and information in an IND.
312.140 Address for correspondence.
312.145 Guidance documents.

Subpart G—Drugs for Investigational Use in Laboratory Research Animals or in Vitro Tests

312.160 Drugs for investigational use in laboratory research animals or in vitro tests.

Subpart H [Reserved]

Subpart I—Expanded Access to Investigational Drugs for Treatment Use

312.300 General.
312.305 Requirements for all expanded access uses.
312.310 Individual patients, including for emergency use.
312.315 Intermediate-size patient populations.
312.320 Treatment IND or treatment protocol.

AUTHORITY: 21 U.S.C. 321, 331, 351, 352, 353, 355, 360bbb, 371; 42 U.S.C. 262.

SOURCE: 52 FR 8831, Mar. 19, 1987, unless otherwise noted.

EDITORIAL NOTE: Nomenclature changes to part 312 appear at 69 FR 13717, Mar. 24, 2004.

Subpart A—General Provisions

§ **312.1 Scope.**

(a) This part contains procedures and requirements governing the use of investigational new drugs, including procedures and requirements for the submission to, and review by, the Food and Drug Administration of investigational new drug applications (IND's). An investigational new drug for which an IND is in effect in accordance with this part is exempt from the premarketing approval requirements that are otherwise applicable and may be shipped lawfully for the purpose of conducting clinical investigations of that drug.

(b) References in this part to regulations in the Code of Federal Regulations are to chapter I of title 21, unless otherwise noted.

§ **312.2 Applicability.**

(a) *Applicability.* Except as provided in this section, this part applies to all clinical investigations of products that are subject to section 505 of the Federal Food, Drug, and Cosmetic Act or to the licensing provisions of the Public Health Service Act (58 Stat. 632, as amended (42 U.S.C. 201 *et seq.*)).

(b) *Exemptions.* (1) The clinical investigation of a drug product that is lawfully marketed in the United States is exempt from the requirements of this part if all the following apply:

(i) The investigation is not intended to be reported to FDA as a well-controlled study in support of a new indication for use nor intended to be used to support any other significant change in the labeling for the drug;

(ii) If the drug that is undergoing investigation is lawfully marketed as a prescription drug product, the investigation is not intended to support a significant change in the advertising for the product;

(iii) The investigation does not involve a route of administration or dosage level or use in a patient population or other factor that significantly increases the risks (or decreases the acceptability of the risks) associated with the use of the drug product;

(iv) The investigation is conducted in compliance with the requirements for institutional review set forth in part 56 and with the requirements for informed consent set forth in part 50; and

(v) The investigation is conducted in compliance with the requirements of § 312.7.

(2)(i) A clinical investigation involving an in vitro diagnostic biological product listed in paragraph (b)(2)(ii) of this section is exempt from the requirements of this part if (*a*) it is intended to be used in a diagnostic procedure that confirms the diagnosis made by another, medically established, diagnostic product or procedure and (*b*) it is shipped in compliance with § 312.160.

(ii) In accordance with paragraph (b)(2)(i) of this section, the following products are exempt from the requirements of this part: (*a*) blood grouping serum; (*b*) reagent red blood cells; and (*c*) anti-human globulin.

(3) A drug intended solely for tests in vitro or in laboratory research animals is exempt from the requirements of this part if shipped in accordance with § 312.160.

(4) FDA will not accept an application for an investigation that is exempt under the provisions of paragraph (b)(1) of this section.

(5) A clinical investigation involving use of a placebo is exempt from the requirements of this part if the investigation does not otherwise require submission of an IND.

(6) A clinical investigation involving an exception from informed consent under §50.24 of this chapter is not exempt from the requirements of this part.

(c) *Bioavailability studies.* The applicability of this part to in vivo bioavailability studies in humans is subject to the provisions of §320.31.

(d) *Unlabeled indication.* This part does not apply to the use in the practice of medicine for an unlabeled indication of a new drug product approved under part 314 or of a licensed biological product.

(e) *Guidance.* FDA may, on its own initiative, issue guidance on the applicability of this part to particular investigational uses of drugs. On request, FDA will advise on the applicability of this part to a planned clinical investigation.

[52 FR 8831, Mar. 19, 1987, as amended at 61 FR 51529, Oct. 2, 1996; 64 FR 401, Jan. 5, 1999]

§312.3 Definitions and interpretations.

(a) The definitions and interpretations of terms contained in section 201 of the Act apply to those terms when used in this part:

(b) The following definitions of terms also apply to this part:

Act means the Federal Food, Drug, and Cosmetic Act (secs. 201–902, 52 Stat. 1040 *et seq.*, as amended (21 U.S.C. 301–392)).

Clinical investigation means any experiment in which a drug is administered or dispensed to, or used involving, one or more human subjects. For the purposes of this part, an experiment is any use of a drug except for the use of a marketed drug in the course of medical practice.

Contract research organization means a person that assumes, as an independent contractor with the sponsor, one or more of the obligations of a sponsor, e.g., design of a protocol, selection or monitoring of investigations, evalua-

tion of reports, and preparation of materials to be submitted to the Food and Drug Administration.

FDA means the Food and Drug Administration.

IND means an investigational new drug application. For purposes of this part, "IND" is synonymous with "Notice of Claimed Investigational Exemption for a New Drug."

Independent ethics committee (IEC) means a review panel that is responsible for ensuring the protection of the rights, safety, and well-being of human subjects involved in a clinical investigation and is adequately constituted to provide assurance of that protection. An institutional review board (IRB), as defined in §56.102(g) of this chapter and subject to the requirements of part 56 of this chapter, is one type of IEC.

Investigational new drug means a new drug or biological drug that is used in a clinical investigation. The term also includes a biological product that is used in vitro for diagnostic purposes. The terms "investigational drug" and "investigational new drug" are deemed to be synonymous for purposes of this part.

Investigator means an individual who actually conducts a clinical investigation (*i.e.*, under whose immediate direction the drug is administered or dispensed to a subject). In the event an investigation is conducted by a team of individuals, the investigator is the responsible leader of the team. "Subinvestigator" includes any other individual member of that team.

Marketing application means an application for a new drug submitted under section 505(b) of the act or a biologics license application for a biological product submitted under the Public Health Service Act.

Sponsor means a person who takes responsibility for and initiates a clinical investigation. The sponsor may be an individual or pharmaceutical company, governmental agency, academic institution, private organization, or other organization. The sponsor does not actually conduct the investigation unless the sponsor is a sponsor-investigator. A person other than an individual that uses one or more of its own employees to conduct an investigation that it has

53

initiated is a sponsor, not a sponsor-investigator, and the employees are investigators.

Sponsor-Investigator means an individual who both initiates and conducts an investigation, and under whose immediate direction the investigational drug is administered or dispensed. The term does not include any person other than an individual. The requirements applicable to a sponsor-investigator under this part include both those applicable to an investigator and a sponsor.

Subject means a human who participates in an investigation, either as a recipient of the investigational new drug or as a control. A subject may be a healthy human or a patient with a disease.

[52 FR 8831, Mar. 19, 1987, as amended at 64 FR 401, Jan. 5, 1999; 64 FR 56449, Oct. 20, 1999; 73 FR 22815, Apr. 28, 2008]

§ 312.6 Labeling of an investigational new drug.

(a) The immediate package of an investigational new drug intended for human use shall bear a label with the statement "Caution: New Drug—Limited by Federal (or United States) law to investigational use."

(b) The label or labeling of an investigational new drug shall not bear any statement that is false or misleading in any particular and shall not represent that the investigational new drug is safe or effective for the purposes for which it is being investigated.

(c) The appropriate FDA Center Director, according to the procedures set forth in §§ 201.26 or 610.68 of this chapter, may grant an exception or alternative to the provision in paragraph (a) of this section, to the extent that this provision is not explicitly required by statute, for specified lots, batches, or other units of a human drug product that is or will be included in the Strategic National Stockpile.

[52 FR 8831, Mar. 19, 1987, as amended at 72 FR 73599, Dec. 28, 2007]

§ 312.7 Promotion of investigational drugs.

(a) *Promotion of an investigational new drug.* A sponsor or investigator, or any person acting on behalf of a sponsor or investigator, shall not represent in a promotional context that an investigational new drug is safe or effective for the purposes for which it is under investigation or otherwise promote the drug. This provision is not intended to restrict the full exchange of scientific information concerning the drug, including dissemination of scientific findings in scientific or lay media. Rather, its intent is to restrict promotional claims of safety or effectiveness of the drug for a use for which it is under investigation and to preclude commercialization of the drug before it is approved for commercial distribution.

(b) *Commercial distribution of an investigational new drug.* A sponsor or investigator shall not commercially distribute or test market an investigational new drug.

(c) *Prolonging an investigation.* A sponsor shall not unduly prolong an investigation after finding that the results of the investigation appear to establish sufficient data to support a marketing application.

[52 FR 8831, Mar. 19, 1987, as amended at 52 FR 19476, May 22, 1987; 67 FR 9585, Mar. 4, 2002; 74 FR 40899, Aug. 13, 2009]

§ 312.8 Charging for investigational drugs under an IND.

(a) *General criteria for charging.* (1) A sponsor must meet the applicable requirements in paragraph (b) of this section for charging in a clinical trial or paragraph (c) of this section for charging for expanded access to an investigational drug for treatment use under subpart I of this part, except that sponsors need not fulfill the requirements in this section to charge for an approved drug obtained from another entity not affiliated with the sponsor for use as part of the clinical trial evaluation (e.g., in a clinical trial of a new use of the approved drug, for use of the approved drug as an active control).

(2) A sponsor must justify the amount to be charged in accordance with paragraph (d) of this section.

(3) A sponsor must obtain prior written authorization from FDA to charge for an investigational drug.

(4) FDA will withdraw authorization to charge if it determines that charging is interfering with the development of a drug for marketing approval or

that the criteria for the authorization are no longer being met.

(b) *Charging in a clinical trial*—(1) *Charging for a sponsor's drug.* A sponsor who wishes to charge for its investigational drug, including investigational use of its approved drug, must:

(i) Provide evidence that the drug has a potential clinical benefit that, if demonstrated in the clinical investigations, would provide a significant advantage over available products in the diagnosis, treatment, mitigation, or prevention of a disease or condition;

(ii) Demonstrate that the data to be obtained from the clinical trial would be essential to establishing that the drug is effective or safe for the purpose of obtaining initial approval of a drug, or would support a significant change in the labeling of an approved drug (e.g., new indication, inclusion of comparative safety information); and

(iii) Demonstrate that the clinical trial could not be conducted without charging because the cost of the drug is extraordinary to the sponsor. The cost may be extraordinary due to manufacturing complexity, scarcity of a natural resource, the large quantity of drug needed (e.g., due to the size or duration of the trial), or some combination of these or other extraordinary circumstances (e.g., resources available to a sponsor).

(2) *Duration of charging in a clinical trial.* Unless FDA specifies a shorter period, charging may continue for the length of the clinical trial.

(c) *Charging for expanded access to investigational drug for treatment use.* (1) A sponsor who wishes to charge for expanded access to an investigational drug for treatment use under subpart I of this part must provide reasonable assurance that charging will not interfere with developing the drug for marketing approval.

(2) For expanded access under §312.320 (treatment IND or treatment protocol), such assurance must include:

(i) Evidence of sufficient enrollment in any ongoing clinical trial(s) needed for marketing approval to reasonably assure FDA that the trial(s) will be successfully completed as planned;

(ii) Evidence of adequate progress in the development of the drug for marketing approval; and

(iii) Information submitted under the general investigational plan (§312.23(a)(3)(iv)) specifying the drug development milestones the sponsor plans to meet in the next year.

(3) The authorization to charge is limited to the number of patients authorized to receive the drug under the treatment use, if there is a limitation.

(4) Unless FDA specifies a shorter period, charging for expanded access to an investigational drug for treatment use under subpart I of this part may continue for 1 year from the time of FDA authorization. A sponsor may request that FDA reauthorize charging for additional periods.

(d) *Costs recoverable when charging for an investigational drug.* (1) A sponsor may recover only the direct costs of making its investigational drug available.

(i) Direct costs are costs incurred by a sponsor that can be specifically and exclusively attributed to providing the drug for the investigational use for which FDA has authorized cost recovery. Direct costs include costs per unit to manufacture the drug (e.g., raw materials, labor, and nonreusable supplies and equipment used to manufacture the quantity of drug needed for the use for which charging is authorized) or costs to acquire the drug from another manufacturing source, and direct costs to ship and handle (e.g., store) the drug.

(ii) Indirect costs include costs incurred primarily to produce the drug for commercial sale (e.g., costs for facilities and equipment used to manufacture the supply of investigational drug, but that are primarily intended to produce large quantities of drug for eventual commercial sale) and research and development, administrative, labor, or other costs that would be incurred even if the clinical trial or treatment use for which charging is authorized did not occur.

(2) For expanded access to an investigational drug for treatment use under §§312.315 (intermediate-size patient populations) and 312.320 (treatment IND or treatment protocol), in addition to the direct costs described in paragraph (d)(1)(i) of this section, a

sponsor may recover the costs of monitoring the expanded access IND or protocol, complying with IND reporting requirements, and other administrative costs directly associated with the expanded access IND.

(3) To support its calculation for cost recovery, a sponsor must provide supporting documentation to show that the calculation is consistent with the requirements of paragraphs (d)(1) and, if applicable, (d)(2) of this section. The documentation must be accompanied by a statement that an independent certified public accountant has reviewed and approved the calculations.

[74 FR 40899, Aug. 13, 2009]

§ 312.10 Waivers.

(a) A sponsor may request FDA to waive applicable requirement under this part. A waiver request may be submitted either in an IND or in an information amendment to an IND. In an emergency, a request may be made by telephone or other rapid communication means. A waiver request is required to contain at least one of the following:

(1) An explanation why the sponsor's compliance with the requirement is unnecessary or cannot be achieved;

(2) A description of an alternative submission or course of action that satisfies the purpose of the requirement; or

(3) Other information justifying a waiver.

(b) FDA may grant a waiver if it finds that the sponsor's noncompliance would not pose a significant and unreasonable risk to human subjects of the investigation and that one of the following is met:

(1) The sponsor's compliance with the requirement is unnecessary for the agency to evaluate the application, or compliance cannot be achieved;

(2) The sponsor's proposed alternative satisfies the requirement; or

(3) The applicant's submission otherwise justifies a waiver.

[52 FR 8831, Mar. 19, 1987, as amended at 52 FR 23031, June 17, 1987; 67 FR 9585, Mar. 4, 2002]

Subpart B—Investigational New Drug Application (IND)

§ 312.20 Requirement for an IND.

(a) A sponsor shall submit an IND to FDA if the sponsor intends to conduct a clinical investigation with an investigational new drug that is subject to § 312.2(a).

(b) A sponsor shall not begin a clinical investigation subject to § 312.2(a) until the investigation is subject to an IND which is in effect in accordance with § 312.40.

(c) A sponsor shall submit a separate IND for any clinical investigation involving an exception from informed consent under § 50.24 of this chapter. Such a clinical investigation is not permitted to proceed without the prior written authorization from FDA. FDA shall provide a written determination 30 days after FDA receives the IND or earlier.

[52 FR 8831, Mar. 19, 1987, as amended at 61 FR 51529, Oct. 2, 1996; 62 FR 32479, June 16, 1997]

§ 312.21 Phases of an investigation.

An IND may be submitted for one or more phases of an investigation. The clinical investigation of a previously untested drug is generally divided into three phases. Although in general the phases are conducted sequentially, they may overlap. These three phases of an investigation are a follows:

(a) *Phase 1.* (1) Phase 1 includes the initial introduction of an investigational new drug into humans. Phase 1 studies are typically closely monitored and may be conducted in patients or normal volunteer subjects. These studies are designed to determine the metabolism and pharmacologic actions of the drug in humans, the side effects associated with increasing doses, and, if possible, to gain early evidence on effectiveness. During Phase 1, sufficient information about the drug's pharmacokinetics and pharmacological effects should be obtained to permit the design of well-controlled, scientifically valid, Phase 2 studies. The total number of subjects and patients included in Phase 1 studies varies with the drug, but is generally in the range of 20 to 80.

(2) Phase 1 studies also include studies of drug metabolism, structure-activity relationships, and mechanism of action in humans, as well as studies in which investigational drugs are used as research tools to explore biological phenomena or disease processes.

(b) *Phase 2.* Phase 2 includes the controlled clinical studies conducted to evaluate the effectiveness of the drug for a particular indication or indications in patients with the disease or condition under study and to determine the common short-term side effects and risks associated with the drug. Phase 2 studies are typically well controlled, closely monitored, and conducted in a relatively small number of patients, usually involving no more than several hundred subjects.

(c) *Phase 3.* Phase 3 studies are expanded controlled and uncontrolled trials. They are performed after preliminary evidence suggesting effectiveness of the drug has been obtained, and are intended to gather the additional information about effectiveness and safety that is needed to evaluate the overall benefit-risk relationship of the drug and to provide an adequate basis for physician labeling. Phase 3 studies usually include from several hundred to several thousand subjects.

§ 312.22 General principles of the IND submission.

(a) FDA's primary objectives in reviewing an IND are, in all phases of the investigation, to assure the safety and rights of subjects, and, in Phase 2 and 3, to help assure that the quality of the scientific evaluation of drugs is adequate to permit an evaluation of the drug's effectiveness and safety. Therefore, although FDA's review of Phase 1 submissions will focus on assessing the safety of Phase 1 investigations, FDA's review of Phases 2 and 3 submissions will also include an assessment of the scientific quality of the clinical investigations and the likelihood that the investigations will yield data capable of meeting statutory standards for marketing approval.

(b) The amount of information on a particular drug that must be submitted in an IND to assure the accomplishment of the objectives described in paragraph (a) of this section depends upon such factors as the novelty of the drug, the extent to which it has been studied previously, the known or suspected risks, and the developmental phase of the drug.

(c) The central focus of the initial IND submission should be on the general investigational plan and the protocols for specific human studies. Subsequent amendments to the IND that contain new or revised protocols should build logically on previous submissions and should be supported by additional information, including the results of animal toxicology studies or other human studies as appropriate. Annual reports to the IND should serve as the focus for reporting the status of studies being conducted under the IND and should update the general investigational plan for the coming year.

(d) The IND format set forth in § 312.23 should be followed routinely by sponsors in the interest of fostering an efficient review of applications. Sponsors are expected to exercise considerable discretion, however, regarding the content of information submitted in each section, depending upon the kind of drug being studied and the nature of the available information. Section 312.23 outlines the information needed for a commercially sponsored IND for a new molecular entity. A sponsor-investigator who uses, as a research tool, an investigational new drug that is already subject to a manufacturer's IND or marketing application should follow the same general format, but ordinarily may, if authorized by the manufacturer, refer to the manufacturer's IND or marketing application in providing the technical information supporting the proposed clinical investigation. A sponsor-investigator who uses an investigational drug not subject to a manufacturer's IND or marketing application is ordinarily required to submit all technical information supporting the IND, unless such information may be referenced from the scientific literature.

§ 312.23 IND content and format.

(a) A sponsor who intends to conduct a clinical investigation subject to this part shall submit an "Investigational New Drug Application" (IND) including, in the following order:

(1) *Cover sheet (Form FDA–1571).* A cover sheet for the application containing the following:

(i) The name, address, and telephone number of the sponsor, the date of the application, and the name of the investigational new drug.

(ii) Identification of the phase or phases of the clinical investigation to be conducted.

(iii) A commitment not to begin clinical investigations until an IND covering the investigations is in effect.

(iv) A commitment that an Institutional Review Board (IRB) that complies with the requirements set forth in part 56 will be responsible for the initial and continuing review and approval of each of the studies in the proposed clinical investigation and that the investigator will report to the IRB proposed changes in the research activity in accordance with the requirements of part 56.

(v) A commitment to conduct the investigation in accordance with all other applicable regulatory requirements.

(vi) The name and title of the person responsible for monitoring the conduct and progress of the clinical investigations.

(vii) The name(s) and title(s) of the person(s) responsible under § 312.32 for review and evaluation of information relevant to the safety of the drug.

(viii) If a sponsor has transferred any obligations for the conduct of any clinical study to a contract research organization, a statement containing the name and address of the contract research organization, identification of the clinical study, and a listing of the obligations transferred. If all obligations governing the conduct of the study have been transferred, a general statement of this transfer—in lieu of a listing of the specific obligations transferred—may be submitted.

(ix) The signature of the sponsor or the sponsor's authorized representative. If the person signing the application does not reside or have a place of business within the United States, the IND is required to contain the name and address of, and be countersigned by, an attorney, agent, or other authorized official who resides or maintains a place of business within the United States.

(2) *A table of contents.*

(3) *Introductory statement and general investigational plan.* (i) A brief introductory statement giving the name of the drug and all active ingredients, the drug's pharmacological class, the structural formula of the drug (if known), the formulation of the dosage form(s) to be used, the route of administration, and the broad objectives and planned duration of the proposed clinical investigation(s).

(ii) A brief summary of previous human experience with the drug, with reference to other IND's if pertinent, and to investigational or marketing experience in other countries that may be relevant to the safety of the proposed clinical investigation(s).

(iii) If the drug has been withdrawn from investigation or marketing in any country for any reason related to safety or effectiveness, identification of the country(ies) where the drug was withdrawn and the reasons for the withdrawal.

(iv) A brief description of the overall plan for investigating the drug product for the following year. The plan should include the following: (*a*) The rationale for the drug or the research study; (*b*) the indication(s) to be studied; (*c*) the general approach to be followed in evaluating the drug; (*d*) the kinds of clinical trials to be conducted in the first year following the submission (if plans are not developed for the entire year, the sponsor should so indicate); (*e*) the estimated number of patients to be given the drug in those studies; and (*f*) any risks of particular severity or seriousness anticipated on the basis of the toxicological data in animals or prior studies in humans with the drug or related drugs.

(4) [Reserved]

(5) *Investigator's brochure.* If required under § 312.55, a copy of the investigator's brochure, containing the following information:

(i) A brief description of the drug substance and the formulation, including the structural formula, if known.

(ii) A summary of the pharmacological and toxicological effects of the drug in animals and, to the extent known, in humans.

(iii) A summary of the pharmacokinetics and biological disposition of the drug in animals and, if known, in humans.

(iv) A summary of information relating to safety and effectiveness in humans obtained from prior clinical studies. (Reprints of published articles on such studies may be appended when useful.)

(v) A description of possible risks and side effects to be anticipated on the basis of prior experience with the drug under investigation or with related drugs, and of precautions or special monitoring to be done as part of the investigational use of the drug.

(6) *Protocols.* (i) A protocol for each planned study. (Protocols for studies not submitted initially in the IND should be submitted in accordance with §312.30(a).) In general, protocols for Phase 1 studies may be less detailed and more flexible than protocols for Phase 2 and 3 studies. Phase 1 protocols should be directed primarily at providing an outline of the investigation—an estimate of the number of patients to be involved, a description of safety exclusions, and a description of the dosing plan including duration, dose, or method to be used in determining dose—and should specify in detail only those elements of the study that are critical to safety, such as necessary monitoring of vital signs and blood chemistries. Modifications of the experimental design of Phase 1 studies that do not affect critical safety assessments are required to be reported to FDA only in the annual report.

(ii) In Phases 2 and 3, detailed protocols describing all aspects of the study should be submitted. A protocol for a Phase 2 or 3 investigation should be designed in such a way that, if the sponsor anticipates that some deviation from the study design may become necessary as the investigation progresses, alternatives or contingencies to provide for such deviation are built into the protocols at the outset. For example, a protocol for a controlled short-term study might include a plan for an early crossover of nonresponders to an alternative therapy.

(iii) A protocol is required to contain the following, with the specific elements and detail of the protocol reflecting the above distinctions depending on the phase of study:

(*a*) A statement of the objectives and purpose of the study.

(*b*) The name and address and a statement of the qualifications (curriculum vitae or other statement of qualifications) of each investigator, and the name of each subinvestigator (e.g., research fellow, resident) working under the supervision of the investigator; the name and address of the research facilities to be used; and the name and address of each reviewing Institutional Review Board.

(*c*) The criteria for patient selection and for exclusion of patients and an estimate of the number of patients to be studied.

(*d*) A description of the design of the study, including the kind of control group to be used, if any, and a description of methods to be used to minimize bias on the part of subjects, investigators, and analysts.

(*e*) The method for determining the dose(s) to be administered, the planned maximum dosage, and the duration of individual patient exposure to the drug.

(*f*) A description of the observations and measurements to be made to fulfill the objectives of the study.

(*g*) A description of clinical procedures, laboratory tests, or other measures to be taken to monitor the effects of the drug in human subjects and to minimize risk.

(7) *Chemistry, manufacturing, and control information.* (i) As appropriate for the particular investigations covered by the IND, a section describing the composition, manufacture, and control of the drug substance and the drug product. Although in each phase of the investigation sufficient information is required to be submitted to assure the proper identification, quality, purity, and strength of the investigational drug, the amount of information needed to make that assurance will vary with the phase of the investigation, the proposed duration of the investigation, the dosage form, and the amount of information otherwise available. FDA recognizes that modifications to the method of preparation of the new drug substance and dosage form and changes in the dosage form itself are likely as

the investigation progresses. Therefore, the emphasis in an initial Phase 1 submission should generally be placed on the identification and control of the raw materials and the new drug substance. Final specifications for the drug substance and drug product are not expected until the end of the investigational process.

(ii) It should be emphasized that the amount of information to be submitted depends upon the scope of the proposed clinical investigation. For example, although stability data are required in all phases of the IND to demonstrate that the new drug substance and drug product are within acceptable chemical and physical limits for the planned duration of the proposed clinical investigation, if very short-term tests are proposed, the supporting stability data can be correspondingly limited.

(iii) As drug development proceeds and as the scale or production is changed from the pilot-scale production appropriate for the limited initial clinical investigations to the larger-scale production needed for expanded clinical trials, the sponsor should submit information amendments to supplement the initial information submitted on the chemistry, manufacturing, and control processes with information appropriate to the expanded scope of the investigation.

(iv) Reflecting the distinctions described in this paragraph (a)(7), and based on the phase(s) to be studied, the submission is required to contain the following:

(a) *Drug substance.* A description of the drug substance, including its physical, chemical, or biological characteristics; the name and address of its manufacturer; the general method of preparation of the drug substance; the acceptable limits and analytical methods used to assure the identity, strength, quality, and purity of the drug substance; and information sufficient to support stability of the drug substance during the toxicological studies and the planned clinical studies. Reference to the current edition of the United States Pharmacopeia—National Formulary may satisfy relevant requirements in this paragraph.

(b) *Drug product.* A list of all components, which may include reasonable alternatives for inactive compounds, used in the manufacture of the investigational drug product, including both those components intended to appear in the drug product and those which may not appear but which are used in the manufacturing process, and, where applicable, the quantitative composition of the investigational drug product, including any reasonable variations that may be expected during the investigational stage; the name and address of the drug product manufacturer; a brief general description of the manufacturing and packaging procedure as appropriate for the product; the acceptable limits and analytical methods used to assure the identity, strength, quality, and purity of the drug product; and information sufficient to assure the product's stability during the planned clinical studies. Reference to the current edition of the United States Pharmacopeia—National Formulary may satisfy certain requirements in this paragraph.

(c) A brief general description of the composition, manufacture, and control of any placebo used in a controlled clinical trial.

(d) *Labeling.* A copy of all labels and labeling to be provided to each investigator.

(e) *Environmental analysis requirements.* A claim for categorical exclusion under § 25.30 or 25.31 or an environmental assessment under § 25.40.

(8) *Pharmacology and toxicology information.* Adequate information about pharmacological and toxicological studies of the drug involving laboratory animals or in vitro, on the basis of which the sponsor has concluded that it is reasonably safe to conduct the proposed clinical investigations. The kind, duration, and scope of animal and other tests required varies with the duration and nature of the proposed clinical investigations. Guidance documents are available from FDA that describe ways in which these requirements may be met. Such information is required to include the identification and qualifications of the individuals who evaluated the results of such studies and concluded that it is reasonably safe to begin the proposed investigations and a statement of where the investigations were conducted and where

the records are available for inspection. As drug development proceeds, the sponsor is required to submit informational amendments, as appropriate, with additional information pertinent to safety.

(i) *Pharmacology and drug disposition.* A section describing the pharmacological effects and mechanism(s) of action of the drug in animals, and information on the absorption, distribution, metabolism, and excretion of the drug, if known.

(ii) *Toxicology.* (*a*) An integrated summary of the toxicological effects of the drug in animals and in vitro. Depending on the nature of the drug and the phase of the investigation, the description is to include the results of acute, subacute, and chronic toxicity tests; tests of the drug's effects on reproduction and the developing fetus; any special toxicity test related to the drug's particular mode of administration or conditions of use (e.g., inhalation, dermal, or ocular toxicology); and any in vitro studies intended to evaluate drug toxicity.

(*b*) For each toxicology study that is intended primarily to support the safety of the proposed clinical investigation, a full tabulation of data suitable for detailed review.

(iii) For each nonclinical laboratory study subject to the good laboratory practice regulations under part 58, a statement that the study was conducted in compliance with the good laboratory practice regulations in part 58, or, if the study was not conducted in compliance with those regulations, a brief statement of the reason for the noncompliance.

(9) *Previous human experience with the investigational drug.* A summary of previous human experience known to the applicant, if any, with the investigational drug. The information is required to include the following:

(i) If the investigational drug has been investigated or marketed previously, either in the United States or other countries, detailed information about such experience that is relevant to the safety of the proposed investigation or to the investigation's rationale. If the drug has been the subject of controlled trials, detailed information on such trials that is relevant to an as-

sessment of the drug's effectiveness for the proposed investigational use(s) should also be provided. Any published material that is relevant to the safety of the proposed investigation or to an assessment of the drug's effectiveness for its proposed investigational use should be provided in full. Published material that is less directly relevant may be supplied by a bibliography.

(ii) If the drug is a combination of drugs previously investigated or marketed, the information required under paragraph (a)(9)(i) of this section should be provided for each active drug component. However, if any component in such combination is subject to an approved marketing application or is otherwise lawfully marketed in the United States, the sponsor is not required to submit published material concerning that active drug component unless such material relates directly to the proposed investigational use (including publications relevant to component-component interaction).

(iii) If the drug has been marketed outside the United States, a list of the countries in which the drug has been marketed and a list of the countries in which the drug has been withdrawn from marketing for reasons potentially related to safety or effectiveness.

(10) *Additional information.* In certain applications, as described below, information on special topics may be needed. Such information shall be submitted in this section as follows:

(i) *Drug dependence and abuse potential.* If the drug is a psychotropic substance or otherwise has abuse potential, a section describing relevant clinical studies and experience and studies in test animals.

(ii) *Radioactive drugs.* If the drug is a radioactive drug, sufficient data from animal or human studies to allow a reasonable calculation of radiation-absorbed dose to the whole body and critical organs upon administration to a human subject. Phase 1 studies of radioactive drugs must include studies which will obtain sufficient data for dosimetry calculations.

(iii) *Pediatric studies.* Plans for assessing pediatric safety and effectiveness.

(iv) *Other information.* A brief statement of any other information that would aid evaluation of the proposed clinical investigations with respect to their safety or their design and potential as controlled clinical trials to support marketing of the drug.

(11) *Relevant information.* If requested by FDA, any other relevant information needed for review of the application.

(b) *Information previously submitted.* The sponsor ordinarily is not required to resubmit information previously submitted, but may incorporate the information by reference. A reference to information submitted previously must identify the file by name, reference number, volume, and page number where the information can be found. A reference to information submitted to the agency by a person other than the sponsor is required to contain a written statement that authorizes the reference and that is signed by the person who submitted the information.

(c) *Material in a foreign language.* The sponsor shall submit an accurate and complete English translation of each part of the IND that is not in English. The sponsor shall also submit a copy of each original literature publication for which an English translation is submitted.

(d) *Number of copies.* The sponsor shall submit an original and two copies of all submissions to the IND file, including the original submission and all amendments and reports.

(e) *Numbering of IND submissions.* Each submission relating to an IND is required to be numbered serially using a single, three-digit serial number. The initial IND is required to be numbered 000; each subsequent submission (e.g., amendment, report, or correspondence) is required to be numbered chronologically in sequence.

(f) *Identification of exception from informed consent.* If the investigation involves an exception from informed consent under § 50.24 of this chapter, the sponsor shall prominently identify on the cover sheet that the investigation is subject to the requirements in § 50.24 of this chapter.

[52 FR 8831, Mar. 19, 1987, as amended at 52 FR 23031, June 17, 1987; 53 FR 1918, Jan. 25, 1988; 61 FR 51529, Oct. 2, 1996; 62 FR 40599, July 29, 1997; 63 FR 66669, Dec. 2, 1998; 65 FR 56479, Sept. 19, 2000; 67 FR 9585, Mar. 4, 2002]

§ 312.30   Protocol amendments.

Once an IND is in effect, a sponsor shall amend it as needed to ensure that the clinical investigations are conducted according to protocols included in the application. This section sets forth the provisions under which new protocols may be submitted and changes in previously submitted protocols may be made. Whenever a sponsor intends to conduct a clinical investigation with an exception from informed consent for emergency research as set forth in § 50.24 of this chapter, the sponsor shall submit a separate IND for such investigation.

(a) *New protocol.* Whenever a sponsor intends to conduct a study that is not covered by a protocol already contained in the IND, the sponsor shall submit to FDA a protocol amendment containing the protocol for the study. Such study may begin provided two conditions are met: (1) The sponsor has submitted the protocol to FDA for its review; and (2) the protocol has been approved by the Institutional Review Board (IRB) with responsibility for review and approval of the study in accordance with the requirements of part 56. The sponsor may comply with these two conditions in either order.

(b) *Changes in a protocol.* (1) A sponsor shall submit a protocol amendment describing any change in a Phase 1 protocol that significantly affects the safety of subjects or any change in a Phase 2 or 3 protocol that significantly affects the safety of subjects, the scope of the investigation, or the scientific quality of the study. Examples of changes requiring an amendment under this paragraph include:

(i) Any increase in drug dosage or duration of exposure of individual subjects to the drug beyond that in the current protocol, or any significant increase in the number of subjects under study.

(ii) Any significant change in the design of a protocol (such as the addition or dropping of a control group).

(iii) The addition of a new test or procedure that is intended to improve monitoring for, or reduce the risk of, a side effect or adverse event; or the dropping of a test intended to monitor safety.

(2)(i) A protocol change under paragraph (b)(1) of this section may be made provided two conditions are met:

(*a*) The sponsor has submitted the change to FDA for its review; and

(*b*) The change has been approved by the IRB with responsibility for review and approval of the study. The sponsor may comply with these two conditions in either order.

(ii) Notwithstanding paragraph (b)(2)(i) of this section, a protocol change intended to eliminate an apparent immediate hazard to subjects may be implemented immediately provided FDA is subsequently notified by protocol amendment and the reviewing IRB is notified in accordance with §56.104(c).

(c) *New investigator.* A sponsor shall submit a protocol amendment when a new investigator is added to carry out a previously submitted protocol, except that a protocol amendment is not required when a licensed practitioner is added in the case of a treatment protocol under §312.315 or §312.320. Once the investigator is added to the study, the investigational drug may be shipped to the investigator and the investigator may begin participating in the study. The sponsor shall notify FDA of the new investigator within 30 days of the investigator being added.

(d) *Content and format.* A protocol amendment is required to be prominently identified as such (*i.e.*, "Protocol Amendment: New Protocol", "Protocol Amendment: Change in Protocol", or "Protocol Amendment: New Investigator"), and to contain the following:

(1)(i) In the case of a new protocol, a copy of the new protocol and a brief description of the most clinically significant differences between it and previous protocols.

(ii) In the case of a change in protocol, a brief description of the change and reference (date and number) to the submission that contained the protocol.

(iii) In the case of a new investigator, the investigator's name, the qualifications to conduct the investigation, reference to the previously submitted protocol, and all additional information about the investigator's study as is required under §312.23(a)(6)(iii)(*b*).

(2) Reference, if necessary, to specific technical information in the IND or in a concurrently submitted information amendment to the IND that the sponsor relies on to support any clinically significant change in the new or amended protocol. If the reference is made to supporting information already in the IND, the sponsor shall identify by name, reference number, volume, and page number the location of the information.

(3) If the sponsor desires FDA to comment on the submission, a request for such comment and the specific questions FDA's response should address.

(e) *When submitted.* A sponsor shall submit a protocol amendment for a new protocol or a change in protocol before its implementation. Protocol amendments to add a new investigator or to provide additional information about investigators may be grouped and submitted at 30-day intervals. When several submissions of new protocols or protocol changes are anticipated during a short period, the sponsor is encouraged, to the extent feasible, to include these all in a single submission.

[52 FR 8831, Mar. 19, 1987, as amended at 52 FR 23031, June 17, 1987; 53 FR 1918, Jan. 25, 1988; 61 FR 51530, Oct. 2, 1996; 67 FR 9585, Mar. 4, 2002; 74 FR 40942, Aug. 13, 2009]

§312.31 Information amendments.

(a) *Requirement for information amendment.* A sponsor shall report in an information amendment essential information on the IND that is not within the scope of a protocol amendment, IND safety reports, or annual report. Examples of information requiring an information amendment include:

(1) New toxicology, chemistry, or other technical information; or

(2) A report regarding the discontinuance of a clinical investigation.

(b) *Content and format of an information amendment.* An information amendment is required to bear prominent identification of its contents (e.g., "Information Amendment: Chemistry, Manufacturing, and Control", "Information Amendment: Pharmacology-Toxicology", "Information Amendment: Clinical"), and to contain the following:

(1) A statement of the nature and purpose of the amendment.

(2) An organized submission of the data in a format appropriate for scientific review.

(3) If the sponsor desires FDA to comment on an information amendment, a request for such comment.

(c) *When submitted.* Information amendments to the IND should be submitted as necessary but, to the extent feasible, not more than every 30 days.

[52 FR 8831, Mar. 19, 1987, as amended at 52 FR 23031, June 17, 1987; 53 FR 1918, Jan. 25, 1988; 67 FR 9585, Mar. 4, 2002]

§ 312.32   IND safety reporting.

(a) *Definitions.* The following definitions of terms apply to this section:

Adverse event means any untoward medical occurrence associated with the use of a drug in humans, whether or not considered drug related.

Life-threatening adverse event or *life-threatening suspected adverse reaction.* An adverse event or suspected adverse reaction is considered "life-threatening" if, in the view of either the investigator or sponsor, its occurrence places the patient or subject at immediate risk of death. It does not include an adverse event or suspected adverse reaction that, had it occurred in a more severe form, might have caused death.

Serious adverse event or *serious suspected adverse reaction.* An adverse event or suspected adverse reaction is considered "serious" if, in the view of either the investigator or sponsor, it results in any of the following outcomes: Death, a life-threatening adverse event, inpatient hospitalization or prolongation of existing hospitalization, a persistent or significant incapacity or substantial disruption of the ability to conduct normal life functions, or a congenital anomaly/birth defect. Important medical events that may not result in death, be life-threatening, or require hospitalization may be considered serious when, based upon appropriate medical judgment, they may jeopardize the patient or subject and may require medical or surgical intervention to prevent one of the outcomes listed in this definition. Examples of such medical events include allergic bronchospasm requiring intensive treatment in an emergency room or at home, blood dyscrasias or convulsions that do not result in inpatient hospitalization, or the development of drug dependency or drug abuse.

Suspected adverse reaction means any adverse event for which there is a reasonable possibility that the drug caused the adverse event. For the purposes of IND safety reporting, "reasonable possibility" means there is evidence to suggest a causal relationship between the drug and the adverse event. Suspected adverse reaction implies a lesser degree of certainty about causality than adverse reaction, which means any adverse event caused by a drug.

Unexpected adverse event or *unexpected suspected adverse reaction.* An adverse event or suspected adverse reaction is considered "unexpected" if it is not listed in the investigator brochure or is not listed at the specificity or severity that has been observed; or, if an investigator brochure is not required or available, is not consistent with the risk information described in the general investigational plan or elsewhere in the current application, as amended. For example, under this definition, hepatic necrosis would be unexpected (by virtue of greater severity) if the investigator brochure referred only to elevated hepatic enzymes or hepatitis. Similarly, cerebral thromboembolism and cerebral vasculitis would be unexpected (by virtue of greater specificity) if the investigator brochure listed only cerebral vascular accidents. "Unexpected," as used in this definition, also refers to adverse events or suspected adverse reactions that are mentioned in the investigator brochure as occurring with a class of drugs or as anticipated from the pharmacological properties of the drug, but are not specifically mentioned as occurring with the particular drug under investigation.

(b) *Review of safety information.* The sponsor must promptly review all information relevant to the safety of the drug obtained or otherwise received by the sponsor from foreign or domestic sources, including information derived from any clinical or epidemiological investigations, animal or in vitro studies, reports in the scientific literature, and unpublished scientific papers, as well as reports from foreign regulatory authorities and reports of foreign commercial marketing experience for drugs that are not marketed in the United States.

(c)(1) *IND safety reports.* The sponsor must notify FDA and all participating investigators (i.e., all investigators to whom the sponsor is providing drug under its INDs or under any investigator's IND) in an IND safety report of potential serious risks, from clinical trials or any other source, as soon as possible, but in no case later than 15 calendar days after the sponsor determines that the information qualifies for reporting under paragraph (c)(1)(i), (c)(1)(ii), (c)(1)(iii), or (c)(1)(iv) of this section. In each IND safety report, the sponsor must identify all IND safety reports previously submitted to FDA concerning a similar suspected adverse reaction, and must analyze the significance of the suspected adverse reaction in light of previous, similar reports or any other relevant information.

(i) *Serious and unexpected suspected adverse reaction.* The sponsor must report any suspected adverse reaction that is both serious and unexpected. The sponsor must report an adverse event as a suspected adverse reaction only if there is evidence to suggest a causal relationship between the drug and the adverse event, such as:

(A) A single occurrence of an event that is uncommon and known to be strongly associated with drug exposure (e.g., angioedema, hepatic injury, Stevens-Johnson Syndrome);

(B) One or more occurrences of an event that is not commonly associated with drug exposure, but is otherwise uncommon in the population exposed to the drug (e.g., tendon rupture);

(C) An aggregate analysis of specific events observed in a clinical trial (such as known consequences of the underlying disease or condition under investigation or other events that commonly occur in the study population independent of drug therapy) that indicates those events occur more frequently in the drug treatment group than in a concurrent or historical control group.

(ii) *Findings from other studies.* The sponsor must report any findings from epidemiological studies, pooled analysis of multiple studies, or clinical studies (other than those reported under paragraph (c)(1)(i) of this section), whether or not conducted under an IND, and whether or not conducted by the sponsor, that suggest a significant risk in humans exposed to the drug. Ordinarily, such a finding would result in a safety-related change in the protocol, informed consent, investigator brochure (excluding routine updates of these documents), or other aspects of the overall conduct of the clinical investigation.

(iii) *Findings from animal or in vitro testing.* The sponsor must report any findings from animal or in vitro testing, whether or not conducted by the sponsor, that suggest a significant risk in humans exposed to the drug, such as reports of mutagenicity, teratogenicity, or carcinogenicity, or reports of significant organ toxicity at or near the expected human exposure. Ordinarily, any such findings would result in a safety-related change in the protocol, informed consent, investigator brochure (excluding routine updates of these documents), or other aspects of the overall conduct of the clinical investigation.

(iv) *Increased rate of occurrence of serious suspected adverse reactions.* The sponsor must report any clinically important increase in the rate of a serious suspected adverse reaction over that listed in the protocol or investigator brochure.

(v) *Submission of IND safety reports.* The sponsor must submit each IND safety report in a narrative format or on FDA Form 3500A or in an electronic format that FDA can process, review, and archive. FDA will periodically issue guidance on how to provide the electronic submission (e.g., method of transmission, media, file formats, preparation and organization of files). The sponsor may submit foreign suspected adverse reactions on a Council for International Organizations of Medical Sciences (CIOMS) I Form instead of a FDA Form 3500A. Reports of overall findings or pooled analyses from published and unpublished in vitro, animal, epidemiological, or clinical studies must be submitted in a narrative format. Each notification to FDA must bear prominent identification of its contents, i.e., "IND Safety Report," and must be transmitted to the review division in the Center for Drug Evaluation and Research or in the Center for Biologics Evaluation and Research that has responsibility for review of the IND. Upon request from FDA, the sponsor must submit to FDA any additional data or information that the agency deems necessary, as soon as possible, but in no case later than 15 calendar days after receiving the request.

(2) *Unexpected fatal or life-threatening suspected adverse reaction reports.* The sponsor must also notify FDA of any unexpected fatal or life-threatening suspected adverse reaction as soon as possible but in no case later than 7 calendar days after the sponsor's initial receipt of the information.

(3) *Reporting format or frequency.* FDA may require a sponsor to submit IND safety reports in a format or at a frequency different than that required under this paragraph. The sponsor may also propose and adopt a different reporting format or frequency if the change is agreed to in advance by the director of the FDA review division that has responsibility for review of the IND.

(4) *Investigations of marketed drugs.* A sponsor of a clinical study of a drug marketed or approved in the United States that is conducted under an IND is required to submit IND safety reports for suspected adverse reactions that are observed in the clinical study, at domestic or foreign study sites. The sponsor must also submit safety information from the clinical study as prescribed by the postmarketing safety reporting requirements (e.g., §§ 310.305, 314.80, and 600.80 of this chapter).

(5) *Reporting study endpoints.* Study endpoints (e.g., mortality or major morbidity) must be reported to FDA by the sponsor as described in the protocol and ordinarily would not be reported under paragraph (c) of this section. However, if a serious and unexpected adverse event occurs for which there is evidence suggesting a causal relationship between the drug and the event (e.g., death from anaphylaxis), the event must be reported under § 312.32(c)(1)(i) as a serious and unexpected suspected adverse reaction even

if it is a component of the study endpoint (e.g., all-cause mortality).

(d) *Followup.* (1) The sponsor must promptly investigate all safety information it receives.

(2) Relevant followup information to an IND safety report must be submitted as soon as the information is available and must be identified as such, i.e., "Followup IND Safety Report."

(3) If the results of a sponsor's investigation show that an adverse event not initially determined to be reportable under paragraph (c) of this section is so reportable, the sponsor must report such suspected adverse reaction in an IND safety report as soon as possible, but in no case later than 15 calendar days after the determination is made.

(e) *Disclaimer.* A safety report or other information submitted by a sponsor under this part (and any release by FDA of that report or information) does not necessarily reflect a conclusion by the sponsor or FDA that the report or information constitutes an admission that the drug caused or contributed to an adverse event. A sponsor need not admit, and may deny, that the report or information submitted by the sponsor constitutes an admission that the drug caused or contributed to an adverse event.

[75 FR 59961, Sept. 29, 2010]

§ 312.33 Annual reports.

A sponsor shall within 60 days of the anniversary date that the IND went into effect, submit a brief report of the progress of the investigation that includes:

(a) *Individual study information.* A brief summary of the status of each study in progress and each study completed during the previous year. The summary is required to include the following information for each study:

(1) The title of the study (with any appropriate study identifiers such as protocol number), its purpose, a brief statement identifying the patient population, and a statement as to whether the study is completed.

(2) The total number of subjects initially planned for inclusion in the study; the number entered into the study to date, tabulated by age group,

gender, and race; the number whose participation in the study was completed as planned; and the number who dropped out of the study for any reason.

(3) If the study has been completed, or if interim results are known, a brief description of any available study results.

(b) *Summary information.* Information obtained during the previous year's clinical and nonclinical investigations, including:

(1) A narrative or tabular summary showing the most frequent and most serious adverse experiences by body system.

(2) A summary of all IND safety reports submitted during the past year.

(3) A list of subjects who died during participation in the investigation, with the cause of death for each subject.

(4) A list of subjects who dropped out during the course of the investigation in association with any adverse experience, whether or not thought to be drug related.

(5) A brief description of what, if anything, was obtained that is pertinent to an understanding of the drug's actions, including, for example, information about dose response, information from controlled trials, and information about bioavailability.

(6) A list of the preclinical studies (including animal studies) completed or in progress during the past year and a summary of the major preclinical findings.

(7) A summary of any significant manufacturing or microbiological changes made during the past year.

(c) A description of the general investigational plan for the coming year to replace that submitted 1 year earlier. The general investigational plan shall contain the information required under §312.23(a)(3)(iv).

(d) If the investigator brochure has been revised, a description of the revision and a copy of the new brochure.

(e) A description of any significant Phase 1 protocol modifications made during the previous year and not previously reported to the IND in a protocol amendment.

(f) A brief summary of significant foreign marketing developments with the drug during the past year, such as

approval of marketing in any country or withdrawal or suspension from marketing in any country.

(g) If desired by the sponsor, a log of any outstanding business with respect to the IND for which the sponsor requests or expects a reply, comment, or meeting.

[52 FR 8831, Mar. 19, 1987, as amended at 52 FR 23031, June 17, 1987; 63 FR 6862, Feb. 11, 1998; 67 FR 9585, Mar. 4, 2002]

§312.38 Withdrawal of an IND.

(a) At any time a sponsor may withdraw an effective IND without prejudice.

(b) If an IND is withdrawn, FDA shall be so notified, all clinical investigations conducted under the IND shall be ended, all current investigators notified, and all stocks of the drug returned to the sponsor or otherwise disposed of at the request of the sponsor in accordance with §312.59.

(c) If an IND is withdrawn because of a safety reason, the sponsor shall promptly so inform FDA, all participating investigators, and all reviewing Institutional Review Boards, together with the reasons for such withdrawal.

[52 FR 8831, Mar. 19, 1987, as amended at 52 FR 23031, June 17, 1987; 67 FR 9586, Mar. 4, 2002]

Subpart C—Administrative Actions

§312.40 General requirements for use of an investigational new drug in a clinical investigation.

(a) An investigational new drug may be used in a clinical investigation if the following conditions are met:

(1) The sponsor of the investigation submits an IND for the drug to FDA; the IND is in effect under paragraph (b) of this section; and the sponsor complies with all applicable requirements in this part and parts 50 and 56 with respect to the conduct of the clinical investigations; and

(2) Each participating investigator conducts his or her investigation in compliance with the requirements of this part and parts 50 and 56.

(b) An IND goes into effect:

(1) Thirty days after FDA receives the IND, unless FDA notifies the sponsor that the investigations described in

the IND are subject to a clinical hold under § 312.42; or

(2) On earlier notification by FDA that the clinical investigations in the IND may begin. FDA will notify the sponsor in writing of the date it receives the IND.

(c) A sponsor may ship an investigational new drug to investigators named in the IND:

(1) Thirty days after FDA receives the IND; or

(2) On earlier FDA authorization to ship the drug.

(d) An investigator may not administer an investigational new drug to human subjects until the IND goes into effect under paragraph (b) of this section.

§ 312.41 Comment and advice on an IND.

(a) FDA may at any time during the course of the investigation communicate with the sponsor orally or in writing about deficiencies in the IND or about FDA's need for more data or information.

(b) On the sponsor's request, FDA will provide advice on specific matters relating to an IND. Examples of such advice may include advice on the adequacy of technical data to support an investigational plan, on the design of a clinical trial, and on whether proposed investigations are likely to produce the data and information that is needed to meet requirements for a marketing application.

(c) Unless the communication is accompanied by a clinical hold order under § 312.42, FDA communications with a sponsor under this section are solely advisory and do not require any modification in the planned or ongoing clinical investigations or response to the agency.

[52 FR 8831, Mar. 19, 1987, as amended at 52 FR 23031, June 17, 1987; 67 FR 9586, Mar. 4, 2002]

§ 312.42 Clinical holds and requests for modification.

(a) *General.* A clinical hold is an order issued by FDA to the sponsor to delay a proposed clinical investigation or to suspend an ongoing investigation. The clinical hold order may apply to one or more of the investigations covered by

an IND. When a proposed study is placed on clinical hold, subjects may not be given the investigational drug. When an ongoing study is placed on clinical hold, no new subjects may be recruited to the study and placed on the investigational drug; patients already in the study should be taken off therapy involving the investigational drug unless specifically permitted by FDA in the interest of patient safety.

(b) *Grounds for imposition of clinical hold*—(1) *Clinical hold of a Phase 1 study under an IND.* FDA may place a proposed or ongoing Phase 1 investigation on clinical hold if it finds that:

(i) Human subjects are or would be exposed to an unreasonable and significant risk of illness or injury;

(ii) The clinical investigators named in the IND are not qualified by reason of their scientific training and experience to conduct the investigation described in the IND;

(iii) The investigator brochure is misleading, erroneous, or materially incomplete; or

(iv) The IND does not contain sufficient information required under § 312.23 to assess the risks to subjects of the proposed studies.

(v) The IND is for the study of an investigational drug intended to treat a life-threatening disease or condition that affects both genders, and men or women with reproductive potential who have the disease or condition being studied are excluded from eligibility because of a risk or potential risk from use of the investigational drug of reproductive toxicity (*i.e.,* affecting reproductive organs) or developmental toxicity (*i.e.,* affecting potential offspring). The phrase "women with reproductive potential" does not include pregnant women. For purposes of this paragraph, "life-threatening illnesses or diseases" are defined as "diseases or conditions where the likelihood of death is high unless the course of the disease is interrupted." The clinical hold would not apply under this paragraph to clinical studies conducted:

(A) Under special circumstances, such as studies pertinent only to one gender (e.g., studies evaluating the excretion of a drug in semen or the effects on menstrual function);

(B) Only in men or women, as long as a study that does not exclude members of the other gender with reproductive potential is being conducted concurrently, has been conducted, or will take place within a reasonable time agreed upon by the agency; or

(C) Only in subjects who do not suffer from the disease or condition for which the drug is being studied.

(2) *Clinical hold of a Phase 2 or 3 study under an IND.* FDA may place a proposed or ongoing Phase 2 or 3 investigation on clinical hold if it finds that:

(i) Any of the conditions in paragraphs (b)(1)(i) through (b)(1)(v) of this section apply; or

(ii) The plan or protocol for the investigation is clearly deficient in design to meet its stated objectives.

(3) *Clinical hold of an expanded access IND or expanded access protocol.* FDA may place an expanded access IND or expanded access protocol on clinical hold under the following conditions:

(i) *Final use.* FDA may place a proposed expanded access IND or treatment use protocol on clinical hold if it is determined that:

(A) The pertinent criteria in subpart I of this part for permitting the expanded access use to begin are not satisfied; or

(B) The expanded access IND or expanded access protocol does not comply with the requirements for expanded access submissions in subpart I of this part.

(ii) *Ongoing use.* FDA may place an ongoing expanded access IND or expanded access protocol on clinical hold if it is determined that the pertinent criteria in subpart I of this part for permitting the expanded access are no longer satisfied.

(4) *Clinical hold of any study that is not designed to be adequate and well-controlled.* FDA may place a proposed or ongoing investigation that is not designed to be adequate and well-controlled on clinical hold if it finds that:

(i) Any of the conditions in paragraph (b)(1) or (b)(2) of this section apply; or

(ii) There is reasonable evidence the investigation that is not designed to be adequate and well-controlled is impeding enrollment in, or otherwise interfering with the conduct or completion of, a study that is designed to be an adequate and well-controlled investigation of the same or another investigational drug; or

(iii) Insufficient quantities of the investigational drug exist to adequately conduct both the investigation that is not designed to be adequate and well-controlled and the investigations that are designed to be adequate and well-controlled; or

(iv) The drug has been studied in one or more adequate and well-controlled investigations that strongly suggest lack of effectiveness; or

(v) Another drug under investigation or approved for the same indication and available to the same patient population has demonstrated a better potential benefit/risk balance; or

(vi) The drug has received marketing approval for the same indication in the same patient population; or

(vii) The sponsor of the study that is designed to be an adequate and well-controlled investigation is not actively pursuing marketing approval of the investigational drug with due diligence; or

(viii) The Commissioner determines that it would not be in the public interest for the study to be conducted or continued. FDA ordinarily intends that clinical holds under paragraphs (b)(4)(ii), (b)(4)(iii) and (b)(4)(v) of this section would only apply to additional enrollment in nonconcurrently controlled trials rather than eliminating continued access to individuals already receiving the investigational drug.

(5) *Clinical hold of any investigation involving an exception from informed consent under §50.24 of this chapter.* FDA may place a proposed or ongoing investigation involving an exception from informed consent under §50.24 of this chapter on clinical hold if it is determined that:

(i) Any of the conditions in paragraphs (b)(1) or (b)(2) of this section apply; or

(ii) The pertinent criteria in §50.24 of this chapter for such an investigation to begin or continue are not submitted or not satisfied.

(6) Clinical hold of any investigation involving an exception from informed consent under §50.23(d) of this chapter.

FDA may place a proposed or ongoing investigation involving an exception from informed consent under § 50.23(d) of this chapter on clinical hold if it is determined that:

(i) Any of the conditions in paragraphs (b)(1) or (b)(2) of this section apply; or

(ii) A determination by the President to waive the prior consent requirement for the administration of an investigational new drug has not been made.

(c) *Discussion of deficiency.* Whenever FDA concludes that a deficiency exists in a clinical investigation that may be grounds for the imposition of clinical hold FDA will, unless patients are exposed to immediate and serious risk, attempt to discuss and satisfactorily resolve the matter with the sponsor before issuing the clinical hold order.

(d) *Imposition of clinical hold.* The clinical hold order may be made by telephone or other means of rapid communication or in writing. The clinical hold order will identify the studies under the IND to which the hold applies, and will briefly explain the basis for the action. The clinical hold order will be made by or on behalf of the Division Director with responsibility for review of the IND. As soon as possible, and no more than 30 days after imposition of the clinical hold, the Division Director will provide the sponsor a written explanation of the basis for the hold.

(e) *Resumption of clinical investigations.* An investigation may only resume after FDA (usually the Division Director, or the Director's designee, with responsibility for review of the IND) has notified the sponsor that the investigation may proceed. Resumption of the affected investigation(s) will be authorized when the sponsor corrects the deficiency(ies) previously cited or otherwise satisfies the agency that the investigation(s) can proceed. FDA may notify a sponsor of its determination regarding the clinical hold by telephone or other means of rapid communication. If a sponsor of an IND that has been placed on clinical hold requests in writing that the clinical hold be removed and submits a complete response to the issue(s) identified in the clinical hold order, FDA shall respond in writing to the sponsor within 30-cal-

endar days of receipt of the request and the complete response. FDA's response will either remove or maintain the clinical hold, and will state the reasons for such determination. Notwithstanding the 30-calendar day response time, a sponsor may not proceed with a clinical trial on which a clinical hold has been imposed until the sponsor has been notified by FDA that the hold has been lifted.

(f) *Appeal.* If the sponsor disagrees with the reasons cited for the clinical hold, the sponsor may request reconsideration of the decision in accordance with § 312.48.

(g) *Conversion of IND on clinical hold to inactive status.* If all investigations covered by an IND remain on clinical hold for 1 year or more, the IND may be placed on inactive status by FDA under § 312.45.

[52 FR 8831, Mar. 19, 1987, as amended at 52 FR 19477, May 22, 1987; 57 FR 13249, Apr. 15, 1992; 61 FR 51530, Oct. 2, 1996; 63 FR 68678, Dec. 14, 1998; 64 FR 54189, Oct. 5, 1999; 65 FR 34971, June 1, 2000; 74 FR 40942, Aug. 13, 2009]

§ 312.44   Termination.

(a) *General.* This section describes the procedures under which FDA may terminate an IND. If an IND is terminated, the sponsor shall end all clinical investigations conducted under the IND and recall or otherwise provide for the disposition of all unused supplies of the drug. A termination action may be based on deficiencies in the IND or in the conduct of an investigation under an IND. Except as provided in paragraph (d) of this section, a termination shall be preceded by a proposal to terminate by FDA and an opportunity for the sponsor to respond. FDA will, in general, only initiate an action under this section after first attempting to resolve differences informally or, when appropriate, through the clinical hold procedures described in § 312.42.

(b) *Grounds for termination*—(1) *Phase 1.* FDA may propose to terminate an IND during Phase 1 if it finds that:

(i) Human subjects would be exposed to an unreasonable and significant risk of illness or unjury.

(ii) The IND does not contain sufficient information required under § 312.23 to assess the safety to subjects of the clinical investigations.

(iii) The methods, facilities, and controls used for the manufacturing, processing, and packing of the investigational drug are inadequate to establish and maintain appropriate standards of identity, strength, quality, and purity as needed for subject safety.

(iv) The clinical investigations are being conducted in a manner substantially different than that described in the protocols submitted in the IND.

(v) The drug is being promoted or distributed for commercial purposes not justified by the requirements of the investigation or permitted by §312.7.

(vi) The IND, or any amendment or report to the IND, contains an untrue statement of a material fact or omits material information required by this part.

(vii) The sponsor fails promptly to investigate and inform the Food and Drug Administration and all investigators of serious and unexpected adverse experiences in accordance with §312.32 or fails to make any other report required under this part.

(viii) The sponsor fails to submit an accurate annual report of the investigations in accordance with §312.33.

(ix) The sponsor fails to comply with any other applicable requirement of this part, part 50, or part 56.

(x) The IND has remained on inactive status for 5 years or more.

(xi) The sponsor fails to delay a proposed investigation under the IND or to suspend an ongoing investigation that has been placed on clinical hold under §312.42(b)(4).

(2) *Phase 2 or 3.* FDA may propose to terminate an IND during Phase 2 or Phase 3 if FDA finds that:

(i) Any of the conditions in paragraphs (b)(1)(i) through (b)(1)(xi) of this section apply; or

(ii) The investigational plan or protocol(s) is not reasonable as a bona fide scientific plan to determine whether or not the drug is safe and effective for use; or

(iii) There is convincing evidence that the drug is not effective for the purpose for which it is being investigated.

(3) FDA may propose to terminate a treatment IND if it finds that:

(i) Any of the conditions in paragraphs (b)(1)(i) through (x) of this section apply; or

(ii) Any of the conditions in §312.42(b)(3) apply.

(c) *Opportunity for sponsor response.* (1) If FDA proposes to terminate an IND, FDA will notify the sponsor in writing, and invite correction or explanation within a period of 30 days.

(2) On such notification, the sponsor may provide a written explanation or correction or may request a conference with FDA to provide the requested explanation or correction. If the sponsor does not respond to the notification within the allocated time, the IND shall be terminated.

(3) If the sponsor responds but FDA does not accept the explanation or correction submitted, FDA shall inform the sponsor in writing of the reason for the nonacceptance and provide the sponsor with an opportunity for a regulatory hearing before FDA under part 16 on the question of whether the IND should be terminated. The sponsor's request for a regulatory hearing must be made within 10 days of the sponsor's receipt of FDA's notification of nonacceptance.

(d) *Immediate termination of IND.* Notwithstanding paragraphs (a) through (c) of this section, if at any time FDA concludes that continuation of the investigation presents an immediate and substantial danger to the health of individuals, the agency shall immediately, by written notice to the sponsor from the Director of the Center for Drug Evaluation and Research or the Director of the Center for Biologics Evaluation and Research, terminate the IND. An IND so terminated is subject to reinstatement by the Director on the basis of additional submissions that eliminate such danger. If an IND is terminated under this paragraph, the agency will afford the sponsor an opportunity for a regulatory hearing under part 16 on the question of whether the IND should be reinstated.

[52 FR 8831, Mar. 19, 1987, as amended at 52 FR 23031, June 17, 1987; 55 FR 11579, Mar. 29, 1990; 57 FR 13249, Apr. 15, 1992; 67 FR 9586, Mar. 4, 2002]

§ 312.45 Inactive status.

(a) If no subjects are entered into clinical studies for a period of 2 years or more under an IND, or if all investigations under an IND remain on clinical hold for 1 year or more, the IND may be placed by FDA on inactive status. This action may be taken by FDA either on request of the sponsor or on FDA's own initiative. If FDA seeks to act on its own initiative under this section, it shall first notify the sponsor in writing of the proposed inactive status. Upon receipt of such notification, the sponsor shall have 30 days to respond as to why the IND should continue to remain active.

(b) If an IND is placed on inactive status, all investigators shall be so notified and all stocks of the drug shall be returned or otherwise disposed of in accordance with § 312.59.

(c) A sponsor is not required to submit annual reports to an IND on inactive status. An inactive IND is, however, still in effect for purposes of the public disclosure of data and information under § 312.130.

(d) A sponsor who intends to resume clinical investigation under an IND placed on inactive status shall submit a protocol amendment under § 312.30 containing the proposed general investigational plan for the coming year and appropriate protocols. If the protocol amendment relies on information previously submitted, the plan shall reference such information. Additional information supporting the proposed investigation, if any, shall be submitted in an information amendment. Notwithstanding the provisions of § 312.30, clinical investigations under an IND on inactive status may only resume (1) 30 days after FDA receives the protocol amendment, unless FDA notifies the sponsor that the investigations described in the amendment are subject to a clinical hold under § 312.42, or (2) on earlier notification by FDA that the clinical investigations described in the protocol amendment may begin.

(e) An IND that remains on inactive status for 5 years or more may be terminated under § 312.44.

[52 FR 8831, Mar. 19, 1987, as amended at 52 FR 23031, June 17, 1987; 67 FR 9586, Mar. 4, 2002]

§ 312.47 Meetings.

(a) *General.* Meetings between a sponsor and the agency are frequently useful in resolving questions and issues raised during the course of a clinical investigation. FDA encourages such meetings to the extent that they aid in the evaluation of the drug and in the solution of scientific problems concerning the drug, to the extent that FDA's resources permit. The general principle underlying the conduct of such meetings is that there should be free, full, and open communication about any scientific or medical question that may arise during the clinical investigation. These meetings shall be conducted and documented in accordance with part 10.

(b) *"End-of-Phase 2" meetings and meetings held before submission of a marketing application.* At specific times during the drug investigation process, meetings between FDA and a sponsor can be especially helpful in minimizing wasteful expenditures of time and money and thus in speeding the drug development and evaluation process. In particular, FDA has found that meetings at the end of Phase 2 of an investigation (end-of-Phase 2 meetings) are of considerable assistance in planning later studies and that meetings held near completion of Phase 3 and before submission of a marketing application ("pre-NDA" meetings) are helpful in developing methods of presentation and submission of data in the marketing application that facilitate review and allow timely FDA response.

(1) *End-of-Phase 2 meetings*—(i) *Purpose.* The purpose of an end-of-phase 2 meeting is to determine the safety of proceeding to Phase 3, to evaluate the Phase 3 plan and protocols and the adequacy of current studies and plans to assess pediatric safety and effectiveness, and to identify any additional information necessary to support a marketing application for the uses under investigation.

(ii) *Eligibility for meeting.* While the end-of-Phase 2 meeting is designed primarily for IND's involving new molecular entities or major new uses of marketed drugs, a sponsor of any IND may request and obtain an end-of-Phase 2 meeting.

(iii) *Timing.* To be most useful to the sponsor, end-of-Phase 2 meetings should be held before major commitments of effort and resources to specific Phase 3 tests are made. The scheduling of an end-of-Phase 2 meeting is not, however, intended to delay the transition of an investigation from Phase 2 to Phase 3.

(iv) *Advance information.* At least 1 month in advance of an end-of-Phase 2 meeting, the sponsor should submit background information on the sponsor's plan for Phase 3, including summaries of the Phase 1 and 2 investigations, the specific protocols for Phase 3 clinical studies, plans for any additional nonclinical studies, plans for pediatric studies, including a time line for protocol finalization, enrollment, completion, and data analysis, or information to support any planned request for waiver or deferral of pediatric studies, and, if available, tentative labeling for the drug. The recommended contents of such a submission are described more fully in FDA Staff Manual Guide 4850.7 that is publicly available under FDA's public information regulations in part 20.

(v) *Conduct of meeting.* Arrangements for an end-of-Phase 2 meeting are to be made with the division in FDA's Center for Drug Evaluation and Research or the Center for Biologics Evaluation and Research which is responsible for review of the IND. The meeting will be scheduled by FDA at a time convenient to both FDA and the sponsor. Both the sponsor and FDA may bring consultants to the meeting. The meeting should be directed primarily at establishing agreement between FDA and the sponsor of the overall plan for Phase 3 and the objectives and design of particular studies. The adequacy of the technical information to support Phase 3 studies and/or a marketing application may also be discussed. FDA will also provide its best judgment, at that time, of the pediatric studies that will be required for the drug product and whether their submission will be deferred until after approval. Agreements reached at the meeting on these matters will be recorded in minutes of the conference that will be taken by FDA in accordance with §10.65 and provided to the sponsor. The minutes along with any other written material provided to the sponsor will serve as a permanent record of any agreements reached. Barring a significant scientific development that requires otherwise, studies conducted in accordance with the agreement shall be presumed to be sufficient in objective and design for the purpose of obtaining marketing approval for the drug.

(2) *"Pre-NDA" and "pre-BLA" meetings.* FDA has found that delays associated with the initial review of a marketing application may be reduced by exchanges of information about a proposed marketing application. The primary purpose of this kind of exchange is to uncover any major unresolved problems, to identify those studies that the sponsor is relying on as adequate and well-controlled to establish the drug's effectiveness, to identify the status of ongoing or needed studies adequate to assess pediatric safety and effectiveness, to acquaint FDA reviewers with the general information to be submitted in the marketing application (including technical information), to discuss appropriate methods for statistical analysis of the data, and to discuss the best approach to the presentation and formatting of data in the marketing application. Arrangements for such a meeting are to be initiated by the sponsor with the division responsible for review of the IND. To permit FDA to provide the sponsor with the most useful advice on preparing a marketing application, the sponsor should submit to FDA's reviewing division at least 1 month in advance of the meeting the following information:

(i) A brief summary of the clinical studies to be submitted in the application.

(ii) A proposed format for organizing the submission, including methods for presenting the data.

(iii) Information on the status of needed or ongoing pediatric studies.

(iv) Any other information for discussion at the meeting.

[52 FR 8831, Mar. 19, 1987, as amended at 52 FR 23031, June 17, 1987; 55 FR 11580, Mar. 29, 1990; 63 FR 66669, Dec. 2, 1998; 67 FR 9586, Mar. 4, 2002]

§ 312.48 Dispute resolution.

(a) *General*. The Food and Drug Administration is committed to resolving differences between sponsors and FDA reviewing divisions with respect to requirements for IND's as quickly and amicably as possible through the cooperative exchange of information and views.

(b) *Administrative and procedural issues*. When administrative or procedural disputes arise, the sponsor should first attempt to resolve the matter with the division in FDA's Center for Drug Evaluation and Research or Center for Biologics Evaluation and Research which is responsible for review of the IND, beginning with the consumer safety officer assigned to the application. If the dispute is not resolved, the sponsor may raise the matter with the person designated as ombudsman, whose function shall be to investigate what has happened and to facilitate a timely and equitable resolution. Appropriate issues to raise with the ombudsman include resolving difficulties in scheduling meetings and obtaining timely replies to inquiries. Further details on this procedure are contained in FDA Staff Manual Guide 4820.7 that is publicly available under FDA's public information regulations in part 20.

(c) *Scientific and medical disputes*. (1) When scientific or medical disputes arise during the drug investigation process, sponsors should discuss the matter directly with the responsible reviewing officials. If necessary, sponsors may request a meeting with the appropriate reviewing officials and management representatives in order to seek a resolution. Requests for such meetings shall be directed to the director of the division in FDA's Center for Drug Evaluation and Research or Center for Biologics Evaluation and Research which is responsible for review of the IND. FDA will make every attempt to grant requests for meetings that involve important issues and that can be scheduled at mutually convenient times.

(2) The "end-of-Phase 2" and "pre-NDA" meetings described in § 312.47(b) will also provide a timely forum for discussing and resolving scientific and medical issues on which the sponsor disagrees with the agency.

(3) In requesting a meeting designed to resolve a scientific or medical dispute, applicants may suggest that FDA seek the advice of outside experts, in which case FDA may, in its discretion, invite to the meeting one or more of its advisory committee members or other consultants, as designated by the agency. Applicants may rely on, and may bring to any meeting, their own consultants. For major scientific and medical policy issues not resolved by informal meetings, FDA may refer the matter to one of its standing advisory committees for its consideration and recommendations.

[52 FR 8831, Mar. 19, 1987, as amended at 55 FR 11580, Mar. 29, 1990]

Subpart D—Responsibilities of Sponsors and Investigators

§ 312.50 General responsibilities of sponsors.

Sponsors are responsible for selecting qualified investigators, providing them with the information they need to conduct an investigation properly, ensuring proper monitoring of the investigation(s), ensuring that the investigation(s) is conducted in accordance with the general investigational plan and protocols contained in the IND, maintaining an effective IND with respect to the investigations, and ensuring that FDA and all participating investigators are promptly informed of significant new adverse effects or risks with respect to the drug. Additional specific responsibilities of sponsors are described elsewhere in this part.

§ 312.52 Transfer of obligations to a contract research organization.

(a) A sponsor may transfer responsibility for any or all of the obligations set forth in this part to a contract research organization. Any such transfer shall be described in writing. If not all obligations are transferred, the writing is required to describe each of the obligations being assumed by the contract research organization. If all obligations are transferred, a general statement that all obligations have been transferred is acceptable. Any obligation not covered by the written description shall be deemed not to have been transferred.

(b) A contract research organization that assumes any obligation of a sponsor shall comply with the specific regulations in this chapter applicable to this obligation and shall be subject to the same regulatory action as a sponsor for failure to comply with any obligation assumed under these regulations. Thus, all references to "sponsor" in this part apply to a contract research organization to the extent that it assumes one or more obligations of the sponsor.

§312.53 Selecting investigators and monitors.

(a) *Selecting investigators.* A sponsor shall select only investigators qualified by training and experience as appropriate experts to investigate the drug.

(b) *Control of drug.* A sponsor shall ship investigational new drugs only to investigators participating in the investigation.

(c) *Obtaining information from the investigator.* Before permitting an investigator to begin participation in an investigation, the sponsor shall obtain the following:

(1) A signed investigator statement (Form FDA–1572) containing:

(i) The name and address of the investigator;

(ii) The name and code number, if any, of the protocol(s) in the IND identifying the study(ies) to be conducted by the investigator;

(iii) The name and address of any medical school, hospital, or other research facility where the clinical investigation(s) will be conducted;

(iv) The name and address of any clinical laboratory facilities to be used in the study;

(v) The name and address of the IRB that is responsible for review and approval of the study(ies);

(vi) A commitment by the investigator that he or she:

(a) Will conduct the study(ies) in accordance with the relevant, current protocol(s) and will only make changes in a protocol after notifying the sponsor, except when necessary to protect the safety, the rights, or welfare of subjects;

(b) Will comply with all requirements regarding the obligations of clinical investigators and all other pertinent requirements in this part;

(c) Will personally conduct or supervise the described investigation(s);

(d) Will inform any potential subjects that the drugs are being used for investigational purposes and will ensure that the requirements relating to obtaining informed consent (21 CFR part 50) and institutional review board review and approval (21 CFR part 56) are met;

(e) Will report to the sponsor adverse experiences that occur in the course of the investigation(s) in accordance with §312.64;

(f) Has read and understands the information in the investigator's brochure, including the potential risks and side effects of the drug; and

(g) Will ensure that all associates, colleagues, and employees assisting in the conduct of the study(ies) are informed about their obligations in meeting the above commitments.

(vii) A commitment by the investigator that, for an investigation subject to an institutional review requirement under part 56, an IRB that complies with the requirements of that part will be responsible for the initial and continuing review and approval of the clinical investigation and that the investigator will promptly report to the IRB all changes in the research activity and all unanticipated problems involving risks to human subjects or others, and will not make any changes in the research without IRB approval, except where necessary to eliminate apparent immediate hazards to the human subjects.

(viii) A list of the names of the subinvestigators (e.g., research fellows, residents) who will be assisting the investigator in the conduct of the investigation(s).

(2) *Curriculum vitae.* A curriculum vitae or other statement of qualifications of the investigator showing the education, training, and experience that qualifies the investigator as an expert in the clinical investigation of the drug for the use under investigation.

(3) *Clinical protocol.* (i) For Phase 1 investigations, a general outline of the planned investigation including the estimated duration of the study and the

maximum number of subjects that will be involved.

(ii) For Phase 2 or 3 investigations, an outline of the study protocol including an approximation of the number of subjects to be treated with the drug and the number to be employed as controls, if any; the clinical uses to be investigated; characteristics of subjects by age, sex, and condition; the kind of clinical observations and laboratory tests to be conducted; the estimated duration of the study; and copies or a description of case report forms to be used.

(4) *Financial disclosure information.* Sufficient accurate financial information to allow the sponsor to submit complete and accurate certification or disclosure statements required under part 54 of this chapter. The sponsor shall obtain a commitment from the clinical investigator to promptly update this information if any relevant changes occur during the course of the investigation and for 1 year following the completion of the study.

(d) *Selecting monitors.* A sponsor shall select a monitor qualified by training and experience to monitor the progress of the investigation.

[52 FR 8831, Mar. 19, 1987, as amended at 52 FR 23031, June 17, 1987; 61 FR 57280, Nov. 5, 1996; 63 FR 5252, Feb. 2, 1998; 67 FR 9586, Mar. 4, 2002]

§ 312.54 Emergency research under § 50.24 of this chapter.

(a) The sponsor shall monitor the progress of all investigations involving an exception from informed consent under § 50.24 of this chapter. When the sponsor receives from the IRB information concerning the public disclosures required by § 50.24(a)(7)(ii) and (a)(7)(iii) of this chapter, the sponsor promptly shall submit to the IND file and to Docket Number 95S–0158 in the Division of Dockets Management (HFA–305), Food and Drug Administration, 5630 Fishers Lane, rm. 1061, Rockville, MD 20852, copies of the information that was disclosed, identified by the IND number.

(b) The sponsor also shall monitor such investigations to identify when an IRB determines that it cannot approve the research because it does not meet the criteria in the exception in § 50.24(a) of this chapter or because of other relevant ethical concerns. The sponsor promptly shall provide this information in writing to FDA, investigators who are asked to participate in this or a substantially equivalent clinical investigation, and other IRB's that are asked to review this or a substantially equivalent investigation.

[61 FR 51530, Oct. 2, 1996, as amended at 68 FR 24879, May 9, 2003]

§ 312.55 Informing investigators.

(a) Before the investigation begins, a sponsor (other than a sponsor-investigator) shall give each participating clinical investigator an investigator brochure containing the information described in § 312.23(a)(5).

(b) The sponsor shall, as the overall investigation proceeds, keep each participating investigator informed of new observations discovered by or reported to the sponsor on the drug, particularly with respect to adverse effects and safe use. Such information may be distributed to investigators by means of periodically revised investigator brochures, reprints or published studies, reports or letters to clinical investigators, or other appropriate means. Important safety information is required to be relayed to investigators in accordance with § 312.32.

[52 FR 8831, Mar. 19, 1987, as amended at 52 FR 23031, June 17, 1987; 67 FR 9586, Mar. 4, 2002]

§ 312.56 Review of ongoing investigations.

(a) The sponsor shall monitor the progress of all clinical investigations being conducted under its IND.

(b) A sponsor who discovers that an investigator is not complying with the signed agreement (Form FDA–1572), the general investigational plan, or the requirements of this part or other applicable parts shall promptly either secure compliance or discontinue shipments of the investigational new drug to the investigator and end the investigator's participation in the investigation. If the investigator's participation in the investigation is ended, the sponsor shall require that the investigator dispose of or return the investigational drug in accordance with the requirements of § 312.59 and shall notify FDA.

(c) The sponsor shall review and evaluate the evidence relating to the safety and effectiveness of the drug as it is obtained from the investigator. The sponsors shall make such reports to FDA regarding information relevant to the safety of the drug as are required under §312.32. The sponsor shall make annual reports on the progress of the investigation in accordance with §312.33.

(d) A sponsor who determines that its investigational drug presents an unreasonable and significant risk to subjects shall discontinue those investigations that present the risk, notify FDA, all institutional review boards, and all investigators who have at any time participated in the investigation of the discontinuance, assure the disposition of all stocks of the drug outstanding as required by §312.59, and furnish FDA with a full report of the sponsor's actions. The sponsor shall discontinue the investigation as soon as possible, and in no event later than 5 working days after making the determination that the investigation should be discontinued. Upon request, FDA will confer with a sponsor on the need to discontinue an investigation.

[52 FR 8831, Mar. 19, 1987, as amended at 52 FR 23031, June 17, 1987; 67 FR 9586, Mar. 4, 2002]

§312.57 Recordkeeping and record retention.

(a) A sponsor shall maintain adequate records showing the receipt, shipment, or other disposition of the investigational drug. These records are required to include, as appropriate, the name of the investigator to whom the drug is shipped, and the date, quantity, and batch or code mark of each such shipment.

(b) A sponsor shall maintain complete and accurate records showing any financial interest in §54.4(a)(3)(i), (a)(3)(ii), (a)(3)(iii), and (a)(3)(iv) of this chapter paid to clinical investigators by the sponsor of the covered study. A sponsor shall also maintain complete and accurate records concerning all other financial interests of investigators subject to part 54 of this chapter.

(c) A sponsor shall retain the records and reports required by this part for 2 years after a marketing application is approved for the drug; or, if an application is not approved for the drug, until 2 years after shipment and delivery of the drug for investigational use is discontinued and FDA has been so notified.

(d) A sponsor shall retain reserve samples of any test article and reference standard identified in, and used in any of the bioequivalence or bioavailability studies described in, §320.38 or §320.63 of this chapter, and release the reserve samples to FDA upon request, in accordance with, and for the period specified in §320.38.

[52 FR 8831, Mar. 19, 1987, as amended at 52 FR 23031, June 17, 1987; 58 FR 25926, Apr. 28, 1993; 63 FR 5252, Feb. 2, 1998; 67 FR 9586, Mar. 4, 2002]

§312.58 Inspection of sponsor's records and reports.

(a) *FDA inspection.* A sponsor shall upon request from any properly authorized officer or employee of the Food and Drug Administration, at reasonable times, permit such officer or employee to have access to and copy and verify any records and reports relating to a clinical investigation conducted under this part. Upon written request by FDA, the sponsor shall submit the records or reports (or copies of them) to FDA. The sponsor shall discontinue shipments of the drug to any investigator who has failed to maintain or make available records or reports of the investigation as required by this part.

(b) *Controlled substances.* If an investigational new drug is a substance listed in any schedule of the Controlled Substances Act (21 U.S.C. 801; 21 CFR part 1308), records concerning shipment, delivery, receipt, and disposition of the drug, which are required to be kept under this part or other applicable parts of this chapter shall, upon the request of a properly authorized employee of the Drug Enforcement Administration of the U.S. Department of Justice, be made available by the investigator or sponsor to whom the request is made, for inspection and copying. In addition, the sponsor shall assure that adequate precautions are taken, including storage of the investigational drug in a securely locked, substantially constructed cabinet, or other securely locked, substantially constructed enclosure, access to which is limited, to prevent theft or diversion of the substance into illegal channels of distribution.

§ 312.59 Disposition of unused supply of investigational drug.

The sponsor shall assure the return of all unused supplies of the investigational drug from each individual investigator whose participation in the investigation is discontinued or terminated. The sponsor may authorize alternative disposition of unused supplies of the investigational drug provided this alternative ‘disposition does not expose humans to risks from the drug. The sponsor shall maintain written records of any disposition of the drug in accordance with § 312.57.

[52 FR 8831, Mar. 19, 1987, as amended at 52 FR 23031, June 17, 1987; 67 FR 9586, Mar. 4, 2002]

§ 312.60 General responsibilities of investigators.

An investigator is responsible for ensuring that an investigation is conducted according to the signed investigator statement, the investigational plan, and applicable regulations; for protecting the rights, safety, and welfare of subjects under the investigator's care; and for the control of drugs under investigation. An investigator shall, in accordance with the provisions of part 50 of this chapter, obtain the informed consent of each human subject to whom the drug is administered, except as provided in §§ 50.23 or 50.24 of this chapter. Additional specific responsibilities of clinical investigators are set forth in this part and in parts 50 and 56 of this chapter.

[52 FR 8831, Mar. 19, 1987, as amended at 61 FR 51530, Oct. 2, 1996]

§ 312.61 Control of the investigational drug.

An investigator shall administer the drug only to subjects under the investigator's personal supervision or under the supervision of a subinvestigator responsible to the investigator. The investigator shall not supply the investigational drug to any person not authorized under this part to receive it.

§ 312.62 Investigator recordkeeping and record retention.

(a) *Disposition of drug.* An investigator is required to maintain adequate records of the disposition of the drug, including dates, quantity, and use by subjects. If the investigation is terminated, suspended, discontinued, or completed, the investigator shall return the unused supplies of the drug to the sponsor, or otherwise provide for disposition of the unused supplies of the drug under § 312.59.

(b) *Case histories.* An investigator is required to prepare and maintain adequate and accurate case histories that record all observations and other data pertinent to the investigation on each individual administered the investigational drug or employed as a control in the investigation. Case histories include the case report forms and supporting data including, for example, signed and dated consent forms and medical records including, for example, progress notes of the physician, the individual's hospital chart(s), and the nurses' notes. The case history for each individual shall document that informed consent was obtained prior to participation in the study.

(c) *Record retention.* An investigator shall retain records required to be maintained under this part for a period of 2 years following the date a marketing application is approved for the drug for the indication for which it is being investigated; or, if no application is to be filed or if the application is not approved for such indication, until 2 years after the investigation is discontinued and FDA is notified.

[52 FR 8831, Mar. 19, 1987, as amended at 52 FR 23031, June 17, 1987; 61 FR 57280, Nov. 5, 1996; 67 FR 9586, Mar. 4, 2002]

§ 312.64 Investigator reports.

(a) *Progress reports.* The investigator shall furnish all reports to the sponsor of the drug who is responsible for collecting and evaluating the results obtained. The sponsor is required under § 312.33 to submit annual reports to FDA on the progress of the clinical investigations.

(b) *Safety reports.* An investigator must immediately report to the sponsor any serious adverse event, whether or not considered drug related, including those listed in the protocol or investigator brochure and must include an assessment of whether there is a reasonable possibility that the drug caused the event. Study endpoints that are serious adverse events (e.g., all-cause mortality) must be reported in accordance with the protocol unless there is evidence suggesting a causal relationship between the drug and the event (e.g., death from anaphylaxis). In that case, the investigator must immediately report the event to the sponsor. The investigator must record nonserious adverse events and report them to the sponsor according to the timetable for reporting specified in the protocol.

(c) *Final report.* An investigator shall provide the sponsor with an adequate report shortly after completion of the investigator's participation in the investigation.

(d) *Financial disclosure reports.* The clinical investigator shall provide the sponsor with sufficient accurate financial information to allow an applicant to submit complete and accurate certification or disclosure statements as required under part 54 of this chapter. The clinical investigator shall promptly update this information if any relevant changes occur during the course of the investigation and for 1 year following the completion of the study.

[52 FR 8831, Mar. 19, 1987, as amended at 52 FR 23031, June 17, 1987; 63 FR 5252, Feb. 2, 1998; 67 FR 9586, Mar. 4, 2002; 75 FR 59963, Sept. 29, 2010]

§312.66 Assurance of IRB review.

An investigator shall assure that an IRB that complies with the requirements set forth in part 56 will be responsible for the initial and continuing review and approval of the proposed clinical study. The investigator shall also assure that he or she will promptly report to the IRB all changes in the research activity and all unanticipated problems involving risk to human subjects or others, and that he or she will not make any changes in the research without IRB approval, except where

necessary to eliminate apparent immediate hazards to human subjects.

[52 FR 8831, Mar. 19, 1987, as amended at 52 FR 23031, June 17, 1987; 67 FR 9586, Mar. 4, 2002]

§312.68 Inspection of investigator's records and reports.

An investigator shall upon request from any properly authorized officer or employee of FDA, at reasonable times, permit such officer or employee to have access to, and copy and verify any records or reports made by the investigator pursuant to §312.62. The investigator is not required to divulge subject names unless the records of particular individuals require a more detailed study of the cases, or unless there is reason to believe that the records do not represent actual case studies, or do not represent actual results obtained.

§312.69 Handling of controlled substances.

If the investigational drug is subject to the Controlled Substances Act, the investigator shall take adequate precautions, including storage of the investigational drug in a securely locked, substantially constructed cabinet, or other securely locked, substantially constructed enclosure, access to which is limited, to prevent theft or diversion of the substance into illegal channels of distribution.

§312.70 Disqualification of a clinical investigator.

(a) If FDA has information indicating that an investigator (including a sponsor-investigator) has repeatedly or deliberately failed to comply with the requirements of this part, part 50 or part 56 of this chapter, or has repeatedly or deliberately submitted to FDA or to the sponsor false information in any required report, the Center for Drug Evaluation and Research or the Center for Biologics Evaluation and Research will furnish the investigator written notice of the matter complained of and offer the investigator an opportunity to explain the matter in writing, or, at the option of the investigator, in an informal conference. If an explanation is offered and accepted by the applicable Center, the Center will discontinue the disqualification proceeding. If an explanation is offered but not accepted by the applicable Center, the investigator will be given an opportunity for a regulatory hearing under part 16 of this chapter on the question of whether the investigator is eligible to receive test articles under this part and eligible to conduct any clinical investigation that supports an application for a research or marketing permit for products regulated by FDA.

(b) After evaluating all available information, including any explanation presented by the investigator, if the Commissioner determines that the investigator has repeatedly or deliberately failed to comply with the requirements of this part, part 50 or part 56 of this chapter, or has repeatedly or deliberately submitted to FDA or to the sponsor false information in any required report, the Commissioner will notify the investigator, the sponsor of any investigation in which the investigator has been named as a participant, and the reviewing institutional review boards (IRBs) that the investigator is not eligible to receive test articles under this part. The notification to the investigator, sponsor, and IRBs will provide a statement of the basis for such determination. The notification also will explain that an investigator determined to be ineligible to receive test articles under this part will be ineligible to conduct any clinical investigation that supports an application for a research or marketing permit for products regulated by FDA, including drugs, biologics, devices, new animal drugs, foods, including dietary supplements, that bear a nutrient content claim or a health claim, infant formulas, food and color additives, and tobacco products.

(c) Each application or submission to FDA under the provisions of this chapter containing data reported by an investigator who has been determined to be ineligible to receive FDA-regulated test articles is subject to examination to determine whether the investigator has submitted unreliable data that are essential to the continuation of an investigation or essential to the approval of a marketing application, or essential to the continued marketing of an FDA-regulated product.

(d) If the Commissioner determines, after the unreliable data submitted by the investigator are eliminated from consideration, that the data remaining are inadequate to support a conclusion that it is reasonably safe to continue the investigation, the Commissioner will notify the sponsor, who shall have an opportunity for a regulatory hearing under part 16 of this chapter. If a danger to the public health exists, however, the Commissioner shall terminate the IND immediately and notify the sponsor and the reviewing IRBs of the termination. In such case, the sponsor shall have an opportunity for a regulatory hearing before FDA under part 16 on the question of whether the IND should be reinstated. The determination that an investigation may not be considered in support of a research or marketing application or a notification or petition submission does not, however, relieve the sponsor of any obligation under any other applicable regulation to submit to FDA the results of the investigation.

(e) If the Commissioner determines, after the unreliable data submitted by the investigator are eliminated from consideration, that the continued approval of the product for which the data were submitted cannot be justified, the Commissioner will proceed to withdraw approval of the product in accordance with the applicable provisions of the relevant statutes.

(f) An investigator who has been determined to be ineligible under paragraph (b) of this section may be reinstated as eligible when the Commissioner determines that the investigator has presented adequate assurances that the investigator will employ all test articles, and will conduct any clinical investigation that supports an application for a research or marketing permit for products regulated by FDA, solely in compliance with the applicable provisions of this chapter.

[77 FR 25359, Apr. 30, 2012]

Subpart E—Drugs Intended to Treat Life-threatening and Severely-debilitating Illnesses

AUTHORITY: 21 U.S.C. 351, 352, 353, 355, 371; 42 U.S.C. 262.

SOURCE: 53 FR 41523, Oct. 21, 1988, unless otherwise noted.

§312.80 Purpose.

The purpose of this section is to establish procedures designed to expedite the development, evaluation, and marketing of new therapies intended to treat persons with life-threatening and severely-debilitating illnesses, especially where no satisfactory alternative therapy exists. As stated §314.105(c) of this chapter, while the statutory standards of safety and effectiveness apply to all drugs, the many kinds of drugs that are subject to them, and the wide range of uses for those drugs, demand flexibility in applying the standards. The Food and Drug Administration (FDA) has determined that it is appropriate to exercise the broadest flexibility in applying the statutory standards, while preserving appropriate guarantees for safety and effectiveness. These procedures reflect the recognition that physicians and patients are generally willing to accept greater risks or side effects from products that treat life-threatening and severely-debilitating illnesses, than they would accept from products that treat less serious illnesses. These procedures also reflect the recognition that the benefits of the drug need to be evaluated in light of the severity of the disease being treated. The procedure outlined in this section should be interpreted consistent with that purpose.

§312.81 Scope.

This section applies to new drug and biological products that are being studied for their safety and effectiveness in treating life-threatening or severely-debilitating diseases.

(a) For purposes of this section, the term "life-threatening" means:

(1) Diseases or conditions where the likelihood of death is high unless the course of the disease is interrupted; and

(2) Diseases or conditions with potentially fatal outcomes, where the end point of clinical trial analysis is survival.

(b) For purposes of this section, the term "severely debilitating" means diseases or conditions that cause major irreversible morbidity.

(c) Sponsors are encouraged to consult with FDA on the applicability of these procedures to specific products.

[53 FR 41523, Oct. 21, 1988, as amended at 64 FR 401, Jan. 5, 1999]

§312.82 Early consultation.

For products intended to treat life-threatening or severely-debilitating illnesses, sponsors may request to meet with FDA-reviewing officials early in the drug development process to review and reach agreement on the design of necessary preclinical and clinical studies. Where appropriate, FDA will invite to such meetings one or more outside expert scientific consultants or advisory committee members. To the extent FDA resources permit, agency reviewing officials will honor requests for such meetings

(a) *Pre-investigational new drug (IND) meetings.* Prior to the submission of the initial IND, the sponsor may request a meeting with FDA-reviewing officials. The primary purpose of this meeting is to review and reach agreement on the design of animal studies needed to initiate human testing. The meeting may also provide an opportunity for discussing the scope and design of phase 1 testing, plans for studying the drug product in pediatric populations, and the best approach for presentation and formatting of data in the IND.

(b) *End-of-phase 1 meetings.* When data from phase 1 clinical testing are available, the sponsor may again request a meeting with FDA-reviewing officials. The primary purpose of this meeting is to review and reach agreement on the design of phase 2 controlled clinical trials, with the goal that such testing will be adequate to provide sufficient data on the drug's safety and effectiveness to support a decision on its approvability for marketing, and to discuss the need for, as well as the design and timing of, studies of the drug in pediatric patients. For drugs for life-threatening diseases, FDA will provide its best judgment, at that time, whether pediatric studies will be required and whether their submission will be deferred until after approval. The procedures outlined in §312.47(b)(1) with respect to end-of-phase 2 conferences, including documentation of agreements reached, would also be used for end-of-phase 1 meetings.

[53 FR 41523, Oct. 21, 1988, as amended at 63 FR 66669, Dec. 2, 1998]

§ 312.83 Treatment protocols.

If the preliminary analysis of phase 2 test results appears promising, FDA may ask the sponsor to submit a treatment protocol to be reviewed under the procedures and criteria listed in §§ 312.305 and 312.320. Such a treatment protocol, if requested and granted, would normally remain in effect while the complete data necessary for a marketing application are being assembled by the sponsor and reviewed by FDA (unless grounds exist for clinical hold of ongoing protocols, as provided in § 312.42(b)(3)(ii)).

[53 FR 41523, Oct. 21, 1988, as amended at 76 FR 13880, Mar. 15, 2011]

§ 312.84 Risk-benefit analysis in review of marketing applications for drugs to treat life-threatening and severely-debilitating illnesses.

(a) FDA's application of the statutory standards for marketing approval shall recognize the need for a medical risk-benefit judgment in making the final decision on approvability. As part of this evaluation, consistent with the statement of purpose in § 312.80, FDA will consider whether the benefits of the drug outweigh the known and potential risks of the drug and the need to answer remaining questions about risks and benefits of the drug, taking into consideration the severity of the disease and the absence of satisfactory alternative therapy.

(b) In making decisions on whether to grant marketing approval for products that have been the subject of an end-of-phase 1 meeting under § 312.82, FDA will usually seek the advice of outside expert scientific consultants or advisory committees. Upon the filing of such a marketing application under § 314.101 or part 601 of this chapter, FDA will notify the members of the relevant standing advisory committee of the application's filing and its availability for review.

(c) If FDA concludes that the data presented are not sufficient for marketing approval, FDA will issue a com-plete response letter under § 314.110 of this chapter or the biological product licensing procedures. Such letter, in describing the deficiencies in the application, will address why the results of the research design agreed to under § 312.82, or in subsequent meetings, have not provided sufficient evidence for marketing approval. Such letter will also describe any recommendations made by the advisory committee regarding the application.

(d) Marketing applications submitted under the procedures contained in this section will be subject to the requirements and procedures contained in part 314 or part 600 of this chapter, as well as those in this subpart.

[53 FR 41523, Oct. 21, 1988, as amended at 73 FR 39607, July 10, 2008]

§ 312.85 Phase 4 studies.

Concurrent with marketing approval, FDA may seek agreement from the sponsor to conduct certain post-marketing (phase 4) studies to delineate additional information about the drug's risks, benefits, and optimal use. These studies could include, but would not be limited to, studying different doses or schedules of administration than were used in phase 2 studies, use of the drug in other patient populations or other stages of the disease, or use of the drug over a longer period of time.

§ 312.86 Focused FDA regulatory research.

At the discretion of the agency, FDA may undertake focused regulatory research on critical rate-limiting aspects of the preclinical, chemical/manufacturing, and clinical phases of drug development and evaluation. When initiated, FDA will undertake such research efforts as a means for meeting a public health need in facilitating the development of therapies to treat life-threatening or severely debilitating illnesses.

§ 312.87 Active monitoring of conduct and evaluation of clinical trials.

For drugs covered under this section, the Commissioner and other agency officials will monitor the progress of the conduct and evaluation of clinical trials and be involved in facilitating their appropriate progress.

§312.88 Safeguards for patient safety.

All of the safeguards incorporated within parts 50, 56, 312, 314, and 600 of this chapter designed to ensure the safety of clinical testing and the safety of products following marketing approval apply to drugs covered by this section. This includes the requirements for informed consent (part 50 of this chapter) and institutional review boards (part 56 of this chapter). These safeguards further include the review of animal studies prior to initial human testing (§312.23), and the monitoring of adverse drug experiences through the requirements of IND safety reports (§312.32), safety update reports during agency review of a marketing application (§314.50 of this chapter), and postmarketing adverse reaction reporting (§314.80 of this chapter).

Subpart F—Miscellaneous

§312.110 Import and export requirements.

(a) *Imports.* An investigational new drug offered for import into the United States complies with the requirements of this part if it is subject to an IND that is in effect for it under §312.40 and: (1) The consignee in the United States is the sponsor of the IND; (2) the consignee is a qualified investigator named in the IND; or (3) the consignee is the domestic agent of a foreign sponsor, is responsible for the control and distribution of the investigational drug, and the IND identifies the consignee and describes what, if any, actions the consignee will take with respect to the investigational drug.

(b) *Exports.* An investigational new drug may be exported from the United States for use in a clinical investigation under any of the following conditions:

(1) An IND is in effect for the drug under §312.40, the drug complies with the laws of the country to which it is being exported, and each person who receives the drug is an investigator in a study submitted to and allowed to proceed under the IND; or

(2) The drug has valid marketing authorization in Australia, Canada, Israel, Japan, New Zealand, Switzerland, South Africa, or in any country in the European Union or the European Economic Area, and complies with the laws of the country to which it is being exported, section 802(b)(1)(A), (f), and (g) of the act, and §1.101 of this chapter; or

(3) The drug is being exported to Australia, Canada, Israel, Japan, New Zealand, Switzerland, South Africa, or to any country in the European Union or the European Economic Area, and complies with the laws of the country to which it is being exported, the applicable provisions of section 802(c), (f), and (g) of the act, and §1.101 of this chapter. Drugs exported under this paragraph that are not the subject of an IND are exempt from the label requirement in §312.6(a); or

(4) Except as provided in paragraph (b)(5) of this section, the person exporting the drug sends a written certification to the Office of International Programs (HFG–1), Food and Drug Administration, 5600 Fishers Lane, Rockville, MD 20857, at the time the drug is first exported and maintains records documenting compliance with this paragraph. The certification shall describe the drug that is to be exported (*i.e.*, trade name (if any), generic name, and dosage form), identify the country or countries to which the drug is to be exported, and affirm that:

(i) The drug is intended for export;

(ii) The drug is intended for investigational use in a foreign country;

(iii) The drug meets the foreign purchaser's or consignee's specifications;

(iv) The drug is not in conflict with the importing country's laws;

(v) The outer shipping package is labeled to show that the package is intended for export from the United States;

(vi) The drug is not sold or offered for sale in the United States;

(vii) The clinical investigation will be conducted in accordance with §312.120;

(viii) The drug is manufactured, processed, packaged, and held in substantial conformity with current good manufacturing practices;

(ix) The drug is not adulterated within the meaning of section 501(a)(1), (a)(2)(A), (a)(3), (c), or (d) of the act;

(x) The drug does not present an imminent hazard to public health, either in the United States, if the drug were to be reimported, or in the foreign country; and

(xi) The drug is labeled in accordance with the foreign country's laws.

(5) In the event of a national emergency in a foreign country, where the national emergency necessitates exportation of an investigational new drug, the requirements in paragraph (b)(4) of this section apply as follows:

(i) *Situations where the investigational new drug is to be stockpiled in anticipation of a national emergency.* There may be instances where exportation of an investigational new drug is needed so that the drug may be stockpiled and made available for use by the importing country if and when a national emergency arises. In such cases:

(A) A person may export an investigational new drug under paragraph (b)(4) of this section without making an affirmation with respect to any one or more of paragraphs (b)(4)(i), (b)(4)(iv), (b)(4)(vi), (b)(4)(vii), (b)(4)(viii), and/or (b)(4)(ix) of this section, provided that he or she:

(*1*) Provides a written statement explaining why compliance with each such paragraph is not feasible or is contrary to the best interests of the individuals who may receive the investigational new drug;

(*2*) Provides a written statement from an authorized official of the importing country's government. The statement must attest that the official agrees with the exporter's statement made under paragraph (b)(5)(i)(A)(*1*) of this section; explain that the drug is to be stockpiled solely for use of the importing country in a national emergency; and describe the potential national emergency that warrants exportation of the investigational new drug under this provision; and

(*3*) Provides a written statement showing that the Secretary of Health and Human Services (the Secretary), or his or her designee, agrees with the findings of the authorized official of the importing country's government. Persons who wish to obtain a written statement from the Secretary should direct their requests to Secretary's Operations Center, Office of Emergency

Operations and Security Programs, Office of Public Health Emergency Preparedness, Office of the Secretary, Department of Health and Human Services, 200 Independence Ave. SW., Washington, DC 20201. Requests may be also be sent by FAX: 202–619–7870 or by e-mail: *HHS.SOC@hhs.gov.*

(B) Exportation may not proceed until FDA has authorized exportation of the investigational new drug. FDA may deny authorization if the statements provided under paragraphs (b)(5)(i)(A)(*1*) or (b)(5)(i)(A)(*2*) of this section are inadequate or if exportation is contrary to public health.

(ii) *Situations where the investigational new drug is to be used for a sudden and immediate national emergency.* There may be instances where exportation of an investigational new drug is needed so that the drug may be used in a sudden and immediate national emergency that has developed or is developing. In such cases:

(A) A person may export an investigational new drug under paragraph (b)(4) of this section without making an affirmation with respect to any one or more of paragraphs (b)(4)(i), (b)(4)(iv), (b)(4)(v), (b)(4)(vi), (b)(4)(vii), (b)(4)(viii), (b)(4)(ix), and/or (b)(4)(xi), provided that he or she:

(*1*) Provides a written statement explaining why compliance with each such paragraph is not feasible or is contrary to the best interests of the individuals who are expected to receive the investigational new drug and

(*2*) Provides sufficient information from an authorized official of the importing country's government to enable the Secretary, or his or her designee, to decide whether a national emergency has developed or is developing in the importing country, whether the investigational new drug will be used solely for that national emergency, and whether prompt exportation of the investigational new drug is necessary. Persons who wish to obtain a determination from the Secretary should direct their requests to Secretary's Operations Center, Office of Emergency Operations and Security Programs, Office of Public Health Emergency Preparedness, Office of the Secretary, Department of Health and Human Services, 200 Independence Ave.

SW., Washington, DC 20201. Requests may be also be sent by FAX: 202–619–7870 or by e-mail: *HHS.SOC@hhs.gov.*

(B) Exportation may proceed without prior FDA authorization.

(c) *Limitations.* Exportation under paragraph (b) of this section may not occur if:

(1) For drugs exported under paragraph (b)(1) of this section, the IND pertaining to the clinical investigation is no longer in effect;

(2) For drugs exported under paragraph (b)(2) of this section, the requirements in section 802(b)(1), (f), or (g) of the act are no longer met;

(3) For drugs exported under paragraph (b)(3) of this section, the requirements in section 802(c), (f), or (g) of the act are no longer met;

(4) For drugs exported under paragraph (b)(4) of this section, the conditions underlying the certification or the statements submitted under paragraph (b)(5) of this section are no longer met; or

(5) For any investigational new drugs under this section, the drug no longer complies with the laws of the importing country.

(d) *Insulin and antibiotics.* New insulin and antibiotic drug products may be exported for investigational use in accordance with section 801(e)(1) of the act without complying with this section.

[52 FR 8831, Mar. 19, 1987, as amended at 52 FR 23031, June 17, 1987; 64 FR 401, Jan. 5, 1999; 67 FR 9586, Mar. 4, 2002; 70 FR 70729, Nov. 23, 2005]

§312.120 Foreign clinical studies not conducted under an IND.

(a) *Acceptance of studies.* (1) FDA will accept as support for an IND or application for marketing approval (an application under section 505 of the act or section 351 of the Public Health Service Act (the PHS Act) (42 U.S.C. 262)) a well-designed and well-conducted foreign clinical study not conducted under an IND, if the following conditions are met:

(i) The study was conducted in accordance with good clinical practice (GCP). For the purposes of this section, GCP is defined as a standard for the design, conduct, performance, monitoring, auditing, recording, analysis, and reporting of clinical trials in a way that provides assurance that the data and reported results are credible and accurate and that the rights, safety, and well-being of trial subjects are protected. GCP includes review and approval (or provision of a favorable opinion) by an independent ethics committee (IEC) before initiating a study, continuing review of an ongoing study by an IEC, and obtaining and documenting the freely given informed consent of the subject (or a subject's legally authorized representative, if the subject is unable to provide informed consent) before initiating a study. GCP does not require informed consent in life-threatening situations when the IEC reviewing the study finds, before initiation of the study, that informed consent is not feasible and either that the conditions present are consistent with those described in §50.23 or §50.24(a) of this chapter, or that the measures described in the study protocol or elsewhere will protect the rights, safety, and well-being of subjects; and

(ii) FDA is able to validate the data from the study through an onsite inspection if the agency deems it necessary.

(2) Although FDA will not accept as support for an IND or application for marketing approval a study that does not meet the conditions of paragraph (a)(1) of this section, FDA will examine data from such a study.

(3) Marketing approval of a new drug based solely on foreign clinical data is governed by §314.106 of this chapter.

(b) *Supporting information.* A sponsor or applicant who submits data from a foreign clinical study not conducted under an IND as support for an IND or application for marketing approval must submit to FDA, in addition to information required elsewhere in parts 312, 314, or 601 of this chapter, a description of the actions the sponsor or applicant took to ensure that the research conformed to GCP as described in paragraph (a)(1)(i) of this section. The description is not required to duplicate information already submitted in the IND or application for marketing approval. Instead, the description must provide either the following information or a cross-reference to another section of the submission where the information is located:

(1) The investigator's qualifications;

(2) A description of the research facilities;

(3) A detailed summary of the protocol and results of the study and, should FDA request, case records maintained by the investigator or additional background data such as hospital or other institutional records;

(4) A description of the drug substance and drug product used in the study, including a description of the components, formulation, specifications, and, if available, bioavailability of the specific drug product used in the clinical study;

(5) If the study is intended to support the effectiveness of a drug product, information showing that the study is adequate and well controlled under §314.126 of this chapter;

(6) The name and address of the IEC that reviewed the study and a statement that the IEC meets the definition in §312.3 of this chapter. The sponsor or applicant must maintain records supporting such statement, including records of the names and qualifications of IEC members, and make these records available for agency review upon request;

(7) A summary of the IEC's decision to approve or modify and approve the study, or to provide a favorable opinion;

(8) A description of how informed consent was obtained;

(9) A description of what incentives, if any, were provided to subjects to participate in the study;

(10) A description of how the sponsor(s) monitored the study and ensured that the study was carried out consistently with the study protocol; and

(11) A description of how investigators were trained to comply with GCP (as described in paragraph (a)(1)(i) of this section) and to conduct the study in accordance with the study protocol, and a statement on whether written commitments by investigators to comply with GCP and the protocol were obtained. Any signed written commitments by investigators must be maintained by the sponsor or applicant and made available for agency review upon request.

(c) *Waivers.* (1) A sponsor or applicant may ask FDA to waive any applicable requirements under paragraphs (a)(1) and (b) of this section. A waiver request may be submitted in an IND or in an information amendment to an IND, or in an application or in an amendment or supplement to an application submitted under part 314 or 601 of this chapter. A waiver request is required to contain at least one of the following:

(i) An explanation why the sponsor's or applicant's compliance with the requirement is unnecessary or cannot be achieved;

(ii) A description of an alternative submission or course of action that satisfies the purpose of the requirement; or

(iii) Other information justifying a waiver.

(2) FDA may grant a waiver if it finds that doing so would be in the interest of the public health.

(d) *Records.* A sponsor or applicant must retain the records required by this section for a foreign clinical study not conducted under an IND as follows:

(1) If the study is submitted in support of an application for marketing approval, for 2 years after an agency decision on that application;

(2) If the study is submitted in support of an IND but not an application for marketing approval, for 2 years after the submission of the IND.

[73 FR 22815, Apr. 28, 2008]

§312.130 Availability for public disclosure of data and information in an IND.

(a) The existence of an investigational new drug application will not be disclosed by FDA unless it has previously been publicly disclosed or acknowledged.

(b) The availability for public disclosure of all data and information in an investigational new drug application for a new drug will be handled in accordance with the provisions established in §314.430 for the confidentiality of data and information in applications submitted in part 314. The availability for public disclosure of all data and information in an investigational new drug application for a biological product will be governed by the provisions of §§601.50 and 601.51.

(c) Notwithstanding the provisions of §314.430, FDA shall disclose upon request to an individual to whom an investigational new drug has been given a copy of any IND safety report relating to the use in the individual.

(d) The availability of information required to be publicly disclosed for investigations involving an exception from informed consent under §50.24 of this chapter will be handled as follows: Persons wishing to request the publicly disclosable information in the IND that was required to be filed in Docket Number 95S–0158 in the Division of Dockets Management (HFA–305), Food and Drug Administration, 5630 Fishers Lane, rm. 1061, Rockville, MD 20852, shall submit a request under the Freedom of Information Act.

[52 FR 8831, Mar. 19, 1987. Redesignated at 53 FR 41523, Oct. 21, 1988, as amended at 61 FR 51530, Oct. 2, 1996; 64 FR 401, Jan. 5, 1999; 68 FR 24879, May 9, 2003]

§312.140 Address for correspondence.

(a) A sponsor must send an initial IND submission to the Center for Drug Evaluation and Research (CDER) or to the Center for Biologics Evaluation and Research (CBER), depending on the Center responsible for regulating the product as follows:

(1) *For drug products regulated by CDER.* Send the IND submission to the Central Document Room, Center for Drug Evaluation and Research, Food and Drug Administration, 5901–B Ammendale Rd., Beltsville, MD 20705–1266; except send an IND submission for an in vivo bioavailability or bioequivalence study in humans to support an abbreviated new drug application to the Office of Generic Drugs (HFD–600), Center for Drug Evaluation and Research, Food and Drug Administration, Metro Park North VII, 7620 Standish Pl., Rockville, MD 20855.

(2) *For biological products regulated by CDER.* Send the IND submission to the CDER Therapeutic Biological Products Document Room, Center for Drug Evaluation and Research, Food and Drug Administration, 12229 Wilkins Ave., Rockville, MD 20852.

(3) *For biological products regulated by CBER.* Send the IND submission to the Document Control Center (HFM–99), Center for Biologics Evaluation and Research, Food and Drug Administration, 1401 Rockville Pike, suite 200N, Rockville, MD 20852–1448.

(b) On receiving the IND, the responsible Center will inform the sponsor which one of the divisions in CDER or CBER is responsible for the IND. Amendments, reports, and other correspondence relating to matters covered by the IND should be sent to the appropriate center at the address indicated in this section and marked to the attention of the responsible division. The outside wrapper of each submission shall state what is contained in the submission, for example, "IND Application", "Protocol Amendment", etc.

(c) All correspondence relating to export of an investigational drug under §312.110(b)(2) shall be submitted to the International Affairs Staff (HFY–50), Office of Health Affairs, Food and Drug Administration, 5600 Fishers Lane, Rockville, MD 20857.

[70 FR 14981, Mar. 24, 2005, as amended at 74 FR 13113, Mar. 26, 2009; 74 FR 55771, Oct. 29, 2009; 75 FR 37295, June 29, 2010]

§312.145 Guidance documents.

(a) FDA has made available guidance documents under §10.115 of this chapter to help you to comply with certain requirements of this part.

(b) The Center for Drug Evaluation and Research (CDER) and the Center for Biologics Evaluation and Research (CBER) maintain lists of guidance documents that apply to the centers' regulations. The lists are maintained on the Internet and are published annually in the FEDERAL REGISTER. A request for a copy of the CDER list should be directed to the Office of Training and Communications, Division of Drug Information, Center for Drug Evaluation and Research, Food and Drug Administration, 10903 New Hampshire Ave., Silver Spring, MD 20993–0002. A request for a copy of the CBER list should be directed to the Office of Communication, Training, and Manufacturers Assistance (HFM–40), Center for Biologics Evaluation and

Research, Food and Drug Administration, 1401 Rockville Pike, Rockville, MD 20852–1448.

[65 FR 56479, Sept. 19, 2000, as amended at 74 FR 13113, Mar. 26, 2009]

Subpart G—Drugs for Investigational Use in Laboratory Research Animals or In Vitro Tests

§ 312.160 Drugs for investigational use in laboratory research animals or in vitro tests.

(a) *Authorization to ship.* (1)(i) A person may ship a drug intended solely for tests in vitro or in animals used only for laboratory research purposes if it is labeled as follows:

CAUTION: Contains a new drug for investigational use only in laboratory research animals, or for tests in vitro. Not for use in humans.

(ii) A person may ship a biological product for investigational in vitro diagnostic use that is listed in § 312.2(b)(2)(ii) if it is labeled as follows:

CAUTION: Contains a biological product for investigational in vitro diagnostic tests only.

(2) A person shipping a drug under paragraph (a) of this section shall use due diligence to assure that the consignee is regularly engaged in conducting such tests and that the shipment of the new drug will actually be used for tests in vitro or in animals used only for laboratory research.

(3) A person who ships a drug under paragraph (a) of this section shall maintain adequate records showing the name and post office address of the expert to whom the drug is shipped and the date, quantity, and batch or code mark of each shipment and delivery. Records of shipments under paragraph (a)(1)(i) of this section are to be maintained for a period of 2 years after the shipment. Records and reports of data and shipments under paragraph (a)(1)(ii) of this section are to be maintained in accordance with § 312.57(b). The person who ships the drug shall upon request from any properly authorized officer or employee of the Food and Drug Administration, at reasonable times, permit such officer or employee to have access to and copy and verify records required to be maintained under this section.

(b) *Termination of authorization to ship.* FDA may terminate authorization to ship a drug under this section if it finds that:

(1) The sponsor of the investigation has failed to comply with any of the conditions for shipment established under this section; or

(2) The continuance of the investigation is unsafe or otherwise contrary to the public interest or the drug is used for purposes other than bona fide scientific investigation. FDA will notify the person shipping the drug of its finding and invite immediate correction. If correction is not immediately made, the person shall have an opportunity for a regulatory hearing before FDA pursuant to part 16.

(c) *Disposition of unused drug.* The person who ships the drug under paragraph (a) of this section shall assure the return of all unused supplies of the drug from individual investigators whenever the investigation discontinues or the investigation is terminated. The person who ships the drug may authorize in writing alternative disposition of unused supplies of the drug provided this alternative disposition does not expose humans to risks from the drug, either directly or indirectly (e.g., through food-producing animals). The shipper shall maintain records of any alternative disposition.

[52 FR 8831, Mar. 19, 1987, as amended at 52 FR 23031, June 17, 1987. Redesignated at 53 FR 41523, Oct. 21, 1988; 67 FR 9586, Mar. 4, 2002]

Subpart H [Reserved]

Subpart I—Expanded Access to Investigational Drugs for Treatment Use

SOURCE: 74 FR 40942, Aug. 13, 2009, unless otherwise noted.

§ 312.300 General.

(a) *Scope.* This subpart contains the requirements for the use of investigational new drugs and approved drugs where availability is limited by a risk evaluation and mitigation strategy

(REMS) when the primary purpose is to diagnose, monitor, or treat a patient's disease or condition. The aim of this subpart is to facilitate the availability of such drugs to patients with serious diseases or conditions when there is no comparable or satisfactory alternative therapy to diagnose, monitor, or treat the patient's disease or condition.

(b) *Definitions.* The following definitions of terms apply to this subpart:

Immediately life-threatening disease or condition means a stage of disease in which there is reasonable likelihood that death will occur within a matter of months or in which premature death is likely without early treatment.

Serious disease or condition means a disease or condition associated with morbidity that has substantial impact on day-to-day functioning. Short-lived and self-limiting morbidity will usually not be sufficient, but the morbidity need not be irreversible, provided it is persistent or recurrent. Whether a disease or condition is serious is a matter of clinical judgment, based on its impact on such factors as survival, day-to-day functioning, or the likelihood that the disease, if left untreated, will progress from a less severe condition to a more serious one.

§ 312.305 Requirements for all expanded access uses.

The criteria, submission requirements, safeguards, and beginning treatment information set out in this section apply to all expanded access uses described in this subpart. Additional criteria, submission requirements, and safeguards that apply to specific types of expanded access are described in §§ 312.310 through 312.320.

(a) *Criteria.* FDA must determine that:

(1) The patient or patients to be treated have a serious or immediately life-threatening disease or condition, and there is no comparable or satisfactory alternative therapy to diagnose, monitor, or treat the disease or condition;

(2) The potential patient benefit justifies the potential risks of the treatment use and those potential risks are not unreasonable in the context of the disease or condition to be treated; and

(3) Providing the investigational drug for the requested use will not interfere with the initiation, conduct, or completion of clinical investigations that could support marketing approval of the expanded access use or otherwise compromise the potential development of the expanded access use.

(b) *Submission.* (1) An expanded access submission is required for each type of expanded access described in this subpart. The submission may be a new IND or a protocol amendment to an existing IND. Information required for a submission may be supplied by referring to pertinent information contained in an existing IND if the sponsor of the existing IND grants a right of reference to the IND.

(2) The expanded access submission must include:

(i) A cover sheet (Form FDA 1571) meeting the requirements of § 312.23(a);

(ii) The rationale for the intended use of the drug, including a list of available therapeutic options that would ordinarily be tried before resorting to the investigational drug or an explanation of why the use of the investigational drug is preferable to the use of available therapeutic options;

(iii) The criteria for patient selection or, for an individual patient, a description of the patient's disease or condition, including recent medical history and previous treatments of the disease or condition;

(iv) The method of administration of the drug, dose, and duration of therapy;

(v) A description of the facility where the drug will be manufactured;

(vi) Chemistry, manufacturing, and controls information adequate to ensure the proper identification, quality, purity, and strength of the investigational drug;

(vii) Pharmacology and toxicology information adequate to conclude that the drug is reasonably safe at the dose and duration proposed for expanded access use (ordinarily, information that would be adequate to permit clinical testing of the drug in a population of the size expected to be treated); and

(viii) A description of clinical procedures, laboratory tests, or other monitoring necessary to evaluate the effects of the drug and minimize its risks.

(3) The expanded access submission and its mailing cover must be plainly marked "EXPANDED ACCESS SUBMISSION." If the expanded access submission is for a treatment IND or treatment protocol, the applicable box on Form FDA 1571 must be checked.

(c) *Safeguards.* The responsibilities of sponsors and investigators set forth in subpart D of this part are applicable to expanded access use under this subpart as described in this paragraph.

(1) A licensed physician under whose immediate direction an investigational drug is administered or dispensed for an expanded access use under this subpart is considered an *investigator,* for purposes of this part, and must comply with the responsibilities for investigators set forth in subpart D of this part to the extent they are applicable to the expanded access use.

(2) An individual or entity that submits an expanded access IND or protocol under this subpart is considered a *sponsor,* for purposes of this part, and must comply with the responsibilities for sponsors set forth in subpart D of this part to the extent they are applicable to the expanded access use.

(3) A licensed physician under whose immediate direction an investigational drug is administered or dispensed, and who submits an IND for expanded access use under this subpart is considered a *sponsor-investigator,* for purposes of this part, and must comply with the responsibilities for sponsors and investigators set forth in subpart D of this part to the extent they are applicable to the expanded access use.

(4) *Investigators.* In all cases of expanded access, investigators are responsible for reporting adverse drug events to the sponsor, ensuring that the informed consent requirements of part 50 of this chapter are met, ensuring that IRB review of the expanded access use is obtained in a manner consistent with the requirements of part 56 of this chapter, and maintaining accurate case histories and drug disposition records and retaining records in a manner consistent with the requirements of §312.62. Depending on the type of expanded access, other investigator responsibilities under subpart D may also apply.

(5) *Sponsors.* In all cases of expanded access, sponsors are responsible for submitting IND safety reports and annual reports (when the IND or protocol continues for 1 year or longer) to FDA as required by §§312.32 and 312.33, ensuring that licensed physicians are qualified to administer the investigational drug for the expanded access use, providing licensed physicians with the information needed to minimize the risk and maximize the potential benefits of the investigational drug (the investigator's brochure must be provided if one exists for the drug), maintaining an effective IND for the expanded access use, and maintaining adequate drug disposition records and retaining records in a manner consistent with the requirements of §312.57. Depending on the type of expanded access, other sponsor responsibilities under subpart D may also apply.

(d) *Beginning treatment*—(1) *INDs.* An expanded access IND goes into effect 30 days after FDA receives the IND or on earlier notification by FDA that the expanded access use may begin.

(2) *Protocols.* With the following exceptions, expanded access use under a protocol submitted under an existing IND may begin as described in §312.30(a).

(i) Expanded access use under the emergency procedures described in §312.310(d) may begin when the use is authorized by the FDA reviewing official.

(ii) Expanded access use under §312.320 may begin 30 days after FDA receives the protocol or upon earlier notification by FDA that use may begin.

(3) *Clinical holds.* FDA may place any expanded access IND or protocol on clinical hold as described in §312.42.

§312.310 Individual patients, including for emergency use.

Under this section, FDA may permit an investigational drug to be used for the treatment of an individual patient by a licensed physician.

(a) *Criteria.* The criteria in §312.305(a) must be met; and the following determinations must be made:

(1) The physician must determine that the probable risk to the person

from the investigational drug is not greater than the probable risk from the disease or condition; and

(2) FDA must determine that the patient cannot obtain the drug under another IND or protocol.

(b) *Submission.* The expanded access submission must include information adequate to demonstrate that the criteria in §312.305(a) and paragraph (a) of this section have been met. The expanded access submission must meet the requirements of §312.305(b).

(1) If the drug is the subject of an existing IND, the expanded access submission may be made by the sponsor or by a licensed physician.

(2) A sponsor may satisfy the submission requirements by amending its existing IND to include a protocol for individual patient expanded access.

(3) A licensed physician may satisfy the submission requirements by obtaining from the sponsor permission for FDA to refer to any information in the IND that would be needed to support the expanded access request (right of reference) and by providing any other required information not contained in the IND (usually only the information specific to the individual patient).

(c) *Safeguards.* (1) Treatment is generally limited to a single course of therapy for a specified duration unless FDA expressly authorizes multiple courses or chronic therapy.

(2) At the conclusion of treatment, the licensed physician or sponsor must provide FDA with a written summary of the results of the expanded access use, including adverse effects.

(3) FDA may require sponsors to monitor an individual patient expanded access use if the use is for an extended duration.

(4) When a significant number of similar individual patient expanded access requests have been submitted, FDA may ask the sponsor to submit an IND or protocol for the use under §312.315 or §312.320.

(d) *Emergency procedures.* If there is an emergency that requires the patient to be treated before a written submission can be made, FDA may authorize the expanded access use to begin without a written submission. The FDA re-

viewing official may authorize the emergency use by telephone.

(1) Emergency expanded access use may be requested by telephone, facsimile, or other means of electronic communications. For investigational biological drug products regulated by the Center for Biologics Evaluation and Research, the request should be directed to the Office of Communication, Outreach and Development, Center for Biologics Evaluation and Research, 301–827–1800 or 1–800–835–4709, e-mail: *ocod@fda.hhs.gov.* For all other investigational drugs, the request for authorization should be directed to the Division of Drug Information, Center for Drug Evaluation and Research, 301–796–3400, e-mail: *druginfo@fda.hhs.gov.* After normal working hours (8 a.m. to 4:30 p.m.), the request should be directed to the FDA Emergency Call Center, 866–300–4374, e-mail: *emergency.operations@fda.hhs.gov.*

(2) The licensed physician or sponsor must explain how the expanded access use will meet the requirements of §§312.305 and 312.310 and must agree to submit an expanded access submission within 15 working days of FDA's authorization of the use.

[74 FR 40942, Aug. 13, 2009, as amended at 75 FR 32659, June 9, 2010]

§312.315 Intermediate-size patient populations.

Under this section, FDA may permit an investigational drug to be used for the treatment of a patient population smaller than that typical of a treatment IND or treatment protocol. FDA may ask a sponsor to consolidate expanded access under this section when the agency has received a significant number of requests for individual patient expanded access to an investigational drug for the same use.

(a) *Need for expanded access.* Expanded access under this section may be needed in the following situations:

(1) *Drug not being developed.* The drug is not being developed, for example, because the disease or condition is so rare that the sponsor is unable to recruit patients for a clinical trial.

(2) *Drug being developed.* The drug is being studied in a clinical trial, but patients requesting the drug for expanded access use are unable to participate in

the trial. For example, patients may not be able to participate in the trial because they have a different disease or stage of disease than the one being studied or otherwise do not meet the enrollment criteria, because enrollment in the trial is closed, or because the trial site is not geographically accessible.

(3) *Approved or related drug.* (i) The drug is an approved drug product that is no longer marketed for safety reasons or is unavailable through marketing due to failure to meet the conditions of the approved application, or

(ii) The drug contains the same active moiety as an approved drug product that is unavailable through marketing due to failure to meet the conditions of the approved application or a drug shortage.

(b) *Criteria.* The criteria in § 312.305(a) must be met; and FDA must determine that:

(1) There is enough evidence that the drug is safe at the dose and duration proposed for expanded access use to justify a clinical trial of the drug in the approximate number of patients expected to receive the drug under expanded access; and

(2) There is at least preliminary clinical evidence of effectiveness of the drug, or of a plausible pharmacologic effect of the drug to make expanded access use a reasonable therapeutic option in the anticipated patient population.

(c) *Submission.* The expanded access submission must include information adequate to satisfy FDA that the criteria in § 312.305(a) and paragraph (b) of this section have been met. The expanded access submission must meet the requirements of § 312.305(b). In addition:

(1) The expanded access submission must state whether the drug is being developed or is not being developed and describe the patient population to be treated.

(2) If the drug is not being actively developed, the sponsor must explain why the drug cannot currently be developed for the expanded access use and under what circumstances the drug could be developed.

(3) If the drug is being studied in a clinical trial, the sponsor must explain why the patients to be treated cannot be enrolled in the clinical trial and under what circumstances the sponsor would conduct a clinical trial in these patients.

(d) *Safeguards.* (1) Upon review of the IND annual report, FDA will determine whether it is appropriate for the expanded access to continue under this section.

(i) If the drug is not being actively developed or if the expanded access use is not being developed (but another use is being developed), FDA will consider whether it is possible to conduct a clinical study of the expanded access use.

(ii) If the drug is being actively developed, FDA will consider whether providing the investigational drug for expanded access use is interfering with the clinical development of the drug.

(iii) As the number of patients enrolled increases, FDA may ask the sponsor to submit an IND or protocol for the use under § 312.320.

(2) The sponsor is responsible for monitoring the expanded access protocol to ensure that licensed physicians comply with the protocol and the regulations applicable to investigators.

§ 312.320 Treatment IND or treatment protocol.

Under this section, FDA may permit an investigational drug to be used for widespread treatment use.

(a) *Criteria.* The criteria in § 312.305(a) must be met, and FDA must determine that:

(1) *Trial status.* (i) The drug is being investigated in a controlled clinical trial under an IND designed to support a marketing application for the expanded access use, or

(ii) All clinical trials of the drug have been completed; and

(2) *Marketing status.* The sponsor is actively pursuing marketing approval of the drug for the expanded access use with due diligence; and

(3) *Evidence.* (i) When the expanded access use is for a serious disease or condition, there is sufficient clinical evidence of safety and effectiveness to support the expanded access use. Such evidence would ordinarily consist of data from phase 3 trials, but could consist of compelling data from completed phase 2 trials; or

(ii) When the expanded access use is for an immediately life-threatening disease or condition, the available scientific evidence, taken as a whole, provides a reasonable basis to conclude that the investigational drug may be effective for the expanded access use and would not expose patients to an unreasonable and significant risk of illness or injury. This evidence would ordinarily consist of clinical data from phase 3 or phase 2 trials, but could be based on more preliminary clinical evidence.

(b) *Submission.* The expanded access submission must include information adequate to satisfy FDA that the criteria in § 312.305(a) and paragraph (a) of this section have been met. The expanded access submission must meet the requirements of § 312.305(b).

(c) *Safeguard.* The sponsor is responsible for monitoring the treatment protocol to ensure that licensed physicians comply with the protocol and the regulations applicable to investigators.

PART 314—APPLICATIONS FOR FDA APPROVAL TO MARKET A NEW DRUG

Subpart A—General Provisions

AUTHORITY: 21 U.S.C. 321, 331, 351, 352, 353, 355, 356, 356a, 356b, 356c, 371, 374, 379e.

EFFECTIVE DATE NOTE: At 79 FR 33088, June 10, 2014, the authority citation for 21 CFR part 314 was revised, effective June 10, 2015. For the convenience of the user, the revised text is set forth as follows:
AUTHORITY: 21 U.S.C. 321, 331, 351, 352, 353, 355, 356, 356a, 356b, 356c, 371, 374, 379e, 379k–1.

SOURCE: 50 FR 7493, Feb. 22, 1985, unless otherwise noted.

EDITORIAL NOTE: Nomenclature changes to part 314 appear at 69 FR 13717, Mar. 24, 2004.

Subpart A—General Provisions

§ 314.1 Scope of this part.

(a) This part sets forth procedures and requirements for the submission to, and the review by, the Food and Drug Administration of applications and abbreviated applications to market a new drug under section 505 of the Federal Food, Drug, and Cosmetic Act, as well as amendments, supplements, and postmarketing reports to them.

(b) This part does not apply to drug products subject to licensing by FDA under the Public Health Service Act (58 Stat. 632 as amended (42 U.S.C. 201 *et seq.*)) and subchapter F of chapter I of title 21 of the Code of Federal Regulations.

(c) References in this part to regulations in the Code of Federal Regulations are to chapter I of title 21, unless otherwise noted.

[50 FR 7493, Feb. 22, 1985, as amended at 57 FR 17981, Apr. 28, 1992; 64 FR 401, Jan. 5, 1999]

§ 314.2 Purpose.

The purpose of this part is to establish an efficient and thorough drug review process in order to: (a) Facilitate the approval of drugs shown to be safe and effective; and (b) ensure the disapproval of drugs not shown to be safe and effective. These regulations are also intended to establish an effective system for FDA's surveillance of marketed drugs. These regulations shall be construed in light of these objectives.

§ 314.3 Definitions.

(a) The definitions and interpretations contained in section 201 of the act apply to those terms when used in this part.

(b) The following definitions of terms apply to this part:

Abbreviated application means the application described under § 314.94, including all amendments and supplements to the application. "Abbreviated application" applies to both an abbreviated new drug application and an abbreviated antibiotic application.

Act means the Federal Food, Drug, and Cosmetic Act (sections 201–901 (21 U.S.C. 301–392)).

Applicant means any person who submits an application or abbreviated application or an amendment or supplement to them under this part to obtain FDA approval of a new drug or an antibiotic drug and any person who owns an approved application or abbreviated application.

Application means the application described under §314.50, including all amendments and supplements to the application.

505(b)(2) Application means an application submitted under section 505(b)(1) of the act for a drug for which the investigations described in section 505(b)(1)(A) of the act and relied upon by the applicant for approval of the application were not conducted by or for the applicant and for which the applicant has not obtained a right of reference or use from the person by or for whom the investigations were conducted.

Approval letter means a written communication to an applicant from FDA approving an application or an abbreviated application.

Assess the effects of the change means to evaluate the effects of a manufacturing change on the identity, strength, quality, purity, and potency of a drug product as these factors may relate to the safety or effectiveness of the drug product.

Authorized generic drug means a listed drug, as defined in this section, that has been approved under section 505(c) of the act and is marketed, sold, or distributed directly or indirectly to retail class of trade with labeling, packaging (other than repackaging as the listed drug in blister packs, unit doses, or similar packaging for use in institutions), product code, labeler code, trade name, or trademark that differs from that of the listed drug.

Class 1 resubmission means the resubmission of an application or efficacy supplement, following receipt of a complete response letter, that contains one or more of the following: Final printed labeling, draft labeling, certain safety updates, stability updates to support provisional or final dating periods, commitments to perform post-marketing studies (including proposals for such studies), assay validation data, final release testing on the last lots used to support approval, minor reanalyses of previously submitted data, and other comparatively minor information.

Class 2 resubmission means the resubmission of an application or efficacy supplement, following receipt of a complete response letter, that includes any item not specified in the definition of "Class 1 resubmission," including any item that would require presentation to an advisory committee.

Complete response letter means a written communication to an applicant from FDA usually describing all of the deficiencies that the agency has identified in an application or abbreviated application that must be satisfactorily addressed before it can be approved.

Drug product means a finished dosage form, for example, tablet, capsule, or solution, that contains a drug substance, generally, but not necessarily, in association with one or more other ingredients.

Drug substance means an active ingredient that is intended to furnish pharmacological activity or other direct effect in the diagnosis, cure, mitigation, treatment, or prevention of disease or to affect the structure or any function of the human body, but does not include intermediates use in the synthesis of such ingredient.

Efficacy supplement means a supplement to an approved application proposing to make one or more related changes from among the following changes to product labeling:

(1) Add or modify an indication or claim;

(2) Revise the dose or dose regimen;

(3) Provide for a new route of administration;

(4) Make a comparative efficacy claim naming another drug product;

(5) Significantly alter the intended patient population;

(6) Change the marketing status from prescription to over-the-counter use;

(7) Provide for, or provide evidence of effectiveness necessary for, the traditional approval of a product originally approved under subpart H of part 314; or

(8) Incorporate other information based on at least one adequate and well-controlled clinical study.

95

FDA means the Food and Drug Administration.

Listed drug means a new drug product that has an effective approval under section 505(c) of the act for safety and effectiveness or under section 505(j) of the act, which has not been withdrawn or suspended under section 505(e)(1) through (e)(5) or (j)(5) of the act, and which has not been withdrawn from sale for what FDA has determined are reasons of safety or effectiveness. Listed drug status is evidenced by the drug product's identification as a drug with an effective approval in the current edition of FDA's "Approved Drug Products with Therapeutic Equivalence Evaluations" (the list) or any current supplement thereto, as a drug with an effective approval. A drug product is deemed to be a listed drug on the date of effective approval of the application or abbreviated application for that drug product.

Newly acquired information means data, analyses, or other information not previously submitted to the agency, which may include (but are not limited to) data derived from new clinical studies, reports of adverse events, or new analyses of previously submitted data (e.g., meta-analyses) if the studies, events or analyses reveal risks of a different type or greater severity or frequency than previously included in submissions to FDA.

Original application means a pending application for which FDA has never issued a complete response letter or approval letter, or an application that was submitted again after FDA had refused to file it or after it was withdrawn without being approved.

Reference listed drug means the listed drug identified by FDA as the drug product upon which an applicant relies in seeking approval of its abbreviated application.

Resubmission means submission by the applicant of all materials needed to fully address all deficiencies identified in the complete response letter. An application or abbreviated application for which FDA issued a complete response letter, but which was withdrawn before approval and later submitted again, is not a resubmission.

Right of reference or use means the authority to rely upon, and otherwise use, an investigation for the purpose of obtaining approval of an application, including the ability to make available the underlying raw data from the investigation for FDA audit, if necessary.

Specification means the quality standard (*i.e.*, tests, analytical procedures, and acceptance criteria) provided in an approved application to confirm the quality of drug substances, drug products, intermediates, raw materials, reagents, components, in-process materials, container closure systems, and other materials used in the production of a drug substance or drug product. For the purpose of this definition, *acceptance criteria* means numerical limits, ranges, or other criteria for the tests described.

The list means the list of drug products with effective approvals published in the current edition of FDA's publication "Approved Drug Products with Therapeutic Equivalence Evaluations" and any current supplement to the publication.

[50 FR 7493, Feb. 22, 1985, as amended at 57 FR 17981, Apr. 28, 1992; 69 FR 18763, Apr. 8, 2004; 73 FR 39607, July 10, 2008; 73 FR 49609, Aug. 22, 2008; 74 FR 37167, July 28, 2009]

Subpart B—Applications

§ 314.50   Content and format of an application.

Applications and supplements to approved applications are required to be submitted in the form and contain the information, as appropriate for the particular submission, required under this section. Three copies of the application are required: An archival copy, a review copy, and a field copy. An application for a new chemical entity will generally contain an application form, an index, a summary, five or six technical sections, case report tabulations of patient data, case report forms, drug samples, and labeling, including, if applicable, any Medication Guide required under part 208 of this chapter. Other applications will generally contain only some of those items, and information will be limited to that needed to support the particular submission. These include an application of the type described in section 505(b)(2) of the act, an amendment, and a supplement. The application is required to contain reports of all investigations of the drug product sponsored by the applicant, and all other information about the drug pertinent to an evaluation of the application that is received or otherwise obtained by the applicant from any source. FDA will maintain guidance documents on the format and content of applications to assist applicants in their preparation.

(a) *Application form.* The applicant shall submit a completed and signed application form that contains the following:

(1) The name and address of the applicant; the date of the application; the application number if previously issued (for example, if the application is a resubmission, an amendment, or a supplement); the name of the drug product, including its established, proprietary, code, and chemical names; the dosage form and strength; the route of administration; the identification numbers of all investigational new drug applications that are referenced in the application; the identification numbers of all drug master files and other applications under this part that are referenced in the application; and the drug product's proposed indications for use.

(2) A statement whether the submission is an original submission, a 505(b)(2) application, a resubmission, or a supplement to an application under §314.70.

(3) A statement whether the applicant proposes to market the drug product as a prescription or an over-the-counter product.

(4) A check-list identifying what enclosures required under this section the applicant is submitting.

(5) The applicant, or the applicant's attorney, agent, or other authorized official shall sign the application. If the person signing the application does not reside or have a place of business within the United States, the application is required to contain the name and address of, and be countersigned by, an attorney, agent, or other authorized official who resides or maintains a place of business within the United States.

(b) *Index.* The archival copy of the application is required to contain a comprehensive index by volume number and page number to the summary

under paragraph (c) of this section, the technical sections under paragraph (d) of this section, and the supporting information under paragraph (f) of this section.

(c) *Summary.* (1) An application is required to contain a summary of the application in enough detail that the reader may gain a good general understanding of the data and information in the application, including an understanding of the quantitative aspects of the data. The summary is not required for supplements under §314.70. Resubmissions of an application should contain an updated summary, as appropriate. The summary should discuss all aspects of the application, and synthesize the information into a well-structured and unified document. The summary should be written at approximately the level of detail required for publication in, and meet the editorial standards generally applied by, refereed scientific and medical journals. In addition to the agency personnel reviewing the summary in the context of their review of the application, FDA may furnish the summary to FDA advisory committee members and agency officials whose duties require an understanding of the application. To the extent possible, data in the summary should be presented in tabular and graphic forms. FDA has prepared a guideline under §10.90(b) that provides information about how to prepare a summary. The summary required under this paragraph may be used by FDA or the applicant to prepare the Summary Basis of Approval document for public disclosure (under §314.430(e)(2)(ii)) when the application is approved.

(2) The summary is required to contain the following information:

(i) The proposed text of the labeling, including, if applicable, any Medication Guide required under part 208 of this chapter, for the drug, with annotations to the information in the summary and technical sections of the application that support the inclusion of each statement in the labeling, and, if the application is for a prescription drug, statements describing the reasons for omitting a section or subsection of the labeling format in §201.57 of this chapter.

(ii) A statement identifying the pharmacologic class of the drug and a discussion of the scientific rationale for the drug, its intended use, and the potential clinical benefits of the drug product.

(iii) A brief description of the marketing history, if any, of the drug outside the United States, including a list of the countries in which the drug has been marketed, a list of any countries in which the drug has been withdrawn from marketing for any reason related to safety or effectiveness, and a list of countries in which applications for marketing are pending. The description is required to describe both marketing by the applicant and, if known, the marketing history of other persons.

(iv) A summary of the chemistry, manufacturing, and controls section of the application.

(v) A summary of the nonclinical pharmacology and toxicology section of the application.

(vi) A summary of the human pharmacokinetics and bioavailability section of the application.

(vii) A summary of the microbiology section of the application (for anti-infective drugs only).

(viii) A summary of the clinical data section of the application, including the results of statistical analyses of the clinical trials.

(ix) A concluding discussion that presents the benefit and risk considerations related to the drug, including a discussion of any proposed additional studies or surveillance the applicant intends to conduct postmarketing.

(d) *Technical sections.* The application is required to contain the technical sections described below. Each technical section is required to contain data and information in sufficient detail to permit the agency to make a knowledgeable judgment about whether to approve the application or whether grounds exist under section 505(d) of the act to refuse to approve the application. The required technical sections are as follows:

(1) *Chemistry, manufacturing, and controls section.* A section describing the composition, manufacture, and specification of the drug substance and the drug product, including the following:

(i) *Drug substance.* A full description of the drug substance including its physical and chemical characteristics and stability; the name and address of its manufacturer; the method of synthesis (or isolation) and purification of the drug substance; the process controls used during manufacture and packaging; and the specifications necessary to ensure the identity, strength, quality, and purity of the drug substance and the bioavailability of the drug products made from the substance, including, for example, tests, analytical procedures, and acceptance criteria relating to stability, sterility, particle size, and crystalline form. The application may provide additionally for the use of alternatives to meet any of these requirements, including alternative sources, process controls, and analytical procedures. Reference to the current edition of the U.S. Pharmacopeia and the National Formulary may satisfy relevant requirements in this paragraph.

(ii)(a) *Drug product.* A list of all components used in the manufacture of the drug product (regardless of whether they appear in the drug product) and a statement of the composition of the drug product; the specifications for each component; the name and address of each manufacturer of the drug product; a description of the manufacturing and packaging procedures and in-process controls for the drug product; the specifications necessary to ensure the identity, strength, quality, purity, potency, and bioavailability of the drug product, including, for example, tests, analytical procedures, and acceptance criteria relating to sterility, dissolution rate, container closure systems; and stability data with proposed expiration dating. The application may provide additionally for the use of alternatives to meet any of these requirements, including alternative components, manufacturing and packaging procedures, in-process controls, and analytical procedures. Reference to the current edition of the U.S. Pharmacopeia and the National Formulary may satisfy relevant requirements in this paragraph.

(b) Unless provided by paragraph (d)(1)(ii)(a) of this section, for each batch of the drug product used to conduct a bioavailability or bioequivalence study described in §320.38 or §320.63 of this chapter or used to conduct a primary stability study: The batch production record; the specification for each component and for the drug product; the names and addresses of the sources of the active and noncompendial inactive components and of the container and closure system for the drug product; the name and address of each contract facility involved in the manufacture, processing, packaging, or testing of the drug product and identification of the operation performed by each contract facility; and the results of any test performed on the components used in the manufacture of the drug product as required by §211.84(d) of this chapter and on the drug product as required by §211.165 of this chapter.

(c) The proposed or actual master production record, including a description of the equipment, to be used for the manufacture of a commercial lot of the drug product or a comparably detailed description of the production process for a representative batch of the drug product.

(iii) *Environmental impact.* The application is required to contain either a claim for categorical exclusion under §25.30 or 25.31 of this chapter or an environmental assessment under §25.40 of this chapter.

(iv) The applicant may, at its option, submit a complete chemistry, manufacturing, and controls section 90 to 120 days before the anticipated submission of the remainder of the application. FDA will review such early submissions as resources permit.

(v) The applicant shall include a statement certifying that the field copy of the application has been provided to the applicant's home FDA district office.

(2) *Nonclinical pharmacology and toxicology section.* A section describing, with the aid of graphs and tables, animal and in vitro studies with drug, including the following:

(i) Studies of the pharmacological actions of the drug in relation to its proposed therapeutic indication and studies that otherwise define the pharma-

cologic properties of the drug or are pertinent to possible adverse effects.

(ii) Studies of the toxicological effects of the drug as they relate to the drug's intended clinical uses, including, as appropriate, studies assessing the drug's acute, subacute, and chronic toxicity; carcinogenicity; and studies of toxicities related to the drug's particular mode of administration or conditions of use.

(iii) Studies, as appropriate, of the effects of the drug on reproduction and on the developing fetus.

(iv) Any studies of the absorption, distribution, metabolism, and excretion of the drug in animals.

(v) For each nonclinical laboratory study subject to the good laboratory practice regulations under part 58 a statement that it was conducted in compliance with the good laboratory practice regulations in part 58, or, if the study was not conducted in compliance with those regulations, a brief statement of the reason for the noncompliance.

(3) *Human pharmacokinetics and bioavailability section.* A section describing the human pharmacokinetic data and human bioavailability data, or information supporting a waiver of the submission of in vivo bioavailability data under subpart B of part 320, including the following:

(i) A description of each of the bioavailability and pharmacokinetic studies of the drug in humans performed by or on behalf of the applicant that includes a description of the analytical procedures and statistical methods used in each study and a statement with respect to each study that it either was conducted in compliance with the institutional review board regulations in part 56, or was not subject to the regulations under §56.104 or §56.105, and that it was conducted in compliance with the informed consent regulations in part 50.

(ii) If the application describes in the chemistry, manufacturing, and controls section tests, analytical procedures, and acceptance criteria needed to assure the bioavailability of the drug product or drug substance, or both, a statement in this section of the rationale for establishing the tests, analytical procedures, and acceptance

99

criteria, including data and information supporting the rationale.

(iii) A summarizing discussion and analysis of the pharmacokinetics and metabolism of the active ingredients and the bioavailability or bioequivalence, or both, of the drug product.

(4) *Microbiology section.* If the drug is an anti-infective drug, a section describing the microbiology data, including the following:

(i) A description of the biochemical basis of the drug's action on microbial physiology.

(ii) A description of the antimicrobial spectra of the drug, including results of in vitro preclinical studies to demonstrate concentrations of the drug required for effective use.

(iii) A description of any known mechanisms of resistance to the drug, including results of any known epidemiologic studies to demonstrate prevalence of resistance factors.

(iv) A description of clinical microbiology laboratory procedures (for example, in vitro sensitivity discs) needed for effective use of the drug.

(5) *Clinical data section.* A section describing the clinical investigations of the drug, including the following:

(i) A description and analysis of each clinical pharmacology study of the drug, including a brief comparison of the results of the human studies with the animal pharmacology and toxicology data.

(ii) A description and analysis of each controlled clinical study pertinent to a proposed use of the drug, including the protocol and a description of the statistical analyses used to evaluate the study. If the study report is an interim analysis, this is to be noted and a projected completion date provided. Controlled clinical studies that have not been analyzed in detail for any reason (e.g., because they have been discontinued or are incomplete) are to be included in this section, including a copy of the protocol and a brief description of the results and status of the study.

(iii) A description of each uncontrolled clinical study, a summary of the results, and a brief statement explaining why the study is classified as uncontrolled.

(iv) A description and analysis of any other data or information relevant to an evaluation of the safety and effectiveness of the drug product obtained or otherwise received by the applicant from any source, foreign or domestic, including information derived from clinical investigations, including controlled and uncontrolled studies of uses of the drug other than those proposed in the application, commercial marketing experience, reports in the scientific literature, and unpublished scientific papers.

(v) An integrated summary of the data demonstrating substantial evidence of effectiveness for the claimed indications. Evidence is also required to support the dosage and administration section of the labeling, including support for the dosage and dose interval recommended. The effectiveness data shall be presented by gender, age, and racial subgroups and shall identify any modifications of dose or dose interval needed for specific subgroups. Effectiveness data from other subgroups of the population of patients treated, when appropriate, such as patients with renal failure or patients with different levels of severity of the disease, also shall be presented.

(vi) A summary and updates of safety information, as follows:

(*a*) The applicant shall submit an integrated summary of all available information about the safety of the drug product, including pertinent animal data, demonstrated or potential adverse effects of the drug, clinically significant drug/drug interactions, and other safety considerations, such as data from epidemiological studies of related drugs. The safety data shall be presented by gender, age, and racial subgroups. When appropriate, safety data from other subgroups of the population of patients treated also shall be presented, such as for patients with renal failure or patients with different levels of severity of the disease. A description of any statistical analyses performed in analyzing safety data should also be included, unless already included under paragraph (d)(5)(ii) of this section.

(*b*) The applicant shall, under section 505(i) of the act, update periodically its pending application with new safety information learned about the drug that may reasonably affect the statement of contraindications, warnings, precautions, and adverse reactions in the draft labeling and, if applicable, any Medication Guide required under part 208 of this chapter. These "safety update reports" are required to include the same kinds of information (from clinical studies, animal studies, and other sources) and are required to be submitted in the same format as the integrated summary in paragraph (d)(5)(vi)(a) of this section. In addition, the reports are required to include the case report forms for each patient who died during a clinical study or who did not complete the study because of an adverse event (unless this requirement is waived). The applicant shall submit these reports (1) 4 months after the initial submission; (2) in a resubmission following receipt of a complete response letter; and (3) at other times as requested by FDA. Prior to the submission of the first such report, applicants are encouraged to consult with FDA regarding further details on its form and content.

(vii) If the drug has a potential for abuse, a description and analysis of studies or information related to abuse of the drug, including a proposal for scheduling under the Controlled Substances Act. A description of any studies related to overdosage is also required, including information on dialysis, antidotes, or other treatments, if known.

(viii) An integrated summary of the benefits and risks of the drug, including a discussion of why the benefits exceed the risks under the conditions stated in the labeling.

(ix) A statement with respect to each clinical study involving human subjects that it either was conducted in compliance with the institutional review board regulations in part 56, or was not subject to the regulations under §56.104 or §56.105, and that it was conducted in compliance with the informed consent regulations in part 50.

(x) If a sponsor has transferred any obligations for the conduct of any clinical study to a contract research organization, a statement containing the name and address of the contract research organization, identification of the clinical study, and a listing of the obligations transferred. If all obliga-

tions governing the conduct of the study have been transferred, a general statement of this transfer—in lieu of a listing of the specific obligations transferred—may be submitted.

(xi) If original subject records were audited or reviewed by the sponsor in the course of monitoring any clinical study to verify the accuracy of the case reports submitted to the sponsor, a list identifying each clinical study so audited or reviewed.

(6) *Statistical section.* A section describing the statistical evaluation of clinical data, including the following:

(i) A copy of the information submitted under paragraph (d)(5)(ii) of this section concerning the description and analysis of each controlled clinical study, and the documentation and supporting statistical analyses used in evaluating the controlled clinical studies.

(ii) A copy of the information submitted under paragraph (d)(5)(vi)(a) of this section concerning a summary of information about the safety of the drug product, and the documentation and supporting statistical analyses used in evaluating the safety information.

(7) *Pediatric use section.* A section describing the investigation of the drug for use in pediatric populations, including an integrated summary of the information (the clinical pharmacology studies, controlled clinical studies, or uncontrolled clinical studies, or other data or information) that is relevant to the safety and effectiveness and benefits and risks of the drug in pediatric populations for the claimed indications, a reference to the full descriptions of such studies provided under paragraphs (d)(3) and (d)(5) of this section, and information required to be submitted under §314.55.

(e) *Samples and labeling.* (1) Upon request from FDA, the applicant shall submit the samples described below to the places identified in the agency's request. FDA will generally ask applicants to submit samples directly to two or more agency laboratories that will perform all necessary tests on the samples and validate the applicant's analytical procedures.

(i) Four representative samples of the following, each sample in sufficient quantity to permit FDA to perform three times each test described in the application to determine whether the drug substance and the drug product meet the specifications given in the application:

(a) The drug product proposed for marketing;

(b) The drug substance used in the drug product from which the samples of the drug product were taken; and

(c) Reference standards and blanks (except that reference standards recognized in an official compendium need not be submitted).

(ii) Samples of the finished market package, if requested by FDA.

(2) The applicant shall submit the following in the archival copy of the application:

(i) Three copies of the analytical procedures and related descriptive information contained in the chemistry, manufacturing, and controls section under paragraph (d)(1) of this section for the drug substance and the drug product that are necessary for FDA's laboratories to perform all necessary tests on the samples and to validate the applicant's analytical procedures. The related descriptive information includes a description of each sample; the proposed regulatory specifications for the drug; a detailed description of the methods of analysis; supporting data for accuracy, specificity, precision and ruggedness; and complete results of the applicant's tests on each sample.

(ii) Copies of the label and all labeling for the drug product (including, if applicable, any Medication Guide required under part 208 of this chapter) for the drug product (4 copies of draft labeling or 12 copies of final printed labeling).

(f) *Case report forms and tabulations.* The archival copy of the application is required to contain the following case report tabulations and case report forms:

(1) *Case report tabulations.* The application is required to contain tabulations of the data from each adequate and well-controlled study under § 314.126 (Phase 2 and Phase 3 studies as described in §§ 312.21 (b) and (c) of this chapter), tabulations of the data from the earliest clinical pharmacology studies (Phase 1 studies as described in

§ 312.21(a) of this chapter), and tabulations of the safety data from other clinical studies. Routine submission of other patient data from uncontrolled studies is not required. The tabulations are required to include the data on each patient in each study, except that the applicant may delete those tabulations which the agency agrees, in advance, are not pertinent to a review of the drug's safety or effectiveness. Upon request, FDA will discuss with the applicant in a "pre-NDA" conference those tabulations that may be appropriate for such deletion. Barring unforeseen circumstances, tabulations agreed to be deleted at such a conference will not be requested during the conduct of FDA's review of the application. If such unforeseen circumstances do occur, any request for deleted tabulations will be made by the director of the FDA division responsible for reviewing the application, in accordance with paragraph (f)(3) of this section.

(2) *Case report forms.* The application is required to contain copies of individual case report forms for each patient who died during a clinical study or who did not complete the study because of an adverse event, whether believed to be drug related or not, including patients receiving reference drugs or placebo. This requirement may be waived by FDA for specific studies if the case report forms are unnecessary for a proper review of the study.

(3) *Additional data.* The applicant shall submit to FDA additional case report forms and tabulations needed to conduct a proper review of the application, as requested by the director of the FDA division responsible for reviewing the application. The applicant's failure to submit information requested by FDA within 30 days after receipt of the request may result in the agency viewing any eventual submission as a major amendment under § 314.60 and extending the review period as necessary. If desired by the applicant, the FDA division director will verify in writing any request for additional data that was made orally.

(4) Applicants are invited to meet with FDA before submitting an application to discuss the presentation and format of supporting information. If

the applicant and FDA agree, the applicant may submit tabulations of patient data and case report forms in a form other than hard copy, for example, on microfiche or computer tapes.

(g) *Other.* The following general requirements apply to the submission of information within the summary under paragraph (c) of this section and within the technical sections under paragraph (d) of this section.

(1) The applicant ordinarily is not required to resubmit information previously submitted, but may incorporate the information by reference. A reference to information submitted previously is required to identify the file by name, reference number, volume, and page number in the agency's records where the information can be found. A reference to information submitted to the agency by a person other than the applicant is required to contain a written statement that authorizes the reference and that is signed by the person who submitted the information.

(2) The applicant shall submit an accurate and complete English translation of each part of the application that is not in English. The applicant shall submit a copy of each original literature publication for which an English translation is submitted.

(3) If an applicant who submits a new drug application under section 505(b) of the act obtains a "right of reference or use," as defined under § 314.3(b), to an investigation described in clause (A) of section 505(b)(1) of the act, the applicant shall include in its application a written statement signed by the owner of the data from each such investigation that the applicant may rely on in support of the approval of its application, and provide FDA access to, the underlying raw data that provide the basis for the report of the investigation submitted in its application.

(h) *Patent information.* The application is required to contain the patent information described under § 314.53.

(i) *Patent certification—*(1) *Contents.* A 505(b)(2) application is required to contain the following:

(i) *Patents claiming drug, drug product, or method of use.* (A) Except as provided in paragraph (i)(2) of this section, a certification with respect to each patent issued by the United States Patent and Trademark Office that, in the opinion of the applicant and to the best of its knowledge, claims a drug (the drug product or drug substance that is a component of the drug product) on which investigations that are relied upon by the applicant for approval of its application were conducted or that claims an approved use for such drug and for which information is required to be filed under section 505(b) and (c) of the act and § 314.53. For each such patent, the applicant shall provide the patent number and certify, in its opinion and to the best of its knowledge, one of the following circumstances:

(*1*) That the patent information has not been submitted to FDA. The applicant shall entitle such a certification "Paragraph I Certification";

(*2*) That the patent has expired. The applicant shall entitle such a certification "Paragraph II Certification";

(*3*) The date on which the patent will expire. The applicant shall entitle such a certification "Paragraph III Certification"; or

(*4*) That the patent is invalid, unenforceable, or will not be infringed by the manufacture, use, or sale of the drug product for which the application is submitted. The applicant shall entitle such a certification "Paragraph IV Certification". This certification shall be submitted in the following form:

I, (*name of applicant*), certify that Patent No. _____ (*is invalid, unenforceable, or will not be infringed by the manufacture, use, or sale of*) (*name of proposed drug product*) for which this application is submitted.

The certification shall be accompanied by a statement that the applicant will comply with the requirements under § 314.52(a) with respect to providing a notice to each owner of the patent or their representatives and to the holder of the approved application for the drug product which is claimed by the patent or a use of which is claimed by the patent and with the requirements under § 314.52(c) with respect to the content of the notice.

(B) If the drug on which investigations that are relied upon by the applicant were conducted is itself a licensed generic drug of a patented drug first approved under section 505(b) of the act, the appropriate patent certification under this section with respect to each patent that claims the first-approved patented drug or that claims an approved use for such a drug.

(ii) *No relevant patents.* If, in the opinion of the applicant and to the best of its knowledge, there are no patents described in paragraph (i)(1)(i) of this section, a certification in the following form:

In the opinion and to the best knowledge of (*name of applicant*), there are no patents that claim the drug or drugs on which investigations are relied upon in this application were conducted or that claim a use of such drug or drugs.

(iii) *Method of use patent.* (A) If information that is submitted under section 505(b) or (c) of the act and § 314.53 is for a method of use patent, and the labeling for the drug product for which the applicant is seeking approval does not include any indications that are covered by the use patent, a statement explaining that the method of use patent does not claim any of the proposed indications.

(B) If the labeling of the drug product for which the applicant is seeking approval includes an indication that, according to the patent information submitted under section 505(b) or (c) of the act and § 314.53 or in the opinion of the applicant, is claimed by a use patent, the applicant shall submit an applicable certification under paragraph (i)(1)(i) of this section.

(2) *Method of manufacturing patent.* An applicant is not required to make a certification with respect to any patent that claims only a method of manufacturing the drug product for which the applicant is seeking approval.

(3) *Licensing agreements.* If a 505(b)(2) application is for a drug or method of using a drug claimed by a patent and the applicant has a licensing agreement with the patent owner, the applicant shall submit a certification under paragraph (i)(1)(i)(A)(*4*) of this section ("Paragraph IV Certification") as to that patent and a statement that it has been granted a patent license. If the patent owner consents to an immediate effective date upon approval of the 505(b)(2) application, the application shall contain a written statement from the patent owner that it has a licens-

ing agreement with the applicant and that it consents to an immediate effective date.

(4) *Late submission of patent information.* If a patent described in paragraph (i)(1)(i)(A) of this section is issued and the holder of the approved application for the patented drug does not submit the required information on the patent within 30 days of issuance of the patent, an applicant who submitted a 505(b)(2) application that, before the submission of the patent information, contained an appropriate patent certification is not required to submit an amended certification. An applicant whose 505(b)(2) application is filed after a late submission of patent information or whose 505(b)(2) application was previously filed but did not contain an appropriate patent certification at the time of the patent submission shall submit a certification under paragraph (i)(1)(i) or (i)(1)(ii) of this section or a statement under paragraph (i)(1)(iii) of this section as to that patent.

(5) *Disputed patent information.* If an applicant disputes the accuracy or relevance of patent information submitted to FDA, the applicant may seek a confirmation of the correctness of the patent information in accordance with the procedures under § 314.53(f). Unless the patent information is withdrawn or changed, the applicant must submit an appropriate certification for each relevant patent.

(6) *Amended certifications.* A certification submitted under paragraphs (i)(1)(i) through (i)(1)(iii) of this section may be amended at any time before the effective date of the approval of the application. An applicant shall submit an amended certification as an amendment to a pending application or by letter to an approved application. If an applicant with a pending application voluntarily makes a patent certification for an untimely filed patent, the applicant may withdraw the patent certification for the untimely filed patent. Once an amendment or letter for the change in certification has been submitted, the application will no longer be considered to be one containing the prior certification.

(i) *After finding of infringement.* An applicant who has submitted a certification under paragraph (i)(1)(i)(A)(*4*) of this section and is sued for patent infringement within 45 days of the receipt of notice sent under §314.52 shall amend the certification if a final judgment in the action is entered finding the patent to be infringed unless the final judgment also finds the patent to be invalid. In the amended certification, the applicant shall certify under paragraph (i)(1)(i)(A)(3) of this section that the patent will expire on a specific date.

(ii) *After removal of a patent from the list.* If a patent is removed from the list, any applicant with a pending application (including a tentatively approved application with a delayed effective date) who has made a certification with respect to such patent shall amend its certification. The applicant shall certify under paragraph (i)(1)(ii) of this section that no patents described in paragraph (i)(1)(i) of this section claim the drug or, if other relevant patents claim the drug, shall amend the certification to refer only to those relevant patents. In the amendment, the applicant shall state the reason for the change in certification (that the patent is or has been removed from the list). A patent that is the subject of a lawsuit under §314.107(c) shall not be removed from the list until FDA determines either that no delay in effective dates of approval is required under that section as a result of the lawsuit, that the patent has expired, or that any such period of delay in effective dates of approval is ended. An applicant shall submit an amended certification as an amendment to a pending application. Once an amendment for the change has been submitted, the application will no longer be considered to be one containing a certification under paragraph (i)(1)(i)(A)(4) of this section.

(iii) *Other amendments.* (A) Except as provided in paragraphs (i)(4) and (i)(6)(iii)(B) of this section, an applicant shall amend a submitted certification if, at any time before the effective date of the approval of the application, the applicant learns that the submitted certification is no longer accurate.

(B) An applicant is not required to amend a submitted certification when information on an otherwise applicable patent is submitted after the effective date of approval for the 505(b)(2) application.

(j) *Claimed exclusivity.* A new drug product, upon approval, may be entitled to a period of marketing exclusivity under the provisions of §314.108. If an applicant believes its drug product is entitled to a period of exclusivity, it shall submit with the new drug application prior to approval the following information:

(1) A statement that the applicant is claiming exclusivity.

(2) A reference to the appropriate paragraph under §314.108 that supports its claim.

(3) If the applicant claims exclusivity under §314.108(b)(2), information to show that, to the best of its knowledge or belief, a drug has not previously been approved under section 505(b) of the act containing any active moiety in the drug for which the applicant is seeking approval.

(4) If the applicant claims exclusivity under §314.108(b)(4) or (b)(5), the following information to show that the application contains "new clinical investigations" that are "essential to approval of the application or supplement" and were "conducted or sponsored by the applicant:"

(i) *"New clinical investigations."* A certification that to the best of the applicant's knowledge each of the clinical investigations included in the application meets the definition of "new clinical investigation" set forth in §314.108(a).

(ii) *"Essential to approval."* A list of all published studies or publicly available reports of clinical investigations known to the applicant through a literature search that are relevant to the conditions for which the applicant is seeking approval, a certification that the applicant has thoroughly searched the scientific literature and, to the best of the applicant's knowledge, the list is complete and accurate and, in the applicant's opinion, such published studies or publicly available reports do not provide a sufficient basis for the approval of the conditions for which the applicant is seeking approval without reference to the new clinical investigation(s) in the application, and an explanation as to why the studies or reports are insufficient.

(iii) *"Conducted or sponsored by."* If the applicant was the sponsor named in the Form FDA–1571 for an investigational new drug application (IND) under which the new clinical investigation(s) that is essential to the approval of its application was conducted, identification of the IND by number. If the applicant was not the sponsor of the IND under which the clinical investigation(s) was conducted, a certification that the applicant or its predecessor in interest provided substantial support for the clinical investigation(s) that is essential to the approval of its application, and information supporting the certification. To demonstrate "substantial support," an applicant must either provide a certified statement from a certified public accountant that the applicant provided 50 percent or more of the cost of conducting the study or provide an explanation of why FDA should consider the applicant to have conducted or sponsored the study if the applicant's financial contribution to the study is less than 50 percent or the applicant did not sponsor the investigational new drug. A predecessor in interest is an entity, e.g., a corporation, that the applicant has taken over, merged with, or purchased, or from which the applicant has purchased all rights to the drug. Purchase of nonexclusive rights to a clinical investigation after it is completed is not sufficient to satisfy this definition.

(k) *Financial certification or disclosure statement.* The application shall contain a financial certification or disclosure statement or both as required by part 54 of this chapter.

(l) *Format of an original application—* (1) *Archival copy.* The applicant must submit a complete archival copy of the application that contains the information required under paragraphs (a) through (f) of this section. FDA will maintain the archival copy during the review of the application to permit individual reviewers to refer to information that is not contained in their particular technical sections of the application, to give other agency personnel access to the application for official business, and to maintain in one place a complete copy of the application. Ex-

cept as required by paragraph (l)(1)(i) of this section, applicants may submit the archival copy on paper or in electronic format provided that electronic submissions are made in accordance with part 11 of this chapter.

(i) *Labeling.* The content of labeling required under § 201.100(d)(3) of this chapter (commonly referred to as the package insert or professional labeling), including all text, tables, and figures, must be submitted to the agency in electronic format as described in paragraph (l)(5) of this section. This requirement is in addition to the requirements of paragraph (e)(2)(ii) of this section that copies of the formatted label and all labeling be submitted. Submissions under this paragraph must be made in accordance with part 11 of this chapter, except for the requirements of § 11.10(a), (c) through (h), and (k), and the corresponding requirements of § 11.30.

(ii) [Reserved]

(2) *Review copy.* The applicant must submit a review copy of the application. Each of the technical sections, described in paragraphs (d)(1) through (d)(6) of this section, in the review copy is required to be separately bound with a copy of the application form required under paragraph (a) of this section and a copy of the summary required under paragraph (c) of this section.

(3) *Field copy.* The applicant must submit a field copy of the application that contains the technical section described in paragraph (d)(1) of this section, a copy of the application form required under paragraph (a) of this section, a copy of the summary required under paragraph (c) of this section, and a certification that the field copy is a true copy of the technical section described in paragraph (d)(1) of this section contained in the archival and review copies of the application.

(4) *Binding folders.* The applicant may obtain from FDA sufficient folders to bind the archival, the review, and the field copies of the application.

(5) *Electronic format submissions.* Electronic format submissions must be in a form that FDA can process, review, and archive. FDA will periodically issue guidance on how to provide the electronic submission (e.g., method of

transmission, media, file formats, preparation and organization of files).

[50 FR 7493, Feb. 22, 1985]

EDITORIAL NOTE: For FEDERAL REGISTER citations affecting §314.50, see the List of CFR Sections Affected, which appears in the Finding Aids section of the printed volume and at *www.fdsys.gov*.

§314.52 Notice of certification of invalidity or noninfringement of a patent.

(a) *Notice of certification.* For each patent which claims the drug or drugs on which investigations that are relied upon by the applicant for approval of its application were conducted or which claims a use for such drug or drugs and which the applicant certifies under §314.50(i)(1)(i)(A)(*4*) that a patent is invalid, unenforceable, or will not be infringed, the applicant shall send notice of such certification by registered or certified mail, return receipt requested to each of the following persons:

(1) Each owner of the patent that is the subject of the certification or the representative designated by the owner to receive the notice. The name and address of the patent owner or its representative may be obtained from the United States Patent and Trademark Office; and

(2) The holder of the approved application under section 505(b) of the act for each drug product which is claimed by the patent or a use of which is claimed by the patent and for which the applicant is seeking approval, or, if the application holder does not reside or maintain a place of business within the United States, the application holder's attorney, agent, or other authorized official. The name and address of the application holder or its attorney, agent, or authorized official may be obtained from the Orange Book Staff, Office of Generic Drugs, 7500 Standish Pl., Rockville, MD 20855.

(3) This paragraph does not apply to a use patent that claims no uses for which the applicant is seeking approval.

(b) *Sending the notice.* The applicant shall send the notice required by paragraph (a) of this section when it receives from FDA an acknowledgment letter stating that its application has

been filed. At the same time, the applicant shall amend its application to include a statement certifying that the notice has been provided to each person identified under paragraph (a) of this section and that the notice met the content requirement under paragraph (c) of this section.

(c) *Content of a notice.* In the notice, the applicant shall cite section 505(b)(3)(B) of the act and shall include, but not be limited to, the following information:

(1) A statement that a 505(b)(2) application submitted by the applicant has been filed by FDA.

(2) The application number.

(3) The established name, if any, as defined in section 502(e)(3) of the act, of the proposed drug product.

(4) The active ingredient, strength, and dosage form of the proposed drug product.

(5) The patent number and expiration date, as submitted to the agency or as known to the applicant, of each patent alleged to be invalid, unenforceable, or not infringed.

(6) A detailed statement of the factual and legal basis of the applicant's opinion that the patent is not valid, unenforceable, or will not be infringed. The applicant shall include in the detailed statement:

(i) For each claim of a patent alleged not to be infringed, a full and detailed explanation of why the claim is not infringed.

(ii) For each claim of a patent alleged to be invalid or unenforceable, a full and detailed explanation of the grounds supporting the allegation.

(7) If the applicant does not reside or have a place of business in the United States, the name and address of an agent in the United States authorized to accept service of process for the applicant.

(d) *Amendment to an application.* If an application is amended to include the certification described in §314.50(i), the applicant shall send the notice required by paragraph (a) of this section at the same time that the amendment to the application is submitted to FDA.

(e) *Documentation of receipt of notice.* The applicant shall amend its application to document receipt of the notice required under paragraph (a) of this section by each person provided the notice. The applicant shall include a copy of the return receipt or other similar evidence of the date the notification was received. FDA will accept as adequate documentation of the date of receipt a return receipt or a letter acknowledging receipt by the person provided the notice. An applicant may rely on another form of documentation only if FDA has agreed to such documentation in advance. A copy of the notice itself need not be submitted to the agency.

(f) *Approval.* If the requirements of this section are met, the agency will presume the notice to be complete and sufficient, and it will count the day following the date of receipt of the notice by the patent owner or its representative and by the approved application holder as the first day of the 45-day period provided for in section 505(c)(3)(C) of the act. FDA may, if the applicant amends its application with a written statement that a later date should be used, count from such later date.

[59 FR 50362, Oct. 3, 1994, as amended at 68 FR 36703, June 18, 2003; 69 FR 11310, Mar. 10, 2004; 74 FR 9766, Mar. 6, 2009; 74 FR 36605, July 24, 2009]

§ 314.53 Submission of patent information.

(a) *Who must submit patent information.* This section applies to any applicant who submits to FDA a new drug application or an amendment to it under section 505(b) of the act and § 314.50 or a supplement to an approved application under § 314.70, except as provided in paragraph (d)(2) of this section.

(b) *Patents for which information must be submitted and patents for which information must not be submitted*—(1) *General requirements.* An applicant described in paragraph (a) of this section shall submit the required information on the declaration form set forth in paragraph (c) of this section for each patent that claims the drug or a method of using the drug that is the subject of the new drug application or amendment or supplement to it and with respect to which a claim of patent infringement could reasonably be asserted if a person not licensed by the owner of the patent engaged in the manufacture, use, or sale of the drug product. For purposes of this part, such patents consist of drug substance (active ingredient) patents, drug product (formulation and composition) patents, and method-of-use patents. For patents that claim the drug substance, the applicant shall submit information only on those patents that claim the drug substance that is the subject of the pending or approved application or that claim a drug substance that is the same as the active ingredient that is the subject of the approved or pending application. For patents that claim a polymorph that is the same as the active ingredient described in the approved or pending application, the applicant shall certify in the declaration forms that the applicant has test data, as set forth in paragraph (b)(2) of this section, demonstrating that a drug product containing the polymorph will perform the same as the drug product described in the new drug application. For patents that claim a drug product, the applicant shall submit information only on those patents that claim a drug product, as is defined in § 314.3, that is described in the pending or approved application. For patents that claim a method of use, the applicant shall submit information only on those patents that claim indications or other conditions of use that are described in the pending or approved application. The applicant shall separately identify each pending or approved method of use and related patent claim. For approved applications, the applicant submitting the method-of-use patent shall identify with specificity the section of the approved labeling that corresponds to the method of use claimed by the patent submitted. Process patents, patents claiming packaging, patents claiming metabolites, and patents claiming intermediates are not covered by this section, and information on these patents must not be submitted to FDA.

(2) *Test Data for Submission of Patent Information for Patents That Claim a Polymorph.* The test data, referenced in paragraph (b)(1) of this section, must include the following:

(i) A full description of the polymorphic form of the drug substance, including its physical and chemical characteristics and stability; the method of synthesis (or isolation) and purification of the drug substance; the process controls used during manufacture and packaging; and such specifications and analytical methods as are necessary to assure the identity, strength, quality, and purity of the polymorphic form of the drug substance;

(ii) The executed batch record for a drug product containing the polymorphic form of the drug substance and documentation that the batch was manufactured under current good manufacturing practice requirements;

(iii) Demonstration of bioequivalence between the executed batch of the drug product that contains the polymorphic form of the drug substance and the drug product as described in the NDA;

(iv) A list of all components used in the manufacture of the drug product containing the polymorphic form and a statement of the composition of the drug product; a statement of the specifications and analytical methods for each component; a description of the manufacturing and packaging procedures and in-process controls for the drug product; such specifications and analytical methods as are necessary to assure the identity, strength, quality, purity, and bioavailability of the drug product, including release and stability data complying with the approved product specifications to demonstrate pharmaceutical equivalence and comparable product stability; and

(v) Comparative in vitro dissolution testing on 12 dosage units each of the executed test batch and the new drug application product.

(c) *Reporting requirements*—(1) *General requirements.* An applicant described in paragraph (a) of this section shall submit the required patent information described in paragraph (c)(2) of this section for each patent that meets the requirements described in paragraph (b) of this section. We will not accept the patent information unless it is complete and submitted on the appropriate forms, FDA Forms 3542 or 3542a. These forms may be obtained on the Internet at *http://www.fda.gov* by searching for "forms".

(2) *Drug substance (active ingredient), drug product (formulation or composition), and method-of-use patents*—(i) *Original Declaration.* For each patent that claims a drug substance (active ingredient), drug product (formulation and composition), or method of use, the applicant shall submit FDA Form 3542a. The following information and verification is required:

(A) New drug application number;

(B) Name of new drug application sponsor;

(C) Trade name (or proposed trade name) of new drug;

(D) Active ingredient(s) of new drug;

(E) Strength(s) of new drug;

(F) Dosage form of new drug;

(G) United States patent number, issue date, and expiration date of patent submitted;

(H) The patent owner's name, full address, phone number and, if available, fax number and e-mail address;

(I) The name, full address, phone number and, if available, fax number and e-mail address of an agent or representative who resides or maintains a place of business within the United States authorized to receive notice of patent certification under sections 505(b)(3) and 505(j)(2)(B) of the act and §§314.52 and 314.95 (if patent owner or new drug application applicant or holder does not reside or have a place of business within the United States);

(J) Information on whether the patent has been submitted previously for the new drug application;

(K) Information on whether the expiration date is a new expiration date if the patent had been submitted previously for listing;

(L) Information on whether the patent is a product-by-process patent in which the product claimed is novel;

(M) Information on the drug substance (active ingredient) patent including the following:

(1) Whether the patent claims the drug substance that is the active ingredient in the drug product described in the new drug application or supplement;

(2) Whether the patent claims a polymorph that is the same active ingredient that is described in the pending application or supplement;

(3) Whether the applicant has test data, described in paragraph (b)(2) of this section, demonstrating that a drug product containing the polymorph will perform the same as the drug product described in the new drug application or supplement, and a description of the polymorphic form(s) claimed by the patent for which such test data exist;

(4) Whether the patent claims only a metabolite of the active ingredient; and

(5) Whether the patent claims only an intermediate;

(N) Information on the drug product (composition/formulation) patent including the following:

(1) Whether the patent claims the drug product for which approval is being sought, as defined in § 314.3; and

(2) Whether the patent claims only an intermediate;

(O) Information on each method-of-use patent including the following:

(1) Whether the patent claims one or more methods of using the drug product for which use approval is being sought and a description of each pending method of use or related indication and related patent claim of the patent being submitted; and

(2) Identification of the specific section of the proposed labeling for the drug product that corresponds to the method of use claimed by the patent submitted;

(P) Whether there are no relevant patents that claim the drug substance (active ingredient), drug product (formulation or composition) or method(s) of use, for which the applicant is seeking approval and with respect to which a claim of patent infringement could reasonably be asserted if a person not licensed by the owner of the patent engaged in the manufacture, use, or sale of the drug product;

(Q) A signed verification which states:

"The undersigned declares that this is an accurate and complete submission of patent information for the NDA, amendment or supplement pending under section 505 of the Federal Food, Drug, and Cosmetic Act. This time-sensitive patent information is submitted pursuant to 21 CFR 314.53. I attest that I am familiar with 21 CFR 314.53 and this submission complies with the requirements of the regulation. I verify under penalty of perjury that the foregoing is true and correct."; and-

(R) Information on whether the applicant, patent owner or attorney, agent, representative or other authorized official signed the form; the name of the person; and the full address, phone number and, if available, the fax number and e-mail address.

(ii) *Submission of patent information upon and after approval.* Within 30 days after the date of approval of its application or supplement, the applicant shall submit FDA Form 3542 for each patent that claims the drug substance (active ingredient), drug product (formulation and composition), or approved method of use. FDA will rely only on the information submitted on this form and will not list or publish patent information if the patent declaration is incomplete or indicates the patent is not eligible for listing. Patent information must also be submitted for patents issued after the date of approval of the new drug application as required in paragraph (c)(2)(ii) of this section. As described in paragraph (d)(4) of this section, patent information must be submitted to FDA within 30 days of the date of issuance of the patent. If the applicant submits the required patent information within the 30 days, but we notify an applicant that a declaration form is incomplete or shows that the patent is not eligible for listing, the applicant must submit an acceptable declaration form within 15 days of FDA notification to be considered timely filed. The following information and verification statement is required:

(A) New drug application number;

(B) Name of new drug application sponsor;

(C) Trade name of new drug;

(D) Active ingredient(s) of new drug;

(E) Strength(s) of new drug;

(F) Dosage form of new drug;

(G) Approval date of new drug application or supplement;

(H) United States patent number, issue date, and expiration date of patent submitted;

(I) The patent owner's name, full address, phone number and, if available, fax number and e-mail address;

(J) The name, full address, phone number and, if available, fax number

and e-mail address of an agent or representative who resides or maintains a place of business within the United States authorized to receive notice of patent certification under sections 505(b)(3) and 505(j)(2)(B) of the act and §§314.52 and 314.95 (if patent owner or new drug application applicant or holder does not reside or have a place of business within the United States);

(K) Information on whether the patent has been submitted previously for the new drug application;

(L) Information on whether the expiration date is a new expiration date if the patent had been submitted previously for listing;

(M) Information on whether the patent is a product-by-process patent in which the product claimed is novel;

(N) Information on the drug substance (active ingredient) patent including the following:

(1) Whether the patent claims the drug substance that is the active ingredient in the drug product described in the approved application;

(2) Whether the patent claims a polymorph that is the same as the active ingredient that is described in the approved application;

(3) Whether the applicant has test data, described at paragraph (b)(2) of this section, demonstrating that a drug product containing the polymorph will perform the same as the drug product described in the approved application and a description of the polymorphic form(s) claimed by the patent for which such test data exist;

(4) Whether the patent claims only a metabolite of the active ingredient; and

(5) Whether the patent claims only an intermediate;

(O) Information on the drug product (composition/formulation) patent including the following:

(1) Whether the patent claims the approved drug product as defined in §314.3; and

(2) Whether the patent claims only an intermediate;

(P) Information on each method-of-use patent including the following:

(1) Whether the patent claims one or more approved methods of using the approved drug product and a description of each approved method of use or indication and related patent claim of the patent being submitted;

(2) Identification of the specific section of the approved labeling for the drug product that corresponds to the method of use claimed by the patent submitted; and

(3) The description of the patented method of use as required for publication;

(Q) Whether there are no relevant patents that claim the approved drug substance (active ingredient), the approved drug product (formulation or composition) or approved method(s) of use and with respect to which a claim of patent infringement could reasonably be asserted if a person not licensed by the owner of the patent engaged in the manufacture, use, or sale of the drug product;

(R) A signed verification which states: "The undersigned declares that this is an accurate and complete submission of patent information for the NDA, amendment or supplement approved under section 505 of the Federal Food, Drug, and Cosmetic Act. This time-sensitive patent information is submitted pursuant to 21 CFR 314.53. I attest that I am familiar with 21 CFR 314.53 and this submission complies with the requirements of the regulation. I verify under penalty of perjury that the foregoing is true and correct."; and

(S) Information on whether the applicant, patent owner or attorney, agent, representative or other authorized official signed the form; the name of the person; and the full address, phone number and, if available, the fax number and e-mail address.

(3) *No relevant patents.* If the applicant believes that there are no relevant patents that claim the drug substance (active ingredient), drug product (formulation or composition), or the method(s) of use for which the applicant has received approval, and with respect to which a claim of patent infringement could reasonably be asserted if a person not licensed by the owner of the patent engaged in the manufacture, use, or sale of the drug product, the applicant will verify this information in the appropriate forms, FDA Forms 3542 or 3542a.

(4) *Authorized signature.* The declarations required by this section shall be signed by the applicant or patent owner, or the applicant's or patent owner's attorney, agent (representative), or other authorized official.

(d) *When and where to submit patent information*—(1) *Original application.* An applicant shall submit with its original application submitted under this part, including an application described in section 505(b)(2) of the act, the information described in paragraph (c) of this section on each drug (ingredient), drug product (formulation and composition), and method of use patent issued before the application is filed with FDA and for which patent information is required to be submitted under this section. If a patent is issued after the application is filed with FDA but before the application is approved, the applicant shall, within 30 days of the date of issuance of the patent, submit the required patent information in an amendment to the application under § 314.60.

(2) *Supplements.* (i) An applicant shall submit patent information required under paragraph (c) of this section for a patent that claims the drug, drug product, or method of use for which approval is sought in any of the following supplements:

(A) To change the formulation;

(B) To add a new indication or other condition of use, including a change in route of administration;

(C) To change the strength;

(D) To make any other patented change regarding the drug, drug product, or any method of use.

(ii) If the applicant submits a supplement for one of the changes listed under paragraph (d)(2)(i) of this section and existing patents for which information has already been submitted to FDA claim the changed product, the applicant shall submit a certification with the supplement identifying the patents that claim the changed product.

(iii) If the applicant submits a supplement for one of the changes listed under paragraph (d)(2)(i) of this section and no patents, including previously submitted patents, claim the changed product, it shall so certify.

(iv) The applicant shall comply with the requirements for amendment of formulation or composition and method of use patent information under paragraphs (c)(2)(ii) and (d)(3) of this section.

(3) *Patent information deadline.* If a patent is issued for a drug, drug product, or method of use after an application is approved, the applicant shall submit to FDA the required patent information within 30 days of the date of issuance of the patent.

(4) *Copies.* The applicant shall submit two copies of each submission of patent information, an archival copy and a copy for the chemistry, manufacturing, and controls section of the review copy, to the Central Document Room, Center for Drug Evaluation and Research, Food and Drug Administration, 5901–B Ammendale Rd., Beltsville, MD 20705–1266. The applicant shall submit the patent information by letter separate from, but at the same time as, submission of the supplement.

(5) *Submission date.* Patent information shall be considered to be submitted to FDA as of the date the information is received by the Central Document Room.

(6) *Identification.* Each submission of patent information, except information submitted with an original application, and its mailing cover shall bear prominent identification as to its contents, *i.e.,* "Patent Information," or, if submitted after approval of an application, "Time Sensitive Patent Information."

(e) *Public disclosure of patent information.* FDA will publish in the list the patent number and expiration date of each patent that is required to be, and is, submitted to FDA by an applicant, and for each use patent, the approved indications or other conditions of use covered by a patent. FDA will publish such patent information upon approval of the application, or, if the patent information is submitted by the applicant after approval of an application as provided under paragraph (d)(2) of this section, as soon as possible after the submission to the agency of the patent information. Patent information submitted by the last working day of a month will be published in that month's supplement to the list. Patent information received by the Agency between monthly publication of supplements to the list will be placed on public display in FDA's Division of Freedom of Information. A request for copies of the file shall be sent in writing to the Freedom of Information Staff at the address listed on the Agency's Web site at *http://www.fda.gov.*

(f) *Correction of patent information errors.* If any person disputes the accuracy or relevance of patent information submitted to the agency under this section and published by FDA in the list, or believes that an applicant has failed to submit required patent information, that person must first notify the agency in writing stating the grounds for disagreement. Such notification should be directed to the Office of Generic Drugs, OGD Document Room, Attention: Orange Book Staff, 7500 Standish Pl., Rockville, MD 20855. The agency will then request of the applicable new drug application holder that the correctness of the patent information or omission of patent information be confirmed. Unless the application holder withdraws or amends its patent information in response to FDA's request, the agency will not change the patent information in the list. If the new drug application holder does not change the patent information submitted to FDA, a 505(b)(2) application or an abbreviated new drug application under section 505(j) of the act submitted for a drug that is claimed by a patent for which information has been submitted must, despite any disagreement as to the correctness of the patent information, contain an appropriate certification for each listed patent.

[59 FR 50363, Oct. 3, 1994, as amended at 68 FR 36703, June 18, 2003; 69 FR 13473, Mar. 23, 2004; 74 FR 9766, Mar. 6, 2009; 74 FR 36605, July 24, 2009; 76 FR 31470, June 1, 2011; 79 FR 68115, Nov. 14, 2014]

§ 314.54 Procedure for submission of an application requiring investigations for approval of a new indication for, or other change from, a listed drug.

(a) The act does not permit approval of an abbreviated new drug application for a new indication, nor does it permit approval of other changes in a listed drug if investigations, other than bioavailability or bioequivalence studies, are essential to the approval of the change. Any person seeking approval of a drug product that represents a modification of a listed drug (e.g., a new indication or new dosage form) and for which investigations, other than bioavailability or bioequivalence studies, are essential to the approval of the changes may, except as provided in paragraph (b) of this section, submit a 505(b)(2) application. This application need contain only that information needed to support the modification(s) of the listed drug.

(1) The applicant shall submit a complete archival copy of the application that contains the following:

(i) The information required under § 314.50(a), (b), (c), (d)(1), (d)(3), (e), and (g), except that § 314.50(d)(1)(ii)(*c*) shall contain the proposed or actual master production record, including a description of the equipment, to be used for the manufacture of a commercial lot of the drug product.

(ii) The information required under § 314.50 (d)(2), (d)(4) (if an anti-infective drug), (d)(5), (d)(6), and (f) as needed to support the safety and effectiveness of the drug product.

(iii) Identification of the listed drug for which FDA has made a finding of safety and effectiveness and on which finding the applicant relies in seeking approval of its proposed drug product by established name, if any, proprietary name, dosage form, strength, route of administration, name of listed drug's application holder, and listed drug's approved application number.

(iv) If the applicant is seeking approval only for a new indication and not for the indications approved for the listed drug on which the applicant relies, a certification so stating.

(v) Any patent information required under section 505(b)(1) of the act with respect to any patent which claims the drug for which approval is sought or a method of using such drug and to which a claim of patent infringement could reasonably be asserted if a person not licensed by the owner of the patent engaged in the manufacture, use, or sale of the drug product.

(vi) Any patent certification or statement required under section 505(b)(2) of the act with respect to any relevant patents that claim the listed drug or that claim any other drugs on which investigations relied on by the applicant for approval of the application were conducted, or that claim a use for the listed or other drug.

(vii) If the applicant believes the change for which it is seeking approval is entitled to a period of exclusivity, the information required under §314.50(j).

(2) The applicant shall submit a review copy that contains the technical sections described in §314.50(d)(1), except that §314.50(d)(1)(ii)(c) shall contain the proposed or actual master production record, including a description of the equipment, to be used for the manufacture of a commercial lot of the drug product, and paragraph (d)(3), and the technical sections described in paragraphs (d)(2), (d)(4), (d)(5), (d)(6), and (f) when needed to support the modification. Each of the technical sections in the review copy is required to be separately bound with a copy of the information required under §314.50 (a), (b), and (c) and a copy of the proposed labeling.

(3) The information required by §314.50 (d)(2), (d)(4) (if an anti-infective drug), (d)(5), (d)(6), and (f) for the listed drug on which the applicant relies shall be satisfied by reference to the listed drug under paragraph (a)(1)(iii) of this section.

(4) The applicant shall submit a field copy of the application that contains the technical section described in §314.50(d)(1), a copy of the information required under §314.50(a) and (c), and certification that the field copy is a true copy of the technical section described in §314.50(d)(1) contained in the archival and review copies of the application.

(b) An application may not be submitted under this section for a drug product whose only difference from the reference listed drug is that:

(1) The extent to which its active ingredient(s) is absorbed or otherwise made available to the site of action is less than that of the reference listed drug; or

(2) The rate at which its active ingredient(s) is absorbed or otherwise made available to the site of action is unintentionally less than that of the reference listed drug.

[57 FR 17982, Apr. 28, 1992; 57 FR 61612, Dec. 28, 1992, as amended at 58 FR 47351, Sept. 8, 1993; 59 FR 50364, Oct. 3, 1994]

§ 314.55 Pediatric use information.

(a) *Required assessment.* Except as provided in paragraphs (b), (c), and (d) of this section, each application for a new active ingredient, new indication, new dosage form, new dosing regimen, or new route of administration shall contain data that are adequate to assess the safety and effectiveness of the drug product for the claimed indications in all relevant pediatric subpopulations, and to support dosing and administration for each pediatric subpopulation for which the drug is safe and effective. Where the course of the disease and the effects of the drug are sufficiently similar in adults and pediatric patients, FDA may conclude that pediatric effectiveness can be extrapolated from adequate and well-controlled studies in adults usually supplemented with other information obtained in pediatric patients, such as pharmacokinetic studies. Studies may not be needed in each pediatric age group, if data from one age group can be extrapolated to another. Assessments of safety and effectiveness required under this section for a drug product that represents a meaningful therapeutic benefit over existing treatments for pediatric patients must be carried out using appropriate formulations for each age group(s) for which the assessment is required.

(b) *Deferred submission.* (1) FDA may, on its own initiative or at the request of an applicant, defer submission of some or all assessments of safety and effectiveness described in paragraph (a) of this section until after approval of the drug product for use in adults. Deferral may be granted if, among other reasons, the drug is ready for approval in adults before studies in pediatric patients are complete, or pediatric studies should be delayed until additional safety or effectiveness data have been collected. If an applicant requests deferred submission, the request must provide a certification from the applicant of the grounds for delaying pediatric studies, a description of the planned or ongoing studies, and evidence that the studies are being or will be conducted with due diligence and at the earliest possible time.

(2) If FDA determines that there is an adequate justification for temporarily delaying the submission of assessments of pediatric safety and effectiveness, the drug product may be approved for use in adults subject to the requirement that the applicant submit the required assessments within a specified time.

(c) *Waivers*—(1) *General.* FDA may grant a full or partial waiver of the requirements of paragraph (a) of this section on its own initiative or at the request of an applicant. A request for a waiver must provide an adequate justification.

(2) *Full waiver.* An applicant may request a waiver of the requirements of paragraph (a) of this section if the applicant certifies that:

(i) The drug product does not represent a meaningful therapeutic benefit over existing treatments for pediatric patients and is not likely to be used in a substantial number of pediatric patients;

(ii) Necessary studies are impossible or highly impractical because, e.g., the number of such patients is so small or geographically dispersed; or

(iii) There is evidence strongly suggesting that the drug product would be ineffective or unsafe in all pediatric age groups.

(3) *Partial waiver.* An applicant may request a waiver of the requirements of paragraph (a) of this section with respect to a specified pediatric age group, if the applicant certifies that:

(i) The drug product does not represent a meaningful therapeutic benefit over existing treatments for pediatric patients in that age group, and is not likely to be used in a substantial number of patients in that age group;

(ii) Necessary studies are impossible or highly impractical because, e.g., the number of patients in that age group is so small or geographically dispersed;

(iii) There is evidence strongly suggesting that the drug product would be ineffective or unsafe in that age group; or

(iv) The applicant can demonstrate that reasonable attempts to produce a pediatric formulation necessary for that age group have failed.

(4) *FDA action on waiver.* FDA shall grant a full or partial waiver, as appropriate, if the agency finds that there is a reasonable basis on which to conclude that one or more of the grounds for waiver specified in paragraphs (c)(2) or (c)(3) of this section have been met. If a waiver is granted on the ground that it is not possible to develop a pediatric formulation, the waiver will cover only those pediatric age groups requiring that formulation. If a waiver is granted because there is evidence that the product would be ineffective or unsafe in pediatric populations, this information will be included in the product's labeling.

(5) *Definition of "meaningful therapeutic benefit".* For purposes of this section and §201.23 of this chapter, a drug will be considered to offer a meaningful therapeutic benefit over existing therapies if FDA estimates that:

(i) If approved, the drug would represent a significant improvement in the treatment, diagnosis, or prevention of a disease, compared to marketed products adequately labeled for that use in the relevant pediatric population. Examples of how improvement might be demonstrated include, for example, evidence of increased effectiveness in treatment, prevention, or diagnosis of disease, elimination or substantial reduction of a treatment-limiting drug reaction, documented enhancement of compliance, or evidence of safety and effectiveness in a new subpopulation; or

(ii) The drug is in a class of drugs or for an indication for which there is a need for additional therapeutic options.

(d) *Exemption for orphan drugs.* This section does not apply to any drug for an indication or indications for which orphan designation has been granted under part 316, subpart C, of this chapter.

[63 FR 66670, Dec. 2, 1998]

§314.60 Amendments to an unapproved application, supplement, or resubmission.

(a) FDA generally assumes that when an original application, supplement to an approved application, or resubmission of an application or supplement is submitted to the agency for review, the applicant believes that the agency can approve the application, supplement, or resubmission as submitted. However, the applicant may submit an amendment to an application that has been filed under § 314.101 but is not yet approved.

(b)(1) Submission of a major amendment to an original application, efficacy supplement, or resubmission of an application or efficacy supplement within 3 months of the end of the initial review cycle constitutes an agreement by the applicant under section 505(c) of the act to extend the initial review cycle by 3 months. (For references to a resubmission of an application or efficacy supplement in paragraph (b) of this section, the timeframe for reviewing the resubmission is the "review cycle" rather than the "initial review cycle.") FDA may instead defer review of the amendment until the subsequent review cycle. If the agency extends the initial review cycle for an original application, efficacy supplement, or resubmission under this paragraph, the division responsible for reviewing the application, supplement, or resubmission will notify the applicant of the extension. The initial review cycle for an original application, efficacy supplement, or resubmission of an application or efficacy supplement may be extended only once due to submission of a major amendment. FDA may, at its discretion, review any subsequent major amendment during the initial review cycle (as extended) or defer review until the subsequent review cycle.

(2) Submission of a major amendment to an original application, efficacy supplement, or resubmission of an application or efficacy supplement more than 3 months before the end of the initial review cycle will not extend the cycle. FDA may, at its discretion, review such an amendment during the initial review cycle or defer review until the subsequent review cycle.

(3) Submission of an amendment to an original application, efficacy supplement, or resubmission of an application or efficacy supplement that is not a major amendment will not extend the initial review cycle. FDA may, at its discretion, review such an amendment during the initial review cycle or defer review until the subsequent review cycle.

(4) Submission of a major amendment to a manufacturing supplement within 2 months of the end of the initial review cycle constitutes an agreement by the applicant under section 505(c) of the act to extend the initial review cycle by 2 months. FDA may instead defer review of the amendment until the subsequent review cycle. If the agency extends the initial review cycle for a manufacturing supplement under this paragraph, the division responsible for reviewing the supplement will notify the applicant of the extension. The initial review cycle for a manufacturing supplement may be extended only once due to submission of a major amendment. FDA may, at its discretion, review any subsequent major amendment during the initial review cycle (as extended) or defer review until the subsequent review cycle.

(5) Submission of an amendment to a supplement other than an efficacy or manufacturing supplement will not extend the initial review cycle. FDA may, at its discretion, review such an amendment during the initial review cycle or defer review until the subsequent review cycle.

(6) A major amendment may not include data to support an indication or claim that was not included in the original application, supplement, or resubmission, but it may include data to support a minor modification of an indication or claim that was included in the original application, supplement, or resubmission.

(7) When FDA defers review of an amendment until the subsequent review cycle, the agency will notify the applicant of the deferral in the complete response letter sent to the applicant under § 314.110 of this part.

(c)(1) An unapproved application may not be amended if all of the following conditions apply:

(i) The unapproved application is for a drug for which a previous application has been approved and granted a period of exclusivity in accordance with section 505(c)(3)(D)(ii) of the act that has not expired;

116

(ii) The applicant seeks to amend the unapproved application to include a published report of an investigation that was conducted or sponsored by the applicant entitled to exclusivity for the drug;

(iii) The applicant has not obtained a right of reference to the investigation described in paragraph (c)(1)(ii) of this section; and

(iv) The report of the investigation described in paragraph (c)(1)(ii) of this section would be essential to the approval of the unapproved application.

(2) The submission of an amendment described in paragraph (c)(1) of this section will cause the unapproved application to be deemed to be withdrawn by the applicant under § 314.65 on the date of receipt by FDA of the amendment. The amendment will be considered a resubmission of the application, which may not be accepted except as provided in accordance with section 505(c)(3)(D)(ii) of the act.

(d) The applicant shall submit a field copy of each amendment to § 314.50(d)(1). The applicant shall include in its submission of each such amendment to FDA a statement certifying that a field copy of the amendment has been sent to the applicant's home FDA district office.

[50 FR 7493, Feb. 22, 1985, as amended at 57 FR 17983, Apr. 28, 1992; 58 FR 47352, Sept. 8, 1993; 63 FR 5252, Feb. 2, 1998; 69 FR 18764, Apr. 8, 2004; 73 FR 39608, July 10, 2008]

§ 314.65 Withdrawal by the applicant of an unapproved application.

An applicant may at any time withdraw an application that is not yet approved by notifying the Food and Drug Administration in writing. If, by the time it receives such notice, the agency has identified any deficiencies in the application, we will list such deficiencies in the letter we send the applicant acknowledging the withdrawal. A decision to withdraw the application is without prejudice to refiling. The agency will retain the application and will provide a copy to the applicant on request under the fee schedule in § 20.45 of FDA's public information regulations.

[50 FR 7493, Feb. 22, 1985, as amended at 68 FR 25287, May 12, 2003; 73 FR 39609, July 10, 2008]

§ 314.70 Supplements and other changes to an approved application.

(a) *Changes to an approved application.* (1)(i) Except as provided in paragraph (a)(1)(ii) of this section, the applicant must notify FDA about each change in each condition established in an approved application beyond the variations already provided for in the application. The notice is required to describe the change fully. Depending on the type of change, the applicant must notify FDA about the change in a supplement under paragraph (b) or (c) of this section or by inclusion of the information in the annual report to the application under paragraph (d) of this section.

(ii) The submission and grant of a written request for an exception or alternative under § 201.26 of this chapter satisfies the applicable requirements in paragraphs (a) through (c) of this section. However, any grant of a request for an exception or alternative under § 201.26 of this chapter must be reported as part of the annual report to the application under paragraph (d) of this section.

(2) The holder of an approved application under section 505 of the act must assess the effects of the change before distributing a drug product made with a manufacturing change.

(3) Notwithstanding the requirements of paragraphs (b) and (c) of this section, an applicant must make a change provided for in those paragraphs in accordance with a regulation or guidance that provides for a less burdensome notification of the change (for example, by submission of a supplement that does not require approval prior to distribution of the product or in an annual report).

(4) The applicant must promptly revise all promotional labeling and advertising to make it consistent with any labeling change implemented in accordance with paragraphs (b) and (c) of this section.

(5) Except for a supplement providing for a change in the labeling, the applicant must include in each supplement and amendment to a supplement providing for a change under paragraph (b) or (c) of this section a statement certifying that a field copy has been provided in accordance with § 314.440(a)(4).

(6) A supplement or annual report must include a list of all changes contained in the supplement or annual report. For supplements, this list must be provided in the cover letter.

(b) *Changes requiring supplement submission and approval prior to distribution of the product made using the change (major changes).* (1) A supplement must be submitted for any change in the drug substance, drug product, production process, quality controls, equipment, or facilities that has a substantial potential to have an adverse effect on the identity, strength, quality, purity, or potency of the drug product as these factors may relate to the safety or effectiveness of the drug product.

(2) These changes include, but are not limited to:

(i) Except those described in paragraphs (c) and (d) of this section, changes in the qualitative or quantitative formulation of the drug product, including inactive ingredients, or in the specifications provided in the approved application;

(ii) Changes requiring completion of studies in accordance with part 320 of this chapter to demonstrate the equivalence of the drug product to the drug product as manufactured without the change or to the reference listed drug;

(iii) Changes that may affect drug substance or drug product sterility assurance, such as changes in drug substance, drug product, or component sterilization method(s) or an addition, deletion, or substitution of steps in an aseptic processing operation;

(iv) Changes in the synthesis or manufacture of the drug substance that may affect the impurity profile and/or the physical, chemical, or biological properties of the drug substance;

(v) The following labeling changes:

(A) Changes in labeling, except those described in paragraphs (c)(6)(iii), (d)(2)(ix), or (d)(2)(x) of this section;

(B) If applicable, any change to a Medication Guide required under part 208 of this chapter, except for changes in the information specified in § 208.20(b)(8)(iii) and (b)(8)(iv) of this chapter; and

(C) Any change to the information required by § 201.57(a) of this chapter, with the following exceptions that may be reported in an annual report under paragraph (d)(2)(x) of this section:

(1) Removal of a listed section(s) specified in § 201.57(a)(5) of this chapter; and

(2) Changes to the most recent revision date of the labeling as specified in § 201.57(a)(15) of this chapter.

(vi) Changes in a drug product container closure system that controls the drug product delivered to a patient or changes in the type (e.g., glass to high density polyethylene (HDPE), HDPE to polyvinyl chloride, vial to syringe) or composition (e.g., one HDPE resin to another HDPE resin) of a packaging component that may affect the impurity profile of the drug product.

(vii) Changes solely affecting a natural product, a recombinant DNA-derived protein/polypeptide, or a complex or conjugate of a drug substance with a monoclonal antibody for the following:

(A) Changes in the virus or adventitious agent removal or inactivation method(s);

(B) Changes in the source material or cell line; and

(C) Establishment of a new master cell bank or seed.

(viii) Changes to a drug product under an application that is subject to a validity assessment because of significant questions regarding the integrity of the data supporting that application.

(3) The applicant must obtain approval of a supplement from FDA prior to distribution of a drug product made using a change under paragraph (b) of this section. Except for submissions under paragraph (e) of this section, the following information must be contained in the supplement:

(i) A detailed description of the proposed change;

(ii) The drug product(s) involved;

(iii) The manufacturing site(s) or area(s) affected;

(iv) A description of the methods used and studies performed to assess the effects of the change;

(v) The data derived from such studies;

(vi) For a natural product, a recombinant DNA-derived protein/polypeptide, or a complex or conjugate of a drug substance with a monoclonal antibody, relevant validation protocols and a list of relevant standard operating procedures must be provided in addition to the requirements in paragraphs (b)(3)(iv) and (b)(3)(v) of this section; and

(vii) For sterilization process and test methodologies related to sterilization process validation, relevant validation protocols and a list of relevant standard operating procedures must be provided in addition to the requirements in paragraphs (b)(3)(iv) and (b)(3)(v) of this section.

(4) An applicant may ask FDA to expedite its review of a supplement for public health reasons or if a delay in making the change described in it would impose an extraordinary hardship on the applicant. Such a supplement and its mailing cover should be plainly marked: "Prior Approval Supplement-Expedited Review Requested."

(c) *Changes requiring supplement submission at least 30 days prior to distribution of the drug product made using the change (moderate changes).* (1) A supplement must be submitted for any change in the drug substance, drug product, production process, quality controls, equipment, or facilities that has a moderate potential to have an adverse effect on the identity, strength, quality, purity, or potency of the drug product as these factors may relate to the safety or effectiveness of the drug product. If the supplement provides for a labeling change under paragraph (c)(6)(iii) of this section, 12 copies of the final printed labeling must be included.

(2) These changes include, but are not limited to:

(i) A change in the container closure system that does not affect the quality of the drug product, except those described in paragraphs (b) and (d) of this section; and

(ii) Changes solely affecting a natural protein, a recombinant DNA-derived protein/polypeptide or a complex or conjugate of a drug substance with a monoclonal antibody, including:

(A) An increase or decrease in production scale during finishing steps that involves different equipment; and

(B) Replacement of equipment with that of a different design that does not affect the process methodology or process operating parameters.

(iii) Relaxation of an acceptance criterion or deletion of a test to comply with an official compendium that is consistent with FDA statutory and regulatory requirements.

(3) A supplement submitted under paragraph (c)(1) of this section is required to give a full explanation of the basis for the change and identify the date on which the change is to be made. The supplement must be labeled "Supplement—Changes Being Effected in 30 Days" or, if applicable under paragraph (c)(6) of this section, "Supplement—Changes Being Effected."

(4) Pending approval of the supplement by FDA, except as provided in paragraph (c)(6) of this section, distribution of the drug product made using the change may begin not less than 30 days after receipt of the supplement by FDA. The information listed in paragraphs (b)(3)(i) through (b)(3)(vii) of this section must be contained in the supplement.

(5) The applicant must not distribute the drug product made using the change if within 30 days following FDA's receipt of the supplement, FDA informs the applicant that either:

(i) The change requires approval prior to distribution of the drug product in accordance with paragraph (b) of this section; or

(ii) Any of the information required under paragraph (c)(4) of this section is missing; the applicant must not distribute the drug product made using the change until the supplement has been amended to provide the missing information.

(6) The agency may designate a category of changes for the purpose of providing that, in the case of a change in such category, the holder of an approved application may commence distribution of the drug product involved upon receipt by the agency of a supplement for the change. These changes include, but are not limited to:

(i) Addition to a specification or changes in the methods or controls to provide increased assurance that the drug substance or drug product will have the characteristics of identity, strength, quality, purity, or potency that it purports or is represented to possess;

(ii) A change in the size and/or shape of a container for a nonsterile drug product, except for solid dosage forms, without a change in the labeled amount of drug product or from one container closure system to another;

(iii) Changes in the labeling to reflect newly acquired information, except for changes to the information required in § 201.57(a) of this chapter (which must be made under paragraph (b)(2)(v)(C) of this section), to accomplish any of the following:

(A) To add or strengthen a contraindication, warning, precaution, or adverse reaction for which the evidence of a causal association satisfies the standard for inclusion in the labeling under § 201.57(c) of this chapter;

(B) To add or strengthen a statement about drug abuse, dependence, psychological effect, or overdosage;

(C) To add or strengthen an instruction about dosage and administration that is intended to increase the safe use of the drug product;

(D) To delete false, misleading, or unsupported indications for use or claims for effectiveness; or

(E) Any labeling change normally requiring a supplement submission and approval prior to distribution of the drug product that FDA specifically requests be submitted under this provision.

(7) If the agency disapproves the supplemental application, it may order the manufacturer to cease distribution of the drug product(s) made with the manufacturing change.

(d) *Changes to be described in an annual report (minor changes).* (1) Changes in the drug substance, drug product, production process, quality controls, equipment, or facilities that have a minimal potential to have an adverse effect on the identity, strength, quality, purity, or potency of the drug product as these factors may relate to the safety or effectiveness of the drug product must be documented by the applicant in the next annual report in accordance with § 314.81(b)(2).

(2) These changes include, but are not limited to:

(i) Any change made to comply with a change to an official compendium, except a change described in paragraph (c)(2)(iii) of this section, that is consistent with FDA statutory and regulatory requirements.

(ii) The deletion or reduction of an ingredient intended to affect only the color of the drug product;

(iii) Replacement of equipment with that of the same design and operating principles except those equipment changes described in paragraph (c) of this section;

(iv) A change in the size and/or shape of a container containing the same number of dosage units for a nonsterile solid dosage form drug product, without a change from one container closure system to another;

(v) A change within the container closure system for a nonsterile drug product, based upon a showing of equivalency to the approved system under a protocol approved in the application or published in an official compendium;

(vi) An extension of an expiration dating period based upon full shelf life data on production batches obtained from a protocol approved in the application;

(vii) The addition or revision of an alternative analytical procedure that provides the same or increased assurance of the identity, strength, quality, purity, or potency of the material being tested as the analytical procedure described in the approved application, or deletion of an alternative analytical procedure;

(viii) The addition by embossing, debossing, or engraving of a code imprint to a solid oral dosage form drug product other than a modified release dosage form, or a minor change in an existing code imprint;

(ix) A change in the labeling concerning the description of the drug product or in the information about how the drug product is supplied, that does not involve a change in the dosage strength or dosage form; and

(x) An editorial or similar minor change in labeling, including a change to the information allowed by paragraphs (b)(2)(v)(C)(*1*) and (*2*) of this section.

(3) For changes under this category, the applicant is required to submit in the annual report:

(i) A statement by the holder of the approved application that the effects of the change have been assessed;

(ii) A full description of the manufacturing and controls changes, including the manufacturing site(s) or area(s) involved;

(iii) The date each change was implemented;

(iv) Data from studies and tests performed to assess the effects of the change; and,

(v) For a natural product, recombinant DNA-derived protein/polypeptide, complex or conjugate of a drug substance with a monoclonal antibody, sterilization process or test methodology related to sterilization process validation, a cross-reference to relevant validation protocols and/or standard operating procedures.

(e) *Protocols.* An applicant may submit one or more protocols describing the specific tests and studies and acceptance criteria to be achieved to demonstrate the lack of adverse effect for specified types of manufacturing changes on the identity, strength, quality, purity, and potency of the drug product as these factors may relate to the safety or effectiveness of the drug product. Any such protocols, if not included in the approved application, or changes to an approved protocol, must be submitted as a supplement requiring approval from FDA prior to distribution of a drug product produced with the manufacturing change. The supplement, if approved, may subsequently justify a reduced reporting category for the particular change because the use of the protocol for that type of change reduces the potential risk of an adverse effect.

(f) *Patent information.* The applicant must comply with the patent information requirements under section 505(c)(2) of the act.

(g) *Claimed exclusivity.* If an applicant claims exclusivity under §314.108 upon approval of a supplement for change to its previously approved drug product, the applicant must include with its supplement the information required under §314.50(j).

[69 FR 18764, Apr. 8, 2004, as amended at 71 FR 3997, Jan. 24, 2006; 72 FR 73600, Dec. 28, 2007; 73 FR 49609, Aug. 22, 2008]

§314.71 Procedures for submission of a supplement to an approved application.

(a) Only the applicant may submit a supplement to an application.

(b) All procedures and actions that apply to an application under §314.50 also apply to supplements, except that the information required in the supplement is limited to that needed to support the change. A supplement is required to contain an archival copy and a review copy that include an application form and appropriate technical sections, samples, and labeling; except that a supplement for a change other than a change in labeling is required also to contain a field copy.

(c) All procedures and actions that apply to applications under this part, including actions by applicants and the Food and Drug Administration, also apply to supplements except as specified otherwise in this part.

[50 FR 7493, Feb. 22, 1985, as amended at 50 FR 21238, May 23, 1985; 58 FR 47352, Sept. 8, 1993; 67 FR 9586, Mar. 4, 2002; 73 FR 39609, July 10, 2008]

§314.72 Change in ownership of an application.

(a) An applicant may transfer ownership of its application. At the time of transfer the new and former owners are required to submit information to the Food and Drug Administration as follows:

(1) The former owner shall submit a letter or other document that states that all rights to the application have been transferred to the new owner.

(2) The new owner shall submit an application form signed by the new owner and a letter or other document containing the following:

(i) The new owner's commitment to agreements, promises, and conditions made by the former owner and contained in the application;

(ii) The date that the change in ownership is effective; and

(iii) Either a statement that the new owner has a complete copy of the approved application, including supplements and records that are required to be kept under §314.81, or a request for a copy of the application from FDA's files. FDA will provide a copy of the application to the new owner under the fee schedule in §20.45 of FDA's public information regulations.

(b) The new owner shall advise FDA about any change in the conditions in the approved application under §314.70, except the new owner may advise FDA in the next annual report about a change in the drug product's label or labeling to change the product's brand or the name of its manufacturer, packer, or distributor.

[50 FR 7493, Feb. 22, 1985; 50 FR 14212, Apr. 11, 1985, as amended at 50 FR 21238, May 23, 1985; 67 FR 9586, Mar. 4, 2002; 68 FR 25287, May 12, 2003]

§314.80 Postmarketing reporting of adverse drug experiences.

(a) *Definitions.* The following definitions of terms apply to this section:

Adverse drug experience. Any adverse event associated with the use of a drug in humans, whether or not considered drug related, including the following: An adverse event occurring in the course of the use of a drug product in professional practice; an adverse event occurring from drug overdose whether accidental or intentional; an adverse event occurring from drug abuse; an adverse event occurring from drug withdrawal; and any failure of expected pharmacological action.

Disability. A substantial disruption of a person's ability to conduct normal life functions.

Life-threatening adverse drug experience. Any adverse drug experience that places the patient, in the view of the initial reporter, at *immediate* risk of death from the adverse drug experience as it occurred, *i.e.,* it does not include an adverse drug experience that, had it occurred in a more severe form, might have caused death.

Serious adverse drug experience. Any adverse drug experience occurring at any dose that results in any of the following outcomes: Death, a life-threatening adverse drug experience, inpatient hospitalization or prolongation of existing hospitalization, a persistent or significant disability/incapacity, or a congenital anomaly/birth defect. Important medical events that may not result in death, be life-threatening, or require hospitalization may be considered a serious adverse drug experience when, based upon appropriate medical judgment, they may jeopardize the patient or subject and may require medical or surgical intervention to prevent one of the outcomes listed in this definition. Examples of such medical events include allergic bronchospasm requiring intensive treatment in an emergency room or at home, blood dyscrasias or convulsions that do not result in inpatient hospitalization, or the development of drug dependency or drug abuse.

Unexpected adverse drug experience. Any adverse drug experience that is not listed in the current labeling for the drug product. This includes events that may be symptomatically and pathophysiologically related to an event listed in the labeling, but differ from the event because of greater severity or specificity. For example, under this definition, hepatic necrosis would be unexpected (by virtue of greater severity) if the labeling only referred to elevated hepatic enzymes or hepatitis. Similarly, cerebral thromboembolism and cerebral vasculitis would be unexpected (by virtue of greater specificity) if the labeling only listed cerebral vascular accidents. "Unexpected," as used in this definition, refers to an adverse drug experience that has not been previously observed (*i.e.,* included in the labeling) rather than from the perspective of such experience not being anticipated from the pharmacological properties of the pharmaceutical product.

(b) *Review of adverse drug experiences.* Each applicant having an approved application under §314.50 or, in the case of a 505(b)(2) application, an effective approved application, shall promptly review all adverse drug experience information obtained or otherwise received by the applicant from any source, foreign or domestic, including information derived from commercial marketing experience, postmarketing clinical investigations, postmarketing epidemiological/surveillance studies, reports in the scientific literature, and unpublished scientific papers. Applicants are not required to resubmit to FDA adverse drug experience reports forwarded to the applicant by FDA; however, applicants must submit all followup information on such reports to FDA. Any person subject to the reporting requirements under paragraph (c) of this section shall also develop written procedures for the surveillance, receipt, evaluation, and reporting of postmarketing adverse drug experiences to FDA.

(c) *Reporting requirements*. The applicant shall report to FDA adverse drug experience information, as described in this section. The applicant shall submit two copies of each report described in this section to the Central Document Room, 5901–B Ammendale Rd., Beltsville, MD 20705–1266. FDA may waive the requirement for the second copy in appropriate instances.

(1)(i) *Postmarketing 15-day "Alert reports"*. The applicant shall report each adverse drug experience that is both serious and unexpected, whether foreign or domestic, as soon as possible but in no case later than 15 calendar days of initial receipt of the information by the applicant.

(ii) *Postmarketing 15-day "Alert reports"—followup*. The applicant shall promptly investigate all adverse drug experiences that are the subject of these postmarketing 15-day Alert reports and shall submit followup reports within 15 calendar days of receipt of new information or as requested by FDA. If additional information is not obtainable, records should be maintained of the unsuccessful steps taken to seek additional information. Postmarketing 15-day Alert reports and followups to them shall be submitted under separate cover.

(iii) *Submission of reports*. The requirements of paragraphs (c)(1)(i) and (c)(1)(ii) of this section, concerning the submission of postmarketing 15-day Alert reports, shall also apply to any person other than the applicant (nonapplicant) whose name appears on the label of an approved drug product as a manufacturer, packer, or distributor. To avoid unnecessary duplication in the submission to FDA of reports required by paragraphs (c)(1)(i) and (c)(1)(ii) of this section, obligations of a nonapplicant may be met by submission of all reports of serious adverse drug experiences to the applicant. If a nonapplicant elects to submit adverse drug experience reports to the applicant rather than to FDA, the non-applicant shall submit each report to the applicant within 5 calendar days of receipt of the report by the nonapplicant, and the applicant shall then comply with the requirements of this section. Under this circumstance, the nonapplicant shall maintain a record of this action which shall include:

(A) A copy of each adverse drug experience report;

(B) The date the report was received by the nonapplicant;

(C) The date the report was submitted to the applicant; and

(D) The name and address of the applicant.

(iv) *Report identification*. Each report submitted under this paragraph shall bear prominent identification as to its contents, *i.e.*, "15-day Alert report," or "15-day Alert report-followup."

(2) *Periodic adverse drug experience reports*. (i) The applicant shall report each adverse drug experience not reported under paragraph (c)(1)(i) of this section at quarterly intervals, for 3 years from the date of approval of the application, and then at annual intervals. The applicant shall submit each quarterly report within 30 days of the close of the quarter (the first quarter beginning on the date of approval of the application) and each annual report within 60 days of the anniversary date of approval of the application. Upon written notice, FDA may extend or reestablish the requirement that an applicant submit quarterly reports, or require that the applicant submit reports under this section at different times than those stated. For example, the agency may reestablish a quarterly reporting requirement following the approval of a major supplement. Followup information to adverse drug experiences submitted in a periodic report may be submitted in the next periodic report.

(ii) Each periodic report is required to contain: (*a*) a narrative summary and analysis of the information in the report and an analysis of the 15-day Alert reports submitted during the reporting interval (all 15-day Alert reports being appropriately referenced by the applicant's patient identification number, adverse reaction term(s), and date of submission to FDA); (*b*) a FDA Form 3500A (Adverse Reaction Report) for each adverse drug experience not reported under paragraph (c)(1)(i) of this section (with an index consisting of a line listing of the applicant's patient identification number and adverse reaction term(s)); and (c) a history of actions taken since the last report because of adverse drug experiences (for example, labeling changes or studies initiated).

(iii) Periodic reporting, except for information regarding 15-day Alert reports, does not apply to adverse drug experience information obtained from postmarketing studies (whether or not conducted under an investigational new drug application), from reports in the scientific literature, and from foreign marketing experience.

(d) *Scientific literature.* (1) A 15-day Alert report based on information from the scientific literature is required to be accompanied by a copy of the published article. The 15-day reporting requirements in paragraph (c)(1)(i) of this section (*i.e.*, serious, unexpected adverse drug experiences) apply only to reports found in scientific and medical journals either as case reports or as the result of a formal clinical trial.

(2) As with all reports submitted under paragraph (c)(1)(i) of this section, reports based on the scientific literature shall be submitted on FDA Form 3500A or comparable format as prescribed by paragraph (f) of this section. In cases where the applicant believes that preparing the FDA Form 3500A constitutes an undue hardship, the applicant may arrange with the Office of Surveillance and Epidemiology for an acceptable alternative reporting format.

(e) *Postmarketing studies.* (1) An applicant is not required to submit a 15-day Alert report under paragraph (c) of this section for an adverse drug experience obtained from a postmarketing study (whether or not conducted under an investigational new drug application) unless the applicant concludes that there is a reasonable possibility that the drug caused the adverse experience.

(2) The applicant shall separate and clearly mark reports of adverse drug experiences that occur during a postmarketing study as being distinct from those experiences that are being reported spontaneously to the applicant.

(f) *Reporting FDA Form 3500A.* (1) Except as provided in paragraph (f)(3) of this section, the applicant shall complete FDA Form 3500A for each report of an adverse drug experience (foreign events may be submitted either on an FDA Form 3500A or, if preferred, on a CIOMS I form).

(2) Each completed FDA Form 3500A should refer only to an individual patient or a single attached publication.

(3) Instead of using FDA Form 3500A, an applicant may use a computer-generated FDA Form 3500A or other alternative format (e.g., a computer-generated tape or tabular listing) provided that:

(i) The content of the alternative format is equivalent in all elements of information to those specified in FDA Form 3500A; and

(ii) The format is agreed to in advance by the Office of Surveillance and Epidemiology.

(4) FDA Form 3500A and instructions for completing the form are available on the Internet at *http://www.fda.gov/ medwatch/index.html.*

(g) *Multiple reports.* An applicant should not include in reports under this section any adverse drug experiences that occurred in clinical trials if they were previously submitted as part of the approved application. If a report applies to a drug for which an applicant holds more than one approved application, the applicant should submit the report to the application that was first approved. If a report refers to more than one drug marketed by an applicant, the applicant should submit the report to the application for the drug listed first in the report.

(h) *Patient privacy.* An applicant should not include in reports under this section the names and addresses of individual patients; instead, the applicant should assign a unique code number to each report, preferably not more than eight characters in length. The applicant should include the name of the reporter from whom the information was received. Names of patients, health care professionals, hospitals, and geographical identifiers in adverse drug experience reports are not releasable to the public under FDA's public information regulations in part 20.

(i) *Recordkeeping*. The applicant shall maintain for a period of 10 years records of all adverse drug experiences known to the applicant, including raw data and any correspondence relating to adverse drug experiences.

(j) *Withdrawal of approval*. If an applicant fails to establish and maintain records and make reports required under this section, FDA may withdraw approval of the application and, thus, prohibit continued marketing of the drug product that is the subject of the application.

(k) *Disclaimer*. A report or information submitted by an applicant under this section (and any release by FDA of that report or information) does not necessarily reflect a conclusion by the applicant or FDA that the report or information constitutes an admission that the drug caused or contributed to an adverse effect. An applicant need not admit, and may deny, that the report or information submitted under this section constitutes an admission that the drug caused or contributed to an adverse effect. For purposes of this provision, the term "applicant" also includes any person reporting under paragraph (c)(1)(iii) of this section.

[50 FR 7493, Feb. 22, 1985; 50 FR 14212, Apr. 11, 1985, as amended at 50 FR 21238, May 23, 1985; 51 FR 24481, July 3, 1986; 52 FR 37936, Oct. 13, 1987; 55 FR 11580, Mar. 29, 1990; 57 FR 17983, Apr. 28, 1992; 62 FR 34168, June 25, 1997; 62 FR 52251, Oct. 7, 1997; 63 FR 14611, Mar. 26, 1998; 67 FR 9586, Mar. 4, 2002; 69 FR 13473, Mar. 23, 2004; 74 FR 13113, Mar. 26, 2009]

EFFECTIVE DATE NOTE: At 79 FR 33088, June 10, 2014, § 314.80 was amended effective June 10, 2015 by:

a. By removing the word "shall" each time it appears and by adding in its place the word "must";

b. In paragraph (a) by alphabetically adding the definitions for "Individual case safety report (ICSR)" and "ICSR attachments";

c. In paragraph (c)(1)(i) by removing the phrase "in no case later than 15 calendar days of" and by adding in its place the phrase "no later than 15 calendar days from";

d. By removing the last sentence of paragraph (c)(1)(ii);

e. By removing paragraph (c)(1)(iv);

f. By revising paragraph (c) introductory text, the first and third sentences of paragraph (c)(1)(iii) introductory text, and paragraph (c)(2)(ii);

g. By removing paragraph (d)(2) and by redesignating paragraph (d)(1) as paragraph (d)

and revising the first sentence of newly redesignated paragraph (d);

h. By removing paragraph (e)(2) and by redesignating paragraph (e)(1) as paragraph (e);

i. By revising paragraph (f);

j. By redesignating paragraph (g) through paragraph (k) as paragraph (h) through paragraph (l); and by revising newly redesignated paragraph (i); and

k. By adding new paragraph (g). For the convenience of the user, the added and revised text is set forth as follows:

§ 314.80 Postmarketing reporting of adverse drug experiences.

(a) * * *

Individual case safety report (ICSR). A description of an adverse drug experience related to an individual patient or subject.

ICSR attachments. Documents related to the adverse drug experience described in an ICSR, such as medical records, hospital discharge summaries, or other documentation.

*   *   *   *   *

(c) *Reporting requirements*. The applicant must submit to FDA adverse drug experience information as described in this section. Except as provided in paragraph (g)(2) of this section, these reports must be submitted to the Agency in electronic format as described in paragraph (g)(1) of this section.

(1) * * *

(iii) *Submission of reports*. The requirements of paragraphs (c)(1)(i) and (c)(1)(ii) of this section, concerning the submission of postmarketing 15-day Alert reports, also apply to any person other than the applicant whose name appears on the label of an approved drug product as a manufacturer, packer, or distributor (nonapplicant). * * * If a nonapplicant elects to submit adverse drug experience reports to the applicant rather than to FDA, the nonapplicant must submit, by any appropriate means, each report to the applicant within 5 calendar days of initial receipt of the information by the nonapplicant, and the applicant must then comply with the requirements of this section. * * *

*   *   *   *   *

(2) * * *

(ii) Each periodic report is required to contain:

(A) *Descriptive information*. (*1*) A narrative summary and analysis of the information in the report;

(*2*) An analysis of the 15-day Alert reports submitted during the reporting interval (all 15-day Alert reports being appropriately referenced by the applicant's patient identification code, adverse reaction term(s), and date of submission to FDA);

(*3*) A history of actions taken since the last report because of adverse drug experiences (for example, labeling changes or studies initiated); and

(4) An index consisting of a line listing of the applicant's patient identification code, and adverse reaction term(s) for all ICSRs submitted under paragraph (c)(2)(ii)(B) of this section.

(B) *ICSRs for serious, expected, and nonserious adverse drug experiences.* An ICSR for each adverse drug experience not reported under paragraph (c)(1)(i) of this section (all serious, expected and nonserious adverse drug experiences). All such ICSRs must be submitted to FDA (either individually or in one or more batches) within the timeframe specified in paragraph (c)(2)(i) of this section. ICSRs must only be submitted to FDA once.

*   *   *   *   *

(d) *Scientific literature.* A 15-day Alert report based on information in the scientific literature must be accompanied by a copy of the published article. * * *

*   *   *   *   *

(f) *Information reported on ICSRs.* ICSRs include the following information:

(1) *Patient information.*

(i) Patient identification code;

(ii) Patient age at the time of adverse drug experience, or date of birth;

(iii) Patient gender; and

(iv) Patient weight.

(2) *Adverse drug experience.*

(i) Outcome attributed to adverse drug experience;

(ii) Date of adverse drug experience;

(iii) Date of ICSR submission;

(iv) Description of adverse drug experience (including a concise medical narrative);

(v) Adverse drug experience term(s);

(vi) Description of relevant tests, including dates and laboratory data; and

(vii) Other relevant patient history, including preexisting medical conditions.

(3) *Suspect medical product(s).*

(i) Name;

(ii) Dose, frequency, and route of administration used;

(iii) Therapy dates;

(iv) Diagnosis for use (indication);

(v) Whether the product is a prescription or nonprescription product;

(vi) Whether the product is a combination product as defined in § 3.2(e) of this chapter;

(vii) Whether adverse drug experience abated after drug use stopped or dose reduced;

(viii) Whether adverse drug experience reappeared after reintroduction of drug;

(ix) Lot number;

(x) Expiration date;

(xi) National Drug Code (NDC) number; and

(xii) Concomitant medical products and therapy dates.

(4) *Initial reporter information.*

(i) Name, address, and telephone number;

(ii) Whether the initial reporter is a health care professional; and

(iii) Occupation, if a health care professional.

(5) *Applicant information.*

(i) Applicant name and contact office address;

(ii) Telephone number;

(iii) Report source, such as spontaneous, literature, or study;

(iv) Date the report was received by applicant;

(v) Application number and type;

(vi) Whether the ICSR is a 15-day "Alert report";

(vii) Whether the ICSR is an initial report or followup report; and

(viii) Unique case identification number, which must be the same in the initial report and any subsequent followup report(s).

(g) *Electronic format for submissions.* (1) Safety report submissions, including ICSRs, ICSR attachments, and the descriptive information in periodic reports, must be in an electronic format that FDA can process, review, and archive. FDA will issue guidance on how to provide the electronic submission (e.g., method of transmission, media, file formats, preparation and organization of files).

(2) An applicant or nonapplicant may request, in writing, a temporary waiver of the requirements in paragraph (g)(1) of this section. These waivers will be granted on a limited basis for good cause shown. FDA will issue guidance on requesting a waiver of the requirements in paragraph (g)(1) of this section.

*   *   *   *   *

(i) *Patient privacy.* An applicant should not include in reports under this section the names and addresses of individual patients; instead, the applicant should assign a unique code for identification of the patient. The applicant should include the name of the reporter from whom the information was received as part of the initial reporter information, even when the reporter is the patient. The names of patients, health care professionals, hospitals, and geographical identifiers in adverse drug experience reports are not releasable to the public under FDA's public information regulations in part 20 of this chapter.

§ 314.81   Other postmarketing reports.

(a) *Applicability.* Each applicant shall make the reports for each of its approved applications and abbreviated applications required under this section and section 505(k) of the act.

(b) *Reporting requirements.* The applicant shall submit to the Food and Drug Administration at the specified times two copies of the following reports:

(1) *NDA—Field alert report.* The applicant shall submit information of the following kinds about distributed drug products and articles to the FDA district office that is responsible for the facility involved within 3 working days of receipt by the applicant. The information may be provided by telephone or other rapid communication means, with prompt written followup. The report and its mailing cover should be plainly marked: "NDA—Field Alert Report."

(i) Information concerning any incident that causes the drug product or its labeling to be mistaken for, or applied to, another article.

(ii) Information concerning any bacteriological contamination, or any significant chemical, physical, or other change or deterioration in the distributed drug product, or any failure of one or more distributed batches of the drug product to meet the specification established for it in the application.

(2) *Annual report.* The applicant shall submit each year within 60 days of the anniversary date of U.S. approval of the application, two copies of the report to the FDA division responsible for reviewing the application. Each annual report is required to be accompanied by a completed transmittal Form FDA 2252 (Transmittal of Periodic Reports for Drugs for Human Use), and must include all the information required under this section that the applicant received or otherwise obtained during the annual reporting interval that ends on the U.S. anniversary date. The report is required to contain in the order listed:

(i) *Summary.* A brief summary of significant new information from the previous year that might affect the safety, effectiveness, or labeling of the drug product. The report is also required to contain a brief description of actions the applicant has taken or intends to take as a result of this new information, for example, submit a labeling supplement, add a warning to the labeling, or initiate a new study. The summary shall briefly state whether labeling supplements for pediatric use have been submitted and whether new studies in the pediatric population to support appropriate labeling for the pediatric population have been initiated. Where possible, an estimate of patient exposure to the drug product, with special reference to the pediatric population (neonates, infants, children, and adolescents) shall be provided, including dosage form.

(ii)(*a*) *Distribution data.* Information about the quantity of the drug product distributed under the approved application, including that distributed to distributors. The information is required to include the National Drug Code (NDC) number, the total number of dosage units of each strength or potency distributed (e.g., 100,000/5 milligram tablets, 50,000/10 milliliter vials), and the quantities distributed for domestic use and the quantities distributed for foreign use. Disclosure of financial or pricing data is not required.

(*b*) *Authorized generic drugs.* If applicable, the date each authorized generic drug (as defined in §314.3) entered the market, the date each authorized generic drug ceased being distributed, and the corresponding trade or brand name. Each dosage form and/or strength is a different authorized generic drug and should be listed separately. The first annual report submitted on or after January 25, 2010 must include the information listed in this paragraph for any authorized generic drug that was marketed during the time period covered by an annual report submitted after January 1, 1999. If information is included in the annual report with respect to any authorized generic drug, a copy of that portion of the annual report must be sent to the Food and Drug Administration, Center for Drug Evaluation and Research, Office of New Drug Quality Assessment, Bldg. 21, rm. 2562, 10903 New Hampshire Ave., Silver Spring, MD 20993–0002, and marked "Authorized Generic Submission" or, by e-mail, to the Authorized Generics electronic mailbox at *AuthorizedGenerics@fda.hhs.gov* with "Authorized Generic Submission" indicated in the subject line. However, at such time that FDA has required that annual reports be submitted in an electronic format, the information required by this paragraph must be submitted as part of the annual report, in the electronic format specified for submission of annual reports at that time, and not as a separate submission under the preceding sentence in this paragraph.

(iii) *Labeling.* (a) Currently used professional labeling, patient brochures or package inserts (if any), and a representative sample of the package labels.

(b) The content of labeling required under § 201.100(d)(3) of this chapter (*i.e.,* the package insert or professional labeling), including all text, tables, and figures, must be submitted in electronic format. Electronic format submissions must be in a form that FDA can process, review, and archive. FDA will periodically issue guidance on how to provide the electronic submission (e.g., method of transmission, media, file formats, preparation and organization of files). Submissions under this paragraph must be made in accordance with part 11 of this chapter, except for the requirements of § 11.10(a), (c) through (h), and (k), and the corresponding requirements of § 11.30.

(c) A summary of any changes in labeling that have been made since the last report listed by date in the order in which they were implemented, or if no changes, a statement of that fact.

(iv) *Chemistry, manufacturing, and controls changes.* (a) Reports of experiences, investigations, studies, or tests involving chemical or physical properties, or any other properties of the drug (such as the drug's behavior or properties in relation to microorganisms, including both the effects of the drug on microorganisms and the effects of microorganisms on the drug). These reports are only required for new information that may affect FDA's previous conclusions about the safety or effectiveness of the drug product.

(b) A full description of the manufacturing and controls changes not requiring a supplemental application under § 314.70 (b) and (c), listed by date in the order in which they were implemented.

(v) *Nonclinical laboratory studies.* Copies of unpublished reports and summaries of published reports of new toxicological findings in animal studies and in vitro studies (e.g., mutagenicity) conducted by, or otherwise obtained by, the applicant concerning the ingredients in the drug product. The applicant shall submit a copy of a published report if requested by FDA.

(vi) *Clinical data.* (a) Published clinical trials of the drug (or abstracts of them), including clinical trials on safety and effectiveness; clinical trials on new uses; biopharmaceutic, pharmacokinetic, and clinical pharmacology studies; and reports of clinical experience pertinent to safety (for example, epidemiologic studies or analyses of experience in a monitored series of patients) conducted by or otherwise obtained by the applicant. Review articles, papers describing the use of the drug product in medical practice, papers and abstracts in which the drug is used as a research tool, promotional articles, press clippings, and papers that do not contain tabulations or summaries of original data should not be reported.

(b) Summaries of completed unpublished clinical trials, or prepublication manuscripts if available, conducted by, or otherwise obtained by, the applicant. Supporting information should not be reported. (A study is considered completed 1 year after it is concluded.)

(c) Analysis of available safety and efficacy data in the pediatric population and changes proposed in the labeling based on this information. An assessment of data needed to ensure appropriate labeling for the pediatric population shall be included.

(vii) *Status reports of postmarketing study commitments.* A status report of each postmarketing study of the drug product concerning clinical safety, clinical efficacy, clinical pharmacology, and nonclinical toxicology that is required by FDA (e.g., accelerated approval clinical benefit studies, pediatric studies) or that the applicant has committed, in writing, to conduct either at the time of approval of an application for the drug product or a supplement to an application, or after approval of the application or a supplement. For pediatric studies, the status report shall include a statement indicating whether postmarketing clinical studies in pediatric populations were required by FDA under §201.23 of this chapter. The status of these post-marketing studies shall be reported annually until FDA notifies the applicant, in writing, that the agency concurs with the applicant's determination that the study commitment has been fulfilled or that the study is either no longer feasible or would no longer provide useful information.

(a) *Content of status report.* The following information must be provided for each postmarketing study reported under this paragraph:

(1) *Applicant's name.*

(2) *Product name.* Include the approved drug product's established name and proprietary name, if any.

(3) *NDA, ANDA, and supplement number.*

(4) *Date of U.S. approval of NDA or ANDA.*

(5) *Date of postmarketing study commitment.*

(6) *Description of postmarketing study commitment.* The description must include sufficient information to uniquely describe the study. This information may include the purpose of the study, the type of study, the patient population addressed by the study and the indication(s) and dosage(s) that are to be studied.

(7) *Schedule for completion and reporting of the postmarketing study commitment.* The schedule should include the actual or projected dates for submission of the study protocol to FDA, completion of patient accrual or initiation of an animal study, completion of the study, submission of the final study report to FDA, and any additional milestones or submissions for which projected dates were specified as part of the commitment. In addition, it should include a revised schedule, as appropriate. If the schedule has been previously revised, provide both the original schedule and the most recent, previously submitted revision.

(8) *Current status of the postmarketing study commitment.* The status of each postmarketing study should be categorized using one of the following terms that describes the study's status on the anniversary date of U.S. approval of the application or other agreed upon date:

(i) *Pending.* The study has not been initiated, but does not meet the criterion for delayed.

(ii) *Ongoing.* The study is proceeding according to or ahead of the original schedule described under paragraph (b)(2)(vii)(a)(7) of this section.

(iii) *Delayed.* The study is behind the original schedule described under paragraph (b)(2)(vii)(a)(7) of this section.

(iv) *Terminated.* The study was ended before completion but a final study report has not been submitted to FDA.

(v) *Submitted.* The study has been completed or terminated and a final study report has been submitted to FDA.

(9) *Explanation of the study's status.* Provide a brief description of the status of the study, including the patient accrual rate (expressed by providing the number of patients or subjects enrolled to date, and the total planned enrollment), and an explanation of the study's status identified under paragraph (b)(2)(vii)(a)(8) of this section. If the study has been completed, include the date the study was completed and the date the final study report was submitted to FDA, as applicable. Provide a revised schedule, as well as the reason(s) for the revision, if the schedule under paragraph (b)(2)(vii)(a)(7) of this section has changed since the last report.

(b) *Public disclosure of information.* Except for the information described in this paragraph, FDA may publicly disclose any information described in paragraph (b)(2)(vii) of this section, concerning a postmarketing study, if the agency determines that the information is necessary to identify the applicant or to establish the status of the study, including the reasons, if any, for failure to conduct, complete, and report the study. Under this section, FDA will not publicly disclose trade secrets, as defined in §20.61 of this chapter, or information, described in §20.63 of this chapter, the disclosure of which would constitute an unwarranted invasion of personal privacy.

(viii) *Status of other postmarketing studies.* A status report of any postmarketing study not included under paragraph (b)(2)(vii) of this section that is being performed by, or on behalf of, the applicant. A status report is to be included for any chemistry, manufacturing, and controls studies that the applicant has agreed to perform and for all product stability studies.

(ix) *Log of outstanding regulatory business.* To facilitate communications between FDA and the applicant, the report may, at the applicant's discretion, also contain a list of any open regulatory business with FDA concerning the drug product subject to the application (e.g., a list of the applicant's unanswered correspondence with the agency, a list of the agency's unanswered correspondence with the applicant).

(3) *Other reporting*—(i) *Advertisements and promotional labeling.* The applicant shall submit specimens of mailing pieces and any other labeling or advertising devised for promotion of the drug product at the time of initial dissemination of the labeling and at the time of initial publication of the advertisement for a prescription drug product. Mailing pieces and labeling that are designed to contain samples of a drug product are required to be complete, except the sample of the drug product may be omitted. Each submission is required to be accompanied by a completed transmittal Form FDA–2253 (Transmittal of Advertisements and Promotional Labeling for Drugs for Human Use) and is required to include a copy of the product's current professional labeling. Form FDA–2253 is available on the Internet at *http://www.fda.gov/opacom/morechoices/fdaforms/cder.html.*

(ii) *Special reports.* Upon written request the agency may require that the applicant submit the reports under this section at different times than those stated.

(iii) *Notification of discontinuance.* (a) An applicant who is the sole manufacturer of an approved drug product must notify FDA in writing at least 6 months prior to discontinuance of manufacture of the drug product if:

(1) The drug product is life supporting, life sustaining, or intended for use in the prevention of a serious disease or condition; and

(2) The drug product was not originally derived from human tissue and replaced by a recombinant product.

(b) Notifications required by paragraph (b)(3)(iii)(a) of this section must be submitted to FDA either electronically or by phone according to instructions on FDA's Drug Shortages Web site at: *http://www.fda.gov/Drugs/DrugSafety/DrugShortages.*

(c) FDA will publicly disclose a list of all drug products to be discontinued under paragraph (b)(3)(iii)(a) of this section. If the notification period is reduced under § 314.91, the list will state the reason(s) for such reduction and the anticipated date that manufacturing will cease.

(d) For purposes of this section and § 314.91, the terms "discontinuance" and "sole manufacturer" are defined as follows:

Discontinuance means any interruption in manufacturing of a drug product described in paragraph (b)(3)(iii)(a) of this section for sale in the United States that could lead to a potential disruption in supply of the drug product, whether the interruption is intended to be temporary or permanent.

Sole manufacturer means an applicant that is the only entity currently manufacturing a drug product of a specific strength, dosage form, or route of administration for sale in the United States, whether the product is manufactured by the applicant or for the applicant under contract with one or more different entities.

(iv) *Withdrawal of approved drug product from sale.* (a) The applicant shall submit on Form FDA 2657 (Drug Product Listing), within 15 working days of the withdrawal from sale of a drug product, the following information:

(1) The National Drug Code (NDC) number.

(2) The identity of the drug product by established name and by proprietary name.

(3) The new drug application or abbreviated application number.

(4) The date of withdrawal from sale. It is requested but not required that the reason for withdrawal of the drug product from sale be included with the information.

(b) The applicant shall submit each Form FDA–2657 to the Records Repository Team (HFD–143), Center for Drug Evaluation and Research, Food and

Drug Administration, 5600 Fishers Lane, Rockville, MD 20857.

(c) Reporting under paragraph (b)(3)(iv) of this section constitutes compliance with the requirements under §207.30(a) of this chapter to report "at the discretion of the registrant when the change occurs."

(c) *General requirements*—(1) *Multiple applications.* For all reports required by this section, the applicant shall submit the information common to more than one application only to the application first approved, and shall not report separately on each application. The submission is required to identify all the applications to which the report applies.

(2) *Patient identification.* Applicants should not include in reports under this section the names and addresses of individual patients; instead, the applicant should code the patient names whenever possible and retain the code in the applicant's files. The applicant shall maintain sufficient patient identification information to permit FDA, by using that information alone or along with records maintained by the investigator of a study, to identify the name and address of individual patients; this will ordinarily occur only when the agency needs to investigate the reports further or when there is reason to believe that the reports do not represent actual results obtained.

(d) *Withdrawal of approval.* If an applicant fails to make reports required under this section, FDA may withdraw approval of the application and, thus, prohibit continued marketing of the drug product that is the subject of the application.

(Collection of information requirements approved by the Office of Management and Budget under control number 0910–0001)

[50 FR 7493, Feb. 22, 1985; 50 FR 14212, Apr. 11, 1985, as amended at 50 FR 21238, May 23, 1985; 55 FR 11580, Mar. 29, 1990; 57 FR 17983, Apr. 28, 1992; 63 FR 66670, Dec. 2, 1998; 64 FR 401, Jan. 5, 1999; 65 FR 64617, Oct. 30, 2000; 66 FR 10815, Feb. 20, 2001; 68 FR 69019, Dec. 11, 2003; 69 FR 18766, Apr. 8, 2004; 69 FR 48775, Aug. 11, 2004; 72 FR 58999, Oct. 18, 2007; 74 FR 13113, Mar. 26, 2009; 74 FR 37167, July 28, 2009; 76 FR 78539, Dec. 19, 2011]

§314.90 Waivers.

(a) An applicant may ask the Food and Drug Administration to waive under this section any requirement that applies to the applicant under §§314.50 through 314.81. An applicant may ask FDA to waive under §314.126(c) any criteria of an adequate and well-controlled study described in §314.126(b). A waiver request under this section is required to be submitted with supporting documentation in an application, or in an amendment or supplement to an application. The waiver request is required to contain one of the following:

(1) An explanation why the applicant's compliance with the requirement is unnecessary or cannot be achieved;

(2) A description of an alternative submission that satisfies the purpose of the requirement; or

(3) Other information justifying a waiver.

(b) FDA may grant a waiver if it finds one of the following:

(1) The applicant's compliance with the requirement is unnecessary for the agency to evaluate the application or compliance cannot be achieved;

(2) The applicant's alternative submission satisfies the requirement; or

(3) The applicant's submission otherwise justifies a waiver.

[50 FR 7493, Feb. 22, 1985, as amended at 50 FR 21238, May 23, 1985; 67 FR 9586, Mar. 4, 2002]

§314.91 Obtaining a reduction in the discontinuance notification period.

(a) *What is the discontinuance notification period?* The discontinuance notification period is the 6-month period required under §314.81(b)(3)(iii)(*a*). The discontinuance notification period begins when an applicant who is the sole manufacturer of certain products notifies FDA that it will discontinue manufacturing the product. The discontinuance notification period ends when manufacturing ceases.

(b) *When can FDA reduce the discontinuance notification period?* FDA can reduce the 6-month discontinuance notification period when it finds good cause exists for the reduction. FDA may find good cause exists based on information certified by an applicant in a request for a reduction of the discontinuance notification period. In limited circumstances, FDA may find good cause exists based on information already known to the agency. These circumstances can include the withdrawal of the drug from the market based upon formal FDA regulatory action (e.g., under the procedures described in §314.150 for the publication of a notice of opportunity for a hearing describing the basis for the proposed withdrawal of a drug from the market) or resulting from the applicant's consultations with the agency.

(c) *How can an applicant request a reduction in the discontinuance notification period?* (1) The applicant must certify in a written request that, in its opinion and to the best of its knowledge, good cause exists for the reduction. The applicant must submit the following certification:

The undersigned certifies that good cause exists for a reduction in the 6-month notification period required in §314.81(b)(3)(iii)(*a*) for discontinuing the manufacture of (*name of the drug product*). The following circumstances establish good cause (*one or more of the circumstances in paragraph (d) of this section*).

(2) The certification must be signed by the applicant or the applicant's attorney, agent (representative), or other authorized official. If the person signing the certification does not reside or have a place of business within the United States, the certification must contain the name and address of, and must also be signed by, an attorney, agent, or other authorized official who resides or maintains a place of business within the United States.

(3) For drugs regulated by the Center for Drug Evaluation and Research (CDER) or the Center for Biologics Evaluation and Research (CBER), one copy of the certification must be submitted to the Drug Shortage Coordinator at the address of the Director of CDER, one copy to the CDER Drug Registration and Listing Team, Division of Compliance Risk Management and Surveillance in CDER, and one copy to either the director of the review division in CDER responsible for reviewing the application, or the director of the office in CBER responsible for reviewing the application.

(d) *What circumstances and information can establish good cause for a reduction in the discontinuance notification period?* (1) A public health problem may result from continuation of manufacturing for the 6-month period. This certification must include a detailed description of the potential threat to the public health.

(2) A biomaterials shortage prevents the continuation of the manufacturing for the 6-month period. This certification must include a detailed description of the steps taken by the applicant in an attempt to secure an adequate supply of biomaterials to enable manufacturing to continue for the 6-month period and an explanation of why the biomaterials could not be secured.

(3) A liability problem may exist for the manufacturer if the manufacturing is continued for the 6-month period. This certification must include a detailed description of the potential liability problem.

(4) Continuation of the manufacturing for the 6-month period may cause substantial economic hardship for the manufacturer. This certification must include a detailed description of the financial impact of continuing to manufacture the drug product over the 6-month period.

(5) The manufacturer has filed for bankruptcy under chapter 7 or 11 of title 11, United States Code (11 U.S.C. 701 *et seq.* and 1101 *et seq.*). This certification must be accompanied by documentation of the filing or proof that the filing occurred.

(6) The manufacturer can continue distribution of the drug product to satisfy existing market need for 6 months. This certification must include a detailed description of the manufacturer's processes to ensure such distribution for the 6-month period.

(7) Other good cause exists for the reduction. This certification must include a detailed description of the need for a reduction.

[72 FR 58999, Oct. 18, 2007]

Subpart C—Abbreviated Applications

SOURCE: 57 FR 17983, Apr. 28, 1992, unless otherwise noted.

§ 314.92 Drug products for which abbreviated applications may be submitted.

(a) Abbreviated applications are suitable for the following drug products within the limits set forth under § 314.93:

(1) Drug products that are the same as a listed drug. A "listed drug" is defined in § 314.3. For determining the suitability of an abbreviated new drug application, the term "same as" means identical in active ingredient(s), dosage form, strength, route of administration, and conditions of use, except that conditions of use for which approval cannot be granted because of exclusivity or an existing patent may be omitted. If a listed drug has been voluntarily withdrawn from or not offered for sale by its manufacturer, a person who wishes to submit an abbreviated new drug application for the drug shall comply with § 314.122.

(2) [Reserved]

(3) Drug products that have been declared suitable for an abbreviated new drug application submission by FDA through the petition procedures set forth under § 10.30 of this chapter and § 314.93.

(b) FDA will publish in the list listed drugs for which abbreviated applications may be submitted. The list is available from the Superintendent of Documents, U.S. Government Printing Office, Washington, DC 20402, 202–783–3238.

[57 FR 17983, Apr. 28, 1992, as amended at 64 FR 401, Jan. 5, 1999]

§ 314.93 Petition to request a change from a listed drug.

(a) The only changes from a listed drug for which the agency will accept a petition under this section are those changes described in paragraph (b) of this section. Petitions to submit abbreviated new drug applications for other changes from a listed drug will not be approved.

(b) A person who wants to submit an abbreviated new drug application for a drug product which is not identical to a listed drug in route of administration, dosage form, and strength, or in which one active ingredient is substituted for one of the active ingredients in a listed combination drug, must first obtain permission from FDA to submit such an abbreviated application.

(c) To obtain permission to submit an abbreviated new drug application for a change described in paragraph (b) of this section, a person must submit and obtain approval of a petition requesting the change. A person seeking permission to request such a change from a reference listed drug shall submit a petition in accordance with § 10.20 of this chapter and in the format specified in § 10.30 of this chapter. The petition shall contain the information specified in § 10.30 of this chapter and any additional information required by this section. If any provision of § 10.20 or § 10.30 of this chapter is inconsistent with any provision of this section, the provisions of this section apply.

(d) The petitioner shall identify a listed drug and include a copy of the proposed labeling for the drug product that is the subject of the petition and a copy of the approved labeling for the listed drug. The petitioner may, under limited circumstances, identify more than one listed drug, for example, when the proposed drug product is a combination product that differs from the combination reference listed drug with regard to an active ingredient, and the different active ingredient is an active ingredient of a listed drug. The petitioner shall also include information to show that:

(1) The active ingredients of the proposed drug product are of the same pharmacological or therapeutic class as those of the reference listed drug.

(2) The drug product can be expected to have the same therapeutic effect as the reference listed drug when administered to patients for each condition of use in the reference listed drug's labeling for which the applicant seeks approval.

(3) If the proposed drug product is a combination product with one different active ingredient, including a different ester or salt, from the reference listed drug, that the different active ingredient has previously been approved in a listed drug or is a drug that does not meet the definition of "new drug" in section 201(b) of the act.

(e) No later than 90 days after the date a petition that is permitted under paragraph (a) of this section is submitted, FDA will approve or disapprove the petition.

(1) FDA will approve a petition properly submitted under this section unless it finds that:

(i) Investigations must be conducted to show the safety and effectiveness of the drug product or of any of its active ingredients, its route of administration, dosage form, or strength which differs from the reference listed drug; or

(ii) For a petition that seeks to change an active ingredient, the drug product that is the subject of the petition is not a combination drug; or

(iii) For a combination drug product that is the subject of the petition and has an active ingredient different from the reference listed drug:

(A) The drug product may not be adequately evaluated for approval as safe and effective on the basis of the information required to be submitted under § 314.94; or

(B) The petition does not contain information to show that the different active ingredient of the drug product is of the same pharmacological or therapeutic class as the ingredient of the reference listed drug that is to be changed and that the drug product can be expected to have the same therapeutic effect as the reference listed drug when administered to patients for each condition of use in the listed drug's labeling for which the applicant seeks approval; or

(C) The different active ingredient is not an active ingredient in a listed drug or a drug that meets the requirements of section 201(p) of the act; or

(D) The remaining active ingredients are not identical to those of the listed combination drug; or

(iv) Any of the proposed changes from the listed drug would jeopardize the safe or effective use of the product so as to necessitate significant labeling changes to address the newly introduced safety or effectiveness problem; or

(v) FDA has determined that the reference listed drug has been withdrawn from sale for safety or effectiveness reasons under § 314.161, or the reference listed drug has been voluntarily withdrawn from sale and the agency has not determined whether the withdrawal is for safety or effectiveness reasons.

(2) For purposes of this paragraph, "investigations must be conducted" means that information derived from animal or clinical studies is necessary to show that the drug product is safe or effective. Such information may be contained in published or unpublished reports.

(3) If FDA approves a petition submitted under this section, the agency's response may describe what additional information, if any, will be required to support an abbreviated new drug application for the drug product. FDA may, at any time during the course of its review of an abbreviated new drug application, request additional information required to evaluate the change approved under the petition.

(f) FDA may withdraw approval of a petition if the agency receives any information demonstrating that the petition no longer satisfies the conditions under paragraph (e) of this section.

§ 314.94 Content and format of an abbreviated application.

Abbreviated applications are required to be submitted in the form and contain the information required under this section. Three copies of the application are required, an archival copy, a review copy, and a field copy. FDA will maintain guidance documents on the format and content of applications to assist applicants in their preparation.

(a) *Abbreviated new drug applications.* Except as provided in paragraph (b) of this section, the applicant shall submit a complete archival copy of the abbreviated new drug application that includes the following:

(1) *Application form.* The applicant shall submit a completed and signed application form that contains the information described under § 314.50(a)(1), (a)(3), (a)(4), and (a)(5). The applicant shall state whether the submission is an abbreviated application under this section or a supplement to an abbreviated application under § 314.97.

(2) *Table of contents.* the archival copy of the abbreviated new drug application is required to contain a table of

contents that shows the volume number and page number of the contents of the submission.

(3) *Basis for abbreviated new drug application submission.* An abbreviated new drug application must refer to a listed drug. Ordinarily, that listed drug will be the drug product selected by the agency as the reference standard for conducting bioequivalence testing. The application shall contain:

(i) The name of the reference listed drug, including its dosage form and strength. For an abbreviated new drug application based on an approverd petition under §10.30 of this chapter or §314.93, the reference listed drug must be the same as the listed drug approved in the petition.

(ii) A statement as to whether, according to the information published in the list, the reference listed drug is entitled to a period of marketing exclusivity under section 505(j)(4)(D) of the act.

(iii) For an abbreviated new drug application based on an approved petition under §10.30 of this chapter or §314.93, a reference to FDA-assigned docket number for the petition and a copy of FDA's correspondence approving the petition.

(4) *Conditions of use.* (i) A statement that the conditions of use prescribed, recommended, or suggested in the labeling proposed for the drug product have been previously approved for the reference listed drug.

(ii) A reference to the applicant's annotated proposed labeling and to the currently approved labeling for the reference listed drug provided under paragraph (a)(8) of this section.

(5) *Active ingredients.* (i) For a single-active-ingredient drug product, information to show that the active ingredient is the same as that of the reference single-active-ingredient listed drug, as follows:

(A) A statement that the active ingredient of the proposed drug product is the same as that of the reference listed drug.

(B) A reference to the applicant's annotated proposed labeling and to the currently approved labeling for the reference listed drug provided under paragraph (a)(8) of this section.

(ii) For a combination drug product, information to show that the active ingredients are the same as those of the reference listed drug except for any different active ingredient that has been the subject of an approved petition, as follows:

(A) A statement that the active ingredients of the proposed drug product are the same as those of the reference listed drug, or if one of the active ingredients differs from one of the active ingredients of the reference listed drug and the abbreviated application is submitted under the approval of a petition under §314.93 to vary such active ingredient, information to show that the other active ingredients of the drug product are the same as the other active ingredients of the reference listed drug, information to show that the different active ingredient is an active ingredient of another listed drug or of a drug that does not meet the definition of "new drug" in section 201(p) of the act, and such other information about the different active ingredient that FDA may require.

(B) A reference to the applicant's annotated proposed labeling and to the currently approved labeling for the reference listed drug provided under paragraph (a)(8) of this section.

(6) *Route of administration, dosage form, and strength.* (i) Information to show that the route of administration, dosage form, and strength of the drug product are the same as those of the reference listed drug except for any differences that have been the subject of an approved petition, as follows:

(A) A statement that the route of administration, dosage form, and strength of the proposed drug product are the same as those of the reference listed drug.

(B) A reference to the applicant's annotated proposed labeling and to the currently approved labeling for the reference listed drug provided under paragraph (a)(8) of this section.

(ii) If the route of administration, dosage form, or strength of the drug product differs from the reference listed drug and the abbreviated application is submitted under an approved petition under § 314.93, such information about the different route of administration, dosage form, or strength that FDA may require.

(7) *Bioequivalence.* (i) Information that shows that the drug product is bioequivalent to the reference listed drug upon which the applicant relies. A complete study report must be submitted for the bioequivalence study upon which the applicant relies for approval. For all other bioequivalence studies conducted on the same drug product formulation as defined in § 320.1(g) of this chapter, the applicant must submit either a complete or summary report. If a summary report of a bioequivalence study is submitted and FDA determines that there may be bioequivalence issues or concerns with the product, FDA may require that the applicant submit a complete report of the bioequivalence study to FDA; or

(ii) If the abbreviated new drug application is submitted under a petition approved under § 314.93, the results of any bioavailability of bioequivalence testing required by the agency, or any other information required by the agency to show that the active ingredients of the proposed drug product are of the same pharmacological or therapeutic class as those in the reference listed drug and that the proposed drug product can be expected to have the same therapeutic effect as the reference listed drug. If the proposed drug product contains a different active ingredient than the reference listed drug, FDA will consider the proposed drug product to have the same therapeutic effect as the reference listed drug if the applicant provides information demonstrating that:

(A) There is an adequate scientific basis for determining that substitution of the specific proposed dose of the different active ingredient for the dose of the member of the same pharmacological or therapeutic class in the reference listed drug will yield a resulting drug product whose safety and effectiveness have not been adversely affected.

(B) The unchanged active ingredients in the proposed drug product are bioequivalent to those in the reference listed drug.

(C) The different active ingredient in the proposed drug product is bioequivalent to an approved dosage form containing that ingredient and approved for the same indication as the proposed drug product or is bioequivalent to a drug product offered for that indication which does not meet the definition of "new drug" under section 201(p) of the act.

(iii) For each in vivo bioequivalence study contained in the abbreviated new drug application, a description of the analytical and statistical methods used in each study and a statement with respect to each study that it either was conducted in compliance with the institutional review board regulations in part 56 of this chapter, or was not subject to the regulations under § 56.104 or § 56.105 of this chapter and that each study was conducted in compliance with the informed consent regulations in part 50 of this chapter.

(8) *Labeling*—(i) *Listed drug labeling.* A copy of the currently approved labeling (including, if applicable, any Medication Guide required under part 208 of this chapter) for the listed drug referred to in the abbreviated new drug application, if the abbreviated new drug application relies on a reference listed drug.

(ii) *Copies of proposed labeling.* Copies of the label and all labeling for the drug product including, if applicable, any Medication Guide required under part 208 of this chapter (4 copies of draft labeling or 12 copies of final printed labeling).

(iii) *Statement on proposed labeling.* A statement that the applicant's proposed labeling including, if applicable, any Medication Guide required under part 208 of this chapter is the same as the labeling of the reference listed drug except for differences annotated and explained under paragraph (a)(8)(iv) of this section.

(iv) *Comparison of approved and proposed labeling.* A side-by-side comparison of the applicant's proposed labeling including, if applicable, any Medication Guide required under part 208 of this chapter with the approved labeling for the reference listed drug with all differences annotated and explained. Labeling (including the container label, package insert, and, if applicable, Medication Guide) proposed for the drug product must be the same as the labeling approved for the reference listed drug, except for changes required because of differences approved under a petition filed under § 314.93 or because the drug product and the reference listed drug are produced or distributed by different manufacturers. Such differences between the applicant's proposed labeling and labeling approved for the reference listed drug may include differences in expiration date, formulation, bioavailability, or pharmacokinetics, labeling revisions made to comply with current FDA labeling guidelines or other guidance, or omission of an indication or other aspect of labeling protected by patent or accorded exclusivity under section 505(j)(5)(F) of the act.

(9) *Chemistry, manufacturing, and controls.* (i) The information required under § 314.50(d)(1), except that § 314.50(d)(1)(ii)(*c*) shall contain the proposed or actual master production record, including a description of the equipment, to be used for the manufacture of a commercial lot of the drug product.

(ii) *Inactive ingredients.* Unless otherwise stated in paragraphs (a)(9)(iii) through (a)(9)(v) of this section, an applicant shall identify and characterize the inactive ingredients in the proposed drug product and provide information demonstrating that such inactive ingredients do not affect the safety or efficacy of the proposed drug product.

(iii) *Inactive ingredient changes permitted in drug products intended for parenteral use.* Generally, a drug product intended for parenteral use shall contain the same inactive ingredients and in the same concentration as the reference listed drug identified by the applicant under paragraph (a)(3) of this section. However, an applicant may seek approval of a drug product that differs from the reference listed drug in preservative, buffer, or antioxidant provided that the applicant identifies and characterizes the differences and provides information demonstrating that the differences do not affect the safety or efficacy of the proposed drug product.

(iv) *Inactive ingredient changes permitted in drug products intended for ophthalmic or otic use.* Generally, a drug product intended for ophthalmic or otic use shall contain the same inactive ingredients and in the same concentration as the reference listed drug identified by the applicant under paragraph (a)(3) of this section. However, an applicant may seek approval of a drug product that differs from the reference listed drug in preservative, buffer, substance to adjust tonicity, or thickening agent provided that the applicant identifies and characterizes the differences and provides information demonstrating that the differences do not affect the safety or efficacy of the proposed drug product, except that, in a product intended for ophthalmic use, an applicant may not change a buffer or substance to adjust tonicity for the purpose of claiming a therapeutic advantage over or difference from the listed drug, e.g., by using a balanced salt solution as a diluent as opposed to an isotonic saline solution, or by making a significant change in the pH or other change that may raise questions of irritability.

(v) *Inactive ingredient changes permitted in drug products intended for topical use.* Generally, a drug product intended for topical use, solutions for aerosolization or nebulization, and nasal solutions shall contain the same inactive ingredients as the reference listed drug identified by the applicant under paragraph (a)(3) of this section. However, an abbreviated application may include different inactive ingredients provided that the applicant identifies and characterizes the differences and provides information demonstrating that the differences do not affect the safety or efficacy of the proposed drug product.

(10) *Samples.* The information required under § 314.50(e)(1) and (e)(2)(i). Samples need not be submitted until requested by FDA.

(11) *Other.* The information required under § 314.50(g).

(12) *Patent certification—*(i) *Patents claiming drug, drug product, or method of use.* (A) Except as provided in paragraph (a)(12)(iv) of this section, a certification with respect to each patent issued by the United States Patent and

137

Trademark Office that, in the opinion of the applicant and to the best of its knowledge, claims the reference listed drug or that claims a use of such listed drug for which the applicant is seeking approval under section 505(j) of the act and for which information is required to be filed under section 505(b) and (c) of the act and § 314.53. For each such patent, the applicant shall provide the patent number and certify, in its opinion and to the best of its knowledge, one of the following circumstances:

(1) That the patent information has not been submitted to FDA. The applicant shall entitle such a certification "Paragraph I Certification";

(2) That the patent has expired. The applicant shall entitle such a certification "Paragraph II Certification";

(3) The date on which the patent will expire. The applicant shall entitle such a certification "Paragraph III Certification"; or

(4) That the patent is invalid, unenforceable, or will not be infringed by the manufacture, use, or sale of the drug product for which the abbreviated application is submitted. The applicant shall entitle such a certification "Paragraph IV Certification". This certification shall be submitted in the following form:

I, (name of applicant), certify that Patent No. _____ (is invalid, unenforceable, or will not be infringed by the manufacture, use, or sale of) (name of proposed drug product) for which this application is submitted.

The certification shall be accompanied by a statement that the applicant will comply with the requirements under § 314.95(a) with respect to providing a notice to each owner of the patent or their representatives and to the holder of the approved application for the listed drug, and with the requirements under § 314.95(c) with respect to the content of the notice.

(B) If the abbreviated new drug application refers to a listed drug that is itself a licensed generic product of a patented drug first approved under section 505(b) of the act, the appropriate patent certification under paragraph (a)(12)(i) of this section with respect to each patent that claims the first-approved patented drug or that claims a use for such drug.

(ii) No relevant patents. If, in the opinion of the applicant and to the best of its knowledge, there are no patents described in paragraph (a)(12)(i) of this section, a certification in the following form:

In the opinion and to the best knowledge of (name of applicant), there are no patents that claim the listed drug referred to in this application or that claim a use of the listed drug.

(iii) Method of use patent. (A) If patent information is submitted under section 505(b) or (c) of the act and § 314.53 for a patent claiming a method of using the listed drug, and the labeling for the drug product for which the applicant is seeking approval does not include any indications that are covered by the use patent, a statement explaining that the method of use patent does not claim any of the proposed indications.

(B) If the labeling of the drug product for which the applicant is seeking approval includes an indication that, according to the patent information submitted under section 505(b) or (c) of the act and § 314.53 or in the opinion of the applicant, is claimed by a use patent, an applicable certification under paragraph (a)(12)(i) of this section.

(iv) Method of manufacturing patent. An applicant is not required to make a certification with respect to any patent that claims only a method of manufacturing the listed drug.

(v) Licensing agreements. If the abbreviated new drug application is for a drug or method of using a drug claimed by a patent and the applicant has a licensing agreement with the patent owner, a certification under paragraph (a)(12)(i)(A)(4) of this section ("Paragraph IV Certification") as to that patent and a statement that it has been granted a patent license.

(vi) Late submission of patent information. If a patent on the listed drug is issued and the holder of the approved application for the listed drug does not submit the required information on the patent within 30 days of issuance of the patent, an applicant who submitted an abbreviated new drug application for that drug that contained an appropriate patent certification before the submission of the patent information is not required to submit an amended certification. An applicant whose abbreviated new drug application is submitted after a late submission of patent information, or whose pending abbreviated application was previously submitted but did not contain an appropriate patent certification at the time of the patent submission, shall submit a certification under paragraph (a)(12)(i) of this section or a statement under paragraph (a)(12)(iii) of this section as to that patent.

(vii) *Disputed patent information.* If an applicant disputes the accuracy or relevance of patent information submitted to FDA, the applicant may seek a confirmation of the correctness of the patent information in accordance with the procedures under §314.53(f). Unless the patent information is withdrawn or changed, the applicant shall submit an appropriate certification for each relevant patent.

(viii) *Amended certifications.* A certification submitted under paragraphs (a)(12)(i) through (a)(12)(iii) of this section may be amended at any time before the effective date of the approval of the application. However, an applicant who has submitted a paragraph IV patent certification may not change it to a paragraph III certification if a patent infringement suit has been filed against another paragraph IV applicant unless the agency has determined that no applicant is entitled to 180-day exclusivity or the patent expires before the lawsuit is resolved or expires after the suit is resolved but before the end of the 180-day exclusivity period. If an applicant with a pending application voluntarily makes a patent certification for an untimely filed patent, the applicant may withdraw the patent certification for the untimely filed patent. An applicant shall submit an amended certification by letter or as an amendment to a pending application or by letter to an approved application. Once an amendment or letter is submitted, the application will no longer be considered to contain the prior certification.

(A) *After finding of infringement.* An applicant who has submitted a certification under paragraph (a)(12)(i)(A)(*4*) of this section and is sued for patent infringement within 45 days of the receipt of notice sent under §314.95 shall amend the certification if a final judgment in the action against the applicant is entered finding the patent to be infringed. In the amended certification, the applicant shall certify under paragraph (a)(12)(i)(A)(*3*) of this section that the patent will expire on a specific date. Once an amendment or letter for the change has been submitted, the application will no longer be considered to be one containing a certification under paragraph (a)(12)(i)(A)(*4*) of this section. If a final judgment finds the patent to be invalid and infringed, an amended certification is not required.

(B) *After removal of a patent from the list.* If a patent is removed from the list, any applicant with a pending application (including a tentatively approved application with a delayed effective date) who has made a certification with respect to such patent shall amend its certification. The applicant shall certify under paragraph (a)(12)(ii) of this section that no patents described in paragraph (a)(12)(i) of this section claim the drug or, if other relevant patents claim the drug, shall amend the certification to refer only to those relevant patents. In the amendment, the applicant shall state the reason for the change in certification (that the patent is or has been removed from the list). A patent that is the subject of a lawsuit under §314.107(c) shall not be removed from the list until FDA determines either that no delay in effective dates of approval is required under that section as a result of the lawsuit, that the patent has expired, or that any such period of delay in effective dates of approval is ended. An applicant shall submit an amended certification. Once an amendment or letter for the change has been submitted, the application will no longer be considered to be one containing a certification under paragraph (a)(12)(i)(A)(4) of this section.

(C) *Other amendments.* (*1*) Except as provided in paragraphs (a)(12)(vi) and (a)(12)(viii)(C)(*2*) of this section, an applicant shall amend a submitted certification if, at any time before the effective date of the approval of the application, the applicant learns that the submitted certification is no longer accurate.

(2) An applicant is not required to amend a submitted certification when information on a patent on the listed drug is submitted after the effective date of approval of the abbreviated application.

(13) *Financial certification or disclosure statement.* An abbreviated application shall contain a financial certification or disclosure statement as required by part 54 of this chapter.

(b) *Drug products subject to the Drug Efficacy Study Implementation (DESI) review.* If the abbreviated new drug application is for a duplicate of a drug product that is subject to FDA's DESI review (a review of drug products approved as safe between 1938 and 1962) or other DESI-like review and the drug product evaluated in the review is a listed drug, the applicant shall comply with the provisions of paragraph (a) of this section.

(c) [Reserved]

(d) *Format of an abbreviated application.* (1) The applicant must submit a complete archival copy of the abbreviated application as required under paragraphs (a) and (c) of this section. FDA will maintain the archival copy during the review of the application to permit individual reviewers to refer to information that is not contained in their particular technical sections of the application, to give other agency personnel access to the application for official business, and to maintain in one place a complete copy of the application.

(i) *Format of submission.* An applicant may submit portions of the archival copy of the abbreviated application in any form that the applicant and FDA agree is acceptable, except as provided in paragraph (d)(1)(ii) of this section.

(ii) *Labeling.* The content of labeling required under § 201.100(d)(3) of this chapter (commonly referred to as the package insert or professional labeling), including all text, tables, and figures, must be submitted to the agency in electronic format as described in paragraph (d)(1)(iii) of this section. This requirement applies to the content of labeling for the proposed drug product only and is in addition to the requirements of paragraph (a)(8)(ii) of this section that copies of the formatted label and all proposed labeling

be submitted. Submissions under this paragraph must be made in accordance with part 11 of this chapter, except for the requirements of § 11.10(a), (c) through (h), and (k), and the corresponding requirements of § 11.30.

(iii) *Electronic format submissions.* Electronic format submissions must be in a form that FDA can process, review, and archive. FDA will periodically issue guidance on how to provide the electronic submission (e.g., method of transmission, media, file formats, preparation and organization of files).

(2) For abbreviated new drug applications, the applicant shall submit a review copy of the abbreviated application that contains two separate sections. One section shall contain the information described under paragraphs (a)(2) through (a)(6), (a)(8), and (a)(9) of this section 505(j)(2)(A)(vii) of the act and one copy of the analytical procedures and descriptive information needed by FDA's laboratories to perform tests on samples of the proposed drug product and to validate the applicant's analytical procedures. The other section shall contain the information described under paragraphs (a)(3), (a)(7), and (a)(8) of this section. Each of the sections in the review copy is required to contain a copy of the application form described under § 314.50(a).

(3) [Reserved]

(4) The applicant may obtain from FDA sufficient folders to bind the archival, the review, and the field copies of the abbreviated application.

(5) The applicant shall submit a field copy of the abbreviated application that contains the technical section described in paragraph (a)(9) of this section, a copy of the application form required under paragraph (a)(1) of this section, and a certification that the field copy is a true copy of the technical section described in paragraph (a)(9) of this section contained in the archival and review copies of the abbreviated application.

[57 FR 17983, Apr. 28, 1992; 57 FR 29353, July 1, 1992, as amended at 58 FR 47352, Sept. 8, 1993; 59 FR 50364, Oct. 3, 1994; 63 FR 5252, Feb. 2, 1998; 63 FR 66399, Dec. 1, 1998; 64 FR 401, Jan. 5, 1999; 65 FR 56479, Sept. 19, 2000; 67 FR 77672, Dec. 19, 2002; 68 FR 69019, Dec. 11, 2003; 69 FR 18766, Apr. 8, 2004; 74 FR 2861, Jan. 16, 2009; 76 FR 13880, Mar. 15, 2011]

§ 314.95 Notice of certification of invalidity or noninfringement of a patent.

(a) *Notice of certification.* For each patent that claims the listed drug or that claims a use for such listed drug for which the applicant is seeking approval and that the applicant certifies under § 314.94(a)(12) is invalid, unenforceable, or will not be infringed, the applicant shall send notice of such certification by registered or certified mail, return receipt requested to each of the following persons:

(1) Each owner of the patent which is the subject of the certification or the representative designated by the owner to receive the notice. The name and address of the patent owner or its representative may be obtained from the United States Patent and Trademark Office; and

(2) The holder of the approved application under section 505(b) of the act for the listed drug that is claimed by the patent and for which the applicant is seeking approval, or, if the application holder does not reside or maintain a place of business within the United States, the application holder's attorney, agent, or other authorized official. The name and address of the application holder or its attorney, agent, or authorized official may be obtained from the Orange Book Staff, Office of Generic Drugs, 7500 Standish Pl., Rockville, MD 20855.

(3) This paragraph does not apply to a use patent that claims no uses for which the applicant is seeking approval.

(b) *Sending the notice.* The applicant shall send the notice required by paragraph (a) of this section when it receives from FDA an acknowledgment letter stating that its abbreviated new drug application is sufficiently complete to permit a substantive review. At the same time, the applicant shall amend its abbreviated new drug application to include a statement certifying that the notice has been provided to each person identified under paragraph (a) of this section and that the notice met the content requirements under paragraph (c) of this section.

(c) *Contents of a notice.* In the notice, the applicant shall cite section 505(j)(2)(B)(ii) of the act and shall include, but not be limited to, the following information:

(1) A statement that FDA has received an abbreviated new drug application submitted by the applicant containing any required bioavailability or bioequivalence data or information.

(2) The abbreviated application number.

(3) The established name, if any, as defined in section 502(e)(3) of the act, of the proposed drug product.

(4) The active ingredient, strength, and dosage form of the proposed drug product.

(5) The patent number and expiration date, as submitted to the agency or as known to the applicant, of each patent alleged to be invalid, unenforceable, or not infringed.

(6) A detailed statement of the factual and legal basis of the applicant's opinion that the patent is not valid, unenforceable, or will not be infringed. The applicant shall include in the detailed statement:

(i) For each claim of a patent alleged not to be infringed, a full and detailed explanation of why the claim is not infringed.

(ii) For each claim of a patent alleged to be invalid or unenforceable, a full and detailed explanation of the grounds supporting the allegation.

(7) If the applicant does not reside or have a place of business in the United States, the name and address of an agent in the United States authorized to accept service of process for the applicant.

(d) *Amendment to an abbreviated application.* If an abbreviated application is amended to include the certification described in § 314.94(a)(12)(i)(A)(4), the applicant shall send the notice required by paragraph (a) of this section at the same time that the amendment to the abbreviated application is submitted to FDA.

(e) *Documentation of receipt of notice.* The applicant shall amend its abbreviated application to document receipt of the notice required under paragraph (a) of this section by each person provided the notice. The applicant shall include a copy of the return receipt or other similar evidence of the date the notification was received. FDA will accept as adequate documentation of the

141

date of receipt a return receipt or a letter acknowledging receipt by the person provided the notice. An applicant may rely on another form of documentation only if FDA has agreed to such documentation in advance. A copy of the notice itself need not be submitted to the agency.

(f) *Approval.* If the requirements of this section are met, FDA will presume the notice to be complete and sufficient, and it will count the day following the date of receipt of the notice by the patent owner or its representative and by the approved application holder as the first day of the 45-day period provided for in section 505(j)(4)(B)(iii) of the act. FDA may, if the applicant provides a written statement to FDA that a later date should be used, count from such later date.

[59 FR 50366, Oct. 3, 1994, as amended at 68 FR 36705, June 18, 2003; 69 FR 11310, Mar. 10, 2004; 74 FR 9766, Mar. 6, 2009; 74 FR 36605, July 24, 2009]

§ 314.96 Amendments to an unapproved abbreviated application.

(a) *Abbreviated new drug application.* (1) An applicant may amend an abbreviated new drug application that is submitted under § 314.94, but not yet approved, to revise existing information or provide additional information. Amendments containing bioequivalence studies must contain reports of all bioequivalence studies conducted by the applicant on the same drug product formulation, unless the information has previously been submitted to FDA in the abbreviated new drug application. A complete study report must be submitted for any bioequivalence study upon which the applicant relies for approval. For all other bioequivalence studies conducted on the same drug product formulation as defined in § 320.1(g) of this chapter, the applicant must submit either a complete or summary report. If a summary report of a bioequivalence study is submitted and FDA determines that there may be bioequivalence issues or concerns with the product, FDA may require that the applicant submit a complete report of the bioequivalence study to FDA.

(2) Submission of an amendment containing significant data or information before the end of the initial review cycle constitutes an agreement between FDA and the applicant to extend the initial review cycle only for the time necessary to review the significant data or information and for no more than 180 days.

(b) The applicant shall submit a field copy of each amendment to § 314.94(a)(9). The applicant, other than a foreign applicant, shall include in its submission of each such amendment to FDA a statement certifying that a field copy of the amendment has been sent to the applicant's home FDA district office.

[57 FR 17983, Apr. 28, 1992, as amended at 58 FR 47352, Sept. 8, 1993; 64 FR 401, Jan. 5, 1999; 73 FR 39609, July 10, 2008; 74 FR 2861, Jan. 16, 2009]

§ 314.97 Supplements and other changes to an approved abbreviated application.

The applicant shall comply with the requirements of §§ 314.70 and 314.71 regarding the submission of supplemental applications and other changes to an approved abbreviated application.

§ 314.98 Postmarketing reports.

(a) Except as provided in paragraph (b) of this section, each applicant having an approved abbreviated new drug application under § 314.94 that is effective shall comply with the requirements of § 314.80 regarding the reporting and recordkeeping of adverse drug experiences.

(b) Each applicant shall submit one copy of each report required under § 314.80 to the Central Document Room, Center for Drug Evaluation and Research, Food and Drug Administration, 5901–B Ammendale Rd., Beltsville, MD 20705–1266.

(c) Each applicant shall make the reports required under § 314.81 and section 505(k) of the act for each of its approved abbreviated applications.

[57 FR 17983, Apr. 28, 1992, as amended at 64 FR 401, Jan. 5, 1999; 74 FR 13113, Mar. 26, 2009]

EFFECTIVE DATE NOTE: At 79 FR 33089, June 10, 2014, § 314.98 was revised, effective June 10, 2015. For the convenience of the user, the revised text is set forth as follows:

§314.98 Postmarketing reports.

(a) Each applicant having an approved abbreviated new drug application under §314.94 that is effective must comply with the requirements of §314.80 regarding the reporting and recordkeeping of adverse drug experiences.

(b) Each applicant must make the reports required under §314.81 and section 505(k) of the Federal Food, Drug, and Cosmetic Act for each of its approved abbreviated applications.

§314.99 Other responsibilities of an applicant of an abbreviated application.

(a) An applicant shall comply with the requirements of §314.65 regarding withdrawal by the applicant of an unapproved abbreviated application and §314.72 regarding a change in ownership of an abbreviated application.

(b) An applicant may ask FDA to waive under this section any requirement that applies to the applicant under §§314.92 through 314.99. The applicant shall comply with the requirements for a waiver under §314.90.

Subpart D—FDA Action on Applications and Abbreviated Applications

SOURCE: 50 FR 7493, Feb. 22, 1985, unless otherwise noted. Redesignated at 57 FR 17983, Apr. 28, 1992.

§314.100 Timeframes for reviewing applications and abbreviated applications.

(a) Except as provided in paragraph (c) of this section, within 180 days of receipt of an application for a new drug under section 505(b) of the act or an abbreviated application for a new drug under section 505(j) of the act, FDA will review it and send the applicant either an approval letter under §314.105 or a complete response letter under §314.110. This 180-day period is called the "initial review cycle."

(b) At any time before approval, an applicant may withdraw an application under §314.65 or an abbreviated application under §314.99 and later submit it again for consideration.

(c) The initial review cycle may be adjusted by mutual agreement between FDA and an applicant or as provided in §§314.60 and 314.96, as the result of a major amendment.

[73 FR 39609, July 10, 2008]

§314.101 Filing an application and receiving an abbreviated new drug application.

(a)(1) Within 60 days after FDA receives an application, the agency will determine whether the application may be filed. The filing of an application means that FDA has made a threshold determination that the application is sufficiently complete to permit a substantive review.

(2) If FDA finds that none of the reasons in paragraphs (d) and (e) of this section for refusing to file the application apply, the agency will file the application and notify the applicant in writing. The date of filing will be the date 60 days after the date FDA received the application. The date of filing begins the 180-day period described in section 505(c) of the act. This 180-day period is called the "filing clock."

(3) If FDA refuses to file the application, the agency will notify the applicant in writing and state the reason under paragraph (d) or (e) of this section for the refusal. If FDA refuses to file the application under paragraph (d) of this section, the applicant may request in writing within 30 days of the date of the agency's notification an informal conference with the agency about whether the agency should file the application. If, following the informal conference, the applicant requests that FDA file the application (with or without amendments to correct the deficiencies), the agency will file the application over protest under paragraph (a)(2) of this section, notify the applicant in writing, and review it as filed. If the application is filed over protest, the date of filing will be the date 60 days after the date the applicant requested the informal conference. The applicant need not resubmit a copy of an application that is filed over protest. If FDA refuses to file the application under paragraph (e) of this section, the applicant may amend the application and resubmit it, and the agency will make a determination under this section whether it may be filed.

(b)(1) An abbreviated new drug application will be reviewed after it is submitted to determine whether the abbreviated application may be received. Receipt of an abbreviated new drug application means that FDA has made a threshold determination that the abbreviated application is sufficiently complete to permit a substantive review.

(2) If FDA finds that none of the reasons in paragraphs (d) and (e) of this section for considering the abbreviated new drug application not to have been received applies, the agency will receive the abbreviated new drug application and notify the applicant in writing.

(3) If FDA considers the abbreviated new drug application not to have been received under paragraph (d) or (e) of this section, FDA will notify the applicant, ordinarily by telephone. The applicant may then:

(i) Withdraw the abbreviated new drug application under § 314.99; or

(ii) Amend the abbreviated new drug application to correct the deficiencies; or

(iii) Take no action, in which case FDA will refuse to receive the abbreviated new drug application.

(c) [Reserved]

(d) FDA may refuse to file an application or may not consider an abbreviated new drug application to be received if any of the following applies:

(1) The application does not contain a completed application form.

(2) The application is not submitted in the form required under § 314.50 or § 314.94.

(3) The application or abbreviated application is incomplete because it does not on its face contain information required under section 505(b), section 505(j), or section 507 of the act and § 314.50 or § 314.94.

(4) The applicant fails to submit a complete environmental assessment, which addresses each of the items specified in the applicable format under § 25.40 of this chapter or fails to provide sufficient information to establish that the requested action is subject to categorical exclusion under § 25.30 or § 25.31 of this chapter.

(5) The application or abbreviated application does not contain an accurate and complete English translation of each part of the application that is not in English.

(6) The application does not contain a statement for each nonclinical laboratory study that it was conducted in compliance with the requirements set forth in part 58 of this chapter, or, for each study not conducted in compliance with part 58 of this chapter, a brief statement of the reason for the noncompliance.

(7) The application does not contain a statement for each clinical study that it was conducted in compliance with the institutional review board regulations in part 56 of this chapter, or was not subject to those regulations, and that it was conducted in compliance with the informed consent regulations in part 50 of this chapter, or, if the study was subject to but was not conducted in compliance with those regulations, the application does not contain a brief statement of the reason for the noncompliance.

(8) The drug product that is the subject of the submission is already covered by an approved application or abbreviated application and the applicant of the submission:

(i) Has an approved application or abbreviated application for the same drug product; or

(ii) Is merely a distributor and/or repackager of the already approved drug product.

(9) The application is submitted as a 505(b)(2) application for a drug that is a duplicate of a listed drug and is eligible for approval under section 505(j) of the act.

(e) The agency will refuse to file an application or will consider an abbreviated new drug application not to have been received if any of the following applies:

(1) The drug product is subject to licensing by FDA under the Public Health Service Act (42 U.S.C. 201 *et seq.*) and subchapter F of this chapter.

(2) In the case of a 505(b)(2) application or an abbreviated new drug application, the drug product contains the same active moiety as a drug that:

(i) Was approved after September 24, 1984, in an application under section 505(b) of the act, and

(ii) Is entitled to a 5-year period of exclusivity under section 505(c)(3)(D)(ii) and (j)(4)(D)(ii) of the act and §314.108(b)(2), unless the 5-year exclusivity period has elapsed or unless 4 years of the 5-year period have elapsed and the application or abbreviated application contains a certification of patent invalidity or noninfringement described in §314.50(i)(1)(i)(A)(4) or §314.94(a)(12)(i)(A)(4).

(f)(1) Within 180 days after the date of filing, plus the period of time the review period was extended (if any), FDA will either:

(i) Approve the application; or

(ii) Issue a notice of opportunity for a hearing if the applicant asked FDA to provide it an opportunity for a hearing on an application in response to a complete response letter.

(2) Within 180 days after the date of receipt, plus the period of time the review clock was extended (if any), FDA will either approve or disapprove the abbreviated new drug application. If FDA disapproves the abbreviated new drug application, FDA will issue a notice of opportunity for hearing if the applicant asked FDA to provide it an opportunity for a hearing on an abbreviated new drug application in response to a complete response letter.

(3) This paragraph does not apply to applications or abbreviated applications that have been withdrawn from FDA review by the applicant.

[57 FR 17987, Apr. 28, 1992; 57 FR 29353, July 1, 1992, as amended at 59 FR 50366, Oct. 3, 1994; 62 FR 40599, July 29, 1997; 64 FR 402, Jan. 5, 1999; 73 FR 39609, July 10, 2008]

§314.102 Communications between FDA and applicants.

(a) *General principles.* During the course of reviewing an application or an abbreviated application, FDA shall communicate with applicants about scientific, medical, and procedural issues that arise during the review process. Such communication may take the form of telephone conversations, letters, or meetings, whichever is most appropriate to discuss the particular issue at hand. Communications shall be appropriately documented in the application in accordance with §10.65 of this chapter. Further details

on the procedures for communication between FDA and applicants are contained in a staff manual guide that is publicly available.

(b) *Notification of easily correctable deficiencies.* FDA reviewers shall make every reasonable effort to communicate promptly to applicants easily correctable deficiencies found in an application or an abbreviated application when those deficiencies are discovered, particularly deficiencies concerning chemistry, manufacturing, and controls issues. The agency will also inform applicants promptly of its need for more data or information or for technical changes in the application or the abbreviated application needed to facilitate the agency's review. This early communication is intended to permit applicants to correct such readily identified deficiencies relatively early in the review process and to submit an amendment before the review period has elapsed. Such early communication would not ordinarily apply to major scientific issues, which require consideration of the entire pending application or abbreviated application by agency managers as well as reviewing staff. Instead, major scientific issues will ordinarily be addressed in a complete response letter.

(c) *Ninety-day conference.* Approximately 90 days after the agency receives the application, FDA will provide applicants with an opportunity to meet with agency reviewing officials. The purpose of the meeting will be to inform applicants of the general progress and status of their applications, and to advise applicants of deficiencies that have been identified by that time and that have not already been communicated. This meeting will be available on applications for all new chemical entities and major new indications of marketed drugs. Such meetings will be held at the applicant's option, and may be held by telephone if mutually agreed upon. Such meetings would not ordinarily be held on abbreviated applications because they are not submitted for new chemical entities or new indications.

(d) *End-of-review conference.* At the conclusion of FDA's review of an NDA as designated by the issuance of a complete response letter, FDA will provide the applicant with an opportunity to meet with agency reviewing officials. The purpose of the meeting will be to discuss what further steps need to be taken by the applicant before the application can be approved. Requests for such meetings must be directed to the director of the division responsible for reviewing the application.

(e) *Other meetings.* Other meetings between FDA and applicants may be held, with advance notice, to discuss scientific, medical, and other issues that arise during the review process. Requests for meetings shall be directed to the director of the division responsible for reviewing the application or abbreviated application. FDA will make every attempt to grant requests for meetings that involve important issues and that can be scheduled at mutually convenient times. However, "drop-in" visits (*i.e.*, an unannounced and unscheduled visit by a company representative) are discouraged except for urgent matters, such as to discuss an important new safety issue.

[57 FR 17988, Apr. 28, 1992; 57 FR 29353, July 1, 1992, as amended at 73 FR 39609, July 10, 2008]

§ 314.103   Dispute resolution.

(a) *General.* FDA is committed to resolving differences between applicants and FDA reviewing divisions with respect to technical requirements for applications or abbreviated applications as quickly and amicably as possible through the cooperative exchange of information and views.

(b) *Administrative and procedural issues.* When administrative or procedural disputes arise, the applicant should first attempt to resolve the matter with the division responsible for reviewing the application or abbreviated application, beginning with the consumer safety officer assigned to the application or abbreviated application. If resolution is not achieved, the applicant may raise the matter with the person designated as ombudsman, whose function shall be to investigate what has happened and to facilitate a timely and equitable resolution. Appropriate issues to raise with the ombudsman include resolving difficulties in scheduling meetings, obtaining timely replies to inquiries, and obtaining timely completion of pending reviews. Further details on this procedure are contained in a staff manual guide that is publicly available under FDA's public information regulations in part 20.

(c) *Scientific and medical disputes.* (1) Because major scientific issues are ordinarily communicated to applicants in a complete response letter pursuant to § 314.110, the "end-of-review conference" described in § 314.102(d) will provide a timely forum for discussing and resolving, if possible, scientific and medical issues on which the applicant disagrees with the agency. In addition, the "ninety-day conference" described in § 314.102(c) will provide a timely forum for discussing and resolving, if possible, issues identified by that date.

(2) When scientific or medical disputes arise at other times during the review process, applicants should discuss the matter directly with the responsible reviewing officials. If necessary, applicants may request a meeting with the appropriate reviewing officials and management representatives in order to seek a resolution. Ordinarily, such meetings would be held first with the Division Director, then with the Office Director, and finally with the Center Director if the matter is still unresolved. Requests for such meetings shall be directed to the director of the division responsible for reviewing the application or abrreviated application. FDA will make every attempt to grant requests for meetings that involve important issues and that can be scheduled at mutually convenient times.

(3) In requesting a meeting designed to resolve a scientific or medical dispute, applicants may suggest that FDA seek the advice of outside experts, in which case FDA may, in its discretion, invite to the meeting one or more of its advisory committee members or other consultants, as designated by the agency. Applicants may also bring their own consultants. For major scientific and medical policy issues not resolved by informal meetings, FDA may refer the matter to one of its standing advisory committees for its consideration and recommendations.

[50 FR 7493, Feb. 22, 1985; 50 FR 14212, Apr. 11, 1985, as amended at 57 FR 17989, Apr. 28, 1992; 73 FR 39609, July 10, 2008]

§314.104 Drugs with potential for abuse.

The Food and Drug Administration will inform the Drug Enforcement Administration under section 201(f) of the Controlled Substances Act (21 U.S.C. 801) when an application or abbreviated application is submitted for a drug that appears to have an abuse potential.

[57 FR 17989, Apr. 28, 1992]

§314.105 Approval of an application and an abbreviated application.

(a) The Food and Drug Administration will approve an application and send the applicant an approval letter if none of the reasons in §314.125 for refusing to approve the application applies. An approval becomes effective on the date of the issuance of the approval letter, except with regard to an approval under section 505(b)(2) of the act with a delayed effective date. An approval with a delayed effective date is tentative and does not become final until the effective date. A new drug product or antibiotic approved under this paragraph may not be marketed until an approval is effective.

(b) FDA will approve an application and issue the applicant an approval letter on the basis of draft labeling if the only deficiencies in the application concern editorial or similar minor deficiencies in the draft labeling. Such approval will be conditioned upon the applicant incorporating the specified labeling changes exactly as directed, and upon the applicant submitting to FDA a copy of the final printed labeling prior to marketing.

(c) FDA will approve an application after it determines that the drug meets the statutory standards for safety and effectiveness, manufacturing and controls, and labeling, and an abbreviated application after it determines that the drug meets the statutory standards for manufacturing and controls, labeling, and, where applicable, bioequivalence. While the statutory standards apply to all drugs, the many kinds of drugs that are subject to the statutory standards and the wide range of uses for those drugs demand flexibility in applying the standards. Thus FDA is required to exercise its scientific judgment to determine the kind and quantity of data and information an applicant is required to provide for a particular drug to meet the statutory standards. FDA makes its views on drug products and classes of drugs available through guidance documents, recommendations, and other statements of policy.

(d) FDA will approve an abbreviated new drug application and send the applicant an approval letter if none of the reasons in §314.127 for refusing to approve the abbreviated new drug application applies. The approval becomes effective on the date of the issuance of the agency's approval letter unless the approval letter provides for a delayed effective date. An approval with a delayed effective date is tentative and does not become final until the effective date. A new drug product approved under this paragraph may not be introduced or delivered for introduction into interstate commerce until approval of the abbreviated new drug application is effective. Ordinarily, the effective date of approval will be stated in the approval letter.

[57 FR 17989, Apr. 28, 1992, as amended at 64 FR 402, Jan. 5, 1999; 65 FR 56479, Sept. 19, 2000; 73 FR 39609, July 10, 2008]

§314.106 Foreign data.

(a) *General.* The acceptance of foreign data in an application generally is governed by §312.120 of this chapter.

(b) *As sole basis for marketing approval.* An application based solely on foreign clinical data meeting U.S. criteria for marketing approval may be approved if: (1) The foreign data are applicable to the U.S. population and U.S. medical practice; (2) the studies have been performed by clinical investigators of recognized competence; and (3) the data may be considered valid without the need for an on-site inspection by FDA or, if FDA considers such an inspection to be necessary, FDA is able to validate the data through an on-site inspection or other appropriate means. Failure of an application to meet any of these criteria will result in the application not being approvable based on the foreign data alone. FDA will apply this policy in a flexible manner according to the nature of the drug and the data being considered.

(c) *Consultation between FDA and applicants.* Applicants are encouraged to meet with agency officials in a "presubmission" meeting when approval based solely on foreign data will be sought.

[50 FR 7493, Feb. 22, 1985, as amended at 55 FR 11580, Mar. 29, 1990]

§ 314.107 Effective date of approval of a 505(b)(2) application or abbreviated new drug application under section 505(j) of the act.

(a) *General.* A drug product may be introduced or delivered for introduction into interstate commerce when approval of the application or abbreviated application for the drug product becomes effective. Except as provided in this section, approval of an application or abbreviated application for a drug product becomes effective on the date FDA issues an approval letter under § 314.105 for the application or abbreviated application.

(b) *Effect of patent on the listed drug.* If approval of an abbreviated new drug application submitted under section 505(j) of the act or of a 505(b)(2) application is granted, that approval will become effective in accordance with the following:

(1) *Date of approval letter.* Except as provided in paragraphs (b)(3), (b)(4), and (c) of this section, approval will become effective on the date FDA issues an approval letter under § 314.105 if the applicant certifies under § 314.50(i) or § 314.94(a)(12) that:

(i) There are no relevant patents; or

(ii) The applicant is aware of a relevant patent but the patent information required under section 505 (b) or (c) of the act has not been submitted to FDA; or

(iii) The relevant patent has expired; or

(iv) The relevant patent is invalid, unenforceable, or will not be infringed.

(2) *Patent expiration.* If the applicant certifies under § 314.50(i) or § 314.94(a)(12) that the relevant patent will expire on a specified date, approval will become effective on the specified date.

(3) *Disposition of patent litigation.* (i)(A) Except as provided in paragraphs (b)(3)(ii), (b)(3)(iii), and (b)(3)(iv) of this section, if the applicant certifies under § 314.50(i) or § 314.94(a)(12) that the relevant patent is invalid, unenforceable, or will not be infringed, and the patent owner or its representative or the exclusive patent licensee brings suit for patent infringement within 45 days of receipt by the patent owner of the notice of certification from the applicant under § 314.52 or § 314.95, approval may be made effective 30 months after the date of the receipt of the notice of certification by the patent owner or by the exclusive licensee (or their representatives) unless the court has extended or reduced the period because of a failure of either the plaintiff or defendant to cooperate reasonably in expediting the action; or

(B) If the patented drug product qualifies for 5 years of exclusive marketing under § 314.108(b)(2) and the patent owner or its representative or the exclusive patent licensee brings suit for patent infringement during the 1-year period beginning 4 years after the date the patented drug was approved and within 45 days of receipt by the patent owner of the notice of certification, the approval may be made effective at the expiration of the 7½ years from the date of approval of the application for the patented drug product.

(ii) If before the expiration of the 30-month period, or 7½ years where applicable, the court issues a final order that the patent is invalid, unenforceable, or not infringed, approval may be made effective on the date the court enters judgment;

(iii) If before the expiration of the 30-month period, or 7½ years where applicable, the court issues a final order or judgment that the patent has been infringed, approval may be made effective on the date the court determines that the patent will expire or otherwise orders; or

(iv) If before the expiration of the 30-month period, or 7½ years where applicable, the court grants a preliminary injunction prohibiting the applicant from engaging in the commercial manufacture or sale of the drug product until the court decides the issues of patent validity and infringement, and if the court later decides that the patent is invalid, unenforceable, or not infringed, approval may be made effective on the date the court enters a final order or judgment that the patent is invalid, unenforceable, or not infringed.

(v) FDA will issue a tentative approval letter when tentative approval is appropriate in accordance with paragraph (b)(3) of this section. In order for an approval to be made effective under paragraph (b)(3) of this section, the applicant must receive an approval letter from the agency indicating that the application has received final approval. Tentative approval of an application does not constitute "approval" of an application and cannot, absent a final approval letter from the agency, result in an effective approval under paragraph (b)(3) of this section.

(4) *Multiple certifications.* If the applicant has submitted certifications under §314.50(i) or §314.94(a)(12) for more than one patent, the date of approval will be calculated for each certification, and the approval will become effective on the last applicable date.

(c) *Subsequent abbreviated new drug application submission.* (1) If an abbreviated new drug application contains a certification that a relevant patent is invalid, unenforceable, or will not be infringed and the application is for a generic copy of the same listed drug for which one or more substantially complete abbreviated new drug applications were previously submitted containing a certification that the same patent was invalid, unenforceable, or would not be infringed, approval of the subsequent abbreviated new drug application will be made effective no sooner than 180 days from whichever of the following dates is earlier:

(i) The date the applicant submitting the first application first commences commercial marketing of its drug product; or

(ii) The date of a decision of the court holding the relevant patent invalid, unenforceable, or not infringed.

(2) For purposes of paragraph (c)(1) of this section, the "applicant submitting the first application" is the applicant that submits an application that is both substantially complete and contains a certification that the patent was invalid, unenforceable, or not infringed prior to the submission of any other application for the same listed drug that is both substantially complete and contains the same certification. A "substantially complete" application must contain the results of any required bioequivalence studies, or, if applicable, a request for a waiver of such studies.

(3) For purposes of paragraph (c)(1) of this section, if FDA concludes that the applicant submitting the first application is not actively pursuing approval of its abbreviated application, FDA will make the approval of subsequent abbreviated applications immediately effective if they are otherwise eligible for an immediately effective approval.

(4) For purposes of paragraph (c)(1)(i) of this section, the applicant submitting the first application shall notify FDA of the date that it commences commercial marketing of its drug product. Commercial marketing commences with the first date of introduction or delivery for introduction into interstate commerce outside the control of the manufacturer of a drug product, except for investigational use under part 312 of this chapter, but does not include transfer of the drug product for reasons other than sale within the control of the manufacturer or application holder. If an applicant does not promptly notify FDA of such date, the effective date of approval shall be deemed to be the date of the commencement of first commercial marketing.

(d) *Delay due to exclusivity.* The agency will also delay the effective date of the approval of an abbreviated new drug application under section 505(j) of the act or a 505(b)(2) application if delay is required by the exclusivity provisions in §314.108. When the effective date of an application is delayed under both this section and §314.108, the effective date will be the later of the 2 days specified under this section and §314.108.

(e) *Notification of court actions.* The applicant shall submit a copy of the entry of the order or judgment to the Office of Generic Drugs (HFD–600), or to the appropriate division in the Office of New Drugs within 10 working days of a final judgment.

149

(f) *Computation of 45-day time clock.* (1) The 45-day clock described in paragraph (b)(3) of this section begins on the day after the date of receipt of the applicant's notice of certification by the patent owner or its representative, and by the approved application holder. When the 45th day falls on Saturday, Sunday, or a Federal holiday, the 45th day will be the next day that is not a Saturday, Sunday, or a Federal holiday.

(2) The abbreviated new drug applicant or the 505(b)(2) applicant shall notify FDA immediately of the filing of any legal action filed within 45 days of receipt of the notice of certification. If the applicant submitting the abbreviated new drug application or the 505(b)(2) application or patent owner or its representative does not notify FDA in writing before the expiration of the 45-day time period or the completion of the agency's review of the application, whichever occurs later, that a legal action for patent infringement was filed within 45 days of receipt of the notice of certification, approval of the abbreviated new drug application or the 505(b)(2) application will be made effective immediately upon expiration of the 45 days or upon completion of the agency's review and approval of the application, whichever is later. The notification to FDA of the legal action shall include:

(i) The abbreviated new drug application or 505(b)(2) application number.

(ii) The name of the abbreviated new drug or 505(b)(2) application applicant.

(iii) The established name of the drug product or, if no established name exists, the name(s) of the active ingredient(s), the drug product's strength, and dosage form.

(iv) A certification that an action for patent infringement identified by number, has been filed in an appropriate court on a specified date.

The applicant of an abbreviated new drug application shall send the notification to FDA's Office of Generic Drugs (HFD–600). A 505(b)(2) applicant shall send the notification to the appropriate division in the Office of New Drugs reviewing the application. A patent owner or its representative may also notify FDA of the filing of any legal action for patent infringement.

The notice should contain the information and be sent to the offices or divisions described in this paragraph.

(3) If the patent owner or approved application holder who is an exclusive patent licensee waives its opportunity to file a legal action for patent infringement within 45 days of a receipt of the notice of certification and the patent owner or approved application holder who is an exclusive patent licensee submits to FDA a valid waiver before the 45 days elapse, approval of the abbreviated new drug application or the 505(b)(2) application will be made effective upon completion of the agency's review and approval of the application. FDA will only accept a waiver in the following form:

(*Name of patent owner or exclusive patent licensee*) has received notice from (*name of applicant*) under (*section 505(b)(3) or 505(j)(2)(B) of the act*) and does not intend to file an action for patent infringement against (*name of applicant*) concerning the drug (*name of drug*) before (*date on which 45 days elapses. (Name of patent owner or exclusive patent licensee*) waives the opportunity provided by (*section 505(c)(3)(C) or 505(j)(B)(iii) of the act*) and does not object to FDA's approval of (*name of applicant*)'s (*505(b)(2) or abbreviated new drug application*) for (*name of drug*) with an immediate effective date on or after the date of this letter.

[59 FR 50367, Oct. 3, 1994, as amended at 63 FR 59712, Nov. 5, 1998; 65 FR 43235, July 13, 2000; 73 FR 39609, July 10, 2008; 74 FR 9766, Mar. 6, 2009]

§ 314.108 New drug product exclusivity.

(a) *Definitions.* The following definitions of terms apply to this section:

Active moiety means the molecule or ion, excluding those appended portions of the molecule that cause the drug to be an ester, salt (including a salt with hydrogen or coordination bonds), or other noncovalent derivative (such as a complex, chelate, or clathrate) of the molecule, responsible for the physiological or pharmacological action of the drug substance.

Approved under section 505(b) means an application submitted under section 505(b) and approved on or after October 10, 1962, or an application that was "deemed approved" under section 107(c)(2) of Pub. L. 87–781.

Clinical investigation means any experiment other than a bioavailability study in which a drug is administered or dispensed to, or used on, human subjects.

Conducted or sponsored by the applicant with regard to an investigation means that before or during the investigation, the applicant was named in Form FDA-1571 filed with FDA as the sponsor of the investigational new drug application under which the investigation was conducted, or the applicant or the applicant's predecessor in interest, provided substantial support for the investigation. To demonstrate "substantial support," an applicant must either provide a certified statement from a certified public accountant that the applicant provided 50 percent or more of the cost of conducting the study or provide an explanation why FDA should consider the applicant to have conducted or sponsored the study if the applicant's financial contribution to the study is less than 50 percent or the applicant did not sponsor the investigational new drug. A predecessor in interest is an entity, e.g., a corporation, that the applicant has taken over, merged with, or purchased, or from which the applicant has purchased all rights to the drug. Purchase of non-exclusive rights to a clinical investigation after it is completed is not sufficient to satisfy this definition.

Date of approval means the date on the letter from FDA stating that the new drug application is approved, whether or not final printed labeling or other materials must yet be submitted as long as approval of such labeling or materials is not expressly required. "Date of approval" refers only to a final approval and not to a tentative approval that may become effective at a later date.

Essential to approval means, with regard to an investigation, that there are no other data available that could support approval of the application.

FDA means the Food and Drug Administration.

New chemical entity means a drug that contains no active moiety that has been approved by FDA in any other application submitted under section 505(b) of the act.

New clinical investigation means an investigation in humans the results of which have not been relied on by FDA to demonstrate substantial evidence of effectiveness of a previously approved drug product for any indication or of safety for a new patient population and do not duplicate the results of another investigation that was relied on by the agency to demonstrate the effectiveness or safety in a new patient population of a previously approved drug product. For purposes of this section, data from a clinical investigation previously submitted for use in the comprehensive evaluation of the safety of a drug product but not to support the effectiveness of the drug product would be considered new.

(b) *Submission of and effective date of approval of an abbreviated new drug application submitted under section 505(j) of the act or a 505(b)(2) application.* (1) [Reserved]

(2) If a drug product that contains a new chemical entity was approved after September 24, 1984, in an application submitted under section 505(b) of the act, no person may submit a 505(b)(2) application or abbreviated new drug application under section 505(j) of the act for a drug product that contains the same active moiety as in the new chemical entity for a period of 5 years from the date of approval of the first approved new drug application, except that the 505(b)(2) application or abbreviated application may be submitted after 4 years if it contains a certification of patent invalidity or non-infringement described in §314.50(i)(1)(i)(A)(*4*) or §314.94(a)(12)(i)(A)(*4*).

(3) The approval of a 505(b)(2) application or abbreviated application described in paragraph (b)(2) of this section will become effective as provided in §314.107(b)(1) or (b)(2), unless the owner of a patent that claims the drug, the patent owner's representative, or exclusive licensee brings suit for patent infringement against the applicant during the 1-year period beginning 48 months after the date of approval of the new drug application for the new chemical entity and within 45 days after receipt of the notice described at §314.52 or §314.95, in which case, approval of the 505(b)(2) application or

abbreviated application will be made effective as provided in §314.107(b)(3).

(4) If an application:

(i) Was submitted under section 505(b) of the act;

(ii) Was approved after September 24, 1984;

(iii) Was for a drug product that contains an active moiety that has been previously approved in another application under section 505(b) of the act; and

(iv) Contained reports of new clinical investigations (other than bioavailability studies) conducted or sponsored by the applicant that were essential to approval of the application, the agency will not make effective for a period of 3 years after the date of approval of the application the approval of a 505(b)(2) application or an abbreviated new drug application for the conditions of approval of the original application, or an abbreviated new drug application submitted pursuant to an approved petition under section 505(j)(2)(C) of the act that relies on the information supporting the conditions of approval of an original new drug application.

(5) If a supplemental application:

(i) Was approved after September 24, 1984; and

(ii) Contained reports of new clinical investigations (other than bioavailability studies) that were conducted or sponsored by the applicant that were essential to approval of the supplemental application, the agency will not make effective for a period of 3 years after the date of approval of the supplemental application the approval of a 505(b)(2) application or an abbreviated new drug application for a change, or an abbreviated new drug application submitted pursuant to an approved petition under section 505(j)(2)(C) of the act that relies on the information supporting a change approved in the supplemental new drug application.

[59 FR 50368, Oct. 3, 1994]

§314.110 Complete response letter to the applicant.

(a) *Complete response letter.* FDA will send the applicant a complete response letter if the agency determines that we will not approve the application or ab-breviated application in its present form for one or more of the reasons given in §314.125 or §314.127, respectively.

(1) *Description of specific deficiencies.* A complete response letter will describe all of the specific deficiencies that the agency has identified in an application or abbreviated application, except as stated in paragraph (a)(3) of this section.

(2) *Complete review of data.* A complete response letter reflects FDA's complete review of the data submitted in an original application or abbreviated application (or, where appropriate, a resubmission) and any amendments that the agency has reviewed. The complete response letter will identify any amendments that the agency has not yet reviewed.

(3) *Inadequate data.* If FDA determines, after an application is filed or an abbreviated application is received, that the data submitted are inadequate to support approval, the agency might issue a complete response letter without first conducting required inspections and/or reviewing proposed product labeling.

(4) *Recommendation of actions for approval.* When possible, a complete response letter will recommend actions that the applicant might take to place the application or abbreviated application in condition for approval.

(b) *Applicant actions.* After receiving a complete response letter, the applicant must take one of following actions:

(1) *Resubmission.* Resubmit the application or abbreviated application, addressing all deficiencies identified in the complete response letter.

(i) A resubmission of an application or efficacy supplement that FDA classifies as a Class 1 resubmission constitutes an agreement by the applicant to start a new 2-month review cycle beginning on the date FDA receives the resubmission.

(ii) A resubmission of an application or efficacy supplement that FDA classifies as a Class 2 resubmission constitutes an agreement by the applicant to start a new 6-month review cycle beginning on the date FDA receives the resubmission.

(iii) A resubmission of an NDA supplement other than an efficacy supplement constitutes an agreement by the applicant to start a new review cycle the same length as the initial review cycle for the supplement (excluding any extension due to a major amendment of the initial supplement), beginning on the date FDA receives the resubmission.

(iv) A major resubmission of an abbreviated application constitutes an agreement by the applicant to start a new 6-month review cycle beginning on the date FDA receives the resubmission.

(v) A minor resubmission of an abbreviated application constitutes an agreement by the applicant to start a new review cycle beginning on the date FDA receives the resubmission.

(2) *Withdrawal.* Withdraw the application or abbreviated application. A decision to withdraw an application or abbreviated application is without prejudice to a subsequent submission.

(3) *Request opportunity for hearing.* Ask the agency to provide the applicant an opportunity for a hearing on the question of whether there are grounds for denying approval of the application or abbreviated application under section 505(d) or (j)(4) of the act, respectively. The applicant must submit the request to the Associate Director for Policy, Center for Drug Evaluation and Research, Food and Drug Administration, 10903 New Hampshire Ave., Silver Spring, MD 20993. Within 60 days of the date of the request for an opportunity for a hearing, or within a different time period to which FDA and the applicant agree, the agency will either approve the application or abbreviated application under §314.105, or refuse to approve the application under §314.125 or abbreviated application under §314.127 and give the applicant written notice of an opportunity for a hearing under §314.200 and section 505(c)(1)(B) or (j)(5)(c) of the act on the question of whether there are grounds for denying approval of the application or abbreviated application under section 505(d) or (j)(4) of the act, respectively.

(c) *Failure to take action.* (1) An applicant agrees to extend the review period under section 505(c)(1) or (j)(5)(A) of the act until it takes any of the actions listed in paragraph (b) of this section. For an application or abbreviated application, FDA may consider an applicant's failure to take any of such actions within 1 year after issuance of a complete response letter to be a request by the applicant to withdraw the application, unless the applicant has requested an extension of time in which to resubmit the application. FDA will grant any reasonable request for such an extension. FDA may consider an applicant's failure to resubmit the application within the extended time period or to request an additional extension to be a request by the applicant to withdraw the application.

(2) If FDA considers an applicant's failure to take action in accordance with paragraph (c)(1) of this section to be a request to withdraw the application, the agency will notify the applicant in writing. The applicant will have 30 days from the date of the notification to explain why the application should not be withdrawn and to request an extension of time in which to resubmit the application. FDA will grant any reasonable request for an extension. If the applicant does not respond to the notification within 30 days, the application will be deemed to be withdrawn.

[73 FR 39609, July 10, 2008]

§314.120 [Reserved]

§314.122 Submitting an abbreviated application for, or a 505(j)(2)(C) petition that relies on, a listed drug that is no longer marketed.

(a) An abbreviated new drug application that refers to, or a petition under section 505(j)(2)(C) of the act and §314.93 that relies on, a listed drug that has been voluntarily withdrawn from sale in the United States must be accompanied by a petition seeking a determination whether the listed drug was withdrawn for safety or effectiveness reasons. The petition must be submitted under §§10.25(a) and 10.30 of this chapter and must contain all evidence available to the petitioner concerning the reasons for the withdrawal from sale.

(b) When a petition described in paragraph (a) of this section is submitted, the agency will consider the evidence in the petition and any other evidence before the agency, and determine whether the listed drug is withdrawn from sale for safety or effectiveness reasons, in accordance with the procedures in § 314.161.

(c) An abbreviated new drug application described in paragraph (a) of this section will be disapproved, under § 314.127(a)(11), and a 505(j)(2)(C) petition described in paragraph (a) of this section will be disapproved, under § 314.93(e)(1)(iv), unless the agency determines that the withdrawal of the listed drug was not for safety or effectiveness reasons.

(d) Certain drug products approved for safety and effectiveness that were no longer marketed on September 24, 1984, are not included in the list. Any person who wishes to obtain marketing approval for such a drug product under an abbreviated new drug application must petition FDA for a determination whether the drug product was withdrawn from the market for safety or effectiveness reasons and request that the list be amended to include the drug product. A person seeking such a determination shall use the petition procedures established in § 10.30 of this chapter. The petitioner shall include in the petition information to show that the drug product was approved for safety and effectiveness and all evidence available to the petitioner concerning the reason that marketing of the drug product ceased.

[57 FR 17990, Apr. 28, 1992; 57 FR 29353, July 1, 1992]

§ 314.125 Refusal to approve an application.

(a) The Food and Drug Administration will refuse to approve the application and for a new drug give the applicant written notice of an opportunity for a hearing under § 314.200 on the question of whether there are grounds for denying approval of the application under section 505(d) of the act, if:

(1) FDA sends the applicant a complete response letter under § 314.110;

(2) The applicant requests an opportunity for hearing for a new drug on the question of whether the application is approvable; and

(3) FDA finds that any of the reasons given in paragraph (b) of this section apply.

(b) FDA may refuse to approve an application for any of the following reasons:

(1) The methods to be used in, and the facilities and controls used for, the manufacture, processing, packing, or holding of the drug substance or the drug product are inadequate to preserve its identity, strength, quality, purity, stability, and bioavailability.

(2) The investigations required under section 505(b) of the act do not include adequate tests by all methods reasonably applicable to show whether or not the drug is safe for use under the conditions prescribed, recommended, or suggested in its proposed labeling.

(3) The results of the tests show that the drug is unsafe for use under the conditions prescribed, recommended, or suggested in its proposed labeling or the results do not show that the drug product is safe for use under those conditions.

(4) There is insufficient information about the drug to determine whether the product is safe for use under the conditions prescribed, recommended, or suggested in its proposed labeling.

(5) There is a lack of substantial evidence consisting of adequate and well-controlled investigations, as defined in § 314.126, that the drug product will have the effect it purports or is represented to have under the conditions of use prescribed, recommended, or suggested in its proposed labeling.

(6) The proposed labeling is false or misleading in any particular.

(7) The application contains an untrue statement of a material fact.

(8) The drug product's proposed labeling does not comply with the requirements for labels and labeling in part 201.

(9) The application does not contain bioavailability or bioequivalence data required under part 320 of this chapter.

(10) A reason given in a letter refusing to file the application under § 314.101(d), if the deficiency is not corrected.

(11) The drug will be manufactured or processed in whole or in part in an establishment that is not registered and

not exempt from registration under section 510 of the act and part 207.

(12) The applicant does not permit a properly authorized officer or employee of the Department of Health and Human Services an adequate opportunity to inspect the facilities, controls, and any records relevant to the application.

(13) The methods to be used in, and the facilities and controls used for, the manufacture, processing, packing, or holding of the drug substance or the drug product do not comply with the current good manufacturing practice regulations in parts 210 and 211.

(14) The application does not contain an explanation of the omission of a report of any investigation of the drug product sponsored by the applicant, or an explanation of the omission of other information about the drug pertinent to an evaluation of the application that is received or otherwise obtained by the applicant from any source.

(15) A nonclinical laboratory study that is described in the application and that is essential to show that the drug is safe for use under the conditions prescribed, recommended, or suggested in its proposed labeling was not conducted in compliance with the good laboratory practice regulations in part 58 of this chapter and no reason for the noncompliance is provided or, if it is, the differences between the practices used in conducting the study and the good laboratory practice regulations do not support the validity of the study.

(16) Any clinical investigation involving human subjects described in the application, subject to the institutional review board regulations in part 56 of this chapter or informed consent regulations in part 50 of this chapter, was not conducted in compliance with those regulations such that the rights or safety of human subjects were not adequately protected.

(17) The applicant or contract research organization that conducted a bioavailability or bioequivalence study described in §320.38 or §320.63 of this chapter that is contained in the application refuses to permit an inspection of facilities or records relevant to the study by a properly authorized officer or employee of the Department of Health and Human Services or refuses to submit reserve samples of the drug products used in the study when requested by FDA.

(18) For a new drug, the application failed to contain the patent information required by section 505(b)(1) of the act.

(c) For drugs intended to treat life-threatening or severely-debilitating illnesses that are developed in accordance with §§312.80 through 312.88 of this chapter, the criteria contained in paragraphs (b) (3), (4), and (5) of this section shall be applied according to the considerations contained in §312.84 of this chapter.

[50 FR 7493, Feb. 22, 1985, as amended at 53 FR 41524, Oct. 21, 1988; 57 FR 17991, Apr. 28, 1992; 58 FR 25926, Apr. 28, 1993; 64 FR 402, Jan. 5, 1999; 73 FR 39610, July 10, 2008; 74 FR 9766, Mar. 6, 2009]

§314.126 Adequate and well-controlled studies.

(a) The purpose of conducting clinical investigations of a drug is to distinguish the effect of a drug from other influences, such as spontaneous change in the course of the disease, placebo effect, or biased observation. The characteristics described in paragraph (b) of this section have been developed over a period of years and are recognized by the scientific community as the essentials of an adequate and well-controlled clinical investigation. The Food and Drug Administration considers these characteristics in determining whether an investigation is adequate and well-controlled for purposes of section 505 of the act. Reports of adequate and well-controlled investigations provide the primary basis for determining whether there is "substantial evidence" to support the claims of effectiveness for new drugs. Therefore, the study report should provide sufficient details of study design, conduct, and analysis to allow critical evaluation and a determination of whether the characteristics of an adequate and well-controlled study are present.

(b) An adequate and well-controlled study has the following characteristics:

(1) There is a clear statement of the objectives of the investigation and a summary of the proposed or actual methods of analysis in the protocol for

the study and in the report of its results. In addition, the protocol should contain a description of the proposed methods of analysis, and the study report should contain a description of the methods of analysis ultimately used. If the protocol does not contain a description of the proposed methods of analysis, the study report should describe how the methods used were selected.

(2) The study uses a design that permits a valid comparison with a control to provide a quantitative assessment of drug effect. The protocol for the study and report of results should describe the study design precisely; for example, duration of treatment periods, whether treatments are parallel, sequential, or crossover, and whether the sample size is predetermined or based upon some interim analysis. Generally, the following types of control are recognized:

(i) *Placebo concurrent control.* The test drug is compared with an inactive preparation designed to resemble the test drug as far as possible. A placebo-controlled study may include additional treatment groups, such as an active treatment control or a dose-comparison control, and usually includes randomization and blinding of patients or investigators, or both.

(ii) *Dose-comparison concurrent control.* At least two doses of the drug are compared. A dose-comparison study may include additional treatment groups, such as placebo control or active control. Dose-comparison trials usually include randomization and blinding of patients or investigators, or both.

(iii) *No treatment concurrent control.* Where objective measurements of effectiveness are available and placebo effect is negligible, the test drug is compared with no treatment. No treatment concurrent control trials usually include randomization.

(iv) *Active treatment concurrent control.* The test drug is compared with known effective therapy; for example, where the condition treated is such that administration of placebo or no treatment would be contrary to the interest of the patient. An active treatment study may include additional treatment groups, however, such as a placebo control or a dose-comparison control. Active treatment trials usu-

ally include randomization and blinding of patients or investigators, or both. If the intent of the trial is to show similarity of the test and control drugs, the report of the study should assess the ability of the study to have detected a difference between treatments. Similarity of test drug and active control can mean either that both drugs were effective or that neither was effective. The analysis of the study should explain why the drugs should be considered effective in the study, for example, by reference to results in previous placebo-controlled studies of the active control drug.

(v) *Historical control.* The results of treatment with the test drug are compared with experience historically derived from the adequately documented natural history of the disease or condition, or from the results of active treatment, in comparable patients or populations. Because historical control populations usually cannot be as well assessed with respect to pertinent variables as can concurrent control populations, historical control designs are usually reserved for special circumstances. Examples include studies of diseases with high and predictable mortality (for example, certain malignancies) and studies in which the effect of the drug is self-evident (general anesthetics, drug metabolism).

(3) The method of selection of subjects provides adequate assurance that they have the disease or condition being studied, or evidence of susceptibility and exposure to the condition against which prophylaxis is directed.

(4) The method of assigning patients to treatment and control groups minimizes bias and is intended to assure comparability of the groups with respect to pertinent variables such as age, sex, severity of disease, duration of disease, and use of drugs or therapy other than the test drug. The protocol for the study and the report of its results should describe how subjects were assigned to groups. Ordinarily, in a concurrently controlled study, assignment is by randomization, with or without stratification.

(5) Adequate measures are taken to minimize bias on the part of the subjects, observers, and analysts of the data. The protocol and report of the

study should describe the procedures used to accomplish this, such as blinding.

(6) The methods of assessment of subjects' response are well-defined and reliable. The protocol for the study and the report of results should explain the variables measured, the methods of observation, and criteria used to assess response.

(7) There is an analysis of the results of the study adequate to assess the effects of the drug. The report of the study should describe the results and the analytic methods used to evaluate them, including any appropriate statistical methods. The analysis should assess, among other things, the comparability of test and control groups with respect to pertinent variables, and the effects of any interim data analyses performed.

(c) The Director of the Center for Drug Evaluation and Research may, on the Director's own initiative or on the petition of an interested person, waive in whole or in part any of the criteria in paragraph (b) of this section with respect to a specific clinical investigation, either prior to the investigation or in the evaluation of a completed study. A petition for a waiver is required to set forth clearly and concisely the specific criteria from which waiver is sought, why the criteria are not reasonably applicable to the particular clinical investigation, what alternative procedures, if any, are to be, or have been employed, and what results have been obtained. The petition is also required to state why the clinical investigations so conducted will yield, or have yielded, substantial evidence of effectiveness, notwithstanding nonconformance with the criteria for which waiver is requested.

(d) For an investigation to be considered adequate for approval of a new drug, it is required that the test drug be standardized as to identity, strength, quality, purity, and dosage form to give significance to the results of the investigation.

(e) Uncontrolled studies or partially controlled studies are not acceptable as the sole basis for the approval of claims of effectiveness. Such studies carefully conducted and documented, may provide corroborative support of well-controlled studies regarding efficacy and may yield valuable data regarding safety of the test drug. Such studies will be considered on their merits in the light of the principles listed here, with the exception of the requirement for the comparison of the treated subjects with controls. Isolated case reports, random experience, and reports lacking the details which permit scientific evaluation will not be considered.

[50 FR 7493, Feb. 22, 1985, as amended at 50 FR 21238, May 23, 1985; 55 FR 11580, Mar. 29, 1990; 64 FR 402, Jan. 5, 1999; 67 FR 9586, Mar. 4, 2002]

§314.127 Refusal to approve an abbreviated new drug application.

(a) FDA will refuse to approve an abbreviated application for a new drug under section 505(j) of the act for any of the following reasons:

(1) The methods used in, or the facilities and controls used for, the manufacture, processing, and packing of the drug product are inadequate to ensure and preserve its identity, strength, quality, and purity.

(2) Information submitted with the abbreviated new drug application is insufficient to show that each of the proposed conditions of use has been previously approved for the listed drug referred to in the application.

(3)(i) If the reference listed drug has only one active ingredient, information submitted with the abbreviated new drug application is insufficient to show that the active ingredient is the same as that of the reference listed drug;

(ii) If the reference listed drug has more than one active ingredient, information submitted with the abbreviated new drug application is insufficient to show that the active ingredients are the same as the active ingredients of the reference listed drug; or

(iii) If the reference listed drug has more than one active ingredient and if the abbreviated new drug application is for a drug product that has an active ingredient different from the reference listed drug:

(A) Information submitted with the abbreviated new drug application is insufficient to show:

(*1*) That the other active ingredients are the same as the active ingredients of the reference listed drug; or

(*2*) That the different active ingredient is an active ingredient of a listed drug or a drug that does not meet the requirements of section 201(p) of the act; or

(B) No petition to submit an abbreviated application for the drug product with the different active ingredient was approved under § 314.93.

(4)(i) If the abbreviated new drug application is for a drug product whose route of administration, dosage form, or strength purports to be the same as that of the listed drug referred to in the abbreviated new drug application, information submitted in the abbreviated new drug application is insufficient to show that the route of administration, dosage form, or strength is the same as that of the reference listed drug; or

(ii) If the abbreviated new drug application is for a drug product whose route of administration, dosage form, or strength is different from that of the listed drug referred to in the application, no petition to submit an abbreviated new drug application for the drug product with the different route of administration, dosage form, or strength was approved under § 314.93.

(5) If the abbreviated new drug application was submitted under the approval of a petition under § 314.93, the abbreviated new drug application did not contain the information required by FDA with respect to the active ingredient, route of administration, dosage form, or strength that is not the same as that of the reference listed drug.

(6)(i) Information submitted in the abbreviated new drug application is insufficient to show that the drug product is bioequivalent to the listed drug referred to in the abbreviated new drug application; or

(ii) If the abbreviated new drug application was submitted under a petition approved under § 314.93, information submitted in the abbreviated new drug application is insufficient to show that the active ingredients of the drug product are of the same pharmacological or therapeutic class as those of the reference listed drug and that the drug product can be expected to have the same therapeutic effect as the reference listed drug when administered to patients for each condition of use approved for the reference listed drug.

(7) Information submitted in the abbreviated new drug application is insufficient to show that the labeling proposed for the drug is the same as the labeling approved for the listed drug referred to in the abbreviated new drug application except for changes required because of differences approved in a petition under § 314.93 or because the drug product and the reference listed drug are produced or distributed by different manufacturers or because aspects of the listed drug's labeling are protected by patent, or by exclusivity, and such differences do not render the proposed drug product less safe or effective than the listed drug for all remaining, nonprotected conditions of use.

(8)(i) Information submitted in the abbreviated new drug application of any other information available to FDA shows that:

(A) The inactive ingredients of the drug product are unsafe for use, as described in paragraph (a)(8)(ii) of this section, under the conditions prescribed, recommended, or suggested in the labeling proposed for the drug product; or

(B) The composition of the drug product is unsafe, as described in paragraph (a)(8)(ii) of this section, under the conditions prescribed, recommended, or suggested in the proposed labeling because of the type or quantity of inactive ingredients included or the manner in which the inactive ingredients are included.

(ii)(A) FDA will consider the inactive ingredients or composition of a drug product unsafe and refuse to approve an abbreviated new drug application under paragraph (a)(8)(i) of this section if, on the basis of information available to the agency, there is a reasonable basis to conclude that one or more of the inactive ingredients of the proposed drug or its composition raises serious questions of safety or efficacy. From its experience with reviewing inactive ingredients, and from other information available to it, FDA may identify changes in inactive ingredients or composition that may adversely affect a drug product's safety or efficacy. The inactive ingredients or composition of a proposed drug product will be considered to raise serious questions of safety or efficacy if the product incorporates one or more of these changes. Examples of the changes that may raise serious questions of safety or efficacy include, but are not limited to, the following:

(1) A change in an inactive ingredient so that the product does not comply with an official compendium.

(2) A change in composition to include an inactive ingredient that has not been previously approved in a drug product for human use by the same route of administration.

(3) A change in the composition of a parenteral drug product to include an inactive ingredient that has not been previously approved in a parenteral drug product.

(4) A change in composition of a drug product for ophthalmic use to include an inactive ingredient that has not been previously approved in a drug for ophthalmic use.

(5) The use of a delivery or a modified release mechanism never before approved for the drug.

(6) A change in composition to include a significantly greater content of one or more inactive ingredients than previously used in the drug product.

(7) If the drug product is intended for topical administration, a change in the properties of the vehicle or base that might increase absorption of certain potentially toxic active ingredients thereby affecting the safety of the drug product, or a change in the lipophilic properties of a vehicle or base, e.g., a change from an oleaginous to a water soluble vehicle or base.

(B) FDA will consider an inactive ingredient in, or the composition of, a drug product intended for parenteral use to be unsafe and will refuse to approve the abbreviated new drug application unless it contains the same inactive ingredients, other than preservatives, buffers, and antioxidants, in the same concentration as the listed drug, and, if it differs from the listed drug in a preservative, buffer, or antioxidant, the application contains sufficient in-

formation to demonstrate that the difference does not affect the safety or efficacy of the drug product.

(C) FDA will consider an inactive ingredient in, or the composition of, a drug product intended for ophthalmic or otic use unsafe and will refuse to approve the abbreviated new drug application unless it contains the same inactive ingredients, other than preservatives, buffers, substances to adjust tonicity, or thickening agents, in the same concentration as the listed drug, and if it differs from the listed drug in a preservative, buffer, substance to adjust tonicity, or thickening agent, the application contains sufficient information to demonstrate that the difference does not affect the safety or efficacy of the drug product and the labeling does not claim any therapeutic advantage over or difference from the listed drug.

(9) Approval of the listed drug referred to in the abbreviated new drug application has been withdrawn or suspended for grounds described in §314.150(a) or FDA has published a notice of opportunity for hearing to withdraw approval of the reference listed drug under §314.150(a).

(10) Approval of the listed drug referred to in the abbreviated new drug application has been withdrawn under §314.151 or FDA has proposed to withdraw approval of the reference listed drug under §314.151(a).

(11) FDA has determined that the reference listed drug has been withdrawn from sale for safety or effectiveness reasons under §314.161, or the reference listed drug has been voluntarily withdrawn from sale and the agency has not determined whether the withdrawal is for safety or effectiveness reasons, or approval of the reference listed drug has been suspended under §314.153, or the agency has issued an initial decision proposing to suspend the reference listed drug under §314.153(a)(1).

(12) The abbreviated new drug application does not meet any other requirement under section 505(j)(2)(A) of the act.

(13) The abbreviated new drug application contains an untrue statement of material fact.

(b) FDA may refuse to approve an abbreviated application for a new drug if the applicant or contract research organization that conducted a bioavailability or bioequivalence study described in § 320.63 of this chapter that is contained in the abbreviated new drug application refuses to permit an inspection of facilities or records relevant to the study by a properly authorized officer of employee of the Department of Health and Human Services or refuses to submit reserve samples of the drug products used in the study when requested by FDA.

[57 FR 17991, Apr. 28, 1992; 57 FR 29353, July 1, 1992, as amended at 58 FR 25927, Apr. 28, 1993; 67 FR 77672, Dec. 19, 2002]

§ 314.150 Withdrawal of approval of an application or abbreviated application.

(a) The Food and Drug Administration will notify the applicant, and, if appropriate, all other persons who manufacture or distribute identical, related, or similar drug products as defined in §§ 310.6 and 314.151(a) of this chapter and for a new drug afford an opportunity for a hearing on a proposal to withdraw approval of the application or abbreviated new drug application under section 505(e) of the act and under the procedure in § 314.200, if any of the following apply:

(1) The Secretary of Health and Human Services has suspended the approval of the application or abbreviated application for a new drug on a finding that there is an imminent hazard to the public health. FDA will promptly afford the applicant an expedited hearing following summary suspension on a finding of imminent hazard to health.

(2) FDA finds:

(i) That clinical or other experience, tests, or other scientific data show that the drug is unsafe for use under the conditions of use upon the basis of which the application or abbreviated application was approved; or

(ii) That new evidence of clinical experience, not contained in the application or not available to FDA until after the application or abbreviated application was approved, or tests by new methods, or tests by methods not deemed reasonably applicable when the application or abbreviated application was approved, evaluated together with the evidence available when the application or abbreviated application was approved, reveal that the drug is not shown to be safe for use under the conditions of use upon the basis of which the application or abbreviated application was approved; or

(iii) Upon the basis of new information before FDA with respect to the drug, evaluated together with the evidence available when the application or abbreviated application was approved, that there is a lack of substantial evidence from adequate and well-controlled investigations as defined in § 314.126, that the drug will have the effect it is purported or represented to have under the conditions of use prescribed, recommended, or suggested in its labeling; or

(iv) That the application or abbreviated application contains any untrue statement of a material fact; or

(v) That the patent information prescribed by section 505(c) of the act was not submitted within 30 days after the receipt of written notice from FDA specifying the failure to submit such information; or

(b) FDA may notify the applicant, and, if appropriate, all other persons who manufacture or distribute identical, related, or similar drug products as defined in § 310.6, and for a new drug afford an opportunity for a hearing on a proposal to withdraw approval of the application or abbreviated new drug application under section 505(e) of the act and under the procedure in § 314.200, if the agency finds:

(1) That the applicant has failed to establish a system for maintaining required records, or has repeatedly or deliberately failed to maintain required records or to make required reports under section 505(k) or 507(g) of the act and § 314.80, § 314.81, or § 314.98, or that the applicant has refused to permit access to, or copying or verification of, its records.

(2) That on the basis of new information before FDA, evaluated together with the evidence available when the application or abbreviated application was approved, the methods used in, or the facilities and controls used for, the manufacture, processing, and packing

of the drug are inadequate to ensure and preserve its identity, strength, quality, and purity and were not made adequate within a reasonable time after receipt of written notice from the agency.

(3) That on the basis of new information before FDA, evaluated together with the evidence available when the application or abbreviated application was approved, the labeling of the drug, based on a fair evaluation of all material facts, is false or misleading in any particular, and the labeling was not corrected by the applicant within a reasonable time after receipt of written notice from the agency.

(4) That the applicant has failed to comply with the notice requirements of section 510(j)(2) of the act.

(5) That the applicant has failed to submit bioavailability or bioequivalence data required under part 320 of this chapter.

(6) The application or abbreviated application does not contain an explanation of the omission of a report of any investigation of the drug product sponsored by the applicant, or an explanation of the omission of other information about the drug pertinent to an evaluation of the application or abbreviated application that is received or otherwise obtained by the applicant from any source.

(7) That any nonclinical laboratory study that is described in the application or abbreviated application and that is essential to show that the drug is safe for use under the conditions prescribed, recommended, or suggested in its labeling was not conducted in compliance with the good laboratory practice regulations in part 58 of this chapter and no reason for the noncompliance was provided or, if it was, the differences between the practices used in conducting the study and the good laboratory practice regulations do not support the validity of the study.

(8) Any clinical investigation involving human subjects described in the application or abbreviated application, subject to the institutional review board regulations in part 56 of this chapter or informed consent regulations in part 50 of this chapter, was not conducted in compliance with those regulations such that the rights or safety of human subjects were not adequately protected.

(9) That the applicant or contract research organization that conducted a bioavailability or bioequivalence study described in §320.38 or §320.63 of this chapter that is contained in the application or abbreviated application refuses to permit an inspection of facilities or records relevant to the study by a properly authorized officer or employee of the Department of Health and Human Services or refuses to submit reserve samples of the drug products used in the study when requested by FDA.

(10) That the labeling for the drug product that is the subject of the abbreviated new drug application is no longer consistent with that for the listed drug referred to in the abbreviated new drug application, except for differences approved in the abbreviated new drug application or those differences resulting from:

(i) A patent on the listed drug issued after approval of the abbreviated new drug application; or

(ii) Exclusivity accorded to the listed drug after approval of the abbreviated new drug application that do not render the drug product less safe or effective than the listed drug for any remaining, nonprotected condition(s) of use.

(c) FDA will withdraw approval of an application or abbreviated application if the applicant requests its withdrawal because the drug subject to the application or abbreviated application is no longer being marketed, provided none of the conditions listed in paragraphs (a) and (b) of this section applies to the drug. FDA will consider a written request for a withdrawal under this paragraph to be a waiver of an opportunity for hearing otherwise provided for in this section. Withdrawal of approval of an application or abbreviated application under this paragraph is without prejudice to refiling.

(d) FDA may notify an applicant that it believes a potential problem associated with a drug is sufficiently serious that the drug should be removed from the market and may ask the applicant to waive the opportunity for hearing otherwise provided for under this section, to permit FDA to withdraw approval of the application or abbreviated application for the product, and to remove voluntarily the product from the market. If the applicant agrees, the agency will not make a finding under paragraph (b) of this section, but will withdraw approval of the application or abbreviated application in a notice published in the FEDERAL REGISTER that contains a brief summary of the agency's and the applicant's views of the reasons for withdrawal.

[57 FR 17993, Apr. 28, 1992, as amended at 58 FR 25927, Apr. 28, 1993; 64 FR 402, Jan. 5, 1999]

§ 314.151 Withdrawal of approval of an abbreviated new drug application under section 505(j)(5) of the act.

(a) Approval of an abbreviated new drug application approved under § 314.105(d) may be withdrawn when the agency withdraws approval, under § 314.150(a) or under this section, of the approved drug referred to in the abbreviated new drug application. If the agency proposed to withdraw approval of a listed drug under § 314.150(a), the holder of an approved application for the listed drug has a right to notice and opportunity for hearing. The published notice of opportunity for hearing will identify all drug products approved under § 314.105(d) whose applications are subject to withdrawal under this section if the listed drug is withdrawn, and will propose to withdraw such drugs. Holders of approved applications for the identified drug products will be provided notice and an opportunity to respond to the proposed withdrawal of their applications as described in paragraphs (b) and (c) of this section.

(b)(1) The published notice of opportunity for hearing on the withdrawal of the listed drug will serve as notice to holders of identified abbreviated new drug applications of the grounds for the proposed withdrawal.

(2) Holders of applications for drug products identified in the notice of opportunity for hearing may submit written comments on the notice of opportunity for hearing issued on the proposed withdrawal of the listed drug. If an abbreviated new drug application holder submits comments on the notice of opportunity for hearing and a hear-

ing is granted, the abbreviated new drug application holder may participate in the hearing as a nonparty participant as provided for in § 12.89 of this chapter.

(3) Except as provided in paragraphs (c) and (d) of this section, the approval of an abbreviated new drug application for a drug product identified in the notice of opportunity for hearing on the withdrawal of a listed drug will be withdrawn when the agency has completed the withdrawal of approval of the listed drug.

(c)(1) If the holder of an application for a drug identified in the notice of opportunity for hearing has submitted timely comments but does not have an opportunity to participate in a hearing because a hearing is not requested or is settled, the submitted comments will be considered by the agency, which will issue an initial decision. The initial decision will respond to the comments, and contain the agency's decision whether there are grounds to withdraw approval of the listed drug and of the abbreviated new drug applications on which timely comments were submitted. The initial decision will be sent to each abbreviated new drug application holder that has submitted comments.

(2) Abbreviated new drug application holders to whom the initial decision was sent may, within 30 days of the issuance of the initial decision, submit written objections.

(3) The agency may, at its discretion, hold a limited oral hearing to resolve dispositive factual issues that cannot be resolved on the basis of written submissions.

(4) If there are no timely objections to the initial decision, it will become final at the expiration of 30 days.

(5) If timely objections are submitted, they will be reviewed and responded to in a final decision.

(6) The written comments received, the initial decision, the evidence relied on in the comments and in the initial decision, the objections to the initial decision, and, if a limited oral hearing has been held, the transcript of that hearing and any documents submitted therein, shall form the record upon which the agency shall make a final decision.

(7) Except as provided in paragraph (d) of this section, any abbreviated new drug application whose holder submitted comments on the notice of opportunity for hearing shall be withdrawn upon the issuance of a final decision concluding that the listed drug should be withdrawn for grounds as described in § 314.150(a). The final decision shall be in writing and shall constitute final agency action, reviewable in a judicial proceeding.

(8) Documents in the record will be publicly available in accordance with § 10.20(j) of this chapter. Documents available for examination or copying will be placed on public display in the Division of Dockets Management (HFA–305), Food and Drug Administration, room. 1–23, 12420 Parklawn Dr., Rockville, MD 20857, promptly upon receipt in that office.

(d) If the agency determines, based upon information submitted by the holder of an abbreviated new drug application, that the grounds for withdrawal of the listed drug are not applicable to a drug identified in the notice of opportunity for hearing, the final decision will state that the approval of the abbreviated new drug application for such drug is not withdrawn.

[57 FR 17994, Apr. 28, 1992]

§ 314.152 Notice of withdrawal of approval of an application or abbreviated application for a new drug.

If the Food and Drug Administration withdraws approval of an application or abbreviated application for a new drug, FDA will publish a notice in the FEDERAL REGISTER announcing the withdrawal of approval. If the application or abbreviated application was withdrawn for grounds described in § 314.150(a) or § 314.151, the notice will announce the removal of the drug from the list of approved drugs published under section 505(j)(6) of the act and shall satisfy the requirement of § 314.162(b).

[57 FR 17994, Apr. 28, 1992]

§ 314.153 Suspension of approval of an abbreviated new drug application.

(a) *Suspension of approval.* The approval of an abbreviated new drug application approved under § 314.105(d)

shall be suspended for the period stated when:

(1) The Secretary of the Department of Health and Human Services, under the imminent hazard authority of section 505(e) of the act or the authority of this paragraph, suspends approval of a listed drug referred to in the abbreviated new drug application, for the period of the suspension;

(2) The agency, in the notice described in paragraph (b) of this section, or in any subsequent written notice given an abbreviated new drug application holder by the agency, concludes that the risk of continued marketing and use of the drug is inappropriate, pending completion of proceedings to withdraw or suspend approval under § 314.151 or paragraph (b) of this section; or

(3) The agency, under the procedures set forth in paragraph (b) of this section, issues a final decision stating the determination that the abbreviated application is suspended because the listed drug on which the approval of the abbreviated new drug application depends has been withdrawn from sale for reasons of safety or effectiveness or has been suspended under paragraph (b) of this section. The suspension will take effect on the date stated in the decision and will remain in effect until the agency determines that the marketing of the drug has resumed or that the withdrawal is not for safety or effectiveness reasons.

(b) *Procedures for suspension of abbreviated new drug applications when a listed drug is voluntarily withdrawn for safety or effectiveness reasons.* (1) If a listed drug is voluntarily withdrawn from sale, and the agency determines that the withdrawal from sale was for reasons of safety or effectiveness, the agency will send each holder of an approved abbreviated new drug application that is subject to suspension as a result of this determination a copy of the agency's initial decision setting forth the reasons for the determination. The initial decision will also be placed on file with the Division of Dockets Management (HFA–305), Food and Drug Administration, room 1–23, 12420 Parklawn Dr., Rockville, MD 20857.

(2) Each abbreviated new drug application holder will have 30 days from the issuance of the initial decision to present, in writing, comments and information bearing on the initial decision. If no comments or information is received, the initial decision will become final at the expiration of 30 days.

(3) Comments and information received within 30 days of the issuance of the initial decision will be considered by the agency and responded to in a final decision.

(4) The agency may, in its discretion, hold a limited oral hearing to resolve dispositive factual issues that cannot be resolved on the basis of written submissions.

(5) If the final decision affirms the agency's initial decision that the listed drug was withdrawn for reasons of safety or effectiveness, the decision will be published in the FEDERAL REGISTER in compliance with § 314.152, and will, except as provided in paragraph (b)(6) of this section, suspend approval of all abbreviated new drug applications identified under paragraph (b)(1) of this section and remove from the list the listed drug and any drug whose approval was suspended under this paragraph. The notice will satisfy the requirement of § 314.162(b). The agency's final decision and copies of materials on which it relies will also be filed with the Division of Dockets Management (address in paragraph (b)(1) of this section).

(6) If the agency determines in its final decision that the listed drug was withdrawn for reasons of safety or effectiveness but, based upon information submitted by the holder of an abbreviated new drug application, also determines that the reasons for the withdrawal of the listed drug are not relevant to the safety and effectiveness of the drug subject to such abbreviated new drug application, the final decision will state that the approval of such abbreviated new drug application is not suspended.

(7) Documents in the record will be publicly available in accordance with § 10.20(j) of this chapter. Documents available for examination or copying will be placed on public display in the Division of Dockets Management (address in paragraph (b)(1) of this sec-

tion) promptly upon receipt in that office.

[57 FR 17995, Apr. 28, 1992]

§ 314.160 Approval of an application or abbreviated application for which approval was previously refused, suspended, or withdrawn.

Upon the Food and Drug Administration's own initiative or upon request of an applicant, FDA may, on the basis of new data, approve an application or abbreviated application which it had previously refused, suspended, or withdrawn approval. FDA will publish a notice in the FEDERAL REGISTER announcing the approval.

[57 FR 17995, Apr. 28, 1992]

§ 314.161 Determination of reasons for voluntary withdrawal of a listed drug.

(a) A determination whether a listed drug that has been voluntarily withdrawn from sale was withdrawn for safety or effectiveness reasons may be made by the agency at any time after the drug has been voluntarily withdrawn from sale, but must be made:

(1) Prior to approving an abbreviated new drug application that refers to the listed drug;

(2) Whenever a listed drug is voluntarily withdrawn from sale and abbreviated new drug applications that referred to the listed drug have been approved; and

(3) When a person petitions for such a determination under §§ 10.25(a) and 10.30 of this chapter.

(b) Any person may petition under §§ 10.25(a) and 10.30 of this chapter for a determination whether a listed drug has been voluntarily withdrawn for safety or effectiveness reasons. Any such petition must contain all evidence available to the petitioner concerning the reason that the drug is withdrawn from sale.

(c) If the agency determines that a listed drug is withdrawn from sale for safety or effectiveness reasons, the agency will, except as provided in paragraph (d) of this section, publish a notice of the determination in the FEDERAL REGISTER.

(d) If the agency determines under paragraph (a) of this section that a listed drug is withdrawn from sale for safety and effectiveness reasons and there are approved abbreviated new drug applications that are subject to suspension under section 505(j)(5) of the act, FDA will initiate a proceeding in accordance with §314.153(b).

(e) A drug that the agency determines is withdrawn for safety or effectiveness reasons will be removed from the list, under §314.162. The drug may be relisted if the agency has evidence that marketing of the drug has resumed or that the withdrawal is not for safety or effectiveness reasons. A determination that the drug is not withdrawn for safety or effectiveness reasons may be made at any time after its removal from the list, upon the agency's initiative, or upon the submission of a petition under §§10.25(a) and 10.30 of this chapter. If the agency determines that the drug is not withdrawn for safety or effectiveness reasons, the agency shall publish a notice of this determination in the FEDERAL REGISTER. The notice will also announce that the drug is relisted, under §314.162(c). The notice will also serve to reinstate approval of all suspended abbreviated new drug applications that referred to the listed drug.

[57 FR 17995, Apr. 28, 1992]

§314.162 Removal of a drug product from the list.

(a) FDA will remove a previously approved new drug product from the list for the period stated when:

(1) The agency withdraws or suspends approval of a new drug application or an abbreviated new drug application under §314.150(a) or §314.151 or under the imminent hazard authority of section 505(e) of the act, for the same period as the withdrawal or suspension of the application; or

(2) The agency, in accordance with the procedures in §314.153(b) or §314.161, issues a final decision stating that the listed drug was withdrawn from sale for safety or effectiveness reasons, or suspended under §314.153(b), until the agency determines that the withdrawal from the market has ceased or is not for safety or effectiveness reasons.

(b) FDA will publish in the FEDERAL REGISTER a notice announcing the removal of a drug from the list.

(c) At the end of the period specified in paragraph (a)(1) or (a)(2) of this section, FDA will relist a drug that has been removed from the list. The agency will publish in the FEDERAL REGISTER a notice announcing the relisting of the drug.

[57 FR 17996, Apr. 28, 1992]

§314.170 Adulteration and misbranding of an approved drug.

All drugs, including those the Food and Drug Administration approves under section 505 of the act and this part, are subject to the adulteration and misbranding provisions in sections 501, 502, and 503 of the act. FDA is authorized to regulate approved new drugs by regulations issued through informal rulemaking under sections 501, 502, and 503 of the act.

[50 FR 7493, Feb. 22, 1985. Redesignated at 57 FR 17983, Apr. 28, 1992, and amended at 64 FR 402, Jan. 5, 1999]

Subpart E—Hearing Procedures for New Drugs

SOURCE: 50 FR 7493, Feb. 22, 1985, unless otherwise noted. Redesignated at 57 FR 17983, Apr. 28, 1992.

§314.200 Notice of opportunity for hearing; notice of participation and request for hearing; grant or denial of hearing.

(a) *Notice of opportunity for hearing.* The Director of the Center for Drug Evaluation and Research, Food and Drug Administration, will give the applicant, and all other persons who manufacture or distribute identical, related, or similar drug products as defined in §310.6 of this chapter, notice and an opportunity for a hearing on the Center's proposal to refuse to approve an application or to withdraw the approval of an application or abbreviated application under section 505(e) of the act. The notice will state the reasons for the action and the proposed grounds for the order.

(1) The notice may be general (that is, simply summarizing in a general way the information resulting in the notice) or specific (that is, either referring to specific requirements in the statute and regulations with which

there is a lack of compliance, or providing a detailed description and analysis of the specific facts resulting in the notice).

(2) FDA will publish the notice in the FEDERAL REGISTER and will state that the applicant, and other persons subject to the notice under § 310.6, who wishes to participate in a hearing, has 30 days after the date of publication of the notice to file a written notice of participation and request for hearing. The applicant, or other persons subject to the notice under § 310.6, who fails to file a written notice of participation and request for hearing within 30 days, waives the opportunity for a hearing.

(3) It is the responsibility of every manufacturer and distributor of a drug product to review every notice of opportunity for a hearing published in the FEDERAL REGISTER to determine whether it covers any drug product that person manufactures or distributes. Any person may request an opinion of the applicability of a notice to a specific product that may be identical, related, or similar to a product listed in a notice by writing to the Division of New Drugs and Labeling Compliance, Office of Compliance, Center for Drug Evaluation and Research, Food and Drug Administration, 10903 New Hampshire Ave., Silver Spring, MD 20993–0002. A person shall request an opinion within 30 days of the date of publication of the notice to be eligible for an opportunity for a hearing under the notice. If a person requests an opinion, that person's time for filing an appearance and request for a hearing and supporting studies and analyses begins on the date the person receives the opinion from FDA.

(b) FDA will provide the notice of opportunity for a hearing to applicants and to other persons subject to the notice under § 310.6, as follows:

(1) To any person who has submitted an application or abbreviated application, by delivering the notice in person or by sending it by registered or certified mail to the last address shown in the application or abbreviated application.

(2) To any person who has not submitted an application or abbreviated application but who is subject to the notice under § 310.6 of this chapter, by

publication of the notice in the FEDERAL REGISTER.

(c)(1) *Notice of participation and request for a hearing, and submission of studies and comments.* The applicant, or any other person subject to the notice under § 310.6, who wishes to participate in a hearing, shall file with the Division of Dockets Management (HFA–305), Food and Drug Administration, 5630 Fishers Lane, rm. 1061, Rockville, MD 20852, (i) within 30 days after the date of the publication of the notice (or of the date of receipt of an opinion requested under paragraph (a)(3) of this section) a written notice of participation and request for a hearing and (ii) within 60 days after the date of publication of the notice, unless a different period of time is specified in the notice of opportunity for a hearing, the studies on which the person relies to justify a hearing as specified in paragraph (d) of this section. The applicant, or other person, may incorporate by reference the raw data underlying a study if the data were previously submitted to FDA as part of an application, abbreviated application, or other report.

(2) FDA will not consider data or analyses submitted after 60 days in determining whether a hearing is warranted unless they are derived from well-controlled studies begun before the date of the notice of opportunity for hearing and the results of the studies were not available within 60 days after the date of publication of the notice. Nevertheless, FDA may consider other studies on the basis of a showing by the person requesting a hearing of inadvertent omission and hardship. The person requesting a hearing shall list in the request for hearing all studies in progress, the results of which the person intends later to submit in support of the request for a hearing. The person shall submit under paragraph (c)(1)(ii) of this section a copy of the complete protocol, a list of the participating investigators, and a brief status report of the studies.

(3) Any other interested person who is not subject to the notice of opportunity for a hearing may also submit comments on the proposal to withdraw approval of the application or abbreviated application. The comments are requested to be submitted within the

time and under the conditions specified in this section.

(d) The person requesting a hearing is required to submit under paragraph (c)(1)(ii) of this section the studies (including all protocols and underlying raw data) on which the person relies to justify a hearing with respect to the drug product. Except, a person who requests a hearing on the refusal to approve an application is not required to submit additional studies and analyses if the studies upon which the person relies have been submitted in the application and in the format and containing the summaries required under § 314.50.

(1) If the grounds for FDA's proposed action concern the effectiveness of the drug, each request for hearing is required to be supported only by adequate and well-controlled clinical studies meeting all of the precise requirements of § 314.126 and, for combination drug products, § 300.50, or by other studies not meeting those requirements for which a waiver has been previously granted by FDA under § 314.126. Each person requesting a hearing shall submit all adequate and well-controlled clinical studies on the drug product, including any unfavorable analyses, views, or judgments with respect to the studies. No other data, information, or studies may be submitted.

(2) The submission is required to include a factual analysis of all the studies submitted. If the grounds for FDA's proposed action concern the effectiveness of the drug, the analysis is required to specify how each study accords, on a point-by-point basis, with each criterion required for an adequate well-controlled clinical investigation established under § 314.126 and, if the product is a combination drug product, with each of the requirements for a combination drug established in § 300.50, or the study is required to be accompanied by an appropriate waiver previously granted by FDA. If a study concerns a drug or dosage form or condition of use or mode of administration other than the one in question, that fact is required to be clearly stated. Any study conducted on the final marketed form of the drug product is required to be clearly identified.

(3) Each person requesting a hearing shall submit an analysis of the data upon which the person relies, except that the required information relating either to safety or to effectiveness may be omitted if the notice of opportunity for hearing does not raise any issue with respect to that aspect of the drug; information on compliance with § 300.50 may be omitted if the drug product is not a combination drug product. A financial certification or disclosure statement or both as required by part 54 of this chapter must accompany all clinical data submitted. FDA can most efficiently consider submissions made in the following format.

I. Safety data.
A. Animal safety data.
1. Individual active components.
a. Controlled studies.
b. Partially controlled or uncontrolled studies.
2. Combinations of the individual active components.
a. Controlled studies.
b. Partially controlled or uncontrolled studies.
B. Human safety data.
1. Individual active components.
a. Controlled studies.
b. Partially controlled or uncontrolled studies.
c. Documented case reports.
d. Pertinent marketing experiences that may influence a determination about the safety of each individual active component.
2. Combinations of the individual active components.
a. Controlled studies.
b. Partially controlled or uncontrolled studies.
c. Documented case reports.
d. Pertinent marketing experiences that may influence a determination about the safety of each individual active component.
II. Effectiveness data.
A. Individual active components: Controlled studies, with an analysis showing clearly how each study satisfies, on a point-by-point basis, each of the criteria required by § 314.126.
B. Combinations of individual active components.
1. Controlled studies with an analysis showing clearly how each study satisfies on a point-by-point basis, each of the criteria required by § 314.126.
2. An analysis showing clearly how each requirement of § 300.50 has been satisfied.
III. A summary of the data and views setting forth the medical rationale and purpose for the drug and its ingredients and the scientific basis for the conclusion that the drug

and its ingredients have been proven safe and/or effective for the intended use. If there is an absence of controlled studies in the material submitted or the requirements of any element of § 300.50 or § 314.126 have not been fully met, that fact is required to be stated clearly and a waiver obtained under § 314.126 is required to be submitted.

IV. A statement signed by the person responsible for such submission that it includes in full (or incorporates by reference as permitted in § 314.200(c)(2)) all studies and information specified in § 314.200(d).

(WARNING: A willfully false statement is a criminal offense, 18 U.S.C. 1001.)

(e) *Contentions that a drug product is not subject to the new drug requirements.* A notice of opportunity for a hearing encompasses all issues relating to the legal status of each drug product subject to it, including identical, related, and similar drug products as defined in § 310.6. A notice of appearance and request for a hearing under paragraph (c)(1)(i) of this section is required to contain any contention that the product is not a new drug because it is generally recognized as safe and effective within the meaning of section 201(p) of the act, or because it is exempt from part or all of the new drug provisions of the act under the exemption for products marketed before June 25, 1938, contained in section 201(p) of the act or under section 107(c) of the Drug Amendments of 1962, or for any other reason. Each contention is required to be supported by a submission under paragraph (c)(1)(ii) of this section and the Commissioner of Food and Drugs will make an administrative determination on each contention. The failure of any person subject to a notice of opportunity for a hearing, including any person who manufactures or distributes an identical, related, or similar drug product as defined in § 310.6, to submit a notice of participation and request for hearing or to raise all such contentions constitutes a waiver of any contentions not raised.

(1) A contention that a drug product is generally recognized as safe and effective within the meaning of section 201(p) of the act is required to be supported by submission of the same quantity and quality of scientific evidence that is required to obtain approval of an application for the product, unless FDA has waived a requirement for ef-

fectiveness (under § 314.126) or safety, or both. The submission should be in the format and with the analyses required under paragraph (d) of this section. A person who fails to submit the required scientific evidence required under paragraph (d) waives the contention. General recognition of safety and effectiveness shall ordinarily be based upon published studies which may be corroborated by unpublished studies and other data and information.

(2) A contention that a drug product is exempt from part or all of the new drug provisions of the act under the exemption for products marketed before June 25, 1938, contained in section 201(p) of the act, or under section 107(c) of the Drug Amendments of 1962, is required to be supported by evidence of past and present quantitative formulas, labeling, and evidence of marketing. A person who makes such a contention should submit the formulas, labeling, and evidence of marketing in the following format.

I. Formulation.

A. A copy of each pertinent document or record to establish the exact quantitative formulation of the drug (both active and inactive ingredients) on the date of initial marketing of the drug.

B. A statement whether such formulation has at any subsequent time been changed in any manner. If any such change has been made, the exact date, nature, and rationale for each change in formulation, including any deletion or change in the concentration of any active ingredient and/or inactive ingredient, should be stated, together with a copy of each pertinent document or record to establish the date and nature of each such change, including, but not limited to, the formula which resulted from each such change. If no such change has been made, a copy of representative documents or records showing the formula at representative points in time should be submitted to support the statement.

II. Labeling.

A. A copy of each pertinent document or record to establish the identity of each item of written, printed, or graphic matter used as labeling on the date the drug was initially marketed.

B. A statement whether such labeling has at any subsequent time been discontinued or changed in any manner. If such discontinuance or change has been made, the exact date, nature, and rationale for each discontinuance or change and a copy of each pertinent document or record to establish each such discontinuance or change should be submitted, including, but not limited to, the labeling which resulted from each such discontinuance or change. If no such discontinuance or change has been made, a copy of representative documents or records showing labeling at representative points in time should be submitted to support the statement.

III. Marketing.

A. A copy of each pertinent document or record to establish the exact date the drug was initially marketed.

B. A statement whether such marketing has at any subsequent time been discontinued. If such marketing has been discontinued, the exact date of each such discontinuance should be submitted, together with a copy of each pertinent document or record to establish each such date.

IV. Verification.

A statement signed by the person responsible for such submission, that all appropriate records have been searched and to the best of that person's knowledge and belief it includes a true and accurate presentation of the facts.

(WARNING: A willfully false statement is a criminal offense, 18 U.S.C. 1001.)

(3) The Food and Drug Administration will not find a drug product, including any active ingredient, which is identical, related, or similar, as described in §310.6, to a drug product, including any active ingredient for which an application is or at any time has been effective or deemed approved, or approved under section 505 of the act, to be exempt from part or all of the new drug provisions of the act.

(4) A contention that a drug product is not a new drug for any other reason is required to be supported by submission of the factual records, data, and information that are necessary and appropriate to support the contention.

(5) It is the responsibility of every person who manufactures or distributes a drug product in reliance upon a "grandfather" provision of the act to maintain files that contain the data and information necessary fully to document and support that status.

(f) *Separation of functions.* Separation of functions commences upon receipt of a request for hearing. The Director of the Center for Drug Evaluation and Research, Food and Drug Administration, will prepare an analysis of the request and a proposed order ruling on the matter. The analysis and proposed order, the request for hearing, and any proposed order denying a hearing and

response under paragraph (g) (2) or (3) of this section will be submitted to the Office of the Commissioner of Food and Drugs for review and decision. When the Center for Drug Evaluation and Research recommends denial of a hearing on all issues on which a hearing is requested, no representative of the Center will participate or advise in the review and decision by the Commissioner. When the Center for Drug Evaluation and Research recommends that a hearing be granted on one or more issues on which a hearing is requested, separation of functions terminates as to those issues, and representatives of the Center may participate or advise in the review and decision by the Commissioner on those issues. The Commissioner may modify the text of the issues, but may not deny a hearing on those issues. Separation of functions continues with respect to issues on which the Center for Drug Evaluation and Research has recommended denial of a hearing. The Commissioner will neither evaluate nor rule on the Center's recommendation on such issues and such issues will not be included in the notice of hearing. Participants in the hearing may make a motion to the presiding officer for the inclusion of any such issue in the hearing. The ruling on such a motion is subject to review in accordance with §12.35(b). Failure to so move constitutes a waiver of the right to a hearing on such an issue. Separation of functions on all issues resumes upon issuance of a notice of hearing. The Office of the General Counsel, Department of Health and Human Services, will observe the same separation of functions.

(g) *Summary judgment.* A person who requests a hearing may not rely upon allegations or denials but is required to set forth specific facts showing that there is a genuine and substantial issue of fact that requires a hearing with respect to a particular drug product specified in the request for hearing.

(1) Where a specific notice of opportunity for hearing (as defined in paragraph (a)(1) of this section) is used, the Commissioner will enter summary judgment against a person who requests a hearing, making findings and conclusions, denying a hearing, if it conclusively appears from the face of

the data, information, and factual analyses in the request for the hearing that there is no genuine and substantial issue of fact which precludes the refusal to approve the application or abbreviated application or the withdrawal of approval of the application or abbreviated application; for example, no adequate and well-controlled clinical investigations meeting each of the precise elements of § 314.126 and, for a combination drug product, § 300.50 of this chapter, showing effectiveness have been identified. Any order entering summary judgment is required to set forth the Commissioner's findings and conclusions in detail and is required to specify why each study submitted fails to meet the requirements of the statute and regulations or why the request for hearing does not raise a genuine and substantial issue of fact.

(2) When following a general notice of opportunity for a hearing (as defined in paragraph (a)(1) of this section) the Director of the Center for Drug Evaluation and Research concludes that summary judgment against a person requesting a hearing should be considered, the Director will serve upon the person requesting a hearing by registered mail a proposed order denying a hearing. This person has 60 days after receipt of the proposed order to respond with sufficient data, information, and analyses to demonstrate that there is a genuine and substantial issue of fact which justifies a hearing.

(3) When following a general or specific notice of opportunity for a hearing a person requesting a hearing submits data or information of a type required by the statute and regulations, and the Director of the Center for Drug Evaluation and Research concludes that summary judgment against the person should be considered, the Director will serve upon the person by registered mail a proposed order denying a hearing. The person has 60 days after receipt of the proposed order to respond with sufficient data, information, and analyses to demonstrate that there is a genuine and substantial issue of fact which justifies a hearing.

(4) If review of the data, information, and analyses submitted show that the grounds cited in the notice are not valid, for example, that substantial evidence of effectiveness exists, the Commissioner will enter summary judgment for the person requesting the hearing, and rescind the notice of opportunity for hearing.

(5) If the Commissioner grants a hearing, it will begin within 90 days after the expiration of the time for requesting the hearing unless the parties otherwise agree in the case of denial of approval, and as soon as practicable in the case of withdrawal of approval.

(6) The Commissioner will grant a hearing if there exists a genuine and substantial issue of fact or if the Commissioner concludes that a hearing would otherwise be in the public interest.

(7) If the manufacturer or distributor of an identical, related, or similar drug product requests and is granted a hearing, the hearing may consider whether the product is in fact identical, related, or similar to the drug product named in the notice of opportunity for a hearing.

(8) A request for a hearing, and any subsequent grant or denial of a hearing, applies only to the drug products named in such documents.

(h) FDA will issue a notice withdrawing approval and declaring all products unlawful for drug products subject to a notice of opportunity for a hearing, including any identical, related, or similar drug product under § 310.6, for which an opportunity for a hearing is waived or for which a hearing is denied. The Commissioner may defer or stay the action pending a ruling on any related request for a hearing or pending any related hearing or other administrative or judicial proceeding.

[50 FR 7493, Feb. 22, 1985; 50 FR 14212, Apr. 11, 1985, as amended at 50 FR 21238, May 23, 1985; 55 FR 11580, Mar. 29, 1990; 57 FR 17996, Apr. 28, 1992; 59 FR 14364, Mar. 28, 1994; 63 FR 5252, Feb. 2, 1998; 67 FR 9586, Mar. 4, 2002; 68 FR 24879, May 9, 2003; 69 FR 48775, Aug. 11, 2004; 74 FR 13113, Mar. 26, 2009]

§ 314.201   Procedure for hearings.

Parts 10 through 16 apply to hearings relating to new drugs under section 505 (d) and (e) of the act.

§314.235 Judicial review.

(a) The Commissioner of Food and Drugs will certify the transcript and record. In any case in which the Commissioner enters an order without a hearing under §314.200(g), the record certified by the Commissioner is required to include the requests for hearing together with the data and information submitted and the Commissioner's findings and conclusion.

(b) A manufacturer or distributor of an identical, related, or similar drug product under §310.6 may seek judicial review of an order withdrawing approval of a new drug application, whether or not a hearing has been held, in a United States court of appeals under section 505(h) of the act.

Subpart F [Reserved]

Subpart G—Miscellaneous Provisions

Source: 50 FR 7493, Feb. 22, 1985, unless otherwise noted. Redesignated at 57 FR 17983, Apr. 28, 1992.

§314.410 Imports and exports of new drugs.

(a) *Imports.* (1) A new drug may be imported into the United States if: (i) It is the subject of an approved application under this part; or (ii) it complies with the regulations pertaining to investigational new drugs under part 312; and it complies with the general regulations pertaining to imports under subpart E of part 1.

(2) A drug substance intended for use in the manufacture, processing, or repacking of a new drug may be imported into the United States if it complies with the labeling exemption in §201.122 pertaining to shipments of drug substances in domestic commerce.

(b) *Exports.* (1) A new drug may be exported if it is the subject of an approved application under this part or it complies with the regulations pertaining to investigational new drugs under part 312.

(2) A new drug substance that is covered by an application approved under this part for use in the manufacture of an approved drug product may be exported by the applicant or any person listed as a supplier in the approved application, provided the drug substance intended for export meets the specification of, and is shipped with a copy of the labeling required for, the approved drug product.

(3) Insulin or an antibiotic drug may be exported without regard to the requirements in section 802 of the act if the insulin or antibiotic drug meets the requirements of section 801(e)(1) of the act.

[50 FR 7493, Feb. 22, 1985. Redesignated at 57 FR 17983, Apr. 28, 1992, and amended at 64 FR 402, Jan. 5, 1999; 69 FR 18766, Apr. 8, 2004]

§314.420 Drug master files.

(a) A drug master file is a submission of information to the Food and Drug Administration by a person (the drug master file holder) who intends it to be used for one of the following purposes: To permit the holder to incorporate the information by reference when the holder submits an investigational new drug application under part 312 or submits an application or an abbreviated application or an amendment or supplement to them under this part, or to permit the holder to authorize other persons to rely on the information to support a submission to FDA without the holder having to disclose the information to the person. FDA ordinarily neither independently reviews drug master files nor approves or disapproves submissions to a drug master file. Instead, the agency customarily reviews the information only in the context of an application under part 312 or this part. A drug master file may contain information of the kind required for any submission to the agency, including information about the following:

(1) [Reserved]

(2) Drug substance, drug substance intermediate, and materials used in their preparation, or drug product;

(3) Packaging materials;

(4) Excipient, colorant, flavor, essence, or materials used in their preparation;

(5) FDA-accepted reference information. (A person wishing to submit information and supporting data in a drug master file (DMF) that is not covered by Types II through IV DMF's must first submit a letter of intent to

the Drug Master File Staff, Food and Drug Administration, 5901–B Ammendale Rd., Beltsville, MD 20705–1266.) FDA will then contact the person to discuss the proposed submission.

(b) An investigational new drug application or an application, abbreviated application, amendment, or supplement may incorporate by reference all or part of the contents of any drug master file in support of the submission if the holder authorizes the incorporation in writing. Each incorporation by reference is required to describe the incorporated material by name, reference number, volume, and page number of the drug master file.

(c) A drug master file is required to be submitted in two copies. The agency has prepared guidance that provides information about how to prepare a well-organized drug master file. If the drug master file holder adds, changes, or deletes any information in the file, the holder shall notify in writing, each person authorized to reference that information. Any addition, change, or deletion of information in a drug master file (except the list required under paragraph (d) of this section) is required to be submitted in two copies and to describe by name, reference number, volume, and page number the information affected in the drug master file.

(d) The drug master file is required to contain a complete list of each person currently authorized to incorporate by reference any information in the file, identifying by name, reference number, volume, and page number the information that each person is authorized to incorporate. If the holder restricts the authorization to particular drug products, the list is required to include the name of each drug product and the application number, if known, to which the authorization applies.

(e) The public availability of data and information in a drug master file, including the availability of data and information in the file to a person authorized to reference the file, is determined under part 20 and § 314.430.

[50 FR 7493, Feb. 22, 1985, as amended at 50 FR 21238, May 23, 1985; 53 FR 33122, Aug. 30, 1988; 55 FR 28380, July 11, 1990; 65 FR 1780, Jan. 12, 2000; 65 FR 56479, Sept. 19, 2000; 67 FR 9586, Mar. 4, 2002; 69 FR 13473, Mar. 23, 2004]

§ 314.430 Availability for public disclosure of data and information in an application or abbreviated application.

(a) The Food and Drug Administration will determine the public availability of any part of an application or abbreviated application under this section and part 20 of this chapter. For purposes of this section, the application or abbreviated application includes all data and information submitted with or incorporated by reference in the application or abbreviated application, including investigational new drug applications, drug master files under § 314.420, supplements submitted under § 314.70 or § 314.97, reports under § 314.80 or § 314.98, and other submissions. For purposes of this section, safety and effectiveness data include all studies and tests of a drug on animals and humans and all studies and tests of the drug for identity, stability, purity, potency, and bioavailability.

(b) FDA will not publicly disclose the existence of an application or abbreviated application before an approval letter is sent to the applicant under § 314.105 or tentative approval letter is sent to the applicant under § 314.107, unless the existence of the application or abbreviated application has been previously publicly disclosed or acknowledged.

(c) If the existence of an unapproved application or abbreviated application has not been publicly disclosed or acknowledged, no data or information in the application or abbreviated application is available for public disclosure.

(d)(1) If the existence of an application or abbreviated application has been publicly disclosed or acknowledged before the agency sends an approval letter to the applicant, no data or information contained in the application or abbreviated application is available for public disclosure before the agency sends an approval letter, but the Commissioner may, in his or her discretion, disclose a summary of selected portions of the safety and effectiveness data that are appropriate for public consideration of a specific pending issue; for example, for consideration of an open session of an FDA advisory committee.

(2) Notwithstanding paragraph (d)(1) of this section, FDA will make available to the public upon request the information in the investigational new drug application that was required to be filed in Docket Number 95S–0158 in the Division of Dockets Management (HFA–305), Food and Drug Administration, 5630 Fishers Lane, rm. 1061, Rockville, MD 20852, for investigations involving an exception from informed consent under § 50.24 of this chapter. Persons wishing to request this information shall submit a request under the Freedom of Information Act.

(e) After FDA sends an approval letter to the applicant, the following data and information in the application or abbreviated application are immediately available for public disclosure, unless the applicant shows that extraordinary circumstances exist. A list of approved applications and abbreviated applications, entitled "Approved Drug Products with Therapeutic Equivalence Evaluations," is available from the Government Printing Office, Washington, DC 20402. This list is updated monthly.

(1) [Reserved]

(2) If the application applies to a new drug, all safety and effectiveness data previously disclosed to the public as set forth in § 20.81 and a summary or summaries of the safety and effectiveness data and information submitted with or incorporated by reference in the application. The summaries do not constitute the full reports of investigations under section 505(b)(1) of the act (21 U.S.C. 355(b)(1)) on which the safety or effectiveness of the drug may be approved. The summaries consist of the following:

(i) For an application approved before July 1, 1975, internal agency records that describe safety and effectiveness data and information, for example, a summary of the basis for approval or internal reviews of the data and information, after deletion of the following:

(a) Names and any information that would identify patients or test subjects or investigators.

(b) Any inappropriate gratuitous comments unnecessary to an objective analysis of the data and information.

(ii) For an application approved on or after July 1, 1975, a Summary Basis of Approval (SBA) document that contains a summary of the safety and effectiveness data and information evaluated by FDA during the drug approval process. The SBA is prepared in one of the following ways:

(a) Before approval of the application, the applicant may prepare a draft SBA which the Center for Drug Evaluation and Research will review and may revise. The draft may be submitted with the application or as an amendment.

(b) The Center for Drug Evaluation and Research may prepare the SBA.

(3) A protocol for a test or study, unless it is shown to fall within the exemption established for trade secrets and confidential commercial information in § 20.61.

(4) Adverse reaction reports, product experience reports, consumer complaints, and other similar data and information after deletion of the following:

(i) Names and any information that would identify the person using the product.

(ii) Names and any information that would identify any third party involved with the report, such as a physician or hospital or other institution.

(5) A list of all active ingredients and any inactive ingredients previously disclosed to the public as set forth in § 20.81.

(6) An assay procedure or other analytical procedure, unless it serves no regulatory or compliance purpose and is shown to fall within the exemption established for trade secrets and confidential commercial information in § 20.61.

(7) All correspondence and written summaries of oral discussions between FDA and the applicant relating to the application, under the provisions of part 20.

(f) All safety and effectiveness data and information which have been submitted in an application and which have not previously been disclosed to the public are available to the public, upon request, at the time any one of the following events occurs unless extraordinary circumstances are shown:

173

(1) No work is being or will be undertaken to have the application approved.

(2) A final determination is made that the application is not approvable and all legal appeals have been exhausted.

(3) Approval of the application is withdrawn and all legal appeals have been exhausted.

(4) A final determination has been made that the drug is not a new drug.

(5) For applications submitted under section 505(b) of the act, the effective date of the approval of the first abbreviated application submitted under section 505(j) of the act which refers to such drug, or the date on which the approval of an abbreviated application under section 505(j) of the act which refers to such drug could be made effective if such an abbreviated application had been submitted.

(6) For abbreviated applications submitted under section 505(j) of the act, when FDA sends an approval letter to the applicant.

(g) The following data and information in an application or abbreviated application are not available for public disclosure unless they have been previously disclosed to the public as set forth in §20.81 of this chapter or they relate to a product or ingredient that has been abandoned and they do not represent a trade secret or confidential commercial or financial information under §20.61 of this chapter:

(1) Manufacturing methods or processes, including quality control procedures.

(2) Production, sales distribution, and similar data and information, except that any compilation of that data and information aggregated and prepared in a way that does not reveal data or information which is not available for public disclosure under this provision is available for public disclosure.

(3) Quantitative or semiquantitative formulas.

(h) The compilations of information specified in §20.117 are available for public disclosure.

[50 FR 7493, Feb. 22, 1985, as amended at 50 FR 21238, May 23, 1985; 55 FR 11580, Mar. 29, 1990; 57 FR 17996, Apr. 28, 1992; 61 FR 51530, Oct. 2, 1996; 64 FR 26698, May 13, 1998; 64 FR 402, Jan. 5, 1999; 66 FR 1832, Jan. 10, 2001; 68 FR 24879, May 9, 2003; 69 FR 18766, Apr. 8, 2004; 73 FR 39610, July 10, 2008]

§ 314.440 Addresses for applications and abbreviated applications.

(a) Applicants shall send applications, abbreviated applications, and other correspondence relating to matters covered by this part, except for products listed in paragraph (b) of this section, to the appropriate office identified below:

(1) Except as provided in paragraph (a)(4) of this section, an application under §314.50 or §314.54 submitted for filing should be directed to the Central Document Room, 5901–B Ammendale Rd., Beltsville, MD 20705–1266. Applicants may obtain information about folders for binding applications on the Internet at *http://www.fda.gov/cder/ddms/binders.htm*. After FDA has filed the application, the agency will inform the applicant which division is responsible for the application. Amendments, supplements, resubmissions, requests for waivers, and other correspondence about an application that has been filed should be addressed to 5901–B Ammendale Rd., Beltsville, MD 20705–1266, to the attention of the appropriate division.

(2) Except as provided in paragraph (a)(4) of this section, an abbreviated application under §314.94, and amendments, supplements, and resubmissions should be directed to the Office of Generic Drugs (HFD–600), Center for Drug Evaluation and Research, Food and Drug Administration, Metro Park North VII, 7620 Standish Pl., Rockville, MD 20855. This includes items sent by parcel post or overnight courier service. Correspondence not associated with an abbreviated application should be addressed specifically to the intended office or division and to the person as follows: Office of Generic Drugs, Center for Drug Evaluation and Research, Food and Drug Administration, Attn: [insert name of person], Metro

Park North II, HFD–[insert mail code of office or division], 7500 Standish Place, rm. 150, Rockville, MD 20855. The mail code for the Office of Generic Drugs is HFD–600, the mail codes for the Divisions of Chemistry I, II, and III are HFD–620, HFD–640, and HFD–630, respectively, and the mail code for the Division of Bioequivalence is HFD–650.

(3) A request for an opportunity for a hearing under § 314.110 on the question of whether there are grounds for denying approval of an application, except an application under paragraph (b) of this section, should be directed to the Associate Director for Policy (HFD–5).

(4) The field copy of an application, an abbreviated application, amendments, supplements, resubmissions, requests for waivers, and other correspondence about an application and an abbreviated application shall be sent to the applicant's home FDA district office, except that a foreign applicant shall send the field copy to the appropriate address identified in paragraphs (a)(1) and (a)(2) of this section.

(b) Applicants shall send applications and other correspondence relating to matters covered by this part for the drug products listed below to the Document Control Center (HFM–99), Center for Biologics Evaluation and Research, 1401 Rockville Pike, suite 200N, Rockville, MD 20852–1448, except applicants shall send a request for an opportunity for a hearing under § 314.110 on the question of whether there are grounds for denying approval of an application to the Director, Center for Biologics Evaluation and Research (HFM–1), at the same address.

(1) Ingredients packaged together with containers intended for the collection, processing, or storage of blood and blood components;

(2) Plasma volume expanders and hydroxyethyl starch for leukapheresis;

(3) Blood component processing solutions and shelf life extenders; and

(4) Oxygen carriers.

[50 FR 7493, Feb. 22, 1985, as amended at 50 FR 21238, May 23, 1985; 55 FR 11581, Mar. 29, 1990; 57 FR 17997, Apr. 28, 1992; 58 FR 47352, Sept. 8, 1993; 62 FR 43639, Aug. 15, 1997; 69 FR 13473, Mar. 23, 2004; 70 FR 14981, Mar. 24, 2005; 73 FR 39610, July 10, 2008; 74 FR 13113, Mar. 26, 2009; 75 FR 37295, June 29, 2010]

§ 314.445 Guidance documents.

(a) FDA has made available guidance documents under § 10.115 of this chapter to help you to comply with certain requirements of this part.

(b) The Center for Drug Evaluation and Research (CDER) maintains a list of guidance documents that apply to CDER's regulations. The list is maintained on the Internet and is published annually in the FEDERAL REGISTER. A request for a copy of the CDER list should be directed to the Office of Training and Communications, Division of Drug Information, Center for Drug Evaluation and Research, Food and Drug Administration, 10903 New Hampshire Ave., Silver Spring, MD 20993–0002.

[65 FR 56480, Sept. 19, 2000, as amended at 74 FR 13113, Mar. 26, 2009]

Subpart H—Accelerated Approval of New Drugs for Serious or Life-Threatening Illnesses

SOURCE: 57 FR 58958, Dec. 11, 1992, unless otherwise noted.

§ 314.500 Scope.

This subpart applies to certain new drug products that have been studied for their safety and effectiveness in treating serious or life-threatening illnesses and that provide meaningful therapeutic benefit to patients over existing treatments (e.g., ability to treat patients unresponsive to, or intolerant of, available therapy, or improved patient response over available therapy).

[57 FR 58958, Dec. 11, 1992, as amended at 64 FR 402, Jan. 5, 1999]

§ 314.510 Approval based on a surrogate endpoint or on an effect on a clinical endpoint other than survival or irreversible morbidity.

FDA may grant marketing approval for a new drug product on the basis of adequate and well-controlled clinical trials establishing that the drug product has an effect on a surrogate endpoint that is reasonably likely, based on epidemiologic, therapeutic, pathophysiologic, or other evidence, to predict clinical benefit or on the basis of an effect on a clinical endpoint other than survival or irreversible morbidity.

Approval under this section will be subject to the requirement that the applicant study the drug further, to verify and describe its clinical benefit, where there is uncertainty as to the relation of the surrogate endpoint to clinical benefit, or of the observed clinical benefit to ultimate outcome. Postmarketing studies would usually be studies already underway. When required to be conducted, such studies must also be adequate and well-controlled. The applicant shall carry out any such studies with due diligence.

§314.520 Approval with restrictions to assure safe use.

(a) If FDA concludes that a drug product shown to be effective can be safely used only if distribution or use is restricted, FDA will require such postmarketing restrictions as are needed to assure safe use of the drug product, such as:

(1) Distribution restricted to certain facilities or physicians with special training or experience; or

(2) Distribution conditioned on the performance of specified medical procedures.

(b) The limitations imposed will be commensurate with the specific safety concerns presented by the drug product.

§314.530 Withdrawal procedures.

(a) For new drugs approved under §§314.510 and 314.520, FDA may withdraw approval, following a hearing as provided in part 15 of this chapter, as modified by this section, if:

(1) A postmarketing clinical study fails to verify clinical benefit;

(2) The applicant fails to perform the required postmarketing study with due diligence;

(3) Use after marketing demonstrates that postmarketing restrictions are inadequate to assure safe use of the drug product;

(4) The applicant fails to adhere to the postmarketing restrictions agreed upon;

(5) The promotional materials are false or misleading; or

(6) Other evidence demonstrates that the drug product is not shown to be safe or effective under its conditions of use.

(b) *Notice of opportunity for a hearing.* The Director of the Center for Drug Evaluation and Research will give the applicant notice of an opportunity for a hearing on the Center's proposal to withdraw the approval of an application approved under §314.510 or §314.520. The notice, which will ordinarily be a letter, will state generally the reasons for the action and the proposed grounds for the order.

(c) *Submission of data and information.* (1) If the applicant fails to file a written request for a hearing within 15 days of receipt of the notice, the applicant waives the opportunity for a hearing.

(2) If the applicant files a timely request for a hearing, the agency will publish a notice of hearing in the FEDERAL REGISTER in accordance with §§12.32(e) and 15.20 of this chapter.

(3) An applicant who requests a hearing under this section must, within 30 days of receipt of the notice of opportunity for a hearing, submit the data and information upon which the applicant intends to rely at the hearing.

(d) *Separation of functions.* Separation of functions (as specified in §10.55 of this chapter) will not apply at any point in withdrawal proceedings under this section.

(e) *Procedures for hearings.* Hearings held under this section will be conducted in accordance with the provisions of part 15 of this chapter, with the following modifications:

(1) An advisory committee duly constituted under part 14 of this chapter will be present at the hearing. The committee will be asked to review the issues involved and to provide advice and recommendations to the Commissioner of Food and Drugs.

(2) The presiding officer, the advisory committee members, up to three representatives of the applicant, and up to three representatives of the Center may question any person during or at the conclusion of the person's presentation. No other person attending the hearing may question a person making a presentation. The presiding officer may, as a matter of discretion, permit questions to be submitted to the presiding officer for response by a person making a presentation.

(f) *Judicial review.* The Commissioner's decision constitutes final agency action from which the applicant may petition for judicial review. Before requesting an order from a court for a stay of action pending review, an applicant must first submit a petition for a stay of action under §10.35 of this chapter.

[57 FR 58958, Dec. 11, 1992, as amended at 64 FR 402, Jan. 5, 1999]

§314.540 Postmarketing safety reporting.

Drug products approved under this program are subject to the postmarketing recordkeeping and safety reporting applicable to all approved drug products, as provided in §§314.80 and 314.81.

§314.550 Promotional materials.

For drug products being considered for approval under this subpart, unless otherwise informed by the agency, applicants must submit to the agency for consideration during the preapproval review period copies of all promotional materials, including promotional labeling as well as advertisements, intended for dissemination or publication within 120 days following marketing approval. After 120 days following marketing approval, unless otherwise informed by the agency, the applicant must submit promotional materials at least 30 days prior to the intended time of initial dissemination of the labeling or initial publication of the advertisement.

§314.560 Termination of requirements.

If FDA determines after approval that the requirements established in §314.520, §314.530, or §314.550 are no longer necessary for the safe and effective use of a drug product, it will so notify the applicant. Ordinarily, for drug products approved under §314.510, these requirements will no longer apply when FDA determines that the required postmarketing study verifies and describes the drug product's clinical benefit and the drug product would be appropriate for approval under traditional procedures. For drug products approved under §314.520, the restrictions would no longer apply when FDA determines that safe use of the drug product can be assured through appropriate labeling. FDA also retains the discretion to remove specific post-approval requirements upon review of a petition submitted by the sponsor in accordance with §10.30.

Subpart I—Approval of New Drugs When Human Efficacy Studies Are Not Ethical or Feasible

SOURCE: 67 FR 37995, May 31, 2002, unless otherwise noted.

§314.600 Scope.

This subpart applies to certain new drug products that have been studied for their safety and efficacy in ameliorating or preventing serious or life-threatening conditions caused by exposure to lethal or permanently disabling toxic biological, chemical, radiological, or nuclear substances. This subpart applies only to those new drug products for which: Definitive human efficacy studies cannot be conducted because it would be unethical to deliberately expose healthy human volunteers to a lethal or permanently disabling toxic biological, chemical, radiological, or nuclear substance; and field trials to study the product's effectiveness after an accidental or hostile exposure have not been feasible. This subpart does not apply to products that can be approved based on efficacy standards described elsewhere in FDA's regulations (e.g., accelerated approval based on surrogate markers or clinical endpoints other than survival or irreversible morbidity), nor does it address the safety evaluation for the products to which it does apply.

§314.610 Approval based on evidence of effectiveness from studies in animals.

(a) FDA may grant marketing approval for a new drug product for which safety has been established and for which the requirements of §314.600 are met based on adequate and well-controlled animal studies when the results of those animal studies establish that the drug product is reasonably likely to produce clinical benefit in humans. In assessing the sufficiency of animal data, the agency may take into account other data, including human data, available to the agency. FDA will rely on the evidence from studies in animals to provide substantial evidence of the effectiveness of these products only when:

(1) There is a reasonably well-understood pathophysiological mechanism of the toxicity of the substance and its prevention or substantial reduction by the product;

(2) The effect is demonstrated in more than one animal species expected to react with a response predictive for humans, unless the effect is demonstrated in a single animal species that represents a sufficiently well-characterized animal model for predicting the response in humans;

(3) The animal study endpoint is clearly related to the desired benefit in humans, generally the enhancement of survival or prevention of major morbidity; and

(4) The data or information on the kinetics and pharmacodynamics of the product or other relevant data or information, in animals and humans, allows selection of an effective dose in humans.

(b) Approval under this subpart will be subject to three requirements:

(1) *Postmarketing studies.* The applicant must conduct postmarketing studies, such as field studies, to verify and describe the drug's clinical benefit and to assess its safety when used as indicated when such studies are feasible and ethical. Such postmarketing studies would not be feasible until an exigency arises. When such studies are feasible, the applicant must conduct such studies with due diligence. Applicants must include as part of their application a plan or approach to postmarketing study commitments in the event such studies become ethical and feasible.

(2) *Approval with restrictions to ensure safe use.* If FDA concludes that a drug product shown to be effective under this subpart can be safely used only if distribution or use is restricted, FDA will require such postmarketing restrictions as are needed to ensure safe use of the drug product, commensurate with the specific safety concerns presented by the drug product, such as:

(i) Distribution restricted to certain facilities or health care practitioners with special training or experience;

(ii) Distribution conditioned on the performance of specified medical procedures, including medical followup; and

(iii) Distribution conditioned on specified recordkeeping requirements.

(3) *Information to be provided to patient recipients.* For drug products or specific indications approved under this subpart, applicants must prepare, as part of their proposed labeling, labeling to be provided to patient recipients. The patient labeling must explain that, for ethical or feasibility reasons, the drug's approval was based on efficacy studies conducted in animals alone and must give the drug's indication(s), directions for use (dosage and administration), contraindications, a description of any reasonably foreseeable risks, adverse reactions, anticipated benefits, drug interactions, and any other relevant information required by FDA at the time of approval. The patient labeling must be available with the product to be provided to patients prior to administration or dispensing of the drug product for the use approved under this subpart, if possible.

§ 314.620 Withdrawal procedures.

(a) *Reasons to withdraw approval.* For new drugs approved under this subpart, FDA may withdraw approval, following a hearing as provided in part 15 of this chapter, as modified by this section, if:

(1) A postmarketing clinical study fails to verify clinical benefit;

(2) The applicant fails to perform the postmarketing study with due diligence;

(3) Use after marketing demonstrates that postmarketing restrictions are inadequate to ensure safe use of the drug product;

(4) The applicant fails to adhere to the postmarketing restrictions applied at the time of approval under this subpart;

(5) The promotional materials are false or misleading; or

(6) Other evidence demonstrates that the drug product is not shown to be safe or effective under its conditions of use.

(b) *Notice of opportunity for a hearing.* The Director of the Center for Drug Evaluation and Research (CDER) will give the applicant notice of an opportunity for a hearing on CDER's proposal to withdraw the approval of an application approved under this subpart. The notice, which will ordinarily be a letter, will state generally the reasons for the action and the proposed grounds for the order.

(c) *Submission of data and information.* (1) If the applicant fails to file a written request for a hearing within 15 days of receipt of the notice, the applicant waives the opportunity for a hearing.

(2) If the applicant files a timely request for a hearing, the agency will publish a notice of hearing in the FEDERAL REGISTER in accordance with §§ 12.32(e) and 15.20 of this chapter.

(3) An applicant who requests a hearing under this section must, within 30 days of receipt of the notice of opportunity for a hearing, submit the data and information upon which the applicant intends to rely at the hearing.

(d) *Separation of functions.* Separation of functions (as specified in § 10.55 of this chapter) will not apply at any point in withdrawal proceedings under this section.

(e) *Procedures for hearings.* Hearings held under this section will be conducted in accordance with the provisions of part 15 of this chapter, with the following modifications:

(1) An advisory committee duly constituted under part 14 of this chapter will be present at the hearing. The committee will be asked to review the issues involved and to provide advice and recommendations to the Commissioner of Food and Drugs.

(2) The presiding officer, the advisory committee members, up to three representatives of the applicant, and up to three representatives of CDER may question any person during or at the conclusion of the person's presentation. No other person attending the hearing may question a person making a presentation. The presiding officer may, as a matter of discretion, permit questions to be submitted to the presiding officer for response by a person making a presentation.

(f) *Judicial review.* The Commissioner of Food and Drugs' decision constitutes final agency action from which the applicant may petition for judicial review. Before requesting an order from a court for a stay of action pending review, an applicant must first submit a petition for a stay of action under § 10.35 of this chapter.

§ 314.630 Postmarketing safety reporting.

Drug products approved under this subpart are subject to the postmarketing recordkeeping and safety reporting requirements applicable to all approved drug products, as provided in §§ 314.80 and 314.81.

§ 314.640 Promotional materials.

For drug products being considered for approval under this subpart, unless otherwise informed by the agency, applicants must submit to the agency for consideration during the preapproval review period copies of all promotional materials, including promotional labeling as well as advertisements, intended for dissemination or publication within 120 days following marketing approval. After 120 days following marketing approval, unless otherwise informed by the agency, the applicant must submit promotional materials at least 30 days prior to the intended time of initial dissemination of the labeling or initial publication of the advertisement.

§ 314.650 Termination of requirements.

If FDA determines after approval under this subpart that the requirements established in §§ 314.610(b)(2), 314.620, and 314.630 are no longer necessary for the safe and effective use of a drug product, FDA will so notify the applicant. Ordinarily, for drug products approved under § 314.610, these requirements will no longer apply when FDA determines that the postmarketing study verifies and describes the drug product's clinical benefit. For drug products approved under § 314.610, the restrictions would no longer apply when FDA determines that safe use of the drug product can be ensured through appropriate labeling. FDA also retains the discretion to remove specific postapproval requirements upon review of a petition submitted by the sponsor in accordance with § 10.30 of this chapter.

PART 315—DIAGNOSTIC RADIOPHARMACEUTICALS

AUTHORITY: 21 U.S.C. 321, 331, 351, 352, 353, 355, 371, 374, 379e; sec. 122, Pub. L. 105–115, 111 Stat. 2322 (21 U.S.C. 355 note).

SOURCE: 64 FR 26667, May 17, 1999, unless otherwise noted.

§ 315.1 Scope.

The regulations in this part apply to radiopharmaceuticals intended for in vivo administration for diagnostic and monitoring use. They do not apply to radiopharmaceuticals intended for therapeutic purposes. In situations where a particular radiopharmaceutical is proposed for both diagnostic and therapeutic uses, the radiopharmaceutical must be evaluated taking into account each intended use.

§ 315.2 Definition.

For purposes of this part, *diagnostic radiopharmaceutical* means:

(a) An article that is intended for use in the diagnosis or monitoring of a disease or a manifestation of a disease in humans and that exhibits spontaneous disintegration of unstable nuclei with the emission of nuclear particles or photons; or

(b) Any nonradioactive reagent kit or nuclide generator that is intended to be used in the preparation of such article as defined in paragraph (a) of this section.

§ 315.3 General factors relevant to safety and effectiveness.

FDA's determination of the safety and effectiveness of a diagnostic radiopharmaceutical includes consideration of the following:

(a) The proposed use of the diagnostic radiopharmaceutical in the practice of medicine,

(b) The pharmacological and toxicological activity of the diagnostic radiopharmaceutical (including any carrier or ligand component of the diagnostic radiopharmaceutical), and

(c) The estimated absorbed radiation dose of the diagnostic radiopharmaceutical.

§ 315.4 Indications.

(a) For diagnostic radiopharmaceuticals, the categories of proposed indications for use include, but are not limited to, the following:

(1) Structure delineation;

(2) Functional, physiological, or biochemical assessment;

(3) Disease or pathology detection or assessment; and

(4) Diagnostic or therapeutic patient management.

(b) Where a diagnostic radiopharmaceutical is not intended to provide disease-specific information, the proposed indications for use may refer to a biochemical, physiological, anatomical, or pathological process or to more than one disease or condition.

§ 315.5 Evaluation of effectiveness.

(a) The effectiveness of a diagnostic radiopharmaceutical is assessed by evaluating its ability to provide useful clinical information related to its proposed indications for use. The method of this evaluation varies depending upon the proposed indication(s) and may use one or more of the following criteria:

(1) The claim of structure delineation is established by demonstrating in a defined clinical setting the ability to locate anatomical structures and to characterize their anatomy.

(2) The claim of functional, physiological, or biochemical assessment is established by demonstrating in a defined clinical setting reliable measurement of function(s) or physiological, biochemical, or molecular process(es).

(3) The claim of disease or pathology detection or assessment is established by demonstrating in a defined clinical setting that the diagnostic radiopharmaceutical has sufficient accuracy in identifying or characterizing the disease or pathology.

(4) The claim of diagnostic or therapeutic patient management is established by demonstrating in a defined clinical setting that the test is useful

in diagnostic or therapeutic patient management.

(5) For a claim that does not fall within the indication categories identified in § 315.4, the applicant or sponsor should consult FDA on how to establish the effectiveness of the diagnostic radiopharmaceutical for the claim.

(b) The accuracy and usefulness of the diagnostic information is determined by comparison with a reliable assessment of actual clinical status. A reliable assessment of actual clinical status may be provided by a diagnostic standard or standards of demonstrated accuracy. In the absence of such diagnostic standard(s), the actual clinical status must be established in another manner, e.g., patient followup.

§ 315.6 Evaluation of safety.

(a) Factors considered in the safety assessment of a diagnostic radiopharmaceutical include, among others, the following:

(1) The radiation dose;

(2) The pharmacology and toxicology of the radiopharmaceutical, including any radionuclide, carrier, or ligand;

(3) The risks of an incorrect diagnostic determination;

(4) The adverse reaction profile of the drug;

(5) Results of human experience with the radiopharmaceutical for other uses; and

(6) Results of any previous human experience with the carrier or ligand of the radiopharmaceutical when the same chemical entity as the carrier or ligand has been used in a previously studied product.

(b) The assessment of the adverse reaction profile includes, but is not limited to, an evaluation of the potential of the diagnostic radiopharmaceutical, including the carrier or ligand, to elicit the following:

(1) Allergic or hypersensitivity responses,

(2) Immunologic responses,

(3) Changes in the physiologic or biochemical function of the target and nontarget tissues, and

(4) Clinically detectable signs or symptoms.

(c)(1) To establish the safety of a diagnostic radiopharmaceutical, FDA

may require, among other information, the following types of data:

(i) Pharmacology data,

(ii) Toxicology data,

(iii) Clinical adverse event data, and

(iv) Radiation safety assessment.

(2) The amount of new safety data required will depend on the characteristics of the product and available information regarding the safety of the diagnostic radiopharmaceutical, and its carrier or ligand, obtained from other studies and uses. Such information may include, but is not limited to, the dose, route of administration, frequency of use, half-life of the ligand or carrier, half-life of the radionuclide, and results of clinical and preclinical studies. FDA will establish categories of diagnostic radiopharmaceuticals based on defined characteristics relevant to risk and will specify the amount and type of safety data that are appropriate for each category (e.g., required safety data may be limited for diagnostic radiopharmaceuticals with a well established, low-risk profile). Upon reviewing the relevant product characteristics and safety information, FDA will place each diagnostic radiopharmaceutical into the appropriate safety risk category.

(d) Radiation safety assessment. The radiation safety assessment must establish the radiation dose of a diagnostic radiopharmaceutical by radiation dosimetry evaluations in humans and appropriate animal models. The maximum tolerated dose need not be established.

PART 316—ORPHAN DRUGS

Subpart A—General Provisions

AUTHORITY: 21 U.S.C. 360aa, 360bb, 360cc, 360dd, 371.

SOURCE: 57 FR 62085, Dec. 29, 1992, unless otherwise noted.

EDITORIAL NOTE: Nomenclature changes to part 316 appear at 69 FR 13717, Mar. 24, 2004.

Subpart A—General Provisions

§ 316.1　Scope of this part.

(a) This part implements sections 525, 526, 527, and 528 of the act and provides procedures to encourage and facilitate the development of drugs for rare diseases or conditions, including biological products and antibiotics. This part sets forth the procedures and requirements for:

(1) Submissions to FDA of:

(i) Requests for recommendations for investigations of drugs for rare diseases or conditions;

(ii) Requests for designation of a drug for a rare disease or condition; and

(iii) Requests for gaining exclusive approval for a drug for a rare disease or condition.

(2) Allowing a sponsor to provide an investigational drug under a treatment protocol to patients who need the drug for treatment of a rare disease or condition.

(b) This part does not apply to food, medical devices, or drugs for veterinary use.

(c) References in this part to regulatory sections of the Code of Federal Regulations are to chapter I of title 21, unless otherwise noted.

[57 FR 62085, Dec. 29, 1992, as amended at 78 FR 35132, June 12, 2013]

§ 316.2　Purpose.

The purpose of this part is to establish standards and procedures for determining eligibility for the benefits provided for in section 2 of the Orphan Drug Act, including written recommendations for investigations of orphan drugs, a 7-year period of exclusive marketing, and treatment use of investigational orphan drugs. This part is also intended to satisfy Congress' requirements that FDA promulgate procedures for the implementation of sections 525(a) and 526(a) of the act.

§ 316.3　Definitions.

(a) The definitions and interpretations contained in section 201 of the act apply to those terms when used in this part.

(b) The following definitions of terms apply to this part:

(1) *Act* means the Federal Food, Drug, and Cosmetic Act as amended by section 2 of the Orphan Drug Act (sections 525–528 (21 U.S.C. 360aa–360dd)).

(2) *Active moiety* means the molecule or ion, excluding those appended portions of the molecule that cause the drug to be an ester, salt (including a salt with hydrogen or coordination bonds), or other noncovalent derivative

(such as a complex, chelate, or clathrate) of the molecule, responsible for the physiological or pharmacological action of the drug substance.

(3) *Clinically superior* means that a drug is shown to provide a significant therapeutic advantage over and above that provided by an approved drug (that is otherwise the same drug) in one or more of the following ways:

(i) Greater effectiveness than an approved drug (as assessed by effect on a clinically meaningful endpoint in adequate and well controlled clinical trials). Generally, this would represent the same kind of evidence needed to support a comparative effectiveness claim for two different drugs; in most cases, direct comparative clinical trials would be necessary; or

(ii) Greater safety in a substantial portion of the target populations, for example, by the elimination of an ingredient or contaminant that is associated with relatively frequent adverse effects. In some cases, direct comparative clinical trials will be necessary; or

(iii) In unusual cases, where neither greater safety nor greater effectiveness has been shown, a demonstration that the drug otherwise makes a major contribution to patient care.

(4) *Director* means the Director of FDA's Office of Orphan Products Development.

(5) *FDA* means the Food and Drug Administration.

(6) *Holder* means the sponsor in whose name an orphan drug is designated and approved.

(7) *IND* means an investigational new drug application under part 312 of this chapter.

(8) *Manufacturer* means any person or agency engaged in the manufacture of a drug that is subject to investigation and approval under the act or the biologics provisions of the Public Health Service Act (42 U.S.C. 262–263).

(9) *Marketing application* means an application for approval of a new drug filed under section 505(b) of the act or an application for a biologics license submitted under section 351 of the Public Health Service Act (42 U.S.C. 262).

(10) *Orphan drug* means a drug intended for use in a rare disease or condition as defined in section 526 of the act.

(11) *Orphan-drug designation* means FDA's act of granting a request for designation under section 526 of the act.

(12) *Orphan-drug exclusive approval* or *exclusive approval* means that, effective on the date of FDA approval as stated in the approval letter of a marketing application for a sponsor of a designated orphan drug, no approval will be given to a subsequent sponsor of the same drug for the same use or indication for 7 years, except as otherwise provided by law or in this part. A designated drug will receive orphan-drug exclusive approval only if the same drug has not already been approved for the same use or indication.

(13) *Orphan subset of a non-rare disease or condition ("orphan subset")* means that use of the drug in a subset of persons with a non-rare disease or condition may be appropriate but use of the drug outside of that subset (in the remaining persons with the non-rare disease or condition) would be inappropriate owing to some property(ies) of the drug, for example, drug toxicity, mechanism of action, or previous clinical experience with the drug.

(14) *Same drug* means:

(i) If it is a drug composed of small molecules, a drug that contains the same active moiety as a previously approved drug and is intended for the same use as the previously approved drug, even if the particular ester or salt (including a salt with hydrogen or coordination bonds) or other noncovalent derivative such as a complex, chelate or clathrate has not been previously approved, except that if the subsequent drug can be shown to be clinically superior to the first drug, it will not be considered to be the same drug.

(ii) If it is a drug composed of large molecules (macromolecules), a drug that contains the same principal molecular structural features (but not necessarily all of the same structural features) and is intended for the same use as a previously approved drug, except that, if the subsequent drug can be shown to be clinically superior, it will not be considered to be the same drug. This criterion will be applied as follows to different kinds of macromolecules:

(A) Two protein drugs would be considered the same if the only differences in structure between them were due to post-translational events or infidelity of translation or transcription or were minor differences in amino acid sequence; other potentially important differences, such as different glycosylation patterns or different tertiary structures, would not cause the drugs to be considered different unless the differences were shown to be clinically superior.

(B) Two polysaccharide drugs would be considered the same if they had identical saccharide repeating units, even if the number of units were to vary and even if there were postpolymerization modifications, unless the subsequent drug could be shown to be clinically superior.

(C) Two polynucleotide drugs consisting of two or more distinct nucleotides would be considered the same if they had an identical sequence of purine and pyrimidine bases (or their derivatives) bound to an identical sugar backbone (ribose, deoxyribose, or modifications of these sugars), unless the subsequent drug were shown to be clinically superior.

(D) Closely related, complex partly definable drugs with similar therapeutic intent, such as two live viral vaccines for the same indication, would be considered the same unless the subsequent drug was shown to be clinically superior.

(15) *Sponsor* means the entity that assumes responsibility for a clinical or nonclinical investigation of a drug, including the responsibility for compliance with applicable provisions of the act and regulations. A sponsor may be an individual, partnership, corporation, or Government agency and may be a manufacturer, scientific institution, or an investigator regularly and lawfully engaged in the investigation of drugs. For purposes of the Orphan Drug Act, FDA considers the real party or parties in interest to be a sponsor.

[57 FR 62085, Dec. 29, 1992, as amended at 64 FR 402, Jan. 5, 1999; 64 FR 56449, Oct. 20, 1999; 78 FR 35132, June 12, 2013]

§ 316.4 Address for submissions.

All correspondence and requests for FDA action under the provisions of this rule should be addressed as follows: Office of Orphan Products Development, Food and Drug Administration, Bldg. 32, Rm. 5271, 10903 New Hampshire Ave., Silver Spring, MD 20993.

[78 FR 35133, June 12, 2013]

Subpart B—Written Recommendations for Investigations of Orphan Drugs

§ 316.10 Content and format of a request for written recommendations.

(a) A sponsor's request for written recommendations from FDA concerning the nonclinical and clinical investigations necessary for approval of a marketing application shall be submitted in the form and contain the information required in this section. FDA may require the sponsor to submit information in addition to that specified in paragraph (b) of this section if FDA determines that the sponsor's initial request does not contain adequate information on which to base recommendations.

(b) A sponsor shall submit two copies of a completed, dated, and signed request for written recommendations that contains the following:

(1) The sponsor's name and address.

(2) A statement that the sponsor is requesting written recommendations on orphan-drug development under section 525 of the act.

(3) The name of the sponsor's primary contact person and/or resident agent, and the person's title, address, and telephone number.

(4) The generic name and trade name, if any, of the drug and a list of the drug product's components or description of the drug product's formulation, and chemical and physical properties.

(5) The proposed dosage form and route of administration.

(6) A description of the disease or condition for which the drug is proposed to be investigated and the proposed indication or indications for use for such disease or condition.

(7) Current regulatory and marketing status and history of the drug product, including:

(i) Whether the product is the subject of an IND or a marketing application (if the product is the subject of an IND or a marketing application, the IND or marketing application numbers should be stated and the investigational or approved indication or indications for use specified);

(ii) Known marketing experience or investigational status outside the United States;

(iii) So far as is known or can be determined, all indications previously or currently under investigation anywhere;

(iv) All adverse regulatory actions taken by the United States or foreign authorities.

(8) The basis for concluding that the drug is for a disease or condition that is rare in the United States, including the following:

(i) The size and other known demographic characteristics of the patient population affected and the source of this information.

(ii) For drugs intended for diseases or conditions affecting 200,000 or more people in the United States, or for a vaccine, diagnostic drug, or preventive drug that would be given to 200,000 or more persons per year, a summary of the sponsor's basis for believing that the disease or condition described in paragraph (b)(6) of this section occurs so infrequently that there is no reasonable expectation that the costs of drug development and marketing will be recovered in future sales of the drug in the United States. The estimated costs and sales data should be submitted as provided for in §316.21(c).

(9) A summary and analysis of available data on the pharmacologic effects of the drug.

(10) A summary and analysis of available nonclinical and clinical data pertinent to the drug and the disease to be studied including copies of pertinent published reports. When a drug proposed for orphan drug designation is intended to treat a life-threatening or severely debilitating illness, especially where no satisfactory alternative therapy exists, the sponsor may wish voluntarily to provide this information. A sponsor of such a drug may be entitled to expeditious development, evaluation, and marketing under 21 CFR part 312, subpart E.

(11) An explanation of how the data summarized and analyzed under paragraphs (b)(9) and (b)(10) of this section

support the rationale for use of the drug in the rare disease or condition.

(12) A definition of the population from which subjects will be identified for clinical trials, if known.

(13) A detailed outline of any protocols under which the drug has been or is being studied for the rare disease or condition and a summary and analysis of any available data from such studies.

(14) The sponsor's proposal as to the scope of nonclinical and clinical investigations needed to establish the safety and effectiveness of the drug.

(15) Detailed protocols for each proposed United States or foreign clinical investigation, if available.

(16) Specific questions to be addressed by FDA in its recommendations for nonclinical laboratory studies and clinical investigations.

[57 FR 62085, Dec. 29, 1992; 58 FR 6167, Jan. 26, 1993]

§316.12 Providing written recommendations.

(a) FDA will provide the sponsor with written recommendations concerning the nonclinical laboratory studies and clinical investigations necessary for approval of a marketing application if none of the reasons described in §316.14 for refusing to do so applies.

(b) When a sponsor seeks written recommendations at a stage of drug development at which advice on any clinical investigations, or on particular investigations would be premature, FDA's response may be limited to written recommendations concerning only nonclinical laboratory studies, or only certain of the clinical studies (e.g., Phase 1 studies as described in §312.21 of this chapter). Prior to providing written recommendations for the clinical investigations required to achieve marketing approval, FDA may require that the results of the nonclinical laboratory studies or completed early clinical studies be submitted to FDA for agency review.

§316.14 Refusal to provide written recommendations.

(a) FDA may refuse to provide written recommendations concerning the nonclinical laboratory studies and clinical investigations necessary for approval of a marketing application for any of the following reasons:

(1) The information required to be submitted by § 316.10(b) has not been submitted, or the information submitted is incomplete.

(2) There is insufficient information about:

(i) The drug to identify the active moiety and its physical and chemical properties, if these characteristics can be determined; or

(ii) The disease or condition to determine that the disease or condition is rare in the United States; or

(iii) The reasons for believing that the drug may be useful for treating the rare disease or condition with that drug; or

(iv) The regulatory and marketing history of the drug to determine the scope and type of investigations that have already been conducted on the drug for the rare disease or condition; or

(v) The plan of study for establishing the safety and effectiveness of the drug for treatment of the rare disease or condition.

(3) The specific questions for which the sponsor seeks the advice of the agency are unclear or are not sufficiently specific.

(4) On the basis of the information submitted and on other information available to the agency, FDA determines that the disease or condition for which the drug is intended is not rare in the United States.

(5) On the basis of the information submitted and on other information available to the agency, FDA determines that there is an inadequate basis for permitting investigational use of the drug under part 312 of this chapter for the rare disease or condition.

(6) The request for information contains an untrue statement of material fact.

(b) A refusal to provide written recommendations will be in writing and will include a statement of the reason for FDA's refusal. Where practicable, FDA will describe the information or material it requires or the conditions the sponsor must meet for FDA to provide recommendations.

(c) Within 90 days after the date of a letter from FDA requesting additional information or material or setting forth the conditions that the sponsor is asked to meet, the sponsor shall either:

(1) Provide the information or material or amend the request for written recommendations to meet the conditions sought by FDA; or

(2) Withdraw the request for written recommendations. FDA will consider a sponsor's failure to respond within 90 days to an FDA letter requesting information or material or setting forth conditions to be met to be a withdrawal of the request for written recommendations.

Subpart C—Designation of an Orphan Drug

§ 316.20 Content and format of a request for orphan-drug designation.

(a) A sponsor that submits a request for orphan-drug designation of a drug for a specified rare disease or condition shall submit each request in the form and containing the information required in paragraph (b) of this section. A sponsor may request orphan-drug designation of a previously unapproved drug, or of a new use for an already marketed drug. In addition, a sponsor of a drug that is otherwise the same drug as an already approved drug may seek and obtain orphan-drug designation for the subsequent drug for the same rare disease or condition if it can present a plausible hypothesis that its drug may be clinically superior to the first drug. More than one sponsor may receive orphan-drug designation of the same drug for the same rare disease or condition, but each sponsor seeking orphan-drug designation must file a complete request for designation as provided in paragraph (b) of this section.

(b) A sponsor shall submit two copies of a completed, dated, and signed request for designation that contains the following:

(1) A statement that the sponsor requests orphan-drug designation for a rare disease or condition, which shall be identified with specificity.

(2) The name and address of the sponsor; the name of the sponsor's primary contact person and/or resident agent including title, address, telephone

number, and email address; the generic and trade name, if any, of the drug, or, if neither is available, the chemical name or a meaningful descriptive name of the drug; and the name and address of the source of the drug if it is not manufactured by the sponsor.

(3) A description of the rare disease or condition for which the drug is being or will be investigated, the proposed use of the drug, and the reasons why such therapy is needed.

(4) A description of the drug, to include the identity of the active moiety if it is a drug composed of small molecules, or of the principal molecular structural features if it is composed of macromolecules; its physical and chemical properties, if these characteristics can be determined; and a discussion of the scientific rationale to establish a medically plausible basis for the use of the drug for the rare disease or condition, including all relevant data from in vitro laboratory studies, preclinical efficacy studies conducted in an animal model for the human disease or condition, and clinical experience with the drug in the rare disease or condition that are available to the sponsor, whether positive, negative, or inconclusive. Animal toxicology studies are generally not relevant to a request for orphan-drug designation. Copies of pertinent unpublished and published papers are also required.

(5) Where the sponsor of a drug that is otherwise the same drug as an already approved drug seeks orphan-drug designation for the subsequent drug for the same rare disease or condition, an explanation of why the proposed variation may be clinically superior to the first drug.

(6) Where a sponsor requests orphan-drug designation for a drug for only a subset of persons with a particular disease or condition that otherwise affects 200,000 or more people ("orphan subset"), a demonstration that, due to one or more properties of the drug, the remaining persons with such disease or condition would not be appropriate candidates for use of the drug.

(7) A summary of the regulatory status and marketing history of the drug in the United States and in foreign countries, e.g., IND and marketing application status and dispositions, what

uses are under investigation and in what countries; for what indication is the drug approved in foreign countries; what adverse regulatory actions have been taken against the drug in any country.

(8) Documentation, with appended authoritative references, to demonstrate that:

(i) The disease or condition for which the drug is intended affects fewer than 200,000 people in the United States or, if the drug is a vaccine, diagnostic drug, or preventive drug, the persons to whom the drug will be administered in the United States are fewer than 200,000 per year as specified in § 316.21(b), or

(ii) For a drug intended for diseases or conditions affecting 200,000 or more people, or for a vaccine, diagnostic drug, or preventive drug to be administered to 200,000 or more persons per year in the United States, there is no reasonable expectation that costs of research and development of the drug for the indication can be recovered by sales of the drug in the United States as specified in § 316.21(c).

(c) Any of the information previously provided by the sponsor to FDA under subpart B of this part may be referenced by specific page or location if it duplicates information required elsewhere in this section.

[57 FR 62085, Dec. 29, 1992, as amended at 78 FR 35133, June 12, 2013]

§ 316.21 Verification of orphan-drug status.

(a) So that FDA can determine whether a drug qualifies for orphan-drug designation under section 526(a) of the act, the sponsor shall include in its request to FDA for orphan-drug designation under § 316.20 either:

(1) Documentation as described in paragraph (b) of this section that the number of people affected by the disease or condition for which the drug is to be developed is fewer than 200,000 persons; or

(2) Documentation as described in paragraph (c) of this section that demonstrates that there is no reasonable expectation that the sales of the drug will be sufficient to offset the costs of developing the drug for the U.S. market and the costs of making the drug available in the United States.

(b) For the purpose of documenting that the number of people affected by the disease or condition for which the drug is to be developed is less than 200,000 persons, "prevalence" is defined as the number of persons in the United States who have been diagnosed as having the disease or condition at the time of the submission of the request for orphan-drug designation. To document the number of persons in the United States who have the disease or condition for which the drug is to be developed, the sponsor shall submit to FDA evidence showing:

(1) The estimated prevalence of the disease or condition for which the drug is being developed, together with a list of the sources (including dates of information provided and literature citations) for the estimate;

(2) Upon request by FDA, the estimated prevalence of any other disease or condition for which the drug has already been approved or for which the drug is currently being developed, together with an explanation of the bases of these estimates; and

(3) The estimated number of people to whom the drug will be administered annually if the drug is a vaccine or is a drug intended for diagnosis or prevention of a rare disease or condition, together with an explanation of the bases of these estimates (including dates of information provided and literature citations).

(c) When submitting documentation that there is no reasonable expectation that costs of research and development of the drug for the disease or condition can be recovered by sales of the drug in the United States, the sponsor shall submit to FDA:

(1) Data on all costs that the sponsor has incurred in the course of developing the drug for the U.S. market. These costs shall include, but are not limited to, nonclinical laboratory studies, clinical studies, dosage form development, record and report maintenance, meetings with FDA, determination of patentability, preparation of designation request, IND/marketing application preparation, distribution of the drug under a "treatment" protocol, licensing costs, liability insurance, and overhead and depreciation. Furthermore, the sponsor shall demonstrate the reasonableness of the cost data. For example, if the sponsor has incurred costs for clinical investigations, the sponsor shall provide information on the number of investigations, the years in which they took place, and on the scope, duration, and number of patients that were involved in each investigation.

(2) If the drug was developed wholly or in part outside the United States, in addition to the documentation listed in paragraph (c)(1) of this section:

(i) Data on and justification for all costs that the sponsor has incurred outside of the United States in the course of developing the drug for the U.S. market. The justification, in addition to demonstrating the reasonableness of the cost data, must also explain the method that was used to determine which portion of the foreign development costs should be applied to the U.S. market, and what percent these costs are of total worldwide development costs. Any data submitted to foreign government authorities to support drug pricing determinations must be included with this information.

(ii) Data that show which foreign development costs were recovered through cost recovery procedures that are allowed during drug development in some foreign countries. For example, if the sponsor charged patients for the drug during clinical investigations, the revenues collected by the sponsor must be reported to FDA.

(3) In cases where the drug has already been approved for marketing for any indication or in cases where the drug is currently under investigation for one or more other indications (in addition to the indication for which orphan-drug designation is being sought), a clear explanation of and justification for the method that is used to apportion the development costs among the various indications.

(4) A statement of and justification for any development costs that the sponsor expects to incur after the submission of the designation request. In cases where the extent of these future development costs are not clear, the sponsor should request FDA's advice and assistance in estimating the scope of nonclinical laboratory studies and clinical investigations and other data

that are needed to support marketing approval. Based on these recommendations, a cost estimate should be prepared.

(5) A statement of and justification for production and marketing costs that the sponsor has incurred in the past and expects to incur during the first 7 years that the drug is marketed.

(6) An estimate of and justification for the expected revenues from sales of the drug in the United States during its first 7 years of marketing. The justification should assume that the total market for the drug is equal to the prevalence of the disease or condition that the drug will be used to treat. The justification should include:

(i) An estimate of the expected market share of the drug in each of the first 7 years that it is marketed, together with an explanation of the basis for that estimate;

(ii) A projection of and justification for the price at which the drug will be sold; and

(iii) Comparisons with sales of similarly situated drugs, where available.

(7) The name of each country where the drug has already been approved for marketing for any indication, the dates of approval, the indication for which the drug is approved, and the annual sales and number of prescriptions in each country since the first approval date.

(8) A report of an independent certified public accountant in accordance with Statement on Standards for Attestation established by the American Institute of Certified Public Accountants on agreed upon procedures performed with respect to the data estimates and justifications submitted pursuant to this section. Cost data shall be determined in accordance with generally accepted accounting principles.

(d) A sponsor that is requesting orphan-drug designation for a drug designed to treat a disease or condition that affects 200,000 or more persons shall, at FDA's request, allow FDA or FDA-designated personnel to examine at reasonable times and in a reasonable manner all relevant financial records

and sales data of the sponsor and manufacturer.

[57 FR 62085, Dec. 29, 1992, as amended at 78 FR 35133, June 12, 2013]

§316.22 Permanent-resident agent for foreign sponsor.

Every foreign sponsor that seeks orphan-drug designation shall name a permanent resident of the United States as the sponsor's agent upon whom service of all processes, notices, orders, decisions, requirements, and other communications may be made on behalf of the sponsor. Notifications of changes in such agents or changes of address of agents should preferably be provided in advance, but not later than 60 days after the effective date of such changes. The permanent-resident agent may be an individual, firm, or domestic corporation and may represent any number of sponsors. The name of the permanent-resident agent, address, telephone number, and email address shall be provided to: Office of Orphan Products Development, Food and Drug Administration, Bldg. 32, rm. 5271, 10903 New Hampshire Ave., Silver Spring, MD 20993.

[78 FR 35133, June 12, 2013]

§316.23 Timing of requests for orphan-drug designation; designation of already approved drugs.

(a) A sponsor may request orphan-drug designation at any time in its drug development process prior to the time that sponsor submits a marketing application for the drug for the same rare disease or condition.

(b) A sponsor may request orphan-drug designation of an already approved drug for an unapproved use without regard to whether the prior marketing approval was for a rare disease or condition.

[78 FR 35133, June 12, 2013]

§316.24 Deficiency letters and granting orphan-drug designation.

(a) FDA will send a deficiency letter to the sponsor if the request for orphan-drug designation lacks information required under §§316.20 and 316.21, or contains inaccurate or incomplete information. FDA may consider a designation request voluntarily withdrawn if the sponsor fails to respond to the deficiency letter within 1 year of issuance of the deficiency letter, unless within that same timeframe the sponsor requests in writing an extension of time to respond. This request must include the reason(s) for the requested extension and the length of time of the requested extension. FDA will grant all reasonable requests for an extension. In the event FDA denies a request for an extension of time, FDA may consider the designation request voluntarily withdrawn. In the event FDA considers a designation request voluntarily withdrawn, FDA will so notify the sponsor in writing.

(b) FDA will grant the request for orphan-drug designation if none of the reasons described in § 316.25 for requiring or permitting refusal to grant such a request applies.

(c) When a request for orphan-drug designation is granted, FDA will notify the sponsor in writing and will publicize the orphan-drug designation in accordance with § 316.28.

(d) A sponsor may voluntarily withdraw an orphan-drug designation request or an orphan-drug designation at any time after the request is submitted or granted, respectively, by submitting a written request for withdrawal to FDA. FDA will acknowledge such withdrawal in a letter to the sponsor. Any benefits attendant to designation (such as orphan-exclusive approval) will cease once designation is voluntarily withdrawn, from the date of FDA's acknowledgement letter. If a sponsor voluntarily withdraws designation, FDA will publicize such withdrawal in accordance with § 316.28.

[57 FR 62085, Dec. 29, 1992, as amended at 78 FR 35133, June 12, 2013]

§ 316.25 Refusal to grant orphan-drug designation.

(a) FDA will refuse to grant a request for orphan-drug designation if any of the following reasons apply:

(1) The drug is not intended for a rare disease or condition because:

(i) There is insufficient evidence to support the estimate that the drug is intended for treatment of a disease or condition in fewer than 200,000 people in the United States, or that the drug is intended for use in prevention or in diagnosis in fewer than 200,000 people annually in the United States; or

(ii) Where the drug is intended for prevention, diagnosis, or treatment of a disease or condition affecting 200,000 or more people in the United States, the sponsor has failed to demonstrate that there is no reasonable expectation that development and production costs will be recovered from sales of the drug for such disease or condition in the United States. A sponsor's failure to comply with § 316.21 shall constitute a failure to make the demonstration required in this paragraph.

(2) There is insufficient information about the drug, or the disease or condition for which it is intended, to establish a medically plausible basis for expecting the drug to be effective in the prevention, diagnosis, or treatment of that disease or condition.

(3) The drug is otherwise the same drug as an already approved drug for the same rare disease or condition and the sponsor has not submitted a medically plausible hypothesis for the possible clinical superiority of the subsequent drug.

(b) FDA may refuse to grant a request for orphan-drug designation if the request for designation contains an untrue statement of material fact or omits material information or if the request is otherwise ineligible under this part.

[57 FR 62085, Dec. 29, 1992, as amended at 78 FR 35133, June 12, 2013]

§ 316.26 Amendment to orphan-drug designation.

(a) At any time prior to approval of a marketing application for a designated orphan drug, the sponsor holding designation may apply for an amendment to the designated use if the proposed change is due to new and unexpected findings in research on the drug, information arising from FDA recommendations, or unforeseen developments in treatment or diagnosis of the disease or condition.

(b) FDA will grant the amendment if it finds that the initial designation request was made in good faith and that the amendment is intended to conform the orphan-drug designation to the results of unanticipated research findings, to unforeseen developments in the treatment or diagnosis of the disease or condition, or to changes based on FDA recommendations, and that, as of the date of the submission of the amendment request, the amendment would not result in exceeding the prevalence or cost recovery thresholds in §316.21(a)(1) or (a)(2) upon which the drug was originally designated.

[78 FR 35134, June 12, 2013]

§316.27 Change in ownership of orphan-drug designation.

(a) A sponsor may transfer ownership of or any beneficial interest in the orphan-drug designation of a drug to a new sponsor. At the time of the transfer, the new and former owners are required to submit the following information to FDA:

(1) The former owner or assignor of rights shall submit a letter or other document that states that all or some rights to the orphan-drug designation of the drug have been transferred to the new owner or assignee and that a complete copy of the request for orphan-drug designation, including any amendments to the request, supplements to the granted request, and correspondence relevant to the orphan-drug designation, has been provided to the new owner or assignee.

(2) The new owner or assignee of rights shall submit a statement accepting orphan-drug designation and a letter or other document containing the following:

(i) The date that the change in ownership or assignment of rights is effective;

(ii) A statement that the new owner has a complete copy of the request for orphan-drug designation including any amendments to the request, supplements to the granted request, and correspondence relevant to the orphan-drug designation; and

(iii) A specific description of the rights that have been assigned and those that have been reserved. This may be satisfied by the submission of either a list of rights assigned and reserved or copies of all relevant agreements between assignors and assignees; and

(iv) The name and address of a new primary contact person or resident agent.

(b) No sponsor may relieve itself of responsibilities under the Orphan Drug Act or under this part by assigning rights to another person without:

(1) Assuring that the sponsor or the assignee will carry out such responsibilities; or

(2) Obtaining prior permission from FDA.

[57 FR 62085, Dec. 29, 1992; 58 FR 6167, Jan. 26, 1993]

§316.28 Publication of orphan-drug designations.

Each month FDA will update a publicly available cumulative posting of all drugs designated as orphan drugs. These postings will contain the following information:

(a) The name and address of the sponsor;

(b) The generic name and trade name, if any, or, if neither is available, the chemical name or a meaningful descriptive name of the drug;

(c) The date of the granting of orphan-drug designation;

(d) The designated use in the rare disease or condition; and

(e) If the drug loses designation after August 12, 2013, the date of it no longer having designation.

[78 FR 35134, June 12, 2013]

§316.29 Revocation of orphan-drug designation.

(a) FDA may revoke orphan-drug designation for any drug if the agency finds that:

(1) The request for designation contained an untrue statement of material fact; or

(2) The request for designation omitted material information required by this part; or

(3) FDA subsequently finds that the drug in fact had not been eligible for orphan-drug designation at the time of submission of the request therefor.

(b) For an approved drug, revocation of orphan-drug designation also suspends or withdraws the sponsor's exclusive marketing rights for the drug but not the approval of the drug's marketing application.

(c) Where a drug has been designated as an orphan drug because the prevalence of a disease or condition (or, in the case of vaccines, diagnostic drugs, or preventive drugs, the target population) is under 200,000 in the United States at the time of designation, its designation will not be revoked on the ground that the prevalence of the disease or condition (or the target population) becomes more than 200,000 persons.

(d) If FDA revokes orphan-drug designation, FDA will publicize that the drug is no longer designated in accordance with § 316.28(e).

[57 FR 62085, Dec. 29, 1992, as amended at 78 FR 35134, June 12, 2013]

§ 316.30 Annual reports of holder of orphan-drug designation.

Within 14 months after the date on which a drug was designated as an orphan drug and annually thereafter until marketing approval, the sponsor of a designated drug shall submit a brief progress report to the FDA Office of Orphan Products Development on the drug that includes:

(a) A short account of the progress of drug development including a review of preclinical and clinical studies initiated, ongoing, and completed and a short summary of the status or results of such studies.

(b) A description of the investigational plan for the coming year, as well as any anticipated difficulties in development, testing, and marketing; and

(c) A brief discussion of any changes that may affect the orphan-drug status of the product. For example, for products nearing the end of the approval process, sponsors should discuss any disparity between the probable marketing indication and the designated indication as related to the need for an amendment to the orphan-drug designation pursuant to § 316.26.

Subpart D—Orphan-drug Exclusive Approval

§ 316.31 Scope of orphan-drug exclusive approval.

(a) FDA may approve a sponsor's marketing application for a designated orphan drug for use in the rare disease or condition for which the drug was designated, or for select indication(s) or use(s) within the rare disease or condition for which the drug was designated. Unless FDA previously approved the same drug for the same use or indication, FDA will not approve another sponsor's marketing application for the same drug for the same use or indication before the expiration of 7 years from the date of such approval as stated in the approval letter from FDA, except that such a marketing application can be approved sooner if, and at such time as, any of the following occurs:

(1) Withdrawal of exclusive approval or revocation of orphan-drug designation by FDA under any provision of this part; or

(2) Withdrawal for any reason of the marketing application for the drug in question; or

(3) Consent by the holder of exclusive approval to permit another marketing application to gain approval; or

(4) Failure of the holder of exclusive approval to assure a sufficient quantity of the drug under section 527 of the act and § 316.36.

(b) Orphan-drug exclusive approval protects only the approved indication or use of a designated drug. If such approval is limited to only particular indication(s) or uses(s) within the rare disease or condition for which the drug was designated, FDA may later approve the drug for additional indication(s) or uses(s) within the rare disease or condition not protected by the exclusive approval. If the sponsor who obtains approval for these new indication(s) or uses(s) has orphan-drug designation for the drug for the rare disease or condition, FDA will recognize a new orphan-drug exclusive approval for these new (not previously approved) indication(s) or use(s) from the date of approval of the drug for such new indication(s) or use(s).

(c) If a sponsor's marketing application for a drug product is determined not to be approvable because approval is barred under section 527 of the Federal Food, Drug, and Cosmetic Act until the expiration of the period of exclusive marketing of another drug,

FDA will so notify the sponsor in writing.

[57 FR 62085, Dec. 29, 1992, as amended at 78 FR 35134, June 12, 2013]

§316.34 FDA recognition of exclusive approval.

(a) FDA will send the sponsor (or, the permanent-resident agent, if applicable) timely written notice recognizing exclusive approval once the marketing application for a designated orphan-drug product has been approved, if the same drug has not already been approved for the same use or indication. The written notice will inform the sponsor of the requirements for maintaining orphan-drug exclusive approval for the full 7-year term of exclusive approval.

(b) When a marketing application is approved under section 505 of the Federal Food, Drug, and Cosmetic Act (21 U.S.C. 355) for a designated orphan drug that qualifies for exclusive approval, FDA will publish in its publication entitled "Approved Drug Products With Therapeutic Equivalence Evaluations" information identifying the sponsor, the drug, and the date of termination of the orphan-drug exclusive approval. A subscription to this publication and its monthly cumulative supplements is available from the Superintendent of Documents, Government Printing Office, Washington, DC 20402–9325, and is also available online at *http://www.accessdata.fda.gov/scripts/cder/ob/default.cfm.*

(c) If a drug is otherwise the same drug as a previously approved drug for the same use or indication, FDA will not recognize orphan-drug exclusive approval if the sponsor fails to demonstrate upon approval that the drug is clinically superior to the previously approved drug.

[78 FR 35135, June 12, 2013]

§316.36 Insufficient quantities of orphan drugs.

(a) Under section 527 of the act, whenever the Director has reason to believe that the holder of exclusive approval cannot assure the availability of sufficient quantities of an orphan drug to meet the needs of patients with the disease or condition for which the drug

was designated, the Director will so notify the holder of this possible insufficiency and will offer the holder one of the following options, which must be exercised by a time that the Director specifies:

(1) Provide the Director in writing, or orally, or both, at the Director's discretion, views and data as to how the holder can assure the availability of sufficient quantities of the orphan drug within a reasonable time to meet the needs of patients with the disease or condition for which the drug was designated; or

(2) Provide the Director in writing the holder's consent for the approval of other marketing applications for the same drug before the expiration of the 7-year period of exclusive approval.

(b) If, within the time that the Director specifies, the holder fails to consent to the approval of other marketing applications and if the Director finds that the holder has not shown that it can assure the availability of sufficient quantities of the orphan drug to meet the needs of patients with the disease or condition for which the drug was designated, the Director will issue a written order withdrawing the drug product's exclusive approval. This order will embody the Director's findings and conclusions and will constitute final agency action. An order withdrawing the sponsor's exclusive marketing rights may issue whether or not there are other sponsors that can assure the availability of alternative sources of supply. Once withdrawn under this section, exclusive approval may not be reinstated for that drug.

Subpart E—Open Protocols for Investigations

§316.40 Treatment use of a designated orphan drug.

Prospective investigators seeking to obtain treatment use of designated orphan drugs may do so as provided in subpart I of this chapter.

[74 FR 40945, Aug. 13, 2009]

Subpart F—Availability of Information

§ 316.50 Guidance documents.

FDA's Office of Orphan Products Development will maintain and make publicly available a list of guidance documents that apply to the regulations in this part. The list is maintained on the Internet and is published annually in the FEDERAL REGISTER. A request for a copy of the list should be directed to the Office of Orphan Products Development, Food and Drug Administration, Bldg. 32, rm. 5271, 10903 New Hampshire Ave., Silver Spring, MD 20993.

[78 FR 35135, June 12, 2013]

§ 316.52 Availability for public disclosure of data and information in requests and applications.

(a) FDA will not publicly disclose the existence of a request for orphan-drug designation under section 526 of the act prior to final FDA action on the request unless the existence of the request has been previously publicly disclosed or acknowledged.

(b) Whether or not the existence of a pending request for designation has been publicly disclosed or acknowledged, no data or information in the request are available for public disclosure prior to final FDA action on the request.

(c) Upon final FDA action on a request for designation, FDA will determine the public availability of data and information in the request in accordance with part 20 and § 314.430 of this chapter and other applicable statutes and regulations.

(d) In accordance with § 316.28, FDA will make a cumulative list of all orphan drug designations available to the public and update such list monthly.

(e) FDA will not publicly disclose the existence of a pending marketing application for a designated orphan drug for the use for which the drug was designated unless the existence of the application has been previously publicly disclosed or acknowledged.

(f) FDA will determine the public availability of data and information contained in pending and approved marketing applications for a designated orphan drug for the use for which the drug was designated in accordance with part 20 and § 314.430 of this chapter and other applicable statutes and regulations.

PART 317—QUALIFYING PATHOGENS

Sec.
317.1 [Reserved]
317.2 List of qualifying pathogens that have the potential to pose a serious threat to public health.

AUTHORITY: 21 U.S.C. 355f, 371.

SOURCE: 79 FR 32480, June 5, 2014, unless otherwise noted.

§ 317.1 [Reserved]

§ 317.2 List of qualifying pathogens that have the potential to pose a serious threat to public health.

The term "qualifying pathogen" in section 505E(f) of the Federal Food, Drug, and Cosmetic Act is defined to mean any of the following:

(a) *Acinetobacter* species.
(b) *Aspergillus* species.
(c) *Burkholderia cepacia* complex.
(d) *Campylobacter* species.
(e) *Candida* species.
(f) *Clostridium difficile*.
(g) *Coccidioides* species.
(h) *Cryptococcus* species.
(i) Enterobacteriaceae.
(j) *Enterococcus* species.
(k) *Helicobacter pylori*.
(l) *Mycobacterium tuberculosis* complex.
(m) *Neisseria gonorrhoeae*.
(n) *Neisseria meningitidis*.
(o) Non-tuberculous mycobacteria species.
(p) *Pseudomonas* species.
(q) *Staphylococcus aureus*.
(r) *Streptococcus agalactiae*.
(s) *Streptococcus pneumoniae*.
(t) *Streptococcus pyogenes*.
(u) *Vibrio cholerae*.

PART 320—BIOAVAILABILITY AND BIOEQUIVALENCE REQUIREMENTS

Subpart A—General Provisions

Subpart B—Procedures for Determining the Bioavailability or Bioequivalence of Drug Products

AUTHORITY: 21 U.S.C. 321, 351, 352, 355, 371.

Subpart A—General Provisions

§320.1 Definitions.

(a) *Bioavailability* means the rate and extent to which the active ingredient or active moiety is absorbed from a drug product and becomes available at the site of action. For drug products that are not intended to be absorbed into the bloodstream, bioavailability may be assessed by measurements intended to reflect the rate and extent to which the active ingredient or active moiety becomes available at the site of action.

(b) *Drug product* means a finished dosage form, e.g., tablet, capsule, or solution, that contains the active drug ingredient, generally, but not necessarily, in association with inactive ingredients.

(c) *Pharmaceutical equivalents* means drug products in identical dosage forms that contain identical amounts of the identical active drug ingredient, *i.e.*, the same salt or ester of the same therapeutic moiety, or, in the case of modified release dosage forms that require a reservoir or overage or such forms as prefilled syringes where residual volume may vary, that deliver identical amounts of the active drug ingredient over the identical dosing period; do not necessarily contain the same inactive ingredients; and meet the identical compendial or other applicable standard of identity, strength, quality, and purity, including potency and, where applicable, content uniformity, disintegration times, and/or dissolution rates.

(d) *Pharmaceutical alternatives* means drug products that contain the identical therapeutic moiety, or its precursor, but not necessarily in the same amount or dosage form or as the same salt or ester. Each such drug product individually meets either the identical or its own respective compendial or other applicable standard of identity, strength, quality, and purity, including potency and, where applicable, content uniformity, disintegration times and/or dissolution rates.

(e) *Bioequivalence* means the absence of a significant difference in the rate and extent to which the active ingredient or active moiety in pharmaceutical equivalents or pharmaceutical alternatives becomes available at the site of drug action when administered at the same molar dose under similar conditions in an appropriately designed study. Where there is an intentional difference in rate (e.g., in certain extended release dosage forms), certain pharmaceutical equivalents or alternatives may be considered bioequivalent if there is no significant difference in the extent to which the active ingredient or moiety from each product becomes available at the site of drug action. This applies only if the difference in the rate at which the active ingredient or moiety becomes available at the site of drug action is intentional and is reflected in the proposed labeling, is not essential to the attainment of effective body drug concentrations on chronic use, and is considered medically insignificant for the drug.

(f) *Bioequivalence requirement* means a requirement imposed by the Food and Drug Administration for in vitro and/or in vivo testing of specified drug products which must be satisfied as a condition of marketing.

(g) *Same drug product formulation* means the formulation of the drug product submitted for approval and any formulations that have minor differences in composition or method of manufacture from the formulation submitted for approval, but are similar enough to be relevant to the agency's determination of bioequivalence.

[42 FR 1634, Jan. 7, 1977, as amended at 42 FR 1648, Jan. 7, 1977; 57 FR 17997, Apr. 28, 1992; 67 FR 77672, Dec. 19, 2002; 74 FR 2861, Jan. 16, 2009]

Subpart B—Procedures for Determining the Bioavailability or Bioequivalence of Drug Products

SOURCE: 42 FR 1648, Jan. 7, 1977, unless otherwise noted.

§ 320.21 Requirements for submission of bioavailability and bioequivalence data.

(a) Any person submitting a full new drug application to the Food and Drug Administration (FDA) shall include in the application either:

(1) Evidence measuring the in vivo bioavailability of the drug product that is the subject of the application; or

(2) Information to permit FDA to waive the submission of evidence measuring in vivo bioavailability.

(b) Any person submitting an abbreviated new drug application to FDA shall include in the application either:

(1) Evidence demonstrating that the drug product that is the subject of the abbreviated new drug application is bioequivalent to the reference listed drug (defined in § 314.3(b) of this chapter). A complete study report must be submitted for the bioequivalence study upon which the applicant relies for approval. For all other bioequivalence studies conducted on the same drug product formulation, the applicant must submit either a complete or summary report. If a summary report of a bioequivalence study is submitted and FDA determines that there may be bioequivalence issues or concerns with the product, FDA may require that the applicant submit a complete report of the bioequivalence study to FDA; or

(2) Information to show that the drug product is bioequivalent to the reference listed drug which would permit FDA to waive the submission of evidence demonstrating in vivo bioequivalence as provided in paragraph (f) of this section.

(c) Any person submitting a supplemental application to FDA shall include in the supplemental application the evidence or information set forth in paragraphs (a) and (b) of this section if the supplemental application proposes any of the following changes:

(1) A change in the manufacturing site or a change in the manufacturing process, including a change in product formulation or dosage strength, beyond the variations provided for in the approved application.

(2) A change in the labeling to provide for a new indication for use of the drug product, if clinical studies are required to support the new indication for use.

(3) A change in the labeling to provide for a new dosage regimen or for an additional dosage regimen for a special patient population, e.g., infants, if clinical studies are required to support the new or additional dosage regimen.

(d) FDA may approve a full new drug application, or a supplemental application proposing any of the changes set forth in paragraph (c) of this section, that does not contain evidence of in vivo bioavailability or information to permit waiver of the requirement for in vivo bioavailability data, if all of the following conditions are met.

(1) The application is otherwise approvable.

(2) The application agrees to submit, within the time specified by FDA, either:

(i) Evidence measuring the in vivo bioavailability and demonstrating the in vivo bioequivalence of the drug product that is the subject of the application; or

(ii) Information to permit FDA to waive measurement of in vivo bioavailability.

(e) Evidence measuring the in vivo bioavailability and demonstrating the in vivo bioequivalence of a drug product shall be obtained using one of the approaches for determining bioavailability set forth in §320.24.

(f) Information to permit FDA to waive the submission of evidence measuring the in vivo bioavailability or demonstrating the in vivo bioequivalence shall meet the criteria set forth in §320.22.

(g) Any person holding an approved full or abbreviated new drug application shall submit to FDA a supplemental application containing new evidence measuring the in vivo bioavailability or demonstrating the in vivo bioequivalence of the drug product that is the subject of the application if notified by FDA that:

(1) There are data demonstrating that the dosage regimen in the labeling is based on incorrect assumptions or facts regarding the pharmacokinetics of the drug product and that following this dosage regimen could potentially result in subtherapeutic or toxic levels; or

(2) There are data measuring significant intra-batch and batch-to-batch variability, e.g., plus or minus 25 percent, in the bioavailability of the drug product.

(h) The requirements of this section regarding the submission of evidence measuring the in vivo bioavailability or demonstrating the in vivo bioequivalence apply only to a full or abbreviated new drug application or a supplemental application for a finished dosage formulation.

[57 FR 17998, Apr. 28, 1992, as amended at 67 FR 77672, Dec. 19, 2002; 74 FR 2862, Jan. 16, 2009]

§320.22 Criteria for waiver of evidence of in vivo bioavailability or bioequivalence.

(a) Any person submitting a full or abbreviated new drug application, or a supplemental application proposing any of the changes set forth in §320.21(c), may request FDA to waive the requirement for the submission of evidence measuring the in vivo bioavailability or demonstrating the in vivo bioequivalence of the drug product that is the subject of the application. An applicant shall submit a request for waiver with the application. Except as provided in paragraph (f) of this section, FDA shall waive the requirement for the submission of evidence of in vivo bioavailability or bioequivalence if the drug product meets any of the provisions of paragraphs (b), (c), (d), or (e) of this section.

(b) For certain drug products, the in vivo bioavailability or bioequivalence of the drug product may be self-evident. FDA shall waive the requirement for the submission of evidence obtained in vivo measuring the bioavailability or demonstrating the bioequivalence of these drug products. A drug product's in vivo bioavailability or bioequivalence may be considered self-evident based on other data in the application if the product meets one of the following criteria:

(1) The drug product:

(i) Is a parenteral solution intended solely for administration by injection, or an ophthalmic or otic solution; and

(ii) Contains the same active and inactive ingredients in the same concentration as a drug product that is the subject of an approved full new drug application or abbreviated new drug application.

(2) The drug product:

(i) Is administered by inhalation as a gas, e.g., a medicinal or an inhalation anesthetic; and

(ii) Contains an active ingredient in the same dosage form as a drug product that is the subject of an approved full new drug application or abbreviated new drug application.

(3) The drug product:

(i) Is a solution for application to the skin, an oral solution, elixir, syrup, tincture, a solution for aerosolization or nebulization, a nasal solution, or similar other solubilized form; and

(ii) Contains an active drug ingredient in the same concentration and dosage form as a drug product that is the subject of an approved full new drug application or abbreviated new drug application; and

(iii) Contains no inactive ingredient or other change in formulation from the drug product that is the subject of the approved full new drug application or abbreviated new drug application that may significantly affect absorption of the active drug ingredient or active moiety for products that are systemically absorbed, or that may significantly affect systemic or local availability for products intended to act locally.

(c) FDA shall waive the requirement for the submission of evidence measuring the in vivo bioavailability or demonstrating the in vivo bioequivalence of a solid oral dosage form (other than a delayed release or extended release dosage form) of a drug product determined to be effective for at least one indication in a Drug Efficacy Study Implementation notice or which is identical, related, or similar to such a drug product under § 310.6 of this chapter unless FDA has evaluated the drug product under the criteria set forth in § 320.33, included the drug product in the Approved Drug Products with Therapeutic Equivalence Evaluations List, and rated the drug product as having a known or potential bioequivalence problem. A drug product so rated reflects a determination by FDA that an in vivo bioequivalence study is required.

(d) For certain drug products, bioavailability may be measured or bioequivalence may be demonstrated by evidence obtained in vitro in lieu of in vivo data. FDA shall waive the requirement for the submission of evidence obtained in vivo measuring the bioavailability or demonstrating the bioequivalence of the drug product if the drug product meets one of the following criteria:

(1) [Reserved]

(2) The drug product is in the same dosage form, but in a different strength, and is proportionally similar in its active and inactive ingredients to another drug product for which the same manufacturer has obtained approval and the conditions in paragraphs (d)(2)(i) through (d)(2)(iii) of this section are met:

(i) The bioavailability of this other drug product has been measured;

(ii) Both drug products meet an appropriate in vitro test approved by FDA; and

(iii) The applicant submits evidence showing that both drug products are proportionally similar in their active and inactive ingredients.

(iv) Paragraph (d) of this section does not apply to delayed release or extended release products.

(3) The drug product is, on the basis of scientific evidence submitted in the application, shown to meet an in vitro test that has been correlated with in vivo data.

(4) The drug product is a reformulated product that is identical, except for a different color, flavor, or preservative that could not affect the bioavailability of the reformulated product, to another drug product for which the same manufacturer has obtained approval and the following conditions are met:

(i) The bioavailability of the other product has been measured; and

(ii) Both drug products meet an appropriate in vitro test approved by FDA.

(e) FDA, for good cause, may waive a requirement for the submission of evidence of in vivo bioavailability or bioequivalence if waiver is compatible with the protection of the public health. For full new drug applications, FDA may defer a requirement for the submission of evidence of in vivo bioavailability if deferral is compatible with the protection of the public health.

(f) FDA, for good cause, may require evidence of in vivo bioavailability or bioequivalence for any drug product if the agency determines that any difference between the drug product and a listed drug may affect the bioavailability or bioequivalence of the drug product.

[57 FR 17998, Apr. 28, 1992, as amended at 67 FR 77673, Dec. 19, 2002]

§ 320.23 Basis for measuring in vivo bioavailability or demonstrating bioequivalence.

(a)(1) The in vivo bioavailability of a drug product is measured if the product's rate and extent of absorption, as determined by comparison of measured parameters, e.g., concentration of the active drug ingredient in the blood, urinary excretion rates, or pharmacological effects, do not indicate a significant difference from the reference material's rate and extent of absorption. For drug products that are not intended to be absorbed into the bloodstream, bioavailability may be assessed by measurements intended to reflect the rate and extent to which the active ingredient or active moiety becomes available at the site of action.

(2) Statistical techniques used shall be of sufficient sensitivity to detect differences in rate and extent of absorption that are not attributable to subject variability.

(3) A drug product that differs from the reference material in its rate of absorption, but not in its extent of absorption, may be considered to be bioavailable if the difference in the rate of absorption is intentional, is appropriately reflected in the labeling, is not essential to the attainment of effective body drug concentrations on chronic use, and is considered medically insignificant for the drug product.

(b) Two drug products will be considered bioequivalent drug products if they are pharmaceutical equivalents or pharmaceutical alternatives whose rate and extent of absorption do not show a significant difference when administered at the same molar dose of the active moiety under similar experimental conditions, either single dose or multiple dose. Some pharmaceutical equivalents or pharmaceutical alternatives may be equivalent in the extent of their absorption but not in their rate of absorption and yet may be considered bioequivalent because such differences in the rate of absorption are intentional and are reflected in the labeling, are not essential to the attainment of effective body drug concentrations on chronic use, and are considered medically insignificant for the particular drug product studied.

[57 FR 17999, Apr. 28, 1992, as amended at 67 FR 77673, Dec. 19, 2002]

§ 320.24 Types of evidence to measure bioavailability or establish bioequivalence.

(a) Bioavailability may be measured or bioequivalence may be demonstrated by several in vivo and in vitro methods. FDA may require in vivo or in vitro testing, or both, to measure the bioavailability of a drug product or establish the bioequivalence of specific drug products. Information on bioequivalence requirements for specific products is included in the current edition of FDA's publication "Approved Drug Products with Therapeutic Equivalence Evaluations" and any current supplement to the publication. The selection of the method used to meet an in vivo or in vitro testing requirement depends upon the purpose of the study, the analytical methods available, and the nature of the drug product. Applicants shall conduct bioavailability and bioequivalence testing using the most accurate, sensitive, and reproducible approach available among those set forth in paragraph (b) of this section. The method used must be capable of measuring bioavailability or establishing bioequivalence, as appropriate, for the product being tested.

(b) The following in vivo and in vitro approaches, in descending order of accuracy, sensitivity, and reproducibility, are acceptable for determining the bioavailability or bioequivalence of a drug product.

(1)(i) An in vivo test in humans in which the concentration of the active ingredient or active moiety, and, when appropriate, its active metabolite(s), in whole blood, plasma, serum, or other appropriate biological fluid is measured as a function of time. This approach is particularly applicable to dosage forms intended to deliver the active moiety to the bloodstream for systemic distribution within the body; or

(ii) An in vitro test that has been correlated with and is predictive of human in vivo bioavailability data; or

(2) An in vivo test in humans in which the urinary excretion of the active moiety, and, when appropriate, its active metabolite(s), are measured as a function of time. The intervals at which measurements are taken should ordinarily be as short as possible so that the measure of the rate of elimination is as accurate as possible. Depending on the nature of the drug product, this approach may be applicable to the category of dosage forms described in paragraph (b)(1)(i) of this section. This method is not appropriate where urinary excretion is not a significant mechanism of elimination.

(3) An in vivo test in humans in which an appropriate acute pharmacological effect of the active moiety, and, when appropriate, its active metabolite(s), are measured as a function of time if such effect can be measured with sufficient accuracy, sensitivity, and reproducibility. This approach is applicable to the category of dosage forms described in paragraph (b)(1)(i) of this section only when appropriate methods are not available for measurement of the concentration of the moiety, and, when appropriate, its active metabolite(s), in biological fluids or excretory products but a method is available for the measurement of an appropriate acute pharmacological effect. This approach may be particularly applicable to dosage forms that are not intended to deliver the active moiety to the bloodstream for systemic distribution.

(4) Well-controlled clinical trials that establish the safety and effectiveness of the drug product, for purposes of measuring bioavailability, or appropriately designed comparative clinical trials, for purposes of demonstrating bioequivalence. This approach is the least accurate, sensitive, and reproducible of the general approaches for measuring bioavailability or demonstrating bioequivalence. For dosage forms intended to deliver the active moiety to the bloodstream for systemic distribution, this approach may be considered acceptable only when analytical methods cannot be developed to permit use of one of the approaches outlined in paragraphs (b)(1)(i) and (b)(2) of this section, when the approaches described in paragraphs (b)(1)(ii), (b)(1)(iii), and (b)(3) of this section are not available. This approach may also be considered sufficiently accurate for measuring bioavailability or demonstrating bioequivalence of dosage forms intended to deliver the active moiety locally, e.g., topical preparations for the skin, eye, and mucous membranes; oral dosage forms not intended to be absorbed, e.g., an antacid or radiopaque medium; and bronchodilators administered by inhalation if the onset and duration of pharmacological activity are defined.

(5) A currently available in vitro test acceptable to FDA (usually a dissolution rate test) that ensures human in vivo bioavailability.

(6) Any other approach deemed adequate by FDA to measure bioavailability or establish bioequivalence.

(c) FDA may, notwithstanding prior requirements for measuring bioavailability or establishing bioequivalence, require in vivo testing in humans of a product at any time if the agency has evidence that the product:

(1) May not produce therapeutic effects comparable to a pharmaceutical equivalent or alternative with which it is intended to be used interchangeably;

(2) May not be bioequivalent to a pharmaceutical equivalent or alternative with which it is intended to be used interchangeably; or

(3) Has greater than anticipated potential toxicity related to pharmacokinetic or other characteristics.

[57 FR 17999, Apr. 28, 1992; 57 FR 29354, July 1, 1992, as amended at 67 FR 77673, Dec. 19, 2002]

§ 320.25 Guidelines for the conduct of an in vivo bioavailability study.

(a) *Guiding principles.* (1) The basic principle in an in vivo bioavailability study is that no unnecessary human research should be done.

(2) An in vivo bioavailability study is generally done in a normal adult population under standardized conditions. In some situations, an in vivo bioavailability study in humans may preferably and more properly be done in suitable patients. Critically ill patients shall not be included in an in vivo bioavailability study unless the attending

physician determines that there is a potential benefit to the patient.

(b) *Basic design.* The basic design of an in vivo bioavailability study is determined by the following:

(1) The scientific questions to be answered.

(2) The nature of the reference material and the dosage form to be tested.

(3) The availability of analytical methods.

(4) Benefit-risk considerations in regard to testing in humans.

(c) *Comparison to a reference material.* In vivo bioavailability testing of a drug product shall be in comparison to an appropriate reference material unless some other approach is more appropriate for valid scientific reasons.

(d) *Previously unmarketed active drug ingredients or therapeutic moieties.* (1) An in vivo bioavailability study involving a drug product containing an active drug ingredient or therapeutic moiety that has not been approved for marketing can be used to measure the following pharmacokinetic data:

(i) The bioavailability of the formulation proposed for marketing; and

(ii) The essential pharmacokinetic characteristics of the active drug ingredient or therapeutic moiety, such as the rate of absorption, the extent of absorption, the half-life of the therapeutic moiety in vivo, and the rate of excretion and/or metabolism. Dose proportionality of the active drug ingredient or the therapeutic moiety needs to be established after single-dose administration and in certain instances after multiple-dose administration. This characterization is a necessary part of the investigation of the drug to support drug labeling.

(2) The reference material in such a bioavailability study should be a solution or suspension containing the same quantity of the active drug ingredient or therapeutic moiety as the formulation proposed for marketing.

(3) The reference material should be administered by the same route as the formulation proposed for marketing unless an alternative or additional route is necessary to answer the scientific question under study. For example, in the case of an active drug ingredient or therapeutic moiety that is poorly absorbed after oral administra-

tion, it may be necessary to compare the oral dosage form proposed for marketing with the active drug ingredient or therapeutic moiety administered in solution both orally and intravenously.

(e) *New formulations of active drug ingredients or therapeutic moieties approved for marketing.* (1) An in vivo bioavailability study involving a drug product that is a new dosage form, or a new salt or ester of an active drug ingredient or therapeutic moiety that has been approved for marketing can be used to:

(i) Measure the bioavailability of the new formulation, new dosage form, or new salt or ester relative to an appropriate reference material; and

(ii) Define the pharmacokinetic parameters of the new formulation, new dosage form, or new salt or ester to establish dosage recommendation.

(2) The selection of the reference material(s) in such a bioavailability study depends upon the scientific questions to be answered, the data needed to establish comparability to a currently marketed drug product, and the data needed to establish dosage recommendations.

(3) The reference material should be taken from a current batch of a drug product that is the subject of an approved new drug application and that contains the same active drug ingredient or therapeutic moiety, if the new formulation, new dosage form, or new salt or ester is intended to be comparable to or to meet any comparative labeling claims made in relation to the drug product that is the subject of an approved new drug application.

(f) *Extended release formulations.* (1) The purpose of an in vivo bioavailability study involving a drug product for which an extended release claim is made is to determine if all of the following conditions are met:

(i) The drug product meets the extended release claims made for it.

(ii) The bioavailability profile established for the drug product rules out the occurrence of any dose dumping.

(iii) The drug product's steady-state performance is equivalent to a currently marketed nonextended release or extended release drug product that contains the same active drug ingredient or therapeutic moiety and that is subject to an approved full new drug application.

(iv) The drug product's formulation provides consistent pharmacokinetic performance between individual dosage units.

(2) The reference material(s) for such a bioavailability study shall be chosen to permit an appropriate scientific evaluation of the extended release claims made for the drug product. The reference material shall be one of the following or any combination thereof:

(i) A solution or suspension of the active drug ingredient or therapeutic moiety.

(ii) A currently marketed noncontrolled release drug product containing the same active drug ingredient or therapeutic moiety and administered according to the dosage recommendations in the labeling of the noncontrolled release drug product.

(iii) A currently marketed extended release drug product subject to an approved full new drug application containing the same active drug ingredient or therapeutic moiety and administered according to the dosage recommendations in the labeling proposed for the extended release drug product.

(iv) A reference material other than one set forth in paragraph (f)(2) (i), (ii) or (iii) of this section that is appropriate for valid scientific reasons.

(g) *Combination drug products.* (1) Generally, the purpose of an in vivo bioavailability study involving a combination drug product is to determine if the rate and extent of absorption of each active drug ingredient or therapeutic moiety in the combination drug product is equivalent to the rate and extent of absorption of each active drug ingredient or therapeutic moiety administered concurrently in separate single-ingredient preparations.

(2) The reference material in such a bioavailability study should be two or more currently marketed, single-ingredient drug products each of which contains one of the active drug ingredients or therapeutic moieties in the combination drug product. The Food and Drug Administration may, for valid scientific reasons, specify that the reference material shall be a combination drug product that is the subject of an approved new drug application.

(3) The Food and Drug Administration may permit a bioavailability study involving a combination drug product to determine the rate and extent of absorption of selected, but not all, active drug ingredients or therapeutic moieties in the combination drug product. The Food and Drug Administration may permit this determination if the pharmacokinetics and the interactions of the active drug ingredients or therapeutic moieties in the combination drug product are well known and the therapeutic activity of the combination drug product is generally recognized to reside in only one of the active drug ingredients or therapeutic moieties, e.g., ampicillin in an ampicillin-probenecid combination drug product.

(h) *Use of a placebo as the reference material.* Where appropriate or where necessary to demonstrate the sensitivity of the test, the reference material in a bioavailability study may be a placebo if:

(1) The study measures the therapeutic or acute pharmacological effect of the active drug ingredient or therapeutic moiety; or

(2) The study is a clinical trial to establish the safety and effectiveness of the drug product.

(i) *Standards for test drug product and reference material.* (1) Both the drug product to be tested and the reference material, if it is another drug product, shall be shown to meet all compendial or other applicable standards of identity, strength, quality, and purity, including potency and, where applicable, content uniformity, disintegration times, and dissolution rates.

(2) Samples of the drug product to be tested shall be manufactured using the same equipment and under the same conditions as those used for full-scale production.

[42 FR 1648, Jan. 7, 1977, as amended at 67 FR 77674, Dec. 19, 2002]

§ 320.26 Guidelines on the design of a single-dose in vivo bioavailability or bioequivalence study.

(a) *Basic principles.* (1) An in vivo bioavailability or bioequivalence study should be a single-dose comparison of the drug product to be tested and the appropriate reference material conducted in normal adults.

(2) The test product and the reference material should be administered to subjects in the fasting state, unless some other approach is more appropriate for valid scientific reasons.

(b) *Study design.* (1) A single-dose study should be crossover in design, unless a parallel design or other design is more appropriate for valid scientific reasons, and should provide for a drug elimination period.

(2) Unless some other approach is appropriate for valid scientific reasons, the drug elimination period should be either:

(i) At least three times the half-life of the active drug ingredient or therapeutic moiety, or its metabolite(s), measured in the blood or urine; or

(ii) At least three times the half-life of decay of the acute pharmacological effect.

(c) *Collection of blood samples.* (1) When comparison of the test product and the reference material is to be based on blood concentration time curves, unless some other approach is more appropriate for valid scientific reasons, blood samples should be taken with sufficient frequency to permit an estimate of both:

(i) The peak concentration in the blood of the active drug ingredient or therapeutic moiety, or its metabolite(s), measured; and

(ii) The total area under the curve for a time period at least three times the half-life of the active drug ingredient or therapeutic moiety, or its metabolite(s), measured.

(2) In a study comparing oral dosage forms, the sampling times should be identical.

(3) In a study comparing an intravenous dosage form and an oral dosage form, the sampling times should be those needed to describe both:

(i) The distribution and elimination phase of the intravenous dosage form; and

(ii) The absorption and elimination phase of the oral dosage form.

(4) In a study comparing drug delivery systems other than oral or intravenous dosage forms with an appropriate reference standard, the sampling times should be based on valid scientific reasons.

(d) *Collection of urine samples.* When comparison of the test product and the reference material is to be based on cumulative urinary excretion-time curves, unless some other approach is more appropriate for valid scientific reasons, samples of the urine should be collected with sufficient frequency to permit an estimate of the rate and extent of urinary excretion of the active drug ingredient or therapeutic moiety, or its metabolite(s), measured.

(e) *Measurement of an acute pharmacological effect.* (1) When comparison of the test product and the reference material is to be based on acute pharmacological effect-time curves, measurements of this effect should be made with sufficient frequency to permit a reasonable estimate of the total area under the curve for a time period at least three times the half-life of decay of the pharmacological effect, unless some other approach is more appropriate for valid scientific reasons.

(2) The use of an acute pharmacological effect to determine bioavailability may further require demonstration of dose-related response. In such a case, bioavailability may be determined by comparison of the dose-response curves as well as the total area under the acute pharmacological effect-time curves for any given dose.

[42 FR 1648, Jan. 7, 1977, as amended at 67 FR 77674, Dec. 19, 2002]

§ 320.27 Guidelines on the design of a multiple-dose in vivo bioavailability study.

(a) *Basic principles.* (1) In selected circumstances it may be necessary for the test product and the reference material to be compared after repeated administration to determine steady-state levels of the active drug ingredient or therapeutic moiety in the body.

(2) The test product and the reference material should be administered to subjects in the fasting or nonfasting state, depending upon the conditions reflected in the proposed labeling of the test product.

(3) A multiple-dose study may be required to determine the bioavailability of a drug product in the following circumstances:

(i) There is a difference in the rate of absorption but not in the extent of absorption.

(ii) There is excessive variability in bioavailability from subject to subject.

(iii) The concentration of the active drug ingredient or therapeutic moiety, or its metabolite(s), in the blood resulting from a single dose is too low for accurate determination by the analytical method.

(iv) The drug product is an extended release dosage form.

(b) *Study design.* (1) A multiple-dose study should be crossover in design, unless a parallel design or other design is more appropriate for valid scientific reasons, and should provide for a drug elimination period if steady-state conditions are not achieved.

(2) A multiple-dose study is not required to be of crossover design if the study is to establish dose proportionality under a multiple-dose regimen or to establish the pharmacokinetic profile of a new drug product, a new drug delivery system, or an extended release dosage form.

(3) If a drug elimination period is required, unless some other approach is more appropriate for valid scientific reasons, the drug elimination period should be either:

(i) At least five times the half-life of the active drug ingredient or therapeutic moiety, or its active metabolite(s), measured in the blood or urine; or

(ii) At least five times the half-life of decay of the acute pharmacological effect.

(c) *Achievement of steady-state conditions.* Whenever a multiple-dose study is conducted, unless some other approach is more appropriate for valid scientific reasons, sufficient doses of the test product and reference material should be administered in accordance with the labeling to achieve steady-state conditions.

(d) *Collection of blood or urine samples.* (1) Whenever comparison of the test product and the reference material is to be based on blood concentration-time curves at steady state, appropriate dosage administration and sampling should be carried out to document attainment of steady state.

(2) Whenever comparison of the test product and the reference material is to be based on cumulative urinary excretion-time curves at steady state, appropriate dosage administration and sampling should be carried out to document attainment of steady state.

(3) A more complete characterization of the blood concentration or urinary excretion rate during the absorption and elimination phases of a single dose administered at steady-state is encouraged to permit estimation of the total area under concentration-time curves or cumulative urinary excretion-time curves and to obtain pharmacokinetic information, e.g., half-life or blood clearance, that is essential in preparing adequate labeling for the drug product.

(e) *Steady-state parameters.* (1) In certain instances, e.g., in a study involving a new drug entity, blood clearances at steady-state obtained in a multiple-dose study should be compared to blood clearances obtained in a single-dose study to support adequate dosage recommendations.

(2) In a linear system, the area under the blood concentration-time curve during a dosing interval in a multiple-dose steady-state study is directly proportional to the fraction of the dose absorbed and is equal to the corresponding "zero to infinity" area under the curve for a single-dose study. Therefore, when steady-state conditions are achieved, a comparison of blood concentrations during a dosing interval may be used to define the fraction of the active drug ingredient or therapeutic moiety absorbed.

(3) Other methods based on valid scientific reasons should be used to determine the bioavailability of a drug product having dose-dependent kinetics (non-linear system).

(f) *Measurement of an acute pharmacological effect.* When comparison of the test product and the reference material is to be based on acute pharmacological effect-time curves, measurements of this effect should be made with sufficient frequency to demonstrate a maximum effect and a lack of significant difference between the test product and the reference material.

[42 FR 1648, Jan. 7, 1977, as amended at 67 FR 77674, Dec. 19, 2002]

§ 320.28 **Correlation of bioavailability with an acute pharmacological effect or clinical evidence.**

Correlation of in vivo bioavailability data with an acute pharmacological effect or clinical evidence of safety and effectiveness may be required if needed to establish the clinical significance of a special claim, e.g., in the case of an extended release preparation.

[42 FR 1648, Jan. 7, 1977, as amended at 67 FR 77674, Dec. 19, 2002]

§ 320.29 **Analytical methods for an in vivo bioavailability or bioequivalence study.**

(a) The analytical method used in an in vivo bioavailability or bioequivalence study to measure the concentration of the active drug ingredient or therapeutic moiety, or its active metabolite(s), in body fluids or excretory products, or the method used to measure an acute pharmacological effect shall be demonstrated to be accurate and of sufficient sensitivity to measure, with appropriate precision, the actual concentration of the active drug ingredient or therapeutic moiety, or its active metabolite(s), achieved in the body.

(b) When the analytical method is not sensitive enough to measure accurately the concentration of the active drug ingredient or therapeutic moiety, or its active metabolite(s), in body fluids or excretory products produced by a single dose of the test product, two or more single doses may be given together to produce higher concentration if the requirements of § 320.31 are met.

[42 FR 1648, Jan. 7, 1977, as amended at 67 FR 77674, Dec. 19, 2002]

§ 320.30 **Inquiries regarding bioavailability and bioequivalence requirements and review of protocols by the Food and Drug Administration.**

(a) The Commissioner of Food and Drugs strongly recommends that, to avoid the conduct of an improper study and unnecessary human research, any person planning to conduct a bioavailability or bioequivalence study submit the proposed protocol for the study to FDA for review prior to the initiation of the study.

(b) FDA may review a proposed protocol for a bioavailability or bioequivalence study and will offer advice with respect to whether the following conditions are met:

(1) The design of the proposed bioavailability or bioequivalence study is appropriate.

(2) The reference material to be used in the bioavailability or bioequivalence study is appropriate.

(3) The proposed chemical and statistical analytical methods are adequate.

(c)(1) General inquiries relating to in vivo bioavailability requirements and methodology shall be submitted to the Food and Drug Administration, Center for Drug Evaluation and Research, Office of Clinical Pharmacology, 10903 New Hampshire Ave., Silver Spring, MD 20993–0002.

(2) General inquiries relating to bioequivalence requirements and methodology shall be submitted to the Food and Drug Administration, Center for Drug Evaluation and Research, Division of Bioequivalence (HFD–650), 7500 Standish Pl., Rockville, MD 20855–2773.

[57 FR 18000, Apr. 28, 1992, as amended at 67 FR 77674, Dec. 19, 2002; 74 FR 13114, Mar. 26, 2009]

§ 320.31 **Applicability of requirements regarding an "Investigational New Drug Application."**

(a) Any person planning to conduct an in vivo bioavailability or bioequivalence study in humans shall submit an "Investigational New Drug Application" (IND) if:

(1) The test product contains a new chemical entity as defined in § 314.108(a) of this chapter; or

(2) The study involves a radioactively labeled drug product; or

(3) The study involves a cytotoxic drug product.

(b) Any person planning to conduct a bioavailability or bioequivalence study in humans using a drug product that contains an already approved, non-new chemical entity shall submit an IND if the study is one of the following:

(1) A single-dose study in normal subjects or patients where either the maximum single or total daily dose exceeds that specified in the labeling of the drug product that is the subject of an approved new drug application or abbreviated new drug application.

(2) A multiple-dose study in normal subjects or patients where either the single or total daily dose exceeds that specified in the labeling of the drug product that is the subject of an approved new drug application or abbreviated new drug application.

(3) A multiple-dose study on an extended release product on which no single-dose study has been completed.

(c) The provisions of parts 50, 56, and 312 of this chapter are applicable to any bioavailability or bioequivalence study in humans conducted under an IND.

(d) A bioavailability or bioequivalence study in humans other than one described in paragraphs (a) through (c) of this section is exempt from the requirements of part 312 of this chapter if the following conditions are satisfied:

(1) If the study is one described under § 320.38(b) or § 320.63, the person conducting the study, including any contract research organization, must retain reserve samples of any test article and reference standard used in the study and release the reserve samples to FDA upon request, in accordance with, and for the period specified in, § 320.38;

(2) An in vivo bioavailability or bioequivalence study in humans must be conducted in compliance with the requirements for institutional review set forth in part 56 of this chapter, and informed consent set forth in part 50 of this chapter; and

(3) The person conducting the study, including any contract research organization, must notify FDA and all participating investigators of any serious adverse event, as defined in § 312.32(a), observed during the conduct of the study as soon as possible but in no case later than 15 calendar days after becoming aware of its occurrence. Each report must be submitted on FDA Form 3500A or in an electronic format that FDA can process, review, and archive. FDA will periodically issue guidance on how to provide the electronic

submission (e.g., method of transmission, media, file formats, preparation and organization of files). Each report must bear prominent identification of its contents, i.e., "bioavailability/bioequivalence safety report." The person conducting the study, including any contract research organization, must also notify FDA of any fatal or life-threatening adverse event from the study as soon as possible but in no case later than 7 calendar days after becoming aware of its occurrence. Each notification under this paragraph must be submitted to the Director, Office of Generic Drugs in the Center for Drug Evaluation and Research at FDA. Relevant followup information to a bioavailability/bioequivalence safety report must be submitted as soon as the information is available and must be identified as such, i.e., "Followup bioavailability/bioequivalence safety report." Upon request from FDA, the person conducting the study, including any contract research organization, must submit to FDA any additional data or information that the agency deems necessary, as soon as possible, but in no case later than 15 calendar days after receiving the request.

[57 FR 18000, Apr. 28, 1992, as amended at 58 FR 25927, Apr. 28, 1993; 67 FR 77674, Dec. 19, 2002; 75 FR 59963, Sept. 29, 2010]

§ 320.32 Procedures for establishing or amending a bioequivalence requirement.

(a) The Food and Drug Administration, on its own initiative or in response to a petition by an interested person, may propose and promulgate a regulation to establish a bioequivalence requirement for a product not subject to section 505(j) of the act if it finds there is well-documented evidence that specific pharmaceutical equivalents or pharmaceutical alternatives intended to be used interchangeably for the same therapeutic effect:

(1) Are not bioequivalent drug products; or

(2) May not be bioequivalent drug products based on the criteria set forth in § 320.33; or

(3) May not be bioequivalent drug products because they are members of

a class of drug products that have close structural similarity and similar physicochemical or pharmacokinetic properties to other drug products in the same class that FDA finds are not bioequivalent drug products.

(b) FDA shall include in a proposed rule to establish a bioequivalence requirement the evidence and criteria set forth in §320.33 that are to be considered in determining whether to issue the proposal. If the rulemaking is proposed in response to a petition, FDA shall include in the proposal a summary and analysis of the relevant information that was submitted in the petition as well as other available information to support the establishment of a bioequivalence requirement.

(c) FDA, on its own initiative or in response to a petition by an interested person, may propose and promulgate an amendment to a bioequivalence requirement established under this subpart.

[57 FR 18000, Apr. 28, 1992]

§320.33 Criteria and evidence to assess actual or potential bioequivalence problems.

The Commissioner of Food and Drugs shall consider the following factors, when supported by well-documented evidence, to identify specific pharmaceutical equivalents and pharmaceutical alternatives that are not or may not be bioequivalent drug products.

(a) Evidence from well-controlled clinical trials or controlled observations in patients that such drug products do not give comparable therapeutic effects.

(b) Evidence from well-controlled bioequivalence studies that such products are not bioequivalent drug products.

(c) Evidence that the drug products exhibit a narrow therapeutic ratio, e.g., there is less than a 2-fold difference in median lethal dose (LD_{50}) and median effective dose (ED_{50}) values, or have less than a 2-fold difference in the minimum toxic concentrations and minimum effective concentrations in the blood, and safe and effective use of the drug products requires careful dosage titration and patient monitoring.

(d) Competent medical determination that a lack of bioequivalence would have a serious adverse effect in the treatment or prevention of a serious disease or condition.

(e) Physicochemical evidence that:

(1) The active drug ingredient has a low solubility in water, e.g., less than 5 milligrams per 1 milliliter, or, if dissolution in the stomach is critical to absorption, the volume of gastric fluids required to dissolve the recommended dose far exceeds the volume of fluids present in the stomach (taken to be 100 milliliters for adults and prorated for infants and children).

(2) The dissolution rate of one or more such products is slow, e.g., less than 50 percent in 30 minutes when tested using either a general method specified in an official compendium or a paddle method at 50 revolutions per minute in 900 milliliters of distilled or deionized water at 37 °C, or differs significantly from that of an appropriate reference material such as an identical drug product that is the subject of an approved full new drug application.

(3) The particle size and/or surface area of the active drug ingredient is critical in determining its bioavailability.

(4) Certain physical structural characteristics of the active drug ingredient, e.g., polymorphic forms, conforms, solvates, complexes, and crystal modifications, dissolve poorly and this poor dissolution may affect absorption.

(5) Such drug products have a high ratio of excipients to active ingredients, e.g., greater than 5 to 1.

(6) Specific inactive ingredients, e.g., hydrophilic or hydrophobic excipients and lubricants, either may be required for absorption of the active drug ingredient or therapeutic moiety or, alternatively, if present, may interfere with such absorption.

(f) Pharmacokinetic evidence that:

(1) The active drug ingredient, therapeutic moiety, or its precursor is absorbed in large part in a particular segment of the gastrointestinal tract or is absorbed from a localized site.

(2) The degree of absorption of the active drug ingredient, therapeutic moiety, or its precursor is poor, e.g., less than 50 percent, ordinarily in comparison to an intravenous dose, even when

it is administered in pure form, e.g., in solution.

(3) There is rapid metabolism of the therapeutic moiety in the intestinal wall or liver during the process of absorption (first-class metabolism) so the therapeutic effect and/or toxicity of such drug product is determined by the rate as well as the degree of absorption.

(4) The therapeutic moiety is rapidly metabolized or excreted so that rapid dissolution and absorption are required for effectiveness.

(5) The active drug ingredient or therapeutic moiety is unstable in specific portions of the gastrointestinal tract and requires special coatings or formulations, e.g., buffers, enteric coatings, and film coatings, to assure adequate absorption.

(6) The drug product is subject to dose dependent kinetics in or near the therapeutic range, and the rate and extent of absorption are important to bioequivalence.

[42 FR 1635, Jan. 7, 1977. Redesignated and amended at 57 FR 18001, Apr. 28, 1992]

§ 320.34 Requirements for batch testing and certification by the Food and Drug Administration.

(a) If the Commissioner determines that individual batch testing by the Food and Drug Administration is necessary to assure that all batches of the same drug product meet an appropriate in vitro test, he shall include in the bioequivalence requirement a requirement for manufacturers to submit samples of each batch to the Food and Drug Administration and to withhold distribution of the batch until notified by the Food and Drug Administration that the batch may be introduced into interstate commerce.

(b) The Commissioner will ordinarily terminate a requirement for a manufacturer to submit samples for batch testing on a finding that the manufacturer has produced four consecutive batches that were tested by the Food and Drug Administration and found to meet the bioequivalence requirement, unless the public health requires that batch testing be extended to additional batches.

[42 FR 1635, Jan. 7, 1977. Redesignated at 57 FR 18001, Apr. 28, 1992]

§ 320.35 Requirements for in vitro testing of each batch.

If a bioequivalence requirement specifies a currently available in vitro test or an in vitro bioequivalence standard comparing the drug product to a reference standard, the manufacturer shall conduct the test on a sample of each batch of the drug product to assure batch-to-batch uniformity.

[42 FR 1635, Jan. 7, 1977. Redesignated at 57 FR 18001, Apr. 28, 1992]

§ 320.36 Requirements for maintenance of records of bioequivalence testing.

(a) All records of in vivo or in vitro tests conducted on any marketed batch of a drug product to assure that the product meets a bioequivalence requirement shall be maintained by the manufacturer for at least 2 years after the expiration date of the batch and submitted to the Food and Drug Administration on request.

(b) Any person who contracts with another party to conduct a bioequivalence study from which the data are intended to be submitted to FDA as part of an application submitted under part 314 of this chapter shall obtain from the person conducting the study sufficient accurate financial information to allow the submission of complete and accurate financial certifications or disclosure statements required under part 54 of this chapter and shall maintain that information and all records relating to the compensation given for that study and all other financial interest information required under part 54 of this chapter for 2 years after the date of approval of the application. The person maintaining these records shall, upon request for any properly authorized officer or employee of the Food and Drug Administration, at reasonable time, permit such officer or employee to have access to and copy and verify these records.

[42 FR 1635, Jan. 7, 1977. Redesignated at 57 FR 18001, Apr. 28, 1992, as amended at 63 FR 5252, Feb. 2, 1998]

§ 320.38 Retention of bioavailability samples.

(a) The applicant of an application or supplemental application submitted under section 505 of the Federal Food, Drug, and Cosmetic Act, or, if bioavailability testing was performed under contract, the contract research organization shall retain an appropriately identified reserve sample of the drug product for which the applicant is seeking approval (test article) and of the reference standard used to perform an in vivo bioavailability study in accordance with and for the studies described in paragraph (b) of this section that is representative of each sample of the test article and reference standard provided by the applicant for the testing.

(b) Reserve samples shall be retained for the following test articles and reference standards and for the studies described:

(1) If the formulation of the test article is the same as the formulation(s) used in the clinical studies demonstrating substantial evidence of safety and effectiveness for the test article's claimed indications, a reserve sample of the test article used to conduct an in vivo bioavailability study comparing the test article to a reference oral solution, suspension, or injection.

(2) If the formulation of the test article differs from the formulation(s) used in the clinical studies demonstrating substantial evidence of safety and effectiveness for the test article's claimed indications, a reserve sample of the test article and of the reference standard used to conduct an in vivo bioequivalence study comparing the test article to the formulation(s) (reference standard) used in the clinical studies.

(3) For a new formulation, new dosage form, or a new salt or ester of an active drug ingredient or therapeutic moiety that has been approved for marketing, a reserve sample of the test article and of the reference standard used to conduct an in vivo bioequivalence study comparing the test article to a marketed product (reference standard) that contains the same active drug ingredient or therapeutic moiety.

(c) Each reserve sample shall consist of a sufficient quantity to permit FDA to perform five times all of the release tests required in the application or supplemental application.

(d) Each reserve sample shall be adequately identified so that the reserve sample can be positively identified as having come from the same sample as used in the specific bioavailability study.

(e) Each reserve sample shall be stored under conditions consistent with product labeling and in an area segregated from the area where testing is conducted and with access limited to authorized personnel. Each reserve sample shall be retained for a period of at least 5 years following the date on which the application or supplemental application is approved, or, if such application or supplemental application is not approved, at least 5 years following the date of completion of the bioavailability study in which the sample from which the reserve sample was obtained was used.

(f) Authorized FDA personnel will ordinarily collect reserve samples directly from the applicant or contract research organization at the storage site during a preapproval inspection. If authorized FDA personnel are unable to collect samples, FDA may require the applicant or contract research organization to submit the reserve samples to the place identified in the agency's request. If FDA has not collected or requested delivery of a reserve sample, or if FDA has not collected or requested delivery of any portion of a reserve sample, the applicant or contract research organization shall retain the sample or remaining sample for the 5-year period specified in paragraph (e) of this section.

(g) Upon release of the reserve samples to FDA, the applicant or contract research organization shall provide a written assurance that, to the best knowledge and belief of the individual executing the assurance, the reserve samples came from the same samples as used in the specific bioavailability or bioequivalence study identified by the agency. The assurance shall be executed by an individual authorized to act for the applicant or contract research organization in releasing the reserve samples to FDA.

(h) A contract research organization may contract with an appropriate, independent third party to provide storage of reserve samples provided that the sponsor of the study has been notified in writing of the name and address of the facility at which the reserve samples will be stored.

(i) If a contract research organization conducting a bioavailability or bioequivalence study that requires reserve sample retention under this section or § 320.63 goes out of business, it shall transfer its reserve samples to an appropriate, independent third party, and shall notify in writing the sponsor of the study of the transfer and provide the study sponsor with the name and address of the facility to which the reserve samples have been transferred.

[58 FR 25927, Apr. 28, 1993, as amended at 64 FR 402, Jan. 5, 1999]

§ 320.63   Retention of bioequivalence samples.

The applicant of an abbreviated application or a supplemental application submitted under section 505 of the Federal Food, Drug, and Cosmetic Act, or, if bioequivalence testing was performed under contract, the contract research organization shall retain reserve samples of any test article and reference standard used in conducting an in vivo or in vitro bioequivalence study required for approval of the abbreviated application or supplemental application. The applicant or contract research organization shall retain the reserve samples in accordance with, and for the period specified in, § 320.38 and shall release the reserve samples to FDA upon request in accordance with § 320.38.

[58 FR 25928, Apr. 28, 1993, as amended at 64 FR 402, Jan. 5, 1999]

PART 328—OVER-THE-COUNTER DRUG PRODUCTS INTENDED FOR ORAL INGESTION THAT CONTAIN ALCOHOL

Subpart A—General Provisions

Subpart C—Labeling

AUTHORITY: Secs. 201, 301, 501, 502, 503, 505, 701 of the Federal Food, Drug, and Cosmetic Act (21 U.S.C. 321, 331, 351, 352, 353, 355, 371).

SOURCE: 60 FR 13595, Mar. 13, 1995, unless otherwise noted.

EDITORIAL NOTE: Nomenclature changes to part 328 appear at 69 FR 13717, Mar. 24, 2004.

Subpart A—General Provisions

§ 328.1   Scope.

Reference in this part to regulatory sections of the Code of Federal Regulations are to chapter I of title 21 unless otherwise noted.

§ 328.3   Definitions.

As used in this part:

(a) *Alcohol* means the substance known as ethanol, ethyl alcohol, or Alcohol, USP.

(b) *Inactive ingredient* means any component of a product other than an active ingredient as defined in § 210.3(b)(7) of this chapter.

Subpart B—Ingredients

§ 328.10   Alcohol.

(a) Any over-the-counter (OTC) drug product intended for oral ingestion shall not contain alcohol as an inactive ingredient in concentrations that exceed those established in this part, unless a specific exemption, as provided in paragraph (e) or (f) of this section, has been approved.

(b) For any OTC drug product intended for oral ingestion and labeled for use by adults and children 12 years of age and over, the amount of alcohol in the product shall not exceed 10 percent.

(c) For any OTC drug product intended for oral ingestion and labeled for use by children 6 to under 12 years of age, the amount of alcohol in the product shall not exceed 5 percent.

(d) For any OTC drug product intended for oral ingestion and labeled for use by children under 6 years of age, the amount of alcohol in the product shall not exceed 0.5 percent.

(e) The Food and Drug Administration will grant an exemption from paragraphs (b), (c), and (d) of this section where appropriate, upon petition under the provisions of §10.30 of this chapter. Appropriate cause, such as a specific solubility or manufacturing problem, must be adequately documented in the petition. Decisions with respect to requests for exemption shall be maintained in a permanent file for public review by the Division of Dockets Management (HFA–305), Food and Drug Administration, 5630 Fishers Lane, rm. 1061, Rockville, MD 20852.

(f) Ipecac syrup is exempt from the provisions of paragraph (d) of this section.

(g) The following drugs are temporarily exempt from the provisions of paragraphs (b), (c), and (d) of this section:

(1) Aromatic Cascara Fluidextract.

(2) Cascara Sagrada Fluidextract.

(3) Orally ingested homeopathic drug products.

[60 FR 13595, Mar. 13, 1995, as amended at 61 FR 58630, Nov. 18, 1996; 68 FR 24879, May 9, 2003]

Subpart C—Labeling

§328.50 Principal display panel of all OTC drug products intended for oral ingestion that contain alcohol.

(a) The amount (percentage) of alcohol present in a product shall be stated in terms of percent volume of absolute alcohol at 60 °F (15.56 °C) in accordance with §201.10(d)(2) of this chapter.

(b) A statement expressing the amount (percentage) of alcohol present in a product shall appear prominently and conspicuously on the "principal display panel," as defined in §201.60 of this chapter. For products whose principal display panel is on the immediate container label and that are not marketed in another retail package (e.g., an outer box), the statement of the percentage of alcohol present in the product shall appear prominently and conspicuously on the "principal display panel" of the immediate container label.

(c) For products whose principal display panel is on the retail package and the retail package is not the immediate container, the statement of the percentage of alcohol present in the product shall also appear on the immediate container label; it may appear anywhere on that label in accord with section 502(e) of the Federal Food, Drug, and Cosmetic Act.

(d) The statement expressing the amount (percentage) of alcohol present in the product shall be in a size reasonably related to the most prominent printed matter on the panel or label on which it appears, and shall be in lines generally parallel to the base on which the package rests as it is designed to be displayed.

(e) For a product to state in its labeling that it is "alcohol free," it must contain no alcohol (0 percent).

(f) For any OTC drug product intended for oral ingestion containing over 5 percent alcohol and labeled for use by adults and children 12 years of age and over, the labeling shall contain the following statement in the directions section: "Consult a physician for use in children under 12 years of age."

(g) For any OTC drug product intended for oral ingestion containing over 0.5 percent alcohol and labeled for use by children ages 6 to under 12 years of age, the labeling shall contain the following statement in the directions section: "Consult a physician for use in children under 6 years of age."

(h) When the direction regarding age in paragraph (e) or (f) of this section differs from an age-limiting direction contained in any OTC drug monograph in this chapter, the direction containing the more stringent age limitation shall be used.

PART 329—NONPRESCRIPTION HUMAN DRUG PRODUCTS SUBJECT TO SECTION 760 OF THE FEDERAL FOOD, DRUG, AND COSMETIC ACT

AUTHORITY: 21 U.S.C. 321, 331, 351, 352, 353, 355, 371, 379aa.

SOURCE: 79 FR 33089, June 10, 2015, unless otherwise noted.

EFFECTIVE DATE NOTE: At 79 FR 33089, June 10, 2014, part 329 was added, effective June 10, 2015.

§ 329.100 Postmarketing reporting of adverse drug events under section 760 of the Federal Food, Drug, and Cosmetic Act.

(a) *Reporting requirements.* Reports of serious adverse events required by section 760 of the Federal Food, Drug, and Cosmetic Act (FD&C Act) must include the information specified in this section, as applicable. Except as provided in paragraph (c)(2) of this section, these reports must be submitted to the Agency in electronic format as described in paragraph (c)(1) of this section.

(b) *Contents of reports.* For purposes of reporting serious adverse events under section 760 of the FD&C Act, an individual case safety report (ICSR) constitutes the MedWatch form required to be submitted by section 760(d) of the FD&C Act. ICSRs include the following information:

(1) *Patient information.*

(i) Patient identification code;

(ii) Patient age at the time of adverse drug experience, or date of birth;

(iii) Patient gender; and

(iv) Patient weight.

(2) *Adverse event.*

(i) Outcome attributed to adverse drug event;

(ii) Date of adverse drug event;

(iii) Date of ICSR submission;

(iv) Description of adverse drug event (including a concise medical narrative);

(v) Adverse drug event term(s);

(vi) Description of relevant tests, including dates and laboratory data; and

(vii) Other relevant patient history, including preexisting medical conditions.

(3) *Suspect medical product(s).*

(i) Name;

(ii) Dose, frequency, and route of administration used;

(iii) Therapy dates;

(iv) Diagnosis for use (indication);

(v) Whether the product is a combination product as defined in § 3.2(e) of this chapter;

(vi) Whether the product is a prescription or nonprescription product;

(vii) Whether adverse drug event abated after drug use stopped or dose reduced;

(viii) Whether adverse drug event reappeared after reintroduction of drug;

(ix) Lot number;

(x) Expiration date;

(xi) National Drug Code (NDC) number; and

(xii) Concomitant medical products and therapy dates.

(4) *Initial reporter information.*

(i) Name, address, and telephone number;

(ii) Whether the initial reporter is a health care professional; and

(iii) Occupation, if a health care professional.

(5) *Responsible person (as defined in section 760(b) of the FD&C Act) information.*

(i) Name and contact office address;

(ii) Telephone number;

(iii) Report source, such as spontaneous;

(iv) Date the report was received by responsible person;

(v) Whether the ICSR is a 15-day report;

(vi) Whether the ICSR is an initial report or followup report; and

(vii) Unique case identification number, which must be the same in the initial report and any subsequent followup report(s).

(c) *Electronic format for submissions.* (1) Each report required to be submitted to FDA under section 760 of the FD&C Act, accompanied by a copy of the label on or within the retail package of the drug and any other documentation (as ICSR attachments), must be in an electronic format that FDA can process, review, and archive. FDA will issue guidance on how to provide the electronic submission (e.g., method of transmission, media, file formats, preparation, and organization of files).

(2) The responsible person may request, in writing, a temporary waiver of the requirements in paragraph (c)(1) of this section. These waivers will be granted on a limited basis for good cause shown. FDA will issue guidance on requesting a waiver of the requirements in paragraph (c)(1) of this section.

(d) *Patient privacy.* The responsible person should not include in reports under this section the names and addresses of individual patients; instead, the responsible person should assign a unique code for identification of the patient. The responsible person should include the name of the reporter from whom the information was received as part of the initial reporter information, even when the reporter is the patient. The names of patients, health care professionals, hospitals, and geographical identifiers in adverse drug event reports are not releasable to the public under FDA's public information regulations in part 20 of this chapter.

PART 330—OVER-THE-COUNTER (OTC) HUMAN DRUGS WHICH ARE GENERALLY RECOGNIZED AS SAFE AND EFFECTIVE AND NOT MISBRANDED

Subpart A—General Provisions

Subpart B—Administrative Procedures

AUTHORITY: 21 U.S.C. 321, 351, 352, 353, 355, 360, 371.

SOURCE: 39 FR 11741, Mar. 29, 1974, unless otherwise noted.

EDITORIAL NOTE: Nomenclature changes to part 330 appear at 69 FR 13717, Mar. 24, 2004.

Subpart A—General Provisions

§330.1 General conditions for general recognition as safe, effective and not misbranded.

An over-the-counter (OTC) drug listed in this subchapter is generally recognized as safe and effective and is not misbranded if it meets each of the conditions contained in this part and each of the conditions contained in any applicable monograph. Any product which fails to conform to each of the conditions contained in this part and in an applicable monograph is liable to regulatory action.

(a) The product is manufactured in compliance with current good manufacturing practices, as established by parts 210 and 211 of this chapter.

(b) The establishment(s) in which the drug product is manufactured is registered, and the drug product is listed, in compliance with part 207 of this chapter. It is requested but not required that the number assigned to the product pursuant to part 207 of this chapter appear on all drug labels and in all drug labeling. If this number is used, it shall be placed in the manner set forth in part 207 of this chapter.

(c)(1) The product is labeled in compliance with chapter V of the Federal Food, Drug, and Cosmetic Act (the act) and subchapter C *et seq.* of this chapter, including the format and content requirements in §201.66 of this chapter. An OTC drug product that is not in compliance with chapter V and subchapter C, including §201.66 of this chapter, is subject to regulatory action. For purposes of §201.61(b) of this chapter, the statement of identity of the product shall be the term or phrase used in the applicable OTC drug monograph established in this part.

(2) The "Uses" section of the label and labeling of the product shall contain the labeling describing the "Indications" that have been established in an applicable OTC drug monograph or alternative truthful and nonmisleading statements describing only those indications for use. that have been established in an applicable monograph, subject to the provisions of section 502 of the act relating to misbranding and the prohibition in section 301(d) of the act against the introduction or delivery for introduction into interstate commerce of unapproved new drugs in violation of section 505(a) of the act. Any other labeling under this subchapter and subchapter C *et seq.* of this chapter shall be stated in the exact language where exact language has been established and identified by quotation marks in

an applicable OTC drug monograph or by regulation (e.g., § 201.63 of this chapter), except as provided in paragraphs (i) and (j) of this section.

(d) The advertising for the product prescribes, recommends, or suggests its use only under the conditions stated in the labeling.

(e) The product contains only suitable inactive ingredients which are safe in the amounts administered and do not interfere with the effectiveness of the preparation or with suitable tests or assays to determine if the product meets its professed standards of identity, strength, quality, and purity. Color additives may be used only in accordance with section 721 of the act and subchapter A of this chapter.

(f) The product container and container components meet the requirements of § 211.94 of this chapter.

(g) The labeling for all drugs contains the general warning: "Keep out of reach of children." [highlighted in bold type]. The labeling of drugs shall also state as follows: For drugs used by oral administration, "In case of overdose, get medical help or contact a Poison Control Center right away"; for drugs used topically, rectally, or vaginally and not intended for oral ingestion, "If swallowed, get medical help or contact a Poison Control Center right away"; and for drugs used topically and intended for oral use, "If more than used for" (insert intended use, e.g., pain) "is accidentally swallowed, get medical help or contact a Poison Control Center right away." The Food and Drug Administration will grant an exemption from these general warnings where appropriate upon petition, which shall be maintained in a permanent file for public review by the Division of Dockets Management, Food and Drug Administration, 5630 Fishers Lane, rm. 1061, Rockville, MD 20852.

(h) Where no maximum daily dosage limit for an active ingredient is established in this part, it is used in a product at a level that does not exceed the amount reasonably required to achieve its intended effect.

(i) The following terms may be used interchangeably in the labeling of OTC drug products, provided such use does not alter the meaning of the labeling that has been established and identified in an applicable monograph or by regulation. The following terms shall not be used to change in any way the title, headings, and subheadings required under § 201.66(c)(1) through (c)(9) of this chapter:

(1) "Abdominal" or "stomach" (in context only).

(2) "Administer" or "give".

(3) "Aggravate(s)" or "make(s) worse".

(4) "Application of this product" or "applying".

(5) "Are uncertain" or "do not know".

(6) "Ask" or "consult" or "contact".

(7) "Asking" or "consulting".

(8) "Assistance" or "help" or "aid".

(9) "Associated with" or "due to" or "caused by".

(10) "Avoid contact with eyes" or "do not get into eyes".

(11) "Avoid inhaling" or "do not inhale".

(12) "Before a doctor is consulted" or "without first consulting your doctor" or "consult your doctor before".

(13) "Beverages" or "drinks".

(14) "Clean" or "cleanse".

(15) "Consulting" or "advising".

(16) "Continue(s)" or "persist(s)" or "is persistent" or "do(es) not go away" or "last(s)".

(17) "Daily" or "every day".

(18) "Develop(s)" or "begin(s)" or "occur(s)".

(19) "Difficulty" or "trouble".

(20) "Difficulty in urination" or "trouble urinating".

(21) "Discard" or "throw away".

(22) "Discontinue" or "stop" or "quit".

(23) "Doctor" or "physician".

(24) "Drowsiness" or "the drowsiness effect".

(25) "Drowsiness may occur" or "you may get drowsy".

(26) "Enlargement of the" or "an enlarged".

(27) "Especially in children" or especially children".

(28) "Exceed" or "use more than" or "go beyond".

(29) "Exceed recommended dosage" or "use more than directed".

(30) "Excessive" or "too much".

(31) "Excitability may occur" or "you may get excited".

(32) "Experience" or "feel".

(33) "For relief of" or "relieves".

(34) "For temporary reduction of" or "temporarily reduces".

(35) "For the temporary relief of" or "temporarily relieves".

(36) "For the treatment of" or "treats".

(37) "Frequently" or "often".

(38) "Give to" or "use in".

(39) "Immediately" or "right away" or "directly".

(40) "Immediately" or "as soon as".

(41) "Immediately following" or "right after".

(42) "Improve(s)" or "get(s) better" or "make(s) better".

(43) "Increased" or "more".

(44) "Increase your risk of" or "cause".

(45) "Indication(s)" or "Use(s)".

(46) "Inhalation" or "puff".

(47) "In persons who" or "if you" or "if the child".

(48) "Instill" or "put".

(49) "Is (are) accompanied by" or "you also have" (in context only) or "(optional: that) occur(s) with".

(50) "Longer" or "more".

(51) "Lung" or "pulmonary".

(52) "Medication(s)" or "medicine(s)" or "drug(s)".

(53) "Nervousness, dizziness, or sleeplessness occurs" or "you get nervous, dizzy, or sleepless".

(54) "Not to exceed" or "do not exceed" or "not more than".

(55) "Obtain(s)" or "get(s)".

(56) "Passages" or "passageways" or "tubes".

(57) "Perforation of" or "hole in".

(58) "Persistent" or "that does not go away" or "that continues" or "that lasts".

(59) "Per day" or "daily".

(60) "Presently" or "now".

(61) "Produce(s)" or "cause(s)".

(62) "Prompt(ly)" or "quick(ly)" or "right away".

(63) "Reduce" or "minimize".

(64) "Referred to as" or "of".

(65) "Sensation" or "feeling".

(66) "Solution" or "liquid".

(67) "Specifically" or "definitely".

(68) "Take" or "use" or "give".

(69) "Tend(s) to recur" or "reoccur(s)" or "return(s)" or "come(s) back".

(70) "To avoid contamination" or "avoid contamination" or "do not contaminate".

(71) "To help" or "helps".

(72) "Unless directed by a doctor" or "except under the advice of a doctor" or "unless told to do so by a doctor".

(73) "Use caution" or "be careful".

(74) "Usually" or "generally" (in context only).

(75) "You" ("Your") or "the child" ("the child's").

(76) "You also have" or "occurs with".

(77) "When practical" or "if possible".

(78) "Whether" or "if".

(79) "Worsen(s)" or "get(s) worse" or "make(s) worse".

(j) The following connecting terms may be deleted from the labeling of OTC drug products, provided such deletion does not alter the meaning of the labeling that has been established and identified in an applicable monograph or by regulation. The following terms shall not be used to change in any way the specific title, headings, and subheadings required under §201.66(c)(1) through (c)(9) of this chapter:

(1) "And".

(2) "As may occur with".

(3) "Associated" or "to be associated".

(4) "Consult a doctor".

(5) "Discontinue use".

(6) "Drug Interaction Precaution".

(7) "Due to".

(8) "Except under the advice and supervision of a physician".

(9) "If this occurs".

(10) "In case of".

(11) "Notice".

(12) "Or".

(13) "Occurring with".

(14) "Or as directed by a doctor".

(15) "Such as".

(16) "Such as occurs with".

(17) "Tends to".

(18) "This product".

(19) "Unless directed by a doctor".

(20) "While taking this product" or "before taking this product".

(21) "Within".

[39 FR 11741, Mar. 29, 1974, as amended at 40 FR 11718, Mar. 13, 1975; 40 FR 13496, Mar. 27, 1975; 42 FR 15674, Mar. 22, 1977; 46 FR 8459, Jan. 27, 1981; 50 FR 8996, Mar. 6, 1985; 51 FR 16266, May 1, 1986; 55 FR 11581, Mar. 29, 1990; 59 FR 4000, Jan. 28, 1994; 59 FR 14365, Mar. 28, 1994; 64 FR 13294, Mar. 17, 1999; 68 FR 24879, May 9, 2003]

§ 330.2 Pregnancy-nursing warning.

A pregnancy-nursing warning for OTC drugs is set forth under § 201.63 of this chapter.

[47 FR 54758, Dec. 3, 1982]

§ 330.3 Imprinting of solid oral dosage form drug products.

A requirement to imprint an identification code on solid oral dosage form drug products is set forth under part 206 of this chapter.

[58 FR 47959, Sept. 13, 1993]

§ 330.5 Drug categories.

Monographs promulgated pursuant to the provisions of this part shall be established in this part 330 and following parts and shall cover the following designated categories:

(a) Antacids.

(b) Laxatives.

(c) Antidiarrheal products.

(d) Emetics.

(e) Antiemetics.

(f) Antiperspirants.

(g) Sunburn prevention and treatment products.

(h) Vitamin-mineral products.

(i) Antimicrobial products.

(j) Dandruff products.

(k) Oral hygiene aids.

(l) Hemorrhoidal products.

(m) Hematinics.

(n) Bronchodilator and antiasthmatic products.

(o) Analgesics.

(p) Sedatives and sleep aids.

(q) Stimulants.

(r) Antitussives.

(s) Allergy treatment products.

(t) Cold remedies.

(u) Antirheumatic products.

(v) Ophthalmic products.

(w) Contraceptive products.

(x) Miscellaneous dermatologic products.

(y) Dentifrices and dental products such as analgesics, antiseptics, etc.

(z) Miscellaneous (all other OTC drugs not falling within one of the above therapeutic categories).

Subpart B—Administrative Procedures

§ 330.10 Procedures for classifying OTC drugs as generally recognized as safe and effective and not misbranded, and for establishing monographs.

For purposes of classifying over-the-counter (OTC) drugs as drugs generally recognized among qualified experts as safe and effective for use and as not misbranded drugs, the following regulations shall apply:

(a) *Procedure for establishing OTC drug monographs*—(1) *Advisory review panels.* The Commissioner shall appoint advisory review panels of qualified experts to evaluate the safety and effectiveness of OTC drugs, to review OTC drug labeling, and to advise him on the promulgation of monographs establishing conditions under which OTC drugs are generally recognized as safe and effective and not misbranded. A single advisory review panel shall be established for each designated category of OTC drugs and every OTC drug category will be considered by a panel. The members of a panel shall be qualified experts (appointed by the Commissioner) and may include persons from lists submitted by organizations representing professional, consumer, and industry interests. The Commissioner shall designate the chairman of each panel. Summary minutes of all meetings shall be made.

(2) *Request for data and views.* The Commissioner will publish a notice in the FEDERAL REGISTER requesting interested persons to submit, for review and evaluation by an advisory review panel, published and unpublished data and information pertinent to a designated category of OTC drugs. Data and information submitted pursuant to a published notice, and falling within the confidentiality provisions of 18 U.S.C. 1905, 5 U.S.C. 552(b), or 21 U.S.C. 331(j), shall be handled by the advisory review panel and the Food and Drug Administration as confidential until publication of a proposed monograph and the full report(s) of the panel or until the Commissioner places the panel's recommendations on public display at the office of the Division of Dockets Management. Thirty days thereafter

such data and information shall be made publicly available and may be viewed at the office of the Division of Dockets Management of the Food and Drug Administration, except to the extent that the person submitting it demonstrates that it still falls within the confidentiality provisions of one or more of those statutes. To be considered, eight copies of the data and/or views on any marketed drug within the class must be submitted, preferably bound, indexed, and on standard sized paper (approximately 8½ × 11 inches). When requested, abbreviated submissions should be sent. All submissions must be in the following format:

OTC DRUG REVIEW INFORMATION

I. Label(s) and all labeling (preferably mounted and filed with the other data—facsimile labeling is acceptable in lieu of actual container labeling).

II. A statement setting forth the quantities of active ingredients of the drug.

III. Animal safety data.

A. Individual active components.

1. Controlled studies.

2. Partially controlled or uncontrolled studies.

B. Combinations of the individual active components.

1. Controlled studies.

2. Partially controlled or uncontrolled studies.

C. Finished drug product.

1. Controlled studies.

2. Partially controlled or uncontrolled studies.

IV. Human safety data.

A. Individual active components.

1. Controlled studies.

2. Partially controlled or uncontrolled studies.

3. Documented case reports. Identify expected or frequently reported side effects.

4. Pertinent marketing experiences that may influence a determination as to the safety of each individual active component.

5. Pertinent medical and scientific literature.

B. Combinations of the individual active components.

1. Controlled studies.

2. Partially controlled or uncontrolled studies.

3. Documented case reports. Identify expected or frequently reported side effects.

4. Pertinent marketing experiences that may influence a determination as to the safety of combinations of the individual active components.

5. Pertinent medical and scientific literature.

C. Finished drug product.

1. Controlled studies.

2. Partially controlled or uncontrolled studies.

3. Documented case reports. Identify expected or frequently reported side effects.

4. Pertinent marketing experiences that may influence a determination as to the safety of the finished drug product.

5. Pertinent medical and scientific literature.

V. Efficacy data.

A. Individual active components.

1. Controlled studies.

2. Partially controlled or uncontrolled studies.

3. Documented case reports. Identify expected or frequently reported side effects.

4. Pertinent marketing experiences that may influence a determination on the efficacy of each individual active component.

5. Pertinent medical and scientific literature.

B. Combinations of the individual active components.

1. Controlled studies.

2. Partially controlled or uncontrolled studies.

3. Documented case reports. Identify expected or frequently reported side effects.

4. Pertinent marketing experiences that may influence a determination on the efficacy of combinations of the individual active components.

5. Pertinent medical and scientific literature.

C. Finished drug product.

1. Controlled studies.

2. Partially controlled or uncontrolled studies.

3. Documented case reports. Identify expected or frequently reported side effects.

4. Pertinent marketing experiences that may influence a determination on the efficacy of the finished drug product.

5. Pertinent medical and scientific literature.

VI. A summary of the data and views setting forth the medical rationale and purpose (or lack thereof) for the drug and its ingredients and the scientific basis (or lack thereof) for the conclusion that the drug and its ingredients have been proven safe and effective for the intended use. If there is an absence of controlled studies in the material submitted, an explanation as to why such studies are not considered necessary must be included.

VII. An official United States Pharmacopeia (USP)–National Formulary (NF) drug monograph for the active ingredient(s) or botanical drug substance(s), or a proposed standard for inclusion in an article to be recognized in an official USP-NF drug monograph for the active ingredient(s) or botanical drug substance(s). Include information showing that the official or proposed compendial monograph for the active ingredient or botanical drug substance is consistent with the active ingredient or botanical drug substance used in the studies establishing safety and effectiveness and with the active ingredient or botanical drug substance marketed in the OTC product(s) to a material extent and for a material time. If differences exist, explain why.

(3) *Deliberations of an advisory review panel.* An advisory review panel will meet as often and for as long as is appropriate to review the data submitted to it and to prepare a report containing its conclusions and recommendations to the Commissioner with respect to the safety and effectiveness of the drugs in a designated category of OTC drugs. A panel may consult any individual or group. Any interested person may request an opportunity to present oral views to the panel; such request may be granted or denied by the panel. Such requests for oral presentations should be in written form including a summarization of the data to be presented to the panel. Any interested person may present written data and views which shall be considered by the panel. This information shall be presented to the panel in the format set forth in paragraph (a)(2) of this section and within the time period established for the drug category in the notice for review by a panel.

(4) *Standards for safety, effectiveness, and labeling.* The advisory review panel, in reviewing the data submitted to it and preparing its conclusions and recommendations, and the Commissioner, in reviewing the conclusions and recommendations of the panel and the published proposed, tentative, and the final monographs, shall apply the following standards to determine general recognition that a category of OTC drugs is safe and effective and not misbranded:

(i) Safety means a low incidence of adverse reactions or significant side effects under adequate directions for use and warnings against unsafe use as well as low potential for harm which may result from abuse under conditions of widespread availability. Proof of safety shall consist of adequate tests by methods reasonably applicable to show the drug is safe under the prescribed, recommended, or suggested conditions of use. This proof shall include results of significant human experience during marketing. General recognition of safety shall ordinarily be based upon published studies which may be corroborated by unpublished studies and other data.

(ii) Effectiveness means a reasonable expectation that, in a significant proportion of the target population, the pharmacological effect of the drug, when used under adequate directions for use and warnings against unsafe use, will provide clinically significant relief of the type claimed. Proof of effectiveness shall consist of controlled clinical investigations as defined in § 314.126(b) of this chapter, unless this requirement is waived on the basis of a showing that it is not reasonably applicable to the drug or essential to the validity of the investigation and that an alternative method of investigation is adequate to substantiate effectiveness. Investigations may be corroborated by partially controlled or uncontrolled studies, documented clinical studies by qualified experts, and reports of significant human experience during marketing. Isolated case reports, random experience, and reports lacking the details which permit scientific evaluation will not be considered. General recognition of effectiveness shall ordinarily be based upon published studies which may be corroborated by unpublished studies and other data.

(iii) The benefit-to-risk ratio of a drug shall be considered in determining safety and effectiveness.

(iv) An OTC drug may combine two or more safe and effective active ingredients and may be generally recognized as safe and effective when each active ingredient makes a contribution to the claimed effect(s); when combining of the active ingredients does not decrease the safety or effectiveness of any of the individual active ingredients; and when the combination, when used under adequate directions for use and warnings against unsafe use, provides rational concurrent therapy for a significant proportion of the target population.

(v) Labeling shall be clear and truthful in all respects and may not be false or misleading in any particular. It shall state the intended uses and results of the product; adequate directions for proper use; and warnings against unsafe use, side effects, and adverse reactions in such terms as to render them likely to be read and understood by the ordinary individual, including individuals of low comprehension, under customary conditions of purchase and use.

(vi) A drug shall be permitted for OTC sale and use by the laity unless, because of its toxicity or other potential for harmful effect or because of the method or collateral measures necessary to its use, it may safely be sold and used only under the supervision of a practitioner licensed by law to administer such drugs.

(5) *Advisory review panel report to the Commissioner.* An advisory review panel may submit to the Commissioner a report containing its conclusions and recommendations with respect to the conditions under which OTC drugs falling within the category covered by the panel are generally recognized as safe and effective and not misbranded. Included within this report shall be:

(i) A recommended monograph or monographs covering the category of OTC drugs and establishing conditions under which the drugs involved are generally recognized as safe and effective and not misbranded (Category I). This monograph may include any conditions relating to active ingredients, labeling indications, warnings and adequate directions for use, prescription or OTC status, and any other conditions necessary and appropriate for the safety and effectiveness of drugs covered by the monograph.

(ii) A statement of active ingredients, labeling claims or other statements, or other conditions reviewed and excluded from the monograph on the basis of the panel's determination that they would result in the drug's not being generally recognized as safe and effective or would result in misbranding (Category II).

(iii) A statement of active ingredients, labeling claims or other statements, or other conditions reviewed and excluded from the monograph on the basis of the panel's determination that the available data are insufficient to classify such condition under either

paragraph (a)(5) (i) or (ii) of this section and for which further testing is therefore required (Category III). The report may recommend the type of further testing required and the time period within which it might reasonably be concluded.

(6) *Proposed monograph.* After reviewing the conclusions and recommendations of the advisory review panel, the Commissioner shall publish in the FEDERAL REGISTER a proposed order containing:

(i) A monograph or monographs establishing conditions under which a category of OTC drugs or a specific or specific OTC drugs are generally recognized as safe and effective and not misbranded (Category I).

(ii) A statement of the conditions excluded from the monograph on the basis of the Commissioner's determination that they would result in the drug's not being generally recognized as safe and effective or would result in misbranding (Category II).

(iii) A statement of the conditions excluded from the monograph on the basis of the Commissioner's determination that the available data are insufficient to classify such conditions under either paragraph (a)(6)(i) or (ii) of this section (Category III).

(iv) The full report(s) of the panel to the Commissioner. The proposed order shall specify a reasonable period of time within which conditions falling within paragraph (a)(6)(iii) of this section may be continued in marketed products while the data necessary to support them are being obtained for evaluation by the Food and Drug Administration. The summary minutes of the panel meetings shall be made available to interested persons upon request. Any interested person may, within 90 days after publication of the proposed order in the FEDERAL REGISTER, file with the Division of Dockets Management of the Food and Drug Administration written comments in triplicate. Comments may be accompanied by a memorandum or brief in support thereof. All comments may be reviewed at the office of the Division of Dockets Management between the hours of 9 a.m. and 4 p.m., Monday through Friday. Within 30 days after the final day for submission of comments, reply comments may be filed with the Division of Dockets Management; these comments shall be utilized to reply to comments made by other interested persons and not to reiterate a position. The Commissioner may satisfy this requirement by publishing in the FEDERAL REGISTER a proposed order summarizing the full report of the advisory review panel, containing its conclusions and recommendations, to obtain full public comment before undertaking his own evaluation and decision on the matters involved.

(7) *Tentative final monograph.* (i) After reviewing all comments, reply comments, and any new data and information or, alternatively, after reviewing a panel's recommendations, the Commissioner shall publish in the FEDERAL REGISTER a tentative order containing a monograph establishing conditions under which a category of OTC drugs or specific OTC drugs are generally recognized as safe and effective and not misbranded. Within 90 days, any interested person may file with the Division of Dockets Management, Food and Drug Administration, written comments or written objections specifying with particularity the omissions or additions requested. These objections are to be supported by a brief statement of the grounds therefor. A request for an oral hearing may accompany such objections.

(ii) The Commissioner may also publish in the FEDERAL REGISTER a separate tentative order containing a statement of those active ingredients reviewed and proposed to be excluded from the monograph on the basis of the Commissioner's determination that they would result in a drug product not being generally recognized as safe and effective or would result in misbranding. This order may be published when no substantive comments in opposition to the panel report or new data and information were received by the Food and Drug Administration under paragraph (a)(6)(iv) of this section or when the Commissioner has evaluated and concurs with a panel's recommendation that a condition be excluded from the monograph. Within 90 days, any interested person may file with the Division of Dockets Management, Food and Drug Administration,

written objections specifying with particularity the provision of the tentative order to which objection is made. These objections are to be supported by a brief statement of the grounds therefor. A request for an oral hearing may accompany such objections.

(iii) Within 12 months after publishing a tentative order pursuant to paragraph (a)(7)(i) of this section, any interested person may file with the Division of Dockets Management, Food and Drug Administration, new data and information to support a condition excluded from the monograph in the tentative order.

(iv) Within 60 days after the final day for submission of new data and information, comments on the new data and information may be filed with the Division of Dockets Management, Food and Drug Administration.

(v) New data and information submitted after the time specified in this paragraph but prior to the establishment of a final monograph will be considered as a petition to amend the monograph and will be considered by the Commissioner only after a final monograph has been published in the FEDERAL REGISTER unless the Commisisoner finds that good cause has been shown that warrants earlier consideration.

(8) *Oral hearing before the Commissioner.* After reviewing objections filed in response to the tentative final monograph, the Commissioner, if he finds reasonable grounds in support thereof, shall by notice in the FEDERAL REGISTER schedule an oral hearing. The notice scheduling an oral hearing shall specify the length of the hearing and how the time shall be divided among the parties requesting the hearing. The hearing shall be conducted by the Commissioner and may not be delegated.

(9) *Final monograph.* After reviewing the objections, the entire administrative record including all new data and information and comments, and considering the arguments made at any oral hearing, the Commissioner shall publish in the FEDERAL REGISTER a final

order containing a monograph establishing conditions under which a category of OTC drugs or a specific or specific OTC drugs are generally recognized as safe and effective and not misbranded. The monograph shall become effective as specified in the order.

(10) *Administrative record.* (i) All data and information to be considered in any proceeding pursuant to this section shall be submitted in response to the request for data and views pursuant to paragraph (a)(2) of this section, in response to any other notice published in the FEDERAL REGISTER, or accepted by the panel during its deliberations pursuant to paragraph (a)(3) of this section or submitted to the Division of Dockets Management as part of the comments during the 90-day period and 30-day rebuttal comment period permitted pursuant to paragraph (a)(6) of this section or submitted to the Division of Dockets Management during the 12-month period or as part of the comments during the 60-day period permitted pursuant to paragraph (a)(7) of this section.

(ii) The Commissioner shall make all decisions and issue all orders pursuant to this section solely on the basis of the administrative record, and shall not consider data or information not included as part of the administrative record.

(iii) The administrative record shall consist solely of the following material: All notices and orders published in the FEDERAL REGISTER, all data and views submitted in response to the request published pursuant to paragraph (a)(2) of this section, in response to any other notice published in the FEDERAL REGISTER, or accepted by the panel during its deliberations pursuant to paragraph (a)(3) of this section, all minutes of panel meetings, the panel report(s), all comments and rebuttal comments submitted on the proposed monograph and all new data and information submitted pursuant to paragraph (a)(6) of this section, all objections submitted on the tentative final monograph and all new data and information and comments submitted pursuant to paragraph (a)(7) of this section, the complete record of any oral public hearing conducted pursuant to paragraph (a)(8) of this section, all

other comments requested at any time by the Commissioner, all data and information for which the Commissioner has reopened the administrative record, and all other material that the Commissioner includes in the administrative record as part of the basis for the Commissioner's decision.

(11) *Court appeal.* The monograph contained in the final order constitutes final agency action from which appeal lies to the courts. The Food and Drug Administration will request consolidation of all appeals in a single court. Upon court appeal, the Commissioner may, at his discretion, stay the effective date for part or all of the monograph pending appeal and final court adjudication.

(12) *Amendment of monographs.* (i) The Commissioner may propose on the Commissioner's own initiative to amend or repeal any monograph established pursuant to this section. Any interested person may petition the Commissioner for such proposal pursuant to § 10.30 of this chapter. The Commissioner may deny the petition if the Commissioner finds a lack of safety or effectiveness employing the standards in paragraph (a)(4) of this section (in which case the appeal provisions of paragraph (a)(11) of this section shall apply), or the Commissioner may publish a proposed amendment or repeal in the FEDERAL REGISTER if the Commissioner finds general recognition of safety and effectiveness employing the standards in paragraph (a)(4) of this section. Any interested person may, within 90 days after publication of the proposed order in the FEDERAL REGISTER, file with the Division of Dockets Management, Food and Drug Administration, written comments in triplicate. Comments may be accompanied by a memorandum or brief in support thereof. All comments may be reviewed in the Division of Dockets Management between the hours of 9 a.m. and 4 p.m., Monday through Friday. After reviewing the comments, the Commissioner shall publish a final order amending the monograph established under the provisions of paragraph (a)(9) of this section or withdraw the proposal if comments opposing the amendment are persuasive. A new drug application

may be submitted in lieu of, or in addition to, a petition under this paragraph.

(ii) A new drug application may be submitted in lieu of a petition to amend the OTC drug monograh only if the drug product with the condition that is the subject of the new drug application has not been marketed on an interim basis (such as under the provisions of paragraph (a)(6)(iii) of this section), all clinical testing has been conducted pursuant to a new drug application plan, and no marketing of the product with the condition for which approval is sought is undertaken prior to approval of the new drug application. The Food and Drug Administration shall handle a new drug application as a petition for amendment of a monograph, and shall review it on that basis, if the provisions of this paragraph preclude approval of a new drug application but permit the granting of such a petition.

(b) *Regulatory action.* Any product which fails to conform to an applicable monograph after its effective date is liable to regulatory action.

(c) Information and data submitted under this section shall include, with respect to each nonclinical laboratory study contained in the application, either a statement that the study was conducted in compliance with the good laboratory practice regulations set forth in part 58 of this chapter, or, if the study was not conducted in compliance with such regulations, a brief statement of the reason for the non-compliance.

(d) [Reserved]

(e) *Institutional review and informed consent.* Information and data submitted under this section after July 27, 1981, shall include statements regarding each clinical investigation involving human subjects, from which the information and data are derived, that it either was conducted in compliance with the requirements for institutional review set forth in part 56 of this chapter, or was not subject to such requirements in accordance with §§ 56.104 or 56.105, and that it was conducted in compliance with the requirements for informed consent set forth in part 50 of this chapter.

(f) *Financial certification or disclosure statement.* Any clinical data submitted under this section must be accompanied by financial certifications or disclosure statements or both as required by part 54 of this chapter.

[39 FR 11741, Mar. 29, 1974, as amended at 39 FR 39556, Nov. 8, 1974; 42 FR 19141, Apr. 12, 1977; 42 FR 54800, Oct. 11, 1977; 46 FR 8460, 8955, Jan. 27, 1981; 46 FR 14340, Feb. 27, 1981; 46 FR 21360, Apr. 10, 1981; 46 FR 47738, Sept. 29, 1981; 50 FR 7516, Feb. 22, 1985; 55 FR 11581, Mar. 29, 1990; 63 FR 5253, Feb. 2, 1998; 67 FR 3073, Jan. 23, 2002]

§ 330.11 NDA deviations from applicable monograph.

A new drug application requesting approval of an OTC drug deviating in any respect from a monograph that has become final shall be in the form required by § 314.50 of this chapter, but shall include a statement that the product meets all conditions of the applicable monograph except for the deviation for which approval is requested and may omit all information except that pertinent to the deviation.

[39 FR 11741, Mar. 29, 1974, as amended at 55 FR 11581, Mar. 29, 1990]

§ 330.12 Status of over-the-counter (OTC) drugs previously reviewed under the Drug Efficacy Study (DESI).

(a) There were 420 OTC drugs reviewed in the Drug Efficacy Study (a review of drugs introduced to the market through new drug procedures between 1938 and 1962). A careful review has been made of the reports on these drugs to determine those drugs for which implementation may be deferred without significant risk to the public health, pending review by appropriate OTC drug advisory review panels and promulgation of a monograph.

(b) On and after April 20, 1972, a number of notices were published in the FEDERAL REGISTER concerning previously unpublished OTC drugs reviewed by the National Academy of Sciences-National Research Council Drug Efficacy Study Group. Only the evaluations and comments of the panels were published, with no conclusions of the Commissioner of Food and Drugs. Those publications were for the purpose of giving interested persons the benefit of the Academy's opinions. For those products, and also for OTC drug products previously published with the Commissioner's conclusions (except for the products listed in paragraphs (b) (1) and (2) of this section, all requests for data, revised labeling, requests for new drug applications, abbreviated new drug applications, updating supplements, data to support less than effective claims, if any, etc., are deferred, and such OTC drug products are instead subject to the OTC drug review in their appropriate classes pursuant to the procedures established in this subpart.

(1) The requirements of the following DESI announcements are not deferred (the reference document may also pertain to prescription drugs):

(i) Certain Surgical Sutures (DESI 4725), published in the FEDERAL REGISTER of November 11, 1971 (36 FR 21612).

(ii) Absorbable Dusting Powder (DESI 6264), published in the FEDERAL REGISTER of May 25, 1971 (36 FR 9475).

(iii) Certain Insulin Preparations (DESI 4286), published in the FEDERAL REGISTER of April 9, 1971 (36 FR 6842).

(iv) Sulfo-Van Ointment (DESI 2230), published in the FEDERAL REGISTER of October 8, 1970 (35 FR 15860).

(v) Antiperspirants and Deodorants Containing Neomycin Sulfate (DESI 11048) for which an order revoking provisions for certification or release was published in the FEDERAL REGISTER of December 5, 1972 (37 FR 25820) and has been stayed by the filing of objections.

(vi) Thorexin Cough Medicine (DESI 11160) for which a notice of opportunity for hearing was published in the FEDERAL REGISTER of February 2, 1973 (38 FR 3210).

(vii) Antibiotic susceptibility discs (DESI 90235) for which an order providing for certain discs to be certified and removing provisions for certification of other discs was published in the FEDERAL REGISTER of September 30, 1972 (37 FR 20525) and has been stayed by the filing of objections notice of which was published in the FEDERAL REGISTER of March 15, 1973 (38 FR 7007).

(2) Deferral of requirements is not appropriate when an announcement has been published and has been followed by a final order classifying a drug either as lacking substantial evidence of effectiveness or as not shown to be safe. These products will be removed from the market, if they have not already been removed. Regulatory action will also be undertaken against identical, similar and related products (21 CFR 310.6). Deferral of requirements is not appropriate for the following (the referenced document may also pertain to prescription drugs):

(i) Certain Sulfonamide-Decongestant Nasal Preparation (DESI 4850), for which notice of withdrawal of approval of new drug applications was published in the FEDERAL REGISTER of October 24, 1970 (35 FR 16605, 16606).

(ii) Eskay's Theranates, containing strychnine, sodium, and calcium glycerophosphates, thiamine hydrochloride, alcohol, and phosphoric acid (DESI 2220), for which notice of withdrawal of approval of the new drug application was published in the FEDERAL REGISTER of February 18, 1971 (36 FR 3152).

(iii) The following topical drugs (DESI 1726), for which notice of withdrawal of new drug applications was published in the FEDERAL REGISTER of August 28, 1971 (36 FR 17368):

(a) Rhulitol Solution, containing tannic acid, chlorobutanol, phenol, camphor, alum, and isopropyl alcohol.

(b) Zirnox Topical Lotion, containing phenyitoloxamine citrate and zirconium oxide.

(iv) Menacyl Tablets, containing aspirin, menadione, and ascorbic acid (DESI 6363), for which notice of withdrawal of approval of the new drug application was published in the FEDERAL REGISTER of July 23, 1970 (35 FR 11827).

(v) Curad Medicated Adhesive Bandage containing sulfathiazole (DESI 4964), for which notice of withdrawal of approval of the new drug application was published in the FEDERAL REGISTER of December 31, 1969 (34 FR 20441).

(vi) Drugs Containing Rutin, Quercetin, Hesperidin, or any Bioflavonoids (DESI 5960), for which notice of withdrawal of approval of new drug applications was published in the FEDERAL REGISTER of July 3, 1970 (35 FR 10872, 10873) and October 17, 1970 (35 FR 16332). A further notice of opportunity for hearing with respect to the drugs covered by the October 17, 1970 FEDERAL REGISTER notice will be published at a later date.

(vii) Antibiotics in Combination with Other Drugs for Nasal Use (DESI 7561), for which an order revoking provision for certification was published in the FEDERAL REGISTER of August 6, 1971 (36 FR 14469) and confirmed in the FEDERAL REGISTER of October 28, 1971 (36 FR 20686).

(viii) Antibiotic Troches (DESI 8328), for which an order revoking provision for certification was published in the FEDERAL REGISTER of July 14, 1971 (36 FR 13089) and confirmed in the FEDERAL REGISTER of October 9, 1971 (36 FR 19695).

(ix) Certain Drugs Containing Oxyphenisatin or Oxyphenisatin Acetate (DESI 10732), for which notices of withdrawal of approval of new drug applications were published in the FEDERAL REGISTER of February 1, 1972 (37 FR 2460), and March 9, 1973 (38 FR 6419).

(x) Curad Medicated Adhesive Bandage containing tyrothricin-nitrofurazone (DESI 6898), for which an order revoking provision for certification was published March 14, 1972 (37 FR 5294), and confirmed in the FEDERAL REGISTER of July 6, 1972 (37 FR 13254).

(xi) Candette Cough Gel (DESI 11562), for which notice of withdrawal of approval of the new drug application was published in the FEDERAL REGISTER of November 19, 1972 (37 FR 25249).

(xii) Certain OTC Multiple-Vitamin Preparations for Oral Use containing excessive amounts of vitamin D and/or vitamin A (DESI 97), for which notice of withdrawal of approval of the new drug applications was published in the FEDERAL REGISTER of November 29, 1972 (37 FR 25249).

(xiii) Certain Sulfonamide-Containing Preparations for Topical Ophthalmic or Otic Use (DESI 368, for which a notice of withdrawal of approval was published in the FEDERAL REGISTER of February 2, 1973 (38 FR 3208).

(xiv) Those parts of the publication entitled "Certain Mouthwash and Gargle Preparations" (DESI 2855) pertaining to Tyrolaris Mouthwash, containing tyrothricin, panthenol, and alcohol, for which an order revoking pro-

vision for certification was published in the FEDERAL REGISTER of February 2, 1967 (32 FR 1172) prior to the drug efficacy study implementation.

(c) Manufacturers and distributors should take notice that the information on OTC drugs provided by the Drug Efficacy Study review is valuable information as to the deficiencies in the data available to support indications for use. They are encouraged to perform studies to obtain adequate evidence of effectiveness for the review of OTC drugs which is already in progress. In the interim it is in the public interest that manufacturers and distributors of all OTC drugs effect changes in their formulations and/or labeling to bring the products into conformity with current medical knowledge and experience.

(d) Manufacturers and distributors of OTC drugs may be reluctant to make appropriate formulation and/or labeling changes for fear of losing the protection of the so-called "grandfather" provisions of the 1938 Federal Food, Drug, and Cosmetic Act (sec. 201(p)(1)) and the 1962 amendments to the act (sec. 107(c) of those amendments). To encourage and facilitate prompt changes, the Food and Drug Administration will not take legal action against any OTC drug, other than those not deferred, based on a charge that the product is a new drug and not grandfathered under the act as a result of the changes if the changes in formulation and/or labeling are of the following kind:

(1) The addition to the labeling of warning, contraindications, side effects, and/or precaution information.

(2) The deletion from the labeling of false, misleading, or unsupported indications for use or claims of effectiveness.

(3) Changes in the components or composition of the drug that will give increased assurance that the drug will have its intended effect, yet not raise or contribute any added safety questions.

(4) Changes in the components or composition of the drug which may reasonably be concluded to improve the safety of the drug, without diminishing its effectiveness.

(e) The forbearance from legal action for lack of grandfather protection is an interim procedure designed to encourage appropriate change in formulation and/or labeling during the time period required to review the various classes of OTC drugs. At such time as an applicable OTC drug monograph becomes effective, the interim procedure will automatically be terminated and any appropriate regulatory action will be initiated.

§ 330.13 Conditions for marketing ingredients recommended for over-the-counter (OTC) use under the OTC drug review.

(a) Before the publication in the FEDERAL REGISTER of an applicable proposed monograph, an OTC drug product that contains: (1) An active ingredient limited, on or after May 11, 1972, to prescription use for the indication and route of administration under consideration by an OTC advisory review panel, and not thereafter exempted from such limitation pursuant to § 310.200 of this chapter, or

(2) An active ingredient at a dosage level higher than that available in an OTC drug product on December 4, 1975, shall be regarded as a new drug within the meaning of section 201(p) of the act for which an approved new drug application is required.

(b)(1) An OTC drug product that contains: (i) An active ingredient limited, on or after May 11, 1972, to prescription use for the indication and route of administration under consideration by an OTC advisory review panel, and not thereafter exempted from such limitation pursuant to § 310.200 of this chapter, or

(ii) An active ingredient at a dosage level higher than that available in an OTC drug product on December 4, 1975, which ingredient and/or dosage level is classified by the panel in category I (conditions subject to § 330.10(a)(6)(i)) shall be regarded as a new drug within the meaning of section 201(p) of the act for which an approved new drug application is required if marketed for OTC use prior to the date of publication in the FEDERAL REGISTER of a proposed monograph.

(2) An OTC drug product covered by paragraph (b)(1) of this section which is marketed after the date of publication in the FEDERAL REGISTER of a proposed monograph but prior to the effective date of a final monograph shall be subject to the risk that the Commissioner may not accept the panel's recommendation and may instead adopt a different position that may require relabeling, recall, or other regulatory action. The Commissioner may state such position at any time by notice in the FEDERAL REGISTER, either separately or as part of another document; appropriate regulatory action will commence immediately and will not await publication of a final monograph. Marketing of such a product with a formulation or labeling not in accord with a proposed monograph or tentative final monograph also may result in regulatory action against the product, the marketer, or both.

(c) An OTC drug product that contains: (1) An active ingredient limited, on or after May 11, 1972, to prescription use for the indication and route of administration under consideration by an OTC advisory review panel, and not thereafter exempted from such limitation pursuant to § 310.200 of this chapter, or

(2) An active ingredient at a dosage level higher than that available in any OTC drug product on December 4, 1975, which ingredient and/or dosage level is classified by the panel in category II (conditions subject to § 330.10(a)(6)(ii)), may be marketed only after:

(i) The Center for Drug Evaluation and Research or the Commissioner tentatively determines that the ingredient is generally recognized as safe and effective, and the Commissioner states by notice in the FEDERAL REGISTER (separately or as part of another document) that marketing under specified conditions will be permitted;

(ii) The ingredient is determined by the Commissioner to be generally recognized as safe and effective and is included in the appropriate published OTC drug final monograph; or

(iii) A new drug application for the product has been approved.

(d) An OTC drug product that contains: (1) An active ingredient limited, on or after May 11, 1972, to prescription use for the indication and route of administration under consideration by an

OTC advisory review panel, and not thereafter exempted from such limitation pursuant to § 310.200 of this chapter, or

(2) An active ingredient at a dosage level higher than that available in any OTC drug product on December 4, 1975, which ingredient and/or dosage level is classified by the panel in category III (conditions subject to § 330.10(a)(6)(iii)), may be marketed only after:

(i) The Center for Drug Evaluation and Research or the Commissioner tentatively determines that the ingredient is generally recognized as safe and effective, and the Commissioner states by notice in the FEDERAL REGISTER (separately or as part of another document) that marketing under specified conditions will be permitted;

(ii) The ingredient is determined by the Commissioner to be generally recognized as safe and effective and is included in the appropriate published OTC drug final monograph; or

(iii) A new drug application for the product has been approved.

(e) This section applies only to conditions under consideration as part of the OTC drug review initiated on May 11, 1972, and evaluated under the procedures set forth in § 330.10. Section 330.14(h) applies to the marketing of all conditions under consideration and evaluated using the criteria and procedures set forth in § 330.14.

[41 FR 32582, Aug. 4, 1976, as amended at 47 FR 17739, Apr. 23, 1982; 50 FR 8996, Mar. 6, 1985; 55 FR 11581, Mar. 29, 1990; 67 FR 3074, Jan. 23, 2002]

§ 330.14 Additional criteria and procedures for classifying OTC drugs as generally recognized as safe and effective and not misbranded.

(a) *Introduction.* This section sets forth additional criteria and procedures by which over the counter (OTC) drugs initially marketed in the United States after the OTC drug review began in 1972 and OTC drugs without any U.S. marketing experience can be considered in the OTC drug monograph system. This section also addresses conditions regulated as a cosmetic or dietary supplement in a foreign country that would be regulated as OTC drugs in the United States. For purposes of this section, "condition" means an active ingredient or botanical drug substance (or a combination of active ingredients or botanical drug substances), dosage form, dosage strength, or route of administration, marketed for a specific OTC use, except as excluded in paragraph (b)(2) of this section. For purposes of this part, "botanical drug substance" means a drug substance derived from one or more plants, algae, or macroscopic fungi, but does not include a highly purified or chemically modified substance derived from such a source.

(b) *Criteria.* To be considered for inclusion in the OTC drug monograph system, the condition must meet the following criteria:

(1) The condition must be marketed for OTC purchase by consumers. If the condition is marketed in another country in a class of OTC drug products that may be sold only in a pharmacy, with or without the personal involvement of a pharmacist, it must be established that this marketing restriction does not indicate safety concerns about the condition's toxicity or other potentiality for harmful effect, the method of its use, or the collateral measures necessary to its use.

(2) The condition must have been marketed OTC for a minimum of 5 continuous years in the same country and in sufficient quantity, as determined in paragraphs (c)(2)(ii), (c)(2)(iii), and (c)(2)(iv) of this section. Depending on the condition's extent of marketing in only one country with 5 continuous years of marketing, marketing in more than one country may be necessary.

(c) *Time and extent application.* Certain information must be provided when requesting that a condition subject to this section be considered for inclusion in the OTC drug monograph system. The following information must be provided in the format of a time and extent application (TEA):

(1) Basic information about the condition that includes a description of the active ingredient(s) or botanical drug substance(s), pharmacologic class(es), intended OTC use(s), OTC strength(s) and dosage form(s), route(s) of administration, directions for use, and the applicable existing OTC drug monograph(s) under which the condition would be marketed or the request

and rationale for creation of a new OTC drug monograph(s).

(i) A detailed chemical description of the active ingredient(s) that includes a full description of the drug substance, including its physical and chemical characteristics, the method of synthesis (or isolation) and purification of the drug substance, and any specifications and analytical methods necessary to ensure the identity, strength, quality, and purity of the drug substance.

(ii) For a botanical drug substance(s), a detailed description of the botanical ingredient (including proper identification of the plant, plant part(s), alga, or macroscopic fungus used; a certificate of authenticity; and information on the grower/supplier; growing conditions, harvest location and harvest time); a qualitative description (including the name, appearance, physical/chemical properties, chemical constituents, active constituent(s) (if known), and biological activity (if known)); a quantitative description of the chemical constituents, including the active constituent(s) or other chemical marker(s) (if known and measurable); the type of manufacturing process (e.g., aqueous extraction, pulverization); and information on any further processing of the botanical substance (e.g., addition of excipients or blending).

(iii) Reference to the current edition of the U.S. Pharmacopeia (USP)–National Formulary (NF) or foreign compendiums may help satisfy the requirements in this section.

(2) A list of all countries in which the condition has been marketed. Include the following information for each country. (For a condition that has been marketed OTC in 5 or more countries with a minimum of 5 continuous years of marketing in at least one country, the sponsor may submit information in accordance with paragraph (c)(4) of this section):

(i) How the condition has been marketed (e.g., OTC general sales direct-to-consumer; sold only in a pharmacy, with or without the personal involvement of a pharmacist; dietary supplement; or cosmetic). If the condition has been marketed as a nonprescription pharmacy-only product, establish that this marketing restriction does not indicate safety concerns about its toxicity or other potentiality for harmful effect, the method of its use, or the collateral measures necessary to its use.

(ii) The cumulative total number of dosage units (e.g., tablets, capsules, ounces) sold for each dosage form of the condition. Manufacturers or suppliers of OTC active ingredients may provide dosage unit information as the total weight of active ingredient sold. List the various package sizes for each dosage form in which the condition is marketed OTC. Provide an estimate of the minimum number of potential consumer exposures to the condition using one of the following calculations:

(A) Divide the total number of dosage units sold by the number of dosage units in the largest package size marketed, or

(B) Divide the total weight of the active ingredient sold by the total weight of the active ingredient in the largest package size marketed.

(iii) A description of the population demographics (percentage of various racial/ethnic groups) and the source(s) from which this information has been compiled, to ensure that the condition's use(s) can be reasonably extrapolated to the U.S. population.

(iv) If the use pattern (*i.e.*, how often it is to be used (according to the label) and for how long) varies between countries based on the condition's packaging and labeling, or changes in use pattern have occurred over time in one or more countries, describe the use pattern for each country and explain why there are differences or changes.

(v) A description of the country's system for identifying adverse drug experiences, especially those found in OTC marketing experience, including method of collection if applicable.

(3) A statement of how long the condition has been marketed in each country and how long the current product labeling has been in use, accompanied by a copy of the current product labeling. All labeling that is not in English must be translated to English in accordance with §10.20(c)(2) of this chapter. State whether the current product labeling has or has not been authorized, accepted, or approved by a regulatory body in each country where the condition is marketed.

(4) For a condition that has been marketed OTC in five or more countries with a minimum of 5 continuous years of marketing in at least one country, the sponsor may select at least five of these countries from which to submit information in accord with paragraphs (c)(2)(i) through (c)(2)(iv) of this section. Selected countries must include the country with a minimum of 5 continuous years of OTC marketing, countries that have the longest duration of marketing, and countries having the most support for extent of marketing, *i.e.*, a large volume of sales with cultural diversity among users of the product. If the condition meets these criteria in countries listed in section 802(b)(1)(A) of the Federal Food, Drug, and Cosmetic Act, some of these countries should be included among the five selected. Sponsors should provide information from more than five countries if they believe that it is needed to support eligibility. Sponsors should explain the basis for the countries selected in the TEA.

(5) A list of all countries where the condition is marketed only as a prescription drug and the reasons why its marketing is restricted to prescription in these countries.

(6) A list of all countries in which the condition has been withdrawn from marketing or in which an application for OTC marketing approval has been denied. Include the reasons for such withdrawal or application denial.

(7) The information requested in paragraphs (c)(2), (c)(2)(i) through (c)(2)(iv), and (c)(3) of this section must be provided in a table format. The labeling required by paragraph (c)(3) of this section must be attached to the table.

(8) For OTC drugs that have been marketed for more than 5 years in the United States under a new drug application, the information requested in paragraphs (c)(2)(i), (c)(2)(iii), (c)(2)(v), (c)(3), and (c)(5) of this section need not be provided.

(d) *Submission of information; confidentiality.* The sponsor must submit three copies of the TEA to the Central Document Room, 5630 Fishers Lane, rm. 1061, Rockville, MD 20852. The Food and Drug Administration will handle the TEA as confidential until such time as

a decision is made on the eligibility of the condition for consideration in the OTC drug monograph system. If the condition is found eligible, the TEA will be placed on public display in the Division of Dockets Management after deletion of information deemed confidential under 18 U.S.C. 1905, 5 U.S.C. 552(b), or 21 U.S.C. 331(j). Sponsors must identify information that is considered confidential under these statutory provisions. If the condition is not found eligible, the TEA will not be placed on public display, but a letter from the agency to the sponsor stating why the condition was not found acceptable will be placed on public display in the Division of Dockets Management.

(e) *Notice of eligibility.* If the condition is found eligible, the agency will publish a notice of eligibility in the FEDERAL REGISTER and provide the sponsor and other interested parties an opportunity to submit data to demonstrate safety and effectiveness. When the notice of eligibility is published, the agency will place the TEA on public display in the Division of Dockets Management.

(f) *Request for data and views.* The notice of eligibility shall request interested persons to submit published and unpublished data to demonstrate the safety and effectiveness of the condition for its intended OTC use(s). These data shall be submitted to a docket established in the Division of Dockets Management and shall be publicly available for viewing at that office, except data deemed confidential under 18 U.S.C. 1905, 5 U.S.C. 552(b), or 21 U.S.C. 331(j). Data considered confidential under these provisions must be clearly identified. Any proposed compendial standards for the condition shall not be considered confidential. The safety and effectiveness submissions shall include the following:

(1) All data and information listed in § 330.10(a)(2) under the outline "OTC Drug Review Information," items III through VII.

(2) All serious adverse drug experiences as defined in §§ 310.305 and 314.80 of this chapter, from each country where the condition has been or is currently marketed as a prescription drug or as an OTC drug or product. Provide

individual adverse drug experience reports (FDA Form 3500A or equivalent) along with a summary of all serious adverse drug experiences and expected or frequently reported side effects for the condition. Individual reports that are not in English must be translated to English in accordance with § 10.20(c)(2) of this chapter.

(g) *Administrative procedures.* The agency may use an advisory review panel to evaluate the safety and effectiveness data in accord with the provisions of § 330.10(a)(3). Alternatively, the agency may evaluate the data in conjunction with the advisory review panel or on its own without using an advisory review panel. The agency will use the safety, effectiveness, and labeling standards in § 330.10(a)(4)(i) through (a)(4)(vi) in evaluating the data.

(1) If the agency uses an advisory review panel to evaluate the data, the panel may submit its recommendations in its official minutes of meeting(s) or by a report under the provisions of § 330.10(a)(5).

(2) The agency may act on an advisory review panel's recommendations using the procedures in §§ 330.10(a)(2) and 330.10(a)(6) through (a)(10).

(3) If the condition is initially determined to be generally recognized as safe and effective for OTC use in the United States, the agency will propose to include it in an appropriate OTC drug monograph(s), either by amending an existing monograph(s) or establishing a new monograph(s), if necessary.

(4) If the condition is initially determined not to be generally recognized as safe and effective for OTC use in the United States, the agency will inform the sponsor and other interested parties who have submitted data of its determination by letter, a copy of which will be placed on public display in the docket established in the Division of Dockets Management. The agency will publish a notice of proposed rulemaking to include the condition in § 310.502 of this chapter.

(5) Interested parties will have an opportunity to submit comments and new data. The agency will subsequently publish a final rule (or reproposal if necessary) in the FEDERAL REGISTER.

(h) *Marketing.* A condition submitted under this section for consideration in the OTC drug monograph system may be marketed in accordance with an applicable final OTC drug monograph(s) only after the agency determines that the condition is generally recognized as safe and effective and includes it in the appropriate OTC drug final monograph(s), and the condition complies with paragraph (i) of this section. When an OTC drug monograph has not been finalized and finalization is not imminent, after the agency has evaluated the comments to a proposed rule to include a new condition in a tentative final monograph as generally recognized as safe and effective and the agency has not changed its position as a result of the comments, and the condition complies with paragraph (i) of this section, the agency may publish a notice of enforcement policy that allows marketing to begin pending completion of the final monograph subject to the risk that the agency may, prior to or in the final monograph, adopt a different position that could require relabeling, recall, or other regulatory action.

(i) *Compendial monograph.* Any active ingredient or botanical drug substance included in a final OTC drug monograph or the subject of an enforcement notice described in paragraph (h) of this section must be recognized in an official USP-NF drug monograph that sets forth its standards of identity, strength, quality, and purity. Sponsors must include an official or proposed compendial monograph as part of the safety and effectiveness data submission listed in § 330.10(a)(2) under item VII of the outline entitled "OTC DRUG REVIEW INFORMATION."

[67 FR 3074, Jan. 23, 2002]

PART 331—ANTACID PRODUCTS FOR OVER-THE-COUNTER (OTC) HUMAN USE

Subpart A—General Provisions

Sec.
331.1 Scope.

Subpart B—Active Ingredients

331.10 Antacid active ingredients.
331.11 Listing of specific active ingredients.

331.15 Combination with nonantacid active ingredients.

Subpart C—Testing Procedures

331.20 Determination of percent contribution of active ingredients.
331.21 Test Modifications.

Subpart D—Labeling

331.30 Labeling of antacid products.
331.80 Professional labeling.

AUTHORITY: 21 U.S.C. 321, 351, 352, 353, 355, 360, 371.

SOURCE: 39 FR 19874, June 4, 1974, unless otherwise noted.

Subpart A—General Provisions

§ 331.1 Scope.

An over-the-counter antacid product in a form suitable for oral administration is generally recognized as safe and effective and is not misbranded if it meets each of the following conditions and each of the general conditions established in § 330.1 of this chapter.

Subpart B—Active Ingredients

§ 331.10 Antacid active ingredients.

(a) The active antacid ingredients of the product consist of one or more of the ingredients permitted in § 331.11 within any maximum daily dosage limit established, each ingredient is included at a level that contributes at least 25 percent of the total acid neutralizing capacity of the product, and the finished product contains at least 5 meq of acid neutralizing capacity as measured by the procedure provided in the United States Pharmacopeia 23/National Formulary 18. The method established in § 331.20 shall be used to determine the percent contribution of each antacid active ingredient.

(b) This section does not apply to an antacid ingredient specifically added as a corrective to prevent a laxative or constipating effect.

[39 FR 19874, June 4, 1974, as amended at 61 FR 4822, Feb. 8, 1996]

§ 331.11 Listing of specific active ingredients.

(a) Aluminum-containing active ingredients:
(1) Basic aluminum carbonate gel.

(2) Aluminum hydroxide (or as aluminum hydroxide-hexitol stabilized polymer, aluminum hydroxide-magnesium carbonate codried gel, aluminum hydroxide-magnesium trisilicate codried gel, aluminum-hydroxide sucrose powder hydrated).

(3) Dihydroxyaluminum aminoacetate and dihydroxyaluminum aminoacetic acid.

(4) Aluminum phosphate gel when used as part of an antacid combination product and contributing at least 25 percent of the total acid neutralizing capacity; maximum daily dosage limit is 8 grams.

(5) Dihydroxyaluminum sodium carbonate.

(b) Bicarbonate-containing active ingredients: Bicarbonate ion; maximum daily dosage limit 200 mEq. for persons up to 60 years old and 100 mEq. for persons 60 years or older.

(c) Bismuth-containing active ingredients:
(1) Bismuth aluminate.
(2) Bismuth carbonate.
(3) Bismuth subcarbonate.
(4) Bismuth subgallate.
(5) Bismuth subnitrate.

(d) Calcium-containing active ingredients: Calcium, as carbonate or phosphate; maximum daily dosage limit 160 mEq. calcium (e.g., 8 grams calcium carbonate).

(e) Citrate-containing active ingredients: Citrate ion, as citric acid or salt; maximum daily dosage limit 8 grams.

(f) Glycine (aminoacetic acid).

(g) Magnesium-containing active ingredients:
(1) Hydrate magnesium aluminate activated sulfate.
(2) Magaldrate.
(3) Magnesium aluminosilicates.
(4) Magnesium carbonate.
(5) Magnesium glycinate.
(6) Magnesium hydroxide.
(7) Magnesium oxide.
(8) Magnesium trisilicate.

(h) Milk solids, dried.

(i) Phosphate-containing active ingredients:
(1) Aluminum phosphate; maximum daily dosage limit 8 grams.
(2) Mono or dibasic calcium salt; maximum daily dosage limit 2 grams.
(3) Tricalcium phosphate; maximum daily dosage limit 24 grams.

(j) Potassium-containing active ingredients:

(1) Potassium bicarbonate (or carbonate when used as a component of an effervescent preparation); maximum daily dosage limit 200 mEq. of bicarbonate ion for persons up to 60 years old and 100 mEq. of bicarbonate ion for persons 60 years or older.

(2) Sodium potassium tartrate.

(k) Sodium-containing active ingredients:

(1) Sodium bicarbonate (or carbonate when used as a component of an effervescent preparation); maximum daily dosage limit 200 mEq. of sodium for persons up to 60 years old and 100 mEq. of sodium for persons 60 years or older, and 200 mEq. of bicarbonate ion for persons up to 60 years old and 100 mEq. of bicarbonate ion for persons 60 years or older. That part of the warning required by § 330.1(g), which states, "Keep this and all drugs out of the reach of children" is not required on a product which contains only sodium bicarbonate powder and which is intended primarily for other than drug uses.

(2) Sodium potassium tartrate.

(l) Silicates:

(1) Magnesium aluminosilicates.

(2) Magnesium trisilicate.

(m) Tartrate-containing active ingredients. Tartaric acid or its salts; maximum daily dosage limit 200 mEq. (15 grams) of tartrate.

[39 FR 19874, June 4, 1974, as amended at 51 FR 27763, Aug. 1, 1986; 55 FR 19859, May 11, 1990]

§ 331.15 Combination with nonantacid active ingredients.

(a) An antacid may contain any generally recognized as safe and effective nonantacid laxative ingredient to correct for constipation caused by the antacid. No labeling claim of the laxative effect may be used for such a product.

(b) An antacid may contain any generally recognized as safe and effective analgesic ingredient(s), if it is indicated for use solely for the concurrent symptoms involved, e.g., headache and acid indigestion, and is marketed in a form intended for ingestion as a solution.

(c) An antacid may contain any generally recognized as safe and effective antiflatulent ingredient if it is indicated for use solely for the concurrent symptoms of gas associated with heartburn, sour stomach or acid indigestion.

Subpart C—Testing Procedures

§ 331.20 Determination of percent contribution of active ingredients.

To determine the percent contribution of an antacid active ingredient, place an accurately weighed amount of the antacid active ingredient equal to the amount present in a unit dose of the product into a 250-milliliter (mL) beaker. If wetting is desired, add not more than 5 mL of alcohol (neutralized to an apparent pH of 3.5), and mix to wet the sample thoroughly. Add 70 mL of water, and mix on a magnetic stirrer at 300 ±30 r.p.m. for 1 minute. Analyze the acid neutralizing capacity of the sample according to the procedure provided in the United States Pharmacopeia 23/National Formulary 18 and calculate the percent contribution of the antacid active ingredient in the total product as follows:

Percent contribution =(Total mEq. Antacid Active Ingredient×100)/(Total mEq. Antacid Product).

[61 FR 4823, Feb. 8, 1996]

§ 331.21 Test modifications.

The formulation or mode of administration of certain products may require a modification of the United States Pharmacopeia 23/National Formulary 18 acid neutralizing capacity test. Any proposed modification and the data to support it shall be submitted as a petition under the rules established in § 10.30 of this chapter. All information submitted will be subject to the disclosure rules in part 20 of this chapter.

[61 FR 4823, Feb. 8, 1996]

Subpart D—Labeling

§ 331.30 Labeling of antacid products.

(a) *Statement of identity.* The labeling of the product contains the established name of the drug, if any, and identifies the product as an "antacid."

(b) *Indications.* The labeling of the product states, under the heading "Indications," the following: "For the relief of" (optional, any or all of the following:) "heartburn," "sour stomach," and/or "acid indigestion" (which may be followed by the optional statement:) "and upset stomach associated with" (optional, as appropriate) "this symptom" or "these symptoms." Other truthful and nonmisleading statements, describing only the indications for use that have been established and listed in this paragraph (b), may also be used, as provided in § 330.1(c)(2) of this chapter, subject to the provisions of section 502 of the act relating to misbranding and the prohibition in section 301(d) of the act against the introduction or delivery for introduction into interstate commerce of unapproved new drugs in violation of section 505(a) of the act.

(c) *Warnings.* The labeling of the product contains the following warnings, under the heading "Warnings", which may be combined but not rearranged to eliminate duplicative words or phrases if the resulting warning is clear and understandable:

(1) "Do not take more than (maximum recommended daily dosage, broken down by age groups if appropriate, expressed in units such as tablets or teaspoonfuls) in a 24–hour period, or use the maximum dosage of this product for more than 2 weeks, except under the advice and supervision of a physician."

(2) For products which cause constipation in 5 percent or more of persons who take the maximum recommended dosage: "May cause constipation."

(3) For products which cause laxation in 5 percent or more of persons who take the maximum recommended dosage: "May have laxative effect."

(4) For products containing more than 5 gm per day lactose in a maximum daily dosage: "Do not use this product except under advice and supervision of a physician if you are allergic to milk or milk products."

(d) *Drug interaction precaution.* The labeling of the product contains the following statement "Ask a doctor or pharmacist before use if you are [bullet][1] presently taking a prescription drug. Antacids may interact with certain prescription drugs."

---

[1] See § 201.66(b)(4) of this chapter.

(e) *Directions for use.* The labeling of the product contains the recommended dosage, under the heading "Directions", per time interval (e.g., every 4 hours) or time period (e.g., 4 times a day) broken down by age groups if appropriate, followed by "or as directed by a physician."

(f) *Exemption from the general accidental overdose warning.* The labeling for antacid drug products containing the active ingredients identified in § 331.11(a), (b), and (d) through (m); permitted combinations of these ingredients provided for in § 331.10; and any of these ingredients or combinations of these ingredients in combination with simethicone (identified in § 332.10 of this chapter and provided for in § 331.15(c)), are exempt from the requirement in § 330.1(g) of this chapter that the labeling bear the general warning statement "In case of accidental overdose, seek professional assistance or contact a poison control center immediately." With the exception of sodium bicarbonate powder products identified in § 331.11(k)(1), the labeling must continue to bear the first part of the general warning in § 330.1(g) of this chapter, which states, "Keep this and all drugs out of the reach of children."

(g) [Reserved]

(h) The word "doctor" may be substituted for the word "physician" in any of the labeling statements in this section.

[39 FR 19874, June 4, 1974, as amended at 47 FR 38484, Aug. 31, 1982; 51 FR 16266, May 1, 1986; 51 FR 27763, Aug. 1, 1986; 52 FR 7830, Mar. 13, 1987; 55 FR 11581, Mar. 29, 1990; 58 FR 45208, Aug. 26, 1993; 59 FR 60556, Nov. 25, 1994; 61 FR 17806, Apr. 22, 1996; 64 FR 13295, Mar. 17, 1999; 69 FR 13734, Mar. 24, 2004]

§ 331.80 Professional labeling.

(a) The labeling of the product provided to health professionals (but not to the general public):

(1) Shall contain the neutralizing capacity of the product as calculated using the procedure set forth in United States Pharmacopeia 23/National Formulary 18 expressed in terms of the dosage recommended per minimum time interval or, if the labeling recommends more than one dosage, in

terms of the minimum dosage recommended per minimum time interval.

(2) May contain an indication for the symptomatic relief of hyperacidity associated with the diagnosis of peptic ulcer, gastritis, peptic esophagitis, gastric hyperacidity, and hiatal hernia.

(3) *For products containing basic aluminum carbonate gel identified in §331.11(a)(1)—Indication.* "For the treatment, control, or management of hyperphosphatemia, or for use with a low phosphate diet to prevent formation of phosphate urinary stones, through the reduction of phosphates in the serum and urine."

(4) *For products containing aluminum identified in §331.11(a)—Warnings.* (i) Prolonged use of aluminum-containing antacids in patients with renal failure may result in or worsen dialysis osteomalacia. Elevated tissue aluminum levels contribute to the development of the dialysis encephalopathy and osteomalacia syndromes. Small amounts of aluminum are absorbed from the gastrointestinal tract and renal excretion of aluminum is impaired in renal failure. Aluminum is not well removed by dialysis because it is bound to albumin and transferrin, which do not cross dialysis membranes. As a result, aluminum is deposited in bone, and dialysis osteomalacia may develop when large amounts of aluminum are ingested orally by patients with impaired renal function.

(ii) Aluminum forms insoluble complexes with phosphate in the gastrointestinal tract, thus decreasing phosphate absorption. Prolonged use of aluminum-containing antacids by normophosphatemic patients may result in hypophosphatemia if phosphate intake is not adequate. In its more severe forms, hypophosphatemia can lead to anorexia, malaise, muscle weakness, and osteomalacia.

(b) Professional labeling for an antacid-antiflatulent combination may contain the information allowed for health professionals for antacids and antiflatulents.

[39 FR 19874, June 4, 1974. Redesignated and amended at 55 FR 19859, May 11, 1990]

PART 332—ANTIFLATULENT PRODUCTS FOR OVER-THE-COUNTER HUMAN USE

Subpart A—General Provisions

Sec.
332.1 Scope.
332.3 Definitions.

Subpart B—Active Ingredients

332.10 Antiflatulent active ingredients.
332.15 Combination with non-antiflatulent active ingredients.

Subpart C—Labeling

332.30 Labeling of antiflatulent products.
332.31 Professional labeling.

AUTHORITY: 21 U.S.C. 321, 351, 352, 353, 355, 360, 371.

SOURCE: 39 FR 19877, June 4, 1974, unless otherwise noted.

Subpart A—General Provisions

§332.1 Scope.

An over-the-counter antiflatulent product in a form suitable for oral administration is generally recognized as safe and effective and is not misbranded if it meets each of the following conditions and each of the general conditions established in §330.1 of this chapter.

§332.3 Definitions.

As used in this part:

Antigas. A term that may be used interchangeably with the term antiflatulent. Neither term should be considered as describing the mechanism of action of the active ingredient contained in the product.

[61 FR 8838, Mar. 5, 1996]

Subpart B—Active Ingredients

§332.10 Antiflatulent active ingredients.

Simethicone; maximum daily dose 500 mg. There is no dosage limitation at this time for professional labeling.

§ 332.15 Combination with non-antiflatulent active ingredients.

An antiflatulent may contain any generally recognized as safe and effective antacid ingredient(s) if it is indicated for use solely for the concurrent symptoms of gas associated with heartburn, sour stomach or acid indigestion.

Subpart C—Labeling

§ 332.30 Labeling of antiflatulent drug products.

(a) *Statement of identity.* The labeling of the product contains the established name of the drug, if any, and identifies the product as an "antiflatulent," "antigas," or "antiflatulent (antigas)."

(b) *Indications.* The labeling of the product states, under the heading "Indications," one or more of the phrases listed in this paragraph (b), as appropriate. Other truthful and nonmisleading statements, describing only the indications for use that have been established and listed in this paragraph (b), may also be used, as provided in § 330.1(c)(2) of this chapter, subject to the provisions of section 502 of the Federal Food, Drug, and Cosmetic Act (the act) relating to misbranding and the prohibition in section 301(d) of the act against the introduction or delivery for introduction into interstate commerce of unapproved new drugs in violation of section 505(a) of the act.

(1) (Select one of the following: "Alleviates or Relieves") "the symptoms referred to as gas."

(2) (Select one of the following: "Alleviates" or "Relieves") (select one or more of the following: "bloating," "pressure," "fullness," or "stuffed feeling") "commonly referred to as gas."

(c) *Exemption from the general accidental overdose warning.* The labeling for antiflatulent drug products containing simethicone identified in § 332.10 and antacid/antiflatulent combination drug products provided for in § 332.15, containing the active ingredients identified in § 331.11(a), (b), and (d) through (m) of this chapter are exempt from the requirement in § 330.1(g) of this chapter that the labeling bear the general warning statement "In case of accidental overdose, seek professional assistance or contact a poison control center immediately." The labeling

must continue to bear the first part of the general warning in § 330.1(g) of this chapter, which states, "Keep this and all drugs out of the reach of children."

[39 FR 19877, June 4, 1974, as amended at 40 FR 11719, Mar. 13, 1975; 51 FR 16266, May 1, 1986; 51 FR 27763, Aug. 1, 1986; 52 FR 7830, Mar. 13, 1987; 61 FR 8838, Mar. 5, 1996]

§ 332.31 Professional labeling.

(a) The labeling of the product provided to health professionals (but not to the general public) may contain as additional indications postoperative gas pain or for use in endoscopic examination.

(b) Professional labeling for an antiflatulent-antacid combination may contain information allowed for health professionals for antacids and antiflatulents.

PART 333—TOPICAL ANTIMICROBIAL DRUG PRODUCTS FOR OVER-THE-COUNTER HUMAN USE

Subpart A [Reserved]

Subpart B—First Aid Antibiotic Drug Products

Subpart C—Topical Antifungal Drug Products

Subpart D—Topical Acne Drug Products

AUTHORITY: 21 U.S.C. 321, 351, 352, 353, 355, 360, 371.

SOURCE: 52 FR 47322, Dec. 11, 1987, unless otherwise noted.

Subpart A [Reserved]

Subpart B—First Aid Antibiotic Drug Products

§333.101 Scope.

(a) An over-the-counter first aid antibiotic drug product in a form suitable for topical administration is generally recognized as safe and effective and is not misbranded if it meets each of the conditions in this subpart and each of the general conditions established in §330.1.

(b) References in this subpart to regulatory sections of the Code of Federal Regulations are to chapter I of title 21 unless otherwise noted.

§333.103 Definitions.

As used in this subpart:

First aid antibiotic. An antibiotic-containing drug product applied topically to the skin to help prevent infection in minor cuts, scrapes, and burns.

[52 FR 47322, Dec. 11, 1987, as amended at 64 FR 403, Jan. 5, 1999]

§333.110 First aid antibiotic active ingredients.

The product consists of any of the following active ingredients within the specified concentration established for each ingredient and in the specified dosage form:

(a) Bacitracin ointment containing, in each gram, 500 units of bacitracin in a suitable ointment base.

(b) Bacitracin zinc ointment containing, in each gram, 500 units of bacitracin zinc in a suitable ointment base.

(c) Chlortetracycline hydrochloride ointment containing, in each gram, 30 milligrams of chlortetracycline hydrochloride in a suitable ointment base.

(d) Neomycin sulfate ointment containing, in each gram, 3.5 milligrams of neomycin in a suitable water soluble or oleaginous ointment base.

(e) Neomycin sulfate cream containing, in each gram, 3.5 milligrams of neomycin in a suitable cream base.

(f) Tetracycline hydrochloride ointment containing, in each gram, 30 milligrams of tetracycline hydrochloride in a suitable ointment base.

[52 FR 47322, Dec. 11, 1987, as amended at 53 FR 18838, May 25, 1988; 64 FR 403, Jan. 5, 1999]

§333.120 Permitted combinations of active ingredients.

The following combinations are permitted provided each active ingredient is present within the established concentration and in the specified dosage form, and the product is labeled in accordance with §333.160.

(a) *Combinations of antibiotic active ingredients.* (1) Bacitracin-neomycin sulfate ointment containing, in each gram, 500 units of bacitracin and 3.5 milligrams of neomycin in a suitable ointment base.

(2) Bacitracin-neomycin sulfate-polymyxin B sulfate ointment containing, in each gram, in a suitable ointment base the following:

(i) 500 units of bacitracin, 3.5 milligrams of neomycin, and 5,000 units of polymyxin B; or

(ii) 400 units of bacitracin, 3.5 milligrams of neomycin, and 5,000 units of polymyxin B;

(3) Bacitracin-polymyxin B sulfate topical aerosol containing, in each gram, 500 units of bacitracin and 5,000 units of polymyxin B in a suitable vehicle, packaged in a pressurized container with suitable inert gases.

(4) Bacitracin zinc-neomycin sulfate ointment containing, in each gram, 500 units of bacitracin and 3.5 milligrams of neomycin in a suitable ointment base.

(5) Bacitracin zinc-neomycin sulfate-polymyxin B sulfate ointment containing, in each gram, in a suitable ointment base the following:

(i) 400 units of bacitracin, 3 milligrams of neomycin, and 8,000 units of polymyxin B; or

(ii) 400 units of bacitracin, 3.5 milligrams of neomycin, and 5,000 units of polymyxin B; or

(iii) 500 units of bacitracin, 3.5 milligrams of neomycin, and 5,000 units of polymyxin B; or

(iv) 500 units of bacitracin, 3.5 milligrams of neomycin, and 10,000 units of polymyxin B;

(6) Bacitracin zinc-polymyxin B sulfate ointment containing, in each gram, 500 units of bacitracin and 10,000 units of polymyxin B in a suitable ointment base.

(7) Bacitracin zinc-polymyxin B sulfate topical aerosol containing, in each gram, 120 units of bacitracin and 2,350 units of polymyxin B in a suitable vehicle, packaged in a pressurized container with suitable inert gases.

(8) Bacitracin zinc-polymyxin B sulfate topical powder containing, in each gram, 500 units of bacitracin and 10,000 units of polymyxin B in a suitable base.

(9) Neomycin sulfate-polymyxin B sulfate ointment containing, in each gram, 3.5 milligrams of neomycin and 5,000 units of polymyxin B in a suitable water miscible base.

(10) Neomycin sulfate-polymyxin B sulfate cream containing, in each gram, 3.5 milligrams of neomycin and 10,000 units of polymyxin B in a suitable vehicle.

(11) Oxytetracycline hydrochloride-polymyxin B sulfate ointment containing, in each gram, 30 milligrams of oxytetracycline and 10,000 units of polymyxin B in a suitable ointment base.

(12) Oxytetracycline hydrochloride-polymyxin B sulfate topical powder containing, in each gram, 30 milligrams of oxytetracycline and 10,000 units of polymyxin B with a suitable filler.

(b) *Combinations of first aid antibiotic active ingredients and local anesthetic active ingredients.* (1) Bacitracin ointment containing, in each gram, 500 units of bacitracin and any single generally recognized as safe and effective amine or "caine"-type local anesthetic active ingredient in a suitable ointment base.

(2) Bacitracin-neomycin sulfate-polymyxin B sulfate ointment containing, in each gram, in a suitable ointment base the following:

(i) 500 units of bacitracin, 3.5 milligrams of neomycin, 5,000 units of polymyxin B, and any single generally recognized as safe and effective amine or "caine"-type local anesthetic active ingredient; or

(ii) 400 units of bacitracin, 3.5 milligrams of neomycin, 5,000 units of polymyxin B, and any single generally rec-

ognized as safe and effective amine or "caine"-type local anesthetic active ingredient.

(3) Bacitracin-polymyxin B sulfate topical aerosol containing, in each gram, 500 units of bacitracin and 5,000 units of polymyxin B and any single generally recognized as safe and effective amine or "caine"-type local anesthetic active ingredient in a suitable vehicle, packaged in a pressurized container with suitable inert gases.

(4) Bacitracin zinc-neomycin sulfate-polymyxin B sulfate ointment containing, in each gram, in a suitable ointment base the following:

(i) 400 units of bacitracin, 3 milligrams of neomycin, 8,000 units of polymyxin B, and any single generally recognized as safe and effective amine or "caine"-type local anesthetic active ingredient; or

(ii) 400 units of bacitracin, 3.5 milligrams of neomycin, 5,000 units of polymyxin B, and any single generally recognized as safe and effective amine or "caine"-type local anesthetic active ingredient; or

(iii) 500 units of bacitracin, 3.5 milligrams of neomycin, 5,000 units of polymyxin B, and any single generally recognized as safe and effective amine or "caine"-type local anesthetic active ingredient; or

(iv) 500 units of bacitracin, 3.5 milligrams of neomycin, 10,000 units of polymyxin B, and any single generally recognized as safe and effective amine or "caine"-type local anesthetic active ingredient;

(5) Bacitracin zinc-polymyxin B sulfate ointment containing, in each gram, 500 units of bacitracin, 10,000 units of polymyxin B, and any single generally recognized as safe and effective amine or "caine"-type local anesthetic active ingredient in a suitable ointment base.

(6) Neomycin sulfate-polymyxin B sulfate cream containing, in each gram, 3.5 milligrams of neomycin, 10,000 units of polymyxin B, and any single generally recognized as safe and effective amine or "caine"-type local

anesthetic active ingredient in a suitable vehicle.

[52 FR 47322, Dec. 11, 1987; 52 FR 48792, Dec. 24, 1987, as amended at 53 FR 18838, May 25, 1988; 55 FR 9722, Mar. 15, 1990; 55 FR 40381, Oct. 3, 1990; 55 FR 50172, Dec. 5, 1990; 64 FR 403, Jan. 5, 1999]

§333.150 Labeling of first aid antibiotic drug products.

(a) *Statement of identity.* The labeling of the product contains the established name of the drug, if any, and identifies the product as a "first aid antibiotic."

(b) *Indications.* The labeling of the product states, under the heading "Indications," the following: "First aid to help" [select one of the following: "prevent," ("decrease" ("the risk of" or "the chance of")), ("reduce" ("the risk of" or "the chance of")), "guard against," or "protect against"] [select one of the following: "infection," "bacterial contamination," or "skin infection"] "in minor cuts, scrapes, and burns." Other truthful and nonmisleading statements describing only the indications for use that have been established and listed in this paragraph (b), may also be used, as provided in §330.1(c)(2), subject to the provisions of section 502 of the act relating to misbranding and the prohibition in section 301(d) of the act against the introduction or delivery for introduction into interstate commerce of unapproved new drugs in violation of section 505(a) of the act.

(c) *Warnings.* The labeling of the product contains the following warnings under the heading "Warnings":

(1) "For external use only. Do not use in the eyes or apply over large areas of the body. In case of deep or puncture wounds, animal bites, or serious burns, consult a doctor."

(2) *For products containing chlortetracycline hydrochloride or tetracycline hydrochloride.* "Stop use and consult a doctor if the condition persists or gets worse. Do not use longer than 1 week unless directed by doctor."

(3) *For any product containing bacitracin, bacitracin zinc, neomycin, neomycin sulfate, polymyxin B, and/or polymyxin B sulfate.* "Stop use and consult a doctor if the condition persists or gets worse, or if a rash or other allergic reaction develops. Do not use if you are allergic to any of the ingredients. Do not use longer than 1 week unless directed by a doctor."

(d) *Directions.* The labeling of the product contains the following statements under the heading "Directions":

(1) *For ointment and cream products.* "Clean the affected area. Apply a small amount of this product (an amount equal to the surface area of the tip of a finger) on the area 1 to 3 times daily. May be covered with a sterile bandage."

(2) *For powder products.* "Clean the affected area. Apply a light dusting of the powder on the area 1 to 3 times daily. May be covered with a sterile bandage."

(3) *For aerosol products.* "Clean the affected area. Spray a small amount of this product on the area 1 to 3 times daily. May be covered with a sterile bandage."

(e) The word "doctor" may be substituted for the word "physician" in any of the labeling statements in this subpart.

[52 FR 47332, Dec. 11, 1987, as amended at 61 FR 58472, Nov. 15, 1996]

§333.160 Labeling of permitted combinations of active ingredients.

Statements of identity, indications, warnings, and directions for use, respectively, applicable to each ingredient in the product may be combined to eliminate duplicative words or phrases so that the resulting information is clear and understandable.

(a) *Statement of identity.* For a combination drug product that has an established name, the labeling of the product states the established name of the combination drug product, followed by the statement of identity for each ingredient in the combination, as established in the statement of identity sections of the applicable OTC drug monographs. For a combination drug product that does not have an established name, the labeling of the product states the statement of identity for each ingredient in the combination, as established in the statement of identity sections of the applicable OTC drug monographs.

(b) *Indications.* The labeling of the product states, under the heading "Indications," the indication(s) for each ingredient in the combination, as established in the "Indications" sections of the applicable OTC drug monographs, unless otherwise stated in this paragraph. Other truthful and nonmisleading statements, describing only the indications for use that have been established and listed in this paragraph (b), may also be used, as provided in § 330.1(c)(2), subject to the provisions of section 502 of the act relating to misbranding and the prohibition in section 301(d) of the act against the introduction or delivery for introduction into interstate commerce of unapproved new drugs in violation of section 505(a) of the act.

(1) *For permitted combinations identified in § 333.120(a).* The indications in § 333.150 should be used.

(2) *For permitted combinations identified in § 333.120(b).* In addition to the required indication identified in § 333.150, the labeling of the product may state, under the heading "Indications," the following additional indication: "First aid for the temporary relief of" (select one of the following: "pain," "discomfort," "pain or discomfort" or "pain and itching") "in minor cuts, scrapes, and burns."

(c) *Warnings.* The labeling of the product states, under the heading "Warnings," the warning(s) for each ingredient in the combination, as established in the warnings sections of the applicable OTC drug monographs.

(d) *Directions.* The labeling of the product states, under the heading "Directions," directions that conform to the directions established for each ingredient in the directions sections of the applicable OTC drug monographs. When the time intervals or age limitations for administrations of the individual ingredients differ, the directions for the combination product may not exceed any maximum dosage limits established for the individual ingredients in the applicable OTC drug monograph.

Subpart C—Topical Antifungal Drug Products

SOURCE: 58 FR 49898, Sept. 23, 1993, unless otherwise noted.

§ 333.201 Scope.

(a) An over-the-counter antifungal drug product in a form suitable for topical administration is generally recognized as safe and effective and is not misbranded if it meets each of the conditions in this subpart and each general condition established in § 330.1 of this chapter.

(b) Reference in this subpart to regulatory sections of the Code of Federal Regulations are to chapter I of title 21 unless otherwise noted.

§ 333.203 Definitions.

As used in this subpart:

(a) *Antifungal.* A drug which inhibits the growth and reproduction of fungal cells and decreases the number of fungi present.

(b) *Athlete's foot.* An infection of the feet caused by certain dermatophytic fungi.

(c) *Dermatophyte.* A fungus that invades and lives upon the skin or in the hair or nails.

(d) *Fungus.* Any of a large division of plants, including dermatophytes, yeasts, and molds, characterized by a simple cell structure and the absence of chlorophyll.

(e) *Jock itch.* A chronic and recurrent infection caused by certain dermatophytic fungi; affects the upper, inner thighs and sometimes extends to the groin and the pubic area; the condition most frequently occurs in men, but may also occur in women.

(f) *Ringworm.* A skin infection caused by certain dermatophytic fungi.

§ 333.210 Antifungal active ingredients.

The active ingredient of the product consists of any one of the following within the specified concentration established for each ingredient:

(a) Clioquinol 3 percent.

(b) Haloprogin 1 percent.

(c) Miconazole nitrate 2 percent.

(d) Povidone-iodine 10 percent.

(e) Tolnaftate 1 percent.

(f) Undecylenic acid, calcium undecylenate, copper undecylenate, and zinc undecylenate may be used individually or in any ratio that provides a total undecylenate concentration of 10 to 25 percent.

(g) Clotrimazole 1 percent.

[58 FR 49898, Sept. 23, 1993, as amended at 67 FR 5943, Feb. 8, 2002]

§333.250 Labeling of antifungal drug products.

(a) *Statement of identity.* The labeling of the product contains the established name of the drug, if any, and identifies the product as an "antifungal."

(b) *Indications.* The labeling of the product states, under the heading "Indications," the phrase listed in paragraph (b)(1)(i) of this section and may contain the additional phrase listed in paragraph (b)(1)(ii) of this section. Other truthful and nonmisleading statements, describing only the indications for use that have been established in paragraph (b) of this section, may also be used, as provided in §330.1(c)(2) of this chapter, subject to the provisions of section 502 of the Federal Food, Drug, and Cosmetic Act (the act) relating to misbranding and the prohibition in section 301(d) of the act against the introduction or delivery for introduction into interstate commerce of unapproved new drugs in violation of section 505(a) of the act.

(1) *For products containing any ingredient identified in §333.210 labeled for the treatment of athlete's foot, jock itch, and ringworm.* (i) (Select one of the following: "Treats," "For the treatment of," "For effective treatment of," "Cures," "For the cure of," "Clears up," or "Proven clinically effective in the treatment of") "most" (select one condition from any one or more of the following groups of conditions:

(A) "Athlete's foot," athlete's foot (dermatophytosis)," "athlete's foot (tinea pedis)," or "tinea pedis (athlete's foot)";

(B) "Jock itch," "jock itch (tinea cruris)," or "tinea cruris (jock itch)"; or

(C) "Ringworm," "ringworm (tinea corporis)," or "tinea corporis (ringworm).")

(ii) In addition to the information identified in paragraph (b)(1)(i) of this section, the labeling of the product may contain the following statement: (Select one of the following: "Relieves," "For relief of," "For effective relief of," or "Soothes,") (select one or more of the following: "Itching,"

"scaling," "cracking," "burning," "redness," "soreness," "irritation," "discomfort," "chafing associated with jock itch," "itchy, scaly skin between the toes," or "itching, burning feet").

(2) *For products containing the ingredient identified in §333.210(e) labeled for the prevention of athlete's foot.* (i) (Select one of the following: "Clinically proven to prevent," "Prevents," "Proven effective in the prevention of," "Helps prevent," "For the prevention of," "For the prophylaxis (prevention) of," "Guards against," or "Prevents the recurrence of") "most" (select one of the following: "Athlete's foot," "athlete's foot (dermatophytosis)," "athlete's foot (tinea pedis)," or "tinea pedis (athlete's foot)") "with daily use."

(ii) In addition to the information identified in paragraph (b)(2)(i) of this section, the labeling of the product may contain the following statement: "Clears up most athlete's foot infection and with daily use helps keep it from coming back."

(c) *Warnings.* The labeling of the product contains the following warnings under the heading "Warnings":

(1) *For products containing any ingredient identified in §330.210.* (i) "Do not use on children under 2 years of age unless directed by a doctor."

(ii) "For external use only."

(iii) "Avoid contact with the eyes."

(2) *For products labeled according to paragraph (b)(1) of this section for the treatment of athlete's foot and ringworm.* "If irritation occurs or if there is no improvement within 4 weeks, discontinue use and consult a doctor."

(3) *For products labeled according to paragraph (b)(1) of this section for the treatment of jock itch.* "If irritation occurs or if there is no improvement within 2 weeks, discontinue use and consult a doctor."

(4) *For products labeled according to paragraph (b)(2) of this section for the prevention of athlete's foot.* "If irritation occurs, discontinue use and consult a doctor."

(5) *For products containing the ingredient identified in §333.210(a) labeled according to paragraph (b)(1) of this section.* The following statements must appear in boldface type as the first

warnings under the "Warnings" heading. (i) "Do not use on children under 2 years of age." (This warning is to be used in place of the warning in paragraph (c)(1)(i) of this section.)

(ii) "Do not use for diaper rash."

(d) *Directions.* The labeling of the product contains the following statements under the heading "Directions":

(1) *For products labeled according to paragraph (b)(1) of this section for the treatment of athlete's foot, jock itch, and ringworm.* [Select one of the following: "Clean" or "Wash"] "the affected area and dry thoroughly. Apply" (the word "spray" may be used to replace the word "apply" for aerosol products) "a thin layer of the product over affected area twice daily (morning and night) or as directed by a doctor. Supervise children in the use of this product. For athlete's foot: Pay special attention to spaces between the toes; wear well-fitting, ventilated shoes, and change shoes and socks at least once daily. For athlete's foot and ringworm, use daily for 4 weeks; for jock itch, use daily for 2 weeks. If condition persists longer, consult a doctor. This product is not effective on the scalp or nails."

(2) *For products labeled according to paragraph (b)(2) of this section for the prevention of athlete's foot.* "To prevent athlete's foot," (select one of the following: "clean" or "wash") "the feet and dry thoroughly. Apply" (the word "spray" may be used to replace the word "apply" for aerosol products) "a thin layer of the product to the feet once or twice daily (morning and/or night). Supervise children in the use of this product. Pay special attention to spaces between the toes; wear well-fitting, ventilated shoes, and change shoes and socks at least once daily."

(e) The word "physician" may be substituted for the word "doctor" in any of the labeling statements in this section.

[58 FR 49898, Sept. 23, 1993, as amended at 65 FR 52305, Aug. 29, 2000]

§ 333.280   Professional labeling.

The labeling provided to health professionals (but not to the general public) may contain the following additional indication:

(a) *For products containing haloprogin or miconazole nitrate identified in* § 333.210 (a) and (c). "For the treatment of superficial skin infections caused by yeast (*Candida albicans*)."

(b) [Reserved]

Subpart D—Topical Acne Drug Products

SOURCE: 56 FR 41019, Aug. 16, 1991, unless otherwise noted.

§ 333.301   Scope.

(a) An over-the-counter acne drug product in a form suitable for topical application is generally recognized as safe and effective and is not misbranded if it meets each of the conditions in this subpart and each general condition established in § 330.1 of this chapter.

(b) References in this subpart to regulatory sections of the Code of Federal Regulations are to chapter I of title 21 unless otherwise noted.

§ 333.303   Definitions.

As used in this subpart:

(a) *Acne.* A disease involving the oil glands and hair follicles of the skin which is manifested by blackheads, whiteheads, acne pimples, and acne blemishes.

(b) *Acne blemish.* A flaw in the skin resulting from acne.

(c) *Acne drug product.* A drug product used to reduce the number of acne blemishes, acne pimples, blackheads, and whiteheads.

(d) *Acne pimple.* A small, prominent, inflamed elevation of the skin resulting from acne.

(e) *Blackhead.* A condition of the skin that occurs in acne and is characterized by a black tip.

(f) *Whitehead.* A condition of the skin that occurs in acne and is characterized by a small, firm, whitish elevation of the skin.

§ 333.310   Acne active ingredients.

The active ingredient of the product consists of any of the following:

(a) Benzoyl peroxide, 2.5 to 10 percent.

(b) Resorcinol, 2 percent, when combined with sulfur in accordance with § 333.320(a).

(c) Resorcinol monoacetate, 3 percent, when combined with sulfur in accordance with §333.320(b).

(d) Salicylic acid, 0.5 to 2 percent.

(e) Sulfur, 3 to 10 percent.

(f) Sulfur, 3 to 8 percent, when combined with resorcinol or resorcinol monoacetate in accordance with §333.320.

[75 FR 9776, Mar. 4, 2010]

§333.320 Permitted combinations of active ingredients.

(a) Resorcinol identified in §333.310(b) may be combined with sulfur identified in §333.310(f).

(b) Resorcinol monoacetate identified in §333.310(c) may be combined with sulfur identified in §333.310(f).

[75 FR 9776, Mar. 4, 2010]

§333.350 Labeling of acne drug products.

(a) *Statement of identity.* The labeling of the product contains the established name of the drug, if any, and identifies the product as an "acne medication," "acne treatment," "acne medication" (insert dosage form, e.g., "cream," "gel," "lotion," or "ointment"), or "acne treatment" (insert dosage form, e.g., "cream," "gel," "lotion," or "ointment").

(b) *Indications.* The labeling of the product states, under the heading "Indications," the phrase listed in paragraph (b)(1) of this section and may contain any of the additional phrases listed in paragraph (b)(2) of this section. Other truthful and nonmisleading statements, describing only the indications for use that have been established and listed in paragraph (b) of this section, may also be used, as provided in §330.1(c)(2) of this chapter, subject to the provisions of section 502 of the Federal Food, Drug, and Cosmetic Act (the act) relating to misbranding and the prohibition in section 301(d) of the act against the introduction or delivery for introduction into interstate commerce of unapproved new drugs in violation of section 505(a) of the act.

(1) "For the" (select one of the following: "management" or "treatment") "of acne."

(2) In addition to the information identified in paragraph (b)(1) of this

section, the labeling of the product may contain any one or more of the following statements:

(i) (Select one of the following: "Clears," "Clears up," "Clears up most," "Dries," "Dries up," "Dries and clears," "Helps clear," "Helps clear up," "Reduces the number of," or "Reduces the severity of") (select one or more of the following: "acne blemishes," "acne pimples," "blackheads," or "whiteheads") which may be followed by "and allows skin to heal."

(ii) "Penetrates pores to" (select one of the following: "eliminate most," "control," "clear most," or "reduce the number of") (select one or more of the following: "acne blemishes," "acne pimples," "blackheads," or "whiteheads").

(iii) "Helps keep skin clear of new" (select one or more of the following: "acne blemishes," "acne pimples," "blackheads," or "whiteheads").

(iv) "Helps prevent new" (select one or more of the following: "acne blemishes," "acne pimples," "blackheads," or "whiteheads") which may be followed by "from forming."

(v) "Helps prevent the development of new" (select one or more of the following: "acne blemishes," "acne pimples," "blackheads," or "whiteheads").

(c) *Warnings.* The labeling of the product contains the following warnings under the heading "Warnings":

(1) *For products containing any ingredients identified in §330.310.*

(i) The labeling states "For external use only."

(ii) The labeling states "When using this product [bullet] skin irritation and dryness is more likely to occur if you use another topical acne medication at the same time. If irritation occurs, only use one topical acne medication at a time."

(2) *For products containing sulfur identified in §333.310(e) and (f).*

(i) The labeling states "Do not use on [bullet] broken skin [bullet] large areas of the skin."

(ii) The labeling states "When using this product [bullet] apply only to areas with acne."

(3) *For products containing any combination identified in §333.320.* (i) The labeling states "When using this product

[bullet] rinse right away with water if it gets in eyes."

(ii) The labeling states "Stop use and ask a doctor [bullet] if skin irritation occurs or gets worse."

(4) *For products containing benzoyl peroxide identified in § 333.310(a).*

(i) The labeling states "Do not use if you [bullet] have very sensitive skin [bullet] are sensitive to benzoyl peroxide."

(ii) The labeling states "When using this product [bullet] avoid unnecessary sun exposure and use a sunscreen [bullet] avoid contact with the eyes, lips, and mouth [bullet] avoid contact with hair and dyed fabrics, which may be bleached by this product [bullet] skin irritation may occur, characterized by redness, burning, itching, peeling, or possibly swelling. Irritation may be reduced by using the product less frequently or in a lower concentration."

(iii) The labeling states "Stop use and ask a doctor if [bullet] irritation becomes severe."

(d) *Directions.* The labeling of the product contains the following information under the heading "Directions":

(1) *For products applied containing any ingredient identified in § 333.310.* The labeling states "[bullet] clean the skin thoroughly before applying this product [bullet] cover the entire affected area with a thin layer one to three times daily [bullet] because excessive drying of the skin may occur, start with one application daily, then gradually increase to two or three times daily if needed or as directed by a doctor [bullet] if bothersome dryness or peeling occurs, reduce application to once a day or every other day."

(2) *For products applied and left on the skin containing benzoyl peroxide identified in § 333.310(a).*

(i) The labeling states the directions in paragraph (d)(1) of this section.

(ii) The labeling states "[bullet] if going outside, apply sunscreen after using this product. If irritation or sensitivity develops, stop use of both products and ask a doctor."

(3) *For products applied and removed from the skin containing any ingredient identified in § 333.310.* Products, such as soaps and masks, may be applied and removed and should include appro-

priate directions. All products containing benzoyl peroxide should include the directions in paragraph (d)(2)(ii) of this section.

(4) *Optional directions.* In addition to the required directions in paragraphs (d)(1) and (d)(2) of this section, the product may contain the following optional labeling: *"Sensitivity Test for a New User.* Apply product sparingly to one or two small affected areas during the first 3 days. If no discomfort occurs, follow the directions stated (select one of the following: 'elsewhere on this label,' 'above,' or 'below')."

[56 FR 41019, Aug. 16, 1991, as amended at 75 FR 9776, Mar. 4, 2010]

PART 335—ANTIDIARRHEAL DRUG PRODUCTS FOR OVER-THE-COUNTER HUMAN USE

Subpart A—General Provisions

Sec.
335.1 Scope.
335.3 Definitions.

Subpart B—Active Ingredients

335.10 Antidiarrheal active ingredients.

Subpart C—Labeling

335.50 Labeling of antidiarrheal drug products.

AUTHORITY: 21 U.S.C. 321, 351, 352, 353, 355, 360, 371.

SOURCE: 68 FR 18881, April 17, 2003, unless otherwise noted.

Subpart A—General Provisions

§ 335.1 Scope.

(a) An over-the-counter antidiarrheal drug product in a form suitable for oral administration is generally recognized as safe and effective and is not misbranded if it meets each condition in this part and each general condition established in § 330.1 of this chapter.

(b) References in this part to regulatory sections of the Code of Federal Regulations are to chapter I of title 21 unless otherwise noted.

§ 335.3 Definitions.

As used in this part:

(a) *Antidiarrheal.* A drug that can be shown by objective measurement to treat or control (stop) the symptoms of diarrhea.

(b) *Diarrhea.* A condition characterized by increased frequency of loose, watery stools (three or more daily) during a limited period (24 to 48 hours), usually with no identifiable cause.

(c) *Travelers' diarrhea.* A subset of diarrhea occurring in travelers that is most commonly caused by an infectious agent.

[68 FR 18881, Apr. 17, 2003, as amended at 69 FR 26302, May 12, 2004]

Subpart B—Active Ingredients

§335.10 Antidiarrheal active ingredients.

The active ingredient of the product consists of any one of the following when used within the dosage limits established for each ingredient in §335.50(d):

(a) Bismuth subsalicylate.

(b) Kaolin.

Subpart C—Labeling

§335.50 Labeling of antidiarrheal drug products.

(a) *Statement of identity.* The labeling of the product contains the established name of the drug, if any, and identifies the product either as an "antidiarrheal" or "for diarrhea."

(b) *Indications.* The labeling of the product states, under the heading "Use," one or more of the phrases listed in this paragraph (b), as appropriate. Other truthful and nonmisleading statements, describing only the indications for use that have been established and listed in this paragraph (b) may also be used, as provided in §330.1(c)(2) of this chapter, subject to the provisions of section 502 of the Federal Food, Drug, and Cosmetic Act (the act) relating to misbranding and the prohibition in section 301(d) of the act against the introduction or delivery for introduction into interstate commerce of unapproved new drugs in violation of section 505(a) of the act.

(1) *For products containing bismuth subsalicylate identified in §335.10(a).* The labeling states [select one of the following: "controls" or "relieves"] [select one or both of the following: "di-arrhea" or "travelers' diarrhea"]. If both "diarrhea" and "travelers' diarrhea" are selected, each shall be preceded by a bullet in accordance with §201.66(b)(4) and (d)(4) of this chapter and the heading "Uses" shall be used.

(2) *For products containing kaolin identified in §335.10(b).* The labeling states "helps firm stool within 24 to 48 hours".

(3) *Additional indications*—(i) When any additional indications are used, the heading "Uses" shall be used and each listed use shall be preceded by a bullet in accord with §201.66(b)(4) of this chapter.

(ii) In addition to the indication in paragraph (b)(1) of this section, one or both of the following may be used for products containing bismuth subsalicylate in §335.10(a): "[bullet] reduces number of bowel movements" "[bullet] helps firm stool".

(c) *Warnings.* The labeling of the product contains the following warnings under the heading "Warnings":

(1) *For products containing any ingredient identified in §335.10.* (i) "Do not use if you have [bullet] bloody or black stool".

(ii) "Ask a doctor before use if you have [bullet] fever [bullet] mucus in the stool".

(2) *For products containing bismuth subsalicylate identified in §335.10(a).* (i) The following shall appear in accordance with §201.66(c)(5)(ii) of this chapter.

(A) The Reye's syndrome warning in §201.314(h) of this chapter.

(B) "Allergy alert: Contains salicylate. Do not take if you are [bullet] allergic to salicylates (including aspirin), [bullet] taking other salicylate products".

(ii) "Do not use if you have [bullet] an ulcer [bullet] a bleeding problem".

(iii) "Ask a doctor or pharmacist before use if you are taking any drug for [bullet] anticoagulation (thinning the blood) [bullet] diabetes [bullet] gout [bullet] arthritis".

(iv) "When using this product a temporary, but harmless, darkening of the stool and/or tongue may occur".

(v) "Stop use and ask a doctor if [bullet] symptoms get worse [bullet] ringing in the ears or loss of hearing occurs [bullet] diarrhea lasts more than 2 days".

(3) *For products containing kaolin identified in § 335.10(b).* (i) "Ask a doctor or pharmacist before use if you are taking any other drugs. Try to use at least 3 hours before or after taking any other drugs."

(ii) "Stop use and ask a doctor if [bullet] symptoms get worse [bullet] diarrhea lasts more than 2 days".

(d) *Directions.* The labeling of the product contains the following information under the heading "Directions":

(1) *For products containing any ingredient identified in § 335.10.* The labeling states "[bullet] drink plenty of clear fluids to help prevent dehydration caused by diarrhea".

(2) *For products containing bismuth subsalicylate identified in § 335.10(a).* The labeling states "[bullet] adults and children 12 years and over:" 525 milligrams "every ½ to 1 hour, or" 1,050 milligrams "every hour as needed [bullet] do not exceed" 4,200 milligrams "in 24 hours [bullet] use until diarrhea stops but not more than 2 days [bullet] children under 12 years: ask a doctor".

(3) *For products containing kaolin identified in § 335.10(b).* The labeling states "[bullet] adults and children 12 years and over:" 26.2 grams "after each loose stool [bullet] continue to take every 6 hours until stool is firm but not more than 2 days [bullet] do not exceed" [262 grams] "in 24 hours [bullet] children under 12 years of age: ask a doctor".

(e) *Products that meet the criteria established in § 201.66(d)(10) of this chapter.* The information described in § 201.66(c) of this chapter shall be printed in accordance with the following specifications.

(1) The labeling shall meet the requirements of § 201.66(c) of this chapter except that the information in § 201.66(c)(3) of this chapter may be omitted, and the information in § 201.66(c)(5) and (c)(6) of this chapter may be presented as follows:

(i) The words "Contains salicylate." may be omitted from the warning in § 335.50(c)(2)(i)(B).

(ii) The subheading "When using this product" in § 335.50(c)(2)(iv) may be omitted.

(iii) The words "continue to" may be omitted from the directions in § 335.50(d)(3).

(2) The labeling shall be printed in accordance with the requirements of § 201.66(d) of this chapter except that any requirements related to § 201.66(c)(3) of this chapter and the bullet in the warning in § 335.50(c)(1)(i) may be omitted.

[68 FR 18881, Apr. 17, 2003, as amended at 69 FR 26302, May 12, 2004]

PART 336—ANTIEMETIC DRUG PRODUCTS FOR OVER-THE-COUNTER HUMAN USE

Subpart A—General Provisions

Sec.
336.1   Scope.
336.3   Definition.

Subpart B—Active Ingredients

336.10   Antiemetic active ingredients.

Subpart C—Labeling

336.50   Labeling of antiemetic drug products.
336.80   Professional labeling.

AUTHORITY: 21 U.S.C. 321, 351, 352, 353, 355, 360, 371.

SOURCE: 52 FR 15892, Apr. 30, 1987, unless otherwise noted.

Subpart A—General Provisions

§ 336.1   Scope.

(a) An over-the-counter antiemetic drug product in a form suitable for oral administration is generally recognized as safe and effective and is not misbranded if it meets each of the conditions in this part and each of the general conditions established in § 330.1.

(b) References in this part to regulatory sections of the Code of Federal Regulations are to chapter I of title 21 unless otherwise noted.

§ 336.3   Definition.

As used in this part:

Antiemetic. An agent that prevents or treats nausea and vomiting.

Subpart B—Active Ingredients

§ 336.10 Antiemetic active ingredients.

The active ingredient of the product consists of any of the following when used within the dosage limits established for each ingredient in § 336.50(d):

(a) Cyclizine hydrochloride.

(b) Dimenhydrinate.

(c) Diphenhydramine hydrochloride.

(d) Meclizine hydrochloride.

Subpart C—Labeling

§ 336.50 Labeling of antiemetic drug products.

(a) *Statement of identity.* The labeling of the product contains the established name of the drug, if any, and identifies the product as an "antiemetic."

(b) *Indications.* The labeling of the product states the following under the heading "Indications," "For the prevention and treatment of the nausea, vomiting, or dizziness associated with motion sickness." Other truthful and nonmisleading statements, describing only the indications for use that have been established and listed in this paragraph (b), may also be used, as provided in § 330.1(c)(2), subject to the provisions of section 502 of the act relating to misbranding and the prohibition in section 301(d) of the act against the introduction or delivery for introduction into interstate commerce of unapproved new drugs in violation of section 505(a) of the act.

(c) *Warnings.* The labeling of the product contains the following warnings under the heading "Warnings:"

(1) *For products containing any ingredient identified in § 336.10*—(i) *When labeled for use in adults and for those products that can be and are labeled for use in children under 12 years of age.* "Do not take this product, unless directed by a doctor, if you have a breathing problem such as emphysema or chronic bronchitis, or if you have glaucoma or difficulty in urination due to enlargement of the prostate gland."

(ii) *For those products that can be and are labeled only for children under 12 years of age.* "Do not give this product to children who have a breathing problem such as chronic bronchitis or who have glaucoma, without first consulting the child's doctor."

(2) *For products containing cyclizine hydrochloride identified in § 336.10(a).* "Do not give to children under 6 years of age unless directed by a doctor."

(3) *For products containing dimenhydrinate identified in § 336.10(b).* "Do not give to children under 2 years of age unless directed by a doctor."

(4) *For products containing diphenhydramine hydrochloride identified in § 336.10(c).* "Do not give to children under 6 years of age unless directed by a doctor."

(5) *For products containing meclizine hydrochloride identified in § 336.10(d).* "Do not give to children under 12 years of age unless directed by a doctor."

(6) *For products containing cyclizine hydrochloride identified in § 336.10(a) or meclizine hydrochloride identified in § 330.10(d).* "May cause drowsiness; alcohol, sedatives, and tranquilizers may increase the drowsiness effect. Avoid alcoholic beverages while taking this product. Do not take this product if you are taking sedatives or tranquilizers, without first consulting your doctor. Use caution when driving a motor vehicle or operating machinery."

(7) *For products containing dimenhydrinate identified in § 336.10(b) or diphenhydramine hydrochloride identified in § 336.10(c).* "May cause marked drowsiness; alcohol, sedatives, and tranquilizers may increase the drowsiness effect. Avoid alcoholic beverages while taking this product. Do not take this product if you are taking sedatives or tranquilizers, without first consulting your doctor. Use caution when driving a motor vehicle or operating machinery."

(8) *For products containing diphenhydramine hydrochloride identified in § 336.10(c).* "Do not use [bullet][1] with any other product containing diphenhydramine, including one used on skin".

(d) *Directions.* The labeling of the product contains the following information under the heading "Directions":

(1) *For products containing cyclizine hydrochloride identified in § 336.10(a).* Adults and children 12 years of age and

---

[1] See § 201.66(b)(4) of this chapter for definition of bullet symbol.

over: Oral dosage is 50 milligrams every 4 to 6 hours, not to exceed 200 milligrams in 24 hours, or as directed by a doctor. Children 6 to under 12 years of age: Oral dosage is 25 milligrams every 6 to 8 hours, not to exceed 75 milligrams in 24 hours, or as directed by a doctor.

(2) *For products containing dimenhydrinate identified in § 336.10(b).* Adults and children 12 years of age and over: Oral dosage is 50 to 100 milligrams every 4 to 6 hours, not to exceed 400 milligrams in 24 hours, or as directed by a doctor. Children 6 to under 12 years of age: Oral dosage is 25 to 50 milligrams every 6 to 8 hours, not to exceed 150 milligrams in 24 hours, or as directed by a doctor. Children 2 to under 6 years of age: Oral dosage is 12.5 to 25 milligrams every 6 to 8 hours, not to exceed 75 milligrams in 24 hours, or as directed by a doctor.

(3) *For products containing diphenhydramine hydrochloride identified in § 336.10(c).* Adults and children 12 years of age and over: Oral dosage is 25 to 50 milligrams every 4 to 6 hours, not to exceed 300 milligrams in 24 hours, or as directed by a doctor. Children 6 to under 12 years of age: Oral dosage is 12.5 to 25 milligrams every 4 to 6 hours, not to exceed 150 milligrams in 24 hours, or as directed by a doctor.

(4) *For products containing meclizine hydrochloride identified in § 336.10(d).* Adults and children 12 years of age and over: Oral dosage is 25 to 50 milligrams once daily, or as directed by a doctor.

(e) The word "physician" may be substituted for the word "doctor" in any of the labeling statements in this section.

[52 FR 15892, Apr. 30, 1987, as amended at 53 FR 35809, Sept. 15, 1988; 59 FR 16982, Apr. 11, 1994; 67 FR 72559, Dec. 6, 2003]

§ 336.80 Professional labeling.

The labeling provided to health professionals (but not to the general public) may contain the following additional indications.

(a) *For products containing cyclizine hydrochloride, dimenhydrinate, and diphenhydramine hydrochloride identified in § 336.10 (a), (b), and (c).* "For the treatment of vertigo of motion sickness."

(b) *For products containing meclizine hydrochloride identified in § 336.10(d).* "For the treatment of vertigo."

PART 338—NIGHTTIME SLEEP-AID DRUG PRODUCTS FOR OVER-THE-COUNTER HUMAN USE

Subpart A—General Provisions

Sec.
338.1 Scope.
338.3 Definition.

Subpart B—Active Ingredients

338.10 Nighttime sleep-aid active ingredients.

Subpart C—Labeling

338.50 Labeling of nighttime sleep-aid drug products.

AUTHORITY: 21 U.S.C. 321, 351, 352, 353, 355, 360, 371.

SOURCE: 54 FR 6826, Feb. 14, 1989, unless otherwise noted.

Subpart A—General Provisions

§ 338.1 Scope.

(a) An over-the-counter nighttime sleep-aid drug product in a form suitable for oral administration is generally recognized as safe and effective and is not misbranded if it meets each condition in this part and each general condition established in § 330.1 of this chapter.

(b) References in this part to regulatory sections of the Code of Federal Regulations are to chapter I of title 21 unless otherwise noted.

§ 338.3 Definition.

As used in this part:
Nighttime sleep-aid. A drug that is useful for the relief of occasional sleeplessness by individuals who have difficulty falling asleep.

Subpart B—Active Ingredients

§ 338.10 Nighttime sleep-aid active ingredients.

The active ingredient of the product consists of any of the following when used within the dosage limits established for each ingredient in § 338.50(d):

(a) Diphenhydramine hydrochloride.

(b) Diphenhydramine citrate.

Subpart C—Labeling

§ 338.50 Labeling of nighttime sleep-aid drug products.

(a) *Statement of identity.* The labeling of the product contains the established name of the drug, if any, and identifies the product as a "nighttime sleep-aid."

(b) *Indications.* The labeling of the product states, under the heading "Indications," one or more of the phrases listed in this paragraph. Other truthful and nonmisleading statements, describing only the indications for use that have been established and listed in this paragraph (b), may also be used, as provided in § 330.1(c)(2) of this chapter, subject to the provisions of section 502 of the act relating to misbranding and the prohibition in section 301(d) of the act against the introduction into delivery for introduction into interstate commerce of unapproved new drugs in violation of section 505(a) of the act.

(1) ("Helps you" or "Reduces time to") "fall asleep if you have difficulty falling asleep."

(2) "For relief of occasional sleeplessness."

(3) "Helps to reduce difficulty falling asleep."

(c) *Warnings.* The labeling of the product contains the following warnings under the heading "Warnings":

(1) "Do not give to children under 12 years of age."

(2) "If sleeplessness persists continuously for more than 2 weeks, consult your doctor. Insomnia may be a symptom of serious underlying medical illness."

(3) "Do not take this product, unless directed by a doctor, if you have a breathing problem such as emphysema or chronic bronchitis, or if you have glaucoma or difficulty in urination due to enlargement of the prostate gland."

(4) "Avoid alcoholic beverages while taking this product. Do not take this product if you are taking sedatives or tranquilizers, without first consulting your doctor."

(5) "Do not use [bullet][1] with any other product containing

---

[1] See § 201.66(b)(4) of this chapter for definition of bullet symbol.

diphenhydramine, even one used on skin".

(d) *Directions.* The labeling of the product contains the following information under the heading "Directions":

(1) *For products containing diphenhydramine hydrochloride identified in § 338.10(a).* Adults and children 12 years of age and over: Oral dosage is 50 milligrams at bedtime if needed, or as directed by a doctor.

(2) *For products containing diphenhydramine citrate identified in § 338.10(b).* Adults and children 12 years of age and over: Oral dosage is 76 milligrams at bedtime if needed, or as directed by a doctor.

(e) The word "physician" may be substituted for the word "doctor" in any of the labeling statements in this section.

[54 FR 6826, Feb. 14, 1989, as amended at 59 FR 16983, Apr. 11, 1994; 67 FR 72559, Dec. 6, 2002]

PART 340—STIMULANT DRUG PRODUCTS FOR OVER-THE-COUNTER HUMAN USE

Subpart A—General Provisions

Subpart B—Active Ingredient

Subpart C—Labeling

AUTHORITY: 21 U.S.C. 321, 351, 352, 353, 355, 360, 371.

SOURCE: 53 FR 6105, Feb. 29, 1988, unless otherwise noted.

Subpart A—General Provisions

§ 340.1 Scope.

(a) An over-the-counter stimulant drug product in a form suitable for oral administration is generally recognized as safe and effective and is not misbranded if it meets each of the conditions in this part and each of the general conditions established in § 330.1.

(b) References in this part to regulatory sections of the Code of Federal

Regulations are to chapter I of title 21 unless otherwise noted.

§ 340.3 Definition.

As used in this part:

Stimulant. A drug which helps restore mental alertness or wakefulness during fatigue or drowsiness.

Subpart B—Active Ingredient

§ 340.10 Stimulant active ingredient.

The active ingredient of the product consists of caffeine when used within the dosage limits established in § 340.50(d).

Subpart C—Labeling

§ 340.50 Labeling of stimulant drug products.

(a) *Statement of identity.* The labeling of the product contains the established name of the drug, if any, and identifies the product as an "altertness aid" or a "stimulant."

(b) *Indications.* The labeling of the product states, under the heading "Indications," the following: "Helps restore mental alertness or wakefulness when experiencing fatigue or drowsiness." Other truthful and nonmisleading statements, describing only the indications for use that have been established and listed in this paragraph (b), may also be used, as provided in § 330.1(c)(2), subject to the provisions of section 502 of the Act relating to misbranding and the prohibition in section 301(d) of the Act against the introduction or delivery for introduction into interstate commerce of unapproved new drugs in violation of section 505(a) of the Act.

(c) *Warnings.* The labeling of the product contains the following warnings under the heading "Warnings":

(1) "The recommended dose of this product contains about as much caffeine as a cup of coffee. Limit the use of caffeine-containing medications, foods, or beverages while taking this product because too much caffeine may cause nervousness, irritability, sleeplessness, and, occasionally, rapid heart beat."

(2) "For occasional use only. Not intended for use as a substitute for sleep. If fatigue or drowsiness persists or continues to recur, consult a" (select one of the following: "physician" or "doctor").

(3) "Do not give to children under 12 years of age."

(d) *Directions.* The labeling of the product contains the following information under the heading "Directions": Adults and children 12 years of age and over: Oral dosage is 100 to 200 milligrams not more often than every 3 to 4 hours.

PART 341—COLD, COUGH, ALLERGY, BRONCHODILATOR, AND ANTIASTHMATIC DRUG PRODUCTS FOR OVER-THE-COUNTER HUMAN USE

Subpart A—General Provisions

AUTHORITY: 21 U.S.C. 321, 351, 352, 353, 355, 360, 371.

EDITORIAL NOTE: Nomenclature changes to part 341 appear at 69 FR 13717, Mar. 24, 2004.

Subpart A—General Provisions

§341.1 Scope.

(a) An over-the-counter cold, cough, allergy, bronchodilator, or anti-asthmatic drug product in a form suitable for oral, inhalant, or topical administration is generally recognized as safe and effective and is not misbranded if it meets each of the conditions in this part and each of the general conditions established in §330.1.

(b) References in this part to regulatory sections of the Code of Federal Regulations are to chapter I of title 21 unless otherwise noted.

[51 FR 35339, Oct. 2, 1986]

§341.3 Definitions.

As used in this part:

(a) *Bronchodilator drug.* A drug used to overcome spasms that cause narrowing of the bronchial air tubes, such as in the symptomatic treatment of the wheezing and shortness of breath of asthma.

(b) *Oral antitussive drug.* A drug that either is taken by mouth or is dissolved in the mouth in the form of a lozenge and acts systemically to relieve cough.

(c) *Topical antitussive drug.* A drug that relieves cough when inhaled after being applied topically to the throat or chest in the form of an ointment or from a steam vaporizer, or when dissolved in the mouth in the form of a lozenge for a local effect.

(d) *Expectorant drug.* A drug taken orally to promote or facilitate the removal of secretions from the respiratory airways.

(e) *Antihistamine drug.* A drug used for the relief of the symptoms of hay fever and upper respiratory allergies (allergic rhinitis).

(f) *Oral nasal decongestant drug.* A drug that is taken by mouth and acts systemically to reduce nasal congestion caused by acute or chronic rhinitis.

(g) *Topical nasal decongestant drug.* A drug that when applied topically inside the nose, in the form of drops, jellies, or sprays, or when inhaled intranasally reduces nasal congestion caused by acute or chronic rhinitis.

(h) *Calibrated dropper.* A dropper calibrated such that the volume error incurred in measuring any liquid does not exceed 15 percent under normal use conditions.

(i) *Effervescent dosage form.* A dosage form intended to be dissolved in water before administration. It contains, in addition to the active ingredient(s), mixtures of acids (citric acid, tartaric acid) and sodium bicarbonate, which release carbon dioxide when dissolved in water.

[51 FR 35339, Oct. 2, 1986, as amended at 54 FR 8509, Feb. 28, 1989; 55 FR 40382, Oct. 3, 1990; 57 FR 58374, Dec. 9, 1992; 59 FR 43409, Aug. 23, 1994; 71 FR 43362, Aug. 1, 2006]

Subpart B—Active Ingredients

§341.12 Antihistamine active ingredients.

The active ingredient of the product consists of any of the following when used within the dosage limits established for each ingredient:

(a) Brompheniramine maleate.
(b) Chlorcyclizine hydrochloride.
(c) Chlorpheniramine maleate.
(d) Dexbrompheniramine maleate.
(e) Dexchlorpheniramine maleate.
(f) Diphenhydramine citrate.
(g) Diphenhydramine hydrochloride.
(h) Doxylamine succinate.
(i) Phenindamine tartrate.
(j) Pheniramine maleate.
(k) Pyrilamine maleate.
(l) Thonzylamine hydrochloride.
(m) Triprolidine hydrochloride.

[57 FR 58374, Dec. 9, 1992, as amended at 59 FR 4218, Jan. 28, 1994]

§341.14 Antitussive active ingredients.

The active ingredients of the product consist of any of the following when used within the dosage limits and in the dosage forms established for each ingredient in §341.74(d):

(a) *Oral antitussives.* (1) Chlophedianol hydrochloride.

(2) *Codeine ingredients.* The following ingredients may be used only in combination in accordance with §290.2 and 21 CFR 1308.15(c).

(i) Codeine.
(ii) Codeine phosphate.
(iii) Codeine sulfate.
(3) Dextromethorphan.
(4) Dextromethorphan hydrobromide.

(5) Diphenhydramine citrate.

(6) Diphenhydramine hydrochloride.

(b) *Topical antitussives.* (1) Camphor.

(2) Menthol.

[52 FR 30055, Aug. 12, 1987, as amended at 59 FR 29174, June 3, 1994; 67 FR 4907, Feb. 1, 2002]

§ 341.16 Bronchodilator active ingredients.

The active ingredients of the product consist of any of the following when used within the dosage limits established for each ingredient:

(a) Ephedrine.

(b) Ephedrine hydrochloride.

(c) Ephedrine sulfate.

(d) Epinephrine.

(e) Epinephrine bitartrate.

(f) Racephedrine hydrochloride.

(g) Racepinephrine hydrochloride.

[51 FR 35339, Oct. 2, 1986]

§ 341.18 Expectorant active ingredient.

The active ingredient of the product is guaifenesin when used within the dosage limits established in § 341.78(d).

[54 FR 8509, Feb. 28, 1989]

§ 341.20 Nasal decongestant active ingredients.

The active ingredient of the product consists of any of the following when used within the dosage limits and in the dosage forms established for each ingredient:

(a) *Oral nasal decongestants.* (1) Phenylephrine hydrochloride.

(2) Pseudoephedrine hydrochloride.

(3) Pseudoephedrine sulfate.

(4) Phenylephrine bitartrate in an effervescent dosage form.

(b) *Topical nasal decongestants.* (1) Levmetamfetamine.

(2) Ephedrine.

(3) Ephedrine hydrochloride.

(4) Ephedrine sulfate.

(5) [Reserved]

(6) Naphazoline hydrochloride.

(7) Oxymetazoline hydrochloride.

(8) Phenylephrine hydrochloride.

(9) Propylhexedrine.

(10) Xylometazoline hydrochloride.

[59 FR 43409, Aug. 23, 1994, as amended at 63 FR 40650, July 30, 1998; 71 FR 43362, Aug. 1, 2006]

§ 341.40 Permitted combinations of active ingredients.

The following combinations are permitted provided each active ingredient is present within the dosage limits established in parts 341, 343, and 356 of this chapter and the product is labeled in accordance with §§ 341.70 or 341.85:

(a) Any single antihistamine active ingredient identified in § 341.12 may be combined with any generally recognized as safe and effective single analgesic-antipyretic active ingredient, or any combination of acetaminophen with other analgesic-antipyretic active ingredients, or any aspirin and antacid combination provided that the product is labeled according to § 341.85.

(b) Any single antihistamine active ingredient identified in § 341.12 may be combined with any single oral nasal decongestant active ingredient identified in § 341.20(a) provided that the product is labeled according to § 341.85.

(c) Any single antihistamine active ingredient identified in § 341.12 may be combined with any single oral nasal decongestant active ingredient identified in § 341.20(a) and any generally recognized as safe and effective single analgesic-antipyretic active ingredient, or any combination of acetaminophen with other analgesic-antipyretic active ingredients, or any aspirin and antacid combination provided that the product is labeled according to § 341.85.

(d) Any single antihistamine active ingredient identified in § 341.12(a) through (e) and (h) through (m) may be combined with any single oral antitussive active ingredient identified in § 341.14(a)(1) through (a)(4) provided that the product is labeled according to § 341.85(c)(4). Diphenhydramine citrate in §§ 341.12(f) and 341.14(a)(5) or diphenhydramine hydrochloride in §§ 341.12(g) and 341.14(a)(6) may be both the antihistamine and the antitussive active ingredient provided that the product is labeled according to § 341.70(a).

(e) Any single antihistamine active ingredient identified in § 341.12(a) through (e) and (h) through (m) may be combined with any single oral antitussive active ingredient identified in § 341.14(a)(1) through (a)(4) and any single oral nasal decongestant active ingredient identified in §341.20(a) provided that the product is labeled according to §341.85(c)(4). Diphenhydramine citrate in §§341.12(f) and 341.14(a)(5) or diphenhydramine hydrochloride in §§341.12(g) and 341.14(a)(6) may be both the antihistamine and the antitussive active ingredient provided that the product is labeled according to §341.70(a).

(f) Any single antihistamine active ingredient identified in §341.12(a) through (e) and (h) through (m) may be combined with any single oral antitussive active ingredient identified in §341.14(a)(1) through (a)(4) and any generally recognized as safe and effective single analgesic-antipyretic active ingredient, or any combination of acetaminophen with other analgesic-antipyretic active ingredients, or any aspirin and antacid combination provided that the product is labeled according to §341.85(c)(4). Diphenhydramine citrate in §§341.12(f) and 341.14(a)(5) or diphenhydramine hydrochloride in §§341.12(g) and 341.14(a)(6) may be both the antihistamine and the antitussive active ingredient provided that the product is labeled according to §341.70(a).

(g) Any single antihistamine active ingredient identified in §341.12(a) through (e) and (h) through (m) may be combined with any single oral antitussive active ingredient identified in §341.14(a)(1) through (a)(4) and any single oral nasal decongestant active ingredient identified in §341.20(a) and any generally recognized as safe and effective single analgesic-antipyretic active ingredient, or any combination of acetaminophen with other analgesic-antipyretic active ingredients, or any aspirin and antacid combination provided that the product is labeled according to §341.85(c)(4). Diphenhydramine citrate in §§341.12(f) and 341.14(a)(5) or diphenhydramine hydrochloride in §§341.12(g) and 341.14(a)(6) may be both the antihistamine and the antitussive active ingredient provided that the product is labeled according to §341.70(a).

(h) Any single oral antitussive active ingredient identified in §341.14(a)(1) through (a)(4) may be combined with any single expectorant active ingredient identified in §341.18 provided that the product is labeled according to §341.85.

(i) Any single oral antitussive active ingredient identified in §341.14(a) may be combined with any single oral nasal decongestant active ingredient identified in §341.20(a) provided that the product is labeled according to §341.85.

(j) Any single oral antitussive active ingredient identified in §341.14(a)(1) through (a)(4) may be combined with any single oral nasal decongestant active ingredient identified in §341.20(a) and any single expectorant active ingredient identified in §341.18 provided that the product is labeled according to §341.85.

(k) Any single antitussive active ingredient identified in §341.14(a) or (b)(2) may be combined with any generally recognized as safe and effective single oral anesthetic/analgesic active ingredient, or any combination of anesthetic/analgesic active ingredients provided that the product is available in either a liquid (to be swallowed) or a solid dosage form (to be dissolved in the mouth and swallowed) and provided that the product is labeled according to §341.85. If the combination contains a topical antitussive, the product must be formulated in a solid dosage form to be dissolved in the mouth. Menthol in §341.14(b)(2) and part 356 of this chapter may be both the antitussive and the anesthetic/analgesic active ingredient provided that the product is labeled according to §341.70(b).

(l) Any single oral antitussive active ingredient identified in §341.14(a) may be combined with any generally recognized as safe and effective single analgesic-antipyretic active ingredient, or any combination of acetaminophen with other analgesic-antipyretic active ingredients, or any aspirin and antacid combination provided that the product is labeled according to §341.85.

(m) Any single oral antitussive active ingredient identified in §341.14(a) may be combined with any single oral nasal decongestant active ingredient identified in §341.20(a) and any generally recognized as safe and effective single analgesic-antipyretic active ingredient, or any combination of acetaminophen with other analgesic-antipyretic active ingredients, or any aspirin and antacid combination provided that the product is labeled according to § 341.85.

(n) Any single oral antitussive active ingredient identified in § 341.14(a)(1) through (a)(4) may be combined with any single oral nasal decongestant active ingredient identified in § 341.20(a) and any single expectorant active ingredient identified in § 341.18 and any generally recognized as safe and effective single analgesic-antipyretic active ingredient, or any combination of acetaminophen with other analgesic-antipyretic active ingredients, or any aspirin and antacid combination provided that the product is labeled according to § 341.85.

(o) Any single expectorant active ingredient identified in § 341.18 may be combined with any generally recognized as safe and effective single analgesic-antipyretic active ingredient, or any combination of acetaminophen with other analgesic-antipyretic active ingredients, or any aspirin and antacid combination provided that the product is labeled according to § 341.85.

(p) Any single expectorant active ingredient identified in § 341.18 may be combined with any single oral nasal decongestant active ingredient identified in § 341.20(a) provided that the product is labeled according to § 341.85.

(q) Any single expectorant active ingredient identified in § 341.18 may be combined with any single oral nasal decongestant active ingredient identified in § 341.20(a) and any generally recognized as safe and effective single analgesic-antipyretic active ingredient, or any combination of acetaminophen with other analgesic-antipyretic active ingredients, or any aspirin and antacid combination provided that the product is labeled according to § 341.85.

(r) Any single oral nasal decongestant active ingredient identified in § 341.20(a) may be combined with any generally recognized as safe and effective single analgesic-antipyretic active ingredient, or any combination of acetaminophen with other analgesic-antipyretic active ingredients, or any aspirin and antacid combination provided that the product is labeled according to § 341.85.

(s) Any single oral nasal decongestant active ingredient identified in § 341.20(a) may be combined with any

generally recognized as safe and effective single oral anesthetic/analgesic active ingredient identified, or any combination of anesthetic/analgesic active ingredients provided that the product is available in either a liquid (to be swallowed) or a solid dosage form (to be dissolved in the mouth and swallowed) and provided that the product is labeled according to § 341.85.

(t) Any single oral nasal decongestant active ingredient identified in § 341.20(a) may be combined with any single antitussive active ingredient identified in § 341.14(a) or (b)(2) and any generally recognized as safe and effective single oral anesthetic/analgesic active ingredient, or any combination of anesthetic/analgesic active ingredients provided that the product is available in either a liquid (to be swallowed) or a solid dosage form (to be dissolved in the mouth and swallowed) and provided that the product is labeled according to § 341.85. If the combination contains a topical antitussive, the product must be formulated in a solid dosage form to be dissolved in the mouth.

(u) Camphor identified in § 341.14(b)(1) may be combined with menthol identified in § 341.14(b)(2) and eucalyptus oil (1.2 to 1.3 percent) provided that the product is available only in a suitable ointment vehicle and provided that the product is labeled according to § 341.85.

(v) Levmetamfetamine identified in § 341.20(b)(1) may be combined with aromatics (camphor (54 milligrams (mg)), menthol (80 mg), methyl salicylate (11 mg), and lavender oil (4 mg)) provided that the product is available only as a nasal inhaler and provided that the product is labeled according to § 341.85.

(w) Any single antitussive active ingredient identified in § 341.14(a) or (b)(2) may be combined with any generally recognized as safe and effective single oral demulcent active ingredient provided that the product is available in either a liquid (to be swallowed) or a solid dosage form (to be dissolved in the mouth and swallowed) and provided that the product is labeled according to § 341.85. If the combination contains a topical antitussive, the product must be formulated in a solid dosage form to be dissolved in the mouth.

(x) Any single oral nasal decongestant active ingredient identified in

§ 341.20(a) may be combined with any generally recognized as safe and effective single oral demulcent active ingredient provided that the product is available in either a liquid (to be swallowed) or a solid dosage form (to be dissolved in the mouth and swallowed) and provided that the product is labeled according to § 341.85.

(y) Any single antitussive active ingredient identified in § 341.14(a) or (b)(2) may be combined with any single oral nasal decongestant active ingredient identified in § 341.20(a) and any generally recognized as safe and effective single oral demulcent active ingredient provided that the product is available in either a liquid (to be swallowed) or a solid dosage form (to be dissolved in the mouth and swallowed) and provided that the product is labeled according to § 341.85. If the combination contains a topical antitussive, the product must be formulated in a solid dosage form to be dissolved in the mouth.

(z) Any single antitussive active ingredient identified in § 341.14(a) or (b)(2) may be combined with any generally recognized as safe and effective single oral anesthetic/analgesic active ingredient or any combination of anesthetic/analgesic active ingredients and any generally recognized as safe and effective single oral demulcent active ingredient provided that the product is available in either a liquid (to be swallowed) or a solid dosage form (to be dissolved in the mouth and swallowed) and provided that the product is labeled according to § 341.85. If the combination contains a topical antitussive, the product must be formulated in a solid dosage form to be dissolved in the mouth.

(aa) Any single oral nasal decongestant active ingredient identified in § 341.20(a) may be combined with any generally recognized as safe and effective single oral anesthetic/analgesic active ingredient or any combination of oral anesthetic/analgesic active ingredients and any generally recognized as safe and effective single oral demulcent active ingredient provided that the product is available in either a liquid (to be swallowed) or a solid dosage form (to be dissolved in the mouth and swallowed) and provided that the product is labeled according to § 341.85.

(bb) Any single antitussive active ingredient identified in § 341.14(a) or (b)(2) may be combined with any single oral nasal decongestant active ingredient identified in § 341.20(a) and any generally recognized as safe and effective single oral anesthetic/analgesic active ingredient identified or any combination of anesthetic/analgesic active ingredients and any generally recognized as safe and effective single oral demulcent active ingredient provided that the product is available in either a liquid (to be swallowed) or a solid dosage form (to be dissolved in the mouth and swallowed) and provided that the product is labeled according to § 341.85. If the combination contains a topical antitussive, the product must be formulated in a solid dosage form to be dissolved in the mouth.

[67 FR 78168, Dec. 23, 2002]

Subpart C—Labeling

§ 341.70 Labeling of OTC drug products containing ingredients that are used for treating concurrent symptoms (in either a single-ingredient or combination drug product).

The statements of identity, indications, warnings, and directions for use, respectively, applicable to each ingredient in the product may be combined to eliminate duplicative words or phrases so that the resulting information is clear and understandable.

(a) *For products containing diphenhydramine citrate and diphenhydramine hydrochloride identified in § 341.14(a)(5) and (a)(6).* The labeling of the product contains the established name of the drug, if any, and identifies the product as an "antihistamine/cough suppressant" or "antihistamine/antitussive (cough suppressant)." The indications shall be combined from §§ 341.72(b) and 341.74(b). The warnings shall be combined from §§ 341.72(c)(1), (c)(2), (c)(4), and (c)(6) and 341.74(c)(1), (c)(2), (c)(3), and (c)(4). Alternatively, all of the warnings in § 341.74(c) shall be used. The directions for OTC labeling shall follow §§ 341.74(d)(1)(iv) or (d)(1)(v), as applicable. The directions for professional labeling shall follow § 341.90(j) or (k), as applicable.

(b) *For products containing menthol identified in §§ 341.14(b)(2) and 356.12(f) of this chapter.* The product contains 5 to 10 milligrams menthol. The labeling of the product contains the established name of the drug, if any, and identifies the product as a "cough suppressant/oral anesthetic" or "antitussive (cough suppressant)/oral anesthetic." The indications shall be combined from § 341.74(b) and part 356 of this chapter. The warnings shall be combined from § 341.74(c)(1), (c)(2), and (c)(3) and part 356 of this chapter. The directions shall be: "Directions [in bold type] [bullet][1] adults and children 2 years and over: dissolve lozenge slowly in the mouth. Repeat every 2 hours as needed or as directed by a doctor. [bullet] children under 2 years of age: ask a doctor".

[61 FR 15703, Apr. 9, 1996, as amended at 67 FR 78170, Dec. 23, 2002; 68 FR 17881, Apr. 14, 2003]

§ 341.72 Labeling of antihistamine drug products.

(a) *Statement of identity.* The labeling of the product contains the established name of the drug, if any, and identifies the product as an "antihistamine."

(b) *Indications.* The labeling of the product states, under the heading "Indications," any of the phrases listed in paragraph (b) of this section, as appropriate. Other truthful and nonmisleading statements, describing only the indications for use that have been established and listed in this paragraph, may also be used, as provided in § 330.1(c)(2) of this chapter, subject to the provisions of section 502 of the Federal Food, Drug, and Cosmetic Act (the act) relating to misbranding and the prohibition in section 301(d) of the act against the introduction or delivery for introduction into interstate commerce of unapproved new drugs in violation of section 505(a) of the act.

(1) "Temporarily" (select one of the following: "relieves," "alleviates," "decreases," "reduces," or "dries") "runny nose and" (select one of the following: "relieves," "alleviates," "decreases," or "reduces") "sneezing, itching of the nose or throat, and itchy, watery eyes due to hay fever" (which may be followed by one or both of the following: "or other upper res-

piratory allergies" or "(allergic rhinitis)").

(2) "For the temporary relief of runny nose, sneezing, itching of the nose or throat, and itchy, watery eyes due to hay fever" (which may be followed by one or both of the following: "or other upper respiratory allergies" or "(allergic rhinitis)").

(c) *Warnings.* The labeling of the product contains the following warnings, under the heading "Warnings":

(1) "May cause excitability especially in children."

(2) "Do not take this product, unless directed by a doctor, if you have a breathing problem such as emphysema or chronic bronchitis, or if you have glaucoma or difficulty in urination due to enlargement of the prostate gland."

(3) *For products containing brompheniramine maleate, chlorcyclizine hydrochloride, chlorpheniramine maleate, dexbrompheniramine maleate, dexchlorpheniramine maleate, phenindamine tartrate, pheniramine maleate, pyrilamine maleate, thonzylamine hydrochloride, or triprolidine hydrochloride identified in § 341.12(a), (b), (c), (d), (e), (i), (j), (k), (l), and (m).* "May cause drowsiness; alcohol, sedatives, and tranquilizers may increase the drowsiness effect. Avoid alcoholic beverages while taking this product. Do not take this product if you are taking sedatives or tranquilizers, without first consulting your doctor. Use caution when driving a motor vehicle or operating machinery."

(4) *For products containing diphenhydramine citrate, diphenhydramine hydrochloride, or doxylamine succinate identified in § 341.12(f), (g), and (h).* "May cause marked drowsiness; alcohol, sedatives, and tranquilizers may increase the drowsiness effect. Avoid alcoholic beverages while taking this product. Do not take this product if you are taking sedatives or tranquilizers, without first consulting your doctor. Use caution when driving a motor vehicle or operating machinery."

(5) *For products containing phenindamine tartrate identified in § 341.12(i).* "May cause nervousness and insomnia in some individuals."

(6) *For products that are labeled only for use by children under 12 years of age.*

---

[1] See § 201.66(b)(4) of this chapter for definition of bullet symbol.

The labeling of the product contains only the warnings identified in paragraphs (c)(1) and (c)(5) of this section as well as the following:

(i) "Do not give this product to children who have a breathing problem such as chronic bronchitis, or who have glaucoma, without first consulting the child's doctor."

(ii) *For products containing brompheniramine maleate, chlorpheniramine maleate, dexbrompheniramine maleate, dexchlorpheniramine maleate, phenindamine tartrate, pheniramine maleate, pyrilamine maleate, thonzylamine hydrochloride, or triprolidine hydrochloride identified in §341.12(a), (c), (d), (e), (i), (j), (k), (l), and (m).* "May cause drowsiness. Sedatives and tranquilizers may increase the drowsiness effect. Do not give this product to children who are taking sedatives or tranquilizers, without first consulting the child's doctor."

(iii) *For products containing diphenhydramine citrate, diphenhydramine hydrochloride, or doxylamine succinate identified in §341.12(f), (g), and (h).* "May cause marked drowsiness. Sedatives and tranquilizers may increase the drowsiness effect. Do not give this product to children who are taking sedatives or tranquilizers, without first consulting the child's doctor."

(iv) *For products containing diphenhydramine citrate or diphenhydramine hydrochloride identified in §341.12(f) and (g).* "Do not use [bullet][1] with any other product containing diphenhydramine, even one used on skin".

(7) *For products containing diphenhydramine citrate or diphenhydramine hydrochloride identified in §341.12(f) and (g).* "Do not use [bullet] with any other product containing diphenhydramine, even one used on skin".

(d) *Directions.* The labeling of the product contains the following information under the heading "Directions":

(1) *For products containing brompheniramine maleate identified in §341.12(a).* Adults and children 12 years of age and over: oral dosage is 4 milligrams every 4 to 6 hours, not to exceed 24 milligrams in 24 hours, or as directed by a doctor. Children 6 to under 12 years of age: oral dosage is 2 milligrams every 4 to 6 hours, not to exceed 12 milligrams in 24 hours, or as directed by a doctor. Children under 6 years of age: consult a doctor.

(2) *For products containing chlorcyclizine hydrochloride identified in §341.12(b).* Adults and children 12 years of age and over: oral dosage is 25 milligrams every 6 to 8 hours, not to exceed 75 milligrams in 24 hours, or as directed by a doctor. Children under 12 years of age: consult a doctor.

(3) *For products containing chlorpheniramine maleate identified in §341.12(c).* Adults and children 12 years of age and over: oral dosage is 4 milligrams every 4 to 6 hours, not to exceed 24 milligrams in 24 hours, or as directed by a doctor. Children 6 to under 12 years of age: oral dosage is 2 milligrams every 4 to 6 hours, not to exceed 12 milligrams in 24 hours, or as directed by a doctor. Children under 6 years of age: consult a doctor.

(4) *For products containing dexbrompheniramine maleate identified in §341.12(d).* Adults and children 12 years of age and over: oral dosage is 2 milligrams every 4 to 6 hours, not to exceed 12 milligrams in 24 hours, or as directed by a doctor. Children 6 to under 12 years of age: oral dosage is 1 milligram every 4 to 6 hours, not to exceed 6 milligrams in 24 hours, or as directed by a doctor. Children under 6 years of age: consult a doctor.

(5) *For products containing dexchlorpheniramine maleate identified in §341.12(e).* Adults and children 12 years of age and over: oral dosage is 2 milligrams every 4 to 6 hours, not to exceed 12 milligrams in 24 hours, or as directed by a doctor. Children 6 to under 12 years of age: oral dosage is 1 milligram every 4 to 6 hours, not to exceed 6 milligrams in 24 hours, or as directed by a doctor. Children under 6 years of age: consult a doctor.

(6) *For products containing diphenhydramine citrate identified in §341.12(f).* Adults and children 12 years of age and over: oral dosage is 38 to 76 milligrams every 4 to 6 hours, not to exceed 456 milligrams in 24 hours, or as

[1] See §201.66(b)(4) of this chapter for definition of bullet symbol.

directed by a doctor. Children 6 to under 12 years of age: oral dosage is 19 to 38 milligrams every 4 to 6 hours, not to exceed 228 milligrams in 24 hours, or as directed by a doctor. Children under 6 years of age: consult a doctor.

(7) *For products containing diphenhydramine hydrochloride identified in § 341.12(g).* Adults and children 12 years of age and over: oral dosage is 25 to 50 milligrams every 4 to 6 hours, not to exceed 300 milligrams in 24 hours, or as directed by a doctor. Children 6 to under 12 years of age: oral dosage is 12.5 to 25 milligrams every 4 to 6 hours, not to exceed 150 milligrams in 24 hours, or as directed by a doctor. Children under 6 years of age: consult a doctor.

(8) *For products containing doxylamine succinate identified in § 341.12(h).* Adults and children 12 years of age and over: oral dosage is 7.5 to 12.5 milligrams every 4 to 6 hours, not to exceed 75 milligrams in 24 hours, or as directed by a doctor. Children 6 to under 12 years of age: oral dosage is 3.75 to 6.25 milligrams every 4 to 6 hours, not to exceed 37.5 milligrams in 24 hours, or as directed by a doctor. Children under 6 years of age: consult a doctor.

(9) *For products containing phenindamine tartrate identified in § 341.12(i).* Adults and children 12 years of age and over: oral dosage is 25 milligrams every 4 to 6 hours, not to exceed 150 milligrams in 24 hours, or as directed by a doctor. Children 6 to under 12 years of age: oral dosage is 12.5 milligrams every 4 to 6 hours, not to exceed 75 milligrams in 24 hours, or as directed by a doctor. Children under 6 years of age: consult a doctor.

(10) *For products containing pheniramine maleate identified in § 341.12(j).* Adults and children 12 years of age and over: oral dosage is 12.5 to 25 milligrams every 4 to 6 hours, not to exceed 150 milligrams in 24 hours, or as directed by a doctor. Children 6 to under 12 years of age: oral dosage is 6.25 to 12.5 milligrams every 4 to 6 hours, not to exceed 75 milligrams in 24 hours, or as directed by a doctor. Children under 6 years of age: consult a doctor.

(11) *For products containing pyrilamine maleate identified in § 341.12(k).* Adults and children 12 years of age and over:

oral dosage is 25 to 50 milligrams every 6 to 8 hours, not to exceed 200 milligrams in 24 hours, or as directed by a doctor. Children 6 to under 12 years of age: oral dosage is 12.5 to 25 milligrams every 6 to 8 hours, not to exceed 100 milligrams in 24 hours, or as directed by a doctor. Children under 6 years of age: consult a doctor.

(12) *For products containing thonzylamine hydrochloride identified in § 341.12(l).* Adults and children 12 years of age and over: oral dosage is 50 to 100 milligrams every 4 to 6 hours, not to exceed 600 milligrams in 24 hours, or as directed by a doctor. Children 6 to under 12 years of age: oral dosage is 25 to 50 milligrams every 4 to 6 hours, not to exceed 300 milligrams in 24 hours, or as directed by a doctor. Children under 6 years of age: consult a doctor.

(13) *For products containing triprolidine hydrochloride identified in § 341.12(m).* Adults and children 12 years of age and over: oral dosage is 2.5 milligrams every 4 to 6 hours, not to exceed 10 milligrams in 24 hours, or as directed by a doctor. Children 6 to under 12 years of age: oral dosage is 1.25 milligrams every 4 to 6 hours, not to exceed 5 milligrams in 24 hours, or as directed by a doctor. Children under 6 years of age: consult a doctor.

(e) The word "physician" may be substituted for the word "doctor" in any of the labeling statements in this section.

[57 FR 58374, Dec. 9, 1992, as amended at 59 FR 4218, Jan. 28, 1994; 67 FR 72559, Dec. 6, 2002]

§ 341.74 Labeling of antitussive drug products.

(a) *Statement of identity.* The labeling of the product contains the established name of the drug, if any, and identifies the product as a "cough suppressant" or an "antitussive (cough suppressant)."

(b) *Indications.* The labeling of the product states, under the heading "Indications," any of the phrases listed in this paragraph (b), as appropriate. Other truthful and nonmisleading statements, describing only the indications for use that have been established and listed in this paragraph, may also be used, as provided in § 330.1(c)(2), subject to the provisions of section 502 of the act relating to misbranding and the prohibition in section 301(d) of the act against the introduction or delivery for introduction into interstate commerce of unapproved new drugs in violation of section 505(a) of the act.

(1) "Temporarily" (select one of the following: "alleviates," "calms," "controls," "decreases," "quiets," "reduces," "relieves," or "suppresses") "cough due to" (select one of the following: "minor bronchial irritation" or "minor throat and bronchial irritation") (select one of the following: "as may occur with," "associated with," or "occurring with") (select one of the following: "A cold" or "the common cold") "or inhaled irritants."

(2) "Temporarily" (select one of the following: "alleviates," "calms," "controls," "decreases," "quiets," "reduces," "relieves," or "suppresses") "cough" (select one of the following: "as may occur with," "associated with," or "occurring with") (select one of the following: "A cold," "the common cold," or "inhaled irritants").

(3) In addition to the required information identified in paragraphs (b) (1) and (2) of this section, the labeling of the product may contain any (one or more) of the following statements:

(i) "Cough suppressant which temporarily" (select one of the following: "Alleviates," "controls," "decreases," "reduces," "relieves," or "suppresses") "the impulse to cough."

(ii) "Temporarily helps you cough less."

(iii) "Temporarily helps to" (select one of the following: "Alleviate," "control," "decrease," "reduce," "relieve," or "suppress") "the cough reflex that causes coughing."

(iv) "Temporarily" (select one of the following: "Alleviates," "controls," "decreases," "reduces," "relieves," or "suppresses") "the intensity of coughing."

(v) (Select one of the following: "Alleviates," "Controls," "Decreases," "Reduces," "Relieves," or "Suppresses") (select one of the following: "Cough," "the impulse to cough," or "your cough") "to help you" (select one of the following: "Get to sleep," "sleep," or "rest").

(vi) *For products containing chlophedianol hydrochloride, codeine in-* gredients, dextromethorphan, or dextromethorphan hydrobromide identified in §341.14(a) (1), (2), (3), and (4). "Calms the cough control center and relieves coughing."

(vii) *For products containing chlophedianol hydrochloride, dextromethorphan, dextromethorphan hydrobromide, camphor, or menthol identified in §341.14(a) (1), (3), (4) and (b) (1) and (2).* (a) "Nonnarcotic cough suppressant for the temporary" (select one of the following: "alleviation," "control," "decrease," "reduction," "relief," or "suppression") "of cough."

(b) (Select one of the following: "Alleviates," "Controls," "Decreases," "Reduces," "Relieves," or "Suppresses") "cough impulses without narcotics."

(c) *Warnings.* The labeling of the product contains the following warnings under the heading "Warnings":

(1) *For oral and topical antitussives.* "A persistent cough may be a sign of a serious condition. If cough persists for more than 1 week, tends to recur, or is accompanied by fever, rash, or persistent headache, consult a doctor."

(2) *For oral and topical antitussives labeled for adults or for adults and children under 12 years of age.* "Do not take this product for persistent or chronic cough such as occurs with smoking, asthma, or emphysema, or if cough is accompanied by excessive phlegm (mucus) unless directed by a doctor."

(3) *For oral and topical antitussives labeled only for children under 12 years of age.* "Do not give this product for persistent or chronic cough such as occurs with asthma or if cough is accompanied by excessive phlegm (mucus) unless directed by a doctor."

(4) *Oral antitussives—*(i) *For products containing codeine ingredients identified in §341.14(a)(2).* "May cause or aggravate constipation."

(ii) *For products containing codeine ingredients identified in §341.14(a)(2) when labeled only for adults.* "Do not take this product if you have a chronic pulmonary disease or shortness of breath unless directed by a doctor."

(iii) *For products containing codeine ingredients identified in §341.14(a)(2) when labeled only for children under 12 years of age.* "Do not give this product to children who have a chronic pulmonary disease, shortness of breath, or who are taking other drugs unless directed by a doctor."

(iv) *For products containing codeine ingredients identified in § 341.14(a)(2) when labeled for use in adults and children under 12 years of age.* "Adults and children who have a chronic pulmonary disease or shortness of breath, or children who are taking other drugs, should not take this product unless directed by a doctor."

(v) *For products containing dextromethorphan or dextromethorphan hydrobromide as identified in § 341.14 (a)(3) and (a)(4) when labeled for adults or for adults and children under 12 years of age. Drug interaction precaution.* "Do not use if you are now taking a prescription monoamine oxidase inhibitor (MAOI) (certain drugs for depression, psychiatric, or emotional conditions, or Parkinson's disease), or for 2 weeks after stopping the MAOI drug. If you do not know if your prescription drug contains an MAOI, ask a doctor or pharmacist before taking this product."

(vi) *For products containing dextromethorphan or dextromethorphan hydrobromide as identified in § 341.14 (a)(3) and (a)(4) when labeled only for children under 12 years of age. Drug interaction precaution.* "Do not use in a child who is taking a prescription monoamine oxidase inhibitor (MAOI) (certain drugs for depression, psychiatric, or emotional conditions, or Parkinson's disease), or for 2 weeks after stopping the MAOI drug. If you do not know if your child's prescription drug contains an MAOI, ask a doctor or pharmacist before giving this product."

(vii) *For products containing diphenhydramine citrate or diphenhydramine hydrochloride identified in § 341.14 (a)(5) and (a)(6).* "May cause excitability especially in children."

(viii) *For products containing diphenhydramine citrate or diphenhydramine hydrochloride identified in § 341.14 (a)(5) and (a)(6) when labeled only for children under 12 years of age—* (A) "Do not give this product to children who have a breathing problem such as chronic bronchitis, or who have glaucoma, without first consulting the child's doctor."

(B) "May cause marked drowsiness. Sedatives and tranquilizers may increase the drowsiness effect. Do not give this product to children who are taking sedatives or tranquilizers, without first consulting the child's doctor."

(C) "Do not use [bullet][1] with any other product containing diphenhydramine, even one used on skin".

(ix) *For products containing diphenhydramine citrate or diphenhydramine hydrochloride identified in § 341.14 (a)(5) and (a)(6) when labeled for use in adults and children under 12 years of age—* (A) "Do not take this product, unless directed by a doctor, if you have a breathing problem such as emphysema or chronic bronchitis, or if you have glaucoma or difficulty in urination due to enlargement of the prostate gland."

(B) "May cause marked drowsiness; alcohol, sedatives, and tranquilizers may increase the drowsiness effect. Avoid alcoholic beverages while taking this product. Do not take this product if you are taking sedatives or tranquilizers, without first consulting your doctor. Use caution when driving a motor vehicle or operating machinery."

(C) "Do not use [bullet] with any other product containing diphenhydramine, even one used on skin".

(5) *Topical antitussives—*(i) *For products containing camphor or menthol identified in § 341.14 (b) (1) and (2) in a suitable ointment vehicle.* "For external use only. Do not take by mouth or place in nostrils."

(ii) *For products containing camphor or menthol identified in § 341.14(b) (1) and (2) for steam inhalation use.* "For steam inhalation only. Do not take by mouth."

(iii) *For any product containing camphor or menthol in a suitable ointment vehicle or for steam inhalation use and meets the definition of one of the signal words ("extremely flammable," "flammable," "combustible") as described in 16 CFR 1500.3(b)(10).* The labeling contains the appropriate flammability signal word(s) followed by a colon and the statement "Keep away from fire or flame."

----

[1] See § 201.66(b)(4) of this chapter for definition of bullet symbol.

(iv) *For any product containing camphor or menthol in a suitable ointment vehicle and that does not contain a flammability signal word as described in 16 CFR 1500.3(b)(10).* "When using this product, do not [bullet][1] heat [bullet] microwave [bullet] add to hot water or any container where heating water. May cause splattering and result in burns." [Information highlighted in bold type.]

(v) *For any product containing camphor or menthol in a suitable ointment vehicle and that contains a flammability signal word as described in 16 CFR 1500.3(b)(10).* "When using this product, do not [bullet] heat [bullet] microwave [bullet] use near an open flame [bullet] add to hot water or any container where heating water. May cause splattering and result in burns." [Information highlighted in bold type.]

(vi) *For any product containing camphor or menthol for steam inhalation use.* "When using this product, do not [bullet] heat [bullet] microwave [bullet] use near an open flame [bullet] add to hot water or any container where heating water except when adding to cold water only in a hot steam vaporizer. May cause splattering and result in burns." [Information highlighted in bold type.]

(vii) *For any product formulated in a volatile vehicle.* The labeling contains the following statement under the heading "Other information": "Close container tightly and store at room temperature away from heat."

(d) *Directions.* The labeling of the product contains the following information under the heading "Directions":

(1) *Oral antitussives—*(i) *For products containing chlophedianol hydrochloride identified in §341.14(a)(1).* Adults and children 12 years of age and over: Oral dosage is 25 milligrams every 6 to 8 hours, not to exceed 100 milligrams in 24 hours, or as directed by a doctor. Children 6 to under 12 years of age: Oral dosage is 12.5 milligrams every 6 to 8 hours, not to exceed 50 milligrams in 24 hours, or as directed by a doctor. Children under 6 years of age: Consult a doctor.

---

[1] For a definition of the term "bullet," see §201.66(b)(4) of this chapter.

(ii) *For products containing codeine ingredients identified in §341.14(a)(2).* Adults and children 12 years of age and over: Oral dosage is 10 to 20 milligrams every 4 to 6 hours, not to exceed 120 milligrams in 24 hours, or as directed by a doctor. Children 6 to under 12 years of age: Oral dosage is 5 to 10 milligrams every 4 to 6 hours, not to exceed 60 milligrams in 24 hours, or as directed by a doctor. Children under 6 years of age: Consult a doctor. A special measuring device should be used to give an accurate dose of this product to children under 6 years of age. Giving a higher dose than recommended by a doctor could result in serious side effects for your child.

(iii) *For products containing dextromethorphan or dextromethorphan hydrobromide identified in §341.14(a) (3) and (4).* The dosage is equivalent to dextromethorphan hydrobromide. Adults and children 12 years of age and over: Oral dosage is 10 to 20 milligrams every 4 hours or 30 milligrams every 6 to 8 hours, not to exceed 120 milligrams in 24 hours, or as directed by a doctor. Children 6 to under 12 years of age: Oral dosage is 5 to 10 milligrams every 4 hours or 15 milligrams every 6 to 8 hours, not to exceed 60 milligrams in 24 hours, or as directed by a doctor. Children 2 to under 6 years of age: Oral dosage is 2.5 to 5 milligrams every 4 hours or 7.5 milligrams every 6 to 8 hours, not to exceed 30 milligrams in 24 hours, or as directed by a doctor. Children under 2 years of age: Consult a doctor.

(iv) *For products containing diphenhydramine citrate identified in §341.14(a)(5).* Adults and children 12 years of age and over: oral dosage is 38 milligrams every 4 hours, not to exceed 228 milligrams in 24 hours, or as directed by a doctor. Children 6 to under 12 years of age: oral dosage is 19 milligrams every 4 hours, not to exceed 114 milligrams in 24 hours, or as directed by a doctor. Children under 6 years of age: consult a doctor.

(v) *For products containing diphenhydramine hydrochloride identified in §341.14(a)(6).* Adults and children 12 years of age and over: oral dosage is 25 milligrams every 4 hours, not to exceed 150 milligrams in 24 hours, or as directed by a doctor. Children 6 to under

12 years of age: oral dosage is 12.5 milligrams every 4 hours, not to exceed 75 milligrams in 24 hours, or as directed by a doctor. Children under 6 years of age: consult a doctor.

(2) *Topical antitussives*—(i) *For products containing camphor identified in § 341.14(b)(1) in a suitable ointment vehicle.* The product contains 4.7 to 5.3 percent camphor. "[bullet] see important warnings under 'When using this product' [appears as the first statement under the heading "Directions" and is highlighted in bold type] [bullet] adults and children 2 years and older: [bullet] rub on the throat and chest in a thick layer [bullet] cover with a warm, dry cloth if desired [bullet] clothing should be loose about throat and chest to help vapors reach the nose and mouth [bullet] use up to three times daily or as directed by a doctor [bullet] children under 2 years of age: Ask a doctor.

(ii) *For products containing menthol identified in § 341.14(b)(2) in a suitable ointment vehicle.* The product contains 2.6 to 2.8 percent menthol. "[bullet] see important warnings under 'When using this product' " [appears as the first statement under the heading "Directions" and is highlighted in bold type] [bullet] adults and children 2 years and older: [bullet] rub on the throat and chest in a thick layer [bullet] cover with a warm, dry cloth if desired [bullet] clothing should be loose about throat and chest to help vapors reach the nose and mouth [bullet] use up to three times daily or as directed by a doctor [bullet] children under 2 years of age: Ask a doctor.

(iii) *For products containing menthol identified in § 341.14(b)(2) in a lozenge.* The product contains 5 to 10 milligrams menthol. Adults and children 2 to under 12 years of age: Allow lozenge to dissolve slowly in the mouth. May be repeated every hour as needed or as directed by a doctor. Children under 2 years of age: Consult a doctor.

(iv) *For products containing camphor identified in § 341.14(b)(1) for steam inhalation use.* The product contains 6.2 percent camphor. "[bullet] see important warnings under 'When using this product' " [appears as the first statement under the heading "Directions" and is highlighted in bold type] [bullet]

adults and children 2 years and older: (select one of the following, as appropriate: *For products formulated to be added directly to cold water inside a hot steam vaporizer.* [bullet] use 1 tablespoonful of solution for each quart of water or 1½ teaspoonsful of solution for each pint of water [bullet] add solution directly to cold water only in a hot steam vaporizer [bullet] follow manufacturer's directions for using vaporizer or *For products formulated to be placed in the medication chamber of a hot steam vaporizer.* [bullet] place water in the vaporizer and follow manufacturer's directions for using vaporizer [bullet] place solution in the medication chamber only) [bullet] breathe in the medicated vapors [bullet] use up to three times daily or as directed by a doctor [bullet] children under 2 years of age: Ask a doctor.

(v) *For products containing menthol identified in § 341.14(b)(2) for steam inhalation use.* The product contains 3.2 percent menthol. "[bullet] see important warnings under 'When using this product' "[appears as the first statement under the heading "Directions" and is highlighted in bold type] [bullet] adults and children 2 years and older: (select one of the following, as appropriate: *For products formulated to be added directly to cold water inside a hot steam vaporizer.* [bullet] use 1 tablespoonful of solution for each quart of water or 1½ teaspoonsful of solution for each pint of water [bullet] add solution directly to cold water only in a hot steam vaporizer [bullet] follow manufacturer's directions for using vaporizer or *For products formulated to be placed in the medication chamber of a hot steam vaporizer.* [bullet] place water in the vaporizer and follow manufacturer's directions for using vaporizer [bullet] place solution in the medication chamber only) [bullet] breathe in the medicated vapors [bullet] use up to three times daily or as directed by a doctor [bullet] children under 2 years of age: Ask a doctor.

(e) The word "physician" may be substituted for the word "doctor" in any of the labeling statements in this section.

(f) *Exemption from the general accidental overdose warning.* The labeling for antitussive drug products containing the active ingredient identified in §341.14(b)(2) marketed in accordance with §341.74(d)(2)(iii) is exempt from the requirement in §330.1(g) of this chapter that the labeling bear the general warning statement "In case of accidental overdose, seek professional assistance or contact a poison control center immediately." The labeling must continue to bear the first part of the general warning in §330.1(g) of this chapter, which states, "Keep this and all drugs out of the reach of children."

[52 FR 30055, Aug. 12, 1987; 52 FR 35610, Sept. 22, 1987; 53 FR 35809, Sept. 15, 1988; 55 FR 27808, July 6, 1990; 55 FR 40383, Oct. 3, 1990; 58 FR 54236, Oct. 20, 1993; 59 FR 29174, June 3, 1994; 59 FR 36051, July 15, 1994; 64 FR 13295, Mar. 17, 1999; 65 FR 8, Jan. 3, 2000; 65 FR 46867, Aug. 1, 2000; 67 FR 72559, Dec. 6, 2002]

§341.76 Labeling of bronchodilator drug products.

(a) *Statement of identity.* The labeling of the product contains the established name of the drug, if any, and identifies the product as a "bronchodilator."

(b) *Indication.* The labeling of the product states the following under the heading "Use": "for temporary relief of mild symptoms of intermittent asthma: [bullet][1] wheezing [bullet] tightness of chest [bullet] shortness of breath". Other truthful and nonmisleading statements, describing only the indication for use that has been established and listed in this paragraph (b) may also be used, as provided in §330.1(c)(2) of this chapter, subject to the provisions of section 502 of the Federal Food, Drug, and Cosmetic Act relating to misbranding and the prohibition in section 301(d) of the Federal Food, Drug, and Cosmetic Act against the introduction or delivery for introduction into interstate commerce of unapproved new drugs in violation of section 505(a) of the Federal Food, Drug, and Cosmetic Act.

(c) *Warnings.* The labeling of the product contains the following warnings under the heading "Warnings":

(1) The following statements shall appear after the subheading "Do not use" [in bold type]:

---

[1] See §201.66(b)(4) of this chapter for the definition of "bullet."

(i) "[Bullet] unless a doctor said you have asthma".

(ii) "[Bullet] if you are now taking a prescription monoamine oxidase inhibitor (MAOI) (certain drugs taken for depression, psychiatric or emotional conditions, or Parkinson's disease), or for 2 weeks after stopping the MAOI drug. If you do not know if your prescription drug contains an MAOI, ask a doctor or pharmacist before taking this product."

(2) The following information shall appear after the subheading "Ask a doctor before use if you have" [in bold type]: "[bullet] ever been hospitalized for asthma [bullet] heart disease [bullet] high blood pressure [bullet] diabetes [bullet] thyroid disease [bullet] seizures [bullet] narrow angle glaucoma [bullet] a psychiatric or emotional condition [bullet] trouble urinating due to an enlarged prostate gland".

(3) The following information shall appear after the subheading "Ask a doctor or pharmacist before use if you are" [in bold type]:

(i) "[Bullet] taking prescription drugs for asthma, obesity, weight control, depression, or psychiatric or emotional conditions".

(ii) "[Bullet] taking any drug that contains phenylephrine, pseudoephedrine, ephedrine, or caffeine (such as for allergy, cough-cold, or pain)".

(4) The following information shall appear after the subheading "When using this product" [in bold type]:

(i) "[Bullet] your blood pressure or heart rate may go up. This could increase your risk of heart attack or stroke, which may cause death." [in bold type]

(ii) "[Bullet] your risk of heart attack or stroke increases if you: [Bullet] have a history of high blood pressure or heart disease [Bullet] take this product more frequently or take more than the recommended dose". [in bold type]

(iii) "[Bullet] avoid foods or beverages that contain caffeine".

(iv) "[Bullet] avoid dietary supplements containing ingredients reported or claimed to have a stimulant effect".

(5) *For products containing ephedrine, ephedrine hydrochloride, ephedrine sulfate, or racephedrine hydrochloride identified in §341.16(a), (b), (c), and (f).* (i)

The following information shall appear after the subheading "Asthma alert: Because asthma may be life threatening, see a doctor if you" [in bold type]:

(A) "[Bullet] are not better in 60 minutes".

(B) "[Bullet] get worse".

(C) "[Bullet] need more than [insert total number of dosage units that equals 150 milligrams] in 24 hours".

(D) "[Bullet] use more than [insert total number of dosage units that equals 100 milligrams] in 24 hours for 3 or more days a week".

(E) "[Bullet] have more than 2 asthma attacks in a week".

(F) "These may be signs that your asthma is getting worse."

(G) "[Bullet] This product will not give you asthma relief as quickly as an inhaled bronchodilator."

(ii) This "Asthma alert" shall appear on any labeling that contains warnings and shall be the first warning statement under the heading "Warnings".

(6) *For products containing epinephrine, epinephrine bitartrate, or racepinephrine hydrochloride identified in § 341.16(d), (e), and (g).* (i) The following information shall appear after the subheading "Asthma alert: Because asthma may be life threatening, see a doctor if you" [in bold type]:

(A) "[Bullet] are not better in 20 minutes".

(B) "[Bullet] get worse".

(C) "[Bullet] need more than 12 inhalations in 24 hours".

(D) "[Bullet] use more than 9 inhalations in 24 hours for 3 or more days a week".

(E) "[Bullet] have more than 2 asthma attacks in a week".

(F) "These may be signs that your asthma is getting worse."

(ii) This "Asthma alert" shall appear on any labeling that contains warnings and shall be the first warning statement under the heading "Warnings."

(iii) *For products intended for use in a hand-held rubber bulb nebulizer.* The following statement shall also appear after the subheading "Do not use" along with the other information in paragraph (c)(1) of this section: "[bullet] if product is brown in color or cloudy".

(7) The following information shall appear after the subheading "Stop use and ask a doctor if" [in bold type]:

(i) "[Bullet] your asthma is getting worse (see Asthma alert)".

(ii) "[Bullet] you have difficulty sleeping".

(iii) "[Bullet] you have a rapid heart beat".

(iv) "[Bullet] you have tremors, nervousness, or seizure".

(d) *Directions.* The labeling of the product contains the following information under the heading "Directions":

(1) *For products containing ephedrine, ephedrine hydrochloride, ephedrine sulfate, or racephedrine hydrochloride identified in § 341.16(a), (b), (c), and (f):* (i) "[Bullet] do not take more than directed" [sentence appears as first bulleted statement under "Directions" and in bold type]

(ii) "[Bullet] adults and children 12 years of age and over: oral dose is 12.5 to 25 milligrams every 4 hours as needed. Do not take more than 150 milligrams in 24 hours".

(iii) "[Bullet] children under 12 years of age: ask a doctor".

(2) *For products containing epinephrine, epinephrine bitartrate, and racepinephrine hydrochloride identified in § 341.16(d), (e), and (g) for use in a hand-held rubber bulb nebulizer.* The ingredient is used in an aqueous solution at a concentration equivalent to 1-percent epinephrine.

(i) "[Bullet] do not use more than directed" [appears as first bulleted statement under "Directions" and in bold type].

(ii) "[Bullet] adults and children 4 years of age and over: 1 to 3 inhalations not more often than every 3 hours. Do not use more than 12 inhalations in 24 hours. The use of this product by children should be supervised by an adult."

(iii) "[Bullet] children under 4 years of age: ask a doctor".

(Collection of information requirement approved by the Office of Management and Budget under control number 0910–0237)

[51 FR 35339, Oct. 2, 1986, as amended at 52 FR 7126, Mar. 9, 1987; 52 FR 7830, Mar. 13, 1987; 53 FR 35810, Sept. 15, 1988; 58 FR 54242, Oct. 20, 1993; 61 FR 25146, May 20, 1996; 62 FR 9684, Mar. 4, 1997; 64 FR 13295, Mar. 17, 1999; 76 FR 44487, July 26, 2011]

§341.78 Labeling of expectorant drug products.

(a) *Statement of identity.* The labeling of the product contains the established name of the drug, if any, and identifies the product as an "expectorant."

(b) *Indications.* The labeling of the product states, under the heading "Indications," the following: "Helps loosen phlegm (mucus) and thin bronchial secretions to" (select one or more of the following: "rid the bronchial passageways of bothersome mucus," "drain bronchial tubes," and "make coughs more productive"). Other truthful and nonmisleading statements, describing only the indications for use that have been established and listed in this paragraph (b), may also be used, as provided in §330.1(c)(2) of this chapter, subject to the provisions of section 502 of the act relating to misbranding and the prohibition in section 301(d) of the act against the introduction or delivery for introduction into interstate commerce of unapproved new drugs in violation of section 505(a) of the act.

(c) *Warnings.* The labeling of the product contains the following warnings, under the heading "Warnings":

(1) "A persistent cough may be a sign of a serious condition. If cough persists for more than 1 week, tends to recur, or is accompanied by a fever, rash, or persistent headache, consult a doctor."

(2) *For expectorant drug products labeled for adults or for adults and children under 12 years of age.* "Do not take this product for persistent or chronic cough such as occurs with smoking, asthma, chronic bronchitis, or emphysema, or where cough is accompanied by excessive phlegm (mucus) unless directed by a doctor."

(3) *For expectorant drug products labeled only for children under 12 years of age.* "Do not give this product for persistent or chronic cough such as occurs with asthma or if cough is accompanied by excessive phlegm (mucus) unless directed by a doctor."

(d) *Directions.* The labeling of the product contains the following information under the heading "Directions" for products containing guaifenesin identified in §341.18: Adults and children 12 years of age and over: oral dosage is 200 to 400 milligrams every 4 hours not to exceed 2,400 milligrams in

24 hours. Children 6 to under 12 years of age: oral dosage is 100 to 200 milligrams every 4 hours not to exceed 1,200 milligrams in 24 hours. Children 2 to under 6 years of age: oral dosage is 50 to 100 milligrams every 4 hours not to exceed 600 milligrams in 24 hours. Children under 2 years of age: consult a doctor.

(e) The word "physician" may be substituted for the word "doctor" in any of the labeling statements in this section.

[54 FR 8509, Feb. 28, 1989, as amended at 57 FR 29177, June 30, 1992]

§341.80 Labeling of nasal decongestant drug products.

(a) *Statement of identity.* The labeling of the product contains the established name of the drug, if any, and identifies the product as a "nasal decongestant."

(b) *Indications.* The labeling of the product states, under the heading "Indications," the phrase listed in paragraph (b)(1) of this section, as appropriate, and may contain any additional phrases listed in paragraph (b)(2) of this section. Other truthful and nonmisleading statements, describing only the indications for use that have been established and listed in paragraphs (b)(1) and (b)(2) of this section, may also be used, as provided in §330.1(c)(2) of this chapter, subject to the provisions of section 502 of the Federal Food, Drug, and Cosmetic Act (the act) relating to misbranding and the prohibition in section 301(d) of the act against the introduction or delivery for introduction into interstate commerce of unapproved new drugs in violation of section 505(a) of the act.

(1) (Select one of the following: "For the temporary relief of nasal congestion" or "Temporarily relieves nasal congestion") (which may be followed by any of the following in paragraphs (b)(1) (i), (ii), and (iii) of this section):

(i) "due to" (select one of the following: "the common cold" or "a cold").

(ii) "due to" (select one of the following: "hay fever," "hay fever (allergic rhinitis)," "hay fever or other upper respiratory allergies," or "hay fever or other upper respiratory allergies (allergic rhinitis)").

(2) In addition to the information identified in paragraph (b)(1) of this

section, the labeling of the product may contain any (one or more) of the following statements:

(i) (Select one of the following: "For the temporary relief of" or "Temporarily relieves") (select one of the following: "stuffy nose," "stopped up nose," "nasal stuffiness," or "clogged up nose.")

(ii) (Select one of the following: "Reduces swelling of," "Decongests," or "Helps clear") "nasal passages; shrinks swollen membranes."

(iii) "Temporarily restores freer breathing through the nose."

(iv) "Helps decongest sinus openings and passages; temporarily relieves sinus congestion and pressure."

(v) "Promotes nasal and/or sinus drainage; temporarily relieves sinus congestion and pressure."

(c) *Warnings.* The labeling of the product contains the following warnings under the heading "Warnings":

(1) *Oral nasal decongestants*—(i) *For products containing phenylephrine hydrochloride, pseudoephedrine hydrochloride, pseudoephedrine sulfate, or phenylephrine bitartrate identified in § 341.20 (a)(1) through (a)(4) when labeled for adults.* (A) "Do not exceed recommended dosage. [first sentence in boldface type] If nervousness, dizziness, or sleeplessness occur, discontinue use and consult a doctor."

(B) "If symptoms do not improve within 7 days or are accompanied by fever, consult a doctor."

(C) "Do not take this product if you have heart disease, high blood pressure, thyroid disease, diabetes, or difficulty in urination due to enlargement of the prostate gland unless directed by a doctor."

(D) *Drug interaction precaution.* "Do not use if you are now taking a prescription monoamine oxidase inhibitor (MAOI) (certain drugs for depression, psychiatric, or emotional conditions, or Parkinson's disease), or for 2 weeks after stopping the MAOI drug. If you do not know if your prescription drug contains an MAOI, ask a doctor or pharmacist before taking this product."

(ii) *For products containing phenylephrine hydrochloride, pseudoephedrine hydrochloride, pseudoephedrine sulfate, or phenylephrine bitartrate identified in § 341.20 (a)(1) through (a)(4) when labeled*

for children under 12 years of age. (A) "Do not exceed recommended dosage. [first sentence in boldface type] If nervousness, dizziness, or sleeplessness occur, discontinue use and consult a doctor."

(B) "If symptoms do not improve within 7 days or are accompanied by fever, consult a doctor."

(C) "Do not give this product to a child who has heart disease, high blood pressure, thyroid disease, or diabetes unless directed by a doctor."

(D) *Drug interaction precaution.* "Do not use in a child who is taking a prescription monoamine oxidase inhibitor (MAOI) (certain drugs for depression, psychiatric, or emotional conditions, or Parkinson's disease), or for 2 weeks after stopping the MAOI drug. If you do not know if your child's prescription drug contains an MAOI, ask a doctor or pharmacist before giving this product."

(iii) *For oral nasal decongestant products labeled for both adults and children under 12 years of age.* The labeling of the product contains the warnings identified in paragraph (c)(1)(i) of this section.

(2) *Topical nasal decongestants*—(i) *For products containing any topical nasal decongestant identified in § 341.20(b) when labeled for adults.* (A) "Do not exceed recommended dosage." [sentence in boldface type]

(B) "This product may cause temporary discomfort such as burning, stinging, sneezing, or an increase in nasal discharge."

(C) "The use of this container by more than one person may spread infection."

(ii) *For products containing levmetamfetamine identified in § 341.20(b)(1) when used in an inhalant dosage form and when labeled for adults.* "Do not use this product for more than 7 days. Use only as directed. Frequent or prolonged use may cause nasal congestion to recur or worsen. If symptoms persist, ask a doctor."

(iii) *For products containing ephedrine, ephedrine hydrochloride, ephedrine sulfate, naphazoline hydrochloride, oxymetazoline hydrochloride, phenylephrine hydrochloride, or xylometazoline hydrochloride identified in § 341.20 (b)(2), (b)(3), (b)(4), (b)(6), (b)(7), (b)(8), and (b)(10) when used as nasal sprays, drops, or jellies and when labeled for adults.* (A) "Do not use this product for more than 3 days. Use only as directed. Frequent or prolonged use may cause nasal congestion to recur or worsen. If symptoms persist, consult a doctor."

(B) "Do not use this product if you have heart disease, high blood pressure, thyroid disease, diabetes, or difficulty in urination due to enlargement of the prostate gland unless directed by a doctor."

(iv) *For products containing naphazoline hydrochloride identified in §341.20(b)(6) at a concentration of 0.05 percent.* "Do not use this product in children under 12 years of age because it may cause sedation if swallowed."

(v) *For products containing propylhexedrine identified in §341.20(b)(9) when used in an inhalant dosage form and when labeled for adults.* "Do not use this product for more than 3 days. Use only as directed. Frequent or prolonged use may cause nasal congestion to recur or worsen. If symptoms persist, consult a doctor."

(vi) *For products containing any topical nasal decongestant identified in §341.20(b) when labeled for children under 12 years of age.* The labeling of the product contains the warnings identified in paragraph (c)(2)(i) of this section.

(vii) *For products containing levmetamfetamine identified in §341.20(b)(1) when used in an inhalant dosage form and when labeled for children under 12 years of age.* "Do not use this product for more than 7 days. Use only as directed. Frequent or prolonged use may cause nasal congestion to recur or worsen. If symptoms persist, ask a doctor."

(viii) *For products containing ephedrine, ephedrine hydrochloride, ephedrine sulfate, naphazoline hydrochloride, oxymetazoline hydrochloride, phenylephrine hydrochloride, or xylometazoline hydrochloride identified in §341.20(b)(2), (b)(3), (b)(4), (b)(6), (b)(7), (b)(8), and (b)(10) when used as nasal sprays, drops, or jellies and when labeled for children under 12 years of age.* (A) "Do not use this product for more than 3 days. Use only as directed. Frequent or prolonged use may cause nasal congestion to recur or worsen. If symptoms persist, consult a doctor."

(B) "Do not use this product in a child who has heart disease, high blood pressure, thyroid disease, or diabetes unless directed by a doctor."

(ix) *For products containing propylhexedrine identified in §341.20(b)(9) when used in an inhalant dosage form and when labeled for children under 12 years of age.* "Do not use this product for more than 3 days. Use only as directed. Frequent or prolonged use may cause nasal congestion to recur or worsen. If symptoms persist, consult a doctor."

(x) *For topical nasal decongestant products labeled for both adults and for children under 12 years of age.* The labeling of the product contains the applicable warnings identified in paragraphs (c)(2)(i), (c)(2)(ii), (c)(2)(iii), and (c)(2)(v) of this section.

(d) *Directions.* The labeling of the product contains the following information under the heading "Directions":

(1) *Oral nasal decongestants*—(i) *For products containing phenylephrine hydrochloride identified in §341.20(a)(1).* Adults and children 12 years of age and over: 10 milligrams every 4 hours not to exceed 60 milligrams in 24 hours. Children 6 to under 12 years of age: 5 milligrams every 4 hours not to exceed 30 milligrams in 24 hours. Children 2 to under 6 years of age: 2.5 milligrams every 4 hours not to exceed 15 milligrams in 24 hours. Children under 2 years of age: consult a doctor.

(ii) *For products containing pseudoephedrine hydrochloride or pseudoephedrine sulfate identified in §341.20 (a)(2) and (a)(3).* Adults and children 12 years of age and over: 60 milligrams every 4 to 6 hours not to exceed 240 milligrams in 24 hours. Children 6 to under 12 years of age: 30 milligrams every 4 to 6 hours not to exceed 120 milligrams in 24 hours. Children 2 to under 6 years of age: 15 milligrams every 4 to 6 hours not to exceed 60 milligrams in 24 hours. Children under 2 years of age: consult a doctor.

(iii) *For products containing phenylephrine bitartrate identified in §341.20(a)(4).* Include information on the number of dosage units and the quantity of water the dosage units are to be dissolved in prior to administration as shown in the following table:

265

Age [1]	Dose [1]
Adults and children 12 years of age and over	15.6 milligrams every 4 hours not to exceed 62.4 milligrams in 24 hours
Children 6 to under 12 years of age	7.8 milligrams every 4 hours not to exceed 31.2 milligrams in 24 hours
Children under 6 years of age	Ask a doctor

[1] Headings are not required to appear in the product's labeling

(2) *Topical nasal decongestants*—(i) *For products containing levmetamfetamine identified in § 341.20(b)(1) when used in an inhalant dosage form.* The product delivers in each 800 milliliters of air 0.04 to 0.150 milligrams of levmetamfetamine. Adults: 2 inhalations in each nostril not more often than every 2 hours. Children 6 to under 12 years of age (with adult supervision): 1 inhalation in each nostril not more often than every 2 hours. Children under 6 years of age: ask a doctor.

(ii) *For products containing ephedrine, ephedrine hydrochloride, or ephedrine sulfate identified in § 341.20(b) (2), (3), and (4)*—(A) *Nasal drops or sprays—For a 0.5-percent aqueous solution.* Adults and children 12 years of age and over: 2 or 3 drops or sprays in each nostril not more often than every 4 hours. Children 6 to under 12 years of age (with adult supervision): 1 or 2 drops or sprays in each nostril not more often than every 4 hours. Children under 6 years of age: consult a doctor.

(B) *Nasal jelly—For a 0.5-percent water-based jelly.* Adults and children 6 to under 12 years of age (with adult supervision): place a small amount in each nostril and inhale well back into the nasal passages. Use not more often than every 4 hours.

(iii) *For products containing naphazoline hydrochloride identified in § 341.20(b)(6)*—(A) *Nasal drops or sprays—(1) For a 0.05-percent aqueous solution.* Adults and children 12 years of age and over: 1 or 2 drops or sprays in each nostril not more often than every 6 hours. Do not give to children under 12 years of age unless directed by a doctor.

(2) *For a 0.025-percent aqueous solution.* Children 6 to under 12 years of age (with adult supervision): 1 or 2 drops or sprays in each nostril not more often

than every 6 hours. Children under 6 years of age: consult a doctor.

(B) *Nasal jelly—(1) For a 0.05-percent water-based jelly.* Adults and children 12 years of age and over: place a small amount in each nostril and inhale well back into the nasal passages. Use not more often than every 6 hours. Do not give to children under 12 years of age unless directed by a doctor.

(2) *For a 0.025-percent water-based jelly.* Children 6 to under 12 years of age (with adult supervision): place a small amount in each nostril and inhale well back into the nasal passages. Use not more often than every 6 hours. Children under 6 years of age: consult a doctor.

(iv) *For products containing oxymetazoline hydrochloride identified in § 341.20(b)(7)*—(A) *Nasal drops or sprays—(1) For a 0.05-percent aqueous solution.* Adults and children 6 to under 12 years of age (with adult supervision): 2 or 3 drops or sprays in each nostril not more often than every 10 to 12 hours. Do not exceed 2 doses in any 24-hour period. Children under 6 years of age: consult a doctor.

(2) *A 0.025-percent aqueous solution in a container having either a calibrated dropper or a metered-dose spray that delivers no more than 0.027 milligrams of oxymetazoline per three drops or three sprays.* Children 2 to under 6 years of age (with adult supervision): 2 or 3 drops or sprays in each nostril not more often than every 10 to 12 hours. Use only recommended amount. Do not exceed 2 doses in any 24-hour period. [previous two sentences in boldface type] Children under 2 years of age: consult a doctor.

(B) *Nasal jelly—For a 0.05-percent water-based jelly.* Adults and children 6 to under 12 years of age (with adult supervision): place a small amount in each nostril and inhale well back into the nasal passages. Use not more often than every 10 to 12 hours. Do not exceed 2 doses in any 24-hour period. Children under 6 years of age: consult a doctor.

(v) *For products containing phenylephrine hydrochloride identified in § 341.20(b)(8)*—(A) *Nasal drops or sprays—(1) For a 1-percent aqueous solution.* Adults and children 12 years of age and over: 2 or 3 drops or sprays in each nostril not more often than every 4 hours. Do not give to children under 12 years of age unless directed by a doctor.

(2) *For a 0.5-percent aqueous solution.* Adults and children 12 years of age and over: 2 or 3 drops or sprays in each nostril not more often than every 4 hours. Do not give to children under 12 years of age unless directed by a doctor.

(3) *For a 0.25-percent aqueous solution.* Adults and children 6 to under 12 years of age (with adult supervision): 2 or 3 drops or sprays in each nostril not more often than every 4 hours. Children under 6 years of age: consult a doctor.

(4) *A 0.125-percent aqueous solution in a container having either a calibrated dropper or a metered-dose spray that delivers no more than 0.135 milligrams of phenylephrine per three drops or three sprays.* Children 2 to under 6 years of age (with adult supervision): **2 or 3 drops or sprays in each nostril not more often than every 4 hours. Use only recommended amount.** [previous sentence in boldface type] Children under 2 years of age: consult a doctor.

(B) *Nasal jelly—(1) For a 1-percent water-based jelly.* Adults and children 12 years of age and over: place a small amount in each nostril and inhale well back into the nasal passages. Use not more often than every 4 hours. Do not give to children under 12 years of age unless directed by a doctor.

(2) *For a 0.5-percent water-based jelly.* Adults and children 12 years of age and over: place a small amount in each nostril and inhale well back into the nasal passages. Use not more often than every 4 hours. Do not give to children under 12 years of age unless directed by a doctor.

(3) *For a 0.25-percent water-based jelly.* Adults and children 6 to under 12 years of age (with adult supervision): place a small amount in each nostril and inhale well back into the nasal passages. Use not more often than every 4 hours. Children under 6 years of age: consult a doctor.

(vi) *For products containing propylhexedrine identified in §341.20(b)(9) when used in an inhalant dosage form.* The product delivers in each 800 milliliters of air 0.40 to 0.50 milligrams of propylhexedrine. Adults and children 6

to under 12 years of age (with adult supervision): 2 inhalations in each nostril not more often than every 2 hours. Children under 6 years of age: consult a doctor.

(vii) *For products containing xylometazoline hydrochloride identified in §341.20(b)(10)—(A) Nasal drops or sprays—(1) For a 0.1-percent aqueous solution.* Adults and children 12 years of age and over: 2 or 3 drops or sprays in each nostril not more often than every 8 to 10 hours. Do not give to children under 12 years of age unless directed by a doctor.

(2) *A 0.05-percent aqueous solution in a container having either a calibrated dropper or a metered-dose spray that delivers no more than 0.054 milligrams of xylometazoline per three drops or three sprays.* Children 6 to under 12 years of age (with adult supervision): 2 or 3 drops or sprays in each nostril not more often than every 8 to 10 hours. Children 2 to under 6 years of age (with adult supervision): **2 or 3 drops or sprays in each nostril not more often than every 8 to 10 hours. Use only recommended amount. Do not exceed 3 doses in any 24-hour period.** [previous two sentences in boldface type] Children under 2 years of age: consult a doctor.

(B) *Nasal jelly—(1) For a 0.1-percent water-based jelly.* Adults and children 12 years of age and over: place a small amount in each nostril and inhale well back into the nasal passages. Use not more often than every 8 to 10 hours. Do not give to children under 12 years of age unless directed by a doctor.

(2) *For a 0.05-percent water-based jelly.* Children 6 to under 12 years of age (with adult supervision): place a small amount in each nostril and inhale well back into the nasal passages. Use not more often than every 8 to 10 hours. Children under 6 years of age: consult a doctor.

(viii) *Other required statements—For products containing levmetamfetamine or propylhexedrine identified in §341.20(b)(1) or (b)(9) when used in an inhalant dosage form.* (A) "This inhaler is effective for a minimum of 3 months after first use."

(B) "Keep inhaler tightly closed."

[59 FR 43409, Aug. 23, 1994, as amended at 63 FR 40650, July 30, 1998; 64 FR 13295, Mar. 17, 1999; 65 FR 8, Jan. 3, 2000; 70 FR 58977, Oct. 11, 2005; 71 FR 43362, Aug. 1, 2006]

§ 341.85 Labeling of permitted combinations of active ingredients.

The statements of identity, indications, warnings, and directions for use, respectively, applicable to each ingredient in the product may be combined to eliminate duplicative words or phrases so that the resulting information is clear and understandable.

(a) *Statement of identity.* For a combination drug product that has an established name, the labeling of the product states the established name of the combination drug product, followed by the statement of identity for each ingredient in the combination, as established in the statement of identity sections of the applicable OTC drug monographs. If there is no established name, the labeling of the product states the statement of identity for each ingredient in the combination, as established in the statement of identity sections of the applicable OTC drug monographs, unless otherwise stated in this paragraph (a).

(1) *For permitted combinations identified in § 341.40(a), (c), (f), (g), (l), (m), (n), (o), (q), and (r) containing an analgesic-antipyretic active ingredient.* The analgesic-antipyretic component of the product shall be identified as a "pain reliever" or "analgesic (pain reliever)." If the product is also labeled to relieve fever, then the analgesic-antipyretic component is identified as a "pain reliever-fever reducer" or "analgesic (pain reliever)-antipyretic (fever reducer)."

(2) [Reserved]

(b) *Indications.* The labeling of the product states, under the heading "Uses," the indication(s) for each ingredient in the combination, as established in the indications sections of the applicable OTC drug monographs, unless otherwise stated in this paragraph (b). Other truthful and nonmisleading statements, describing only the indications for use that have been established and listed in the applicable OTC drug monographs or listed in this paragraph (b), may also be used, as provided in

§ 330.1(c)(2) of this chapter, subject to the provisions of section 502 of the Federal Food, Drug, and Cosmetic Act (the act) relating to misbranding and the prohibition in section 301(d) of the act against the introduction or delivery for introduction into interstate commerce of unapproved new drugs in violation of section 505(a) of the act.

(1) *For permitted combinations containing an analgesic-antipyretic active ingredient identified in § 341.40(a), (c), (f), (g), (l), (m), (n), (o), (q), and (r) when labeled for relief of general cough-cold symptoms and/or the common cold.* (i) The labeling for the analgesic-antipyretic ingredients states "[bullet] temporarily relieves [bullet] minor aches and pains [bullet] headache" and "[bullet] temporarily reduces fever".

(ii) The labeling for the cough-cold ingredient(s) may follow a separate bullet(s) or may be combined with the relieves part of the indication in paragraph (b)(1)(i) of this section.

(2) *For permitted combinations containing an analgesic-antipyretic active ingredient identified in § 341.40(a), (c), (f), (g), (m), (q), and (r) when labeled for relief of hay fever/allergic rhinitis and/or nasal congestion symptoms.* (i) The labeling for the analgesic-antipyretic ingredients states "[bullet] temporarily relieves [bullet] minor aches and pains [bullet] headache".

(ii) The indication(s) for the cough-cold ingredient(s) consists of the labeling for antihistamines in § 341.72(b)(1) or (b)(2) and/or nasal decongestants in § 341.80(b)(1)(ii), as appropriate, and the labeling for any other cough-cold combination. This labeling may follow a separate bullet(s) or may be combined with the indication in paragraph (b)(2)(i) of this section.

(3) *For permitted combinations containing an oral analgesic-antipyretic active ingredient identified in § 341.40(a), (c), (f), (g), (m), (q), and (r) when labeled for relief of general cough-cold symptoms and/or the common cold and for relief of hay fever/allergic rhinitis and/or nasal congestion symptoms.* The labeling states both indications in paragraphs (b)(1) and (b)(2) of this section.

(4) *For permitted combinations containing an oral anesthetic-analgesic active ingredient identified in § 341.40(k), (s), (t), (z), (aa), and (bb).* The labeling for

the anesthetic-analgesic ingredients in part 356 of this chapter should be used.

(5) *For permitted combinations containing camphor, menthol, and eucalyptus oil identified in §341.40(u).* The labeling for antitussive ingredients in §341.74(b) should be used.

(6) *For permitted combinations containing levmetamfetamine with aromatics identified in §341.40(v).* The labeling for nasal decongestant ingredients in §341.80(b) should be used.

(7) *Other allowable statements.* In addition to the required information identified in paragraph (b) of this section, the labeling of the combination drug product may contain any of the "other allowable statements" (if any), that are identified in the applicable OTC drug monographs, provided such statements are neither placed in direct conjunction with information required to appear in the labeling nor occupy labeling space with greater prominence or conspicuousness than the required information.

(c) *Warnings.* The labeling of the product states, under the heading "Warnings," the warning(s) for each ingredient in the combination, as established in the warnings sections of the applicable OTC drug monographs, unless otherwise stated in paragraph (c) of this section.

(1) *For permitted combinations containing an antitussive and an analgesic-antipyretic identified in §341.40(f), (g), (l), and (m).* The labeling states the following warnings:

(i) *For products labeled only for adults.* The following warning should be used instead of the warnings in §341.74(c)(1) and part 343 of this chapter: "Stop use and ask a doctor if [in bold type] [bullet] pain or cough gets worse or lasts more than 7 days [bullet] fever gets worse or lasts more than 3 days [bullet] redness or swelling is present [bullet] new symptoms occur [bullet] cough comes back or occurs with rash or headache that lasts. These could be signs of a serious condition."

(ii) *For products labeled only for children under 12 years of age.* The following warning should be used instead of the warnings in §341.74(c)(3) and part 343 of this chapter: "Stop use and ask a doctor if [in bold type] [bullet] pain or cough gets worse or lasts more than 5 days [bullet] fever gets worse or lasts more than 3 days [bullet] redness or swelling is present [bullet] new symptoms occur [bullet] cough comes back or occurs with rash or headache that lasts. These could be signs of a serious condition."

(iii) *For products labeled for both adults and for children under 12 years of age.* The following warning should be used instead of the warnings in §341.74(c)(2) and part 343 of this chapter: "Stop use and ask a doctor if [in bold type] [bullet] pain or cough gets worse or lasts more than 5 days (children) or 7 days (adults) [bullet] fever gets worse or lasts more than 3 days [bullet] redness or swelling is present [bullet] new symptoms occur [bullet] cough comes back or occurs with rash or headache that lasts. These could be signs of a serious condition."

(2) *For permitted combinations containing an expectorant and an analgesic-antipyretic identified in §341.40(o).* The labeling states the following warnings:

(i) *For products labeled only for adults.* The warning in paragraph (c)(1)(i) of this section should be used instead of the warnings in §341.78(c)(3) and part 343 of this chapter.

(ii) *For products labeled only for children under 12 years of age.* The warning in paragraph (c)(1)(ii) of this section should be used instead of the warnings in §341.78(c)(3) and part 343 of this chapter.

(iii) *For products labeled for both adults and for children under 12 years of age.* The warning in paragraph (c)(1)(iii) of this section should be used instead of the warnings in §341.78(c)(3) and part 343 of this chapter.

(3) *For permitted combinations containing a nasal decongestant and an analgesic-antipyretic identified in §341.40(c), (g), (m), (n), (q), and (r).* The labeling states the following warnings:

(i) *For products labeled only for adults.* The following warning should be used instead of the warnings in §341.80(c)(1)(i)(B) and part 343 of this chapter: "Stop use and ask a doctor if [in bold type] [bullet] pain or nasal congestion gets worse or lasts more than 7 days [bullet] fever gets worse or lasts more than 3 days [bullet] redness or swelling is present [bullet] new symptoms occur".

(ii) *For products labeled for only children under 12 years of age.* The following warning should be used instead of the warnings in § 341.80(c)(1)(ii)(B) and part 343 of this chapter: "Stop use and ask a doctor if [in bold type] [bullet] pain or nasal congestion gets worse or lasts more than 5 days [bullet] fever gets worse or lasts more than 3 days [bullet] redness or swelling is present [bullet] new symptoms occur".

(iii) *For products labeled for both adults and children under 12 years of age.* The following warning should be used instead of the warnings in § 341.80(c)(1)(iii) and part 343 of this chapter: "Stop use and ask a doctor if [in bold type] [bullet] pain or nasal congestion gets worse or lasts more than 5 days (children) or 7 days (adults) [bullet] fever gets worse or lasts more than 3 days [bullet] redness or swelling is present [bullet] new symptoms occur".

(4) *For permitted combinations containing an antihistamine combined with an oral antitussive.* The labeling states the warning "When using this product [in bold type] [bullet] may cause marked drowsiness." The word "marked" may be deleted from the warning upon petition under the provisions of § 10.30 of this chapter provided adequate data are submitted to demonstrate that the combination product does not cause a significant increase in drowsiness as compared with each active ingredient when tested alone. The petition and the data it contains will be maintained in a permanent file for public review in the Division of Dockets Management (HFA–305), Food and Drug Administration, 5630 Fishers Lane, rm. 1061, Rockville, MD 20852.

(5) *For permitted combinations containing camphor, menthol, and eucalyptus oil identified in § 341.40(u).* The labeling states the warnings for topical antitussive ingredients in § 341.74(c).

(6) *For permitted combinations containing levmetamfetamine with aromatics identified in § 341.40(v).* The labeling states the warnings for topical nasal decongestant ingredients in § 341.80(c)(2).

(d) *Directions.* The labeling of the product states, under the heading "Directions," directions that conform to the directions established for each ingredient in the directions sections of the applicable OTC drug monographs, unless otherwise stated in paragraph (d) of this section. When the time intervals or age limitations for administration of the individual ingredients differ, the directions for the combination product may not exceed any maximum dosage limits established for the individual ingredients in the applicable OTC drug monograph.

(1) *For permitted combinations containing an anesthetic/analgesic and/or a demulcent in a liquid dosage form identified in § 341.40(k), (s), (t), (w), (x), (y), (z), (aa), and (bb).* The labeling states "[optional, bullet] gargle, swish around, or keep in the mouth for at least 1 minute and then swallow. Do not spit out."

(2) *For permitted combinations containing camphor, menthol, and eucalyptus oil identified in § 341.40(u).* The labeling states the directions for topical antitussive ingredients in § 341.74(d).

(3) *For permitted combinations containing levmetamfetamine with aromatics identified in § 341.40(v).* The labeling states the directions for topical nasal decongestant ingredients in § 341.80(d)(2)(i) and (d)(2)(viii).

[67 FR 78170, Dec. 23, 2002, as amended at 70 FR 58977, Oct. 11, 2005; 71 FR 43362, Aug. 1, 2006]

§ 341.90 Professional labeling.

The labeling of the product provided to health professionals (but not to the general public) may contain the following additional dosage information for products containing the active ingredients identified below:

(a) *For products containing ephedrine, ephedrine hydrochloride, ephedrine sulfate, or racephedrine hydrochloride identified in § 341.16 (a), (b), (c), and (f).* Children 6 to under 12 years of age: oral dosage is 6.25 to 12.5 milligrams every 4 hours, not to exceed 75 milligrams in 24 hours. Children 2 to under 6 years of age: oral dosage is 0.3 to 0.5 milligram per kilogram of body weight every 4 hours, not to exceed 2 milligrams per kilogram of body weight in 24 hours.

(b) *For products containing chlophedianol hydrochloride identified in 341.14(a)(1).* Children 2 to under 6 years of age: oral dosage is 12.5 milligrams every 6 to 8 hours, not to exceed 50 milligrams in 24 hours.

(c) *For products containing codeine ingredients identified in §341.14(a)(2)*. (1) Children 2 to under 6 years of age: Oral dosage is 1 milligram per kilogram body weight per day administered in four equal divided doses. The average body weight for each age may also be used to determine dosage as follows: For children 2 years of age (average body weight, 12 kilograms), the oral dosage is 3 milligrams every 4 to 6 hours, not to exceed 12 milligrams in 24 hours; for children 3 years of age (average body weight, 14 kilograms), the oral dosage is 3.5 milligrams every 4 to 6 hours, not to exceed 14 milligrams in 24 hours; for children 4 years of age (average body weight, 16 kilograms), the oral dosage is 4 milligrams every 4 to 6 hours, not to exceed 16 milligrams in 24 hours: for children 5 years of age (average body weight, 18 kilograms), the oral dosage is 4.5 milligrams every 4 to 6 hours, not to exceed 18 milligrams in 24 hours. The manufacturer must relate these dosages for its specific product dosages for its specific product to the use of the calibrated measuring device discussed in paragraph (c)(3) of this section. If age is used to determine the dose, the directions must include instructions to reduce the dose for low-weight children.

(2) Parents should be instructed to obtain and use a calibrated measuring device for administering the drug to the child, to use extreme care in measuring the dosage, and not exceed the recommended daily dosage.

(3) A dispensing device (such as a dropper calibrated for age or weight) should be dispensed along with the product when it is intended for use in children 2 to under 6 years of age to prevent possible overdose due to improper measuring of the dose.

(4) Codeine is not recommended for use in children under 2 years of age. Children under 2 years may be more susceptible to the respiratory depressant effects of codeine, including respiratory arrest, coma, and death.

(d) *The following labeling indication may be used for products containing guaifenesin identified in §341.18 when used as a single ingredient product.* "Helps loosen phlegm and thin bronchial secretions in patients with stable chronic bronchitis."

(e) *For products containing brompheniramine maleate identified in §341.12(a)*. Children 2 to under 6 years of age: oral dosage is 1 milligram every 4 to 6 hours, not to exceed 6 milligrams in 24 hours.

(f) *For products containing chlorcyclizine hydrochloride identified in §341.12(b)*. Children 6 to under 12 years of age: oral dosage is 12.5 milligrams every 6 to 8 hours, not to exceed 37.5 milligrams in 24 hours. Children 2 to under 6 years of age: oral dosage is 6.25 milligrams every 6 to 8 hours, not to exceed 18.75 milligrams in 24 hours.

(g) *For products containing chlorpheniramine maleate identified in §341.12(c)*. Children 2 to under 6 years of age: oral dosage is 1 milligram every 4 to 6 hours, not to exceed 6 milligrams in 24 hours.

(h) *For products containing dexbrompheniramine maleate identified in §341.12(d)*. Children 2 to under 6 years of age: oral dosage is 0.5 milligram every 4 to 6 hours, not to exceed 3 milligrams in 24 hours.

(i) *For products containing dexchlorpheniramine maleate identified in §341.12(e)*. Children 2 to under 6 years: oral dosage is 0.5 milligram every 4 to 6 hours, not to exceed 3 milligrams in 24 hours.

(j) *For products containing diphenhydramine citrate identified in §341.12(f)*. Children 2 to under 6 years of age: oral dosage is 9.5 milligrams every 4 to 6 hours, not to exceed 57 milligrams in 24 hours.

(k) *For products containing diphenhydramine hydrochloride identified in §341.12(g)*. Children 2 to under 6 years of age: oral dosage is 6.25 milligrams every 4 to 6 hours, not to exceed 37.5 mg in 24 hours.

(l) *For products containing doxylamine succinate identified in §341.12(h)*. Children 2 to under 6 years of age: oral dosage is 1.9 to 3.125 milligrams every 4 to 6 hours, not to exceed 18.75 milligrams in 24 hours.

(m) *For products containing phenindamine tartrate identified in §341.12(i)*. Children 2 to under 6 years of age: oral dosage is 6.25 milligrams every 4 to 6 hours, not to exceed 37.5 milligrams in 24 hours.

(n) *For products containing pheniramine maleate identified in*

§ 341.12(j). Children 2 to under 6 years of age: oral dosage is 3.125 to 6.25 milligrams every 4 to 6 hours, not to exceed 37.5 milligrams in 24 hours.

(o) *For products containing pyrilamine maleate identified in § 341.12(k).* Children 2 to under 6 years of age: oral dosage is 6.25 to 12.5 milligrams every 6 to 8 hours, not to exceed 50 milligrams in 24 hours.

(p) *For products containing thonzylamine hydrochloride identified in § 341.12(l).* Children 2 to under 6 years of age: oral dosage is 12.5 to 25 milligrams every 4 to 6 hours, not to exceed 150 milligrams in 24 hours.

(q) *For products containing triprolidine hydrochloride identified in § 341.12(m).* Children 4 to under 6 years of age: oral dosage is 0.938 milligram every 4 to 6 hours, not to exceed 3.744 milligrams in 24 hours. Children 2 to under 4 years of age: oral dosage is 0.625 milligram every 4 to 6 hours, not to exceed 2.5 milligrams in 24 hours. Infants 4 months to under 2 years of age: oral dosage is 0.313 milligram every 4 to 6 hours, not to exceed 1.252 milligrams in 24 hours.

(r) *For products containing diphenhydramine citrate identified in § 341.14(a)(5).* Children 2 to under 6 years of age: oral dosage is 9.5 milligrams every 4 hours, not to exceed 57 milligrams in 24 hours.

(s) *For products containing diphenhydramine hydrochloride identified in § 341.14(a)(6).* Children 2 to under 6 years of age: oral dosage is 6.25 milligrams every 4 hours, not to exceed 37.5 milligrams in 24 hours.

[51 FR 35339, Oct. 2, 1986, as amended at 52 FR 30057, Aug. 12, 1987; 54 FR 8509, Feb. 28, 1989; 57 FR 58376, Dec. 9, 1992; 59 FR 4218, Jan. 28, 1994; 59 FR 29174, June 3, 1994; 59 FR 36051, July 15, 1994]

PART 343—INTERNAL ANALGESIC, ANTIPYRETIC, AND ANTIRHEUMATIC DRUG PRODUCTS FOR OVER-THE-COUNTER HUMAN USE

Subpart A—General Provisions

Subpart B—Active Ingredients

Subpart C—Labeling

Subpart D—Testing Procedures

AUTHORITY: 21 U.S.C. 321, 351, 352, 353, 355, 360, 371.

SOURCE: 63 FR 56814, Oct. 23, 1998, unless otherwise noted.

Subpart A—General Provisions

§ 343.1   Scope.

(a) An over-the-counter analgesic-antipyretic drug product in a form suitable for oral administration is generally recognized as safe and effective and is not misbranded if it meets each of the conditions in this part in addition to each of the general conditions established in § 330.1 of this chapter.

(b) References in this part to regulatory sections of the Code of Federal Regulations are to chapter I of title 21 unless otherwise noted.

§ 343.3   Definitions.

As used in this part:

Analgesic—antipyretic drug. An agent used to alleviate pain and to reduce fever.

Cardiovascular drug. An agent used to prevent ischemic events.

Rheumatologic drug. An agent used for the treatment of rheumatologic disorders.

Subpart B—Active Ingredients

§ 343.10   [Reserved]

§ 343.12   Cardiovascular active ingredients.

(a) Aspirin.

(b) Buffered aspirin. Aspirin identified in paragraph (a) of this section may be buffered with any antacid ingredient(s) identified in § 331.11 of this chapter provided that the finished product contains at least 1.9 milli-equivalents of acid-neutralizing capacity per 325 milligrams of aspirin as measured by the procedure provided in the United States Pharmacopeia 23/National Formulary 18.

§ 343.13 Rheumatologic active ingredients.

(a) Aspirin.

(b) Buffered aspirin. Aspirin identified in paragraph (a) of this section may be buffered with any antacid ingredient(s) identified in §331.11 of this chapter provided that the finished product contains at least 1.9 milli-equivalents of acid-neutralizing capacity per 325 milligrams of aspirin as measured by the procedure provided in the United States Pharmacopeia 23/National Formulary 18.

§ 343.20 [Reserved]

§ 343.22 Permitted combinations of active ingredients for cardiovascular-rheumatologic use.

Combinations containing aspirin must meet the standards of an acceptable dissolution test, as set forth in §343.90. The following combinations are permitted: Aspirin identified in §§343.12 and 343.13 may be combined with any antacid ingredient identified in §331.11 of this chapter or any combination of antacids permitted in accordance with §331.10(a) of this chapter provided that the finished product meets the requirements of §331.10 of this chapter and is marketed in a form intended for ingestion as a solution.

Subpart C—Labeling

§§ 343.50–343.60 [Reserved]

§ 343.80 Professional labeling.

The labeling of an over-the-counter drug product written for health professionals (but not for the general public) shall consist of the following:

(a) *For products containing aspirin identified in §§343.12 and 343.13 or permitted combinations identified in §343.22.* (These products must meet United States Pharmacopeia (USP) standards for dissolution or drug release in §343.90.)

(1) The labeling contains the following prescribing information under the heading "Comprehensive Prescribing Information" and the subheadings "Description," "Clinical Pharmacology," "Clinical Studies," "Animal Toxicology," "Indications and Usage," "Contraindications," "Warnings," "Precautions," "Adverse Reactions," "Drug Abuse and Dependence," "Overdosage," "Dosage and Administration," and "How Supplied" in the exact language and the exact order provided as follows:

COMPREHENSIVE PRESCRIBING
INFORMATION

DESCRIPTION

(*Insert the proprietary name and the established name (if any) of the drug, type of dosage form (followed by the phrase "for oral administration"), the established name(s) and quantity of the active ingredient(s) per dosage unit, the total sodium content in milligrams per dosage unit if the sodium content of a single recommended dose is 5 milligrams or more, the established name(s) (in alphabetical order) of any inactive ingredient(s) which may cause an allergic hypersensitivity reaction, the pharmacological or therapeutic class of the drug, and the chemical name(s) and structural formula(s) of the drug.*) Aspirin is an odorless white, needle-like crystalline or powdery substance. When exposed to moisture, aspirin hydrolyzes into salicylic and acetic acids, and gives off a vinegary-odor. It is highly lipid soluble and slightly soluble in water.

CLINICAL PHARMACOLOGY

Mechanism of Action: Aspirin is a more potent inhibitor of both prostaglandin synthesis and platelet aggregation than other salicylic acid derivatives. The differences in activity between aspirin and salicylic acid are thought to be due to the acetyl group on the aspirin molecule. This acetyl group is responsible for the inactivation of cyclooxygenase via acetylation.

PHARMACOKINETICS

Absorption: In general, immediate release aspirin is well and completely absorbed from the gastrointestinal (GI) tract. Following absorption, aspirin is hydrolyzed to salicylic acid with peak plasma levels of salicylic acid occurring within 1–2 hours of dosing (see PHARMACOKINETICS—*Metabolism*). The rate of absorption from the GI tract is dependent upon the dosage form, the presence or absence of food, gastric pH (the presence or absence of GI antacids or buffering agents), and other physiologic factors. Enteric coated aspirin products are erratically absorbed from the GI tract.

Distribution: Salicylic acid is widely distributed to all tissues and fluids in the body including the central nervous system (CNS), breast milk, and fetal tissues. The highest concentrations are found in the plasma, liver, renal cortex, heart, and lungs. The protein binding of salicylate is concentration-dependent, *i.e.,* nonlinear. At low concentrations (<100 micrograms/milliliter (μg/mL)), approximately 90 percent of plasma salicylate is bound to albumin while at higher concentrations (>400 μg/mL), only about 75 percent is bound. The early signs of salicylic overdose (salicylism), including tinnitus (ringing in the ears), occur at plasma concentrations approximating 200 μg/mL. Severe toxic effects are associated with levels >400 μg/mL. (See ADVERSE REACTIONS and OVERDOSAGE.)

Metabolism: Aspirin is rapidly hydrolyzed in the plasma to salicylic acid such that plasma levels of aspirin are essentially undetectable 1–2 hours after dosing. Salicylic acid is primarily conjugated in the liver to form salicyluric acid, a phenolic glucuronide, an acyl glucuronide, and a number of minor metabolites. Salicylic acid has a plasma half-life of approximately 6 hours. Salicylate metabolism is saturable and total body clearance decreases at higher serum concentrations due to the limited ability of the liver to form both salicyluric acid and phenolic glucuronide. Following toxic doses (10–20 grams (g)), the plasma half-life may be increased to over 20 hours.

Elimination: The elimination of salicylic acid follows zero order pharmacokinetics; (*i.e.,* the rate of drug elimination is constant in relation to plasma concentration). Renal excretion of unchanged drug depends upon urine pH. As urinary pH rises above 6.5, the renal clearance of free salicylate increases from <5 percent to >80 percent. Alkalinization of the urine is a key concept in the management of salicylate overdose. (See OVERDOSAGE.) Following therapeutic doses, approximately 10 percent is found excreted in the urine as salicylic acid, 75 percent as salicyluric acid, and 10 percent phenolic and 5 percent acyl glucuronides of salicylic acid.

Pharmacodynamics Aspirin affects platelet aggregation by irreversibly inhibiting prostaglandin cyclo-oxygenase. This effect lasts for the life of the platelet and prevents the formation of the platelet aggregating factor thromboxane A2. Nonacetylated salicylates do not inhibit this enzyme and have no effect on platelet aggregation. At somewhat higher doses, aspirin reversibly inhibits the formation of prostaglandin I_2 (prostacyclin), which is an arterial vasodilator and inhibits platelet aggregation.

At higher doses aspirin is an effective anti-inflammatory agent, partially due to inhibition of inflammatory mediators via cyclo-oxygenase inhibition in peripheral tissues. In vitro studies suggest that other mediators of inflammation may also be suppressed by aspirin administration, although the precise mechanism of action has not been elucidated. It is this nonspecific suppression of cyclo-oxygenase activity in peripheral tissues following large doses that leads to the primary side effect of gastric irritation. (See ADVERSE REACTIONS.)

CLINICAL STUDIES

Ischemic Stroke and Transient Ischemic Attack (TIA): In clinical trials of subjects with TIA's due to fibrin platelet emboli or ischemic stroke, aspirin has been shown to significantly reduce the risk of the combined endpoint of stroke or death and the combined endpoint of TIA, stroke, or death by about 13–18 percent.

Suspected Acute Myocardial Infarction (MI): In a large, multi-center study of aspirin, streptokinase, and the combination of aspirin and streptokinase in 17,187 patients with suspected acute MI, aspirin treatment produced a 23-percent reduction in the risk of vascular mortality. Aspirin was also shown to have an additional benefit in patients given a thrombolytic agent.

Prevention of Recurrent MI and Unstable Angina Pectoris: These indications are supported by the results of six large, randomized, multi-center, placebo-controlled trials of predominantly male post-MI subjects and one randomized placebo-controlled study of men with unstable angina pectoris. Aspirin therapy in MI subjects was associated with a significant reduction (about 20 percent) in the risk of the combined endpoint of subsequent death and/or nonfatal reinfarction in these patients. In aspirin-treated unstable angina patients the event rate was reduced to 5 percent from the 10 percent rate in the placebo group.

Chronic Stable Angina Pectoris: In a randomized, multi-center, double-blind trial designed to assess the role of aspirin for prevention of MI in patients with chronic stable angina pectoris, aspirin significantly reduced the primary combined endpoint of nonfatal MI, fatal MI, and sudden death by 34 percent. The secondary endpoint for vascular events (first occurrence of MI, stroke, or vascular death) was also significantly reduced (32 percent).

Revascularization Procedures: Most patients who undergo coronary artery revascularization procedures have already had symptomatic coronary artery disease for which aspirin is indicated. Similarly, patients with lesions of the carotid bifurcation sufficient to require carotid endarterectomy are likely to have had a precedent event. Aspirin is recommended for patients who undergo revascularization procedures if there is a preexisting condition for which aspirin is already indicated.

Rheumatologic Diseases: In clinical studies in patients with rheumatoid arthritis, juvenile rheumatoid arthritis, ankylosing spondylitis and osteoarthritis, aspirin has been shown to be effective in controlling various indices of clinical disease activity.

ANIMAL TOXICOLOGY

The acute oral 50 percent lethal dose in rats is about 1.5 g/kilogram (kg) and in mice 1.1 g/kg. Renal papillary necrosis and decreased urinary concentrating ability occur in rodents chronically administered high doses. Dose-dependent gastric mucosal injury occurs in rats and humans. Mammals may develop aspirin toxicosis associated with GI symptoms, circulatory effects, and central nervous system depression. (See OVERDOSAGE.)

INDICATIONS AND USAGE

Vascular Indications (Ischemic Stroke, TIA, Acute MI, Prevention of Recurrent MI, Unstable Angina Pectoris, and Chronic Stable Angina Pectoris): Aspirin is indicated to: (1) Reduce the combined risk of death and nonfatal stroke in patients who have had ischemic stroke or transient ischemia of the brain due to fibrin platelet emboli, (2) reduce the risk of vascular mortality in patients with a suspected acute MI, (3) reduce the combined risk of death and nonfatal MI in patients with a previous MI or unstable angina pectoris, and (4) reduce the combined risk of MI and sudden death in patients with chronic stable angina pectoris.

Revascularization Procedures (Coronary Artery Bypass Graft (CABG), Percutaneous Transluminal Coronary Angioplasty (PTCA), and Carotid Endarterectomy): Aspirin is indicated in patients who have undergone revascularization procedures (*i.e.*, CABG, PTCA, or carotid endarterectomy) when there is a preexisting condition for which aspirin is already indicated.

Rheumatologic Disease Indications (Rheumatoid Arthritis, Juvenile Rheumatoid Arthritis, Spondyloarthropathies, Osteoarthritis, and the Arthritis and Pleurisy of Systemic Lupus Erythematosus (SLE)): Aspirin is indicated for the relief of the signs and symptoms of rheumatoid arthritis, juvenile rheumatoid arthritis, osteoarthritis, spondyloarthropathies, and arthritis and pleurisy associated with SLE.

CONTRAINDICATIONS

Allergy: Aspirin is contraindicated in patients with known allergy to nonsteroidal anti-inflammatory drug products and in patients with the syndrome of asthma, rhinitis, and nasal polyps. Aspirin may cause severe urticaria, angioedema, or bronchospasm (asthma).

Reye's Syndrome: Aspirin should not be used in children or teenagers for viral infections, with or without fever, because of the risk of Reye's syndrome with concomitant use of aspirin in certain viral illnesses.

WARNINGS

Alcohol Warning: Patients who consume three or more alcoholic drinks every day should be counseled about the bleeding risks involved with chronic, heavy alcohol use while taking aspirin.

Coagulation Abnormalities: Even low doses of aspirin can inhibit platelet function leading to an increase in bleeding time. This can adversely affect patients with inherited (hemophilia) or acquired (liver disease or vitamin K deficiency) bleeding disorders.

GI Side Effects: GI side effects include stomach pain, heartburn, nausea, vomiting, and gross GI bleeding. Although minor upper GI symptoms, such as dyspepsia, are common and can occur anytime during therapy, physicians should remain alert for signs of ulceration and bleeding, even in the absence of previous GI symptoms. Physicians should inform patients about the signs and symptoms of GI side effects and what steps to take if they occur.

Peptic Ulcer Disease: Patients with a history of active peptic ulcer disease should avoid using aspirin, which can cause gastric mucosal irritation and bleeding.

PRECAUTIONS

General

Renal Failure: Avoid aspirin in patients with severe renal failure (glomerular filtration rate less than 10 mL/minute).

Hepatic Insufficiency: Avoid aspirin in patients with severe hepatic insufficiency.

Sodium Restricted Diets: Patients with sodium-retaining states, such as congestive heart failure or renal failure, should avoid sodium-containing buffered aspirin preparations because of their high sodium content.

Laboratory Tests

Aspirin has been associated with elevated hepatic enzymes, blood urea nitrogen and serum creatinine, hyperkalemia, proteinuria, and prolonged bleeding time.

Drug Interactions

Angiotensin Converting Enzyme (ACE) Inhibitors: The hyponatremic and hypotensive effects of ACE inhibitors may be diminished by the concomitant administration of aspirin due to its indirect effect on the renin-angiotensin conversion pathway.

Acetazolamide: Concurrent use of aspirin and acetazolamide can lead to high serum concentrations of acetazolamide (and toxicity) due to competition at the renal tubule for secretion.

Anticoagulant Therapy (Heparin and Warfarin): Patients on anticoagulation therapy are at increased risk for bleeding because of drug-drug interactions and the effect on platelets. Aspirin can displace warfarin from protein binding sites, leading to prolongation of both the prothrombin time and the bleeding time. Aspirin can increase the anticoagulant activity of heparin, increasing bleeding risk.

Anticonvulsants: Salicylate can displace protein-bound phenytoin and valproic acid, leading to a decrease in the total concentration of phenytoin and an increase in serum valproic acid levels.

Beta Blockers: The hypotensive effects of beta blockers may be diminished by the concomitant administration of aspirin due to inhibition of renal prostaglandins, leading to decreased renal blood flow, and salt and fluid retention.

Diuretics: The effectiveness of diuretics in patients with underlying renal or cardiovascular disease may be diminished by the concomitant administration of aspirin due to inhibition of renal prostaglandins, leading to decreased renal blood flow and salt and fluid retention.

Methotrexate: Salicylate can inhibit renal clearance of methotrexate, leading to bone marrow toxicity, especially in the elderly or renal impaired.

Nonsteroidal Anti-inflammatory Drugs (NSAID's): The concurrent use of aspirin with other NSAID's should be avoided because this may increase bleeding or lead to decreased renal function.

Oral Hypoglycemics: Moderate doses of aspirin may increase the effectiveness of oral hypoglycemic drugs, leading to hypoglycemia.

Uricosuric Agents (Probenecid and Sulfinpyrazone): Salicylates antagonize the uricosuric action of uricosuric agents.

Carcinogenesis, Mutagenesis, Impairment of Fertility: Administration of aspirin for 68 weeks at 0.5 percent in the feed of rats was not carcinogenic. In the Ames Salmonella assay, aspirin was not mutagenic; however, aspirin did induce chromosome aberrations in cultured human fibroblasts. Aspirin inhibits ovulation in rats. (See *Pregnancy.*)

Pregnancy: Pregnant women should only take aspirin if clearly needed. Because of the known effects of NSAID's on the fetal cardiovascular system (closure of the ductus arteriosus), use during the third trimester of pregnancy should be avoided. Salicylate products have also been associated with alterations in maternal and neonatal hemostasis mechanisms, decreased birth weight, and with perinatal mortality.

Labor and Delivery: Aspirin should be avoided 1 week prior to and during labor and delivery because it can result in excessive blood loss at delivery. Prolonged gestation and prolonged labor due to prostaglandin inhibition have been reported.

Nursing Mothers: Nursing mothers should avoid using aspirin because salicylate is excreted in breast milk. Use of high doses may lead to rashes, platelet abnormalities, and bleeding in nursing infants.

Pediatric Use: Pediatric dosing recommendations for juvenile rheumatoid arthritis are based on well-controlled clinical studies. An initial dose of 90–130 mg/kg/day in divided doses, with an increase as needed for anti-inflammatory efficacy (target plasma salicylate levels of 150–300 µg/mL) are effective. At high doses (*i.e.*, plasma levels of greater than 200 µg/mL), the incidence of toxicity increases.

ADVERSE REACTIONS

Many adverse reactions due to aspirin ingestion are dose-related. The following is a list of adverse reactions that have been reported in the literature. (See WARNINGS.)

Body as a Whole: Fever, hypothermia, thirst.

Cardiovascular: Dysrhythmias, hypotension, tachycardia.

Central Nervous System: Agitation, cerebral edema, coma, confusion, dizziness, headache, subdural or intracranial hemorrhage, lethargy, seizures.

Fluid and Electrolyte: Dehydration, hyperkalemia, metabolic acidosis, respiratory alkalosis.

Gastrointestinal: Dyspepsia, GI bleeding, ulceration and perforation, nausea, vomiting, transient elevations of hepatic enzymes, hepatitis, Reye's Syndrome, pancreatitis.

Hematologic: Prolongation of the prothrombin time, disseminated intravascular coagulation, coagulopathy, thrombocytopenia.

Hypersensitivity: Acute anaphylaxis, angioedema, asthma, bronchospasm, laryngeal edema, urticaria.

Musculoskeletal: Rhabdomyolysis.

Metabolism: Hypoglycemia (in children), hyperglycemia.

Reproductive: Prolonged pregnancy and labor, stillbirths, lower birth weight infants, antepartum and postpartum bleeding.

Respiratory: Hyperpnea, pulmonary edema, tachypnea.

Special Senses: Hearing loss, tinnitus. Patients with high frequency hearing loss may have difficulty perceiving tinnitus. In these patients, tinnitus cannot be used as a clinical indicator of salicylism.

Urogenital: Interstitial nephritis, papillary necrosis, proteinuria, renal insufficiency and failure.

DRUG ABUSE AND DEPENDENCE

Aspirin is nonnarcotic. There is no known potential for addiction associated with the use of aspirin.

OVERDOSAGE

Salicylate toxicity may result from acute ingestion (overdose) or chronic intoxication. The early signs of salicylic overdose (salicylism), including tinnitus (ringing in the ears), occur at plasma concentrations approaching 200 µg/mL. Plasma concentrations of aspirin above 300 µg/mL are clearly toxic. Severe toxic effects are associated with levels above 400 µg/mL. (See CLINICAL PHARMACOLOGY.) A single lethal dose of aspirin in adults is not known with certainty but death may be expected at 30 g. For real or suspected overdose, a Poison Control Center should be contacted immediately. Careful medical management is essential.

Signs and Symptoms: In acute overdose, severe acid-base and electrolyte disturbances may occur and are complicated by hyperthermia and dehydration. Respiratory alkalosis occurs early while hyperventilation is present, but is quickly followed by metabolic acidosis.

Treatment: Treatment consists primarily of supporting vital functions, increasing salicylate elimination, and correcting the acid-base disturbance. Gastric emptying and/or lavage is recommended as soon as possible after ingestion, even if the patient has vomited spontaneously. After lavage and/or emesis, administration of activated charcoal, as a slurry, is beneficial, if less than 3 hours have passed since ingestion. Charcoal adsorption should not be employed prior to emesis and lavage.

Severity of aspirin intoxication is determined by measuring the blood salicylate level. Acid-base status should be closely followed with serial blood gas and serum pH measurements. Fluid and electrolyte balance should also be maintained.

In severe cases, hyperthermia and hypovolemia are the major immediate threats to life. Children should be sponged with tepid water. Replacement fluid should be administered intravenously and augmented with correction of acidosis. Plasma electrolytes and pH should be monitored to promote alkaline diuresis of salicylate if renal function is normal. Infusion of glucose may be required to control hypoglycemia.

Hemodialysis and peritoneal dialysis can be performed to reduce the body drug content. In patients with renal insufficiency or in cases of life-threatening intoxication, dialysis is usually required. Exchange transfusion may be indicated in infants and young children.

DOSAGE AND ADMINISTRATION

Each dose of aspirin should be taken with a full glass of water unless patient is fluid restricted. Anti-inflammatory and analgesic dosages should be individualized. When aspirin is used in high doses, the development of tinnitus may be used as a clinical sign of elevated plasma salicylate levels except in patients with high frequency hearing loss.

Ischemic Stroke and TIA: 50–325 mg once a day. Continue therapy indefinitely.

Suspected Acute MI: The initial dose of 160–162.5 mg is administered as soon as an MI is suspected. The maintenance dose of 160–162.5 mg a day is continued for 30 days post-infarction. After 30 days, consider further therapy based on dosage and administration for prevention of recurrent MI.

Prevention of Recurrent MI: 75–325 mg once a day. Continue therapy indefinitely.

Unstable Angina Pectoris: 75–325 mg once a day. Continue therapy indefinitely.

Chronic Stable Angina Pectoris: 75–325 mg once a day. Continue therapy indefinitely.

CABG: 325 mg daily starting 6 hours post-procedure. Continue therapy for 1 year post-procedure.

PTCA: The initial dose of 325 mg should be given 2 hours pre-surgery. Maintenance dose is 160–325 mg daily. Continue therapy indefinitely.

Carotid Endarterectomy: Doses of 80 mg once daily to 650 mg twice daily, started presurgery, are recommended. Continue therapy indefinitely.

Rheumatoid Arthritis: The initial dose is 3 g a day in divided doses. Increase as needed for anti-inflammatory efficacy with target plasma salicylate levels of 150–300 µg/mL. At high doses (*i.e.,* plasma levels of greater than 200 µg/mL), the incidence of toxicity increases.

Juvenile Rheumatoid Arthritis: Initial dose is 90–130 mg/kg/day in divided doses. Increase as needed for anti-inflammatory efficacy with target plasma salicylate levels of 150–300 µg/mL. At high doses (*i.e.,* plasma levels of greater than 200 µg/mL), the incidence of toxicity increases.

Spondyloarthropathies: Up to 4 g per day in divided doses.

Osteoarthritis: Up to 3 g per day in divided doses.

Arthritis and Pleurisy of SLE: The initial dose is 3 g a day in divided doses. Increase as needed for anti-inflammatory efficacy with target plasma salicylate levels of 150–300 µg/mL. At high doses (*i.e.,* plasma levels of greater than 200 mµ/mL), the incidence of toxicity increases.

HOW SUPPLIED

(*Insert specific information regarding, strength of dosage form, units in which the dosage form is generally available, and information to facilitate identification of the dosage form as required under §201.57(k)(1), (k)(2), and (k)(3).)*

Store in a tight container at 25 °C (77 °F); ex-cursions permitted to 15–30 °C (59–86 °F).

REV: October 23, 1998.

(2) In addition to, and immediately preceding, the labeling required under paragraph (a)(1) of this section, the professional labeling may contain the following highlights of prescribing information in the exact language and exact format provided, but only when accompanied by the comprehensive prescribing information required in paragraph (a)(1) of this section.

HIGHLIGHTS OF PRESCRIBING INFORMATION
ASPIRIN (FORMULATION)
(acetylsalicylic acid)

PROFESSIONAL INDICATIONS AND USAGE
Vascular Indications:
· Ischemic Strokes and Transient Ischemic Attacks (TIA)
· Suspected Acute Myocardial Infarction (MI)
· Prevention of Recurrent MI
· Unstable Angina Pectoris
· Chronic Stable Angina Pectoris
Revascularization Procedures in Select Patients:[1]
· Coronary Artery Bypass Graft (CABG)
· Percutaneous Transluminal Coronary Angioplasty (PTCA)
· Carotid Endarterectomy
Rheumatologic Disease Indications:
· Rheumatoid Arthritis
· Juvenile Rheumatoid Arthritis
· Spondyloarthropathies
· Osteoarthritis
· Arthritis and Pleurisy of Systemic Lupus Erythematosus (SLE)

Warnings Regarding Use In Pregnancy
Pregnant women should only take aspirin if clearly needed. Because of the known effects of nonsteroidal anti-inflammatory drugs on the fetal cardiovascular system (closure of the ductus arteriosus), use during the third trimester of pregnancy should be avoided. Salicylate products have also been associated with alterations in maternal and neonatal hemostasis mechanisms, decreased birth weight, and with perinatal mortality. Salicylate is excreted in breast milk. (See "Pregnancy," "Labor and Delivery" and "Nursing Mothers" in the "Precautions" section of the Comprehensive Prescribing Information.)

[1]Patients with a pre-existing condition for which aspirin is already indicated. See "Revascularization Procedures" under the "Indications and Usage" and "Clinical Studies" sections in the Comprehensive Prescribing Information.

....Dosage and Administration..
General: Each dose should be taken with a full glass of water unless contraindicated. Doses may need to be individualized depending on indication.

Indications	Recommended Daily Dose	Duration of Therapy
Vascular Indications:		
Ischemic Strokes and TIA	50-325 milligrams (mg) daily	Indefinitely
Suspected Acute MI	160-162.5 mg taken as soon as infarction is suspected; then once daily	For 30 days post infarction (after 30 days consider further treatment based on indication for previous MI)
Prevention of Recurrent MI	75-325 mg daily	Indefinitely
Unstable Angina Pectoris	75-325 mg daily	Indefinitely
Chronic Stable Angina Pectoris	75-325 mg daily	Indefinitely
Revascularization Procedures in Select Patients:		
CABG	325 mg daily starting 6 hrs. postprocedure	1 year
PTCA	325 mg 2 hours presurgery Maintenance therapy: 160-325 mg daily	Indefinitely
Carotid Endarterectomy	80 mg daily to 650 mg twice a day started presurgery	Indefinitely
Rheumatologic Disease Indications:		
Rheumatoid Arthritis	Initial dose 3 g daily. Target plasma salicylate levels 150-300 micrograms/milliliter (μg/mL)	As indicated
Juvenile Rheumatoid Arthritis	Initial dose 90-130 mg/kilograms/day. Target plasma salicylate levels 150-300 μg/mL	As indicated
Spondyloarthropathies	Up to 4 grams (g) daily	As indicated
Osteoarthritis	Up to 3 g daily	As indicated
Arthritis and Pleurisy of SLE	Initial dose 3 g daily. Target plasma salicylate levels 150-300 μg/mL	As indicated

CONTRAINDICATIONS
Aspirin is contraindicated in patients with known allergy to nonsteroidal anti-inflammatory drugs and in patients with the syndrome of asthma, rhinitis, and nasal polyps. Aspirin should not be used in children or teenagers for viral infections, with or without fever, because of the risk of Reye's syndrome with concomitant use of aspirin in certain viral illnesses.
PRECAUTIONS
General
· Renal Failure
· Hepatic Insufficiency
· Sodium Restricted Diets
Laboratory Tests
Drug Interactions:
· Angiotensin Converting Enzyme (ACE) Inhibitors
· Acetazolamide
· Anticoagulant Therapy
· Anticonvulsants
· Beta Blockers
· Diuretics
· Methotrexate
· Nonsteroidal Anti-inflammatory Drugs (NSAID's)
· Oral Hypoglycemics
· Uricosuric Agents
Carcinogenesis, Mutagenesis, Impairment of Fertility
Pregnancy, Labor and Delivery, Nursing Mothers
Pediatric Use

WARNINGS
· Alcohol Warning
· Coagulation Abnormalities
· Gastrointestinal Side Effects
· Peptic Ulcer Disease
ADVERSE REACTIONS (Most common)
· Gastrointestinal (Abdominal Pain, Ulceration, Bleeding)
· Inhibition of Platelet Aggregation (Bleeding)
· Tinnitus
· Dizziness
· Hearing Loss
To report SERIOUS adverse drug reactions, call (manufacturer) at (phone number) or MEDWATCH at 1-800-FDA-1088
HOW SUPPLIED
(Insert specific information regarding, strength of dosage form, units in which the dosage form is generally available, and information to facilitate identification of the dosage form.) Store in a tight container at 25 °C (77 °F); excursions permitted to 15-30 °C (59-86 °F).

These highlights do not include all the information needed to prescribe aspirin safely and effectively. See aspirin's comprehensive prescribing information.

(b) [Reserved]

[63 FR 56814, Oct. 23, 1998; 63 FR 66015, 66016, Dec. 1, 1998, as amended at 64 FR 49653, Sept. 14, 1999]

Subpart D—Testing Procedures

§ 343.90 Dissolution and drug release testing.

(a) [Reserved]

(b) *Aspirin capsules.* Aspirin capsules must meet the dissolution standard for aspirin capsules as contained in the United States Pharmacopeia (USP) 23 at page 132.

(c) *Aspirin delayed-release capsules and aspirin delayed-release tablets.* Aspirin delayed-release capsules and aspirin delayed-release tablets must meet the drug release standard for aspirin delayed-release capsules and aspirin delayed-release tablets as contained in USP 23 at pages 133 and 136 respectively.

(d) *Aspirin tablets.* Aspirin tablets must meet the dissolution standard for aspirin tablets as contained in USP 23 at page 134.

(e) *Aspirin, alumina, and magnesia tablets.* Aspirin in combination with alumina and magnesia in a tablet dosage form must meet the dissolution standard for aspirin, alumina, and magnesia tablets as contained in USP 23 at page 138.

(f) *Aspirin, alumina, and magnesium oxide tablets.* Aspirin in combination with alumina, and magnesium oxide in a tablet dosage form must meet the dissolution standard for aspirin, alumina, and magnesium tablets as contained in USP 23 at page 139.

(g) *Aspirin effervescent tablets for oral solution.* Aspirin effervescent tablets for oral solution must meet the dissolution standard for aspirin effervescent tablets for oral solution as contained in USP 23 at page 137.

(h) *Buffered aspirin tablets.* Buffered aspirin tablets must meet the dissolution standard for buffered aspirin tablets as contained in USP 23 at page 135.

PART 344—TOPICAL OTIC DRUG PRODUCTS FOR OVER-THE-COUNTER HUMAN USE

Subpart A—General Provisions

Sec.
344.1 Scope.
344.3 Definitions.

Subpart B—Active Ingredients

344.10 Earwax removal aid active ingredient.
344.12 Ear drying aid active ingredient.

Subpart C—Labeling

344.50 Labeling of earwax removal aid drug products.
344.52 Labeling of ear drying aid drug products.

AUTHORITY: 21 U.S.C. 321, 351, 352, 353, 355, 360, 371.

SOURCE: 51 FR 28660, Aug. 8, 1986, unless otherwise noted.

Subpart A—General Provisions

§ 344.1 Scope.

(a) An over-the-counter topical otic drug product in a form suitable for topical administration is generally recognized as safe and effective and is not misbranded if it meets each of the conditions in this part in addition to each of the general conditions established in § 330.1.

(b) References in this part to regulatory sections of the Code of Federal Regulations are to chapter I of title 21 unless otherwise noted.

§ 344.3 Definitions.

As used in this part:

(a) *Anhydrous glycerin.* An ingredient that may be prepared by heating glycerin U.S.P. at 150 °C for 2 hours to drive off the moisture content.

(b) *Earwax removal aid.* A drug used in the external ear canal that aids in the removal of excessive earwax.

(c) *Water-clogged ears.* The retention of water in the external ear canal, thereby causing discomfort and a sensation of fullness or hearing impairment.

(d) *Ear drying aid.* A drug used in the external ear canal to help dry water-clogged ears.

[51 FR 28660, Aug. 8, 1986, as amended at 65 FR 48905, Aug. 10, 2000]

Subpart B—Active Ingredients

§ 344.10 Earwax removal aid active ingredient.

The active ingredient of the product consists of carbamide peroxide 6.5 percent formulated in an anhydrous glycerin vehicle.

[51 FR 28660, Aug. 8, 1986, as amended at 65 FR 48905, Aug. 10, 2000]

§ 344.12 Ear drying aid active ingredient.

The active ingredient of the product consists of isopropyl alcohol 95 percent in an anhydrous glycerin 5 percent base.

[65 FR 48905, Aug. 10, 2000]

Subpart C—Labeling

§ 344.50 Labeling of earwax removal aid drug products.

(a) *Statement of identity.* The labeling of the product contains the established name of the drug, if any, and identifies the product as an "earwax removal aid."

(b) *Indication.* The labeling of the product states, under the heading "Indication," the following: "For occasional use as an aid to" (which may be followed by: "soften, loosen, and") "remove excessive earwax." Other truthful and nonmisleading statements, describing only the indications for use that have been established and listed in this paragraph (b), may also be used, as provided in § 330.1(c)(2), subject to the provisions of section 502 of the act relating to misbranding and the prohibition in section 301(d) of the act against the introduction or delivery for introduction into interstate commerce of unapproved new drugs in violation of section 505(a) of the act.

(c) *Warnings.* The labeling of the product contains the following warnings under the heading "Warnings":

(1) "Do not use if you have ear drainage or discharge, ear pain, irritation, or rash in the ear or are dizzy; consult a doctor."

(2) "Do not use if you have an injury or perforation (hole) of the ear drum or after ear surgery unless directed by a doctor."

(3) "Do not use for more than 4 days; if excessive earwax remains after use of this product, consult a doctor."

(4) "Avoid contact with the eyes."

(d) *Directions.* The labeling of the product contains the following statement under the heading "Directions": FOR USE IN THE EAR ONLY. Adults and children over 12 years of age: tilt head sideways and place 5 to 10 drops into ear. Tip of applicator should not enter ear canal. Keep drops in ear for several minutes by keeping head tilted or placing cotton in the ear. Use twice daily for up to 4 days if needed, or as directed by a doctor. Any wax remaining after treatment may be removed by gently flushing the ear with warm water, using a soft rubber bulb ear syringe. Children under 12 years of age: consult a doctor.

[51 FR 28660, Aug. 8, 1986; 52 FR 7830, Mar. 13, 1987; 65 FR 48905, Aug. 10, 2000]

§ 344.52 Labeling of ear drying aid drug products.

(a) *Statement of identity.* The labeling of the product contains the established name of the drug, if any, and identifies the product as an "ear drying aid."

(b) *Indications.* The labeling of the product states, under the heading "Use," the following: "dries water in the ears" (optional, which may be followed by: "and relieves water-clogged ears") (which may be followed by any or all of the following: "after: [bullet][1] swimming [bullet] showering [bullet] bathing [bullet] washing the hair"). Other truthful and nonmisleading statements, describing only the indications for use that have been established and listed in paragraph (b) of this section, may also be used, as provided in § 330.1(c)(2) of this chapter, subject to the provisions of section 502 of the Federal Food, Drug, and Cosmetic Act (the act) relating to misbranding and the prohibition in section 301(d) of the act against the introduction or delivery for introduction into interstate commerce of unapproved new drugs in violation of section 505(a) of the act.

(c) *Warnings.* The labeling of the product contains the following warnings under the heading "Warnings":

---

[1] See § 201.66(b)(4) of this chapter.

(1) "Flammable [in bold type]: Keep away from fire or flame."

(2) "Do not use [in bold type] in the eyes."

(3) "Ask a doctor before use if you have [in bold type] [bullet] ear drainage or discharge [bullet] pain, irritation, or rash in the ear [bullet] had ear surgery [bullet] dizziness."

(4) "Stop use and ask a doctor if [in bold type] irritation (too much burning) or pain occurs."

(d) *Directions.* The labeling of the product contains the following statement under the heading "Directions": [optional, bullet] "apply 4 to 5 drops in each affected ear."

[65 FR 48905, Aug. 10, 2000]

PART 346—ANORECTAL DRUG PRODUCTS FOR OVER-THE-COUNTER HUMAN USE

Subpart A—General Provisions

AUTHORITY: 21 U.S.C. 321, 351, 352, 353, 355, 360, 371.

SOURCE: 55 FR 31779, Aug. 3, 1990, unless otherwise noted.

Subpart A—General Provisions

§ 346.1 Scope.

(a) An over-the-counter anorectal drug product in a form suitable for external (topical) or intrarectal (rectal) administration is generally recognized as safe and effective and is not misbranded if it meets each condition in this part and each general condition established in § 330.1 of this chapter.

(b) References in this part to regulatory sections of the Code of Federal Regulations are to chapter I of title 212 unless otherwise noted.

§ 346.3 Definitions.

As used in this part:

(a) *Analgesic, anesthetic drug.* A topically (externally) applied drug that relieves pain by depressing cutaneous sensory receptors.

(b) *Anorectal drug.* A drug that is used to relieve symptoms caused by anorectal disorders in the anal canal, perianal area, and/or the lower rectal areas.

(c) *Antipruritic drug.* A topically (externally) applied drug that relieves itching by depressing cutaneous sensory receptors.

(d) *Astringent drug.* A drug that is applied topically (externally) to the skin or mucous membranes for a local and limited protein coagulant effect.

(e) *External use.* Topical application of an anorectal drug product to the skin of the perianal area and/or the skin of the anal canal.

(f) *Intrarectal use.* Topical application of an anorectal drug product to the mucous membrane of the rectum.

(g) *Keratolytic drug.* A drug that causes desquamation (loosening) and debridement or sloughing of the surface cells of the epidermis.

(h) *Local anesthetic drug.* A drug that produces local disappearance of pain, burning, itching, irritation, and/or discomfort by reversibly blocking nerve conduction when applied to nerve tissue in appropriate concentrations.

(i) *Protectant drug.* A drug that provides a physical barrier, forming a protective coating over skin or mucous membranes.

(j) *Vasoconstrictor.* A drug that causes temporary constriction of blood vessels.

Subpart B—Active Ingredients

§ 346.10 Local anesthetic active ingredients.

The active ingredient of the product consists of any of the following when used in the concentration or within the concentration range established for each ingredient:

(a) Benzocaine 5 to 20 percent.

(b) Benzyl alcohol 1 to 4 percent.

(c) Dibucaine 0.25 to 1 percent.

(d) Dibucaine hydrochloride 0.25 to 1 percent.

(e) Dyclonine hydrochloride 0.5 to 1 percent.

(f) Lidocaine 2 to 5 percent.

(g) Pramoxine hydrochloride 1 percent.

(h) Tetracaine 0.5 to 1 percent.

(i) Tetracaine hydrochloride 0.5 to 1 percent.

§346.12 Vasoconstrictor active ingredients.

The active ingredient of the product consists of any of the following when used in the concentration or within the concentration range established for each ingredient.

(a) Ephedrine sulfate 0.1 to 1.25 percent.

(b) Epinephrine 0.005 to 0.01 percent.

(c) Epinephrine hydrochloride 0.005 to 0.01 percent.

(d) Phenylephrine hydrochloride 0.25 percent.

§346.14 Protectant active ingredients.

(a) The following active ingredients may be used as the sole protectant active ingredient in a product if the ingredient as identified constitutes 50 percent or more by weight of the final product. In addition, the following active ingredients may be used in concentrations of less than 50 percent by weight only when used in combinations in accordance with §346.22 (a), (b), or (n).

(1) Aluminum hydroxide gel.

(2) Cocoa butter.

(3) Glycerin in a 20- to 45-percent (weight/weight) aqueous solution so that the final product contains not less than 10 and not more than 45 percent glycerin (weight/weight). Any combination product containing glycerin must contain at least this minimum amount of glycerin.

(4) Hard fat.

(5) Kaolin.

(6) Lanolin.

(7) Mineral oil.

(8) Petrolatum.

(9) Topical starch.

(10) White petrolatum.

(b) The following active ingredients may not be used as a sole protectant ingredient but may be used in combination with one, two, or three other protectant active ingredients in accordance with §346.22 (a), (b), (n), and (o) and with the following limitations:

(1) Calamine not to exceed 25 percent by weight per dosage unit (based on the zinc oxide content of calamine).

(2) Cod liver oil, provided that the product is labeled so that the amount of the product that is used in a 24-hour period represents a quantity that provides 10,000 U.S.P. units of vitamin A and 400 U.S.P. units of cholecalciferol.

(3) Shark liver oil, provided that the product is labeled so that the amount of the product that is used in a 24-hour period represents a quantity that provides 10,000 U.S.P. units of vitamin A and 400 U.S.P. units of cholecalciferol.

(4) Zinc oxide not to exceed 25 percent by weight per dosage unit.

§346.16 Analgesic, anesthetic, and antipruritic active ingredients.

The active ingredient of the product consists of any of the following when used within the concentration range established for each ingredient:

(a) Camphor 0.1 to 3 percent.

(b) Juniper tar 1 to 5 percent.

(c) Menthol 0.1 to 1 percent.

§346.18 Astringent active ingredients.

The active ingredient of the product consists of any of the following when used within the concentration range established for each ingredient:

(a) Calamine, within a concentration range of 5 to 25 percent by weight per dosage unit (based on the zinc oxide content of calamine).

(b) Witch hazel, 10 to 50 percent.

(c) Zinc oxide, within a concentration range of 5 to 25 percent by weight per dosage unit.

[55 FR 31779, Aug. 3, 1990, as amended at 59 FR 28767, June 3, 1994]

§346.20 Keratolytic active ingredients.

The active ingredient of the product consists of any of the following when used within the concentration range established for each ingredient:

(a) Alcloxa 0.2 to 2 percent.

(b) Resorcinol 1 to 3 percent.

§ 346.22 Permitted combinations of anorectal active ingredients.

(a) Any two, three, or four protectants identified in § 346.14(a) may be combined, except aluminum hydroxide gel in § 346.14(a)(1) and kaolin in § 346.14(a)(5) may not be combined with any ingredient in § 346.14(a) (2), (4), (6), (7), (8) and (10), and (b) (2) and (3), provided that the combined percentage by weight of all protectants in the combination is at least 50 percent of the final product (e.g., 1 gram of a 2-gram dosage unit). Any protectant ingredient included in the combination must be present at a level that contributes at least 12.5 percent by weight (e.g., 0.25 gram of a 2-gram dosage unit), except cod liver oil and shark liver oil. If an ingredient in § 346.14(b) is included in the combination, it must not exceed the concentration limit specified in § 346.14(b).

(b) Any single anorectal ingredient identified in § 346.10, 346.12, 346.16, 346.18, or 346.20 may be combined with up to four protectants in accordance with paragraph (a) of this section.

(c) Any single local anesthetic identified in § 346.10 may be combined with any single vasoconstrictor identified in § 346.12.

(d) Any single local anesthetic identified in § 346.10 may be combined with any single astringent identified in § 346.18.

(e) Any single local anesthetic identified in § 346.10 may be combined with any single keratolytic identified in § 346.20.

(f) Any single vasoconstrictor identified in § 346.12 may be combined with any single astringent identified in § 346.18.

(g) Any single analgesic, anesthetic, and antipruritic identified in § 346.16 may be combined with any single astringent identified in § 346.18.

(h) Any single analgesic, anesthetic, and antipruritic identified in § 346.16 may be combined with any single keratolytic identified in § 346.18.

(i) Any single astringent identified in § 346.18 may be combined with any single keratolytic identified in § 346.20.

(j) Any single local anesthetic identified in § 346.10 may be combined with any single vasoconstrictor identified in § 346.12 and with any single astringent identified in § 346.18.

(k) Any single local anesthetic identified in § 346.10 may be combined with any single astringent identified in § 346.18 and with any single keratolytic identified in § 346.20.

(l) Any single vasoconstrictor identified in § 346.12 may be combined with any single analgesic, anesthetic, and antipruritic identified in § 346.16 and with any single astringent identified in § 346.18.

(m) Any single analgesic, anesthetic, and antipruritic identified in § 346.16 may be combined with any single astringent identified in § 346.18 and with any single keratolytic identified in § 346.20.

(n) Any combination of ingredients listed in paragraphs (c) through (m) of this section may be combined with up to four protectants in accordance with paragraph (a) of this section.

(o) Any product containing calamine for use as a protectant and/or as an astringent and/or containing zinc oxide for use as a protectant and/or as an astringent may not have a total weight of zinc oxide exceeding 25 percent by weight per dosage unit.

Subpart C—Labeling

§ 346.50 Labeling of anorectal drug products.

The labeling of the product contains the following information for anorectal ingredients identified in §§ 346.10, 346.12, 346.14, 346.16, 346.18, and 346.20, and for combinations of anorectal ingredients identified in § 346.22. Unless otherwise specified, the labeling in this subpart is applicable to anorectal drug products for both external and intrarectal use.

(a) *Statement of identity.* The labeling of the product contains the established name of the drug, if any, and identifies the product as "anorectal (hemorrhoidal)," "hemorrhoidal," "hemorrhoidal (anorectal) (insert dosage form, e.g., cream, lotion, or ointment)."

(b) *Indications.* The labeling of the product states, under the heading "Indications," any of the phrases listed in paragraph (b) of this section, as appropriate. Other truthful and nonmisleading statements, describing only the indications for use that have been established and listed in this paragraph, may also be used, as provided in §330.1(c)(2) of this chapter, subject to the provisions of section 502 of the Federal Food, Drug, and Cosmetic Act (the act) relating to misbranding and the prohibition in section 301(d) of the act against the introduction or delivery for introduction into interstate commerce of unapproved new drugs in violation of section 505(a) of the act.

(1) ("For the temporary relief of," "Gives temporary relief of," or "Helps relieve the") (As an option, select one or both of the following: "local" or "anorectal") [select one or more of the following: "discomfort," "itching," or "itching and discomfort," followed by: "in the perianal area" or "associated with" (select one or more of the following: "hemorrhoids," "anorectal disorders," "inflamed hemorrhoidal tissues," "anorectal inflammation," "hemorrhoidal tissues," or "piles (hemorrhoids)."]]

(2) *Additional indications.* Indications applicable to each active ingredient of the product may be combined to eliminate duplicative words or phrases so that the resulting indication is clear and understandable. In addition to the indication identified in paragraph (b)(1) of this section, the labeling of the product intended for external or intrarectal use may also contain the following indications, as appropriate.

(i) *For products for external use only containing any ingredient identified in §346.10.* "For the temporary relief of" (select one or more of the following: "pain," "soreness," or "burning").

(ii) *For products containing epinephrine or epinephrine hydrochloride identified in §346.12 (b) and (c) for external use only, and for products containing ephedrine sulfate or phenylephrine hydrochloride identified in §346.12 (a) and (d).*

(A) "Temporarily reduces the swelling associated with" (select one of the following: "irritated hemorrhoidal tissue and other anorectal disorders" or "irritation in hemorrhoids and other anorectal disorders").

(B) "Temporarily shrinks hemorrhoidal tissue."

(iii) *For products for external use only containing glycerin identified in §346.14(a)(3) and for products for external*

and/or intrarectal use containing any protectant identified in §346.14(a) (2), (4), (6) through (10), and (b) (1) through (4).

(A) "Temporarily forms a protective coating over inflamed tissues to help prevent drying of tissues."

(B) "Temporarily protects irritated areas."

(C) "Temporarily relieves burning."

(D) "Provides temporary relief from skin irritations."

(E) "Temporarily provides a coating for relief of anorectal discomforts."

(F) "Temporarily protects the inflamed, irritated anorectal surface" (select one of the following: "to help make bowel movements less painful" or "from irritation and abrasion during bowel movement").

(G) "Temporarily protects inflamed perianal skin."

(H) "Temporarily relieves the symptoms of perianal skin irritation."

(iv) *For products containing aluminum hydroxide gel identified in §346.14(a)(1) and for products containing kaolin identified in §346.14(a)(5).* "For the temporary relief of itching associated with moist anorectal conditions."

(v) *For products for external use only containing any analgesic, anesthetic, and antipruritic identified in §346.16.*

(A) "For the temporary relief of" (select one or both of the following: "pain" or "burning").

(B) "Can help distract from pain."

(C) "May provide a cooling sensation."

(vi) *For products for external use only containing witch hazel identified in §346.18(b), and for products for external use and/or intrarectal use containing calamine or zinc oxide identified in §346.18 (a) and (c).*

(A) "Aids in protecting irritated anorectal areas."

(B) "Temporary relief of" (select one or both of the following: "irritation" or "burning").

(vii) *For products for external use only containing any ingredient identified in §346.20.* The indication in paragraph (b)(1) of this section applies.

(c) *Warnings.* Warnings applicable to each active ingredient of the product may be combined to eliminate duplicative words or phrases so that the resulting warning is clear and understandable. The labeling of the product

285

contains the following warnings under the heading "Warnings":

(1) "If condition worsens or does not improve within 7 days, consult a doctor."

(2) "Do not exceed the recommended daily dosage unless directed by a doctor."

(3) "In case of bleeding, consult a doctor promptly."

(4) *For products for external use only.* "Do not put this product into the rectum by using fingers or any mechanical device or applicator."

(5) *For products for intrarectal use to be used with a special applicator such as a pile pipe or other mechanical device.* "Do not use this product with an applicator if the introduction of the applicator into the rectum causes additional pain. Consult a doctor promptly."

(6) *For products for external use only containing any local anesthetic identified in § 346.10, menthol identified in § 346.16(c), or resorcinol identified in § 346.20(b).* "Certain persons can develop allergic reactions to ingredients in this product. If the symptom being treated does not subside or if redness, irritation, swelling, pain, or other symptoms develop or increase, discontinue use and consult a doctor."

(7) *For products containing any vasoconstrictor identified in § 346.12.* (i) "Do not use this product if you have heart disease, high blood pressure, thyroid disease, diabetes, or difficulty in urination due to enlargement of the prostate gland unless directed by a doctor."

(ii) "Ask a doctor or pharmacist before use if you are [bullet][1] presently taking a prescription drug for high blood pressure or depression."

(iii) *For products containing ephedrine sulfate identified in § 346.12(a).* "Some users of this product may experience nervousness, tremor, sleeplessness, nausea, and loss of appetite. If these symptoms persist or become worse, consult your doctor."

(8) *For products containing aluminum hydroxide gel identified in § 346.14(a)(1) and for products containing kaolin identified in § 346.14(a)(5).* "Remove petrolatum or greasy ointment before using this product because they interfere

with the ability of this product to adhere properly to the skin area."

(9) *For products for external use only containing resorcinol identified in § 346.20(b).* "Do not use on open wounds near the anus."

(d) *Directions.* Directions applicable to each active ingredient of the product may be combined to eliminate duplicative words or phrases so that the resulting information is clear and understandable. The labeling of the product contains the following information under the heading "Directions":

(1) *"Adults:* When practical, cleanse the affected area" (select one or both of the following: "with mild soap and warm water and rinse thoroughly" or "by patting or blotting with an appropriate cleansing pad"). "Gently dry by patting or blotting with toilet tissue or a soft cloth before application of this product." [Other appropriate directions in this section may be inserted here.] "Children under 12 years of age: consult a doctor."

(2) *For products for external use only.* "Apply externally to the affected area" (insert appropriate time interval of administration as identified in paragraphs (d)(6), (7), (8), or (9) of this section).

(3) *For products for external use that are pads containing anorectal ingredients.* "Gently apply to the affected area by patting and then discard."

(4) *For products for intrarectal use that are wrapped suppositories.* "Remove wrapper before inserting into the rectum."

(5) *For products for intrarectal use that are to be used with a special applicator such as a pile pipe or other mechanical device.* "FOR INTRARECTAL USE: Attach applicator to tube. Lubricate applicator well, then gently insert applicator into the rectum."

(6) *For products for external use only containing any of the local anesthetics identified in § 346.10; analgesics, anesthetics, and antipruritics identified in § 346.16; or alcloxa or resorcinol identified in § 346.20.* Apply to the affected area up to 6 times daily.

(i) *For products for external use only containing dibucaine or dibucaine hydrochloride identified in § 346.10 (c) and (d).* Apply to the affected area up to 3 or 4 times daily.

---

[1] See § 201.66(b)(4) of this chapter.

(ii) *For products for external use only containing pramoxine hydrochloride identified in § 346.10(g)*. Apply to the affected area up to 5 times daily.

(7) *For products containing vasoconstrictors identified in § 346.12*. Apply to the affected area up to 4 times daily.

(8) *For products for external use only containing glycerin identified in § 346.14(a)(3) or witch hazel identified in § 346.18(b), and for products for external and/or intrarectal use containing any protectant identified in § 346.14(a)(1), (2), (4), (5), (6), (7), and (9), and (b)(1), (2), (3), and (4), or any astringent identified in § 346.18(a) and (c)*. Apply to the affected area up to 6 times daily or after each bowel movement.

(9) *For products containing petrolatum or white petrolatum identified in § 346.14(a)(8) and (10)*. Apply liberally to the affected area as often as necessary.

(e) The word "physician" may be substituted for the word "doctor" in any of the labeling statements in this section.

[55 FR 31779, Aug. 3, 1990, as amended at 59 FR 28767, June 3, 1994; 64 FR 13295, Mar. 17, 1999]

§ 346.52 Labeling of permitted combinations of anorectal active ingredients.

Indications, warnings, and directions for use, respectively, applicable to each ingredient in the product may be combined to eliminate duplicative words or phrases so that the resulting information is clear and understandable.

(a) *Statement of identity.* For a combination drug product that has an established name, the labeling of the product states the established name of the combination drug product, followed by the statement of identity established in § 346.50(a). For a combination drug product that does not have an established name, the labeling of the product states the statement of identity established in § 346.50(a).

(b) *Indications.* The labeling of the product states, under the heading "Indications," the indication(s) for each ingredient in the combination, as established in the indications sections of this subpart.

(c) *Warnings.* The labeling of the product states, under the heading "Warnings," the warning(s) for each ingredient in the combination, as established in the warnings sections of this subpart.

(d) *Directions.* The labeling of the product states, under the heading "Directions," directions that conform to the directions established for each ingredient in the directions sections of this subpart. When the time intervals or age limitations for administration of the individual ingredients differ, the directions for the combination product may not exceed any maximum dosage limits established for the individual ingredients in the applicable OTC drug monograph.

PART 347—SKIN PROTECTANT DRUG PRODUCTS FOR OVER-THE-COUNTER HUMAN USE

Subpart A—General Provisions

AUTHORITY: 21 U.S.C. 321, 351, 352, 353, 355, 360, 371.

SOURCE: 58 FR 54462, Oct. 21, 1993, unless otherwise noted.

Subpart A—General Provisions

§ 347.1 Scope.

(a) An over-the-counter skin protectant drug product in a form suitable for topical administration is generally recognized as safe and effective and is not misbranded if it meets each condition in this part and each general condition established in § 330.1 of this chapter.

(b) References in this part to regulatory sections of the Code of Federal Regulations are to chapter I of title 21 unless otherwise noted.

§ 347.3 Definitions.

As used in this part:

Astringent drug product. A drug product applied to the skin or mucous membranes for a local and limited protein coagulant effect.

Lip protectant drug product. A drug product that temporarily prevents dryness and helps relieve chapping of the exposed surfaces of the lips; traditionally called "lip balm."

Poison ivy, oak, sumac dermatitis. An allergic contact dermatitis due to exposure to plants of the genus Rhus (poison ivy, poison oak, poison sumac), which contain urushiol, a potent skin-sensitizer.

Skin protectant drug product. A drug product that temporarily protects injured or exposed skin or mucous membrane surfaces from harmful or annoying stimuli, and may help provide relief to such surfaces.

[68 FR 33376, June 4, 2003]

Subpart B—Active Ingredients

SOURCE: 68 FR 33377, June 4, 2003, unless otherwise noted.

§ 347.10 Skin protectant active ingredients.

The active ingredients of the product consist of any of the following, within the concentration specified for each ingredient:

(a) Allantoin, 0.5 to 2 percent.

(b) Aluminum hydroxide gel, 0.15 to 5 percent.

(c) Calamine, 1 to 25 percent.

(d) Cocoa butter, 50 to 100 percent.

(e) Cod liver oil, 5 to 13.56 percent, in accordance with § 347.20(a)(1) or (a)(2), provided the product is labeled so that the quantity used in a 24-hour period does not exceed 10,000 U.S.P. Units vitamin A and 400 U.S.P. Units cholecalciferol.

(f) Colloidal oatmeal, 0.007 percent minimum; 0.003 percent minimum in combination with mineral oil in accordance with § 347.20(a)(4).

(g) Dimethicone, 1 to 30 percent.

(h) Glycerin, 20 to 45 percent.

(i) Hard fat, 50 to 100 percent.

(j) Kaolin, 4 to 20 percent.

(k) Lanolin, 12.5 to 50 percent.

(l) Mineral oil, 50 to 100 percent; 30 to 35 percent in combination with colloidal oatmeal in accordance with § 347.20(a)(4).

(m) Petrolatum, 30 to 100 percent.

(n) [Reserved]

(o) Sodium bicarbonate.

(p) [Reserved]

(q) Topical starch, 10 to 98 percent.

(r) White petrolatum, 30 to 100 percent.

(s) Zinc acetate, 0.1 to 2 percent.

(t) Zinc carbonate, 0.2 to 2 percent.

(u) Zinc oxide, 1 to 25 percent.

§ 347.12 Astringent active ingredients.

The active ingredient of the product consists of any one of the following within the specified concentration established for each ingredient:

(a) Aluminum acetate, 0.13 to 0.5 percent (depending on the formulation and concentration of the marketed product, the manufacturer must provide adequate directions so that the resulting solution to be used by the consumer contains 0.13 to 0.5 percent aluminum acetate).

(b) Aluminum sulfate, 46 to 63 percent (the concentration is based on the anhydrous equivalent).

(c) Witch hazel.

§ 347.20 Permitted combinations of active ingredients.

(a) *Combinations of skin protectant active ingredients.* (1) Any two or more of the ingredients identified in § 347.10(a), (d), (e), (i), (k), (l), (m), and (r) may be combined provided the combination is labeled according to § 347.50(b)(1) and provided each ingredient in the combination is within the concentration specified in § 347.10.

(2) Any two or more of the ingredients identified in § 347.10(a), (d), (e), (g), (h), (i), (k), (l), (m), and (r) may be combined provided the combination is labeled according to § 347.50(b)(2) and provided each ingredient in the combination is within the concentration specified in § 347.10.

(3) Any two or more of the ingredients identified in § 347.10(b), (c), (j), (s), (t), and (u) may be combined provided the combination is labeled according to § 347.50(b)(3) and provided each ingredient in the combination is within the concentration specified in § 347.10.

(4) The ingredients identified in §347.10(f) and (l) may be combined provided the combination is labeled according to §347.50(b)(7) and provided each ingredient in the combination is within the concentration specified in §347.10.

(b) *Combination of ingredients to prepare an aluminum acetate solution.* Aluminum sulfate tetradecahydrate may be combined with calcium acetate monohydrate in powder or tablet form to provide a 0.13 to 0.5 percent aluminum acetate solution when the powder or tablet is dissolved in the volume of water specified in "Directions."

(c) *Combinations of skin protectant and external analgesic active ingredients.* Any one (two when required to be in combination) or more of the active ingredients identified in §347.10(a), (d), (e), (i), (k), (l), (m), and (r) may be combined with any of the following generally recognized as safe and effective external analgesic active ingredients: Single amine and "caine"-type local anesthetics, alcohols and ketones, antihistamines, or any permitted combination of these ingredients, but not with hydrocortisone, provided the product is labeled according to §347.60(b)(1).

(d) *Combinations of skin protectant and first aid antiseptic active ingredients.* Any one (two when required to be in combination) or more of the active ingredients identified in §347.10(a), (d), (e), (i), (k), (l), (m), and (r) may be combined with any generally recognized as safe and effective single first aid antiseptic active ingredient, or any permitted combination of these ingredients, provided the product is labeled according to §347.60(b)(2).

(e) *Combinations of skin protectant and sunscreen active ingredients.* Any one (two when required to be in combination) or more of the skin protectant active ingredients identified in §347.10(a), (d), (e), (g), (h), (i), (k), (l), (m), and (r) may be combined with any generally recognized as safe and effective single sunscreen active ingredient, or any permitted combination of these ingredients, provided the product meets the conditions in §352.20(b) of this chapter and is labeled according to

§§347.60(b)(3) and 352.60(b) of this chapter.

[68 FR 33377, June 4, 2003, as amended at 74 FR 9765, Mar. 6, 2009]

EFFECTIVE DATE NOTE: At 68 FR 33377, June 4, 2003, in §347.20 paragraph (d) was stayed until further notice, effective June 4, 2004. At 74 FR 9765, Mar. 6, 2009, in §347.20, paragraph (d) was redesignated as paragraph (e).

Subpart C—Labeling

SOURCE: 68 FR 33377, June 4, 2003, unless otherwise noted.

§347.50 Labeling of skin protectant drug products.

A skin protectant drug product may have more than one labeled use and labeling appropriate to different uses may be combined to eliminate duplicative words or phrases as long as the labeling is clear and understandable. When the labeling of the product contains more than one labeled use, the appropriate statement(s) of identity, indications, warnings, and directions must be stated in the labeling.

(a) *Statement of identity.* The labeling of the product contains the established name of the drug, if any, and identifies the product with one or more of the following:

(1) *For any product.* "Skin protectant" (optional, may add dosage form, e.g., "cream," "gel," "lotion," or "ointment").

(2) *For any product formulated as a lip protectant.* "Skin protectant," "lip protectant," or "lip balm" (optional, may add dosage form, e.g., "cream," "gel," "lotion," or "ointment").

(3) *For products containing any ingredient in §347.10(b), (c), (j), (s), (t), and (u).* "Poison ivy, oak, sumac drying" (optional, may add dosage form, e.g., "cream," "gel," "lotion," or "ointment").

(4) *For products containing any ingredient in §347.10(b), (c), (f), (j), (o), (s), (t), and (u).* "Poison ivy, oak, sumac protectant."

(b) *Indications.* The labeling of the product states, under the heading "Uses," one or more of the phrases listed in this paragraph (b), as appropriate. Other truthful and nonmisleading statements, describing only the uses that have been established and listed in this paragraph (b), may also be used, as provided in § 330.1(c)(2) of this chapter, subject to the provisions of section 502 of the Federal Food, Drug, and Cosmetic Act (the act) relating to misbranding and the prohibition in section 301(d) of the act against the introduction or delivery for introduction into interstate commerce of unapproved new drugs in violation of section 505(a) of the act.

(1) *For products containing any ingredient in § 347.10(a), (d), (e), (i), (k), (l), (m), and (r).* The labeling states "temporarily protects minor: [bullet][1] cuts [bullet] scrapes [bullet] burns".

(2) *For products containing any ingredient in § 347.10(a), (d), (e), (g), (h), (i), (k), (l), (m), and (r)—*(i) *The labeling states* (optional: "helps prevent and") "temporarily protects" (optional: "and helps relieve") (optional: "chafed,") "chapped or cracked skin" (optional: "and lips"). This statement may be followed by the optional statement: "helps" (optional: "prevent and") "protect from the drying effects of wind and cold weather". [If both statements are used, each is preceded by a bullet.]

(ii) *For products formulated as a lip protectant.* The labeling states (optional: "helps prevent and") "temporarily protects" (optional: "and helps relieve") (optional: "chafed,") "chapped or cracked lips". This statement may be followed by the optional statement: "helps" (optional: "prevent and") "protect from the drying effects of wind and cold weather". [If both statements are used, each is preceded by a bullet.]

(3) *For products containing any ingredient in § 347.10(b), (c), (j), (s), (t), and (u).* The labeling states "dries the oozing and weeping of poison: [bullet] ivy [bullet] oak [bullet] sumac".

(4) *For products containing colloidal oatmeal identified in § 347.10(f).* The labeling states "temporarily protects and helps relieve minor skin irritation and itching due to: [select one or more of the following: '[bullet] rashes' '[bullet] eczema' '[bullet] poison ivy, oak, or sumac' '[bullet] insect bites']."

---

[1] *See* § 201.66(b)(4) of this chapter for definition of bullet symbol.

(5) *For products containing sodium bicarbonate identified in § 347.10(o).* The labeling states "temporarily protects and helps relieve minor skin irritation and itching due to: [bullet] poison ivy, oak, or sumac [bullet] insect bites".

(6) *For products containing topical starch identified in § 347.10(q).* The labeling states "temporarily protects and helps relieve minor skin irritation".

(7) *For products containing the combination of ingredients in § 347.20(a)(4).* The labeling states "temporarily protects and helps relieve minor skin irritation and itching due to: [select one or more of the following: 'rashes' or 'eczema']." [If both conditions are used, each is preceded by a bullet.]

(c) *Warnings.* The labeling of the product contains the following warnings under the heading "Warnings":

(1) "For external use only" in accord with § 201.66(c)(5)(i) of this chapter. For products containing only mineral oil in § 347.10(l) or sodium bicarbonate in § 347.10(o), this warning may be omitted if labeling for oral use of the product is also provided.

(2) "When using this product [bullet] do not get into eyes".

(3) "Stop use and ask a doctor if [bullet] condition worsens [bullet] symptoms last more than 7 days or clear up and occur again within a few days".

(4) For products labeled according to § 347.50(b)(1) or (b)(2): "Do not use on [bullet] deep or puncture wounds [bullet] animal bites [bullet] serious burns".

(5) For products containing colloidal oatmeal identified in § 347.10(f) when labeled for use as a soak in a tub. "When using this product [bullet] to avoid slipping, use mat in tub or shower".

(6) For powder products containing kaolin identified in § 347.10(j) or topical starch identified in § 347.10(q)—(i) "Do not use on [bullet] broken skin".

(ii) "When using this product [bullet] keep away from face and mouth to avoid breathing it".

(7) For products containing colloidal oatmeal identified in § 347.10(f) or sodium bicarbonate identified in § 347.10(o) when labeled for use as a soak, compress, or wet dressing. "When using this product [bullet] in some skin conditions, soaking too long may overdry".

(d) *Directions.* The labeling of the product contains the following statements, as appropriate, under the heading "Directions":

(1) *For products labeled according to §347.50(b)(1), (b)(2), (b)(3), (b)(5), or (b)(6).* The labeling states "apply as needed".

(2) *For products containing colloidal oatmeal identified in §347.10(f)*—(i) *For products requiring dispersal in water.* The labeling states "[bullet] turn warm water faucet on to full force [bullet] slowly sprinkle" (manufacturer to insert quantity to be used) "of colloidal oatmeal directly under the faucet into the tub or container [bullet] stir any colloidal oatmeal settled on the bottom".

(A) *For products used as a soak in a bath.* The manufacturer must provide adequate directions to obtain a solution containing a minimum of 0.007 percent colloidal oatmeal or 0.003 percent colloidal oatmeal in the oilated form for a tub bath, sitz bath, or infant bath, or a minimum of 0.25 percent colloidal oatmeal for a foot bath. "For use as a soak in a bath: [bullet] soak affected area for 15 to 30 minutes as needed, or as directed by a doctor [bullet] pat dry (do not rub) to keep a thin layer on the skin".

(B) *For products used as a compress or wet dressing.* The manufacturer must provide adequate directions to obtain a solution containing a minimum of 0.25 percent colloidal oatmeal. "For use as a compress or wet dressing: [bullet] soak a clean, soft cloth in the mixture [bullet] apply cloth loosely to affected area for 15 to 30 minutes [bullet] repeat as needed or as directed by a doctor [bullet] discard mixture after each use".

(ii) *For topical products intended for direct application.* The labeling states "apply as needed".

(3) *For products containing sodium bicarbonate identified in §347.10(o).* The labeling states "[bullet] adults and children 2 years of age and over:"

(i) The labeling states "For use as a paste: [bullet] add enough water to the sodium bicarbonate to form a paste [bullet] apply to the affected area of the skin as needed, or as directed by a doctor".

(ii) The labeling states "For use as a soak in a bath: [bullet] dissolve 1 to 2 cupfuls in a tub of warm water [bullet] soak for 10 to 30 minutes as needed, or as directed by a doctor [bullet] pat dry (do not rub) to keep a thin layer on the skin".

(iii) The labeling states "For use as a compress or wet dressing: [bullet] add sodium bicarbonate to water to make a mixture in a container [bullet] soak a clean, soft cloth in the mixture [bullet] apply cloth loosely to affected area for 15 to 30 minutes [bullet] repeat as needed or as directed by a doctor [bullet] discard mixture after each use".

(iv) Any of the directions in paragraphs (d)(3)(i), (d)(3)(ii), or (d)(3)(iii) of this section shall be followed by the statement: "[bullet] children under 2 years: ask a doctor".

(4) *For products containing aluminum hydroxide gel identified in §347.10(b).* The labeling states "[bullet] children under 6 months: ask a doctor".

(5) *For products containing glycerin identified in §347.10(h).* The labeling states "[bullet] children under 6 months: ask a doctor".

(6) *For products containing zinc acetate identified in §347.10(s).* The labeling states "[bullet] children under 2 years: ask a doctor".

(e) *Products formulated and labeled as a lip protectant and that meet the criteria established in §201.66(d)(10) of this chapter.* The title, headings, subheadings, and information described in §201.66(c) of this chapter shall be printed in accordance with the following specifications:

(1) The labeling shall meet the requirements of §201.66(c) of this chapter except that the title, headings, and information described in §201.66(c)(1), (c)(3), (c)(6), and (c)(7) may be omitted, and the headings, subheadings, and information described in §201.66(c)(2), (c)(4), and (c)(5) may be presented as follows:

(i) The active ingredients (§201.66(c)(2) of this chapter) shall be listed in alphabetical order.

(ii) The heading and the indication required by §201.66(c)(4) of this chapter may be limited to: "Use [in bold type] helps" (optional: "prevent and") "protect" (optional: "and relieve") "chapped lips". If both optional terms are used, the indication may be limited to: "Use [in bold type] helps prevent, protect, and relieve chapped lips".

(iii) The "external use only" warning in § 347.50(c)(1) and in § 201.66(c)(5)(i) of this chapter may be omitted. The warnings in § 347.50(c)(2), (c)(3), and (c)(4) are not required.

(iv) The subheadings in § 201.66(c)(5)(iii) through (c)(5)(vi) of this chapter may be omitted, provided the information after the heading "Warning" contains the warning in § 347.50(e)(1)(iii).

(v) The warnings in § 201.66(c)(5)(x) of this chapter may be omitted.

(2) The labeling shall be printed in accordance with the requirements of § 201.66(d) of this chapter except that any requirements related to § 201.66(c)(1), (c)(3), (c)(6), and (c)(7), and the horizontal barlines and hairlines described in § 201.66(d)(8), may be omitted.

(f) *Products containing only cocoa butter, petrolatum, or white petrolatum identified in § 347.10(d), (m), and (r), singly or in combination with each other, and marketed other than as a lip protectant.* (1) The labeling shall meet the requirements of § 201.66(c) of this chapter except that the headings and information described in § 201.66(c)(3) and (c)(7) may be omitted, and the headings, subheadings, and information described in § 201.66(c)(2), (c)(4), and (c)(5) may be presented as follows:

(i) The active ingredients (§ 201.66(c)(2) of this chapter) shall be listed in alphabetical order.

(ii) The heading and the indication required by § 201.66(c)(4) of this chapter may be limited to "Use [in bold type] helps protect minor cuts and burns" or "Use [in bold type] helps" (optional: "prevent and") "protect chapped skin" or "Use [in bold type] helps protect minor cuts and burns and" (optional: "prevent and protect") "chapped skin".

(iii) The warning in § 347.50(c)(3) may be revised to read "*See* a doctor if condition lasts more than 7 days."

(iv) The subheadings in § 201.66(c)(5)(iv) through (c)(5)(vii) of this chapter may be omitted, provided the information after the heading "Warnings" contains the warnings in § 347.50(c)(2), (c)(4), and (f)(1)(iii).

(2) The labeling shall be printed in accordance with the requirements of § 201.66(d) of this chapter except that any requirements related to § 201.66(c)(3) and (c)(7) may be omitted.

[68 FR 33377, June 4, 2003, as amended at 68 FR 68511, Dec. 9, 2003; 73 FR 6017, Feb. 1, 2008]

§ 347.52 Labeling of astringent drug products.

(a) *Statement of identity.* The labeling of the product contains the established name of the drug, if any, and identifies the product as an "astringent." *For products containing the combination of aluminum sulfate tetradecahydrate and calcium acetate monohydrate identified in § 347.20(b),* under the "Purpose" heading identified in § 201.66(c)(3) of this chapter, the labeling of each active ingredient in the product states "Astringent*", which is followed by the statements "* When combined together in water, these ingredients form the active ingredient aluminum acetate. See [the following in bold italic type] Directions."

(b) *Indications.* The labeling of the product states, under the heading "Uses" any of the phrases listed in this paragraph (b), as appropriate. Other truthful and nonmisleading statements describing only the indications for use that have been established and listed in this paragraph (b) may also be used, as provided in § 330.1(c)(2) of this chapter, subject to the provisions of section 502 of the Federal Food, Drug, and Cosmetic Act (the act) relating to misbranding and the prohibition of section 301(d) of the act against the introduction or delivery for introduction into interstate commerce of unapproved new drugs in violation of section 505(a) of the act.

(1) *For products containing aluminum acetate identified in § 347.12(a) or the combination of aluminum sulfate tetradecahydrate and calcium acetate monohydrate identified in § 347.20(b).* "For temporary relief of minor skin irritations due to: [select one or more of the following: 'poison ivy,' 'poison oak,' 'poison sumac,' 'insect bites,' 'athlete's foot,' or 'rashes caused by soaps, detergents, cosmetics, or jewelry']."

(2) *For products containing aluminum sulfate identified in § 347.12(b) for use as a*

styptic pencil. "Stops bleeding caused by minor surface cuts and abrasions as may occur during shaving."

(3) *For products containing witch hazel identified in § 347.12(c).* "Relieves minor skin irritations due to: [select one or more of the following: 'insect bites,' 'minor cuts,' or 'minor scrapes']." [If more than one condition is used, each is preceded by a bullet.]

(c) *Warnings.* The labeling of the product contains the following warnings under the heading "Warnings":

(1) *For all products*—(i) The labeling states "For external use only".

(ii) The labeling states "When using this product [bullet] avoid contact with eyes. If contact occurs, rinse thoroughly with water."

(2) *For products containing aluminum acetate identified in § 347.12(a), witch hazel identified in § 347.12(c), or the combination of aluminum sulfate tetradecahydrate and calcium acetate monohydrate identified in § 347.20(b).* The labeling states "Stop use and ask a doctor if [bullet] condition worsens or symptoms last more than 7 days".

(3) *For products containing aluminum acetate identified in § 347.12(a) or the combination of aluminum sulfate tetradecahydrate and calcium acetate monohydrate identified in § 347.20(b) when labeled for use as a compress or wet dressing.* The labeling states "When using this product [bullet] do not cover compress or wet dressing with plastic to prevent evaporation".

(4) *For products containing aluminum acetate identified in § 347.12(a) or the combination of aluminum sulfate tetradecahydrate and calcium acetate monohydrate identified in § 347.20(b) when labeled for use as a soak, compress, or wet dressing.* The labeling states "When using this product [bullet] in some skin conditions, soaking too long may overdry".

(d) *Directions.* The labeling of the product contains the following information under the heading "Directions":

(1) *For products containing aluminum acetate identified in § 347.12(a) or the combination of aluminum sulfate tetradecahydrate and calcium acetate monohydrate identified in § 347.20(b)*—(i) *For products used as a soak.* "For use as a soak: [preceding words in bold type] [bullet] soak affected area for 15 to 30 minutes as needed, or as directed by a doctor [bullet] repeat 3 times a day or as directed by a doctor [bullet] discard solution after each use".

(ii) *For products used as a compress or wet dressing.* "For use as a compress or wet dressing: [preceding words in bold type] [bullet] soak a clean, soft cloth in the solution [bullet] apply cloth loosely to affected area for 15 to 30 minutes [bullet] repeat as needed or as directed by a doctor [bullet] discard solution after each use".

(2) *For products containing aluminum sulfate identified in § 347.12(b) for use as a styptic pencil.* "Moisten tip of pencil with water and apply to the affected area. Dry pencil after use."

(3) *For products containing witch hazel identified in § 347.12(c).* "Apply as often as needed".

(4) *For products containing the combination of aluminum sulfate tetradecahydrate and calcium acetate monohydrate identified in § 347.20(b)*—(i) *For powder dosage form.* The labeling states "[bullet] dissolve 1 to 3 packets in [insert volume] of cool or warm water [bullet] stir until fully dissolved; do not strain or filter. The resulting mixture contains [insert percent] (1 packet), [insert percent] (2 packets), or [insert percent] (3 packets) aluminum acetate and is ready for use." These statements shall be the first statements under the heading "Directions".

(ii) *For tablet dosage form.* The labeling states "[bullet] dissolve 1 to 3 tablets in [insert volume] of cool or warm water [bullet] stir until fully dissolved; do not strain or filter. The resulting mixture contains [insert percent] (1 tablet), [insert percent] (2 tablets), or [insert percent] (3 tablets) aluminum acetate and is ready for use." These statements shall be the first statements under the heading "Directions".

(e) *Products formulated and labeled as a styptic pencil and that meet the criteria established in § 201.66(d)(10) of this chapter.* The title, headings, subheadings, and information described in § 201.66(c) of this chapter shall be printed in accordance with the following specifications:

(1) The labeling shall meet the requirements of § 201.66(c) of this chapter

293

except that the headings and information described in § 201.66(c)(3) and (c)(7) may be omitted, and the headings, subheadings, and information described in § 201.66(c)(4) and (c)(5) may be presented as follows:

(i) The heading and indication required by § 201.66(c)(4) of this chapter may be limited to: "Use [in bold type] stops bleeding of minor cuts from shaving".

(ii) The "external use only" warning in § 347.52(c)(1) and in § 201.66(c)(5)(i) of this chapter may be omitted. The second warning in § 347.52(c)(1) may state: "avoid contact with eyes". The warning in § 201.66(c)(5)(x) may be limited to the following: "Keep out of reach of children." The subheadings in § 201.66(c)(5)(iii) through (c)(5)(vii) may be omitted, provided the information after the heading "Warning" contains the warnings in this paragraph.

(2) The labeling shall be printed in accordance with the requirements of § 201.66(d) of this chapter except that any requirements related to § 201.66(c)(3) and (c)(7), and the horizontal barlines and hairlines described in § 201.66(d)(8), may be omitted.

[68 FR 33377, June 4, 2003, as amended at 68 FR 35293, June 13, 2003; 69 FR 3005, Jan. 22, 2004; 74 FR 9765, Mar. 6, 2009]

§ 347.60 Labeling of permitted combinations of active ingredients.

The statement of identity, indications, warnings, and directions for use, respectively, applicable to each ingredient in the product may be combined to eliminate duplicative words or phrases so that the resulting information is clear and understandable.

(a) *Statement of identity.* For a combination drug product that has an established name, the labeling of the product states the established name of the combination drug product, followed by the statement of identity for each ingredient in the combination, as established in the statement of identity sections of the applicable OTC drug monographs. For a combination drug product that does not have an established name, the labeling of the product states the statement of identity for each ingredient in the combination, as established in the statement of iden-

tity sections of the applicable OTC drug monographs.

(b) *Indications.* The labeling of the product states, under the heading "Uses," the indication(s) for each ingredient in the combination as established in the indications sections of the applicable OTC drug monographs, unless otherwise stated in this paragraph (b). Other truthful and nonmisleading statements, describing only the indications for use that have been established in the applicable OTC drug monographs or listed in this paragraph (b) may also be used, as provided in § 330.1(c)(2) of this chapter, subject to the provisions of section 502 of the Federal Food, Drug, and Cosmetic Act (the act) relating to misbranding and the prohibition in section 301(d) of the act against the introduction or delivery for introduction into interstate commerce of unapproved new drugs in violation of section 505(a) of the act. In addition to the required information identified in this paragraph (b), the labeling of the product may contain any of the "other allowable statements" that are identified in the applicable monographs, provided such statements are neither placed in direct conjunction with information required to appear in the labeling nor occupy labeling space with greater prominence or conspicuousness than the required information.

(1) *Combinations of skin protectant and external analgesic active ingredients in § 347.20(b).* In addition to any or all of the indications for skin protectant drug products in § 347.50(b)(1), any or all of the allowable indications for external analgesic drug products may be used if the product is labeled for concurrent symptoms.

(2) *Combinations of skin protectant and first aid antiseptic active ingredients in § 347.20(c).* In addition to any or all of the indications for skin protectant drug products in § 347.50(b)(1), the required indications for first aid antiseptic drug products should be used.

(3) *Combinations of skin protectant and sunscreen active ingredients in § 347.20(d).* In addition to any or all of the indications for skin protectant drug products in § 347.50(b)(2)(i), the required indications for sunscreen drug products

should be used and any or all of the additional indications for sunscreen drug products may be used.

(c) *Warnings.* The labeling of the product states, under the heading "Warnings," the warning(s) for each ingredient in the combination, as established in the warnings section of the applicable OTC drug monographs unless otherwise stated in this paragraph (c).

(1) *For combinations containing a skin protectant and a sunscreen identified in §§ 347.20(d) and 352.20(b).* The warnings for sunscreen drug products in § 352.60(c) of this chapter are used.

(2) [Reserved]

(d) *Directions.* The labeling of the product states, under the heading "Directions," directions that conform to the directions established for each ingredient in the directions sections of the applicable OTC drug monographs, unless otherwise stated in this paragraph (d). When the time intervals or age limitations for administration of the individual ingredients differ, the directions for the combination product may not contain any dosage that exceeds those established for any individual ingredient in the applicable OTC drug monograph(s), and may not provide for use by any age group lower than the highest minimum age limit established for any individual ingredient.

(1) *For combinations containing a skin protectant and a sunscreen identified in §§ 347.20(d) and 352.20(b).* The directions for sunscreen drug products in § 352.60(d) of this chapter are used.

(2) [Reserved]

PART 348—EXTERNAL ANALGESIC DRUG PRODUCTS FOR OVER-THE-COUNTER HUMAN USE

Subpart A—General Provisions

AUTHORITY: 21 U.S.C. 321, 351, 352, 353, 355, 360, 371.

SOURCE: 57 FR 27656, June 19, 1992, unless otherwise noted.

Subpart A—General Provisions

§ 348.1 Scope.

(a) An over-the-counter external analgesic drug product in a form suitable for topical administration is generally recognized as safe and effective and is not misbranded if it meets each condition in this part and each general condition established in § 330.1 of this chapter.

(b) References in this part to regulatory sections of the Code of Federal Regulations are to chapter I of title 21 unless otherwise noted.

§ 348.3 Definitions.

As used in this part:

(a) *Male genital desensitizing drug product.* A drug product applied to the penis to help in temporarily slowing the onset of ejaculation.

(b) [Reserved]

Subpart B—Active Ingredients

§ 348.10 Analgesic, anesthetic, and antipruritic active ingredients.

The active ingredient of the product consists of any of the following within the specified concentration established for each ingredient:

(a) *Male genital desensitizers.* (1) Benzocaine, 3 to 7.5 percent in a water-soluble base.

(2) Lidocaine in a metered spray with approximately 10 milligrams per spray.

(b) [Reserved]

Subpart C—Labeling

§ 348.50 Labeling of external analgesic drug products.

(a) *Statement of identity.* The labeling of the product contains the established name of the drug, if any, and identifies the product as follows:

(1) *For products containing any ingredient identified in § 348.10(a).* "Male genital desensitizer."

(2) [Reserved]

(b) *Indications.* The labeling of the product states, under the heading "Indications," any of the phrases listed in paragraph (b) of this section. Other truthful and nonmisleading statements, describing only the indications for use that have been established and listed in paragraph (b) of this section, may also be used, as provided in § 330.1(c)(2) of this chapter, subject to the provisions of section 502 of the Federal Food, Drug, and Cosmetic Act (the act) relating to misbranding and the prohibition in section 301(d) of the act against the introduction or delivery for introduction into interstate commerce of unapproved new drugs in violation of section 505(a) of the act.

(1) *For products containing any ingredient identified in § 348.10(a).* (i) "Helps in the prevention of premature ejaculation."

(ii) "For temporary male genital desensitization, helping to slow the onset of ejaculation."

(iii) "Helps in temporarily" (select one of the following: "retarding the onset of," "slowing the onset of," or "prolonging the time until") followed by "ejaculation."

(iv) "For reducing oversensitivity in the male in advance of intercourse."

(2) [Reserved]

(c) *Warnings.* The labeling of the product contains the following warnings under the heading "Warnings":

(1) *For products containing any ingredient identified in § 348.10(a).* (i) "Premature ejaculation may be due to a condition requiring medical supervision. If this product, used as directed, does not provide relief, discontinue use and consult a doctor."

(ii) "Avoid contact with the eyes."

(iii) "If you or your partner develop a rash or irritation, such as burning or itching, discontinue use. If symptoms persist, consult a doctor."

(2) [Reserved]

(d) *Directions.* The labeling of the product contains the following information under the heading "Directions":

(1) *For products containing any ingredient identified in § 348.10(a)*—(i) *For products containing benzocaine identified in § 348.10(a)(1).* "Apply a small amount to head and shaft of penis before inter-

course, or use as directed by a doctor. Wash product off after intercourse."

(ii) *For products containing lidocaine identified in § 348.10(a)(2).* "Apply 3 or more sprays, not to exceed 10, to head and shaft of penis before intercourse, or use as directed by a doctor. Wash product off after intercourse."

(2) [Reserved]

(e) The word "physician" may be substituted for the word "doctor" in any of the labeling statements in this section.

PART 349—OPHTHALMIC DRUG PRODUCTS FOR OVER-THE-COUNTER HUMAN USE

Subpart A—General Provisions

Sec.
349.1 Scope.
349.3 Definitions.

Subpart B—Active Ingredients

349.10 Ophthalmic astringent.
349.12 Ophthalmic demulcents.
349.14 Ophthalmic emollients.
349.16 Ophthalmic hypertonicity agent.
349.18 Ophthalmic vasoconstrictors.
349.20 Eyewashes.
349.30 Permitted combinations of active ingredients.

Subpart C—Labeling

349.50 Labeling of ophthalmic drug products.
349.55 Labeling of ophthalmic astringent drug products.
349.60 Labeling of ophthalmic demulcent drug products.
349.65 Labeling of ophthalmic emollient drug products.
349.70 Labeling of ophthalmic hypertonicity drug products.
349.75 Labeling of ophthalmic vasoconstrictor drug products.
349.78 Labeling of eyewash drug products.
349.79 Labeling of permitted combinations of active ingredients.
349.80 Professional labeling.

AUTHORITY: 21 U.S.C. 321, 351, 352, 353, 355, 360, 371.

SOURCE: 53 FR 7090, Mar. 4, 1988, unless otherwise noted.

Subpart A—General Provisions

§349.1 Scope.

(a) An over-the-counter ophthalmic drug product in a form suitable for topical administration is generally recognized as safe and effective and is not misbranded if it meets each of the conditions in this part and each of the general conditions established in §330.1.

(b) References in this part to regulatory sections of the Code of Federal Regulations are to chapter I of title 21 unless otherwise noted.

§349.3 Definitions.

As used in this part:

(a) *Ophthalmic drug product.* A drug product, which should be sterile in accordance with §200.50, to be applied to the eyelid or instilled in the eye.

(b) *Astringent.* A locally acting pharmacologic agent which, by precipitating protein, helps to clear mucus from the outer surface of the eye.

(c) *Buffering agent.* A substance which stabilizes the pH of solutions against changes produced by introduction of acids or bases from such sources as drugs, body fluids, tears, etc.

(d) *Demulcent.* An agent, usually a water-soluble polymer, which is applied topically to the eye to protect and lubricate mucous membrane surfaces and relieve dryness and irritation.

(e) *Emollient.* An agent, usually a fat or oil, which is applied locally to eyelids to protect or soften tissues and to prevent drying and cracking.

(f) *Eyewash, eye lotion, irrigating solution.* A sterile aqueous solution intended for washing, bathing, or flushing the eye.

(g) *Hypertonicity agent.* An agent which exerts an osmotic gradient greater than that present in body tissues and fluids, so that water is drawn from the body tissues and fluids across semipermeable membranes. Applied topically to the eye, a hypertonicity agent creates an osmotic gradient which draws water out of the cornea.

(h) *Isotonicity.* A state or quality in which the osmotic pressure in two fluids is equal.

(i) *Vasoconstrictor.* A pharmacologic agent which, when applied topically to the mucous membranes of the eye, causes transient constriction of conjunctival blood vessels.

Subpart B—Active Ingredients

§349.10 Ophthalmic astringent.

The active ingredient and its concentration in the product is as follows: Zinc sulfate, 0.25 percent.

§349.12 Ophthalmic demulcents.

The active ingredients of the product consist of any of the following, within the established concentrations for each ingredient:

(a) Cellulose derivatives:

(1) Carboxymethylcellulose sodium, 0.2 to 2.5 percent.

(2) Hydroxyethyl cellulose, 0.2 to 2.5 percent.

(3) Hypromellose, 0.2 to 2.5 percent.

(4) Methylcellulose, 0.2 to 2.5 percent.

(b) Dextran 70, 0.1 percent when used with another polymeric demulcent agent in this section.

(c) Gelatin, 0.01 percent.

(d) Polyols, liquid:

(1) Glycerin, 0.2 to 1 percent.

(2) Polyethylene glycol 300, 0.2 to 1 percent.

(3) Polyethylene glycol 400, 0.2 to 1 percent.

(4) Polysorbate 80, 0.2 to 1 percent.

(5) Propylene glycol, 0.2 to 1 percent.

(e) Polyvinyl alcohol, 0.1 to 4 percent.

(f) Povidone, 0.1 to 2 percent.

[53 FR 7090, Mar. 4, 1988, as amended at 68 FR 32982, June 3, 2003]

§349.14 Ophthalmic emollients.

The active ingredients of the product consist of any of the following:

(a) Lanolin preparations:

(1) Anhydrous lanolin, 1 to 10 percent in combination with one or more oleaginous emollient agents included in the monograph.

(2) Lanolin, 1 to 10 percent in combination with one or more oleaginous emollient agents included in the monograph.

(b) Oleaginous ingredients:

(1) Light mineral oil, up to 50 percent in combination with one or more other emollient agents included in the monograph.

(2) Mineral oil, up to 50 percent in combination with one or more other

emollient agents included in the monograph.

(3) Paraffin, up to 5 percent in combination with one or more other emollient agents included in the monograph.

(4) Petrolatum, up to 100 percent.

(5) White ointment, up to 100 percent.

(6) White petrolatum, up to 100 percent.

(7) White wax, up to 5 percent in combination with one or more other emollient agents included in the monograph.

(8) Yellow wax, up to 5 percent in combination with one or more other emollient agents included in the monograph.

§ 349.16 Ophthalmic   hypertonicity agent.

The active ingredient and its concentration in the product is as follows: Sodium chloride, 2 to 5 percent.

§ 349.18 Ophthalmic vasoconstrictors.

The active ingredient of the product consists of one of the following, within the established concentration for each ingredient:

(a) Ephedrine hydrochloride, 0.123 percent.

(b) Naphazoline hydrochloride, 0.01 to 0.03 percent.

(c) Phenylephrine hydrochloride, 0.08 to 0.2 percent.

(d) Tetrahydrozoline hydrochloride, 0.01 to 0.05 percent.

§ 349.20 Eyewashes.

The active ingredient of the product is purified water. The product also contains suitable tonicity agents to establish isotonicity with tears, suitable agents for establishing pH and buffering to achieve the same pH as tears, and a suitable preservative agent.

[68 FR 7921, Feb. 19, 2003]

§ 349.30 Permitted combinations of active ingredients.

The following combinations are permitted provided each active ingredient is present within the established concentration, and the product is labeled in accordance with § 349.79.

(a) Any single ophthalmic astringent active ingredient identified in § 349.10

may be combined with any single ophthalmic vasoconstrictor active ingredient identified in § 349.18.

(b) Any two or three ophthalmic demulcent active ingredients identified in § 349.12 may be combined.

(c) Any single ophthalmic demulcent active ingredient identified in § 349.12 or any ophthalmic demulcent combination identified in paragraph (b) of this section may be combined with any single ophthalmic vasoconstrictor identified in § 349.18.

(d) Any single ophthalmic astringent active ingredient identified in § 349.10 may be combined with any single ophthalmic vasoconstrictor active ingredient identified in § 349.18 and any single ophthalmic demulcent identified in § 349.12 or ophthalmic demulcent combination identified in paragraph (b) of this section.

(e) Any two or more emollient active ingredients identified in § 349.14 may be combined as necessary to give the product proper consistency for application to the eye.

Subpart C—Labeling

§ 349.50 Labeling of ophthalmic drug products.

(a) The word "physician" may be substituted for the word "doctor" in any of the labeling statements in this part.

(b) Where applicable, indications in this part applicable to each ingredient in the product may be combined to eliminate duplicative words or phrases so that the resulting information is clear and understandable. Other truthful and nonmisleading statements, describing only the indications for use that have been established and listed in this part, may also be used, as provided in § 330.1(c)(2), subject to the provisions of section 502 of the act relating to misbranding and the prohibition in section 301(d) of the act against the introduction or delivery for introduction into interstate commerce of unapproved new drugs in violation of section 505(a) of the act.

(c) The labeling of the product contains the following warnings, under the heading "Warnings":

(1) *For ophthalmic drug products packaged in multi-use containers.* "To avoid

contamination, do not touch tip of container to any surface. Replace cap after using."

(2) *For ophthalmic drug products packaged in single-use containers.* "To avoid contamination, do not touch tip of container to any surface. Do not reuse. Once opened, discard."

(3) *For ophthalmic drug products containing mercury compounds used as a preservative.* "This product contains (name and quantity of mercury-containing ingredient) as a preservative. Do not use this product if you are sensitive to" (select one of the following: "mercury" or "(insert name of mercury-containing ingredient) or any other ingredient containing mercury)."

§349.55 Labeling of ophthalmic astringent drug products.

(a) *Statement of identity.* The labeling of the product contains the established name of the drug, if any, and identifies the product as an "astringent" (select one of the following: "eye" or "ophthalmic") "(insert dosage form, e.g., drops)."

(b) *Indications.* The labeling of the product states, under the heading "Indications," the following phrase: "For the temporary relief of discomfort from minor eye irritations."

(c) *Warnings.* In addition to the warnings in §349.50, the labeling of the product contains the following warnings under the heading "Warnings" for products containing any ingredient identified in §349.10:

(1) "If you experience eye pain, changes in vision, continued redness or irritation of the eye, or if the condition worsens or persists for more than 72 hours, discontinue use and consult a doctor."

(2) "If solution changes color or becomes cloudy, do not use."

(d) *Directions.* The labeling of the product contains the following information under the heading "Directions": Instill 1 to 2 drops in the affected eye(s) up to four times daily.

§349.60 Labeling of ophthalmic demulcent drug products.

(a) *Statement of identity.* The labeling of the product contains the established name of the drug(s), if any, and identifies the product as a "lubricant" or "demulcent (lubricant)" (select one of the following: "eye" or "ophthalmic") "(insert dosage form, e.g., drops)."

(b) *Indications.* The labeling of the product states, under the heading "Indications," one or more of the following phrases:

(1) "For the temporary relief of burning and irritation due to dryness of the eye."

(2) "For the temporary relief of discomfort due to minor irritations of the eye or to exposure to wind or sun."

(3) "For use as a protectant against further irritation or to relieve dryness of the eye."

(4) "For use as a lubricant to prevent further irritation or to relieve dryness of the eye."

(c) *Warnings.* In addition to the warnings in §349.50, the labeling of the product contains the following warnings under the heading "Warnings" for products containing any ingredient identified in §349.12:

(1) "If you experience eye pain, changes in vision, continued redness or irritation of the eye, or if the condition worsens or persists for more than 72 hours, discontinue use and consult a doctor."

(2) "If solution changes color or becomes cloudy, do not use."

(d) *Directions.* The labeling of the product contains the following information under the heading "Directions": Instill 1 or 2 drops in the affected eye(s) as needed.

§349.65 Labeling of ophthalmic emollient drug products.

(a) *Statement of identity.* The labeling of the product contains the established name of the drug(s), if any, and identifies the product as a "lubricant" or "emollient (lubricant)" (select one of the following: "eye" or "ophthalmic") "(insert dosage form, e.g., ointment)."

(b) *Indications.* The labeling of the product states, under the heading "Indications," one or more of the following phrases:

(1) "For the temporary relief of burning and irritation due to dryness of the eye."

(2) "For the temporary relief of discomfort due to minor irritations of the eye or to exposure to wind or sun."

(3) "For use as a protectant against further irritation or to relieve dryness of the eye."

(4) "For use as a lubricant to prevent further irritation or to relieve dryness of the eye."

(c) *Warnings.* In addition to the warnings in § 349.50, the labeling of the product contains the following warnings under the heading "Warnings" for products containing any ingredient identified in § 349.14: "If you experience eye pain, changes in vision, continued redness or irritation of the eye, or if the condition worsens or persists for more than 72 hours, discontinue use and consult a doctor."

(d) *Directions.* The labeling of the product contains the following information under the heading "Directions": Pull down the lower lid of the affected eye and apply a small amount (one-fourth inch) of ointment to the inside of the eyelid.

§ 349.70 Labeling of ophthalmic hypertonicity drug products.

(a) *Statement of identity.* The labeling of the product contains the established name of the drug, if any, and identifies the product as a "hypertonicity" (select one of the following: "eye" or "ophthalmic") "(insert dosage form, e.g., drops)."

(b) *Indications.* The labeling of the product states, under the heading "Indications," the following phrase: "For the temporary relief of corneal edema."

(c) *Warnings.* In addition to the warnings in § 349.50, the labeling of the product contains the following warnings under the heading "Warnings" for products containing any ingredient identified in § 349.16:

(1) "Do not use this product except under the advice and supervision of a doctor. If you experience eye pain, changes in vision, continued redness or irritation of the eye, or if the condition worsens or persists, consult a doctor."

(2) "This product may cause temporary burning and irritation on being instilled into the eye."

(3) "If solution changes color or becomes cloudy, do not use."

(d) *Directions.* The labeling of the product contains the following information under the heading "Direc-

tions": Instill 1 or 2 drops in the affected eye(s) every 3 or 4 hours, or as directed by a doctor.

§ 349.75 Labeling of ophthalmic vaso-constrictor drug products.

(a) *Statement of identity.* The labeling of the product contains the established name of the drug(s), if any, and identifies the product as a "redness reliever" or "vasoconstrictor (redness reliever)" (select one of the following: "eye" or "ophthalmic") "(insert dosage form, e.g., drops)."

(b) *Indications.* The labeling of the product states, under the heading "Indications," the following phrase: "Relieves redness of the eye due to minor eye irritations."

(c) *Warnings.* In addition to the warnings in § 349.50, the labeling of the product contains the following warnings under the heading "Warnings" for products containing any ingredient identified in § 349.18:

(1) "If you experience eye pain, changes in vision, continued redness or irritation of the eye, or if the condition worsens or persists for more than 72 hours, discontinue use and consult a doctor."

(2) "Ask a doctor before use if you have [in bold type] narrow angle glaucoma."

(3) "Overuse of this product may produce increased redness of the eye."

(4) "If solution changes color or becomes cloudy, do not use."

(5) "When using this product [in bold type] pupils may become enlarged temporarily."

(d) *Directions.* The labeling of the product contains the following information under the heading "Directions": Instill 1 to 2 drops in the affected eye(s) up to four times daily.

[53 FR 7090, Mar. 4, 1988, as amended at 65 FR 38428, June 21, 2000]

§ 349.78 Labeling of eyewash drug products.

(a) *Statement of identity.* The labeling of the product identifies the product with one or more of the following terms: "eyewash," "eye irrigation," or "eye irrigating solution."

(b) *Indications.* The labeling of the product states, under the heading "Indications," one of the following phrases:

(1) "For" (select one of the following: "flushing," "irrigating," "cleansing," "washing," or "bathing") "the eye to remove" (select one or more of the following: "loose foreign material," "air pollutants (smog or pollen)," or "chlorinated water").

(2) "For" (select one of the following: "flushing," "irrigating," "cleansing," "washing," or "bathing") "the eye to help relieve" (select one or more of the following: "irritation," "discomfort," "burning," "stinging," "smarting," or "itching") "by removing" (select one or more of the following: "loose foreign material," "air pollutants (smog or pollen)," or "chlorinated water").

(c) *Warnings.* In addition to the warnings in §349.50, the labeling of the product contains the following warnings under the heading "Warnings" for all eyewash products:

(1) "If you experience eye pain, changes in vision, continued redness or irritation of the eye, or if the condition worsens or persists, consult a doctor."

(2) "Obtain immediate medical treatment for all open wounds in or near the eyes."

(3) "If solution changes color or becomes cloudy, do not use."

(d) *Directions.* The labeling of the product contains the following information under the heading "Directions":

(1) *For eyewash products intended for use with an eyecup.* Rinse cup with clean water immediately before each use. Avoid contamination of rim and inside surfaces of cup. Fill cup half full and apply the cup to the affected eye, pressing tightly to prevent the escape of the liquid, and tilt the head backward. Open eyelids wide and rotate eyeball to ensure thorough bathing with the wash or lotion. Rinse cup with clean water after each use.

(2) *For eyewash products intended for use with a nozzle applicator.* Flush the affected eye as needed, controlling the rate of flow of solution by pressure on the bottle.

[53 FR 7090, Mar. 4, 1988, as amended at 68 FR 7921, Feb. 19, 2003]

§349.79 Labeling of permitted combinations of active ingredients.

Statements of identity, indications, warnings, and directions for use, respectively, applicable to each ingredient in the product may be combined to eliminate duplicative words or phrases so that the resulting information is clear and understandable.

(a) *Statement of identity.* For a combination drug product that has an established name, the labeling of the product states the established name of the combination drug product, followed by the statement of identity for each ingredient in the combination, as established in the statement of identity sections of this part. For a combination drug product that does not have an established name, the labeling of the product states the statement of identity for each ingredient in the combination, as established in the statement of identity sections of this part.

(b) *Indications.* The labeling of the product states, under the heading "Indications," the indication(s) for each ingredient in the combination, as established in the indications sections of this part.

(c) *Warnings.* The labeling of the product states, under the heading "Warnings," the warning(s) for each ingredient in the combination, as established in the warnings sections of this part.

(d) *Directions.* The labeling of the product states, under the heading "Directions," directions that conform to the directions established for each ingredient in the directions sections of this part. When the time intervals or age limitations for administration of the individual ingredients differ, the directions for the combination product may not exceed any maximum dosage limits established for the individual ingredients in the applicable OTC drug monograph.

§349.80 Professional labeling.

The labeling of any OTC ophthalmic demulcent drug product provided to health professionals (but not to the general public) may contain instructions for the use of these products in professional eye examinations (*i.e.,* gonioscopy, electroretinography).

PART 350—ANTIPERSPIRANT DRUG PRODUCTS FOR OVER-THE-COUNTER HUMAN USE

Subpart A—General Provisions

Sec.
350.1 Scope.
350.3 Definition.

Subpart B—Active Ingredients

350.10 Antiperspirant active ingredients.

Subpart C—Labeling

350.50 Labeling of antiperspirant drug products.

Subpart D—Guidelines for Effectiveness Testing

350.60 Guidelines for effectiveness testing of antiperspirant drug products.

AUTHORITY: 21 U.S.C. 321, 351, 352, 353, 355, 360, 371.

SOURCE: 68 FR 34291, June 9, 2003, unless otherwise noted.

Subpart A—General Provisions

§ 350.1 Scope.

(a) An over-the-counter antiperspirant drug product in a form suitable for topical administration is generally recognized as safe and effective and is not misbranded if it meets each condition in this part and each general condition established in § 330.1 of this chapter.

(b) References in this part to regulatory sections of the Code of Federal Regulations are to chapter I of title 21 unless otherwise noted.

§ 350.3 Definition.

As used in this part:
Antiperspirant. A drug product applied topically that reduces the production of perspiration (sweat) at that site.

Subpart B—Active Ingredients

§ 350.10 Antiperspirant active ingredients.

The active ingredient of the product consists of any of the following within the established concentration and dosage formulation. Where applicable, the ingredient must meet the aluminum to chloride, aluminum to zirconium, and aluminum plus zirconium to chloride atomic ratios described in the U.S. Pharmacopeia-National Formulary. The concentration of ingredients in paragraphs (b) through (j) of this section is calculated on an anhydrous basis, omitting from the calculation any buffer component present in the compound, in an aerosol or nonaerosol dosage form. The concentration of ingredients in paragraphs (k) through (r) of this section is calculated on an anhydrous basis, omitting from the calculation any buffer component present in the compound, in a nonaerosol dosage form. The labeled declaration of the percentage of the active ingredient should exclude any water, buffer components, or propellant.

(a) Aluminum chloride up to 15 percent, calculated on the hexahydrate form, in an aqueous solution nonaerosol dosage form.

(b) Aluminum chlorohydrate up to 25 percent.

(c) Aluminum chlorohydrex polyethylene glycol up to 25 percent.

(d) Aluminum chlorohydrex propylene glycol up to 25 percent.

(e) Aluminum dichlorohydrate up to 25 percent.

(f) Aluminum dichlorohydrex polyethylene glycol up to 25 percent.

(g) Aluminum dichlorohydrex propylene glycol up to 25 percent.

(h) Aluminum sesquichlorohydrate up to 25 percent.

(i) Aluminum sesquichlorohydrex polyethylene glycol up to 25 percent.

(j) Aluminum sesquichlorohydrex propylene glycol up to 25 percent.

(k) Aluminum zirconium octachlorohydrate up to 20 percent.

(l) Aluminum zirconium octachlorohydrex gly up to 20 percent.

(m) Aluminum zirconium pentachlorohydrate up to 20 percent.

(n) Aluminum zirconium pentachlorohydrex gly up to 20 percent.

(o) Aluminum zirconium tetrachlorohydrate up to 20 percent.

(p) Aluminum zirconium tetrachlorohydrex gly up to 20 percent.

(q) Aluminum zirconium trichlorohydrate up to 20 percent.

(r) Aluminum zirconium trichlorohydrex gly up to 20 percent.

Subpart C—Labeling

§350.50 Labeling of antiperspirant drug products.

(a) *Statement of identity.* The labeling of the product contains the established name of the drug, if any, and identifies the product as an "antiperspirant."

(b) *Indications.* The labeling of the product states, under the heading "Uses," the phrase listed in paragraph (b)(1) of this section and may contain any additional phrases listed in paragraphs (b)(2) through (b)(5) of this section, as appropriate. Other truthful and nonmisleading statements, describing only the uses that have been established and listed in paragraphs (b)(1) through (b)(5) of this section, may also be used, as provided in §330.1(c)(2) of this chapter, subject to the provisions of section 502 of the Federal Food, Drug, and Cosmetic Act (the act) relating to misbranding and the prohibition in section 301(d) of the act against the introduction or delivery for introduction into interstate commerce of unapproved new drugs in violation of section 505(a) of the act.

(1) For any product, the labeling states [select one of the following: "decreases," "lessens," or "reduces"] "underarm" [select one of the following: "dampness," "perspiration," "sweat," "sweating," or "wetness"].

(2) The labeling may state "also [select one of the following: 'decreases,' 'lessens,' or 'reduces'] underarm [select one of the following: 'dampness,' 'perspiration,' 'sweat,' 'sweating,' or 'wetness'] due to stress".

(3) For products that demonstrate standard effectiveness (20 percent sweat reduction) over a 24-hour period, the labeling may state [select one of the following: "all day protection," "lasts all day," "lasts 24 hours," or "24 hour protection"].

(4) For products that demonstrate extra effectiveness (30 percent sweat reduction), the labeling may state "extra effective".

(5) Products that demonstrate extra effectiveness (30 percent sweat reduction) sustained over a 24-hour period may state the claims in paragraphs (b)(3) and (b)(4) of this section either individually or combined, e.g., "24 hour extra effective protection", "all day extra effective protection," "extra effective protection lasts 24 hours," or "extra effective protection lasts all day".

(c) *Warnings.* The labeling of the product contains the following statements under the heading "Warnings":

(1) "Do not use on broken skin".

(2) "Stop use if rash or irritation occurs".

(3) "Ask a doctor before use if you have kidney disease".

(4) *For products in an aerosolized dosage form.* (i) "When using this product [bullet][1] keep away from face and mouth to avoid breathing it".

(ii) The warning required by §369.21 of this chapter for drugs in dispensers pressurized by gaseous propellants.

(d) *Directions.* The labeling of the product contains the following statement under the heading "Directions": "apply to underarms only".

EFFECTIVE DATE NOTE: At 69 FR 61149, Oct. 15, 2004, the limitation of the enhanced duration claim to 24 hours (21 CFR 350.50 (b)(3) and (b) (5)) was stayed until further notice.

Subpart D—Guidelines for Effectiveness Testing

§350.60 Guidelines for effectiveness testing of antiperspirant drug products.

An antiperspirant in finished dosage form may vary in degree of effectiveness because of minor variations in formulation. To assure the effectiveness of an antiperspirant, the Food and Drug Administration is providing guidelines that manufacturers may use in testing for effectiveness. These guidelines are on file in the Dockets Management Branch (HFA–305), Food and Drug Administration, 5630 Fishers Lane, rm. 1061, Rockville, MD 20852. These guidelines are available on the FDA's web site at *http://www.fda.gov/cder/otc/index.htm* or on request for a nominal charge by submitting a Freedom of Information (FOI) request in writing to FDA's Division of Freedom of Information (address is located on

[1] See §201.66(b)(4) of this chapter for definition of bullet.

303

the agency's web site at *http://www.fda.gov.*

[68 FR 34291, June 9, 2003, as amended at 76 FR 31470, June 1, 2011; 79 FR 68115, Nov. 14, 2014]

PART 352—SUNSCREEN DRUG PRODUCTS FOR OVER-THE-COUNTER HUMAN USE [STAYED INDEFINITELY]

AUTHORITY: 21 U.S.C. 321, 351, 352, 353, 355, 360, 371.

SOURCE: 64 FR 27687, May 21, 1999, unless otherwise noted.

EFFECTIVE DATE NOTE: At 68 FR 33381, June 4, 2003, part 352 was stayed until further notice, effective June 4, 2004.

Subpart A—General Provisions

§ 352.1   Scope.

(a) An over-the-counter sunscreen drug product in a form suitable for topical administration is generally recognized as safe and effective and is not misbranded if it meets each condition in this part and each general condition established in § 330.1 of this chapter.

(b) References in this part to regulatory sections of the Code of Federal Regulations are to Chapter I of Title 21 unless otherwise noted.

§ 352.3   Definitions.

As used in this part:

(a) *Minimal erythema dose (MED).* The quantity of erythema-effective energy (expressed as Joules per square meter) required to produce the first perceptible, redness reaction with clearly defined borders.

(b) *Product category designation (PCD).* A labeling designation for sunscreen drug products to aid in selecting the type of product best suited to an individual's complexion (pigmentation) and desired response to ultraviolet (UV) radiation.

(1) *Minimal sun protection product.* A sunscreen product that provides a sun protection factor (SPF) value of 2 to under 12.

(2) *Moderate sun protection product.* A sunscreen product that provides an SPF value of 12 to under 30.

(3) *High sun protection product.* A sunscreen product that provides an SPF value of 30 or above.

(c) *Sunscreen active ingredient.* An active ingredient listed in § 352.10 that absorbs, reflects, or scatters radiation in the UV range at wavelengths from 290 to 400 nanometers.

(d) *Sun protection factor (SPF) value.* The UV energy required to produce an MED on protected skin divided by the UV energy required to produce an MED on unprotected skin, which may also be defined by the following ratio: SPF value =MED (protected skin (PS))/MED (unprotected skin (US)), where MED (PS) is the minimal erythema dose for protected skin after application of 2 milligrams per square centimeter of the final formulation of the sunscreen product, and MED (US) is the minimal erythema dose for unprotected skin, *i.e.,* skin to which no sunscreen product has been applied. In effect, the SPF value is the reciprocal of the effective transmission of the product viewed as a UV radiation filter.

Subpart B—Active Ingredients

§ 352.10   Sunscreen active ingredients.

The active ingredient of the product consists of any of the following, within the concentration specified for each ingredient, and the finished product provides a minimum SPF value of not less than 2 as measured by the testing procedures established in subpart D of this part:

(a) Aminobenzoic acid (PABA) up to 15 percent.

(b) Avobenzone up to 3 percent.

(c) Cinoxate up to 3 percent.

(d) [Reserved]

(e) Dioxybenzone up to 3 percent.

(f) Homosalate up to 15 percent.

(g) [Reserved]

(h) Menthyl anthranilate up to 5 percent.

(i) Octocrylene up to 10 percent.

(j) Octyl methoxycinnamate up to 7.5 percent.

(k) Octyl salicylate up to 5 percent.

(l) Oxybenzone up to 6 percent.

(m) Padimate O up to 8 percent.

(n) Phenylbenzimidazole sulfonic acid up to 4 percent.

(o) Sulisobenzone up to 10 percent.

(p) Titanium dioxide up to 25 percent.

(q) Trolamine salicylate up to 12 percent.

(r) Zinc oxide up to 25 percent.

[64 FR 27687, May 21, 1999]

EFFECTIVE DATE NOTE: At 67 FR 41823, June 20, 2002, §352.10 was amended by revising paragraphs (f) through (n), effective Sept. 1, 2002. This amendment could not be incorporated because at 66 FR 67485, Dec. 31, 2001 the effective date was stayed until further notice. For the convenience of the user, the revised text is set forth as follows:

§352.10 Sunscreen active ingredients.

*   *   *   *   *

(f) Ensulizole up to 4 percent.

(g) Homosalate up to 15 percent.

(h) [Reserved]

(i) Meradimate up to 5 percent.

(j) Octinoxate up to 7.5 percent.

(k) Octisalate up to 5 percent.

(l) Octocrylene up to 10 percent.

(m) Oxybenzone up to 6 percent.

(n) Padimate O up to 8 percent.

*   *   *   *   *

§352.20 Permitted combinations of active ingredients.

The SPF of any combination product is measured by the testing procedures established in subpart D of this part.

(a) *Combinations of sunscreen active ingredients.* (1) Two or more sunscreen active ingredients identified in §352.10(a), (c), (e), (f), and (h) through (r) may be combined with each other in a single product when used in the concentrations established for each ingredient in §352.10. The concentration of each active ingredient must be sufficient to contribute a minimum SPF of not less than 2 to the finished product. The finished product must have a minimum SPF of not less than the number of sunscreen active ingredients used in the combination multiplied by 2.

(2) Two or more sunscreen active ingredients identified in §352.10(b), (c), (e), (f), (i) through (l), (o), and (q) may be combined with each other in a single product when used in the concentrations established for each ingredient in §352.10. The concentration of each active ingredient must be sufficient to contribute a minimum SPF of not less than 2 to the finished product. The finished product must have a minimum SPF of not less than the number of sunscreen active ingredients used in the combination multiplied by 2.

(b) *Combinations of sunscreen and skin protectant active ingredients.* Any single sunscreen active ingredient or any permitted combination of sunscreen active ingredients when used in the concentrations established for each ingredient in §352.10 may be combined with one or more skin protectant active ingredients identified in §347.10(a), (d), (e), (g), (h), (i), (k), (l), (m), and (r) of this chapter. The concentration of each sunscreen active ingredient must be sufficient to contribute a minimum SPF of not less that 2 to the finished product. The finished product must have a minimum SPF of not less than the number of sunscreen active ingredients used in the combination multiplied by 2, and the product must be labeled according to §352.60.

(c) [Reserved]

[64 FR 27687, May 21, 1999, as amended at 68 FR 33380, June 4, 2003]

EFFECTIVE DATE NOTE: At 67 FR 41823, June 20, 2002, §352.20 was amended by revising paragraphs (a)(1) through (a)(2), effective Sept. 1, 2002. This amendment could not be incorporated because at 66 FR 67485, Dec. 31, 2001 the effective date was stayed until further notice. For the convenience of the user, the text is set forth as follows:

§ 352.20 Permitted combinations of active ingredients.

*   *   *   *   *

(a) *Combinations of sunscreen active ingredients.* (1) Two or more sunscreen active ingredients identified in § 352.10(a), (c), (e), (f), (g), and (i) through (r) may be combined with each other in a single product when used in the concentrations established for each ingredient in § 352.10. The concentration of each active ingredient must be sufficient to contribute a minimum SPF of not less than 2 to the finished product. The finished product must have a minimum SPF of not less than the number of sunscreen active ingredients used in the combination multiplied by 2.

(2) Two or more sunscreen active ingredients identified in § 352.10(b), (c), (e), (g), (j) through (m), (o), and (q) may be combined with each other in a single product when used in the concentrations established for each ingredient in § 352.10. The concentration of each active ingredient must be sufficient to contribute a minimum SPF of not less than 2 to the finished product. The finished product must have a minimum SPF of not less than the number of sunscreen active ingredients used in the combination multiplied by 2.

*   *   *   *   *

Subpart C—Labeling

§ 352.50 Principal display panel of all sunscreen drug products.

In addition to the statement of identity required in § 352.52, the following labeling statements shall be prominently placed on the principal display panel:

(a) *For products that do not satisfy the water resistant or very water resistant sunscreen product testing procedures in § 352.76—*(1) *For products with SPF values up to 30.* "SPF (insert tested SPF value of the product up to 30)."

(2) *For products with SPF values over 30.* "SPF 30" (select one of the following: "plus" or "+"). Any statement accompanying the marketed product that states a specific SPF value above 30 or similar language indicating a person can stay in the sun more than 30 times longer than without sunscreen will cause the product to be misbranded under section 502 of the Federal Food, Drug, and Cosmetic Act (the act).

(b) *For products that satisfy the water resistant sunscreen product testing procedures in § 352.76.* (1) (Select one of the following: "Water," "Water/Sweat," or "Water/Perspiration") "Resistant."

(2) "SPF (insert SPF value of the product, as stated in paragraph (a)(1) or (a)(2) of this section, after it has been tested using the water resistant sunscreen product testing procedures in § 352.76)."

(c) *For products that satisfy the very water resistant sunscreen product testing procedures in § 352.76.* (1) "Very" (select one of the following: "Water," "Water/Sweat," or "Water/Perspiration") "Resistant."

(2) "SPF (insert SPF value of the product, as stated in paragraph (a)(1) or (a)(2) of this section, after it has been tested using the very water resistant sunscreen product testing procedures in § 352.76)."

§ 352.52 Labeling of sunscreen drug products.

(a) *Statement of identity.* The labeling of the product contains the established name of the drug, if any, and identifies the product as a "sunscreen."

(b) *Indications.* The labeling of the product states, under the heading "Uses," all of the phrases listed in paragraph (b)(1) of this section that are applicable to the product and may contain any of the additional phrases listed in paragraph (b)(2) of this section, as appropriate. Other truthful and nonmisleading statements, describing only the uses that have been established and listed in this paragraph (b), may also be used, as provided in § 330.1(c)(2) of this chapter, subject to the provisions of section 502 of the act relating to misbranding and the prohibition in section 301(d) of the act against the introduction or delivery for introduction into interstate commerce of unapproved new drugs in violation of section 505(a) of the act.

(1) *For products containing any ingredient in § 352.10.* (i) "[bullet][1] helps prevent sunburn [bullet] higher SPF gives more sunburn protection".

(ii) *For products that satisfy the water resistant testing procedures identified in § 352.76.* "[bullet] retains SPF after 40

---

[1] See § 201.66(b)(4) of this chapter.

minutes of'' (select one or more of the following: "activity in the water," "sweating," or "perspiring").

(iii) *For products that satisfy the very water resistant testing procedures identified in §352.76.* "[bullet] retains SPF after 80 minutes of" (select one or more of the following: "activity in the water," "sweating," or "perspiring").

(2) *Additional indications.* In addition to the indications provided in paragraph (b)(1) of this section, the following may be used for products containing any ingredient in §352.10:

(i) *For products that provide an SPF of 2 to under 12.* Select one or both of the following: ["[bullet]" (select one of the following: "provides minimal," "provides minimum," "minimal," or "minimum") "protection against" (select one of the following: "sunburn" or "sunburn and tanning")], or "[bullet] for skin that sunburns minimally".

(ii) *For products that provide an SPF of 12 to under 30.* Select one or both of the following: ["[bullet]" (select one of the following: "provides moderate" or "moderate") "protection against" (select one of the following: "sunburn" or "sunburn and tanning")], or "[bullet] for skin that sunburns easily".

(iii) *For products that provide an SPF of 30 or above.* Select one or both of the following: ["[bullet]" (select one of the following: "provides high" or "high") "protection against" (select one of the following: "sunburn" or "sunburn and tanning")], or "[bullet] for skin highly sensitive to sunburn".

(c) *Warnings.* The labeling of the product contains the following warnings under the heading "Warnings:"

(1) *For products containing any ingredient in §352.10.* (i) "When using this product [bullet] keep out of eyes. Rinse with water to remove."

(ii) "Stop use and ask a doctor if [bullet] rash or irritation develops and lasts".

(2) *For products containing any ingredient identified in §352.10 marketed as a lip protectant or lipstick.* The external use only warning in §201.66(c)(5)(i) of this chapter and the warning in paragraph (c)(1)(i) of this section are not required.

(d) *Directions.* The labeling of the product contains the following statements, as appropriate, under the head-

ing "Directions." More detailed directions applicable to a particular product formulation (e.g., cream, gel, lotion, oil, spray, etc.) may also be included.

(1) *For products containing any ingredient in §352.10.* (i) "[bullet] apply" (select one or more of the following, as applicable: "liberally," "generously," "smoothly," or "evenly") "(insert appropriate time interval, if a waiting period is needed) before sun exposure and as needed".

(ii) "[bullet] children under 6 months of age: ask a doctor".

(2) *In addition to the directions provided in §352.52(d)(1), the following may be used for products containing any ingredient in §352.10.* "[bullet] reapply as needed or after towel drying, swimming, or" (select one of the following: "sweating" or "perspiring").

(3) *If the additional directions provided in §352.52(d)(2) are used, the phrase "and as needed" in §352.52(d)(1) is not required.*

(4) *For products marketed as a lip protectant or lipstick.* The directions in paragraphs (d)(1) and (d)(2) of this section are not required.

(e) *Statement on product performance—* (1) *For products containing any ingredient identified in §352.10, the following PCD labeling claims may be used under the heading "Other information" or anywhere outside of the "Drug Facts" box or enclosure.*

(i) *For products containing active ingredient(s) that provide an SPF value of 2 to under 12.* (Select one of the following: "minimal" or "minimum") "sun protection product."

(ii) *For products containing active ingredient(s) that provide an SPF value of 12 to under 30.* "moderate sun protection product."

(iii) *For products containing active ingredient(s) that provide an SPF value of 30 or above.* "high sun protection product."

(2) *For products containing any ingredient identified in §352.10, the following labeling statement may be used under the heading "Other information" or anywhere outside of the "Drug Facts" box or enclosure.* "Sun alert: Limiting sun exposure, wearing protective clothing, and using sunscreens may reduce the risks of skin aging, skin cancer, and other harmful effects of the sun." Any

variation of this statement will cause the product to be misbranded under section 502 of the act.

(f) *Products labeled for use only on specific small areas of the face (e.g., lips, nose, ears, and/or around eyes) and that meet the criteria established in § 201.66(d)(10) of this chapter.* The title, headings, subheadings, and information described in § 201.66(c) of this chapter shall be printed in accordance with the following specifications:

(1) The labeling shall meet the requirements of § 201.66(c) of this chapter except that the title, headings, and information described in § 201.66(c)(1), (c)(3), and (c)(7) may be omitted, and the headings, subheadings, and information described in § 201.66(c)(2), (c)(4), (c)(5), and (c)(6) may be presented as follows:

(i) The active ingredients (§ 201.66(c)(2) of this chapter) shall be listed in alphabetical order.

(ii) The heading and the indication required by § 201.66(c)(4) of this chapter may be limited to: "Use [in bold type] helps protect against sunburn." For a lip protectant product, the heading and the indication required by § 201.66(c)(4) may be limited to: "Use [in bold type] helps protect against sunburn and chapped lips."

(iii) The "external use only" warning in § 201.66(c)(5)(i) of this chapter may be omitted.

(iv) The subheadings in § 201.66(c)(5)(iii) through (c)(5)(vii) of this chapter may be omitted, provided the information after the heading "Warnings" states: "Keep out of eyes." and "Stop use if skin rash occurs."

(v) The warning in § 201.66(c)(5)(x) of this chapter may be limited to the following: "Keep out of reach of children."

(vi) For a lip protectant product or lipstick, the warnings "Keep out of eyes" in § 352.52(f)(1)(iv) and "Keep out of reach of children" in § 352.52(f)(1)(v) and the directions in § 352.52(d) may be omitted.

(2) The labeling shall be printed in accordance with the requirements of § 201.66(d) of this chapter except that any requirements related to § 201.66(c)(1), (c)(3), and (c)(7), and the

horizontal barlines and hairlines described in § 201.66(d)(8), may be omitted.

[64 FR 27687, May 21, 1999, as amended at 68 FR 33380, June 4, 2003]

§ 352.60 Labeling of permitted combinations of active ingredients.

Statements of identity, indications, warnings, and directions for use, respectively, applicable to each ingredient in the product may be combined to eliminate duplicative words or phrases so that the resulting information is clear and understandable.

(a) *Statement of identity.* For a combination drug product that has an established name, the labeling of the product states the established name of the combination drug product, followed by the statement of identity for each ingredient in the combination, as established in the statement of identity sections of the applicable OTC drug monographs. For a combination drug product that does not have an established name, the labeling of the product states the statement of identity for each ingredient in the combination, as established in the statement of identity sections of the applicable OTC drug monographs.

(b) *Indications.* The labeling of the product states, under the heading "Uses," the indication(s) for each ingredient in the combination as established in the indications sections of the applicable OTC drug monographs, unless otherwise stated in this paragraph. Other truthful and nonmisleading statements, describing only the indications for use that have been established in the applicable OTC drug monographs or listed in this paragraph (b), may also be used, as provided by § 330.1(c)(2) of this chapter, subject to the provisions of section 502 of the Federal Food, Drug, and Cosmetic Act (the act) relating to misbranding and the prohibition in section 301(d) of the act against the introduction or delivery for introduction into interstate commerce of unapproved new drugs in violation of section 505(a) of the act.

(1) In addition, the labeling of the product may contain any of the "other allowable statements" that are identified in the applicable monographs.

(2) For permitted combinations containing a sunscreen and a skin protectant identified in §352.20(b), any or all of the applicable indications for sunscreens in §352.52(b) and the indication for skin protectants in §347.50(b)(2)(i) of this chapter should be used. For products marketed as a lip protectant, the indication in §352.52(f)(1)(ii) should be used.

(c) *Warnings.* The labeling of the product states, under the heading "Warnings," the warning(s) for each ingredient in the combination, as established in the warnings section of the applicable OTC drug monographs, except that the warning for skin protectants in §347.50(c)(3) of this chapter is not required for permitted combinations containing a sunscreen and a skin protectant identified in §352.20(b). For products marketed as a lip protectant or lipstick, §352.52(f)(1)(iii), (f)(1)(iv) (except "Keep out of eyes," which may be omitted), and (f)(1)(vi) apply.

(d) *Directions.* The labeling of the product states, under the heading "directions," directions that conform to the directions established for each ingredient in the directions sections of the applicable OTC drug monographs, unless otherwise stated in this paragraph. When the time intervals or age limitations for administration of the individual ingredients differ, the directions for the combination product may not contain any dosage that exceeds those established for any individual ingredient in the applicable OTC drug monograph(s), and may not provide for use by any age group lower than the highest minimum age limit established for any individual ingredient. For permitted combinations containing a sunscreen and a skin protectant identified in §352.20(b), the directions for sunscreens in §352.52(d) should be used. For products marketed as a lip protectant or lipstick, §352.52(d)(4) applies.

[64 FR 27687, May 21, 1999, as amended at 68 FR 33380, June 4, 2003]

Subpart D—Testing Procedures

§352.70   Standard sunscreen.

(a) *Laboratory validation.* A standard sunscreen shall be used concomitantly in the testing procedures for determining the SPF value of a sunscreen drug product to ensure the uniform evaluation of sunscreen drug products. The standard sunscreen shall be an 8-percent homosalate preparation with a mean SPF value of 4.47 (standard deviation =1.279). In order for the SPF determination of a test product to be considered valid, the SPF of the standard sunscreen must fall within the standard deviation range of the expected SPF (*i.e.*, 4.47 ±1.279) and the 95-percent confidence interval for the mean SPF must contain the value 4.

(b) *Preparation of the standard homosalate sunscreen.* (1) The standard homosalate sunscreen is prepared from two different preparations (preparation A and preparation B) with the following compositions:

COMPOSITION OF PREPARATION A AND PREPARATION B OF THE STANDARD SUNSCREEN

Ingredients	Percent by weight
Preparation A	
Lanolin	5.00
Homosalate	8.00
White petrolatum	2.50
Stearic acid	4.00
Propylparaben	0.05
Preparation B	
Methylparaben	0.10
Edetate disodium	0.05
Propylene glycol	5.00
Triethanolamine	1.00
Purified water U.S.P	74.30

(2) Preparation A and preparation B are heated separately to 77 to 82 °C, with constant stirring, until the contents of each part are solubilized. Add preparation A slowly to preparation B while stirring. Continue stirring until the emulsion formed is cooled to room temperature (15 to 30 °C). Add sufficient purified water to obtain 100 grams of standard sunscreen preparation.

(c) *Assay of the standard homosalate sunscreen.* Assay the standard homosalate sunscreen preparation by the following method to ensure proper concentration:

(1) *Preparation of the assay solvent.* The solvent consists of 1 percent glacial acetic acid (V/V) in denatured ethanol. The denatured ethanol should not contain a UV radiation absorbing denaturant.

(2) *Preparation of a 1-percent solution of the standard homosalate sunscreen*

preparation. Accurately weigh 1 gram of the standard homosalate sunscreen preparation into a 100-milliliter volumetric flask. Add 50 milliliters of the assay solvent. Heat on a steam bath and mix well. Cool the solution to room temperature (15 to 30 °C). Then dilute the solution to volume with the assay solvent and mix well to make a 1-percent solution.

(3) *Preparation of the test solution (1:50 dilution of the 1-percent solution).* Filter a portion of the 1-percent solution through number 1 filter paper. Discard the first 10 to 15 milliliters of the filtrate. Collect the next 20 milliliters of the filtrate (second collection). Add 1 milliliter of the second collection of the filtrate to a 50-milliliter volumetric flask. Dilute this solution to volume with assay solvent and mix well. This is the test solution (1:50 dilution of the 1-percent solution).

(4) *Spectrophotometric determination.* The absorbance of the test solution is measured in a suitable double beam spectrophotometer with the assay solvent and reference beam at a wavelength near 306 nanometers.

(5) *Calculation of the concentration of homosalate.* The concentration of homosalate is determined by the following formula which takes into consideration the absorbance of the sample of the test solution, the dilution of the 1-percent solution (1:50), the weight of the sample of the standard homosalate sunscreen preparation (1 gram), and the standard absorbance value (172) of homosalate as determined by averaging the absorbance of a large number of batches of raw homosalate:

Concentration of homosalate
=absorbance × 50 × 100 × 172
=percent concentration by weight.

§ 352.71   **Light source (solar simulator).**

A solar simulator used for determining the SPF of a sunscreen drug product should be filtered so that it provides a continuous emission spectrum from 290 to 400 nanometers similar to sunlight at sea level from the sun at a zenith angle of 10° it has less than 1 percent of its total energy output contributed by nonsolar wavelengths shorter than 290 nanometers; and it has not more than 5 percent of its total energy output contributed by wavelengths longer than 400 nanometers. In addition, a solar simulator should have no significant time-related fluctuations in radiation emissions after an appropriate warmup time, and it should have good beam uniformity (within 10 percent) in the exposure plane. To ensure that the solar simulator delivers the appropriate spectrum of UV radiation, it must be measured periodically with an accurately-calibrated spectroradiometer system or equivalent instrument.

§ 352.72   **General testing procedures.**

(a) *Selection of test subjects (male and female).* (1) Only fair-skin subjects with skin types I, II, and III using the following guidelines shall be selected:

Selection of Fair-skin Subjects
Skin Type and Sunburn and Tanning History (Based on first 30 to 45 minutes sun exposure after a winter season of no sun exposure.)
I—Always burns easily; never tans (sensitive).
II—Always burns easily; tans minimally (sensitive).
III—Burns moderately; tans gradually (light brown) (normal).
IV—Burns minimally; always tans well (moderate brown) (normal).
V—Rarely burns; tans profusely (dark brown) (insensitive).
VI—Never burns; deeply pigmented (insensitive).

(2) A medical history shall be obtained from all subjects with emphasis on the effects of sunlight on their skin. Ascertain the general health of the individual, the individual's skin type (I, II, or III), whether the individual is taking medication (topical or systemic) that is known to produce abnormal sunlight responses, and whether the individual is subject to any abnormal responses to sunlight, such as a phototoxic or photoallergic response.

(b) *Test site inspection.* The physical examination shall determine the presence of sunburn, suntan, scars, active dermal lesions, and uneven skin tones on the areas of the back to be tested. The presence of nevi, blemishes, or moles will be acceptable if in the physician's judgment they will not interfere with the study results. Excess hair on the back is acceptable if the hair is clipped or shaved.

(c) *Informed consent.* Legally effective written informed consent must be obtained from all individuals.

(d) *Test site delineation*—(1) *Test site area.* A test site area serves as an area for determining the subject's MED after application of either the sunscreen standard or the test sunscreen product, or for determining the subject's MED when the skin is unprotected (control site). The area to be tested shall be the back between the beltline and the shoulder blade (scapulae) and lateral to the midline. Each test site area for applying a product or the standard sunscreen shall be a minimum of 50-square centimeters, e.g., 5 × 10 centimeters. The test site areas are outlined with ink. If the person is to be tested in an upright position, the lines shall be drawn on the skin with the subject upright. If the subject is to be tested while prone, the markings shall be made with the subject prone.

(2) *Test subsite area.* Each test site area shall be divided into at least three test subsite areas that are at least 1 square centimeter. Usually four or five subsites are employed. Each test subsite within a test site area is subjected to a specified dosage of UV radiation, in a series of UV radiation exposures, in which the test site area is exposed for the determination of the MED.

(e) *Application of test materials.* To ensure standardized reporting and to define a product's SPF value, the application of the product shall be expressed on a weight basis per unit area which establishes a standard film. Both the test sunscreen product and the standard sunscreen application shall be 2 milligrams per square centimeter. For oils and most lotions, the viscosity is such that the material can be applied with a volumetric syringe. For creams, heavy gels, and butters, the product shall be warmed slightly so that it can be applied volumetrically. On heating, care shall be taken not to alter the product's physical characteristics, especially separation of the formulations. Pastes and ointments shall be weighed, then applied by spreading on the test site area. A product shall be spread by using a finger cot. If two or more sunscreen drug products are

being evaluated at the same time, the test products and the standard sunscreen, as specified in § 352.70, should be applied in a blinded, randomized manner. If only one sunscreen drug product is being tested, the testing subsites should be exposed to the varying doses of UV radiation in a randomized manner.

(f) *Waiting period.* Before exposing the test site areas after applying a product, a waiting period of at least 15 minutes is required.

(g) *Number of subjects.* A test panel shall consist of not more than 25 subjects with the number fixed in advance by the investigator. From this panel, at least 20 subjects must produce valid data for analysis.

(h) *Response criteria.* In order that the person who evaluates the MED responses does not know which sunscreen formulation was applied to which site or what doses of UV radiation were administered, he/she must not be the same person who applied the sunscreen drug product to the test site or administered the doses of UV radiation. After UV radiation exposure from the solar simulator is completed, all immediate responses shall be recorded. These include several types of typical responses such as the following: An immediate darkening or tanning, typically greyish or purplish in color, fading in 30 to 60 minutes, and attributed to photo-oxidation of existing melanin granules; immediate reddening, fading rapidly, and viewed as a normal response of capillaries and venules to heat, visible and infrared radiation; and an immediate generalized heat response, resembling prickly heat rash, fading in 30 to 60 minutes, and apparently caused by heat and moisture generally irritating to the skin's surface. After the immediate responses are noted, each subject shall shield the exposed area from further UV radiation for the remainder of the test day. The MED is determined 22 to 24 hours after exposure. The erythema responses of the test subject should be evaluated under the following conditions: The source of illumination should be either a tungsten light bulb or a warm white fluorescent light bulb that provides a level of illumination at the test site within the

311

range of 450 to 550 lux, and the test subject should be in the same position used when the test site was irradiated. Testing depends upon determining the smallest dose of energy that produces redness reaching the borders of the exposure site at 22 to 24 hours postexposure for each series of exposures. To determine the MED, somewhat more intense erythemas must also be produced. The goal is to have some exposures that produce absolutely no effect, and of those exposures that produce an effect, the maximal exposure should be no more than twice the total energy of the minimal exposure.

(i) *Rejection of test data.* Test data shall be rejected if the exposure series fails to elicit an MED response on either the treated or unprotected skin sites, or if the responses on the treated sites are randomly absent (which indi-

cates the product was not spread evenly), or if the subject was noncompliant (e.g., subject withdraws from the test due to illness or work conflicts, subject does not shield the exposed testing sites from further UV radiation until the MED is read, etc.).

§ 352.73 Determination of SPF value.

(a)(1) The following erythema action spectrum shall be used to calculate the erythema effective exposure of a solar simulator:

$V_i (\lambda) = 1.0$ (250 < λ < 298 nm)
$V_i (\lambda) = 1.0^{0.094 (298 - \lambda)}$ (298 < λ < 328 nanometers)
$V_i (\lambda) = 1.0^{0.015 (139 - \lambda)}$ (328 < λ < 400 nanometers)

(2) The data contained in this action spectrum are to be used as spectral weighting factors to calculate the erythema effective exposure of a solar simulator as follows:

$$E = \sum_{250}^{400} V_i (\lambda) * I (\lambda) * t_{exp}$$

where: E = Erythema Effective Exposure (dose: Joules per square meter)

V_i = Weighting Factor (Erythema Action Spectrum)

I = Spectral Irradiance (Watts per square meter per nanometer)

t_{exp} = exposure time (seconds)

(b) *Determination of MED of the unprotected skin.* A series of UV radiation exposures expressed as Joules per square meter (adjusted to the erythema action spectrum calculated according to § 352.73(a)) is administered to the subsite areas on each subject with an accurately calibrated solar simulator. A series of five exposures shall be administered to the untreated, unprotected skin to determine the subject's

inherent MED. The doses selected shall be a geometric series represented by (1.25^n), wherein each exposure time interval is 25 percent greater than the previous time to maintain the same relative uncertainty (expressed as a constant percentage), independent of the subject's sensitivity to UV radiation, regardless of whether the subject has a high or low MED. Usually, the MED of a person's unprotected skin is determined the day prior to testing a product. This MED(US) shall be used in the determination of the series of UV radiation exposures to be administered to the protected site in subsequent testing. The MED(US) should be determined again on the same day as the standard and test sunscreens and this MED(US) should be used in calculating the SPF.

(c) *Determination of individual SPF values.* A series of UV radiation exposures expressed as Joules per square meter (adjusted to the erythema action spectrum calculated according to §352.73(a)) is administered to the subsite areas on each subject with an accurately-calibrated solar simulator. A series of seven exposures shall be administered to the protected test sites to determine the MED of the protected skin (MED(PS)). The doses selected shall consist of a geometric series of five exposures, where the middle exposure is placed to yield the expected SPF plus two other exposures placed symmetrically around the middle exposure. The exact series of exposures to be given to the protected skin shall be determined by the previously established MED(US) and the expected SPF of the test sunscreen. For products with an expected SPF less than 8, the exposures shall be the MED(US) times 0.64X, 0.80X, 0.90X, 1.00X, 1.10X, 1.25X, and 1.56X, where X equals the expected SPF of the test product. For products with an expected SPF between 8 and 15, the exposures shall be the MED(US) times 0.69X, 0.83X, 0.91X, 1.00X, 1.09X, 1.20X, and 1.44X, where X equals the expected SPF of the test product. For products with an expected SPF greater that 15, the exposures shall be the MED(US) times 0.76X, 0.87X, 0.93X, 1.00X, 1.07X, 1.15X, and 1.32X, where X equals the expected SPF of the test product. The MED is the quantity of erythema-effective energy required to produce the first perceptible, unambiguous redness reaction with clearly defined borders at 22 to 24 hours postexposure. The SPF value of the test sunscreen is then calculated from the dose of UV radiation required to produce the MED of the protected skin and from the dose of UV radiation required to produce the MED of the unprotected skin (control site) as follows:

SPF value =the ratio of erythema effective exposure (Joules per square meter) (MED(PS)) to the erythema effective exposure (Joules per square meter) (MED(US)).

(d) *Determination of the test product's SPF value and PCD.* Use data from at least 20 test subjects with n representing the number of subjects used. First, for each subject, compute the SPF value as stated in §352.73(b) and (c). Second, compute the mean SPF value, $\bar{x}$, and the standard deviation, s, for these subjects. Third, obtain the upper 5-percent point from the t distribution table with n-1 degrees of freedom. Denote this value by t. Fourth, compute ts/$\sqrt{n}$. Denote this quantity by A (*i.e.*, A =ts/$\sqrt{n}$). Fifth, calculate the SPF value to be used in labeling as follows: the label SPF equals the largest whole number less than $\bar{x}$. - A. Sixth and last, the drug product is classified into a PCD as follows: if 30 + A <$\bar{x}$, the PCD is High; if 12 + A <$\bar{x}$ <30 + A, the PCD is Moderate; if 2 + A <$\bar{x}$ <12 + A, the PCD is Minimal; if $\bar{x}$ <2 + A, the product shall not be labeled as a sunscreen drug product and shall not display an SPF value.

§352.76 Determination if a product is water resistant or very water resistant.

The general testing procedures in §352.72 shall be used as part of the following tests, except where modified in this section. An indoor fresh water pool, whirlpool, and/or jacuzzi maintained at 23 to 32 °C shall be used in these testing procedures. Fresh water is clean drinking water that meets the standards in 40 CFR part 141. The pool and air temperature and the relative humidity shall be recorded.

(a) *Procedure for testing the water resistance of a sunscreen product.* For sunscreen products making the claim of "water resistant," the label SPF shall be the label SPF value determined after 40 minutes of water immersion using the following procedure for the water resistance test:

(1) Apply sunscreen product (followed by the waiting period after application of the sunscreen product indicated on the product labeling).

(2) 20 minutes moderate activity in water.

(3) 20-minute rest period (do not towel test sites).

(4) 20 minutes moderate activity in water.

(5) Conclude water test (air dry test sites without toweling).

(6) Begin solar simulator exposure to test site areas as described in § 352.73.

(b) *Procedure for testing a very water resistant sunscreen product.* For sunscreen products making the claim of "very water resistant," the label SPF shall be the label SPF value determined after 80 minutes of water immersion using the following procedure for the very water resistant test:

(1) Apply sunscreen product (followed by the waiting period after application of the sunscreen product indicated on the product labeling).

(2) 20 minutes moderate activity in water.

(3) 20-minute rest period (do not towel test sites).

(4) 20 minutes moderate activity in water.

(5) 20-minute rest period (do not towel test sites).

(6) 20 minutes moderate activity in water.

(7) 20-minute rest period (do not towel test sites).

(8) 20 minutes moderate activity in water.

(9) Conclude water test (air dry test sites without toweling).

(10) Begin solar simulator exposure to test site areas as described in § 352.73.

§ 352.77 Test modifications.

The formulation or mode of administration of certain products may require modification of the testing procedures in this subpart. In addition, alternative methods (including automated or in vitro procedures) employing the same basic procedures as those described in this subpart may be used. Any proposed modification or alternative procedure shall be submitted as a petition in accord with § 10.30 of this chapter. The petition should contain data to support the modification or data demonstrating that an alternative procedure provides results of equivalent accuracy. All information submitted will be subject to the disclosure rules in part 20 of this chapter.

PART 355—ANTICARIES DRUG PRODUCTS FOR OVER-THE-COUNTER HUMAN USE

Subpart A—General Provisions

Subpart B—Active Ingredients

Subpart C—Labeling

Subpart D—Testing Procedures

AUTHORITY: 21 U.S.C. 321, 351, 352, 353, 355, 360, 371.

SOURCE: 60 FR 52507, Oct. 6, 1995, unless otherwise noted.

EDITORIAL NOTE: Nomenclature changes to part 355 appear at 69 FR 13717, Mar. 24, 2004.

Subpart A—General Provisions

§ 355.1 Scope.

(a) An over-the-counter anticaries drug product in a form suitable for topical administration to the teeth is generally recognized as safe and effective and is not misbranded if it meets each condition in this part and each general condition established in § 330.1 of this chapter.

(b) References in this part to regulatory sections of the Code of Federal Regulations are to chapter I of title 21 unless otherwise noted.

§ 355.3 Definitions.

As used in this part:

(a) *Abrasive.* Solid materials that are added to dentifrices to facilitate mechanical removal of dental plaque, debris, and stain from tooth surfaces.

(b) *Anhydrous glycerin.* An ingredient that may be prepared by heating glycerin U.S.P. at 150 °C for 2 hours to drive off the moisture content.

(c) *Anticaries drug.* A drug that aids in the prevention and prophylactic treatment of dental cavities (decay, caries).

(d) *Dental caries.* A disease of calcified tissues of teeth characterized by demineralization of the inorganic portion and destruction of the organic matrix.

(e) *Dentifrice.* An abrasive-containing dosage form (gel, paste, or powder) for delivering an anticaries drug to the teeth.

(f) *Fluoride.* The inorganic form of the chemical element fluorine in combination with other elements.

(g) *Fluoride ion.* The negatively charged atom of the chemical element fluorine.

(h) *Fluoride supplement.* A special treatment rinse dosage form that is intended to be swallowed, and is promoted to health professionals for use in areas where the water supply contains 0 to 0.7 parts per million (ppm) fluoride ion.

(i) *Preventive treatment gel.* A dosage form for delivering an anticaries drug to the teeth. Preventive treatment gels are formulated in an anhydrous glycerin base with suitable thickening agents included to adjust viscosity. Preventive treatment gels do not contain abrasives.

(j) *Treatment rinse.* A liquid dosage form for delivering an anticaries drug to the teeth.

(k) *Treatment rinse concentrated solution.* A fluoride treatment rinse in a concentrated form to be mixed with water before using to result in the appropriate fluoride concentration specified in the monograph.

(l) *Treatment rinse effervescent tablets.* A fluoride treatment rinse prepared by adding an effervescent tablet (a concentrated solid dosage form) to water before using to result in the appropriate fluoride concentration specified in the monograph.

(m) *Treatment rinse powder.* A fluoride treatment rinse prepared by adding the powder (a concentrated solid dosage form) to water before using to result in the appropriate fluoride concentration specified in the monograph.

[60 FR 52507, Oct. 6, 1995, as amended at 61 FR 52286, Oct. 7, 1996]

Subpart B—Active Ingredients

§355.10 Anticaries active ingredients.

The active ingredient of the product consists of any of the following when used in the concentration and dosage form established for each ingredient:

(a) *Sodium fluoride*—(1) *Dentifrices containing 850 to 1,150 ppm theoretical total fluorine in a gel or paste dosage form.* Sodium fluoride 0.188 to 0.254 percent with an available fluoride ion concentration ≥650 parts per million (ppm).

(2) *Dentifrices containing 850 to 1,150 ppm theoretical total fluorine in a powdered dosage form.* Sodium fluoride 0.188 to 0.254 percent with an available fluoride ion concentration of ≥850 ppm for products containing the abrasive sodium bicarbonate and a poured-bulk density of 1.0 to 1.2 grams per milliliter.

(3) *Treatment rinses.* (i) An aqueous solution of acidulated phosphate fluoride derived from sodium fluoride acidulated with a mixture of sodium phosphate, monobasic, and phosphoric acid to a level of 0.1 molar phosphate ion and a pH of 3.0 to 4.5 and which yields an effective fluoride ion concentration of 0.02 percent.

(ii) An aqueous solution of acidulated phosphate fluoride derived from sodium fluoride acidulated with a mixture of sodium phosphate, dibasic, and phosphoric acid to a pH of 3.5 and which yields an effective fluoride ion concentration of 0.01 percent.

(iii) Sodium fluoride 0.02 percent aqueous solution with a pH of approximately 7.

(iv) Sodium fluoride 0.05 percent aqueous solution with a pH of approximately 7.

(v) Sodium fluoride concentrate containing adequate directions for mixing with water before using to result in a 0.02-percent or 0.05-percent aqueous solution with a pH of approximately 7.

(b) *Sodium monofluorophosphate*—(1) *Dentifrices containing 850 to 1,150 ppm theoretical total fluorine in a gel or paste dosage form.* Sodium monofluorophosphate 0.654 to 0.884 percent with an available fluoride ion concentration (consisting of $PO_3F^=$ and F^- combined) ≥800 ppm.

(2) *Dentifrices containing 1,500 ppm theoretical total fluorine in a gel or paste*

dosage form. Sodium monofluorophosphate 1.153 percent with an available fluoride ion concentration (consisting of PO_3 $F^=$ and F^- combined) ≥1,275 ppm.

(c) *Stannous fluoride*—(1) *Dentifrices containing 850 to 1,150 ppm theoretical total fluorine in a gel or paste dosage form.* (i) Stannous fluoride 0.351 to 0.474 percent with an available fluoride ion concentration ≥700 ppm for products containing abrasives other than calcium pyrophosphate.

(ii) Stannous fluoride 0.351 to 0.474 percent with an available fluoride ion concentration ≥290 ppm for products containing the abrasive calcium pyrophosphate.

(2) *Preventive treatment gel.* Stannous fluoride 0.4 percent in an anhydrous glycerin gel, made from anhydrous glycerin and the addition of suitable thickening agents to adjust viscosity.

(3) *Treatment rinse.* Stannous fluoride concentrate marketed in a stable form and containing adequate directions for mixing with water immediately before using to result in a 0.1-percent aqueous solution.

[60 FR 52507, Oct. 6, 1995, as amended at 61 FR 52286, Oct. 7, 1996]

§ 355.20 Packaging conditions.

(a) *Package size limitation.* Due to the toxicity associated with fluoride active ingredients, the following package size limitations are required for anticaries drug products:

(1) *Dentifrices.* Dentifrice (toothpastes and tooth powders) packages shall not contain more than 276 milligrams (mg) total fluorine per package.

(2) *Preventive treatment gels and treatment rinses.* Preventive treatment gel and treatment rinse packages shall not contain more than 120 mg total fluorine per package.

(3) *Exception.* Package size limitations do not apply to anticaries drug products marketed for professional office use only and labeled in accord with § 355.60.

(b) *Tight container packaging.* To minimize moisture contamination, all fluoride powdered dentifrices shall be packaged in a tight container as defined as a container that protects the contents from contamination by extraneous liquids, solids, or vapors, from loss of the article, and from efflorescence, deliquescence, or evaporation under the ordinary or customary conditions of handling, shipment, storage, and distribution, and is capable of tight reclosure.

Subpart C—Labeling

§ 355.50 Labeling of anticaries drug products.

(a) *Statement of identity.* The labeling of the product contains the established name of the drug, if any, and identifies the product as: (select one or both of the following: 'anticavity' or 'fluoride') (select one of the following as appropriate: "dentifrice," "toothpaste," "tooth polish," "tooth powder;" (optional: "dental") "preventive treatment gel;" or (optional: "treatment" or "dental")) (select one of the following: "rinse," "concentrated solution," "rinse powder," or "rinse effervescent tablets"). The word "mouthwash" may be substituted for the word "rinse" in this statement of identity if the product also has a cosmetic use, as defined in section 201(i) of the Federal Food, Drug, and Cosmetic Act (the act) (21 U.S.C. 321(i)).

(b) *Indication.* The labeling of the product states, under the heading "Indication," the following: "Aids in the prevention of dental (select one of the following: "cavities," "decay," "caries (decay)," or "caries (cavities)"). Other truthful and nonmisleading statements, describing only the indication for use that has been established and listed in this paragraph (b), may also be used, as provided in § 330.1(c)(2) of this chapter, subject to the provisions of section 502 of the Federal Food, Drug, and Cosmetic Act (the act) relating to misbranding and the prohibition in section 301(d) of the act against the introduction or delivery for introduction into interstate commerce of unapproved new drugs in violation of section 505(a) of the act.

(c) *Warning.* The labeling of the product contains the following warning under the heading "Warning":

(1) *For all fluoride dentifrice (gel, paste, and powder) products.* "Keep out of reach of children under 6 years of age. [highlighted in bold type] If more than used for brushing is accidentally swallowed, get medical help or contact a

Poison Control Center right away." These warnings shall be used in place of the general warning statements required by §330.1(g) of this chapter.

(2) *For all fluoride rinse and preventive treatment gel products.* "Keep out of reach of children. [highlighted in bold type] If more than used for" (select appropriate word: "brushing" or "rinsing") "is accidentally swallowed, get medical help or contact a Poison Control Center right away." These warnings shall be used in place of the general warning statements required by §330.1(g) of this chapter.

(d) *Directions.* The labeling of the product contains the following statements under the heading "Directions":

(1) *For anticaries dentifrice products—* (i) *Gel or paste dosage form with a theoretical total fluorine concentration of 850 to 1,150 ppm identified in §355.10(a)(1), (b)(1), and (c)(1).* Adults and children 2 years of age and older: Brush teeth thoroughly, preferably after each meal or at least twice a day, or as directed by a dentist or doctor. Instruct children under 6 years of age in good brushing and rinsing habits (to minimize swallowing). Supervise children as necessary until capable of using without supervision. Children under 2 years of age: Consult a dentist or doctor.

(ii) *Gel or paste dosage form with a theoretical total fluorine concentration of 1,500 ppm identified in §355.10(b)(2).* Adults and children 6 years of age and older: Brush teeth thoroughly, preferably after each meal or at least twice a day, or as directed by a dentist or doctor. Instruct children under 12 years of age in good brushing and rinsing habits (to minimize swallowing). Supervise children as necessary until capable of using without supervision. Children under 6 years of age: Do not use unless directed by a dentist or doctor.

(iii) *Powdered dosage form with a theoretical total fluorine concentration of 850 to 1,150 ppm identified in §355.10(a)(2).* Adults and children 6 years of age and older: Apply powder to a wet toothbrush; completely cover all bristles. Brush for at least 30 seconds. Reapply powder as before and brush again. Rinse and spit out thoroughly. Brush teeth, preferably after each meal or at

least twice a day, or as directed by a dentist or doctor. Instruct children under 12 years of age in good brushing and rinsing habits (to minimize swallowing). Supervise children as necessary until capable of using without supervision. Children under 6 years of age: Do not use unless directed by a dentist or doctor.

(2) *For anticaries treatment rinse products—*(i) *For acidulated phosphate fluoride solution containing 0.02 percent fluoride ion, sodium fluoride 0.05 percent, sodium fluoride concentrate, and stannous fluoride concentrate identified in §355.10(a)(3)(i), (a)(3)(iv), (a)(3)(v), and (c)(3).* Adults and children 6 years of age and older: Use once a day after brushing your teeth with a toothpaste. Vigorously swish 10 milliliters of rinse between your teeth for 1 minute and then spit out. Do not swallow the rinse. Do not eat or drink for 30 minutes after rinsing. Instruct children under 12 years of age in good rinsing habits (to minimize swallowing). Supervise children as necessary until capable of using without supervision. Children under 6 years of age: Consult a dentist or doctor.

(ii) *For acidulated phosphate fluoride solution containing 0.01 percent fluoride ion and sodium fluoride 0.02 percent aqueous solution identified in §355.10(a)(3)(ii) and (a)(3)(iii).* Adults and children 6 years of age and older: Use twice a day after brushing your teeth with a toothpaste. Vigorously swish 10 milliliters of rinse between your teeth for 1 minute and then spit out. Do not swallow the rinse. Do not eat or drink for 30 minutes after rinsing. Instruct children under 12 years of age in good rinsing habits (to minimize swallowing). Supervise children as necessary until capable of using without supervision. Children under 6 years of age: consult a dentist or doctor.

(3) *For stannous fluoride treatment rinse products.* (i) "Use immediately after preparing the rinse."

(ii) *For powder or effervescent tablets used to prepare treatment rinses.* "Do not use as a rinse until all the" (select one of the following: "powder" or "tablet") "has dissolved."

(4) *For anticaries preventive treatment gel products.* Adults and children 6 years of age and older: Use once a day

after brushing your teeth with a toothpaste. Apply the gel to your teeth and brush thoroughly. Allow the gel to remain on your teeth for 1 minute and then spit out. Do not swallow the gel. Do not eat or drink for 30 minutes after brushing. Instruct children under 12 years of age in the use of this product (to minimize swallowing). Supervise children as necessary until capable of using without supervision. Children under 6 years of age: consult a dentist or doctor.

(5) *For all concentrated treatment rinse solutions, powders, and effervescent tablets.* The following statement shall appear as the first statement under directions: "Do not use before mixing with water."

(e) *Additional labeling statements for anticaries drug products.* The following statements need not appear under warnings, but are required to appear on the label of anticaries drugs products as applicable.

(1) *For all preventive treatment gels.* "This is a(n)" (select one or both of the following: "anticavity" or "fluoride") "preventive treatment gel, not a toothpaste. Read directions carefully before using."

(2) *For all stannous fluoride treatment rinse, preventive treatment gel, and dentifrice products.* "This product may produce surface staining of the teeth. Adequate toothbrushing may prevent these stains which are not harmful or permanent and may be removed by your dentist."

(f) *Optional additional labeling statements—(1) For fluoride treatment rinses and preventive treatment gels.* The following labeling statement may appear in the required boxed area designated "APPROVED USES": "The combined daily use of a fluoride preventive treatment" (select one of the following: "rinse" or "gel") "and a fluoride toothpaste can help reduce the incidence of dental cavities."

(2) *For dentifrice products containing 1,500 ppm theoretical total fluorine.* "Adults and children over 6 years of age may wish to use this extra-strength fluoride dentifrice if they reside in a nonfluoridated area or if they

have a greater tendency to develop cavities."

[60 FR 52507, Oct. 6, 1995; 60 FR 57927, Nov. 24, 1995; 61 FR 51187, Oct. 7, 1996; 64 FR 13296, Mar. 17, 1999]

§ 355.55 Principal display panel of all fluoride rinse drug products.

In addition to the statement of identity required in § 355.50, the following statement shall be prominently placed on the principal display panel: "IMPORTANT: Read directions for proper use."

§ 355.60 Professional labeling.

(a) The labeling for anticaries fluoride treatment rinses identified in § 355.10(a)(3) and (c)(3) that are specially formulated so they may be swallowed (fluoride supplements) and are provided to health professionals (but not to the general public) may contain the following additional dosage information: Children 3 to under 14 years of age: As a supplement in areas where the water supply is nonfluoridated (less than 0.3 parts per million (ppm)), clean the teeth with a toothpaste and rinse with 5 milliliters (mL) of 0.02 percent or 10 mL of 0.01 percent fluoride ion rinse daily, then swallow. When the water supply contains 0.3 to 0.7 ppm fluoride ion, reduce the dose to 2.5 mL of 0.02 percent or 5 mL of 0.01 percent fluoride ion rinse daily.

(b) The labeling for products marketed to health to health professionals in package sizes larger than those specified in § 355.20 shall include the statements: "For Professional Office Use Only" and "This product is not intended for home or unsupervised consumer use."

Subpart D—Testing Procedures

§ 355.70 Testing procedures for fluoride dentifrice drug products.

(a) A fluoride dentifrice drug product shall meet the biological test requirements for animal caries reduction and one of the following tests: Enamel solubility reduction or fluoride enamel uptake. The testing procedures for these biological tests are labeled *Biological Testing Procedures for Fluoride Dentifrices*; these testing procedures are on file under Docket No. 80N–0042 in the Division of Dockets Management (HFA–305), Food and Drug Administration, 5630 Fishers Lane, rm. 1061, Rockville, MD 20852, and are available on request to that office.

(b) The United States Pharmacopeia fluoride dentifrice reference standards along with reference standard stability profiles (total fluoride, available fluoride ion, pH, and specific gravity) required to be used in the biological tests are available to any purchaser upon written request to the United States Pharmacopeial Convention, Inc., 1260 Twinbrook Parkway, Rockville, MD 20852.

(c) Alternative testing procedures may be used. Any proposed modification or alternative testing procedures shall be submitted as a petition in accord with § 10.30 of this chapter. The petition should contain data to support the modification or data demonstrating that an alternative testing procedure provides results of equivalent accuracy. All information submitted will be subjected to the disclosure rules in part 20 of this chapter.

[60 FR 52507, Oct. 6, 1995, as amended at 68 FR 24879, May 9, 2003]

PART 357—MISCELLANEOUS INTERNAL DRUG PRODUCTS FOR OVER-THE-COUNTER HUMAN USE

AUTHORITY: 21 U.S.C. 321, 351, 352, 353, 355, 360, 371.

Subpart A [Reserved]

Subpart B—Anthelmintic Drug Products

SOURCE: 51 FR 27759, Aug. 1, 1986, unless otherwise noted.

§ 357.101 Scope.

(a) An over-the-counter anthelmintic drug product in a form suitable for oral administration is generally recognized as safe and effective and is not misbranded if it meets each condition in this subpart and each general condition established in § 330.1.

(b) References in this subpart to regulatory sections of the Code of Federal Regulations are to chapter I of title 21 unless otherwise noted.

§ 357.103 Definition.

As used in this subpart:

Anthelmintic. An agent that is destructive to worms.

§ 357.110 Anthelmintic active ingredient.

The active ingredient of the product is pyrantel pamoate when used within the dosage limits established in § 357.150(d)(1).

§ 357.150 Labeling of anthelmintic drug products.

(a) *Statement of identity.* The labeling of the product contains the established name of the drug, if any, and identifies the product as a "pinworm treatment."

(b) *Indication.* The labeling of the product states, under the heading "Indication," the following: "For the treatment of pinworms." Other truthful and nonmisleading statements, describing only the indications for use that have been established and listed in this paragraph (b), may also be used, as provided in § 330.1(c)(2), subject to the provisions of section 502 of the act relating to misbranding and the prohibition in section 301(d) of the act against the introduction or delivery for introduction into interstate commerce of unapproved new drugs in violation of section 505(a) of the act.

(c) *Warnings.* The labeling of the product contains the following warnings under the heading "Warnings":

(1) "Abdominal cramps, nausea, vomiting, diarrhea, headache, or dizziness sometimes occur after taking this drug. If any of these conditions persist consult a doctor."

(2) "If you are pregnant or have liver disease, do not take this product unless directed by a doctor."

(d) *Directions.* The labeling of the product contains the following information under the heading "Directions":

(1) Adults, children 12 years of age and over, and children 2 years to under 12 years of age: Oral dosage is a single dose of 5 milligrams of pyrantel base per pound, or 11 milligrams per kilogram, of body weight not to exceed 1 gram. Dosing information should be converted to easily understood directions for the consumer using the following dosage schedule:

Weight	Dosage (taken as a single dose) [1]
Less than 25 pounds or under 2 years old.	Do not use unless directed by a doctor.
25 to 37 pounds	125 milligrams.
38 to 62 pounds	250 milligrams.
63 to 87 pounds	375 milligrams.
88 to 112 pounds	500 milligrams.
113 to 137 pounds	625 milligrams.
138 to 162 pounds	750 milligrams.
163 to 187 pounds	875 milligrams.
188 pounds and over	1,000 milligrams.

[1] Depending on the product, the label should state the quantity of drug as a liquid measurement (e.g., teaspoonsful) or as the number of dosage units (e.g., tablets) to be taken for the varying body weights. (If appropriate, it is recommended that a measuring cup graduated by body weight and/or liquid measurement be provided with the product.) Manufacturers should present this information as appropriate for their product and may vary the format of this chart as necessary.

(2) "Read package insert carefully before taking this medication. Take only according to directions and do not exceed the recommended dosage unless directed by a doctor. Medication should only be taken on time as a single dose; do not repeat treatment unless directed by a doctor. When one individual in a household has pinworms, the entire household should be treated unless otherwise advised. See Warnings. If any worms other than pinworms are present before or after treatment, consult a doctor. If any symptoms or pinworms are still present after treatment, consult a doctor.

(3) "This product can be taken any time of day, with or without meals. It may be taken alone or with milk or fruit juice. Use of a laxative is not necessary prior to, during, or after medication."

(e) *Optional wording.* The word "physician" may be substituted for the word "doctor" in any of the labeling statements in this section.

[51 FR 27759, Aug. 1, 1986; 52 FR 7831, Mar. 13, 1987, as amended at 53 FR 35810, Sept. 15, 1988]

§ 357.152 Package inserts for anthelmintic drug products.

The labeling of the product contains a consumer package insert which includes the following information:

(a) A discussion of the symptoms suggestive of pinworm infestation, including a statement that pinworms must be visually identified before taking this medication.

(b) A detailed description of how to find and identify the pinworm.

(c) A commentary on the life cycle of the pinworm.

(d) A commentary on the ways in which pinworms may be spread from person to person and hygienic procedures to follow to avoid such spreading.

(e) The appropriate labeling information contained in § 357.150

(Collection of information requirement approved by the Office of Management and Budget under control number 0910–0232)

[51 FR 27759, Aug. 1, 1986, as amended at 52 FR 2515, Jan. 23, 1987]

§ 357.180 Professional labeling.

The labeling provided to health professionals (but not to the general public) may contain an additional indication: "For the treatment of common roundworm infestation."

Subpart C—Cholecystokinetic Drug Products

§ 357.201 Scope.

(a) An over-the-counter cholecystokinetic drug product in a form suitable for oral administration is generally recognized as safe and effective and is not misbranded if it meets each of the conditions in this subpart in addition to each of the general conditions established in § 330.1.

(b) References in this subpart to regulatory sections of the Code of Federal Regulations are to chapter I of title 21 unless otherwise noted.

[48 FR 27005, June 10, 1983]

§ 357.203 Definition.

As used in this subpart:

Cholecystokinetic drug product. A drug product that causes contraction of the gallbladder and is used during the course of diagnostic gallbladder studies (cholecystography).

[48 FR 27005, June 10, 1983]

§ 357.210 Cholecystokinetic active ingredients.

The active ingredient of the product consists of any of the following when used within the specified concentration and dosage form established for each ingredient:

(a) 50-percent aqueous emulsion of corn oil.

(b) Hydrogenated soybean oil in a suitable, water-dispersible powder. The hydrogenated soybean oil is food-grade, partially hydrogenated with a melting point of 41 to 43.5 °C, an iodine value of 65 to 69, and a fatty acid composition as follows:

Fatty acid	Percent composition
Myristic acid	0.1
Palmitic acid	10.0
Palmitoleic acid	0.1
Stearic acid	13.5
Oleic acid	72.0
Linoleic acid	3.8
Linolenic acid	0.1
Arachidic acid	0.5
Behenic acid	0.2

[54 FR 8321, Feb. 28, 1989]

§ 357.250 Labeling of cholecystokinetic drug products.

(a) *Statement of identity.* The labeling of the product contains the established name of the drug, if any, and identifies the product as a "gallbladder diagnostic agent."

(b) *Indications.* The labeling of the product states, under the heading "Indications," the following: "For the contraction of the gallbladder during diagnostic gallbladder studies." Other truthful and nonmisleading statements, describing only the indications for use that have been established and listed in this paragraph (b), may also be used, as provided in § 330.1(c)(2), subject to the provisions of section 502 of the act relating to misbranding and the prohibition in section 301(d) of the act against the introduction or delivery for introduction into interstate commerce of unapproved new drugs in violation of section 505(a) of the act.

(c) *Warnings.* [Reserved]

(d) *Directions.* The labeling of the product contains the following statements under the heading "Directions":

(1) "Take only when instructed by a doctor:"

(2) *For products containing 50-percent aqueous emulsion of corn oil.*

(i) "Shake well before using."

(ii) Oral dosage is 60 milliliters 20 minutes before diagnostic gallbladder x-ray or as directed by a doctor.

(3) *For products containing hydrogeneated soybean oil.* Oral dosage is 12.4 grams in a suitable, water-dispersible powder in 2 to 3 ounces of water. Stir briskly to prepare a suspension before using. Drink 20 minutes before diagnostic gallbladder x-ray or as directed by a doctor.

(e) The word "physician" may be substituted for the word "doctor" in any of the labeling statements in this section.

[48 FR 27005, June 10, 1983, as amended at 51 FR 16267, May 1, 1986; 52 FR 7830, Mar. 13, 1987; 54 FR 8321, Feb. 28, 1989]

§ 357.280 Professional labeling.

The labeling provided to health professionals (but not to the general public) may contain the following information for ingredients identified in § 357.210: *Indication.* "For visualization of biliary ducts during cholecystography.''

[54 FR 8321, Feb. 28, 1989]

Subparts D-H [Reserved]

Subpart I—Deodorant Drug Products for Internal Use

SOURCE: 55 FR 19865, May 11, 1990, unless otherwise noted.

§ 357.801   Scope.

(a) An over-the-counter deodorant drug product for internal use in a form suitable for oral administration is generally recognized as safe and effective and is not misbranded if it meets each condition in this subpart and each general condition established in § 330.1 of this chapter.

(b) References in this subpart to regulatory sections of the Code of Federal Regulations are to chapter I of title 21 unless otherwise noted.

§ 357.803   Definitions.

As used in this subpart:

(a) *Colostomy.* An external operative opening of the colon.

(b) *Deodorant for internal use.* An ingredient taken internally to reduce odors arising from conditions such as colostomies, ileostomies, or fecal incontinence.

(c) *Ileostomy.* An external operative opening from the ileum.

(d) *Incontinence.* An inability to retain urine or feces.

§ 357.810   Active ingredients for deodorant drug products for internal use.

The active ingredient of the product consists of either of the following when used within the dosage limits established for each ingredient in § 357.850(d):

(a) Bismuth subgallate.

(b) Chlorophyllin copper complex.

§ 357.850   Labeling of deodorant drug products for internal use.

(a) *Statement of identity.* The labeling of the product contains the established name of the drug, if any, and identifies the product as a "deodorant for internal use" or as a "colostomy or ileostomy deodorant."

(b) *Indications.* The labeling of the product states, under the heading "Indications," any of the phrases listed in paragraph (b) of this section as appropriate. Other truthful and nonmisleading statements, describing only the indications for use that have been established and listed in paragraph (b) of this section may also be used, as provided in § 330.1(c)(2) of this chapter, subject to the provisions of section 502 of the Federal Food, Drug, and Cosmetic Act (the act) relating to misbranding and the prohibition in section 301(d) of the act against the introduction or delivery for introduction into interstate commerce of unapproved new drugs in violation of section 505(a) of the act.

(1) *For products containing bismuth subgallate identified in § 357.810(a).* "An aid to reduce odor from a colostomy or ileostomy."

(2) *For products containing chlorophyllin copper complex identified in § 357.810(b).* (i) "An aid to reduce odor from a colostomy or ileostomy."

(ii) "An aid to reduce fecal odor due to incontinence."

(c) *Warnings.* The labeling of the product contains the following warnings under the heading "Warnings": (1) *For products containing chlorophyllin copper complex identified in § 357.810(b).* (i) "If cramps or diarrhea occurs, reduce the dosage. If symptoms persist, consult your doctor."

(ii) The warning required by § 330.1(g) of this chapter concerning overdose is not required on products containing chlorophyllin copper complex identified in § 357.810(b).

(2) [Reserved]

(d) *Directions.* The labeling of the product contains the following information under the heading "Directions."

(1) *For products containing bismuth subgallate identified in § 357.810(a).* Adults and children 12 years of age and over: Oral dosage is 200 to 400 milligrams up to 4 times daily. Children under 12 years of age: consult a doctor.

(2) *For products containing chlorophyllin copper complex identified in § 357.810(b).* Adults and children 12 years of age and over: Oral dosage is 100 to 200 milligrams daily in divided doses as required. If odor is not controlled, take

up to an additional 100 milligrams daily in divided doses as required. The smallest effective dose should be used. Do not exceed 300 milligrams daily. Children under 12 years of age: consult a doctor.

PART 358—MISCELLANEOUS EXTERNAL DRUG PRODUCTS FOR OVER-THE-COUNTER HUMAN USE

AUTHORITY: 21 U.S.C. 321, 351, 352, 353, 355, 360, 371.

SOURCE: 55 FR 33255, Aug. 14, 1990, unless otherwise noted.

Subpart A [Reserved]

Subpart B—Wart Remover Drug Products

§ 358.101 Scope.

(a) An over-the-counter wart remover drug product in a form suitable for topical application is generally recognized as safe and effective and is not misbranded if it meets each of the conditions in this subpart and each of the general conditions established in § 330.1 of this chapter.

(b) References in this subpart to regulatory sections of the Code of Federal Regulations are to chapter I of title 21 unless otherwise noted.

§ 358.103 Definitions.

As used in this subpart:

(a) *Wart remover drug product.* A topical agent used for the removal of common or plantar warts.

(b) *Collodion-like vehicle.* A solution containing pyroxylin (nitrocellulose) in an appropriate nonaqueous solvent that leaves a transparent cohesive film when applied to the skin in a thin layer.

(c) *Plaster vehicle.* A fabric, plastic, or other suitable backing material in which medication is usually incorporated for topical application to the skin.

§ 358.110 Wart remover active ingredients.

The product consists of any of the following active ingredients within the specified concentration and in the dosage form established for each ingredient.

(a) Salicylic acid 12 to 40 percent in a plaster vehicle.

(b) Salicylic acid 5 to 17 percent in a collodion-like vehicle.

(c) Salicylic acid 15 percent in a karaya gum, glycol plaster vehicle.

§ 358.150 Labeling of wart remover drug products.

(a) *Statement of identity.* The labeling of the product contains the established name of the drug, if any, and identifies the product as a "wart remover."

(b) *Indications.* The labeling of the product states, under the heading "Indications," any of the phrases listed in paragraph (b) of this section. Other truthful and nonmisleading statements, describing only the indications for use that have been established in paragraph (b) of this section, may also be used, as provided in § 330.1(c)(2) of this chapter, subject to the provisions of section 502 of the Federal Food, Drug, and Cosmetic Act (the act) relating to misbranding and the prohibition in section 301(d) of the act against the introduction or delivery for introduction into interstate commerce of unapproved new drugs in violation of section 505(a) of the act.

(1) "For the removal of common warts. The common wart is easily recognized by the rough 'cauliflower-like' appearance of the surface."

(2) "For the removal of plantar warts on the bottom of the foot. The plantar wart is recognized by its location only on the bottom of the foot, its tenderness, and the interruption of the footprint pattern."

(c) *Warnings.* The labeling of the product contains the following warnings under the heading "Warnings":

(1) *For products containing any ingredient identified in § 358.110.* (i) "For external use only."

(ii) "Do not use this product on irritated skin, on any area that is infected or reddened, if you are a diabetic, or if you have poor blood circulation."

(iii) "If discomfort persists, see your doctor."

(iv) "Do not use on moles, birthmarks, warts with hair growing from them, genital warts, or warts on the face or mucous membranes."

(2) *For any product formulated in a flammable vehicle.* (i) The labeling should contain an appropriate flammability signal word, e.g. "extremely

flammable," "flammable," "combustible," consistent with 16 CFR 1500.3(b)(10).

(ii) "Keep away from fire or flame."

(3) *For any product formulated in a volatile vehicle.* "Cap bottle tightly and store at room temperature away from heat."

(4) *For any product formulated in a collodion-like vehicle.* (i) "If product gets into the eye, flush with water for 15 minutes."

(ii) "Avoid inhaling vapors."

(d) *Directions.* The labeling of the product contains the following information under the heading "Directions":

(1) *For products containing salicylic acid identified in § 358.110(a).* "Wash affected area." (Optional: "May soak wart in warm water for 5 minutes.") "Dry area thoroughly." (If appropriate: "Cut plaster to fit wart.") "Apply medicated plaster. Repeat procedure every 48 hours as needed (until wart is removed) for up to 12 weeks."

(2) *For products containing salicylic acid identified in § 358.110(b).* "Wash affected area." (Optional: "May soak wart in warm water for 5 minutes.") "Dry area thoroughly. Apply" (select one of the following, as appropriate: "one drop" or "small amount") "at a time with" (select one of the following, as appropriate: "applicator" or "brush") "to sufficiently cover each wart. Let dry. Repeat this procedure once or twice daily as needed (until wart is removed) for up to 12 weeks."

(3) *For products containing salicylic acid identified in § 358.110(c).* "Wash affected area." (Optional: "May soak wart in warm water for 5 minutes.") "Dry area thoroughly. Gently smooth wart surface with emery file supplied." (If appropriate: "Cut plaster to fit wart.") "Apply a drop of warm water to the wart, keeping the surrounding skin dry. Apply medicated plaster at bedtime and leave in place for at least 8 hours. In the morning, remove plaster and discard. Repeat procedure every 24 hours as needed (until wart is removed) for up to 12 weeks."

(e) The word "physician" may be substituted for the word "doctor" in any of the labeling statements in this section.

(f) The phrase "or podiatrist" may be used in addition to the word "doctor" in any of the labeling statements in this section when a product is labeled with the indication identified in § 358.150(b)(2).

[55 FR 33255, Aug. 14, 1990; 55 FR 37403, Sept. 11, 1990, as amended at 57 FR 44495, Sept. 28, 1992; 59 FR 60317, Nov. 23, 1994]

Subpart C [Reserved]

Subpart D—Ingrown Toenail Relief Drug Products

SOURCE: 68 FR 24348, May 7, 2003, unless otherwise noted.

§ 358.301 Scope.

(a) An over-the-counter ingrown toenail relief drug product in a form suitable for topical administration is generally recognized as safe and effective and is not misbranded if it meets each condition in this subpart and each general condition established in § 330.1 of this chapter.

(b) References in this subpart to regulatory sections of the Code of Federal Regulations are to chapter 1 of title 21 unless otherwise noted.

§ 358.303 Definitions.

As used in this subpart:

(a) *Ingrown toenail relief drug product.* A drug product applied to an ingrown toenail that relieves pain or discomfort either by softening the nail or by hardening the nail bed.

(b) *Retainer ring.* A die cut polyethylene foam pad coated on one side with medical grade acrylic pressure-sensitive adhesive. The retainer ring has slots, center-cut completely through the foam with the cut of sufficient size to allow for localization of an active ingredient in a gel vehicle to a specific target area. The retainer ring is used with adhesive bandage strips to place over the retainer ring to hold it in place.

§ 358.310 Ingrown toenail relief active ingredient.

The active ingredient of the product is sodium sulfide 1 percent in a gel vehicle. The gel vehicle is an aqueous, semisolid system with large organic molecules interpenetrated with a liquid.

§ 358.350 Labeling of ingrown toenail relief drug products.

(a) *Statement of identity.* The labeling of the product contains the established name of the product, if any, and identifies the product as an "ingrown toenail relief product" or as an "ingrown toenail discomfort reliever."

(b) *Indications.* The labeling of the product states, under the heading "Use," the following: "for temporary relief of" [select one or both of the following: 'pain' or 'discomfort'] "from ingrown toenails". Other truthful and nonmisleading statements, describing only the use that has been established and listed in this paragraph (b), may also be used, as provided in § 330.1(c)(2) of this chapter, subject to the provisions of section 502 of the Federal Food, Drug, and Cosmetic Act (the act) relating to misbranding and the prohibition in section 301(d) of the act against the introduction or delivery for introduction into interstate commerce of unapproved new drugs in violation of section 505(a) of the act.

(c) *Warnings.* The labeling of the product contains the following warnings under the heading "Warnings":

(1) "For external use only" in accord with § 201.66(c)(5)(i) of this chapter.

(2) "Do not use [bullet][1] on open sores".

(3) "Ask a doctor before use if you have [bullet] diabetes [bullet] poor circulation [bullet] gout".

(4) "When using this product [bullet] use with a retainer ring".

(5) "Stop use and ask a doctor if [bullet] redness or swelling of your toe increases [bullet] discharge is present around the nail [bullet] symptoms last more than 7 days or clear up and occur again within a few days".

(d) *Directions.* The labeling of the product contains the following statements under the heading "Directions":

(1) "[Bullet] adults and children 12 years and over:"

(i) "[Bullet] wash the affected area and dry thoroughly [bullet] place retainer ring on toe with slot over the

---

[1] See § 201.66(b)(4) of this chapter for definition of bullet.

area where the ingrown nail and the skin meet. Smooth ring down firmly. [bullet] apply enough gel product to fill the slot in the ring [bullet] place round center section of bandage strip directly over the gel-filled ring to seal the gel in place. Smooth ends of bandage strip around toes.''

(ii) ''[Bullet] repeat twice daily (morning and night) for up to 7 days until discomfort is relieved or until the nail can be lifted out of the nail groove and easily trimmed''.

(2) ''[Bullet] children under 12 years: ask a doctor''.

Subpart E [Reserved]

Subpart F—Corn and Callus Remover Drug Products

SOURCE: 55 FR 33261, Aug. 14, 1990, unless otherwise noted.

§ 358.501 Scope.

(a) An over-the-counter corn and callus remover drug product in a form suitable for topical application is generally recognized as safe and effective and is not misbranded if it meets each of the conditions in this subpart and each of the general conditions established in § 330.1 of this chapter.

(b) References in this subpart to regulatory sections of the Code of Federal Regulations are to chapter I of title 21 unless otherwise noted.

§ 358.503 Definitions.

As used in this subpart:

(a) *Corn and callus remover drug product.* A topical agent used for the removal of corns and calluses.

(b) *Collodion-like vehicle.* A solution containing pyroxylin (nitrocellulose) in an appropriate nonaqueous solvent that leaves a transparent cohesive film when applied to the skin in a thin layer.

(c) *Plaster vehicle.* A fabric, plastic, or other suitable backing material in which medication is usually incorporated for topical application to the skin.

§ 358.510 Corn and callus remover active ingredients.

The product consists of any of the following active ingredients within the specified concentrations and in the dosage form established for each ingredient.

(a) Salicylic acid 12 to 40 percent in a plaster vehicle.

(b) Salicylic acid 12 to 17.6 percent in a collodion-like vehicle.

§ 358.550 Labeling of corn and callus remover drug products.

(a) *Statement of identity.* The labeling of the product contains the established name of the drug, if any, and identifies the product as a ''corn and callus remover.''

(b) *Indications.* The labeling of the product states, under the heading ''Indications,'' the phrase listed in paragraph (b)(1) of this section and may contain the additional phrase listed in paragraph (b)(2) of this section. Other truthful and nonmisleading statements, describing only the indications for use that have been established in paragraph (b) of this section, may also be used, as provided in § 330.1(c)(2) of this chapter, subject to the provisions of section 502 of the Federal Food, Drug, and Cosmetic Act (the act) relating to misbranding and the prohibition in section 301(d) of the act against the introduction or delivery for introduction into interstate commerce of unapproved new drugs in violation of section 505(a) of the act.

(1) ''For the removal of corns and calluses.''

(2) In addition to the information identified in paragraph (b)(1) of this section, the labeling of the product may contain the following statement: ''Relieves pain by removing corns and calluses.''

(c) *Warnings.* The labeling of the product contains the following warnings under the heading ''Warnings'':

(1) *For products containing any ingredient identified in § 358.510.* (i) ''For external use only.''

(ii) ''Do not use this product on irritated skin, on any area that is infected or reddened, if you are a diabetic, or if you have poor blood circulation.''

(iii) ''If discomfort persists, see your doctor or podiatrist.''

(2) *For any product formulated in a flammable vehicle.* (i) The labeling should contain an appropriate flammability signal word, e.g., "extremely flammable," "flammable," "combustible," consistent with 16 CFR 1500.3(b)(10).

(ii) "Keep away from fire or flame."

(3) *For any product formulated in a volatile vehicle.* "Cap bottle tightly and store at room temperature away from heat."

(4) *For any product formulated in a collodion-like vehicle.* (i) "If product gets into the eye, flush with water for 15 minutes."

(ii) "Avoid inhaling vapors."

(d) *Directions.* The labeling of the product contains the following information under the heading "Directions":

(1) *For products containing salicylic acid identified in § 358.510(a).* "Wash affected area and dry thoroughly." (If appropriate: "Cut plaster to fit corn/callus.") "Apply medicated plaster. After 48 hours remove the medicated plaster. Repeat this procedure every 48 hours as needed for up to 14 days (until corn/callus is removed)." (Optional: "May soak corn/callus in warm water for 5 minutes to assist in removal.")

(2) *For products containing salicylic acid identified in § 358.510(b).* "Wash affected area and dry thoroughly. Apply" (select one of the following, as appropriate: "one drop" or "small amount") "at a time with" (select one of the following, as appropriate: "applicator" or "brush") "to sufficiently cover each corn/callus. Let dry. Repeat this procedure once or twice daily as needed for up to 14 days (until corn/callus is removed)." (Optional: "May soak corn/callus in warm water for 5 minutes to assist in removal.")

(e) The word "physician" may be substituted for the word "doctor" in any of the labeling statements in this section.

[55 FR 33261, Aug. 14, 1990, as amended at 57 FR 44494, Sept. 28, 1992]

Subpart G—Pediculicide Drug Products

SOURCE: 58 FR 65455, Dec. 14, 1993, unless otherwise noted.

§ 358.601 Scope.

(a) An over-the-counter pediculicide drug product in a form suitable for topical application is generally recognized as safe and effective and is not misbranded if it meets each condition in this subpart and each general condition established in § 330.1 of this chapter.

(b) References in this subpart to regulatory sections of the Code of Federal Regulations are to chapter I of title 21 unless otherwise noted.

§ 358.603 Definition.

As used in this subpart:

Pediculicide drug product. A drug product for the treatment of head, pubic (crab), and body lice.

§ 358.610 Pediculicide active ingredients.

The active ingredients of the product consist of the combination of pyrethrum extract (providing a concentration of pyrethrins of 0.17 to 0.33 percent) with piperonyl butoxide (2 to 4 percent) in a nonaerosol dosage formulation.

[63 FR 43303, Aug. 13, 1998]

§ 358.650 Labeling of pediculicide drug products.

(a) *Statement of identity.* The labeling of the product contains the established name of the drug, if any, and identifies the product as a "lice treatment."

(b) *Indications.* The labeling of the product states, under the heading "Uses," the following: "treats head, pubic (crab), and body lice." Other truthful and nonmisleading statements, describing only the uses that have been established and listed in this paragraph (b), may also be used, as provided in § 330.1(c)(2) of this chapter, subject to the provisions of section 502 of the Federal Food, Drug, and Cosmetic Act (the act) relating to misbranding and the prohibition in section 301(d) of the act against the introduction or delivery for introduction into interstate commerce of unapproved new drugs in violation of section 505(a) of the act.

(c) *Warnings.* The labeling of the product contains the following warnings under the heading "Warnings":

(1) "For external use only" in accord with § 201.66(c)(5)(i) of this chapter.

(2) "Do not use [bullet][1] near eyes [bullet] inside nose, mouth, or vagina [bullet] on lice in eyebrows or eyelashes. See a doctor if lice are present in these areas."

(3) "Ask a doctor before use if you are [bullet] allergic to ragweed. May cause breathing difficulty or an asthmatic attack."

(4) "When using this product [bullet] keep eyes tightly closed and protect eyes with a washcloth or towel [bullet] if product gets in eyes, flush with water right away [bullet] scalp itching or redness may occur".

(5) "Stop use and ask a doctor if [bullet] breathing difficulty occurs [bullet] eye irritation occurs [bullet] skin or scalp irritation continues or infection occurs".

(d) *Directions.* The labeling of the product contains the following information under the heading "Directions":

(1) The labeling states "[bullet] Important: Read warnings before use" [statement shall appear first and in bold type].

(2) The labeling states "adults and children 2 years and over:" [in bold type].

(3) For head lice treatment products "Inspect [in bold type] [bullet] check each household member with a magnifying glass in bright light for lice/nits (eggs) [bullet] look for tiny nits near scalp, beginning at back of neck and behind ears [bullet] examine small sections of hair at a time [bullet] unlike dandruff which moves when touched, nits stick to the hair [bullet] if either lice or nits are found, treat with this product".

(4) Select one of the following:

(i) *For shampoo products* "Treat [in bold type] [bullet] apply thoroughly to (optional, may add "dry") hair or other affected area. For head lice, first apply behind ears and to back of neck. [bullet] allow product to remain for 10 minutes, but no longer [bullet] use warm water to form a lather, shampoo, then thoroughly rinse [bullet] for head lice, towel dry hair and comb out tangles".

---

[1] See § 201.66(b)(4) of this chapter for definition of bullet symbol.

(ii) *For nonshampoo products* "Treat [in bold type] [bullet] apply thoroughly to (optional, may add "dry") hair or other affected area. For head lice, first apply behind ears and to back of neck. [bullet] allow product to remain for 10 minutes, but no longer [bullet] wash area thoroughly with warm water and soap or shampoo [bullet] for head lice, towel dry hair and comb out tangles".

(5) "Remove lice and their eggs (nits) [in bold type] [bullet] use a fine-tooth or special lice/nit comb. Remove any remaining nits by hand (using a throwaway glove). [bullet] hair should remain slightly damp while removing nits [bullet] if hair dries during combing, dampen slightly with water [bullet] for head lice, part hair into sections. Do one section at a time starting on top of head. Longer hair may take 1 to 2 hours. [bullet] lift a 1- to 2-inch wide strand of hair. Place comb as close to scalp as possible and comb with a firm, even motion away from scalp. [bullet] pin back each strand of hair after combing [bullet] clean comb often. Wipe nits away with tissue and discard in a plastic bag. Seal bag and discard to prevent lice from coming back. [bullet] after combing, thoroughly recheck for lice/nits. Repeat combing if necessary. [bullet] check daily for any lice/nits that you missed".

(6) The labeling states "[bullet] a second treatment must be done in 7 to 10 days to kill any newly hatched lice".

(7) The labeling states "[bullet] if infestation continues, see a doctor for other treatments".

(8) The labeling states "children under 2 years:" [in bold type] "ask a doctor".

(e) *Other information.* The labeling of the product contains the following statements, as appropriate, under the heading "Other information." This information may appear in a package insert. If a package insert is used, the "Other information" section on the outer carton or container label shall include a statement referring to the package insert for additional information.

(1) "Head lice [highlighted in bold type] [bullet] lay small white eggs (nits) on hair shaft close to scalp [bullet] nits are most easily found on back

of neck or behind ears [bullet] disinfect hats, hair ribbons, scarves, coats, towels, and bed linens by machine washing in hot water (above 54 °C (130 °F)), then using hottest dryer cycle for at least 20 minutes [bullet] items that cannot be washed (bedspreads, blankets, pillows, stuffed toys, etc.) should be dry-cleaned or sealed in a plastic bag for 4 weeks, then removed outdoors and shaken out very hard before using again [bullet] items that cannot be washed, dry-cleaned, or stored may be sprayed with a product designed for this purpose [bullet] soak all combs and brushes in hot water (above 54 °C (130 °F)) for at least 10 minutes [bullet] vacuum all carpets, mattresses, upholstered furniture, and car seats that may have been used by affected people''.

(2) "Pubic (crab) lice [highlighted in bold type] [bullet] may be transmitted by sexual contact. Sexual partners should be treated simultaneously to avoid reinfestation [bullet] lice are very small and look like brown or grey dots on skin [bullet] usually cause intense itching and lay small white eggs (nits) on the hair shaft generally close to the skin surface [bullet] may be present on the short hairs of groin, thighs, trunk, and underarms, and occasionally on the beard and mustache [bullet] disinfect underwear by machine washing in hot water (above 54 °C (130 °F)), then using hottest dryer cycle for at least 20 minutes''.

(3) "Body lice [highlighted in bold type] [bullet] body lice and their eggs (nits) are generally found in the seams of clothing particularly in waistline and armpit area [bullet] body lice feed on skin then return to clothing to lay their eggs [bullet] disinfect clothing by machine washing in hot water (above 54 °C (130 °F)), then using hottest dryer cycle for at least 20 minutes [bullet] do not seal clothing in a plastic bag because nits can remain dormant for up to 30 days''.

[68 FR 75417, Dec. 31, 2003]

Subpart H—Drug Products for the Control of Dandruff, Seborrheic Dermatitis, and Psoriasis

SOURCE: 56 FR 63568, Dec. 4, 1991, unless otherwise noted.

§ 358.701 Scope.

(a) An over-the-counter dandruff, seborrheic dermatitis, or psoriasis drug product in a form suitable for topical application is generally recognized as safe and effective and is not misbranded if it meets each of the conditions in this subpart and each general condition established in § 330.1 of this chapter.

(b) References in this subpart to regulatory sections of the Code of Federal Regulations are to chapter I of title 21 unless otherwise noted.

§ 358.703 Definitions.

As used in this subpart:

(a) *Coal tar.* The tar used for medicinal purposes that is obtained as a by-product during the destructive distillation of bituminous coal at temperatures in the range of 900 °C to 1,100 °C. It may be further processed using either extraction with alcohol and suitable dispersing agents and maceration times or fractional distillation with or without the use of suitable organic solvents.

(b) *Dandruff.* A condition involving an increased rate of shedding of dead epidermal cells of the scalp.

(c) *Psoriasis.* A condition of the scalp or body characterized by irritation, itching, redness, and extreme excess shedding of dead epidermal cells.

(d) *Seborrheic dermatitis.* A condition of the scalp or body characterized by irritation, itching, redness, and excess shedding of dead epidermal cells.

(e) *Selenium sulfide, micronized.* Selenium sulfide that has been finely ground and that has a median particle size of approximately 5 micrometers (μm), with not more than 0.1 percent of the particles greater than 15 μm and not more than 0.1 percent of the particles less than 0.5 μm.

[56 FR 63568, Dec. 4, 1991, as amended at 59 FR 4001, Jan. 28, 1994]

§ 358.710 Active ingredients for the control of dandruff, seborrheic dermatitis, or psoriasis.

The active ingredient of the product consists of any of the following within the specified concentration established for each ingredient:

(a) *Active ingredients for the control of dandruff.* (1) Coal tar, 0.5 to 5 percent. When a coal tar solution, derivative, or fraction is used as the source of the coal tar, the labeling shall specify the identity and concentration of the coal tar source used and the concentration of the coal tar present in the final product.

(2) Pyrithione zinc, 0.3 to 2 percent when formulated to be applied and then washed off after brief exposure.

(3) Pyrithione zinc, 0.1 to 0.25 percent when formulated to be applied and left on the skin or scalp.

(4) Salicylic acid, 1.8 to 3 percent.

(5) Selenium sulfide, 1 percent.

(6) Selenium sulfide, micronized, 0.6 percent.

(7) Sulfur, 2 to 5 percent.

(b) *Active ingredients for the control of seborrheic dermatitis.* (1) Coal tar, 0.5 to 5 percent. When a coal tar solution, derivative, or fraction is used as the source of the coal tar, the labeling shall specify the identity and concentration of the coal tar source used and the concentration of the coal tar present in the final product.

(2) Pyrithione zinc, 0.95 to 2 percent when formulated to be applied and then washed off after brief exposure.

(3) Pyrithione zinc, 0.1 to 0.25 percent when formulated to be applied and left on the skin or scalp.

(4) Salicylic acid, 1.8 to 3 percent.

(5) Selenium sulfide, 1 percent.

(c) *Active ingredients for the control of psoriasis.* (1) Coal tar, 0.5 to 5 percent. When a coal tar solution, derivative, or fraction is used as the source of the coal tar, the labeling shall specify the identity and concentration of the coal tar source used and the concentration of the coal tar present in the final product.

(2) Salicylic acid, 1.8 to 3 percent.

[56 FR 63568, Dec. 4, 1991, as amended at 59 FR 4001, Jan. 28, 1994]

§ 358.720 Permitted combinations of active ingredients.

(a) *Combination of active ingredients for the control of dandruff.* Salicylic acid identified in § 358.710(a)(4) may be combined with sulfur identified in § 358.710(a)(7) provided each ingredient is present within the established concentration and the product is labeled according to § 358.750.

(b) *Combination of control of dandruff and external analgesic active ingredients.* Coal tar identified in § 358.710(a)(1) may be used at a concentration of 1.8 percent coal tar solution, on a weight to volume basis, in combination with menthol, 1.5 percent, in a shampoo formulation provided the product is labeled according to § 358.760.

[72 FR 9852, Mar. 6, 2007]

§ 358.750 Labeling of drug products for the control of dandruff, seborrheic dermatitis, or psoriasis.

(a) *Statement of identity.* The labeling of the product contains the established name of the drug, if any, and identifies the product with one or more of the following, as appropriate:

(1) "Dandruff (insert product form)" or "antidandruff (insert product form)".

(2) "Seborrheic dermatitis (insert product form)".

(3) "Psoriasis (insert product form)".

(b) *Indications.* The labeling of the product states, under the heading "Indications," the phrase listed in paragraph (b)(1) of this section and may contain any of the terms listed in paragraph (b)(2) or (b)(3) of this section. Other truthful and nonmisleading statements, describing only the indications for use that have been established and listed in paragraph (b) of this section, may also be used, as provided in § 330.1(c)(2) of this chapter, subject to the provisions of section 502 of the Federal Food, Drug, and Cosmetic Act (the act) relating to misbranding and the prohibition in section 301(d) of the act against the introduction or delivery for introduction into interstate commerce of unapproved new drugs in violation of section 505(a) of the act.

(1) ("For relief of" or "Controls") "the symptoms of" (select one or more

of the following, as appropriate: "dandruff," "seborrheic dermatitis," and/or "psoriasis.")

(2) The following terms or phrases may be used in place of or in addition to the words "For the relief of" or "Controls" in the indications in paragraph (b)(1) of this section: "fights," "reduces," "helps eliminate," "helps stop," "controls recurrence of," "fights recurrence of," "helps prevent recurrence of," "reduces recurrence of," "helps eliminate recurrence of," "helps stop recurrence of."

(3) The following terms may be used in place of the words "the symptoms of" in the indications in paragraph (b)(1) of this section: ("skin" and/or "scalp," as appropriate) (select one or more of the following: "itching," "irritation," "redness," "flaking," "scaling,") "associated with."

(c) *Warnings.* The labeling of the product contains the following warnings under the heading "Warnings":

(1) *For products containing any ingredient identified in §358.710.* (i) "For external use only."

(ii) "Avoid contact with the eyes. If contact occurs, rinse eyes thoroughly with water."

(iii) "If condition worsens or does not improve after regular use of this product as directed, consult a doctor."

(2) *For any product containing coal tar identified in §358.710(a), (b), or (c).* (i) "Use caution in exposing skin to sunlight after applying this product. It may increase your tendency to sunburn for up to 24 hours after application."

(ii) "Do not use for prolonged periods without consulting a doctor."

(3) *For products containing coal tar when formulated to be applied and left on the skin (e.g., creams, ointments, lotions).* "Do not use this product in or around the rectum or in the genital area or groin except on the advice of a doctor."

(4) *For products containing coal tar identified in §358.710(c) for the control of psoriasis.* "Do not use this product with other forms of psoriasis therapy such as ultraviolet radiation or prescription drugs unless directed to do so by a doctor."

(5) *For products containing any ingredient identified in §358.710(b) or (c) for the control of seborrheic dermatitis or psoriasis.* "If condition covers a large area

of the body, consult your doctor before using this product."

(d) *Directions.* The labeling of the product contains the following information under the heading "Directions." More detailed directions applicable to a particular product formulation may also be included.

(1) *For products containing active ingredients for the control of dandruff, seborrheic dermatitis, or psoriasis when formulated to be applied and then washed off after brief (a few minutes) exposure (e.g, shampoos, preshampoo rinses, postshampoo rinses).* "For best results use at least twice a week or as directed by a doctor."

(2) *For products containing active ingredients for the control of dandruff, seborrheic dermatitis, or psoriasis when formulated so as to be applied and left on the skin or scalp (e.g., creams, ointments, lotions, hairgrooms).* "Apply to affected areas one to four times daily or as directed by a doctor."

(3) *For products containing active ingredients for the control of seborrheic dermatitis or psoriasis of the skin when formulated as soaps.* "Use on affected areas in place of your regular soap."

(e) The word "physician" may be substituted for the word "doctor" in any of the labeling statements in this section.

§358.760 **Labeling of permitted combinations of active ingredients for the control of dandruff.**

The statement of identity, indications, warnings, and directions for use, respectively, applicable to each ingredient in the product may be combined to eliminate duplicative words or phrases so that the resulting information is clear and understandable.

(a) *Statement of identity.* For a combination drug product that has an established name, the labeling of the product states the established name of the combination drug product, followed by the statement of identity for each ingredient in the combination, as established in the statement of identity sections of the applicable OTC drug monographs.

(1) *Combinations of control of dandruff and external analgesic active ingredients*

in §358.720(b). The label states "dandruff/anti-itch shampoo" or "anti-dandruff/anti-itch shampoo".

(2) [Reserved]

(b) *Indications*. The labeling of the product states, under the heading "Uses," one or more of the phrases listed in this paragraph (b), as appropriate. Other truthful and nonmisleading statements, describing only the uses that have been established and listed in this paragraph (b), may also be used, as provided in §330.1(c)(2) of this chapter, subject to the provisions of section 502 of the Federal Food, Drug, and Cosmetic Act (the act) relating to misbranding and the prohibition in section 301(d) of the act against the introduction or delivery for introduction into interstate commerce of unapproved new drugs in violation of section 505(a) of the act.

(1) *Combinations of control of dandruff and external analgesic active ingredients in §358.720(b)*. The labeling states "[bullet] [select one of the following: 'for relief of' or 'controls'] the symptoms of dandruff [bullet] [select one of the following: 'additional' or 'extra'] relief of itching due to dandruff".

(2) The following terms or phrases may be used in place of or in addition to the words "for the relief of" or "controls" in the indications in paragraph (b)(1) of this section: "fights," "reduces," "helps eliminate," "helps stop," "controls recurrence of," "fights recurrence of," "helps prevent recurrence of," "reduces recurrence of," "helps eliminate recurrence of," "helps stop recurrence of."

(3) The following terms may be used in place of the words "the symptoms of" in the indication in paragraph (b)(1) of this section: "scalp" (select one or more of the following: "itching," "irritation," "redness," "flaking," "scaling") "associated with".

(c) *Warnings*. The labeling of the product states, under the heading "Warnings," the warning(s) listed in §358.750(c)(1) and (c)(2).

(d) *Directions*. The labeling of the product states, under the heading "Directions," directions that conform to the directions established for each ingredient in the directions sections of the applicable OTC drug monographs, unless otherwise stated in this para-

graph (d). When the time intervals or age limitations for administration of the individual ingredients differ, the directions for the combination product may not contain any dosage that exceeds those established for any individual ingredient in the applicable OTC drug monograph(s), and may not provide for use by any age group lower than the highest minimum age limit established for any individual ingredient.

(1) *Combinations of control of dandruff and external analgesic active ingredients in §358.720(b)*. The labeling states "[bullet] wet hair [bullet] apply shampoo and work into a lather [bullet] rinse thoroughly [bullet] for best results, use at least twice a week or as directed by a doctor".

(2) [Reserved]

[72 FR 9852, Mar. 6, 2007]

PART 361—PRESCRIPTION DRUGS FOR HUMAN USE GENERALLY RECOGNIZED AS SAFE AND EFFECTIVE AND NOT MISBRANDED: DRUGS USED IN RESEARCH

AUTHORITY: 21 U.S.C. 321, 351, 352, 353, 355, 371; 42 U.S.C. 262.

§361.1 Radioactive drugs for certain research uses.

(a) Radioactive drugs (as defined in §310.3(n) of this chapter) are generally recognized as safe and effective when administered, under the conditions set forth in paragraph (b) of this section, to human research subjects during the course of a research project intended to obtain basic information regarding the metabolism (including kinetics, distribution, and localization) of a radioactively labeled drug or regarding human physiology, pathophysiology, or biochemistry, but not intended for immediate therapeutic, diagnostic, or similar purposes or to determine the safety and effectiveness of the drug in humans for such purposes (*i.e.*, to carry out a clinical trial). Certain basic research studies, e.g., studies to determine whether a drug localizes in a particular organ or fluid space and to describe the kinetics of that localization, may have eventual therapeutic or diagnostic implications, but the initial studies are considered to be basic research within the meaning of this section.

(b) The conditions under which use of radioactive drugs for research are considered safe and effective are:

(1) *Approval by Radioactive Drug Research Committee.* A Radioactive Drug Research Committee, composed and approved by the Food and Drug Administration in accordance with paragraph (c) of this section, has determined, in accordance with the standards set forth in paragraph (d) of this section, that:

(i) The pharmacological dose is within the limits set forth in paragraph (b)(2) of this section;

(ii) The radiation dose is within the limits set forth in paragraph (b)(3) of this section;

(iii) The radiation exposure is justified by the quality of the study being undertaken and the importance of the information it seeks to obtain;

(iv) The study meets the other requirements set forth in paragraph (d) of this section regarding qualifications of the investigator, proper licensure for handling radioactive materials, selection and consent of research subjects, quality of radioactive drugs used, research protocol design, reporting of adverse reactions, and approval by an appropriate Institutional Review Committee; and

(v) The use of the radioactive drug in human subjects has the approval of the Radioactive Drug Research Committee.

(2) *Limit on pharmacological dose.* The amount of active ingredient or combination of active ingredients to be administered shall be known not to cause any clinically detectable pharmacological effect in human beings. If the same active ingredients (exclusive of the radionuclide) are to be administered simultaneously, e.g., under a "Investigational New Drug Application" or for a therapeutic use in accordance with labeling for a drug approved under part 314 of this chapter, the total amount of active ingredients including the radionuclide shall be known not to exceed the dose limitations applicable to the separate administration of the active ingredients excluding the radionuclide.

(3) *Limit on radiation dose.* The amount of radioactive material to be administered shall be such that the subject receives the smallest radiation dose with which it is practical to perform the study without jeopardizing the benefits to be obtained from the study.

(i) Under no circumstances may the radiation dose to an adult research subject from a single study or cumulatively from a number of studies conducted within 1 year be generally recognized as safe if such dose exceeds the following:

Whole body, active blood-forming organs, lens of the eye, and gonads:

	Rems
Single dose	3
Annual and total dose commitment	5
Other organs:	
Single dose	5
Annual and total dose commitment	15

(ii) For a research subject under 18 years of age at his last birthday, the radiation dose shall not exceed 10 percent of that set forth in paragraph (b)(3)(i) of this section.

(iii) All radioactive material included in the drug either as essential material or as a significant contaminant or impurity shall be included when determining the total radiation doses and dose commitments. Radiation doses from x-ray procedures that are part of the research study (*i.e.*, would not have occurred but for the study) shall also be included. The possibility of followup studies shall be considered for inclusion in the dose calculations.

(iv) Numerical definitions of dose shall be based on an absorbed fraction method of radiation absorbed dose calculation, such as the system set forth by the Medical Internal Radiation Dose Committee of the Society of Nuclear Medicine, or the system set forth by the International Commission on Radiological Protection.

(c) A Radioactive Drug Research Committee, in order to comply with paragraph (b)(1) of this section, shall be composed, shall function, and shall obtain and maintain approval of the Food and Drug Administration in conformity with the following:

(1) *Membership.* A Radioactive Drug Research Committee shall consist of at

least five individuals. Each committee shall include the following three individuals: (i) A physician recognized as a specialist in nuclear medicine, (ii) a person qualified by training and experience to formulate radioactive drugs, and (iii) a person with special competence in radiation safety and radiation dosimetry. The remainder of the committee shall consist of individuals qualified in various disciplines pertinent to the field of nuclear medicine (e.g., radiology, internal medicine, clinical pathology, hematology, endocrinology, radiation therapy, radiation physics, radiation biophysics, health physics, and radiopharmacy). Membership shall be sufficiently diverse to permit expert review of the technical and scientific aspects of proposals submitted to the committee. The addition of consultants in other pertinent medical disciplines is encouraged. A Radioactive Drug Research Committee shall be either associated with a medical institution operated for care of patients and with sufficient scientific expertise to allow for selection of committee members from its faculty, or with a committee established by a State authority to provide advice on radiation health matters. Joint committees involving more than one medical institution which have been established in order to achieve a high level and diversity of experience will be acceptable. The Director of the Center for Drug Evaluation and Research may modify any of the foregoing requirements in a particular situation where alternative factors provide substantially the same composition and association.

(2) *Function.* Each Radioactive Drug Research Committee shall select a chairman, who shall sign all applications, minutes, and reports of the committee. Each committee shall meet at least once each quarter in which research activity has been authorized or conducted. A quorum consisting of more than 50 percent of the membership must be present with appropriate representation of the required fields of specialization. Minutes shall be kept and shall include the numerical results of votes on protocols involving use in human subjects. No member shall vote on a protocol in which he is an investigator.

(3) *Reports.* Each Radioactive Drug Research Committee shall submit an annual report on or before January 31 of each year to the Food and Drug Administration, Center for Drug Evaluation and Research, HFD–160, 5600 Fishers Lane, Rockville, MD 20857. The annual report shall include the names and qualifications of the members of, and of any consultants used by, the Radioactive Drug Research Committee, and, for each study conducted during the preceding year, a summary of information presented in the following format:

REPORT ON RESEARCH USE OF RADIOACTIVE DRUG

1. Title of the research project.
2. Brief description of the purpose of the research project.
3. Name of the investigator responsible.
4. Pharmacological dose:
a. Active ingredients.
b. Maximum amount administered per subject.
5. Name of the radionuclide(s) used, including any present, as significant contaminants or impurities.
6. Radiation absorbed dose. Provide the maximum dose commitement to the whole body and each organ specified in 21 CFR 361.1(b)(3)(i) that was received by a representative subject and the calculations or references that were used to estimate these maximum dose commitments. The report shall include the dose contribution of both the administered radionuclide(s) and any X-ray procedures associated with the study. If the study elicits data on the uptake or excretion of the radioactive drug pertinent to the estimation of dose commitment, report the mean value and range of values. For each subject provide:
(a) Age, sex, and approximate weight.
(b) Total activity of each radionuclide administered for each radioactive drug used in the study. Report each X-ray procedure used in conjunction with the study.
(c) If the subject has participated in other radioactive drug research studies, report the name of the radioactive drug used in these other studies, the date of administration, and the total activity of each radionuclide administered. If any X-ray procedures were used, identify the X-ray procedure(s) and include an estimate of the absorbed radiation doses.
(d) If more than one administration of a radioactive drug per subject, cumulative radiation dose and dose commitment, expressed as whole body, active blood-forming organs, lens of the eye, gonads, and other organ doses from the administered radionuclides.

7. A claim of confidentiality, if any.

NOTE: Contents of this report are available for public disclosure unless confidentiality is requested by the investigator and it is adequately shown by the investigator that the report constitutes a trade secret or confidential commercial information as defined in 21 CFR 20.61.

_____ Investigator

_____
Chairman, Radioactive Drug
Research Committee

At any time a proposal is approved which involves exposure either of more than 30 research subjects, or of any research subject under 18 years of age, the committee shall immediately submit to the Food and Drug Administration a special summary of information in the format shown in this paragraph. Contents of these reports are available for public disclosure, unless confidentiality is requested by the investigator and it is adequately shown by the investigator that the report constitutes a trade secret or confidential commercial information as defined in §20.61 of this chapter.

(4) *Approval.* Each Radioactive Drug Research Committee shall be specifically approved by the Center for Drug Evaluation and Research of the Food and Drug Administration. Applications shall be submitted to the Food and Drug Administration, Center for Drug Evaluation and Research, HFD–160, 5600 Fishers Lane, Rockville, MD 20857, and shall contain the names and qualifications of the members of the committee, and a statement that the committee agrees to comply with the requirements set forth in this section. Approval shall be based upon an assessment of the qualifications of the members of the committee, and the assurance that all necessary fields of expertise are covered. Approval of a committee may be withdrawn at any time for failure of the committee to comply with any of the requirements of this section. Approval of a committee shall remain effective unless and until the FDA withdraws such approval. Changes in membership and applications for new members shall be submitted to the Food and Drug Administration as soon as, or before, vacancies occur on the committee.

(5) *Monitoring.* The Food and Drug Administration shall conduct periodic reviews of approved committees. Monitoring of the activities of the committee shall be conducted through review of its annual report, through review of minutes and full protocols for certain studies, and through on-site inspections.

(d) In making the determination required in paragraph (b)(1) of this section, a Radioactive Drug Research Committee shall consider the following requirements and assure that each is met:

(1) *Radiation dose to subjects.* To assure that the radiation dose to research subjects is as low as practicable to perform the study and meet the criteria of §361.1(b)(3), the Radioactive Drug Research Committee shall require that:

(i) The investigator provide absorbed dose calculations based on biologic distribution data available from published literature or from other valid studies.

(ii) The investigator provide for an acceptable method of radioassay of the radioactive drug prior to its use to assure that the dose calculations actually reflect the administered dose.

(iii) The radioactive drug chosen for the study has that combination of half-life, types of radiations, radiation energy, metabolism, chemical properties, etc., which results in the lowest dose to the whole body or specific organs with which it is possible to obtain the necessary information.

(iv) The investigator utilize adequate and appropriate instrumentation for the detection and measurement of the specific radionuclide.

(2) *Pharmacological dosage.* To determine that the amount of active ingredients to be administered does not exceed the limitations set forth in paragraph (b)(2) of this section, the committee shall require that the investigator provide pharmacological dose calculations based on data available from published literature or from other valid human studies.

(3) *Qualifications of investigators.* Each investigator shall be qualified by training and experience to conduct the proposed research studies.

(4) *License to handle radioactive materials.* The responsible investigator or

institutions shall, in the case of reactor-produced isotopes, be licensed by the Nuclear Regulatory Commission or Agreement State to possess and use the specific radionuclides for research use or be a listed investigator under a broad license, or in the case of non-reactor-produced isotopes, be licensed by other appropriate State or local authorities, when required by State or local law, to possess and use the specific radionuclides for research use.

(5) *Human research subjects.* Each investigator shall select appropriate human subjects and shall obtain the review and approval of an institutional review committee that conforms to the requirements of part 56 of this chapter, and shall obtain the consent of the subjects or their legal representatives in accordance with part 50 of this chapter. The research subjects shall be at least 18 years of age and legally competent. Exceptions are permitted only in those special situations when it can be demonstrated to the committee that the study presents a unique opportunity to gain information not currently available, requires the use of research subjects less than 18 years of age, and is without significant risk to the subject. Studies involving minors shall be supported with review by qualified pediatric consultants to the Radioactive Drug Research Committee. Each female research subject of childbearing potential shall state in writing that she is not pregnant, or, on the basis of a pregnancy test be confirmed as not pregnant, before she may participate in any study.

(6) *Quality of radioactive drug.* The radioactive drug used in the research study shall meet appropriate chemical, pharmaceutical, radiochemical, and radionuclidic standards of identity, strength, quality, and purity as needed for safety and be of such uniform and reproducible quality as to give significance to the research study conducted. The Radioactive Drug Research Committee shall determine that radioactive materials for parenteral use are prepared in sterile and pyrogen-free form.

(7) *Research protocol.* No matter how small the amount of radioactivity, no study involving administration of a radioactive drug, as defined in § 310.3(n) of this chapter, to research subjects under this section, shall be permitted unless the Radioactive Drug Research Committee concludes, in its judgment, that scientific knowledge and benefit is likely to result from that study. Therefore, the protocol shall be based upon a sound rationale derived from appropriate animal studies or published literature and shall be of sound design such that information of scientific value may result. The radiation dose shall be both sufficient and no greater than necessary to obtain valid measurement. The projected number of subjects shall be sufficient but no greater than necessary for the purpose of the study. The number of subjects shall also reflect the fact that the study is intended to obtain basic research information referred to in paragraph (a) of this section and not intended for immediate therapeutic, diagnostic or similar purposes or to determine the safety and effectiveness of the drug in humans for such purposes (*i.e.*, to carry out a clinical trial).

(8) *Adverse reactions.* The investigator shall immediately report to the Radioactive Drug Research Committee all adverse effects associated with the use of the radioactive drug in the research study. All adverse reactions probably attributable to the use of the radioactive drug in the research study shall be immediately reported by the Radioactive Drug Research Committee to the Food and Drug Administration, Center for Drug Evaluation and Research, HFD–160, 5600 Fishers Lane, Rockville, MD 20857.

(9) *Approval by an institutional review board.* The investigator shall obtain the review and approval of an institutional review board that conforms to the requirements of part 56 of this chapter.

(e) The results of any research conducted pursuant to this section as part of the evaluation of a drug pursuant to part 312 of this chapter shall be included in the submissions required under part 312 of this chapter.

(f) A radioactive drug prepared, packaged, distributed, and primarily intended for use in accordance with the requirements of this section shall be exempt from section 502(f)(1) of the act and §§ 201.5 and 201.100 of this chapter if the packaging, label, and labeling are in compliance with Federal, State, and local law regarding radioactive materials and if the label of the immediate container and shielded container, if any, either separate from or as part of any label and labeling required for radioactive materials by the Nuclear Regulatory Commission or by State or local radiological health authorities bear the following:

(1) The statement "Rx only";

(2) The statement "To be administered in compliance with the requirements of Federal regulations regarding radioactive drugs for research use (21 CFR 361.1)";

(3) The established name of the drug, if any;

(4) The established name and quantity of each active ingredient;

(5) The name and half-life of the radionuclide, total quantity of radioactivity in the drug product's immediate container, and amount of radioactivity per unit volume or unit mass at a designated referenced time;

(6) The route of administration, if it is for the other than oral use;

(7) The net quantity of contents;

(8) An identifying lot or control number from which it is possible to determine the complete manufacturing history of the package of the drug;

(9) The name and address of the manufacturer, packer, or distributor;

(10) The expiration date, if any;

(11) If the drug is intended for parenteral use, a statement as to whether the contents are sterile;

(12) If the drug is for other than oral use, the names of all inactive ingredients, except that:

(i) Trace amounts of harmless substances added solely for individual product identification need not be named.

(ii) If the drug is intended for parenteral use, the quantity or proportion of all inactive ingredients, except that ingredients added to adjust pH or to make the drug isotonic may be declared by name and a statement of their effect; if the vehicle is water for injection, it need not be named. *Provided, however,* That in the case of containers too small or otherwise unable to accommodate a label with sufficient space to bear all such information, the information required by paragraphs (f)

(1) and (12) of this section may be placed on the shielded container only.

[40 FR 31308, July 25, 1975, as amended at 40 FR 44543, Sept. 29, 1975; 42 FR 15674, Mar. 22, 1977; 43 FR 14646, Apr. 7, 1978; 46 FR 8955, Jan. 27, 1981; 49 FR 44460, Nov. 7, 1984; 50 FR 8996, Mar. 6, 1985; 55 FR 11582, Mar. 29, 1990; 56 FR 10806, Mar. 14, 1991; 67 FR 4907, Feb. 1, 2002]

PART 369—INTERPRETATIVE STATEMENTS RE WARNINGS ON DRUGS AND DEVICES FOR OVER-THE-COUNTER SALE

Subpart A—Definitions and Interpretations

AUTHORITY: 21 U.S.C. 321, 331, 351, 352, 353, 355, 371.

SOURCE: 39 FR 11745, Mar. 29, 1974, unless otherwise noted.

EDITORIAL NOTE: Nomenclature changes to part 369 appear at 69 FR 13717, Mar. 24, 2004.

Subpart A—Definitions and Interpretations

§369.1 Purpose of issuance.

The warning and caution statements suggested in subparts B and C of this part, for inclusion in the label or labeling of drugs and devices subject to section 502(d) and (f)(2) and other relevant provisions of the Federal Food, Drug, and Cosmetic Act are issued for the purpose of assisting industry in preparing proper labeling for these articles for over-the-counter sale and in meeting the legal requirements of the act that the label or labeling of drugs and devices bear adequate warnings, in such manner and form as are necessary for the protection of users. Only section 502(d) of the act requires use of the specific language included in these suggested warning and caution statements. These suggested warning or caution statements are illustrative of those that may be necessary or desirable. It is the responsibility of the manufacturer, packer, shipper, or distributor in interstate commerce to see that such statements are adequate for compliance with the provisions of the law. Omission of any article from this suggested list does not relieve drugs and devices subject to provisions of the act from bearing adequate warning or caution statements where such statements are necessary or desirable for the protection of the user.

§ 369.2 Definitions.

(a) As used in this part, the term *act* means the Federal Food, Drug, and Cosmetic Act.

(b) The terms *drugs* and *devices* are defined in section 201(g) and (k) of the act.

(c) Official compendia are defined in section 201(j) of the act.

§ 369.3 Warnings required on drugs exempted from prescription-dispensing requirements of section 503(b)(1)(C).

Drugs exempted from prescription-dispensing requirements under section 503(b)(1)(C) of the act are subject to the labeling requirements prescribed in § 310.201(a) of this chapter. Although, for convenience, warning and caution statements for a number of the drugs named in § 310.201 of this chapter (cross-referenced in the text of this part) are included in subpart B of this part, the inclusion of such drugs in §§ 369.20, 369.21, 369.22 in no way affects the requirements for compliance with § 310.201(a) of this chapter, or the provisions of an effective application pursuant to section 505(b) of the act.

§ 369.4 Warnings suggested for drugs by formal or informal statements of policy.

The warning and caution statements included in subpart B of this part in no way affect any warning statement suggested for such drugs or devices by any statement of policy or interpretation in subchapter C of this chapter.

[39 FR 11745, Mar. 29, 1974, as amended at 40 FR 13496, Mar. 27, 1975]

§ 369.6 [Reserved]

§ 369.7 Warnings required by official compendia.

Any drug included in the official compendia defined by the act shall bear such warning or caution statement as may be required by such compendia, and no statement in subpart B or subpart C of this part is intended to alter, modify, or permit the omission of any such statement required by such compendia.

§ 369.8 Warning statements in relation to conditions for use.

The mention in any warning or caution statement included in subparts A, B, and C of this part, of a disease condition does not imply a finding on the part of the Food and Drug Administration that any drug or device is efficacious in such condition; nor is any drug or device bearing labeling referring to such disease condition precluded from regulatory action under the applicable provisions of the act if such claim is considered to be misbranding.

§ 369.9 General warnings re accidental ingestion by children.

Section 369.20 includes under certain items, but not all medicines, the statement: "Keep this and all medicines out of children's reach. In case of overdose, get medical help or contact a Poison Control Center right away," or "Keep out of reach of children." However, in view of the possibility of accidental ingestion of drugs, it is not only suggested but is recommended that one of these statements be used on the label of all drug products.

[64 FR 13296, Mar. 17, 1999]

§369.10 Conspicuousness of warning statements.

Necessary warning statements should appear in the labeling prominently and conspicuously as compared to other words, statements, designs, and devices, and in bold type on clearly contrasting background, in order to comply with the provisions of section 502(c) and (f)(2) of the act. The warning statements should be placed in the labeling in juxtaposition with the directions for use and, in any case, should appear on the label when there is sufficient label space in addition to mandatory label information.

Subpart B—Warning and Caution Statements for Drugs

§369.20 Drugs; recommended warning and caution statements.

ACETANILID.

Warning—Do not exceed recommended dosage. Overdosage or continued use may result in serious blood disturbances.

ACETOPHENETIDIN CONTAINING PREPARATIONS. (See §201.309 of this chapter.)

Warning—This medication may damage the kidneys when used in large amounts or for a long period of time. Do not take more than the recommended dosage, nor take regularly for longer than 10 days without consulting your physician.

ANESTHETICS FOR EXTERNAL USE (LOCAL ANESTHETICS). (See also §310.201(a)(19) and (23) of this chapter.)

Caution—Do not use in the eyes. Not for prolonged use. If the condition for which this preparation is used persists or if a rash or irritation develops, discontinue use and consult physician.

ANTIHISTAMINICS FOR EXTERNAL USE (EXCEPT PREPARATIONS FOR OPHTHALMIC USE).

Caution—Do not use in the eyes. If the condition for which this preparation is used persists or if a rash or irritation develops, discontinue use and consult physician.

ANTIHISTAMINICS, ORAL. (See also §310.201(a)(4) and (a)(24) of this chapter.)

Caution—This preparation may cause drowsiness. Do not drive or operate machinery while taking this medication. Do not give to children under 6 years of age or exceed the recommended dosage unless directed by physician.

The reference to drowsiness is not required on preparations for the promotion of sleep or on preparations that are shown not to produce drowsiness.

ANTIPYRINE.

Warning—Do not exceed recommended dosage. If skin rash appears, discontinue use and consult physician.

ANTISEPTICS FOR EXTERNAL USE.

Caution—In case of deep or puncture wounds or serious burns, consult physician. If redness, irritation, swelling, or pain persists or increases or if infection occurs discontinue use and consult physician.

The reference to wounds and burns is not required on preparations intended solely for diaper rash.

ARSENIC PREPARATIONS.

Warning—Frequent or prolonged use may cause serious injury. Do not exceed recommended dosage. Keep out of the reach of children.

BELLADONNA PREPARATIONS AND PREPARATIONS OF ITS ALKALOIDS (ATROPINE, HYOSCYAMINE, AND SCOPOLAMINE (HYOSCINE); HYOSCYAMUS, STRAMONIUM, THEIR DERIVATIVES, AND RELATED DRUG PREPARATIONS.

Warning—Not to be used by persons having glaucoma or excessive pressure within the eye, by elderly persons (where undiagnosed glaucoma or excessive pressure within the eye occurs most frequently), or by children under 6 years of age, unless directed by a physician. Discontinue use if blurring of vision, rapid pulse, or dizziness occurs. Do not exceed recommended dosage. Not for frequent or prolonged use. If dryness of the mouth occurs, decrease dosage. If eye pain occurs, discontinue use and see your physician immediately as this may indicate undiagnosed glaucoma.

In the case of scopolamine or scopolamine aminoxide preparations indicated for insomnia, the portion of the above warning that reads "children under 6 years of age" should read instead "children under 12 years of age".

BORIC ACID (POWDERED, CRYSTALLINE, OR GRANULAR).

Warning—Do not use as a dusting powder, especially on infants, or take internally. Use only as a solution. Do not apply to badly broken or raw skin, or to large areas of the body.

BROMIDES.

Caution—Use only as directed. Do not give to children or use in the presence of kidney disease. If skin rash appears or if nervous symptoms persist, recur frequently, or are unusual, discontinue use and consult physician.

CARBOLIC ACID (PHENOL) PREPARATIONS (MORE THAN 0.5 PERCENT) FOR EXTERNAL USE.

Warning—Use according to directions. Do not apply to large areas of the body. If applied to fingers or toes, do not bandage.

CATHARTICS AND LAXATIVES—IRRITANTS AND OTHER PERISTALTIC STIMULANTS.

Warning—Do not use when abdominal pain, nausea, or vomiting are present. Frequent or prolonged use of this preparation may result in dependence on laxatives.

Mercury preparations should have added to the "frequent use" statement, the words "and serious mercury poisoning".

Phenolphthalein preparations should bear, in addition to the general warning, the following statement:

Caution—If skin rash appears, do not use this or any other preparation containing phenolphthalein.

See also Mineral Oil Laxatives.

CHLORATES: MOUTH WASH OR GARGLE.

Avoid swallowing.

COBALT PREPARATIONS (See also § 250.106 of this chapter.)

Warning—Do not exceed the recommended dosage. Do not administer to children under 12 years of age unless directed by physician. Do not use for more than 2 months unless directed by physician.

This warning is not required on articles containing not more than 0.5 milligram of cobalt as a cobalt salt per dosage unit and which recommend administration of not more than 0.5 milligram per dose and not more than 2 milligrams per 24-hour period.

"COUGH-DUE-TO-COLD" PREPARATIONS. (See also § 310.201(a)(20) of this chapter.)

Warning—Persons with a high fever or persistent cough should not use this preparation unless directed by physician.

COUNTERIRRITANTS AND RUBEFACIENTS.

Caution—Do not apply to irritated skin or if excessive irritation develops. Avoid getting into the eyes or on mucous membranes.

If offered for use in arthritis or rheumatism, in juxtaposition therewith, the statement:

Caution—If pain persists for more than 10 days, or redness is present, or in conditions affecting children under 12 years of age consult a physician immediately.

See also "Salicylates" in this section for additional warnings for preparations containing methyl salicylate.

CREOSOTE, CRESOLS, GUAIACOL, AND SIMILAR SUBSTANCES IN PREPARATIONS FOR EXTERNAL USE.

Caution—Do not apply to large areas of the body.

CREOSOTE, CRESOLS, GUAIACOL, AND SIMILAR SUBSTANCES IN DOUCHE PREPARATIONS.

Warning—The use of solutions stronger than those recommended may result in severe local irritation, burns, or serious poisoning. Mix as directed before pouring into douche bag. Do not use more often than twice weekly unless directed by physician.

DENTURE RELINERS, PADS, AND CUSHIONS.

Warning—*For temporary use only.* Long-term use of this product may lead to faster bone loss, continuing irritation, sores, and tumors. For Use Only Until a Dentist Can Be Seen.

DENTURE REPAIR KITS.

Warning—For emergency repairs only. Long-term use of home-repaired dentures may cause faster bone loss, continuing irritation, sores, and tumors. This kit for emergency use only. See Dentist Without Delay.

DOUCHE PREPARATIONS.

*Warning—*Do not use more often than twice weekly unless directed by physician.

See also Creosote * * * Douche for additional warning.

DRESSINGS, PROTECTIVE SPRAY-ON TYPE. (See also §310.201(a) (11) and (18) of this chapter.)

*Warning—*In case of deep or puncture wounds or serious burns consult physician. If redness, irritation, swelling or pain persists or increases or if infection occurs consult physician. Keep away from eyes or other mucous membranes. Avoid inhaling.

See also Dispensers Pressurized by Gaseous Propellants * * * for additional warnings to be included for products under pressure.

IODINE AND IODIDES (ORAL).

*Caution—*If a skin rash appears, discontinue use and consult physician.

MERCURY PREPARATIONS FOR EXTERNAL USE.

*Warning—*Discontinue use if rash or irritation develops or if condition for which used persists. Frequent or prolonged use, or application to large areas may cause serious mercury poisoning.

MINERAL OIL LAXATIVES. (See also §201.302 of this chapter.)

*Caution—*Take only at bedtime. Avoid prolonged use. Do not administer to infants or young children, in pregnancy, or to bedridden or aged patients unless directed by physician.

NASAL PREPARATIONS: VASOCONSTRICTORS (PHENYLPROPANOLAMINE).

*Caution—*Do not exceed recommended dosage.

NUX VOMICA AND STRYCHNINE PREPARATIONS.

"Do not use more than the recommended dosage. Keep out of reach of children. In case of overdose, get medical help or contact a Poison Control Center right away."

OPHTHALMIC PREPARATIONS. (See also §200.50 of this chapter.)

Boric acid offered for use in the preparation of ophthalmic solutions should bear the statement: Prepare solution by boiling in water. Store in a sterile container. Prepare sufficient for one day's use and discard unused portion.

PHENACETIN-CONTAINING PREPARATION. (See acetophenetidin.)

PHENYLPROPANOLAMINE HYDROCHLORIDE PREPARATIONS, ORAL.

*Caution—*Individuals with high blood pressure, heart disease, diabetes, or thyroid disease should use only as directed by physician.

POTASSIUM PERMANGANATE AQUEOUS SOLUTIONS (CONTAINING NOT MORE THAN 0.04 PERCENT POTASSIUM PERMANGANATE). (See §250.108 of this chapter.)

*Warning—*For external use on the skin only. Severe injury may result from use internally or as a douche. Avoid contact with mucous membranes.

QUININE AND OTHER CINCHONA DERIVATIVES (EXCEPT FOR USE IN MALARIA).

*Caution—*Discontinue use if ringing in the ears, deafness, skin rash, or visual disturbances occur.

RESINS, OLEORESINS, AND VOLATILE OILS.

*Caution—*If nausea, vomiting, abdominal discomfort, diarrhea, or skin rash occurs, discontinue use and consult physician.

RESORCINOL (NOT THE MONOACETATE) HAIR PREPARATIONS.

*Caution—*Excessive use of this preparation may temporarily discolor blond, white, or red hair.

SALICYLATES, INCLUDING ASPIRIN AND SALICYLAMIDE (EXCEPT METHYL SALICYLATE, EFFERVESCENT SALICYLATE PREPARATIONS, AND PREPARATIONS OF AMINOSALICYLIC ACID AND ITS

SALTS). (See also § 201.314 of this chapter.)

"Keep out of reach of children. In case of overdose, get medical help or contact a Poison Control Center right away;" or "Keep out of reach of children."

If the article is an aspirin preparation, it should bear the first of the above two warning statements. In either case, the above information should appear on the label.

Caution—For children under 3 years of age, consult your physician; or

Caution—For younger children, consult your physician.

One of the two immediately preceding caution statements is required on the label of all aspirin tablets, but such a statement is not required on the labels of other salicylates clearly offered for administration to adults only.

If offered for use in arthritis or rheumatism, in juxtaposition therewith, the statement:

Caution—If pain persists for more than 10 days, or redness is present, or in conditions affecting children under 12 years of age, consult a physician immediately.

SALICYLATES: METHYL SALICYLATE (WINTERGREEN OIL). (See also §§ 201.303 and 201.314 of this chapter.)

"Do not use otherwise than as directed. Keep out of reach of children to avoid accidental poisoning. If swallowed, get medical help or contact a Poison Control Center right away."

If the preparation is a counter-irritant or rubefacient the statement:

Caution—Discontinue use if excessive irritation of the skin develops. Avoid getting into the eyes or on mucous membranes.

If offered for use in arthritis or rheumatism, in juxtaposition therewith, the statement:

Caution—If pain persists for more than 10 days, or redness is present, or in conditions affecting children under 12 years of age consult a physician immediately.

SILVER.

Caution—Frequent or prolonged use of this preparation may result in permanent discoloration of skin and mucous membranes.

SODIUM PERBORATE MOUTHWASH AND GARGLE AND TOOTHPASTE.

Caution—Discontinue use if irritation or inflammation develops, or increases. Avoid swallowing.

SULFONAMIDE NOSE DROPS.

Caution—Do not use if a known allergy to sulfonamide drugs exists.

SULFUR PREPARATION FOR EXTERNAL USE.

Caution—If undue skin irritation develops or increases, discontinue use and consult physician.

THROAT PREPARATIONS FOR TEMPORARY RELIEF OF MINOR SORE THROAT: LOZENGES, TROCHES, WASHES, GARGLES, ETC. (See also § 201.315 of this chapter.)

Warning—Severe or persistent sore throat or sore throat accompanied by high fever, headache, nausea, and vomiting may be serious. Consult physician promptly. Do not use more than 2 days or administer to children under 3 years of age unless directed by physician.

TOOTHACHE PREPARATIONS.

For temporary use only until a dentist can be consulted.

ZINC STEARATE DUSTING POWDERS.

"Keep out of reach of children; avoid inhaling. If swallowed, get medical help or contact a Poison Control Center right away."

[39 FR 11745, Mar. 29, 1974, as amended at 40 FR 8917, Mar. 3, 1975; 40 FR 13496, Mar. 27, 1975; 41 FR 10885, Mar. 15, 1976; 51 FR 27760, Aug. 1, 1986; 51 FR 35340, Oct. 2, 1986; 52 FR 15893, Apr. 30, 1987; 52 FR 30057, Aug. 12, 1987; 52 FR 47324, Dec. 11, 1987; 53 FR 7093, Mar. 4, 1988; 55 FR 31783, Aug. 3, 1990; 57 FR 58376, Dec. 9, 1992; 59 FR 43412, Aug. 23, 1994; 64 FR 13296, Mar. 17, 1999; 68 FR 18882, Apr. 17, 2003; 68 FR 34293, June 9, 2003]

§ 369.21   Drugs; warning and caution statements required by regulations.

ACETAMINOPHEN (N-ACETYL-*p*-AMINOPHENOL) (See § 310.201(a)(1) of this chapter.)

Warning—Do not give to children under 3 years of age or use for more than 10 days unless directed by a physician.

If offered for use in arthritis, or rheumatism, in juxtaposition therewith, the statement:

Caution—If pain persists for more than 10 days, or redness is present, or in conditions affecting children under 12 years of age consult a physician immediately.

ALCOHOL RUBBING COMPOUND. (See 26 CFR 182.855(a)(5); The National Formulary, Tenth Edition 1955, pp. 27–28; and section 502(g) of the act).

Warning—For external use only. If taken internally serious gastric distrubances will result.

ANTIHISTAMINICS, ORAL (PHENYL-TOLOXAMINE DIHYDROGEN CITRATE AND CHLOROTHEN CITRATE PREPARATIONS). (See §310.201(a)(4) and (a)(24) of this chapter.)

Caution—This preparation may cause drowsiness. Do not drive or operate machinery while taking this medication. Do not give to children under 6 years of age or exceed the recommended dosage unless directed by physician.

If offered for symptoms of colds, the statement:

Caution—If relief does not occur within 3 days, discontinue use and consult physician.

DICYCLOMINE HYDROCHLORIDE WITH AN ANTACID. (See §310.201(a)(8) of this chapter.)

Warning—Do not exceed the recommended dosage. Do not administer to children under 12 years of age or use for a prolonged period unless directed by physician, since persistent or recurring symptoms may indicate a serious disease requiring medical attention.

DIPHEMANIL METHYLSULFATE FOR EXTERNAL USE. (See §310.201(a)(22) of this chapter.)

Caution—If redness, irritation, swelling, or pain persists or increases, discontinue use and consult physician.

DRUGS IN DISPENSERS PRESSURIZED BY GASEOUS PROPELLANTS. (See also §310.201(a) (11) and (18) of this chapter.)

The warnings herein shall appear prominently and conspicuously, but in no case may the letters be less than 1/16 inch in height.

If the label of any package is too small to accommodate the warnings, the Commissioner may establish by regulation an acceptable alternative method, e.g., a type size smaller than 1/16 inch in height. A petition requesting such a regulation, as an amendment to this paragraph, shall be submitted to the Division of Dockets Management in the form established in part 10 of this chapter.

Warning—Avoid spraying in eyes. Contents under pressure. Do not puncture or incinerate. Do not store at temperature above 120 °F. Keep out of reach of children.

In the case of products packaged in glass containers, the word "break" may be substituted for the word "puncture."

The words "Avoid spraying in eyes" may be deleted from the warning in the case of a product not expelled as a spray, or that is intended to be used in the eyes.

In addition to the above warning, the label of a drug packaged in a self-pressurized container in which the propellant consists in whole or in part of a halocarbon or hydrocarbon shall bear the following warning:

Warning—Use only as directed. Intentional misuse by deliberately concentrating and inhaling the contents can be harmful or fatal.

The warning is not required for the following products:

(a) Products expelled in the form of a foam or cream, which contain less than ten percent propellant in the container;

(b) Products in a container with a physical barrier that prevents escape of the propellant at the time of use;

(c) Products of a net quantity of contents of less than 2 ozs. that are designed to release a measured amount of product with each valve actuation;

(d) Products of a net quantity of contents of less than 1/2 oz.

DYCLONINE HYDROCHLORIDE. (See §310.201(a)(23) of this chapter.)

Caution—Do not use in the eyes. Not for prolonged use. Do not apply to large areas of the body. If redness, irritation, swelling, or pain persists or increases, discontinue use unless directed by physician. Do not use, but consult physician for deep or puncture wounds

343

or serious burns. Do not use in case of rectal bleeding, as this may indicate serious disease.

HEXADENOL. (See § 310.201(a)(11) of this chapter.)

Caution—Do not use for treatment of serious burns or skin conditions or for conditions which persist for prolonged periods. In such cases, consult your physician. Do not spray in vicinity of eyes, mouth, nose, or ears. Do not store above 120 °F.

IPECAC SYRUP IN ONE-FLUID OUNCE CONTAINERS FOR EMERGENCY TREATMENT OF POISONING, TO INDUCE VOMITING. (See § 201.308 of this chapter.)

Ipecac syrup packaged for over-the-counter sale must bear statements to the following effect, in a prominent and conspicuous manner:

The following statement (boxed and in red letters):

"For emergency use to cause vomiting in poisoning. Before using, call physician, the Poison Control Center, or hospital emergency room immediately for advice."

The following warning: Warning— Keep out of reach of children. Do not use in unconscious persons. Ordinarily, this drug should not be used if strychnine, corrosives such as alkalies (lye) and strong acids, or petroleum distillates such as kerosene, gasoline, coal oil, fuel oil, paint thinner, or cleaning fluid have been ingested.

ISOAMYLHYRDOCUPREINE AND ZOLAMINE HYDROCHLORIDE RECTAL PREPARATIONS FOR EXTERNAL USE (See § 310.201(a)(3) of this chapter.)

Warning—Do not use this preparation in case of rectal bleeding, as this may indicate serious disease.

NEOMYCIN SULFATE WITH A VASOCONSTRICTOR, IN NASAL PREPARATIONS (SPRAY OR DROPS).

Caution—Do not exceed recommended dosage. Do not administer to children under 3 years of age unless directed by physician.

PRAMOXINE HYDROCHLORIDE FOR EXTERNAL USE. (See § 310.201(a)(19) of this chapter.)

Caution—Do not use in the eyes or nose. Not for prolonged use. Do not apply to large areas of the body. If redness, irritation, swelling, or pain persists or increases, discontinue use unless directed by a physician.

SODIUM GENTISATE. (See §§ 201.314 and 310.301(a)(2) of this chapter.)

Warning—Do not use in children under 6 years of age or use for prolonged period unless directed by physician.

"Keep out of reach of children. In case of overdose, get medical help or contact a Poison Control Center right away."

If offered for use in arthritis or rheumatism, in juxtaposition therewith, the statement:

Caution—If pain persists for more than 10 days, or redness is present, or in conditions affecting children under 12 years of age, consult a physician immediately.

TUAMINOHEPTANE SULFATE NASAL PREPARATIONS. (See § 310.201(a)(16) of this chapter.)

Caution—Do not exceed recommended dosage. Overdosage may cause nervousness, restlessness, or sleeplessness. Individuals with high blood pressure, heart disease, diabetes, or thyroid disease should use only as directed by physician. Do not use for more than 3 or 4 consecutive days unless directed by physician.

VIBESATE PREPARATIONS. (See § 310.201(a)(18) of this chapter.)

Caution—Do not use but consult physician for deep or puncture wounds or serious burns. If redness, irritation, swelling, or pain persists or increases, discontinue use and consult physician.

Warning—Contents under pressure. Do not puncture. Do not use or store near heat or open flame. Exposure to temperatures above 130 °Fahrenheit may cause bursting. Never throw container into fire or incinerator.

[39 FR 11745, Mar. 29, 1974]

EDITORIAL NOTE: For FEDERAL REGISTER citations affecting § 369.21, see the List of CFR Sections Affected, which appears in the Finding Aids section of the printed volume and at *www.fdsys.gov.*

PARTS 370–499 [RESERVED]

FINDING AIDS

A list of CFR titles, subtitles, chapters, subchapters and parts and an alphabetical list of agencies publishing in the CFR are included in the CFR Index and Finding Aids volume to the Code of Federal Regulations which is published separately and revised annually.

Table of CFR Titles and Chapters

(Revised as of April 1, 2015)

Title 1—General Provisions

Title 2—Grants and Agreements

Title 8—Aliens and Nationality

Title 9—Animals and Animal Products

Title 10—Energy

Title 11—Federal Elections

Title 12—Banks and Banking

Title 24—Housing and Urban Development

Title 25—Indians

Title 25—Indians—Continued

Title 26—Internal Revenue

Title 27—Alcohol, Tobacco Products and Firearms

Title 28—Judicial Administration

Title 29—Labor

Title 29—Labor—Continued

Title 30—Mineral Resources

Title 31—Money and Finance: Treasury

Title 39—Postal Service

Title 40—Protection of Environment

Title 41—Public Contracts and Property Management

Title 42—Public Health

Title 43—Public Lands: Interior

Title 44—Emergency Management and Assistance

Title 45—Public Welfare

Title 46—Shipping

Title 47—Telecommunication

Title 48—Federal Acquisition Regulations System

Title 49—Transportation

Title 50—Wildlife and Fisheries

Alphabetical List of Agencies Appearing in the CFR

(Revised as of April 1, 2015)

Agency	CFR Title, Subtitle or Chapter
Administrative Committee of the Federal Register	1, I
Administrative Conference of the United States	1, III
Advisory Council on Historic Preservation	36, VIII
Advocacy and Outreach, Office of	7, XXV
Afghanistan Reconstruction, Special Inspector General for	22, LXXXIII
African Development Foundation	22, XV
Federal Acquisition Regulation	48, 57
Agency for International Development	2, VII; 22, II
Federal Acquisition Regulation	48, 7
Agricultural Marketing Service	7, I, IX, X, XI
Agricultural Research Service	7, V
Agriculture Department	2, IV; 5, LXXIII
Advocacy and Outreach, Office of	7, XXV
Agricultural Marketing Service	7, I, IX, X, XI
Agricultural Research Service	7, V
Animal and Plant Health Inspection Service	7, III; 9, I
Chief Financial Officer, Office of	7, XXX
Commodity Credit Corporation	7, XIV
Economic Research Service	7, XXXVII
Energy Policy and New Uses, Office of	2, IX; 7, XXIX
Environmental Quality, Office of	7, XXXI
Farm Service Agency	7, VII, XVIII
Federal Acquisition Regulation	48, 4
Federal Crop Insurance Corporation	7, IV
Food and Nutrition Service	7, II
Food Safety and Inspection Service	9, III
Foreign Agricultural Service	7, XV
Forest Service	36, II
Grain Inspection, Packers and Stockyards Administration	7, VIII; 9, II
Information Resources Management, Office of	7, XXVII
Inspector General, Office of	7, XXVI
National Agricultural Library	7, XLI
National Agricultural Statistics Service	7, XXXVI
National Institute of Food and Agriculture	7, XXXIV
Natural Resources Conservation Service	7, VI
Operations, Office of	7, XXVIII
Procurement and Property Management, Office of	7, XXXII
Rural Business-Cooperative Service	7, XVIII, XLII, L
Rural Development Administration	7, XLII
Rural Housing Service	7, XVIII, XXXV, L
Rural Telephone Bank	7, XVI
Rural Utilities Service	7, XVII, XVIII, XLII, L
Secretary of Agriculture, Office of	7, Subtitle A
Transportation, Office of	7, XXXIII
World Agricultural Outlook Board	7, XXXVIII
Air Force Department	32, VII
Federal Acquisition Regulation Supplement	48, 53
Air Transportation Stabilization Board	14, VI
Alcohol and Tobacco Tax and Trade Bureau	27, I
Alcohol, Tobacco, Firearms, and Explosives, Bureau of	27, II
AMTRAK	49, VII
American Battle Monuments Commission	36, IV
American Indians, Office of the Special Trustee	25, VII

373

374

Agency	CFR Title, Subtitle or Chapter
Science and Technology Policy, Office of, and National Security Council	47, II
Secret Service	31, IV
Securities and Exchange Commission	5, XXXIV; 17, II
Selective Service System	32, XVI
Small Business Administration	2, XXVII; 13, I
Smithsonian Institution	36, V
Social Security Administration	2, XXIII; 20, III; 48, 23
Soldiers' and Airmen's Home, United States	5, XI
Special Counsel, Office of	5, VIII
Special Education and Rehabilitative Services, Office of	34, III
State Department	2, VI; 22, I; 28, XI
Federal Acquisition Regulation	48, 6
Surface Mining Reclamation and Enforcement, Office of	30, VII
Surface Transportation Board	49, X
Susquehanna River Basin Commission	18, VIII
Technology Administration	15, XI
Technology Policy, Assistant Secretary for	37, IV
Tennessee Valley Authority	5, LXIX; 18, XIII
Thrift Supervision Office, Department of the Treasury	12, V
Trade Representative, United States, Office of	15, XX
Transportation, Department of	2, XII; 5, L
Commercial Space Transportation	14, III
Contract Appeals, Board of	48, 63
Emergency Management and Assistance	44, IV
Federal Acquisition Regulation	48, 12
Federal Aviation Administration	14, I
Federal Highway Administration	23, I, II
Federal Motor Carrier Safety Administration	49, III
Federal Railroad Administration	49, II
Federal Transit Administration	49, VI
Maritime Administration	46, II
National Highway Traffic Safety Administration	23, II, III; 47, IV; 49, V
Pipeline and Hazardous Materials Safety Administration	49, I
Saint Lawrence Seaway Development Corporation	33, IV
Secretary of Transportation, Office of	14, II; 49, Subtitle A
Surface Transportation Board	49, X
Transportation Statistics Bureau	49, XI
Transportation, Office of	7, XXXIII
Transportation Security Administration	49, XII
Transportation Statistics Bureau	49, XI
Travel Allowances, Temporary Duty (TDY)	41, 301
Treasury Department	2, X; 5, XXI; 12, XV; 17, IV; 31, IX
Alcohol and Tobacco Tax and Trade Bureau	27, I
Community Development Financial Institutions Fund	12, XVIII
Comptroller of the Currency	12, I
Customs and Border Protection	19, I
Engraving and Printing, Bureau of	31, VI
Federal Acquisition Regulation	48, 10
Federal Claims Collection Standards	31, IX
Federal Law Enforcement Training Center	31, VII
Financial Crimes Enforcement Network	31, X
Fiscal Service	31, II
Foreign Assets Control, Office of	31, V
Internal Revenue Service	26, I
Investment Security, Office of	31, VIII
Monetary Offices	31, I
Secret Service	31, IV
Secretary of the Treasury, Office of	31, Subtitle A
Thrift Supervision, Office of	12, V
Truman, Harry S. Scholarship Foundation	45, XVIII
United States and Canada, International Joint Commission	22, IV
United States and Mexico, International Boundary and Water Commission, United States Section	22, XI
U.S. Copyright Office	37, II
Utah Reclamation Mitigation and Conservation Commission	43, III

List of CFR Sections Affected

All changes in this volume of the Code of Federal Regulations (CFR) that were made by documents published in the FEDERAL REGISTER since January 1, 2010 are enumerated in the following list. Entries indicate the nature of the changes effected. Page numbers refer to FEDERAL REGISTER pages. The user should consult the entries for chapters, parts and subparts as well as sections for revisions.

For changes to this volume of the CFR prior to this listing, consult the annual edition of the monthly List of CFR Sections Affected (LSA). The LSA is available at *www.fdsys.gov*. For changes to this volume of the CFR prior to 2001, see the "List of CFR Sections Affected, 1949–1963, 1964–1972, 1973–1985, and 1986–2000" published in 11 separate volumes. The "List of CFR Sections Affected 1986–2000" is available at *www.fdsys.gov*.